FROM
JULIA CHILD'S
KITCHEN

Other cookbooks from Random House Value Publishing:

MARION CUNNINGHAM'S GOOD EATING

THE FRUGAL GOURMET

LEE BAILEY'S COOKING FOR FRIENDS

THE FANNIE FARMER BAKING BOOK

FROM
JULIA CHILD'S
KITCHEN

JULIA CHILD

Photographs and drawings by Paul Child

Additional technical photographs by Albie Walton

GRAMERCY BOOKS
NEW YORK

This 1999 edition is published by Gramercy Books™, an imprint of Random House Value Publishing, Inc., 201 East 50th Street, New York, NY 10021, by arrangement with Alfred A. Knopf, Inc.

Gramercy Books™ and design are trademarks of Random House Value Publishing, Inc.

Some of this material has previously been published in a slightly different form in McCall's Magazine.

Drawings on pages 649, 656, 658, and 661, courtesy of the National Live Stock and Meat Board, Chicago.

Drawings on pages 173 and 176 by Geo. Price; © 1953 and 1971 The New Yorker Magazine, Inc. Copyright renewed 1981 by The New Yorker Magazine, Inc.

The author would like to thank the Ritz Carlton of Boston for permitting Albie Walton to photograph the duck press on page 244.

Printed in the United States of America

Random House
New York • Toronto • London • Sydney • Auckland
http://www.randomhouse.com/

A CIP catalog record for this title is available from the Library of Congress.

ISBN: 0-517-20712-5

This book
is dedicated to

Ruth Lockwood

Producer of
The French Chef

in gratitude for those years working with me in
planning that other "Julia's Kitchen" in our WGBH-Boston
television studio. The preliminary thinking, the
stop-watch counting, the wild witticisms, the verbal
stumbles caught in time, the encouragements main-
tained, the hard work—always steady, even-tempered,
able, astute—she has been my ever-loving friend.

Contents

Introduction

———————◆———————

*W*hat is this book about? Well, it started out as a record of the 72 *French Chef* television shows in our color series—our second series, which was a continuation of our 119 black-and-white programs. But, as I went along in a leisurely manner, I found that almost every recipe gave rise to variations and other ideas, or to tangents, comments, anecdotes, personal trials and discoveries, and the result is this rather large and rambling book—a summation, really, of my 25 years in the kitchen. In contrast to the formality of the two *Mastering the Art of French Cooking* volumes, which are intended to be textbooks of classical French cuisine and were, furthermore, written in collaboration, this book is very personal and informal. Where *The French Chef Cookbook* takes all the recipes for the black-and-white shows and sets them forth as they were shown on the air, in order and without further comment, this book pulls the new color shows apart and sets their subject matter into categories: soups, fish, meats, and so forth. Again, where the other books are almost entirely French in their inspiration, this one has burst out into other directions as well.

It's more than just French this time

After all, although my formal culinary training was entirely French, and while I am constantly building it during our months in France every year, I remain very American indeed. I always look at French cuisine from an American point of view: How can we make that pastry here? What can we use to duplicate that *Loup Flambé au Fenouil* in the way of fish, flames, and fennel? How can we make that French bread, or that chick-pea pancake, or that *Canard à la Presse?* But now, in addition to French concerns, I feel free to delve into New England chowders, Belgian cookie doughs, personal fruit cakes, curries, pastas. I've gone into experiments with the pressure cooker, for example, the micro-wave oven, and the electric super-blender-food-processor. I've worked out studies with cake batters and the electric mixer and am, in other words, putting my cooking vocabulary to work in all directions. I hope, in turn, if you are not already of the same persuasion, to encourage the same attitude in you, my fellow cook.

Those long long recipes—for the novice—but for the expert, too

As is my wont, I have unabashedly gone into great detail about such subjects as the hard-boiling of eggs, the boning of chicken breasts and fish, the opening of oysters, the various types of chocolate on the market and what to do when you don't have the brand that's called for, and, in general, taken up whatever hows, whys, whats, and wheres that I believe we should all know about. For example, I don't think a plain recipe for souffléed potatoes is nearly enough. Not for me, anyway. They're tricky little busters, and we should know every detail about how they work, why they don't work, and what the general pitfalls are. The same with those sometimes frustrating egg-yolk sauces: what makes them curdle or thin out, how can troubles be avoided, what can you do when all has failed?

Detailed recipes, furthermore, are teaching recipes, and I consider this book to be a private cooking school. Anyone who already knows cooking needs no recipes at all, only a description of processes, such as the following for the *Soufflé de Homard Plaza Athenée* of the *grande cuisine.* "Cook two 1½-pound live lobsters *à l'Américaine;* with the lobster cooking juices make a *sauce velouté* enriched with the lobster tomalley and butter; arrange the lobster meat and half of the sauce in a baking dish, cover with a light cheese soufflé mixture, bake, and serve accompanied by the rest of the lobster sauce enriched with cream." The directions could perhaps indicate that the recipe was for 8 servings, and be more specific about the lobsters, mentioning, parenthetically, that they are cut up, sautéed, and flamed in Cognac before being simmered 15 minutes with white wine, *mirepoix,* tarragon, and a cup of fresh tomato pulp; the soufflé proportions might be outlined as, a white *roux,* ¾ cup milk, 4 eggs, 2 egg whites, and ½ cup grated Swiss cheese. For the non-cook such descriptions are, of course, mind-boggling and meaningless, but for even a moderately accomplished performer the directions are perfectly clear: it is but an assemblage of standard cookery procedures and nothing more is needed in the way of explanation. How well the soufflé turns out depends on the cook's training, dexterity, and sense of taste.

But what a problem for cookery bookery writers. How are we to know the extent of our reader's experience? I, for one, have solved that riddle by deciding to tell all. And I hope that by the clever use of headings in the main text such as *"For the sauce velouté," "Beating the egg whites," "Clarifying the stock,"* and so forth, that the experienced cook will know where to skip along fast through the verbiage. But the full explanations are there for those who need them.

A goodly number of beginner's recipes

Some of the recipes are deliberately written for the beginner cook, such as the Chocolate Mousse on page 524, the Apples Rosie on page 494, the Beef Stew on page 260, the Cheese Soufflé on page 106, as well as the Strawberry Soufflé on page 528. This is true also for the basic Béchamel and Velouté sauces on page 617, for the Mayonnaise on page 439, and the Hollandaise on page 622. Furthermore, in a series of recipes such as those for the sautéed chickens or for the fish fillets poached in wine, the introductory recipe is the detailed master, and those following it are derivations, variations, and sometimes merely sketched suggestions. The point being that once you've done the master and digested the techniques involved it should, after a time or two, be definitely part of your cooking fundamentals. And when one is seriously interested in cooking, that is the way to go about it: think what you are doing, relate it to other recipes you have done, and categorize it in your memory bank.

How to become a cook—and a thrifty and speedy one, too

With your memory bank plugged in, then, you don't have to look up the directions for braised beef, as an example; you know how to do it, and you'll do it your own way, now, with white wine rather than red, and no onions, only garlic and pepper in the braising sauce, and perhaps a little curry powder. Or you've some leftover poached salmon and you decide you'll turn it into a quiche; you don't need a recipe for that because you can whip up a pastry shell blindfolded and you know the quiche proportions by heart: 3 eggs in a measure, plus enough cream or milk and salmon to come up to the 1¾ cup mark. Then you might well decide to add a little diced oinion cooked in butter, some fresh dill and parsley plus a sprinkling of Swiss cheese, and you easily produce a first-rate dish. Again, with your leftover poached fish be it salmon, or bass, or even flounder, you may wish to serve it cold with mayonnaise; you don't need a recipe for that, either, since mayonnaise is engraved upon your heart. Or you'd like it hot *au gratin* on a bed of cooked chopped spinach and a sliced hard-boiled egg or two tucked around the fish to flesh it out; a white wine sauce perked up with cheese and enriched with cream would both flavor the spinach and serve as a cloak to cover the ensemble, and you don't need a recipe for any part of the dish since it is an assembly of standard everyday elements. These are examples of being a cook, and one is not born knowing how; one learns by doing.

Learn how to cook! That's my invariable answer when I am asked to give forth with money-saving recipes, economy tips, budget gourmet dinner menus for six people under ten dollars, and the like. Learn how to cook! That's the way to save money. You don't save it buying hamburger helpers, and prepared foods; you save it buying fresh foods in season or in large supply, when they are cheapest and usually best, and you prepare them from scratch at home. Why pay for some one else's work, when if you know how to do it, you can save all that money for yourself? Knowing how to do it also means doing it fast, and preparing parts of a dish or a meal whenever you have a spare moment in the kitchen. That way, cooking well doesn't take a great deal of time, and when you cook well, you'll be eating far better meals than you could buy from the freezer, or at a restaurant.

French cooking isn't fancy cooking, it's just good cooking

Cooking well, too, doesn't mean cooking fancy, it just means that anything you set your hand to makes good eating, be it mashed potatoes, chicken soup, meat balls, or a twelve-layer cake. French food, by the way, isn't fancy unless, like other cooking, it wants to be fancy; perhaps it sounds so because it is in a foreign language, but a *Coq au Vin* is a chicken stew, a *Pot-au-feu* is a boiled dinner, a *Mayonnaise de Volaille* is a chicken salad, *Soubise* is plain old rice cooked with onions, and there is nothing fancy about any of them. But what is continually pleasing about the French way of cooking is that you *do* something with the food. You don't just boil it, butter it, and dish it out. Not usually. You arrange your cooked broccoli spears like the spokes of a wheel in a round shallow baking dish, you sprinkle them with cheese and butter, and you brown them lightly in the oven. Those very few minutes of effort turn them from a plain vegetable into "a dish." You don't serve your hamburgers plain. No! After sautéing them you swirl some wine and shallots into the pan, and perhaps a chopped tomato along with a good pinch of herbs. There—with a few seconds' rapid boil, a swirl, and a seasoning, you spoon the sauce over the meat, and they aren't just hamburgers any more, they have taken a far more serious and deliciously gastronomic significance. Again, for a quick dessert, you gather a modest variety of canned fruits, boil them a few minutes in their own syrup with strips of lemon peel and a stick of cinnamon; then, while their syrup is boiling down to a glaze, you arrange the fruits beautifully in a serving dish, interspersing them, perhaps, with thinly sliced bananas and a sprinkling of supermarket sliced almonds (always on hand in your freezer for such occasions) . When you spoon the glaze over the fruits, you have a lovely looking dessert that, also, has a certain sophistication of taste. Yet how very simple it is. These few examples are typical of the French approach, that of taking ordinary everyday ingredients, and with a little bit of love and imagination, turning them into something appealing, even exciting, and certainly fun to make as well as to serve and to eat.

A great variety of dishes

I hope, then, to have achieved most of the foregoing points in the following pages, which include a great variety of dishes, but no exotic ingredients. Some are everyday cooking, some are dressy, and the recipes range from soups and main courses to desserts and cakes. There are beans and lentils in various ways, plain consommés to dress up for chic first courses, numerous appetizers from toasted French cheese sandwiches to a fancy ham tart, new ways with eggs from hard-boiling and poaching through omelettes and soufflé-*roulades*. The fish section includes directions on how to keep it fine and fresh at home, then takes up *brochettes,* poached trout, thick steaks, whole fish flamed, mousses and *terrines,* shellfish delicacies, and concludes with old-fashioned salt codfish. The poultry chapter treats whole chickens, sautéed chickens, an illustrated section on chicken breasts, boiled fowl, all about roasting a turkey, and the secrets of pressed duck and goose ragout. Beef is stewed in a number of ways, braised, stuffed, boiled, and a tenderloin is roasted luxuriously before being served with a truffled sauce. Lamb is roasted, curried, and skewered, while pork and ham go through their paces, as do burgers of many sorts. Leftovers go into stuffed cabbage, and tripe is cooked *à la mode* with wine and aromatic vegetables. A whole chapter deals with the earthy alternatives to meaty main courses, featuring legumes, rice, and pasta dishes.

The chapter on French *charcuterie* gives you illustrated directions on making your own sausages, and describes in detail the art of the French *pâté.* These delicious French meat products are almost impossible to buy here and when you do find them in a big-city market or restaurant, they cost a fortune. Yet they are no more difficult and only slightly more expensive to concoct than the average American meat loaf. The fresh vegetable chapter is a large one, as it should be, with new ways for artichokes, asparagus, broccoli, cauliflower to name but a few of them, and not forgetting eggplant, green beans, zucchini, and potatoes. Then, you will not want to miss the true story of Caesar and his famous salad of the 1920's, nor that all-time American favorite, cole slaw. Among the breads you will find a marvelous yeast-batter method for making a great big country-style rye loaf, and you can use the same system for French brioche dough which, surprisingly, turns out to produce the best kind of American doughnuts and coffeecakes. There is French bread, of course, duplicating as far as possible the real French bread of France, and illustrated directions on how to form those long loaves. You have directions, too, on how to turn your home oven into a simulated baker's oven. Then, using that same oven system, you can also produce your own magnificent homemade pizza.

Grand finales are the desserts and cakes, with free-form shells for glittering fruit tarts, fruits poached in wine, and a meringue fantasy, custards, molded desserts, and mousses, and a spectacular strawberry soufflé. Crêpes are cooked right side up and upside down with illustrated directions, while sherbets and ice creams freeze by themselves—no special equipment required. Cakes include one with a halo, another in a cage, and a delicious easy-to-make group done in the mixer. There is a *génoise* jelly roll that transforms itself into a Christmas log or into a *grande bouffe* layer cake with chocolate butter cream and almonds. A famous fruit cake is revealed, as are *Madeleines* done two ways, cookies, and gingerbread, and we end with one of French puff pastry's greats, *Le Pithiviers.*

Meat cuts, metrics, and a culinary gazetteer

In the Appendix, you will find a detailed section on meat cuts, giving the location of each piece as related to the human body so you will visualize it more clearly, also the official name, the aliases, and the French equivalents. Then, because the metric system is, I hope, almost upon us, I have put in several charts relating metrics to our present ounce-cup-spoon system and to French measurements. Finally, as a catch-all to supplement the Index, there is a Culinary Gazetteer that groups together and defines various terms and processes such as how to fold, how to beat egg whites, what to look for in an electric beater, terms for sugars, herb information, and so forth and so on.

Recipes with stopovers—for the chef-host serving 6 to 8

Because this is a book for the home cook who is also bottle washer, waiter, and host or hostess, as I am in my own house, all the recipes have stopping points where a delay is possible; they are indicated by this symbol ☼ —meaning you can complete the dish up to this point—with directions for how to hold it and how, then, to continue. I have tried, also, wherever possible, to tell you how you can see when the chicken is done, or when the fish is cooked through, or when the cake is baked—how it should look or feel, so that you know where and what to observe.

I have not gone into the business of doubling or tripling recipes because that is a very special technique. I like to cook for 2, or for 4 or 6 or at the most 8 people. Beyond that you get into quantity cooking and that is just not my field at all. The last time we had 12 for a sit-down dinner and I did all the cooking, and Paul and I did all the setting up, serving, and washing up afterwards, I said never again. I'll do a buffet, but I don't consider that civilized dining; it is feeding, and I like to sit down at a well-set table.

In sum, this is a personal and informal collection of recipes and general information, but it has no pretensions of being a complete treatise on cookery. It is complete in itself, however, meaning that you will not need to plow through other sources to cook any of the dishes involved. You will find some repeats from (my) other books, inevitably, since how could one have a cookbook at all without the basic sauces, and some of the primary dishes like beef stew, pie doughs, and the like? But in every case of repetition I have come up with a different angle or an expanded conception, since it is useful indeed to know several paths to the same dish.

Sincere thanks

None of the following pages were conceived in solitude. Far from it! In addition to sound advice along the way from my producer, Ruthie Lockwood, on all the television recipes as we did them together, our associate cooks, Bess Coughlin, Liz Bishop, Bess Hopkins, Mary O'Brien, Rita Rains, and Edith Seltzer have contributed enormously to all the dishes done on our *French Chef* shows, by their testing, pre-cooking, and helpful suggestions. My friend Rosie Manell, who, with Liz Bishop, has been with me on the stage at most of my public cooking demonstrations, has also contributed generously from her knowledge and expertise, as well as from her store of recipes. My wonderful secretary, Gladys Christopherson, has ever enthusiastically typed and typed, and re-typed. Avis DeVoto also typed, as well as lending her expert eye to the proofreading. And my favorite editor, Judith Jones, with her fine judgment, her encouraging words, her admonitions, her blue pencilings, and her overall conception of what the book should be-my admiration and gratitude to her are without measure.

Illustrations from a cook's eye view

What a beautiful looking book this is! My editor, and the designers and technical people at Knopf are responsible for that. I love the headings, the use of space, the way the titles and ingredients are set off from the text. It is a stylish and distinguished example of the bookmaker's art, I think, and one that is easy and pleasant to use, as well. Of course, I am delighted with the photographs and drawings, and the way they fit perfectly into the text. Notice when you look at the illustrated directions on how to carve a roast chicken, or how to toss an omelette or to form a loaf of French bread that you are looking at the picture from the angle at which you will be doing the work. This useful how-to photographic technique was perfected by my husband, Paul, who used it when he took all the photographs on which Sidonie Coryn based her drawings for the two volumes of *Mastering the Art of French Cooking*. It is, in fact, the only way that technical illustrations make sense: you don't have to hold the book upside down or do cumbersome mental reversals to arrive at what the picture is all about. You, as cook, place that chicken or hold that pan just the way you see it angled in the illustration, because it was drawn or photographed from your point of view. Half the technical photographs in these pages are Paul's; the others are by Albie Walton, who ably completed the roster. The drawings are Paul's, too, except for the sketch of fennel flowers on page 147, and the handsome rendition of a mackerel type bone structure on page 121, both by our friend and neighbor, the scientific illustrator, Elmer W. Smith.

Finally, those romantic photographic spreads at the beginning of each chapter, those picture that so much capture the atmosphere of La Belle France, the lovely land that made this book possible—they also are Paul's, a handful collected from his years of observing France with his fond artist-photographer's eye.

It now only remains for me to say in conclusion: Be a fearless cook! Try out new ideas and new recipes, but always buy the freshest and finest of ingredients, whatever they may be. Furnish your kitchen with the most solid and workmanlike equipment you can find. Keep your knives ever sharp and—*toujours bon appétit!*

> *J.C.*
> *Cambridge, Massachusetts*
> *April 2, 1975*

From Julia Child's Kitchen

Soupes du jour

Potages

Potage Parmentier; potage bonne femme
—leek and potato soup
Soupe du jour—potato soup with leeks
or onions and leftover vegetables
Soupe au cresson—watercress soup
Vichyssoise—cold cream of potato soup
with leeks or onions
Pressure cooker soup

Pistou

Soupe au pistou verte—green zucchini
soup with a garlic and basil garnish

Meal-in-a-pot soups with lentils or beans

Potage purée de lentilles;
potage purée Conti—old-fashioned
lentil soup
Lentil soup made in the pressure cooker
Serving suggestions for lentil soup
Potage purée de haricots—bean soup
Potage crème de haricots—
white bean soup with herbs and lemon

Bouillons and fancy consommés

Bouillon ordinaire; bouillon
du pot-au-feu—beef bouillon
Bouillon aux légumes—vegetable soup
Croûte au pot—bouillon with hard-toasted
French bread, with cheese, and with
poached eggs
Consommé double—rich, strong,
crystal-clear consommé
Garnitures for consommé
Canned consommé dissembled
Some classic consommé combinations

French fish chowders

Fish to choose
Soupe de poissons provençale—
clear fish soup, and soup base
for bouillabaisse

Rouille—garlic and pepper sauce
for fish soups
Bouillabaisse à la marseillaise

New England fish chowder

Fish stock for chowders
New England fresh fish chowder;
chowder with salt codfish; with finnan
haddie or smoked cod or hake

*W*hy a whole chapter on homemade soups when all of us can find such a variety of canned, frozen, and dehydrated soups on every grocery shelf? Why manufacture all that trouble? Well, most soups are no trouble, but the main reason for making one's own is that homemade soups taste wonderfully homemade; they are fresh, and full, and natural. Just a plain beef bouillon, for instance, the cooking liquid from a beef shank simmered in water with fresh vegetables and seasonings, has that delicious honest quality that makes you want to linger over every mouthful. Homemade soup, then, can be your perfect answer to that always nagging question—how to begin a dinner party. Why not serve a sparkling consommé garnished with royal custard cutouts and a julienne of chicken breasts and mushrooms? Or start the dinner with a cup of *Soupe de Poissons Provençale*, the fragrant Mediterranean fish soup, or serve a purée of leeks and potatoes speckled with fresh watercress leaves and laced with sour cream.

For family meals, or an informal Sunday lunch or brunch, give them a hearty soup as the main course, one made from beans or lentils, or a codfish chowder. And don't forget that soup puts extra vegetables to work (I shall not call them leftovers!) , as well as giving a place of significance to cooked meats, small portions of gravy, and savory juices, to say nothing of meaty bones, goose necks, and gizzards.

Finally, an economical note: since a brimming bowlful of nourishing soup will blunt the edge off ravening appetites, you can cut down considerably on the copiousness of the meat course.

This is not an enormous soup chapter, merely a selective one, including a few recipes you may have seen in our other books, like the ubiquitous leek and potato all-time French favorite, and *Bouillabaisse*. But these several familiars come to you with new twists, and the new recipes are entirely new, such as the green *Pistou,* the bean soup with lemon, the bouillons, the consommés with their myriad garnitures, and the New England fish chowders.

Potages

Potage Parmentier; potage bonne femme

LEEK AND POTATO SOUP

What a delicious soup, you cannot help saying to yourself as you breathe in its appetizing aroma, and then its full homey flavor fills your mouth. There is nothing to mask the taste of those fresh vegetables—no canned chicken stock, no enhancers, preservatives, additives—nothing but the vegetables themselves and a final enriching fillip of cream or butter. This is homemade soup in its primal beauty, to me, and although I love many others, it is leek and potato that I dream of. And it couldn't be simpler to make—sauté the leeks briefly in butter to release their flavor, stir in a little flour to make the light liaison that will hold the vegetables in suspension, add potatoes, water, and salt, and cook until done, as the old books used to say—30 to 40 minutes in a saucepan, or 5 minutes in the pressure cooker. Purée the soup if you wish, or serve it in peasanty chunks; add a dollop of cream for each serving, and that's all there is to it.

Although *Potage Parmentier* is in our other books, it is here again with a few changes in technique—the leek sauté and the flour *roux*—plus a piece of absolutely vital information, namely: If, rather than slicing the vegetables, you mince the leeks nicely, and tailor the potatoes into neat

⅜-inch dice, you are then empowered and entitled to call the soup by a new name—*Potage Bonne Femme*. By the way, if you cannot find leeks you can use onions, but leeks are best because of their very special onion-taste-with-a-difference.

Note: Directions for the pressure cooker are on page 7.

Directions for the pressure cooker are on page 7.

For about 8 cups, serving 6 to 8	3 Tb butter in a 3- to 4-quart heavy-bottomed saucepan

3 cups sliced or minced leeks (white part only) , or onions, or a combination of both

3 Tb flour

2 quarts hot water (or 4 to 6 cups water plus milk added at end of cooking)

1 Tb salt; pepper to taste

Optional: A cup or so of tender green part of the leeks, sliced or minced

4 cups (about 1½ pounds) potatoes, peeled, and roughly chopped or neatly diced— in this latter case use "boiling" potatoes that keep their shape

⅓ to ½ cup heavy cream or sour cream, and/or 2 to 3 Tb butter

2 to 3 Tb minced fresh parsley and/or chives

The soup base. Melt butter over moderate heat, stir in the leeks and/or onions, cover pan, and cook slowly for 5 minutes without browning. Then blend in the flour, and stir over moderate heat for 2 minutes to cook the flour without browning it either. Remove from heat, let cool a moment, and gradually beat in a cup or so of hot water. Blend thoroughly with the flour and vegetables, then stir in the rest of the water. (If you want to use milk, add it at the end of the cooking—it will curdle if you add it now.) Stir in the salt and pepper, optional green of leek, and the potatoes. Bring to a boil, and simmer partially covered for about 40 minutes, until vegetables are thoroughly tender.

For a peasant-type soup, mash the vegetables in the pan with a mixing fork or potato masher. For a smoother texture, put through medium blade of a food mill.

☼ Soup base may be completed hours or even a day ahead to this point: when cool, cover and refrigerate; reheat to simmer before proceeding.

Final enrichments. To serve the soup as is, stir in milk if you are using it, bring to the simmer, and blend in as much of the cream as you wish. Taste carefully, adding more salt and pepper, as needed. Off heat, and by table-spoons if you wish, stir in the butter. Decorate each serving with a spoon-ful more cream, again if you wish to, and a sprinkling of herbs.

"Any word as to the nature of the soupe du jour?"

Soup of the day—the standby of all good family-style restaurants, as George Price's vagrant gastronome so well knows.

ADDITIONS AND VARIATIONS

Soupe du jour (*Potato soup with leeks or onions and leftover vegetables*).
Simmer the preceding soup base until the potatoes, onions, and leeks are tender, then add one or all of such cooked vegetables as a cup of squash, a handful of chopped Brussels sprouts, broccoli, cauliflower, or beans, mashed green peas, lettuce leaves from last night's salad, washed and shredded. Simmer 2 to 3 minutes to warm them through. Complete the soup as in the master recipe, mashing the big vegetables into the soup or puréeing all of it through a vegetable mill, and enriching with milk, cream, and/or butter.

Soupe au cresson (*Watercress soup*). Wash a bunch of watercress 2 to 2½ inches in diameter; pull off most of the leaves and reserve them. Chop the rest, including stems, roughly; stir into the potato and leek soup base after it has simmered about 30 minutes and vegetables are almost tender. Simmer 5 minutes, then purée through a food mill. Stir in the reserved leaves when reheating soup just before serving, and enrich with milk, cream, and/or butter. (This soup is also delicious when served cold; follow general idea of the following recipe for vichyssoise.)

Vichyssoise (*Cold cream of potato soup with leeks or onions*). Simmer the potato and leek or onion soup base (omitting green of leek) in 6 cups of water until vegetables are tender. Purée through fine blade of food mill, or through medium blade and then through a sieve, or through a blender and sieve. Stir in milk and cream to desired consistency, and season carefully with white pepper and salt—oversalt slightly, because chilled soup loses savor. Cover and chill. Taste again for seasoning just before serving, and stir in more chilled cream if you wish; sprinkle each portion with minced fresh chives or parsley.

Since Chef Louis Diat created this soup at the old Hotel Ritz-Carlton in New York, there have been many versions and many additions of chicken stock from the can. I do prefer Diat's simple base of fresh leeks and potatoes, water, milk, cream, and seasonings.

Pressure cooker soup. Use the proportions in the main recipe, *Potage Parmentier.* After sautéing the leeks and onions in your pressure cooker, uncovered, blend in the flour, cook it, and blend in the liquid, salt, and potatoes as described. Then cover the pan, bring rapidly to full pressure, and cook exactly 5 minutes. Release pressure at once. If you taste the soup at this point it will have little flavor: for some reason I am ignorant of, it now must simmer 5 minutes or so (or simply sit 15 minutes) for it to develop its taste. Then complete the soup as described in the main recipe or in any of the preceding variations.

Pistou

Soupe au pistou verte

GREEN ZUCCHINI
SOUP WITH A
GARLIC AND
BASIL GARNISH

The Italians have their *pesto*, while the Mediterranean French have their *pistou*, a fragrant paste of pounded garlic, basil, cheese, and olive oil. You use it as a sauce on spaghetti, noodles, broiled fish, and snails, or beat it into soups just before serving. The classic *Soupe au Pistou* is a vegetable mixture like a minestrone, and the recipe for it is in both *The French Chef Cookbook* and in Volume I of *Mastering*. This soup is all green. The first time I had it was in a small restaurant in Grimaud, an old village in the coastal hills north and east of Saint-Tropez. I have no idea what their mixture was, but suspect it contained a purée of chard, spinach, and perhaps green beans, along with the usual base of potatoes and onions. When we were doing our show "A Vegetable for All Seasons," featuring zucchini, I remembered that delicious green soup and here is my version, starting with cooked onions, and grated and squeezed raw zucchini, then a purée of peas and lima beans; the green juices extracted from the zucchini are added at the last minute so they will not lose their color. The *pistou* flavoring, made separately, tops each serving.

The soup

For about 6 cups
of soup,
serving 4 to 6

*1 lb. zucchini (about two, 8 inches by 1¾ to
    2 inches in diameter)*
½ tsp salt
3 Tb butter or olive oil
1½ cups sliced onions (2 medium onions)
*6 cups water boiling in a 2½- to 3-quart
    saucepan*
1 tsp salt
2 cups shelled lima beans, fresh or frozen
*1 cup shelled green peas, preferably fresh
    but frozen will do*

The pistou flavoring

1 Tb fresh pork fat, or 1 thin strip
*   blanched bacon (simmer it 10 minutes in*
*   1 quart boiling water)*
1 or 2 large cloves garlic
10 to 12 leaves fresh basil, minced; or
*   ½ Tb fragrant dried basil*
3 Tb chopped fresh parsley
2 egg yolks
⅓ cup (about 1½ ounces) freshly grated
*   Parmesan cheese*
⅓ cup olive oil

The zucchini and onions. Wash and scrub the zucchini. Do not peel it, but shave off the two ends. Using the large holes of a grater, grate the zucchini into a colander set over a bowl. Toss with the salt, and let drain. Meanwhile, in a medium frying pan, heat the butter or oil, blend in the onions, cover, and cook slowly for 8 to 10 minutes, stirring occasionally, until tender and translucent. While onions are cooking, squeeze the juices out of the zucchini into the bowl either by handfuls or through a potato ricer. Pour the green juices into a glass measure or small bowl and reserve. Stir the squeezed zucchini into the cooked onions, raise heat to moderately high, and toss and turn for several minutes until zucchini is fairly tender. Set aside.

The purée of lima beans and peas. With the 6 cups of water at a rolling boil, add the salt and the lima beans; boil slowly, uncovered, and add the peas in time for them to finish cooking with the lima beans. Purée the vegetables with their cooking liquid through a vegetable mill or electric blender, and return to saucepan. Scrape in the cooked onions and zucchini; simmer 5 minutes or more, until zucchini is tender.

The pistou flavoring. While the soup ingredients are cooking, mince the pork fat or blanched bacon into a fine purée; place in a small mortar or small solid bowl. Purée the garlic through a press into the mortar, and pound vigorously together with a pestle or the end of a wooden spoon. When a smooth paste, add the basil and parsley, pounding thoroughly. Stir in and mash the raw egg yolks to make a sticky thick mass. Stir in the cheese, and finally, by droplets, stir in and mix the olive oil. You will have a heavy, fragrant, green, mayonnaiselike sauce; set it aside, covered.

☼ All of this may be prepared hours in advance of serving. Refrigerate the soup, cover and refrigerate the zucchini juices and the *pistou*.

Serving. Just before serving, bring the soup to the simmer. Blend in the green zucchini juices, bring to the simmer again, and correct seasoning. If you wish to serve from a tureen, scoop the *pistou* into the bottom of it, stir in a cupful or so of the hot soup by dribbles, and blend in the rest by ladlefuls. Or ladle the soup into bowls and top each serving with a spoonful of *pistou*.

Meal-in-a-pot soups with lentils or beans

Nourishing soups from legumes, as dried lentils and beans are called, can easily be the main course of a meal. A cup of cooked lentils, for instance, contains over 20 grams of protein, or two thirds as much as an equal amount of beefsteak or roast chicken, plus most of the necessary vitamins and minerals needed for a healthy diet. Add to this the other vegetables that cook with lentil soup plus, if you use them, homemade meat stock and a garnishing of sausages or ham, and you have a very sustaining as well as economical mess of Esau's potage to ladle out to your family. Since all these leguminous soups follow the same general pattern of ingredients and flavoring, I shall let lentil soup be the pattern, and discuss beans at the end of the lentil recipe, along with remarks on the ever-useful pressure cooker.

In preparation for our show "How About Lentils?" which included lentils as a vegetable garnish, page 336, and the lentil *cassoulet* on page 337, I had fun looking up old French recipes and found, of course, that just as the lentil is one of the ancient vegetables, lentil soup goes back to Biblical times, and continues right up into the elegant cuisines of the eighteenth and nineteenth centuries and beyond. In the early 1800's the great chef Carême called his a *Potage de Purée de Lentilles à la Conti*.

Conti, as far as we know, was Louis-François de Conti, Grand Prior of the Knights Templars near the end of the eighteenth century. It has not been revealed whether it was he or his chef who was a lover of lentil purées, or the Templars themselves. But any time you run into something *à la Conti,* whether it be a soup, a vegetable garnish, or an egg dish, you can be sure what it is. Just as Florentine means spinach and Cardinal means lobster, Conti and lentils are linked forevermore.

Along with some 1½ quarts of lentils, then, Carême directs that you put into the pot a carrot, an onion, a turnip, and 2 leeks tied together with a bunch of celery. Along with a goodly quantity of excellent bouillon, you are to add to the pot a slice of lean ham and a mature partridge. After a slow simmer of 3 hours or so, you strain out the liquid, purée the lentils, and return liquid to lentils. You simmer a bit and skim assiduously, season carefully, and serve up your soup with croutons tossed in butter. And the ham and the partridge? He never mentions them again; we must conclude they are expendable like soup bones, having given their all to the *potage.*

On the other hand, you can use your partridge and eat it too, following the suggestion of Henri Babinski—Ali-Bab—well-known gourmand and amateur cook in the Paris of the 1920's. Roast it, he suggests in his splendid tome of 1,281 pages, *Gastronomie Pratique,* slice the breast meat into julienne to garnish the soup, then put the remains of the bird through a duck press, adding the juices to the soup along with a goodly quantity of heavy cream. (The heroic task of translating Babinski into English has finally been accomplished by Elizabeth Benson—*Ali-Bab: Encyclopedia of Practical Gastronomy* [New York: McGraw-Hill, 1974.])

The lentil soup resulting from my research follows along classic lines, including Carême's turnip, which I find gives a most pleasantly subtle something of flavor, but there must not be too much or it will not remain incognito. Then for those who do not have partridge, I have suggested Polish or Italian sausage. Finally, since the modern lentil has less binding power than the lentil of yore and of Carême, the purée will sink to the bottom of the soup bowls unless you provide a liaison of some sort; a little flour, cooked along with the preliminary vegetable flavoring, does the trick.

Potage purée de lentilles; potage purée Conti

OLD-FASHIONED
LENTIL SOUP

2 celery stalks
1 medium carrot
1 medium onion
1 medium leek, or another onion
3 Tb butter, cooking oil, or olive oil
3 Tb flour
6 cups hot liquid (ham stock, or poultry or
    meat stock, or water)
1 bay leaf
¼ tsp thyme
Optional: ⅓ cup diced turnip or rutabaga
1½ cups washed lentils
2 tsp salt

Cooking time: About 1½ hours in an open pot; see end of recipe for speedier timing in the pressure cooker

For about 2 quarts, serving 4 to 6 people

Wash, peel and/or otherwise prepare the celery, carrot, onion, and leek, and chop roughly. Heat butter or oil in a 4- to 5-quart saucepan, stir in the vegetables, and cook, covered, over moderately low heat; stir occasionally, until vegetables are tender and just beginning to brown lightly—10 minutes or so. Blend in the flour, stirring, and cook for 2 minutes; remove pan from heat. Gradually blend in 1 cup of the hot liquid, stirring vigorously to mix flour and liquid thoroughly. Pour in the rest of the liquid, and bring to the simmer, adding herbs and optional diced turnip. Stir in the lentils and salt, cover pan loosely, and simmer slowly 1¼ to 1½ hours, or until lentils are very tender.

Purée the soup through a vegetable mill or in an electric blender, and return over heat; carefully correct seasoning, and add a little more liquid if soup seems too thick.

☼ May be cooked in advance: let cool uncovered, then cover and refrigerate. Bring to the simmer shortly before continuing.

Lentil soup made in the pressure cooker. This will take you 30 to 40 minutes in all. Following the master recipe for lentil soup, melt the butter with a little oil in the pressure cooker, stir in the chopped vegetables, and sauté over moderately high heat for several minutes, stirring frequently, to brown the vegetables lightly. Lower heat, blend in and cook the flour 2 minutes. Remove from heat, let cool a moment, then blend in the liquid, and finally the lentils and other ingredients. Pressure

cook 5 minutes, remove from heat, and let pressure go down by itself—
15 to 20 minutes. Uncover, and either simmer 5 minutes or so, or let sit
15 to 20 minutes, allowing flavor to develop. Serve, using any of the following suggestions.

SERVING SUGGESTIONS FOR LENTIL SOUP

Herb-butter garnish with croutons. While soup is simmering beat together 6 to 8 tablespoons soft butter, 2 tablespoons finely minced parsley,
salt and pepper to taste, and a big pinch or two of thyme, oregano, or
basil. Place a spoonful in each bowl as you serve the soup, and garnish
with little croutons (white bread cut in ⅜-inch dice, dried out in the
oven, tossed in a frying pan with clear melted butter to brown lightly,
then seasoned with salt and pepper).

Sausage garnish. Here just a little bit of sausage gives a meaty impression.
Whatever you decide on quantity, prick the sausage in several places
with a sharp skewer; for Polish or Italian sausage, simmer in the soup
30 minutes. Follow package directions for frankfurters. Slice into thin
rounds, and reheat in soup just before serving. You may also wish to include the preceding herb butter with or without the croutons.

Ham garnish. You may have made the lentil-cooking liquid from a ham
bone still containing meat; in that case remove the meat from the bone
before it is stringy and overcooked. Or you may have some leftover ham
or a thick ham slice. Again, even a small amount gives a good impression,
a tablespoon or two per person. Dice the ham into ¼-inch pieces and
sauté in butter with a bit of oil, until very lightly browned. Season with
salt and pepper and set aside. Stir into the soup just before serving. Again,
you may also wish to add the herb butter and/or croutons, depending on
how much ham you have.

Potage purée de haricots

BEAN SOUP

For about 2 quarts,
serving 4 to 6 people

The lentil soup recipe also makes a delicious bean
soup; however, unless you are using the special
quick-cooking type, beans need presoaking. In the
old days, you put them in water overnight, but the
quick-soak method developed by our Department
of Agriculture people takes only an hour, as follows:

1½ cups dried beans, picked over and washed
6 cups boiling liquid (meat stock; or
water and 1 tsp salt)

Drop the beans into the boiling liquid, bring rapidly back to the boil, and boil exactly 2 minutes. Remove from heat, cover pan, and let sit for 1 hour. Then proceed with the recipe, using the soaking-liquid for the soup. Simmer the soup 1½ to 2 hours in an open pot or use the pressure cooker, which takes a third the time. (I find the pressure cooker wonderfully successful for beans and, in addition, I think white beans discolor less in the pressure cooker than they do in the open pot.) Follow the lentil soup recipe on page 12 with these two exceptions: Omit the flour, since puréed beans have enough body in themselves and thus need no liaison, and for white beans, do not brown the preliminary vegetables; simply cook them slowly until limp. Besides this lentil formula and its variations, you might also try the following delicious and quite different formula, using white beans or the small pale-green French ones called *flageolets.*

Potage crème de haricots

———

**WHITE BEAN SOUP
WITH HERBS
AND LEMON**

For about 2 quarts,
serving 4 to 6 people

This delicious soup, served in fancy cups, would be good even at a formal dinner, especially when you use the cream enrichment with herbs and lemon at the end of the recipe.

2 celery stalks, sliced
1 medium onion, sliced
1 medium leek, or another onion, sliced
3 Tb butter
6 cups liquid (chicken stock, or water,
*   or a combination)*
1½ cups washed white beans of any type,
*   or flageolets*
1 bay leaf
2 tsp salt
Optional: 1 or more cloves garlic, unpeeled

In an uncovered pressure cooker, or in a heavy 3- to 4-quart saucepan, sauté the sliced vegetables in the butter 5 minutes until fairly limp, but not browned. Add the liquid, bring to the boil, then add the beans, bay leaf, salt, and optional garlic. Bring rapidly to the boil again, uncovered, and boil exactly 2 minutes. Remove from heat, cover pan, and set aside for 1 hour. Then bring to the boil again. Either pressure cook exactly 5 minutes at full pressure; let pressure go down by itself—15 to 20 minutes. Or simmer slowly, partially covered, for 1½ to 2 hours, until beans are thoroughly tender, adding a little boiling water if liquid has evaporated below top level of beans.

Drain in a colander set over a bowl. Discard bay leaf. Squeeze contents of optional garlic cloves into beans, and purée beans and other vegetables either through a vegetable mill or in an electric blender. Return purée and cooking liquid to pan. Now you may thin out the soup with milk, enrich it with cream, season it to taste, and serve it forth, or try the following:

Egg yolk and cream enrichment with herbs and lemon

2 egg yolks in a mixing bowl
½ cup heavy cream plus more cream, or milk, if needed
4 to 6 Tb soft butter blended with:
  The grated rind and strained juice of 1 lemon
  3 to 4 Tb fresh minced herbs such as basil, or tarragon and parsley, or summer savory and parsley, or fresh parsley and ½ tsp dried tarragon
Big pinches each of salt, white pepper, nutmeg
Optional: Toasted and buttered croutons (as for lentil soup, page 13)

Just before serving, bring the soup to the simmer, carefully correct seasoning with salt and white pepper. Then, beating the yolks with a wire whip, blend in ½ cup cream and, by dribbles, several ladlesful of hot soup. Pour this mixture back into the soup, and bring to just below the simmer. If soup seems too thick, thin out with spoonfuls of cream or milk. Remove from heat, and beat in the herbal lemon butter by spoonfuls. Serve immediately, accompanied, if you wish, with toasted and buttered croutons.

Cold bean soup. The preceding bean soup with its herb and lemon fillip is also very good cold. Overseason it slightly, chill it, and when you are ready to serve, stir in a bit of chilled medium cream; top each serving with a sprinkling of fresh green herbs, or with a slice of lemon and slices of hard-boiled egg sprinkled with herbs.

Bouillons and fancy consommés

Bouillon comes from *bouillir*, to boil, and a bouillon is any liquid that meats or vegetables have cooked in. In France, when you are feeling a little picky, they will inevitably prescribe for you a *bouillon de légumes,* a vegetable broth, to settle your stomach, along with a glass of warm milk, since milk drinking is for babies and invalids. But when, in *cuisine,* one speaks of bouillon, it is assumed one means a beef broth, a *bouillon du pot-au-feu,* that marvelous cooking liquid resulting from a French boiled dinner, smacking of long-simmering beef, marrow bones, and fresh vegetables.

Bouillon simple; bouillon du pot-au-feu

BEEF BOUILLON

When we did our show "Pot-au-feu," described on page 273, I had that lovely broth but no time to do anything with it. Now I can fill this gaping lacuna. So, take that priceless bouillon, strain it through a fine sieve and, if you have none of the degreasing devices illustrated on page 635, chill it, and peel all the congealed fat off the top. You now have a bouillon you can use just as it is in a number of simple and delicious ways. Or you can clarify it—meaning to render it clear and sparkling—and, at the same time, enrich it with more meat and flavorings. Clarified and enriched bouillon then becomes not only consommé, but also in official French culinary language, *consommé double. Consommé double* can be an elegant cup of soup for the beginning of a chic dinner; it can also be turned into jellied consommé or into an aspic, simply with the addition of gelatin. Bouillon, consommé, *consommé double,* jellied consommé, and aspic all can be frozen, and will keep for months. What better reason can there be for a boiled dinner except for the dinner itself? Here, then, are suggestions for serving bouillon, and for turning bouillon into consommé.

Fonds de volaille (*Chicken, turkey, and poultry stocks and broths*). The recipe for turkey stock on page 234 serves for all poultry stocks, and you can substitute poultry stock for beef bouillon in any of the following recipes.

Bouillon aux légumes

VEGETABLE SOUP

For about 2 quarts, serving 6 people

2 quarts thoroughly degreased beef bouillon from a boiled dinner (Pot-au-feu, page 273), or a good beef stock, or a combination of canned beef broth and chicken broth plus any homemade stock on hand
About 2 cups mixed vegetables left over from the dinner, or ½ cup each sliced carrots, onions, celery, turnips, and shredded cabbage
Optional: 1 cup or so boiled beef left over from the dinner, trimmed and diced
2 medium tomatoes, peeled, seeded, juiced, and diced
Salt and pepper to taste
2 or more tablespoons minced fresh herbs, such as parsley, basil, and chives, or parsley only

If your vegetables are already cooked, slice or dice them, and place in a 3-quart saucepan with the bouillon, the optional diced meat, and the diced fresh tomato; heat to simmering, correct seasoning, skim off any scum if it appears, stir in the herbs, and serve. If your vegetables are raw, simmer them 15 to 20 minutes with 2 cups of the bouillon, add the rest of the bouillon, the optional meat, and the tomato; bring to the simmer, correct seasoning, skim if necessary, stir in the herbs, and serve. (You can also add tapioca, rice, noodles, dried beans, or barley, which you could cook in some of the bouillon or separately, and fresh green vegetables like peas or diced green beans, which would either cook separately or with the bouillon.)

Croûte
au pot

—————

BOUILLON WITH
HARD-TOASTED
FRENCH BREAD,
WITH CHEESE,
AND WITH
POACHED EGGS

The age-old way to make a meal out of a bouillon is to serve it over hard-toasted bread rounds. To make them, take a regular long loaf of French bread —making sure it is of the good-quality, rather chewy type, the kind you can make yourself on page 461—limp, textureless bread will disintegrate in the soup. Either cut it in rounds about ¾ inch thick or split the loaf lengthwise, and cut each half into pieces 3 inches long. Arrange on a baking sheet and dry out in a 325-degree oven until the bread is hard through and a light golden brown— 25 to 30 minutes or more. Baste it while it bakes, if you wish, with olive oil or butter—in the old days they used the fat skimmed off the bouillon itself or fat saved from roasting meat. The *croûtes* are now ready to use, and you place 2 or 3 in the bottom of each soup plate as you serve the bouillon. Or spread them with a quarter-inch coating of grated Swiss or Parmesan cheese, baste with oil or butter, and brown under the broiler. Another old French idea is to spread them with a purée of cooked vegetables left over from the boiled dinner, then sprinkle with cheese and brown. A final thought, and a delicious one, is to place a poached egg on the *croûte,* ladle on the bouillon, and sprinkle each serving with a heaping spoonful of freshly grated Parmesan cheese.

Consommé
double

—————

RICH, STRONG,
CRYSTAL-CLEAR
CONSOMMÉ
TO BE SERVED
HOT OR
JELLIED, OR
FOR ASPICS

To turn a regular homemade beef bouillon into sparkling consommé, you mix it with raw egg whites, agitate it with a whip until it comes barely to the simmer, and hold it at just below the simmer 10 to 15 minutes. The egg whites rise, drawing into themselves and imprisoning all the cloudy particles. Then, when you very gently strain the mixture through cheesecloth, a beautifully clear consommé drains through, leaving the egg whites and sediments behind. It is fun and easy to do, and especially rewarding because it has that incomparable homemade taste. Follow exactly the detailed directions for clarification in the *Trout in Aspic* recipe, page 447, using the following ingredients. (To give added strength and flavor, additional meat and aromatic ingredients are mixed with the egg whites. There are no fixed proportions here; put in more or fewer ingredients depending on your opinion of the original bouillon.)

For about 2 quarts

2½ quarts beef bouillon from a boiled dinner, Pot-au-feu, page 273, very thoroughly degreased

⅔ cup (about 5) egg whites

1 lb. (2 cups) very lean beef with no traces of fat (shin, neck, or heel of the round, for instance), finely ground

About 1 cup finely minced green of leek, or a combination of whole minced scallions and celery leaves

¼ cup minced parsley stems

A branch or so of fresh tarragon or a handful of chervil, or ½ Tb fragrant dried tarragon

Optional wine flavoring to be added after clarification: ½ cup dry Madeira or Port wine, or Cognac

Optional gelatin, to be dissolved in the preceding wine

For jellied consommé: 2½ envelopes (2½ Tb) plain unflavored gelatin (1 envelope for each 3 cups)

For plain aspic coatings: 1 envelope for each 2 cups of consommé

For aspic to line a mold: 1 envelope for each 1½ cups of consommé

GARNITURES FOR CONSOMMÉ

The *Escoffier Cook Book* (New York: Crown, 1941) lists 88 ways to serve consommé, while the chef's handbook of recipe résumés, *La Répertoire de la Cuisine,* by Gringoire and Saulnier (Paris: Dupont et Malgat, 9th edition, 1947, and reprints) describes 189. These range from the simple addition of tapioca, poached fresh tomato pulp, or buttered asparagus tips to essence of wild mushrooms, truffle juices, boned and stuffed chicken wings, and *quenelles* of *foie gras* with julienne of wild game, especially partridge. (That bird again—we borrowed a stuffed one from the Audubon Society for our lentil show, when discussing Carême's soup.) Always, reading over the contents of these consommés, I picture the cavernous formal hotel dining rooms of bygone days, where dinner consisted of 5 courses at least, with a sherbet somewhere in between. I remember the vivid cinematic re-creation of that epoque in the dining scenes of *Death in Venice*. And I remember, too, a splendid evening at the Hotel de Paris in Monte Carlo in the early 1950's, when their magnificent downstairs dining room was still functioning. We were having a gustatory bash with our favorite English traveling companions, almost weeping over the end-of-an-era elegance of the room, with its string orchestra hidden in a balcony, its marble columns, its gilt encrustations everywhere, its flocks of frock-coated waiters, and its diners in evening dress.

We were also marveling over the *petite friture de soles* that both Paul and Peter had ordered, real baby soles 3 inches long, deep fried and crisp. Suddenly, through their enticing aroma of very fresh fish impeccably fried, we became aware of a slight murmur and rustle in the room, a turning of heads. Our waiter leaned over. "It's Colette," he hissed to us. Already a legendary figure as well as an immensely popular novelist, her gray-white hair moplike and flying in its unmistakable way, she was over eighty and in a wheelchair. But she had vigorous movements, an imperial look to her eyes, and one of those rapidly moving wide mouths that also purse in a particularly French way. The *maître d'hôtel* pushed her at a stately pace in front of the marble columns, under the orchestra, then right by our table, and to the other side of the room. As she slowly passed table after table, she looked intently at what everyone was eating, and when she came to us her glance flickered over the *petite friture,* and rested several seconds on Mari's *feuilleté aux crevettes,* whose little shrimp forms were clearly visible under a winey creamy sauce with bits of truffle. Did she linger with special interest over the elaborate consommé I had ordered? I like to think she did.

I happened to be working on consommés at the time, and had been thrilled to find that the large menu listed half a dozen under the heading of *consommé en tasse.* I would love to have ordered a cup of each, but our warmly gracious table captain was happy to describe what some of them were. *Consommé Chasseur,* for instance? Yes, flavored with the *fumet,* or essence, of game birds (that ubiquitous partridge probably) and Port wine, garnished with a julienne of mushrooms and *pluches de cerfeuil*—leaves of chervil, that most typical ingredient of French soupery. A side dish of tiny *profiterole* puffs stuffed with a purée of game comes with it. Sounds delicious. How about *Sévigné?* I was engulfed in her memoirs and felt, as a grateful reader, I owed her some small recognition. Ah, that is a chicken consommé with *quenelles,* a julienne of lettuce, and asparagus tips. Not too exciting. I would then have preferred a *Consommé Balzac,* had there been one, but settled on *George Sand,* a friend of Balzac's anyway. She had been honored by a fish consommé garnished with crayfish *quenelles* and morel mushrooms. On a covered silver salver came the accompaniment—*croûtes* spread, so he said, with the white roe of carp. It was very good indeed. It had a wonderfully worldly taste—the taste of Colette's world and of *La Belle Époque*—and I knew as I savored it slowly that I'd probably never see the like again.

How true. When Paul and I returned to Monte Carlo with James Beard some years later, our minds aglow with old memories, all had changed. The great main dining room was a dreary relic, and the action had moved up to a modern rooftop restaurant. Not a trace was left of bygone atmosphere, and only *Consommé Madrilène* was on the menu. A pity, but it is useless to cry over lost loves and lacunae in modern restaurant menus. One can, however, revive for one's own pleasure some of those consommé combinations, and serve them forth as elegant first courses. I offer you the following nostalgic suggestions.

You certainly need not be as elaborate as these examples, but a little clever garnishing gives you an easy and elegant first course. You will find that most are in your cooking repertoire anyway, or appear elsewhere in this book, and the following are simply to give you some ideas. All of them may usually be prepared well in advance, and that makes serving easy indeed. You need not use your own homemade brand of consommé either, of course, but you should most certainly disguise canned consommé: a short simmer with some tasteful additions, and it becomes your own.

Canned consommé dissembled

About 8 cups strong, concentrated canned consommé
⅓ to ½ cup minced fresh mushroom stems (save the caps for something else)
2 to 3 Tb each of minced celery, leek or scallion, and carrot
6 or more parsley stems, minced

For 2 quarts,
serving 6 to 8

1 bay leaf
⅛ tsp thyme or tarragon, more if needed
1 cup dry white wine, or ⅔ cup dry white
*   French Vermouth*
2 or more Tb Madeira, Port, or Sherry,
*   for final flavoring*

Simmer the consommé in a covered saucepan with the vegetables, herbs, and the white wine or Vermouth for 10 to 15 minutes. Season carefully, strain, and stir in the Madeira, Port, or Sherry to taste.

☼ May be refrigerated for several days, or frozen for several months.

Tapioca

FOR THICKENINGS

This homely item is one of the very oldest foods known. Produced in the tropics from the roots of manioc (cassava) plants, it has long been used in soups and puddings. Tapioca's role in a consommé is to thicken the soup lightly without clouding it; tapioca also gives clear soup a certain consistency. For example, you may want a thickened effect for a *Consommé Printanier* with fresh vegetables, so that your attractive garnish will remain in suspension rather than sinking down into a mass at the bottom of the cups.

For each quart
of consommé

5 to 6 Tb quick-cooking tapioca

Bring the consommé to the boil, sprinkle in the tapioca, and boil slowly until the tapioca is transparent, usually about 10 minutes. Skim as necessary, and you can serve the soup just as it is with perhaps a sprinkling of fresh green herbs, or make more of a show by adding the following tomato garnish.

Dés de tomates

POACHED DICED
TOMATO PULP,
FOR COLOR

Little flecks of tomato add color and a welcome suggestion of acidity to consommé, used either alone or in combination with other items. Here the tomato is simmered separately so it won't cloud the soup.

For 2 quarts
of consommé

2 medium-size firm, ripe, red tomatoes

Peel, seed, and juice the tomatoes; cut them into neat even pieces ⅜ inch to a side. Bring about 1 quart of salted water to the simmer, drop in the tomato pieces, and simmer very slowly for several minutes, until the tomato is just tender but the pieces have kept their shape. Remove with a skimmer, letting each group drain, and arrange on a plate. Float the tomato in the consommé just before serving.

Crêpes

PAPER-THIN
FRENCH
PANCAKES, FOR
AMUSEMENT AND
NOURISHMENT

Crêpes make a simple garnish, and you might keep this in mind the next time you are doing a batch; save out a few, freeze them, and you have instant access since they thaw very quickly. Use them as is, or fill with a stuffing as suggested here.

For 2 quarts
of consommé

2 or 3 crêpes 5 inches or so in diameter

Use the all-purpose recipe on page 531 for the crêpes, and you can substitute bouillon or consommé for the liquid in the recipe, and add 3 tablespoons minced green herbs like fresh parsley and chives. Roll the cooked crêpes into tight cylinders, and slice into strips less than ¼ inch wide. Stir into the hot consommé just before serving, and sprinkle on some fresh green herbs; include also, if you wish, the preceding poached tomato pieces.

Fillings for crêpes

Keep the following kind of a stuffing in mind also, when you are making a thick sauce base and have a little left over, or have a bit of chicken or ham or minced sautéed mushrooms. Store them in your freezer, and make the filling suggested here.

For 2 quarts
of consommé

About ½ cup leftover bouillie sauce base,
    (page 69) warmed, or the following:
3 Tb flour
½ cup beef broth or chicken bouillon
1 Tb butter
1 egg yolk
2 Tb freshly grated Parmesan or Swiss cheese
1 to 2 Tb minced or puréed cooked chicken,
    chicken livers, liver paste, ham, spinach,
    broccoli, onions, mushrooms, or whatever
    would go with the consommé

Salt and pepper
4 cooked crêpes about 5 inches in diameter

Make the sauce as follows: Place the flour in a small heavy-bottomed saucepan and gradually beat in the liquid with a wire whip. When blended and smooth, beat slowly over heat; as it comes near the boil it will get lumpy—beat vigorously to smooth it, then beat in the butter and egg yolk and let boil again for a minute, beating. The sauce will be very thick. Beat in the cheese, the mince or purée, and salt and pepper to taste.

To stuff the crêpes: lay one, its worst side up, on your work surface; spread with a ⅛-inch layer of the filling. Lay a second, its worst side down, over the first, and press together quite firmly. Fill the 2 other crêpes in the same manner. Wrap and refrigerate before cutting, to firm and set the filling. Cut into strips or fancy shapes, and add to the consommé for a moment, to heat, before serving. Another obvious system is to spread each crêpe with the filling, roll up tight, refrigerate, and cut into thin strips for serving; 2 crêpes would then be enough.

Omelettes *(For amusement and nourishment)*. Rather than crêpes, use a very thin one-egg flat omelette, like the ones in the Omni-Omelette recipe, page 104. It may be plain, cheese, or herb-filled; roll into a cylinder and cut into strips less than ¼ inch wide. Stir into the hot consommé just before serving, adding a sprinkling of fresh herbs and/or poached tomato pulp, if you wish.

Quenelles *(Forcemeat balls, for grand occasions)*. These are made from fish, veal, or chicken dumpling or mousse mixtures, forced through a pastry bag held over simmering salted water, and cut off to make little balls of ⅜-inch size. Poach at below the simmer for 5 minutes, drain, and heat in the consommé just before serving. If you are making a fish consommé, following the poached trout recipe on page 131, you could use the shrimp mousse mixture on page 153. Or substitute raw veal or the white meat of chicken for the shrimp when you want *quenelles* for chicken or beef consommé. Recipes for *quenelles* are also in Volume I of *Mastering* and in *The French Chef Cookbook*. (Don't forget that both raw and cooked *quenelle* and mousse mixtures freeze. Thus when you are making them initially, save the leftovers for soup garnishings, cutting them into dice or fancy shapes before freezing, if you wish.)

Profiteroles *(Tiny cream puffs, for chic)*. Make very small baked puffs less than half an inch in size, as small as possible—using the *pâte à choux* recipe on page 160. Serve them as is in a side dish, to be sprinkled in the

soup, or fill them with a chicken liver purée, *foie gras,* or the cheese filling for croquettes on page 45. (Again, this is a perfect use for that little
leftover dab of *choux* pastry—form it into baby puffs, bake them, and
freeze them.)

Les royales (*Custard cutouts, for flavor and class*). These are firm cup
custards, baked, cooled, then cut into dice or fancy designs. They are
either plain, consisting of eggs and bouillon, or they contain eggs, a
thick sauce, and a purée such as tomato, spinach, *foie gras,* and so forth.
Baked in a buttered mold or pan in a *bain-marie* they take 15 to 20
minutes in the oven, and must be done a good 2 hours before using so
they will set and can then be cut. Here are two formulae.

Plain royal custard

AN EASY GARNISH

For 2 quarts
of consommé

1 "*large*" egg and 2 egg yolks
¾ cup hot bouillon or consommé
Salt and pepper to taste

Preheat oven to 325 degrees. Choose a 1- to 1½-cup
custard or soufflé mold or fireproof dish of some
sort, and butter it heavily. Blend the egg and yolks
in a mixing bowl, then by dribbles beat in the hot
liquid. Taste, and correct seasoning. Skim off bubbles, and pour through a fine strainer into buttered
mold; again skim any bubbles off surface. Place in
a *bain-marie* (pan of boiling water), and bake 15
to 20 minutes, making sure water in pan is never
quite simmering. (Too high heat causes custards to
become grainy or to separate.) Custard is done
when a knife or skewer, plunged through center,
comes out clean. Remove from hot water, set in
cold water, and put in the refrigerator.

In about 2 hours, or when custard is thoroughly chilled and set, run
a knife around edge of baking dish, and unmold the custard upside
down on a clean cutting board. Cut into horizontal slices about ⅛ inch
thick, then into dice, squares, or diamonds, or use fancy truffle cutters
with special designs. Refrigerate until you are ready to add them to the
hot consommé just before serving.

☼ *Royales* will keep several days under refrigeration.

Royal custard with a purée

FOR COLOR AND
VARIETY, AND A
USE FOR LEFTOVERS

This is slightly different in makeup than the plain royal, in that you have a thick flour-based sauce, a very thick purée of any cooked meat or vegetable you wish, and raw egg yolks. However, you cook it just like the plain custard. An electric blender is useful here; otherwise you will have to force your purée through a sieve.

For 2 quarts
of consommé

1 Tb flour in a small saucepan
⅓ cup bouillon or consommé
1 Tb butter
¼ cup concentrated cooked tomato pulp, or
*   thoroughly drained and sieved canned*
*   Italian plum tomatoes; or cooked chopped*
*   spinach, broccoli, or asparagus tips; or*
*   carrots and onions cooked in butter;*
*   or the meat from cooked chicken or game;*
*   or foie gras or liver paste*
3 egg yolks

Blending the flour with a small wire whip, dribble in the bouillon or consommé, beating vigorously to be sure mixture is perfectly smooth. Add the butter, and beat over moderate heat until sauce has come to the boil and thickened. Put into blender with the vegetable or meat mixture, and the egg yolks; purée several seconds, until perfectly smooth. (Tomato paste, *foie gras,* and liver paste need no blender treatment, of course, since they are already smooth enough.)

Turn into a heavily buttered 1- to 1½-cup baking dish, and proceed as for the preceding plain royal custard.

SOME CLASSIC
CONSOMMÉ COMBINATIONS

Here are just a few of the traditional consommés. It is always rather impressive, I think, to name off something fancy as you serve it forth. Other combinations abound in Escoffier and numerous standard books on classical cuisine. As for proportions, 1 to 2 tablespoons of garnish per serving are usually about right.

Consommé Alsacienne. Beef consommé with thin noodles cooked separately, and accompanied by *profiteroles* stuffed with *foie gras.*

Consommé Ambassadrice. Chicken consommé with three royal custards: plain with minced truffles, red with tomato, and green with a purée of green peas; plus a julienne of mushrooms and breast of chicken.

Consommé Aurore. Consommé flavored with tomato, lightly thickened with tapioca, and garnished with a julienne of chicken breast.

Consommé Brunoise. Beef consommé garnished with very very finely and evenly minced vegetables such as carrots, turnips, leeks, celery, onions, mushrooms, all cooked in butter, seasoned, then added to the soup at the last minute, plus fresh peas if you wish, and herbs, and diced poached tomato.

Consommé Célestine. Beef consommé lightly thickened with tapioca, and garnished with a julienne of crêpes made from a batter containing minced green herbs and/or minced truffles.

Consommé Colbert. Beef consommé with diced cooked vegetables, poached eggs, and minced fresh herbs.

Consommé Crécy. Chicken consommé lightly thickened with tapioca, garnished with lozenge-shaped royal custard made with purée of carrots, and also diced cooked carrots and fresh green herbs.

Consommé Dubarry. Beef or chicken consommé lightly thickened with tapioca, garnished with rounds of plain royal custard, tiny cauliflower flowerets cooked separately in salted water, and fresh green herbs.

Consommé Julienne. Beef consommé garnished with very thin and evenly cut julienne matchsticks of carrots, turnips, leeks or onions, and cabbage cooked slowly in butter with seasonings and a pinch of sugar, plus boiled julienned green beans, whole small green peas, and fresh green herbs.

Consommé Madrilène. Beef consommé brought to the simmer and, for 6 cups, take 2 medium-sized very ripe and red tomatoes, peel them, and push through a sieve into the consommé; simmer a moment, strain, season, and garnish with diced red pimiento or poached diced tomato pulp, Cayenne pepper, and fresh green herbs.

Consommé Mimosa. Chicken consommé garnished wth red, yellow, and green, which can be royal custards with various purées plus a sprinkling of fresh green herbs, or, as an easier alternative, force a hard-boiled egg through the holes of a colander and mix with salt and pepper, finely diced cooked green beans, fresh green herbs, and diced cooked tomato pulp. Sprinkle over each serving.

Consommé Parisienne. Chicken consommé garnished with finely diced carrots, turnips, green beans, and asparagus tips, all cooked separately, and with fresh green peas, plus diced royal custard and fresh green herbs.

Consommé Printanier. Same as Parisienne, but the vegetables are usually formed with a special vegetable-ball cutter to match the size of the peas. No royal custard.

Consommé Royale. Consommé with any type of royal custard or a mixture.

Consommé Windsor. Consommé made from calf's foot bouillon flavored with *herbes à tortue*—basil, bay leaf, marjoram, and thyme. Garnished with the tendons of the calf's foot in julienne, and chicken *quenelles* with hard-boiled eggs. (No *pluches de cerfeuil* or fresh green herbs? I put this in for your amusement and, who knows, you may want to play around with a calf's foot.)

Consommé Xavier. Beef consommé with diced royal custard made from chicken purée, fresh green peas, and fresh green herbs—chervil, if possible.

French fish chowders

From *bouillabaisse* in the Mediterranean, *marmites* and *chaudrées* in the Atlantic, and fresh-water *meurettes, pauchouses,* and *matelotes* in the interior, France abounds in recipes for hearty fish chowders, any one of which is a meal in itself. Praises be, also, for our own New England fish chowder. Whether or not you live where the fish are caught, you can make them anywhere first-class fish are to be found, and here are two chowders, one from each side of the Atlantic.

"Bouillabaisse à la marseillaise" was the first show of our new color series, and we'd filmed part of it in Marseille itself, at the open public market, and at the Criée aux Poissons, the wholesale market on the Old Port—fishwives screaming, the stands teeming with the morning's catch. Although we have *bouillabaisse* in Volume I of *Mastering* as well as in *The French Chef Cookbook,* here it is again, in a slightly different guise, since there is always more to say about it. You cannot, of course, expect to transport all the essences of Marseille to a *bouillabaisse* made in Birmingham, Boston, Buffalo, Boise, or San Bernardino because the fish are different. But you do have those hearty flavors of Provence that give the soup its particular character—the tomatoes, onions, garlic, saffron, olive oil, and herbs. Using these and a strong fish stock, which you can make out of bottled clam juice if you've no fresh trimmings, you can produce a marvelous dish, and rather quickly, too. It doesn't have to be a fancy production; remember that it originated as a simple fisherman's soup and not a high-priced restaurant fantasy.

FISH TO CHOOSE

Whatever fish you use, fresh or frozen, it must smell absolutely fresh, as though it had just swum in from the sea; your nose is the best indicator of this. Under ideal conditions for a *bouillabaisse,* where a real selection of fresh fish is available to you, buy as large a variety of lean (non-oily) fish as you can find, since it is the variety that gives both texture and special flavor to the soup. Flimsy fish like flounder and whiting thicken the broth as they flake into it, while firm fish like halibut, cod, and eel give out gelatin and body. Also, if you are where the fish are caught and cleaned, pick up a large fish frame or two—the bones and head from filleted cod, hake, haddock, or whatever is around. These are frequently thrown out, or given away if you've bought something else to establish friendly relations; it is the frames that make a great fish stock base for any fish soup. Usually, too, fish frames contain enough meat to garnish a simple soup or chowder.

> Bass, both sea bass and fresh-water bass
>   (*bar* or *loup de mer*)
> Cod (*cabillaud*)
> Conger eel—sea eel (*congre*)
> Cusk
> Flounder and sole (*carrelet, plie, limande,*
>   *Saint-Pierre,* etc.)
> Goosefish—monkfish (*baudroie*)
> Grouper
> Grunt
> Haddock
> Hake (equivalents: *merluche, lieu jaune, colin*)
> Halibut (*flétan*)

Ocean whitefish
Perch (*perche*)
Pollack (equivalents: *lieu jaune, églefin jaune,
    merluche blanche*)
Rockfish, any lean edible variety (*poissons de
    roche*)
Sculpin (same family as Mediterranean *rascasse*)
Snapper
Trout, both sea and fresh-water (*truite*)
Whiting (equivalent: *merlan*)
SHELLFISH—these are not necessary, but are
    always welcome: crabs, lobster, mussels,
    scallops

PREPARATION OF THE FISH. Have whole fish cleaned, gilled, scaled; save heads, bones, and trimmings for soup base. For chowder, have all the fish filleted and cut into large serving pieces. For *bouillabaisse*, cut large fish into serving slices, leaving skin on and bones in. Leave small fish whole. Scrub and beard mussels, wash scallops. If you are using live crab or lobster, split them just before cooking; remove sand sacks and intestines.

Soupe de poissons provençale

CLEAR FISH SOUP,
AND SOUP BASE
FOR BOUILLABAISSE

When you are in Mediterranean France you will see far more *soupes de poissons* than you will *bouillabaisses* because the latter is an elaborate production and the former is really a kind of fish bouillon. Ideally you use handfuls of tiny fresh rockfish and boil them up with garlic, onions, leeks, and tomatoes, then strain the rich broth and serve it with a garlic and pepper sauce—*rouille*—and hard-toasted French bread rounds. Actually and most frequently, the soup is made with fresh fish trimmings or fish frames—the head, tail, and bony frame remaining after the fish has been filleted. Whether from fish, frames, or trimmings, it is a marvelously fragrant and hearty brew that could begin an equally hearty meal of roast meat or fish, or pasta.

About 2½ quarts,
for 6 to 8 people

1 cup sliced onions
1 cup sliced white of leek (or 1 cup more onions)

> ½ *cup olive oil*
> 6 *to 8 unpeeled tomatoes,*
> *washed and roughly chopped*
> 4 *to 6 large cloves unpeeled garlic, crushed*
> 8 *sprigs parsley*
> ½ *tsp thyme*
> ¼ *tsp fennel seeds*
> 3 *big pinches saffron threads*
> ½ *tsp dried orange peel*
> *Either: 2 quarts of trimmings from fresh fish*
> *or shellfish, 2½ quarts water, and 1 Tb salt*
> *Or: 1 quart clam juice, 1½ quarts water,*
> *and no salt*
>
> *Equipment: A heavy 8-quart kettle or casserole and*
> *a large sieve or colander*

Stir into the kettle or casserole the onions, leeks, and olive oil; simmer 5 minutes without browning. Stir in the tomatoes and garlic, and cook 5 minutes more. Then add the rest of the ingredients listed and bring to the boil. Skim, and boil slowly, uncovered, for 40 minutes. Strain, pressing juices out of ingredients, correct seasoning, and set aside uncovered. When cool, if you are not proceeding immediately, cover and refrigerate.

Serving suggestions. Serve the soup just as it is, accompanied by rounds of hard-toasted French bread, *croûtes,* page 18, a bowl of freshly grated Parmesan cheese, and the *rouille* described below. Or, you may want to incorporate the *rouille* in the soup to thicken it before serving; to do so, scoop it into a mixing bowl or soup tureen, stir in a cup or so of hot soup by dribbles, then pour in the rest, and decorate with chopped green herbs. A final suggestion to make a more nourishing soup: simmer in the cooked, strained broth 2 cups of diced potatoes or a handful of pasta; or serve *croûtes* and poached eggs in the soup, along with grated cheese and the *rouille.*

Rouille

GARLIC AND
PEPPER SAUCE
FOR FISH SOUPS

This is especially recommended for those times when you are using one or two kinds of fish, such as cod or perch, or scallops only. The bread crumbs will thicken the soup while the egg yolks and oil enrich it. (Although this appeared in the newspaper recipe for the *bouillabaisse* show, I didn't do it on the screen, and some woman wrote in, furiously upbraiding us for showing all those foreigners and those foreign fish that didn't exist over here, when I could have made that sauce instead!)

For 1 cup or so, enough for 6 to 8 people

4 large cloves peeled garlic
2 egg yolks
1 dozen large leaves fresh basil or
    1 Tb dried, or 1 tsp thyme or savory
¼ cup canned red pimientos, drained
½ cup fresh crumbs (pressed down) from
    unsweetened homemade-type white bread
2 to 3 Tb hot soup base
⅔ to ¾ cup olive oil
Drops of hot pepper sauce, or
    a big pinch Cayenne pepper
Salt and pepper to taste

Equipment: A heavy bowl, and a pestle or pounding
    instrument of some sort, like the
    wrong end of a wooden spoon

Purée the garlic into a small, heavy bowl and add the egg yolks and herbs. Pound and stir into a thick sticky paste; pound in the pimientos, incorporating thoroughly. Then pound in the bread crumbs, adding drops of soup base to moisten them. When all is thick, sticky, and smooth, begin adding the oil by droplets, as though you were making mayonnaise —pound and stir, and change from pestle to a small whip while adding the final oil. Beat in the seasonings. Sauce should be thick and strong. Cover airtight until serving time.

Bouillabaisse à la marseillaise

When you have your fish-soup base done, and your fish prepared, the actual making of the bouillabaisse itself is a matter of only 20 minutes or so. Then be ready to serve immediately, although you will find that any leftover soup and fish will be delicious when warmed up the next day. You may wish to add a side dish of boiled potatoes when this is your main course, and follow with a dessert of fresh fruit, or a fruit tart. Serve a young red wine like Beaujolais, or a rosé, or a strong dry white wine like a Chablis or Côtes du Rhône.

For 6 to 8 people
The 2½ quarts prepared, strained, and perfectly seasoned soupe de poissons base, in a kettle large enough to hold all the fish easily
The prepared fish—1 lb. whole fish per person, or ½ lb. filleted fish, as large a variety as possible, although only one kind will do if that is all you can get (list and directions on page 29)
A cup or so rouille, preceding recipe
⅓ cup chopped fresh parsley
2 to 3 croûtes per person—hard-toasted French bread (page 18)

Be sure to provide yourself with a large hot platter for the fish, and a tureen or large serving bowl for the soup, plus a ladle, and wide soup plates.

About 20 minutes before serving, bring soup base to a rolling boil. Add lobsters and crabs if you are using them, and firm-fleshed fish such as halibut or eel, and boil 5 minutes. Then add the other fish (cod, hake, perch, flounder), and the mussels or scallops. Bring rapidly back to the boil, and boil slowly about 5 minutes. Fish is done when it is opaque, and springy rather than squashy—do not overcook. Lift out the fish and arrange it attractively on the platter.

(If you have used only 1 or 2 kinds of fish, the *rouille,* rather than being passed separately, should now go into the soup tureen; correct seasoning of soup and, beating *rouille* with a whip, gradually ladle the hot soup into it until about 2 cups have gone in, then pour in the rest, stirring to blend.)

Ladle a bit of soup over the platter of fish, decorate both soup and fish with chopped parsley, and bring to the table.

To serve, place 2 *croûtes* of French bread into each soup plate, arrange a selection of fish over and around them, and ladle in the soup. Pass the *rouille* separately if you have not already beaten it into the soup.

New England fish chowder

Salt pork, onions, potatoes, milk, and fish are the basic ingredients for a New England fish chowder, and there are as many ways of combining them in the region as there are cooks. One item I do find of great importance is a good fish stock; it gives clout and personality to the chowder, and if I don't have fish trimmings to make it with, I use a little clam juice. Then my general recipe goes like this: blanch and dice salt pork, brown lightly to render its fat, add sliced onions and cook until tender, drain out the fat, and stir in a little flour to make a liaison for the soup later; in go stock and potatoes to simmer until tender, then the fish, milk, and final seasonings. Served with a big dollop of sour cream, a sprinkling of fresh parsley, and buttered croutons, this fish chowder makes a whole meal, and you need nothing but a bowl of fresh fruit or a slice of blueberry pie to top it off. Although wine is certainly not typical of New England chowder parties, we serve a strong dry white like a Rhône or a jug of Pinot Chardonnay (California Chablis).

FISH STOCK FOR CHOWDERS
(For 2 quarts, serving 4 to 6 people)

USING FRESH FISH. Save all fish heads, bones, and tails, and ask for extra if they are available. Remove gills and viscera, and discard; wash all ingredients, and chop into a size to fit a large saucepan or small kettle. You should have 1½ quarts or so. Cover with 2½ quarts of cold water, bring to the boil, skim off scum, and boil slowly 25 to 30 minutes. Strain, and that is all there is to it. When cool, cover and refrigerate or freeze until you are ready to use the stock.

USING LARGE FISH FRAMES—COD, HADDOCK, SEA BASS, HALIBUT. When you have friendly relations with a fish filleting operation, you can often pick up fish frames free. Let us say you have 2 fine fresh fish frames 20 inches long, including head, tail, and some meat. Discard the gills and any viscera, chop up the frames to fit your kettle, wash them, and cover with cold water. Boil slowly 4 to 5 minutes, just to cook the meat in the heads and the meat attached to the bones. Then remove and reserve the meat, return the bones to the pot and boil slowly 20 minutes longer. Strain, and you have both the fish stock and the fish for your chowder.

USING FROZEN FISH. Frozen fish is fine for chowders. Just be very sure it smells perfectly fresh—it is the lovely fresh quality of the fish that makes the chowder.

USING BOTTLED OR CANNED CLAM JUICE. Be careful with canned or bottled clam juice: be sure it tastes fresh and fine, remember it is naturally salty, and use it in diluted form. When you need 1 quart of fish stock, for instance, use 1½ to 2 cups of clam juice and add plain water; start with the smaller amount of clam juice and add a little more if you think it needed.

THE PRESSURE COOKER. The pressure cooker is great when you are in a hurry to cook up a chowder, and is given as an alternate in each step where you can use it in the following recipes.

New England fresh fish chowder

For 4 people, as a main course

4 ounces (a 1½-inch square) lean salt pork diced into ⅜-inch pieces and blanched (boiled 5 minutes in 2 quarts of water, and drained)
3½ cups sliced onions
3 Tb flour
1 cup hot water
4 cups fish stock (preceding recipe)
4 cups sliced "boiling" potatoes
½ tsp thyme or sage
1 large imported bay leaf
¼ tsp freshly ground pepper
Salt as needed
Either: 2 lbs. cod, hake, haddock, halibut, or sea bass fillets (see also list of fish, page 29)
Or: 2 large fresh fish frames
2 or more cups milk
½ cup or more sour cream
2 cups toasted croutons, tossed in butter, salt, and pepper
⅓ cup roughly chopped fresh parsley

The salt pork and onions. Sauté the blanched salt pork for several minutes in a heavy-bottomed 3-quart saucepan (or uncovered pressure cooker), to brown very lightly and to render its fat. Add the onions and cook 8 to 10 minutes, stirring frequently, until tender but not browned (or pressure cook 2 minutes and release pressure). Pour pork and onions into a sieve set over a bowl to drain out fat, then return them to pan. Blend in the flour, adding a little of the pork fat if mixture is stiff, and cook slowly 2 minutes, stirring; remove from heat. Vigorously blend in the cup of hot water, being sure all flour is cleaned from bottom and sides of pan and absorbed into liquid, and beat in the fish stock, blending thoroughly. Add the sliced potatoes, herbs, pepper and salt. Boil slowly about 15 minutes, until potatoes are tender (or pressure cook 2 minutes, and release pressure).

☼ May be completed in advance to this point. Refrigerate uncovered, then cover when cool. Will keep 2 days, if need be.

Adding the fish. Shortly before you are ready to serve, bring chowder base to the simmer, and add the fresh (or frozen) fish; simmer about 5 minutes for fresh fish, just until texture has changed from squashy to lightly springy, or a few minutes longer for frozen fish. (If you are using cooked fish-frame meat, add it when the chowder is at the simmer.) Pour in 2 or more cups of milk—it tends to curdle if added sooner—let come to the simmer, and correct seasoning.

☼ May be completed in advance. Set partially covered on an electric warming device. Or refrigerate uncovered, and cover when cool—chowders often have even more flavor when cooked in advance. Bring just to the simmer before proceeding.

To serve. Ladle chowder into big soup plates, top each with a large spoonful of sour cream, a handful of croutons, and sprinkle the parsley over all.

VARIATIONS

New England fish chowder with salt codfish

Salt codfish and salt pork, as well as onions and potatoes, are old-fashioned staples that are good to have on hand for emergencies. Both the cod and the pork will keep for months in the back of your refrigerator, but you do need to soak cod a good 24 hours before you can put it to use. Once soaked, however, it can be frozen for a few weeks—this seems an odd double preservation, but you may change your plans in 24 hours, and it is useful to know the system. Use the master recipe for chowder, but treat the cod as follows:

<table>
<tr><td>For 4 people,
as a main course</td><td>1 lb. salt cod fillets, de-salted for 24 hours
as directed on page 478
1 quart milk
4 large cloves garlic, puréed
1 imported bay leaf
⅛ tsp crushed peppercorns
Salt, for later, as needed</td></tr>
</table>

Drain the soaked cod and place in a saucepan with the milk, garlic, bay leaf, and peppercorns. Bring slowly to just below the simmer, where liquid is moving but not bubbling. Cover, and maintain at below the simmer for 10 minutes. Set aside, covered, until you are ready to combine it with the rest of the ingredients—but in 10 minutes or so, taste it and stir in a little salt if you feel it necessary.

Cook the pork, onions, and potatoes as described in the master recipe, then add the cod and its cooking liquid. Heat to just below the simmer and maintain at below simmer for 5 minutes to blend flavors. Correct seasoning, remove bay leaf, and serve as in the preceding recipe.

New England fish chowder with finnan haddie or smoked cod or hake. These make delicious chowders. Proceed exactly as for the salt cod, above, but the smoked fish needs no presoaking or de-salting—simply the poaching in milk, as described.

Entrées and appetizers

Cheese appetizers

Croque Monsieur and Croque Madame—
   two French versions of the toasted ham
   and cheese sandwich

Croquettes

Petites fondues frites—cheese croquettes

Appetizers using pastry dough

Petites bouchées au Chester; tartelettes
   Bugnard—cheddar cheese tartlets
Demi-feuilletée—mock puff pastry
   made from pie dough
Amuse-gueule aux anchois—
   anchovy appetizers
Amuse-gueule au fromage—round
   appetizers, with cheese or anchovy filling
Talmouses au fromage—four-cornered
   cheese puff pastries

Quiche Lorraine & Co.—
   all-purpose rules

Quiche Lorraine—cream and bacon quiche
Quiche au gruyère; quiche au fromage—
   Swiss cheese quiche and
   mixed cheese quiche
Other quiches—smoked salmon, eggplant
   and cheese, broccoli or spinach,
   and more ideas

Pastry turnovers and
   covered tarts

Pantin aux épinards, Simone Beck—
   Simca's spinach turnover with ham
   and mushrooms
Other fillings for turnovers

Covered tarts made with
   French puff pastry

Feuilleté au jambon—ham tart made with
   French puff pastry

*I*n the old days of elaborate dinners and kitchens stocked with well-trained personnel, the entrée stood apart from the soup course and the fish, and served to usher in the roast wild boar, pheasant in plumage, or whatever the main course happened to be. In our day those dishes—those handsome pastry concoctions and cheese fantasies—are entrées no more, at least in this country, but they have other uses. They can be the beginning of a dinner party. They can be the main course for a luncheon —what could be more appetizing than a quiche or a puff pastry tart, a salad, and a bottle of wine? Or, made smaller or cut into bite-size pieces, these same entrées serve as elegant cocktail appetizers. It is particularly here, in the realm of the small party-size hors d'oeuvre, that most of us need a little inspiration. Why not, for example, make a *Croque Monsieur*, the delicious French version of a toasted ham and cheese sandwich, cut it into slivers, and serve it hot, pierced with toothpicks? Tiny cheese tartlets are charming on a silver platter; they are easy to prepare ahead, and 15 minutes in the oven makes them ready for serving. Cocktail time is also the time I like to put my puff pastry to work, with small cheese or anchovy mouthfuls, or a single puffed splendor that I bear in on a serving board and cut to order. And the quiche, of course. I like to make a free-form large rectangular one out of Camembert, smoked salmon, lobster, or onions and olives, and cut it, also, to order.

Most of the suggestions here are ones you can do in advance, or freeze, or otherwise arrange in preparation so that you are not harried at the last minute. And that is the way they should be, since being able to present something unusual and attractive to your guests is proof that you honor them. You care about them so much that you have made a real effort to please them, and that spirit immediately makes it a party when people come to your house—not only for them, but for you too.

Cheese appetizers

TWO FRENCH VERSIONS OF THE TOASTED
HAM AND CHEESE SANDWICH

Where do those names come from, *Croque Monsieur* and *Croque Madame? Croque* means "crusty," "crackly," but that seems to be as far as anyone goes except to note that *Croque Monsieur* did not begin to appear in any of the annals of French gastronomy until the early 1900's. Thus it was not made for Louis XIV's wastrel brother in the seventeenth century, but because his name, Monsieur, is a living part of French history, he could well have had an influence. Perhaps the chef who created it felt a crusty toasted sandwich had a masculine appeal, and out popped the catchy title that certainly has given this otherwise quite ordinary combination much of its popularity. *Croque Madame,* which came much later, was presumably softer and more womanly.

Serve either one cut into bite-sized pieces for cocktails. Or serve them whole or halved as a first course, or as luncheon or supper dishes, along with a good bottle of white Riesling wine, and a tossed salad.

Croque Monsieur

HAM AND CHEESE
SANDWICH SAUTÉED
IN BUTTER

Famous recipes like *bouillabaisse* and the upside-down apple tart Tatin tend to take on frills through the years. Who is to say, for example, among the many existing versions, what was the original of *Croque Monsieur?* I suspect it was the simple one —a slice of ham between 2 slices of cheese then sandwiched between 2 slices of fresh white bread, and slowly sautéed in butter. But there are more elaborate methods, such as grating the cheese and blending it with a thick cream sauce, or dipping the assembled sandwich in beaten egg, either sautéing or deep-frying it, and serving it with a cheese sauce. Since there is no known classical rule to guide us, however, the cook should feel free to adapt to circumstance, cheese, and mood. I prefer Mozzarella to Swiss cheese, by the way, since I find its softer consistency blends more meltingly with the ham, the butter, and the bread. But if all I have is stale, hard, under-aged Swiss, I have no hesitation in grating it, and I combine it with Dijon mustard, butter, droplets of *crème fraîche,* pepper, Tabasco, and Worces-tershire. Here is the plain version, with its delicious primal taste of ham, cheese, and bread all browned leisurely in the best butter.

For each sandwich

> *2 thin slices (¼ inch thick) fresh white sandwich bread of best homemade-type quality, such as the Pain de Mie on page 471*
> *2 to 3 Tb clarified butter (butter melted, skimmed, the clear liquid poured off the milky residue—have a small saucepan of it for several sandwiches)*
> *2 thin slices (⅛ inch thick) Mozzarella cheese or rather soft Swiss*
> *1 thin slice (⅛ inch thick) cooked ham, the dimensions of the bread*

For each sandwich, lay a slice of bread on your work surface, brush it with clarified butter, cover with a slice of cheese, a slice of ham, another slice of cheese, then brush one side of the second slice of bread with butter, and lay it buttered side down to top the sandwich. Now press the sandwich together firmly, leaning on it with the palm of your hand. Trim off crusts, and press down again on sandwich.

Film a frying pan with ⅛ inch of the clarified butter, heat to bubbling, and brown the sandwiches rather slowly (2 to 3 minutes) on each side, so the cheese will melt; add more butter as needed. For appetizers, cut the sandwiches in quarters or eighths.

☼ If done ahead, arrange on a baking sheet and set aside, covered with plastic wrap. Uncover and heat in a 375-degree oven 5 minutes or so before serving.

Croque Madame

OPEN-FACED HAM
AND CHEESE
SANDWICH, BAKED
IN THE OVEN

Some say *Croque Madame* is cheese flavoring only, some make it like *Monsieur* but substitute chicken for ham. I like ham and cheese, myself, but you should feel free to do what you wish since there is no set recipe, and the process is the same whatever you choose. Here is an amusing presentation—a giant sandwich made from a fat long-oval loaf of French or Italian bread cut lengthwise. Present it whole, and cut it in crosswise pieces. The beer and cheese topping, by the way, came from my colleague, Simca; she sent me the recipe years ago, and now may not even remember her genial conception.

For each slice

For 3 lengthwise slices of bread about 14 inches long, each making from 4 to 12 or more portions

1 Tb flour (instant-blending flour useful here)
⅓ cup beer
1 Tb Cognac
1 egg
1 cup (3½ to 4 ounces) coarsely grated Swiss cheese
Salt, pepper, and Cayenne pepper
2 to 3 Tb melted butter
3 or 4 thin slices cooked ham

Cut the bread lengthwise into slices about ¾ inch thick and lay on a baking sheet. Dry out for 20 minutes or so in a 350-degree oven, until quite hard and just beginning to color. (If you want to use only 1 slice, for instance, cool, wrap, and freeze the rest for another time.)

Place the flour in a small mixing bowl, gradually beat in the beer, then the Cognac and egg; stir in the cheese, and seasonings to taste, exaggerating a bit on the pepper. Brush the top of each slice of bread with melted butter, cover with slices of ham, then mask completely, out to the edges all around, with the cheese topping.

Bake in upper third of a preheated 450-degree oven 15 to 20 minutes, until cheese topping has puffed and browned.

To serve as a first course, cut in half lengthwise and crosswise, to make 4 pieces. To serve for cocktail appetizers, cut in half lengthwise, then crosswise into pieces of whatever size you wish.

☼ As a first course, serve immediately; for appetizers, cut and reheat as necessary.

Croquettes

Petites fondues frites

CHEESE
CROQUETTES

Croquettes are a carefully flavored very thick sauce containing ground cooked meat, fish, mushrooms, chicken livers, or simply cheese. When the mixture is chilled and firm, you cut it into squares or roll it into balls or sausage shapes, dip these in egg and fresh bread crumbs, and fry to a fine golden brown in very fresh oil or fat. For cocktail mouthfuls, make them about an inch in size; double or triple them for a first course or luncheon dish.

For 24 to 30 1-inch cocktail pieces

Timing note: You will have to start these at least 2 hours before serving, since the initial mixture must chill before being crumbed, and the crumbed croquettes need an hour to set. It is a good idea to make them a day ahead, so you won't feel rushed; then fry at leisure. Fried croquettes may be reheated in the oven.

For the thick sauce base: bouillie
1¼ cups milk
½ cup flour (instant-blending recommended)
*   in a 2½-quart pan*
2 Tb butter
2 egg yolks
1 cup lightly pressed down (3½ to 4 ounces)
*   grated cheese (a mixture of Swiss and*
*   Parmesan, or cheddar)*
½ tsp ground sage
Salt, pepper, nutmeg

For crumbing—panure à l'anglaise— and frying
1 cup flour on a plate
1 egg and 2 egg whites blended on a plate
*   with 1 Tb oil and 1 tsp water*
2 cups fresh white bread crumbs on a plate
Sufficient fresh new oil for frying
*   (I suggest peanut oil)*

Gradually beat the milk into the flour with a wire whip. When perfectly smooth, beat slowly over heat; as sauce comes near the boil it will get lumpy—beat vigorously to smooth it out. It will be very thick. With a wooden spoon, beat in the butter, egg yolks, cheese, and seasonings. Cover surface with plastic wrap and chill an hour or so, or overnight.

When cold and thick, proceed one by one to dip out tablespoon gobs with a rubber spatula, drop into the flour, and roll into a ball or cylinder with your fingers. Drop into beaten egg, lift with 2 forks and let drain, then drop into the crumbs, patting them evenly into entire surface, and remove to a plate. When all are done, refrigerate for an hour, or cover and leave overnight; although you can fry them immediately, it is safer to let the crumbs have time to set.

When you are ready to fry the croquettes, fill a deep fat fryer with 3 inches of fresh new oil (or pour sufficient oil into an electric frying pan, or use a wide saucepan and frying thermometer). Heat oil to 400 degrees, set beside you a roasting pan or tray lined with several layers of crumpled paper, and have a slotted spoon or skimmer at hand. Lower 4 or 5 croquettes into the hot oil and fry 2 to 3 minutes, until nicely browned (larger ones, 3 inches long and 1½ inches wide, will take 5 to 6 minutes to fry). Drain on the paper towels and continue with the rest until all are done.

✿ May be fried an hour or so in advance.

Shortly before serving, arrange the croquettes on a baking sheet and reheat 3 minutes in a 450-degree oven—watch them, since they will break and leak if overheated.

Additions. Blend other ingredients into the sauce base, such as ground or finely minced cooked poultry, fish, chicken livers, ham, mushrooms, plus herb and onion flavoring, more seasonings as you feel necessary, and a little cheese. Use, for instance, ¼ cup of cheese and ¾ cup of other ingredients, then proceed exactly as for the cheese croquettes.

Appetizers using pastry dough

Pastry appetizers are good to have in your repertoire because you can make a lot while you're at it, and keep the extras in the freezer. The tiny tartlet is a specialty of Simca's, and I think her favorite is the easy and delicious little cheese one that we call *Les Tartelettes Bugnard*, after our wonderful chef and teacher, Max Bugnard, who died in the spring of 1974, at the age of ninety-one. You can see him on the back of the book jacket for Volume I of *Mastering*, his white chef's hat nicely floppy in the old manner, his fine French mustache, and his thoughtful look as we *Trois Gourmandes*, Simca, Louisette, and I, ponder our sauce.

Petites bouchées au Chester; tartelettes Bugnard

CHEDDAR CHEESE TARTLETS

For 24 to 30 tartlets, 2½ to 2¾ inches in diameter

The pastry dough recipe on page 602, using
1¾ cups flour (or enough ready-mix
for an 8-inch 2-crust pie)
1 lb. sharp cheddar cheese cut into ¼-inch dice
1⅓ cups heavy cream
2 "large" eggs
Drops of hot pepper sauce or Cayenne pepper,
and Worcestershire sauce
Salt and pepper to taste

Equipment: 24 to 30 buttered tartlet molds
about 2¾ inches top diameter and ½ inch
deep, or muffin tins; a round cookie cutter
3 inches in diameter; baking sheet

Preheat oven to 425 degrees in time for baking.

Roll out dough less than ⅛ inch thick, cut it, and line the buttered molds with it; prick all over with the tines of a fork. Place a tablespoon of diced cheese in each mold. Blend the cream in a bowl with the eggs, and season to taste. Pour a spoonful over the cheese in each mold, and arrange molds on a baking sheet (or 2 sheets, if need be).

☼ May be prepared ahead to this point; cover and refrigerate.

Bake about 15 minutes in the middle level (or upper- and lower-middle levels) of preheated, 425-degree oven, until nicely browned and puffed. Unmold onto cookie sheet, and keep warm. Or you may reheat them.

Other tartlet fillings. In addition to or instead of the diced cheddar cheese, use diced cooked ham, chicken livers, mushrooms, shrimp, crab, or lobster, flaked canned tuna, salmon, or sardines, or canned liver paste, or other cheese such as Roquefort or blue. Then pour on the egg and cream mixture, and bake as for the preceding cheese tartlets.

MOCK PUFF PASTRY

Take an ordinary pie-crust dough, roll it out, spread it with a little soft butter, fold it in three, roll and fold it several more times, and you have created several dozen paper-thin layers of dough sandwiched between several dozen paper-thin layers of butter. Now it's a pastry that will puff up in the oven, because each of the many layers of dough rises separately as it bakes. The result has a deliciously light and flaky quality that makes it ideal for all kinds of little cocktail mouthfuls. Its official name is *demi-feuilletée,* mock puff pastry—*feuille* means leaf or layer. (Classic puff pastry is just another way of achieving the same result, and the recipe is on page 611.)

Demi-feuilletée

———◆———

MOCK PUFF PASTRY
MADE FROM PIE
DOUGH

For about 24 appetizers

Your own chilled pie dough (pâte brisée fine), made from 1¾ cups flour, page 602 (or enough ready-mix dough for an 8-inch 2-crust pie)

4 Tb butter, soft enough to be easily spreadable, but still cold

Roll the dough out in front of you into a rectangle about 20 inches long and 8 inches wide. Spread 2 tablespoons of butter down two thirds of the length of the dough. Then, as though you were folding a business letter, bring the unbuttered bottom third up to the middle, and fold the remaining buttered third face down to cover it; rotate the dough so its top flap opens to your right, like a book. (Each of these roll-outs and fold-ups is called a turn.)

Rapidly roll out the dough again, spread on the remaining 2 tablespoons of butter as before, fold again into three, then wrap and chill the pastry for an hour to firm up the butter and relax the gluten in the dough. Give two final turns, rolling out the dough but omitting the butter; fold as before. Wrap and chill again for an hour, or until you are ready to use it.

✿ Dough may be frozen at this point and will keep perfectly for several months.

Amuse-gueule aux anchois

ANCHOVY
APPETIZERS

Timing note: Plan to work fast here so your dough doesn't lose its chill; once it softens it becomes impossible to work with. In that case stop immediately, shove a pastry sheet under all, and refrigerate for half an hour to firm the dough; then continue. Thus, if this kind of pastry work is new to you, give yourself plenty of time.

For about 2 dozen 3- by 1½-inch pastries that may be cut in half after baking

Amuse-gueule means to amuse the mouth, to give gustatory pleasure in a bite-sized cocktail-appetizer way. This is a piece of French slang that has managed to enter the *salon,* since *gueule* is an inelegant word: it means an animal's maw. Another popular example of the maw is *"Ta gueule!"*—ordering you to shut your trap or else. So you pull a long face, *vous faites la gueule,* and are then prompted to have yourself a *gueuleton*—to grossly overindulge at the cocktail party. You wake up the next morning with a *gueule de bois,* wooden mawed—which only serves you right. But if you had indulged in these *amuse-gueule* (always written in the singular however many you eat), made of French puff pastry, it would have been worth your while. They have a marvelous melt-in-the-mouth effect when you bite into them: you expect to find some resistance, but your mouth fills with the tender buttery leaves of pastry until the surprise ending is revealed to you—the anchovy.

The preceding chilled pastry
Dijon-type prepared mustard
Three 1¾-ounce cans flat anchovy fillets
    packed in olive oil, or sufficient de-salted
    anchovies of your own make, page 437
Egg glaze (1 egg beaten with 1 tsp water)

Equipment: A buttered baking sheet, wax paper,
    a pastry brush, a table fork

This first recipe has illustrated
directions for making
amuse-gueule the easiest way—
in a long rectangle, which you cut
like this after baking.

They can also be made
in individual rounds
like these—dressier but longer
in the construction. Directions
for this method, filling the pastry
with cheese or anchovy begin on
page 53, following the master
recipe.

Roll the chilled pastry into a rectangle about 20 by 8 inches, cut in
half crosswise, and chill one piece for your second batch.

Butter the baking sheet and place the wax paper over two thirds of its
width, to help you flip over the pastry when the time comes. Roll the remaining piece of dough into a rectangle about 8 by 10 inches, and ¼
inch thick.

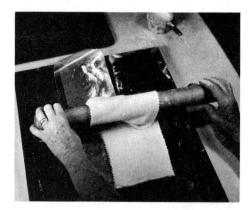

Roll the pastry up on your pin,
and unroll it so half its width
rests on the paper—this half is the
one you will flip over to cover
the filling later.

Rapidly paint this side
of the dough with a light coating
of cold water, and proceed
at once with the next steps,
so dough will not soften.

Spread finger-shaped blobs of
mustard ⅛ inch thick down
half the width of the pastry
(the part not on the wax paper),
spacing the blobs 1½ inches
apart.

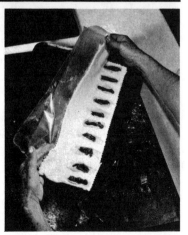

Lay an anchovy over each blob of
mustard; then, using the paper
to help you, flip this plain side
over onto the anchovy side,
covering it completely. You
now have a long, narrow
rectangle of pastry.

With your finger, press edges of dough rectangle together around the
3 sides where they join. Then, feeling for the lines of anchovies with your
fingers, press dough to seal it together between them.

With the tines of a table fork, press decorative sealing marks around the 3 edges, and between the anchovies.

Cover and refrigerate the pastry for 30 minutes before baking; this rests the dough and minimizes its baking out of shape. (Prepare second half of dough, if you are using it, in the same way, and on the same baking sheet or on a separate one, whichever is easier for you.)

☼ Pastry may be refrigerated for a day, or covered airtight and frozen for several weeks. You may bake it in its frozen state.

Preheat oven to 450 degrees. Just before baking, paint top of pastry with egg glaze; in one minute, paint on a second coat. With the back of a sharp-pointed knife, make decorative crosshatch marks through the glaze.

Baking. Set baking sheet in upper-middle level (or upper- and lower-middle levels if you have 2 sheets) of preheated oven. Bake about 20 minutes, until pastry has puffed and browned; turn thermostat down to 350 degrees and bake 10 to 15 minutes more, until edges feel firm and crisp.

☼ If you are not ready to serve, slide pastry onto a rack and keep in turned-off oven with door ajar, or in a warming oven at around 120 degrees. Although you may let the pastry cool and reheat before serving, it is at its best when freshly made. However, if you must bake a day or so ahead, let cool, wrap airtight, and freeze; to reheat, place on a buttered baking sheet in a 450-degree oven, then turn oven off to let pastry thaw and recrisp for 5 minutes or so.

Other fillings. Use strips of smoked salmon or boneless and skinless sardines or herring fillets instead of anchovies, laying them on top of the mustard blobs. Or use fingers of sharp cheddar, Roquefort, or blue cheese.

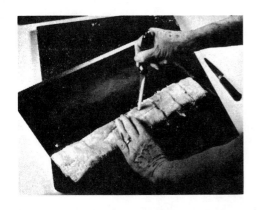

To serve. Using a serrated knife, cut the pastry strip crosswise, between the anchovies. Cut each of these pieces crosswise, in half, if you wish.

Amuse-gueule au fromage

ROUND APPETIZERS, WITH CHEESE OR ANCHOVY FILLING

Here, in brief illustrated form, is the system for making round appetizers.

Use a round blob of mustard and top with a ball of cheese or a curled anchovy. Roll the dough into a wide rectangle ¼ inch thick, and paint surface with cold water.

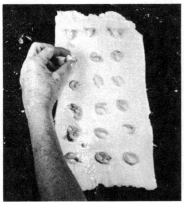

Space blobs of Dijon-type prepared mustard about an inch in diameter, ¼ inch thick, 3 inches apart on the dough. Cover with teaspoon-size balls of Roquefort, blue cheese, or sharp cheddar—or a rolled anchovy fillet.

Roll a second sheet of dough up on your pin and unroll gently over the first.

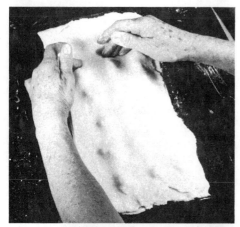

With fingers, press dough all
around cheese blobs to seal.
(If dough has softened, chill it.)

Choose a fluted round cutter
about 2½ inches in diameter
(and one slightly smaller for next
step) . Cut out the cheese-blob
sections of the dough.

Transfer the cut pastries to a
wet baking sheet (wet to make
the dough grip, so it can rise) .
Press smaller cutter upside down
into pastries, letting its rounded
top seal the 2 layers of dough
firmly.

Chill, glaze, and bake as for the preceding anchovy appetizers.

Talmouses au fromage

FOUR-CORNERED
CHEESE PUFF
PASTRIES

Plop a spoonful of filling in the center of a puff-pastry square, gather the four corners together in a point on top, and your pastry bakes into the shape of a bishop's hat. At least that is what the medieval bakers, *les Talemeliers,* of Sarcelles, north of Paris, are said to have offered the archbishop on occasion. The dictionary of the Académie des Gastronomes suggests this possibility, anyway, also remarking that the *Talmouses* of Saint-Denis, a Paris suburb, were celebrated throughout pre-revolutionary France. As is usual with recipes from ancient history, many versions have come down to us, some of which call for a thick *bouillie* sauce filling, like that for the croquettes on page 45, while others use *choux* pastry. Sometimes the flavoring is only cottage cheese, or cottage cheese and Brie cheese mixed. The first *Talmouses* I had were in a restaurant in the little hill town of Biot, in Provence, and were filled with Roquefort cheese. To me, that is a perfect combination, and I like the simplicity of it—cheese, egg, and sour cream. The idea, however, is more important here than the actual recipe. The following is for cocktail-size *Talmouses;* make them twice as big if they are a first or main course, and serve two or three per person.

For about 4 dozen
cocktail pastries
1½ inches across
when baked

¼ cup (2 ounces) Roquefort or blue cheese
1 egg beaten in a small bowl
Drops of Worcestershire sauce
Salt and pepper
1 Tb sour cream or crème fraîche, more
if needed
The chilled mock puff-pastry dough, page 48

For the filling, cream the cheese with half the egg, season to taste, and thin out a little with the cream, to make a fairly thick paste that holds its shape. Roll the dough out into a rectangle 8 by 24 inches and ¼ inch thick. Cut it into 2-inch squares.

Place a teaspoon of cheese mixture in the center of each square. Moisten the 4 corners of each with cold water.

Pick up 2 opposite corners of a square in your fingers and press them together.

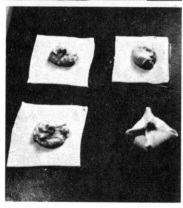

Then gather the opposite corners and press together over the first. You now have a neat package. Continue rapidly with the rest.

Arrange the pastries on a buttered baking sheet, cover loosely, and chill 30 minutes before baking.

☼ May be refrigerated for a day or two before baking; may be covered airtight and frozen, then baked in their frozen state.

Baking. Preheat oven to 450 degrees. When ready to bake, blend a teaspoon of water into the remaining egg and brush over the pastries; in 1

minute, glaze again. Bake 12 to 15 minutes, until puffed and brown —the corners spread open during baking, but should stay upright to hold the filling as pictured here. (For details on holding, freezing, and reheating, see directions for Anchovy Appetizers, page 52.)

Quiche Lorraine & Co.

Open-faced tarts for entrées and appetizers

"French cooking is not complicated," I keep telling those who insist it is. At least it does not have to be. I think it is the foreign-sounding names of dishes that often strike terror in the hearts of innocent cooks. *Quiche Lorraine* is an example. I used to think most people knew all about it, but I was wrong. Just before we did our show on the subject, we were setting out for the local market as our neighbor, Jean, was getting into her car. When she saw us she sprang out of it. "Oh, Julia and Paul!" she said rapturously. "Last night I made a quiche, my first quiche. It was so good. Everyone was so impressed." "Maybe next time," remarked her thirteen-year-old son, coming up behind her, "she'll make the pie dough, too." She kicked him in a motherly way, and we went on to discuss ready-made pie shells. She was so immensely pleased with herself and her quiche, and left in such a glow of happiness, it became clear to me that frozen store-bought ready-made shells would definitely be a part of our show. After all, the important thing is to make and bake a quiche, and to get that thrill of accomplishment. Homemade pie shells can come later.

Although quiches are in two other books of mine, and appeared twice on television, I make no apologies at all for repeating them here. There is always more to say in the way of recent observations and techniques, and remedies for trouble spots noted by readers and viewers. But, and most important to me, quiches and pastry in general are fundamental to French cooking. So many simple ingredients can appear exotic merely by being dressed up in a pastry crust, like a meat loaf masquerading as a *Pâté en Croûte*. Or take the blob of cheddar cheese that turns into an *Amuse-gueule*, and, in this instance, baby's custard transformed into a *Quiche Lorraine*. As soon as you perceive that a quiche is only a custard plus a flavoring, you can make one out of anything you want. A custard means liquid blended with eggs, and when this combination heats in the oven it coagulates into a soft mass that holds its shape. Since the coagulation process happens automatically, quiches are the most foolproof of the fancy-sounding foods, and you can make yourself a foolproof rule for the proportions. Here it is:

ALL-PURPOSE QUICHE FILLING PROPORTIONS

For 8- to 9-inch shells *3 "large" eggs broken into a 4-cup measure*
¼ tsp salt
Pinch each of pepper and nutmeg
Either: For liquid quiches like cheese or bacon—
½ cup cream, or enough to fill measure to
the 1¼-cup level
Or: For quiches with solid or puréed fillings like
vegetables or shellfish—½ to ¾ cup cooked
spinach, chicken livers, crab, or etc., plus
¼ cup liquid (cream, milk, or etc.), or
enough to fill measure to the 1½- to
1¾-cup level

Beat all ingredients together in the measure with a fork or whisk; taste, and add more seasonings if needed. Cover and refrigerate until you are ready to bake the quiche, then beat briefly to reblend ingredients. If, for instance, you find you need more liquid to fill the shell, another 2 to 3 tablespoons of cream will not upset the proportions. But if you need more than that, add also another egg.

PIE SHELLS

Notice most people eating even Mother's own apple pie, and you will usually see them leave the bottom crust on the plate. It's soggy; that's why. But if you prebake your shell first, whether it is homemade or store-bought, the bottom is already cooked when the filling goes in, and you get a fully edible shell all around as well as underneath. Directions for prebaking shells are on page 608, for making your own dough, on page 602, and for forming your own shells, on page 606. Baked pie shells freeze perfectly, and you take them right from the freezer, fill them, and set them in the oven.

MASTER RECIPE FOR QUICHES

All quiches are baked in the same way, and they all take 30 to 35 minutes in the oven. Thus you may time your serving almost exactly when you have all your ingredients at the ready. Here, if you have never done one before, are detailed directions; after you have made a quiche or two you should never have to look at the recipe again. You will confidently throw your filling together, pour it into the shell, shove it into the oven, and come back for your quiche when the kitchen timer sounds its klaxon.

Quiche Lorraine

———◆———

CREAM AND BACON
QUICHE

The original genuine classic *Quiche Lorraine* has no cheese, although many people add it. Do try it in its original form because I think you will find, as I do, that the subtle flavor of bacon blended with eggs, cream, and butter is so wonderfully good it is a shame to mask it with other things.

Serving and menu suggestions. Serve a quiche as a first course, and pick a menu containing no other eggs, cream, or pastry; for instance, you might follow the quiche with something like a roast, broiled or baked fish, or a stew, and a fruit dessert. Quiches are lovely luncheon dishes, along with a salad, or artichokes, or fresh asparagus; again, have a simple dessert of fruit or sherbet. Dry white wines go with quiches, such as Chablis, Pouilly Fumé, Pouilly Fuissé, or Pinot Blanc. (For cocktails, cut the quiche into a dozen or more thin wedges and let guests serve themselves on plates or small cocktail napkins; see also the rectangular shapes that are easy to serve in small pieces, page 609.)

For 4 to 6 people,
as a first
or main course

Timing: 35 minutes
at 375 degrees

*An 8- to 9-inch prebaked pie shell on a buttered
baking sheet, pages 602–608*
5 or 6 thick slices bacon, cooked and crisp
*The 1¼ cups all-purpose quiche filling
(3 "large" eggs, ¼ tsp salt, pinches of pepper
and nutmeg, and about ½ cup heavy cream)*
1½ Tb butter

Preliminaries. Preheat oven to 375 degrees in time for baking, and place rack in upper-middle level. Prepare the ingredients listed. Choose an appropriate serving dish or board.

Assembling. About 40 minutes before you wish to serve, crumble the bacon into the bottom of the pastry shell, beat up the filling to be sure all is blended, and pour enough into the shell to come ¼ inch from its rim at its lowest point. It is better to use too little than too much, since an overfill will swell up and spill a large part of your custard into the oven. Hold the butter over the top of the quiche, cutting it into quarter-inch bits and dropping them onto the surface.

Baking. Immediately place the quiche (on a baking sheet) in the pre-heated oven, and set your timer for 15 minutes. Normally the quiche mixture will slowly begin to set, rising to about double as it does so; when it has risen completely, in 30 to 35 minutes, and the top is nicely browned, it is done. You can double check by plunging a skewer down through the center of the quiche, and the skewer should emerge as clean as it went in—if bits of wet custard cling to it, bake 3 or 4 minutes longer.

Trouble-shooting. When you are new to quiches, or have any doubts about your pie shell, keep a roll of aluminum foil handy and take quick peeks at the quiche after 15 minutes of baking, and every 3 minutes or so, until you can see that the filling has begun to swell and then to set—a very very gentle shake of the oven rack will make the filling sway like custard rather than ripple like liquid. Until it has set (and sways like custard) it can spill over at a low spot in the shell. If you think there is the slightest chance of an accident, rapidly slip a double thickness of foil under the shell at that point and press it against the edge of the quiche, then brace it with a bread pan, a pyrex jar, or anything fireproof and handy. You can almost always avoid trouble when you are aware of what might happen and are ready to take bold instant action.

Serving. When the quiche is done, you can keep it puffed and warm in the turned-off oven with door ajar for 5 to 10 minutes, but after the quiche has baked its puff gradually subsides. To serve, slide it onto a serving dish or board, and cut into wedges, like a pie.

Reheating. You can reheat a quiche, but it will never puff again.

Cold quiche. Cold quiche can be delicious picnic food, served with a salad, or with pickles and cold cuts.

Frozen quiche. You can wrap baked quiche airtight and freeze, then re-heat on a buttered baking sheet. It will never puff again nor will it ever be the magnificent creation it was when it first appeared, but it will be pleasantly edible, particularly if the crust was of your own making. A topping of fresh grated Swiss cheese and dribble of melted butter could freshen it, however, browning nicely as the quiche reheats in a 425-degree oven.

Quiche au gruyère; quiche au fromage

SWISS CHEESE QUICHE AND MIXED CHEESE QUICHE

The usual combination here is Swiss cheese, milk or light cream, plus the usual eggs and seasonings. However, I find the quiche an elegant way to use up miscellaneous cheese bits of any type, including blue cheese, Roquefort, Gorgonzola, Camembert, Brie, Liederkranz, cream cheese, cottage cheese, cheddar, Parmesan, and so forth, and you may mix them if you wish. Actually it is a good idea to grate together leftover bits of cheddar, Swiss, and other like cheeses, and freeze them in a covered jar; this horde can also serve for grated cheese toppings on baked dishes. Lump the blue cheese family together and freeze separately, and do the same for the Camembert and Brie type of soft cheese, since you might wish special effects. You may, of course, add crumbled cooked bacon to the quiche filling, but I do think you need it only when the cheese is too mild and uninteresting to stand by itself. Here is the plain Swiss cheese quiche, followed by suggestions for other cheeses.

For 4 to 6 people

Timing: 35 minutes at 375 degrees

An 8- to 9-inch prebaked pie shell on a buttered baking sheet, page 602
The 1¼ cups all-purpose quiche filling (3 "large" eggs, ¼ tsp salt, pinches of pepper and nutmeg, and about ½ cup milk or light cream)
About 3 ounces (¾ cup lightly pressed down) coarsely grated Swiss cheese
1½ Tb butter, cut into ¼-inch bits

Preheat oven and have all ingredients ready about 40 minutes before serving. Strew two thirds of the grated cheese in the bottom of the shell, pour on the filling liquid, strew rest of cheese and the butter bits on top. Bake in upper-middle level of oven for 30 to 35 minutes, or until filling has puffed and browned.

OTHER CHEESE COMBINATIONS

Use the same proportions and ingredients, but substitute for the Swiss cheese one of the following:

Mixed cheese. ¾ cup grated mixed cheese of any sort.

Blue, Roquefort, or Gorgonzola cheese. These are strong, and you use ¼ to ⅓ cup; or make it blue and half a cup of cream cheese or cottage cheese.

Cottage cheese. ¾ cup cottage cheese plus dashes of Worcestershire and Tabasco, plus some herbs like 2 Tb fresh chives, or very finely minced scallion and parsley, or ½ tsp dried oregano, thyme, or sage.

Camembert, Brie, or Liederkranz. ¾ cup cheese plus extra grinds of pepper and dashes of Tabasco, and 2 to 3 Tb minced fresh parsley if you wish.

OTHER QUICHES

Again, use the same proportions as those given in the master recipe for *Quiche Lorraine,* page 59, with the 1¼ to 1½ cups all-purpose filling that includes 3 eggs, milk or cream, salt and pepper, and the special ingredients that follow.

Quiche au saumon fumé (Smoked salmon quiche). Smoked salmon makes an extremely good quiche, and is an idea for the leftover scraps when you have been fortunate enough to slice up a whole side of it. Save all bits, trimmings, and scrapings from the salmon, and keep them frozen until it is time for your quiche. Just a quarter cup of minced salmon is enough—more can make too strong a taste. Strew the salmon bits in the bottom of your quiche shell, pour on the 1¼ cups all-purpose filling (made with heavy cream), adding some minced fresh parsley or dill, if you wish, dot with butter, and bake as usual in a 375-degree oven for 30 to 35 minutes.

Quiche à l'aubergine

EGGPLANT AND
CHEESE QUICHE

This pleasantly unusual quiche shows you what you can do with the general idea. You could serve it with a salad of sliced tomatoes and watercress, or with a fine tomato sauce, such as the one on page 351, plus a tossed green salad.

For an 8- to 9-inch
quiche

A fine shiny firm eggplant (½ pound should
be enough, but if larger, turn the sautéed
extra amount into the eggplant caviar
on page 400)
½ tsp salt
Olive oil
2 Tb minced shallots or scallions
1 clove garlic, finely minced or puréed
3 Tb fresh chopped parsley
¼ tsp thyme, or an herb mixture
like Italian seasoning
⅓ cup grated Swiss and Parmesan cheese combined
The all-purpose quiche filling (3 "large" eggs,
cream, pepper, and salt if needed)
An 8- to 9-inch prebaked pie shell set on a
buttered pastry sheet, pages 602–608
1½ Tb butter, cut into ¼-inch bits

Preparing the eggplant. Peel the eggplant and cut into ¾-inch dice. Toss in a bowl with the salt, and let stand 20 to 30 minutes, to drain out excess moisture and to neutralize bitterness. Drain, and pat dry with paper towels. Heat a ⅛-inch layer of olive oil in a large frying pan. When very hot but not smoking, add the eggplant; toss and turn frequently for 5 to 8 minutes, until tender and very lightly browned. Toss in the shallots or scallions and garlic, shaking pan over heat for a minute to cook them, then turn the eggplant into a large sieve set over a bowl to drain off excess oil. (You will want 1 loosely packed cup for your quiche, approximately.)

Baking the quiche. Preheat oven to 375 degrees. Turn the sautéed eggplant into the pastry shell and delicately blend with the parsley, herbs, and half the cheese. Pour over it the filling mixture—as much as will come to within ⅛ inch of rim of shell—spread on the remaining cheese, and the butter. Bake 30 to 35 minutes in upper-middle level of preheated oven, until puffed and brown.

Quiche aux
brocoli ou
aux épinards

BROCCOLI OR
SPINACH QUICHE

½ to ¾ cup cooked chopped broccoli or spinach
  (squeezed dry if spinach)
2 Tb butter
1 Tb sliced shallots or scallions
Salt, pepper, and a pinch of nutmeg
The all-purpose quiche filling (3 "large" eggs,
  cream, salt, and pepper)
¼ cup grated Swiss and Parmesan cheese
An 8- to 9-inch prebaked pie shell set on a
  buttered pastry sheet, pages 602–608
1½ Tb butter, cut into ¼-inch bits

Preheat oven to 375 degrees. Sauté the broccoli or spinach in the butter with the shallots, turning and tossing over moderate heat for several minutes to impregnate with the butter; season carefully with salt, pepper, and nutmeg. Let cool to tepid, turn into a 4-cup measure, blend in the eggs, and enough cream to come to the 1½- to 1¾-cup mark. Season again, blend in three-quarters of the cheese, and pour into pastry shell. Top with the rest of the cheese, and the butter. Bake 30 to 35 minutes in upper-middle level of preheated oven, until puffed and brown.

OTHER QUICHE IDEAS

Use the broccoli or spinach system for chicken livers or mushrooms, quartering them and sautéing in butter with shallots or scallions. Or warm peeled and cooked asparagus tips in butter and seasonings; these you can arrange attractively in the shell, pour the quiche filling over, and sprinkle with cheese. Treat cooked crab, lobster, and shrimp the same way, warming them in butter and seasonings before combining them with the filling. Onion quiche is marvelous too; adapt the *Pissaladière* idea on page 486, mixing the cooked onions with eggs and cream, and decorating the quiche with olives and anchovies. Anything goes, in other words.

Pastry turnovers and covered tarts

Pantin aux épinards, Simone Beck

SIMCA'S SPINACH
TURNOVER WITH
HAM AND
MUSHROOMS

Perhaps you saw my friend Simca do this attractive pastry on "The Spinach Twins," when we filmed her in action while she created it one spring afternoon in our French kitchen. She uses a filling of spinach creamed with onions, and makes her turnover into a hearty main course by adding mushrooms, ham, and cheese. She serves it with a creamy cheese sauce, a platter of sliced tomatoes and cucumbers garnished with small black olives, and a fresh white wine like a Chablis or Riesling, or a rosé.

Amount of dough. I am suggesting more dough than you need here, since I find it difficult to work with too little, and any extra can go into the freezer to be used again or to be combined with more dough of the same type.

For a 16- by 5-inch
pastry, serving 6 as
a main course

2 Tb butter
1 cup minced onions
1½ lbs. fresh spinach (or 2 packages frozen leaf spinach—20 ounces)
½ cup flour
1⅔ cups milk; more if needed
1 "large" egg
Salt, white pepper, and nutmeg
½ to ¾ cup light cream
⅓ cup coarsely grated Swiss cheese (1½ ounces)
Chilled pastry dough:
    Either: A pâte brisée
    (3 cups flour, 2¼ sticks butter, 4½ Tb lard or shortening, 1¾ tsp salt, and ½ to ¾ cup water, page 602)
    Or: Enough ready-mix for two 9-inch pies
Optional additions to filling (one or all of the following) :
    ½ cup diced sautéed ham
    ½ cup diced sautéed mushrooms

> *½ cup diced Swiss cheese*
> *Egg glaze: 1 egg beaten in a small bowl*
> *with 1 tsp water*
>
> *Equipment: The usual saucepans, whips, spatulas,*
> *a baking sheet, dough-rolling setup, pastry*
> *brush, a kettle for boiling the spinach, and a*
> *platter or board long enough to hold a*
> *16-inch tart 5 inches wide*

Onion flavoring for spinach and sauce. Melt the butter in a medium-sized heavy-bottomed saucepan, blend in the onions, cover and cook slowly about 10 minutes, stirring occasionally, until onions are tender and translucent but not browned. While onions are cooking, prepare the spinach.

Cooked chopped spinach. For fresh spinach, wash it, strip off stems, boil leaves in a large kettle of water 2 to 3 minutes until limp, refresh in cold water, and drain; for frozen spinach, thaw in a large basin of cold water, and drain. By handfuls, squeeze out as much water from the spinach as you can, chop fine with a stainless steel knife, and scrape into another medium-sized heavy saucepan that is stainless or of enamelware. Stir half the cooked onions into the spinach, and set aside to await the following sauce.

The sauce base. Stir the ½ cup of flour into the first saucepan with the remaining cooked onions. Using a wire whip, vigorously beat in the milk by droplets at first, to blend with flour; then add in a steady stream. Set over moderately high heat, stirring and reaching all over bottom of pan until sauce begins to thicken. Then beat vigorously to smooth out floury lumps. Boil 1 minute, stirring and reaching all over bottom of pan. Sauce will be very thick. Remove from heat, and break the egg into the hot sauce; beat it in. Beat in ¼ teaspoon salt, several grinds of white pepper, and a speck of nutmeg. Stir a quarter of the sauce (about ½ cup) into the spinach; then complete the sauce as follows.

Finishing the sauce soubise au Gruyère (to serve with the turnover). Blend ½ cup of the cream into the sauce and simmer slowly 10 to 15 minutes or so, stirring frequently, and adding a little more cream if sauce thickens too much—it should coat a spoon lightly. Correct seasoning, and remove from heat. To prevent a skin from forming on the surface while the sauce is waiting, clean sauce off sides of pan with a rubber spatula, and spread the grated cheese over the surface.

Finishing the spinach—spinach creamed with onions. While the previous sauce is cooking, stir ¼ tsp salt into the spinach, bring to the simmer, cover, and cook slowly, stirring frequently, for 8 to 10 minutes or until spinach is tender. Very carefully correct seasoning and set aside uncovered. If you are to assemble the tart at once, stir over cold water to cool the spinach quickly.

Forming the turnover. Preheat the oven to 400 degrees if you are to bake immediately. Lightly butter a baking sheet at least 12 by 20 inches, and lay a sheet of wax paper over one third its length—this will help you turn the pastry dough over the filling later. Work speedily from now on, so dough will not soften. Roll dough into a rectangle about ⅛ inch thick, and trim with a knife or pastry wheel to 12 by 18 inches. Reserve dough scraps. Roll dough rectangle up on your pin, and unroll it so that half of its width rests on the wax paper and the other half on the baking sheet. The half of the dough on the sheet is the bottom of the turnover. Leaving a ½-inch border of dough all around, spread bottom of turnover with a ¼-inch layer of cooled spinach. Spread on top of this the optional ham, mushrooms, and cheese; cover with another ¼-inch layer of cooled spinach. Paint the half-inch border of dough with cold water, and, using the wax paper to help you, flip the other half of the dough over the filling. Seal edges by pressing with the balls of your fingers. (If at this point the dough has become soft and sticky, refrigerate it and dough scraps for 20 minutes or so, then continue.)

To further seal the dough, roll the three joined sides up against the turnover, and press a design upon them with the tines of a table fork. Cut thin strips or fancy shapes out of dough scraps, paint top of turnover lightly with cold water, and affix the decorations. Spacing them one third the way from each end of turnover, poke 2 steam holes ¼ inch in diameter through top of dough into filling, and circle with thin strips of dough.

✿ May be prepared ahead to this point. Cover with wax paper or plastic and refrigerate for a day, or freeze for several weeks. (If you freeze, of course, you would also have to cover and freeze the sauce base.) If frozen, you may proceed from freezer to oven, but allow 5 to 15 minutes additional baking time.

Baking: 30 to 40 minutes at 400 degrees. About 40 minutes before serving time, paint top of dough with the egg glaze, wait 1 minute, and paint with a second coat. Draw the point of a knife or the tines of a fork over the glaze into the dough to make close crosshatch marks all over surface.

Immediately set in upper middle of preheated oven and bake until pastry is crisp and brown; filling should be bubbling up at steam holes, and you can smell its welcoming aroma. If you are not quite ready to serve, turn off oven and leave door ajar, or leave in a warming oven at 120 degrees; but do not overcook and do not overwarm or you will lose the fresh color and taste of the spinach.

Serving. Bring the *sauce soubise* to the simmer, stirring; thin out again with cream or milk if necessary. Turn into a warm sauce bowl. Slide the turnover onto a board or platter, and cut slices straight across from one of the short sides.

Leftovers. You can wrap and refrigerate or freeze leftover tart, and reheat it; or serve cold tart for a picnic lunch.

OTHER FILLINGS FOR TURNOVERS

Use the preceding system for other cooked vegetables like broccoli or Swiss chard. Here is the same general idea with the same type of sauce for a cheddar cheese tart, and you can adapt it as an all-purpose technique for Roquefort cheese, chicken livers, shellfish, and so forth. I am particularly partial to the cheese tart for cocktails; I bring it in whole, on a board, and cut across its rectangular shape, making thin pieces that I again cut into halves or thirds.

Pantin au Chester

CHEDDAR CHEESE TURNOVER

Cheese note: Cheddar, Cheshire, and Chester cheeses are very much alike. In France you would be most likely to find Chester, as it is made there in the Lot in a deliberate effort to reproduce the old English Cheshire, and in America you would rely on the good native cheddar. Use any of the three for this recipe, and use the same proportions for pastry dough and filling and the same baking method described in the preceding recipe, page 65. Make the filling as follows:

For a 16- by 5-inch pastry

⅓ cup flour
¾ to 1 cup milk
2 Tb butter
¼ to ⅓ cup heavy cream
1 whole egg and 1 egg yolk
Salt, nutmeg, drops of Worcestershire or
  Tabasco sauce, white pepper

8 to 10 ounces sharp (cheddar, Cheshire, or Chester)
cheese cut into ⅜-inch dice

Bouillie sauce base. Place the flour in a medium-sized heavy-bottomed saucepan. Using a wire whip, beat in dribbles of milk until you have added ¾ cup. Add the butter, and stir over moderately high heat, beating vigorously as sauce comes to the boil, to smooth it out. Sauce will be very thick; beat in dribbles of heavy cream and/or milk, simmering, to thin out the sauce slightly—it should coat a spoon heavily, and you should let it boil slowly for several minutes, stirring all the while, to cook the flour. Then remove from heat, at once beat in the whole egg, then the yolk. Season very carefully with ¼ teaspoon or so of salt, a pinch of nutmeg, Worcestershire or Tabasco, and a good amount of white pepper. (If not to be used at once, clean off sides of pan, and float a thin film of cream on top to prevent a skin from forming.)

When you have rolled out the pastry, spoon half the sauce over the bottom of the turnover, spread on the diced cheese, and cover with the rest of the sauce. Proceed to finish the tart and bake it as described on page 67.

Covered tarts made with French puff pastry

Feuilletés

While a turnover made with *pâte brisée* pie dough is a lovely creation, one made from French puff pastry is even more special, since the high rise of the dough is as dramatic as its texture is light and airy. To make one, use either the regular puff-pastry recipe on page 611 or the mock puff pastry made from pie dough on page 48. Again, as with plain dough, I would far rather have too much to work with than too little, and have specified more than you need. This is because you must roll the dough at least ¼ inch thick or you will not get the puff you should have—a rule I learned to my dismay during our show "Flaky Pastry." The *feuilleté* I removed from the oven to take to the dining room was rather flat, but the standby, that went in later but no one saw, puffed like a dream. I had rolled the first one too thin, and therefore I reaped me my woe, but did learn my lesson.

This is how a successful *feuilleté* should look, although seeing it from above as you do here, it does not reveal its full puffy glory.

Spelling note: A *feuilleté* is a noun with single "é," but in *pâte feuille-tée* it is an adjective modifying *la pâte,* and has the "ée" ending. Same with *bouillie,* where the "e" refers to the unwritten but understood *la sauce; bouilli* without the "e," however, refers to *le boeuf* that has been boiled. Many are the mistakes on those two, including some committed in print by a certain Mrs. J. C.

Feuilleté au jambon

———◆———

HAM TART MADE
WITH FRENCH
PUFF PASTRY

When you are working with puff pastry, you are safest, I think, to have a fairly solid filling that will not run during baking. The puff pastry swells in all directions, and might push a loose filling out. At least that has been my experience, and now I don't take any chances. The binder here, then, is our familiar *bouillie,* but it is thicker than in the previous recipes because you boil the sauce again, after the egg has gone in.

Ham seems most appropriate as a main-course luncheon or supper dish, and you could serve a white Burgundy or Pinot Blanc with it, followed by a combination salad or a lone vegetable, such as fresh string beans tossed with butter and lemon, or fresh asparagus or artichokes. Dessert could be fresh pears, a fruit compote, or sherbet, and walnut wafers.

The filling

For a rectangular
tart 16 inches long,
serving 4 to 6 people

2 Tb flour
About ¾ cup light cream
1 whole egg and 1 egg yolk
Salt and pepper
¼ cup (about 1 ounce) coarsely grated
Swiss cheese
About 6 ounces (1½ cups) cooked ham
2 Tb butter
½ Tb minced shallots or scallions

The dough

Either: Double the recipe for mock puff pastry,
page 48;
Or: The recipe for regular
puff pastry, page 611
Egg glaze (1 egg beaten in a small bowl
with 1 tsp water)

Equipment: The usual saucepans, whip,
spatulas, baking sheet, dough-rolling setup,
and pastry brush

Timing. Tart will take 10 minutes or so to assemble, and should rest 30 minutes or more before baking, to relax the dough. Baking is about 1 hour; it can be kept warm another hour or so, but is best freshly baked. Thus you will need about 2 hours from assembly to serving, but you may assemble the tart in advance and refrigerate or freeze before baking.

The bouillie sauce. Place flour in a smallish heavy-bottomed saucepan, and gradually beat in ½ cup of the cream with a wire whip. Bring to simmer, stirring and blending to make a smooth, thick sauce; boil slowly 1 minute, stirring. Remove from heat and beat in the egg, then the egg yolk. Bring to the simmer again, stirring; thin out with droplets of cream to make a quite thick sauce that coats a spoon heavily. Remove from heat, season with salt and pepper, and clean sauce off sides of pan with a rubber spatula. Spread the cheese over the surface to prevent a skin from forming, and set aside.

The ham. Cut the ham either into ¼-inch slices 1 inch across, or into ⅜-inch dice, whichever is easier. Sauté briefly (2 minutes) in the butter with the minced shallots or scallions. Set aside.

The puff pastry. This will create a wide bottom strip, the edges of which fold up to make a border around the filling, and a top strip that lies over it and falls down around the bottom to cover it entirely. Remember that you have to work fast with puff pastry; don't hesitate to stop the instant it softens, and refrigerate everything for 20 minutes or so to firm the dough before proceeding. Choose a pastry sheet about 12 by 20 inches long, and rinse surface in cold water but do not dry it—pastry is to adhere, giving it a footing to puff. Roll the puff pastry into a rectangle ¼ to ⅜ inch thick, and cut it to make a rectangle 20 by 15 inches. Cut a strip 8 inches wide from the rectangle (this is for the top), place on lightly floured wax paper, and refrigerate on a tray or baking sheet along with trimmings.

Enlarge remaining piece of dough an inch or so, bottom and sides, then roll up on pin and unroll upside down on dampened pastry sheet. With a table fork, prick entire surface, going down to pastry sheet, at ¼-inch intervals—this is to discourage bottom of pastry from rising too much during baking. Stir the ham into the *bouillie* sauce, and rapidly spread it down the middle of the pastry, leaving an inch free border all around.

Fold ends and sides of dough up onto filling all around. (If by this time your dough has begun to soften too much for easy manipulation, place the whole thing in the refrigerator for 20 minutes or so, then continue.)

Paint top of dough edging with cold water. Remove reserved 8-inch strip of pastry from refrigerator and lay it over bottom strip, which it should cover completely, falling down all around.

Press in place with the balls of your fingers, then press the sides of the pastry all around with the back of a table fork held vertically, to make a design as you complete the sealing of the dough.

☼ At this point, it is wise to let the pastry rest and chill for half an hour to ensure even baking, or cover and refrigerate it for a day, or freeze it. You may take it directly from freezer to oven, but allow 10 minutes or so extra baking time.

Glazing and decorating. Here the decorations are knife cuts made in the dough through the glaze; if you wish pastry cutouts made from leftover dough, see the directions for *pâté en croûte,* page 375. Paint entire surface of pastry with egg glaze. Make 2 steam holes ¼ inch in diameter in top, one third the way from each end. Paint surface of dough again with glaze. Then cut decorative designs in dough with the point of a knife, going down $\frac{1}{16}$ inch deep—such as a long curling branch from top to bottom, and big curlicues reaching out from it. Insert funnels in steam holes, such as buttered metal tubes from a pastry bag, or buttered aluminum foil twisted around the end of a pencil; funnels should reach right down into filling. Tart should now be baked immediately.

Baking: about 1 hour at 450 degrees. Bake in lower-middle level of oven for 20 to 30 minutes, or until pastry has swelled and browned. Then turn down to 400 degrees and continue baking another 20 to 30 minutes, until sides are crisp; if tart seems to be browning too much, cover very loosely with aluminum foil and/or reduce heat to 350 degrees. Large puff pastries like this often take longer to bake than you would think, since all those interior leaves of dough must bake or the pastry will be soggy.

☼ If you are not serving immediately, turn oven off and leave door ajar; or keep in warming oven at around 120 degrees. *Pâte feuilletée* loses some of its glory when you let it cool and then reheat it; the sooner you can serve it, the lighter and more delicious it will be.

Other fillings. Use the same sauce and system for diced cheddar cheese, Roquefort, sautéed mushrooms or chicken livers, shellfish, and so forth.

Other shapes. You can, of course, make *feuilletés* of any size and shape you wish. The large round one 10 inches or so in diameter is particularly attractive, and directions for it are on page 595, the *Pithiviers.*

Egg dishes

Hard-boiled eggs—
the whys and hows

The straight simmer method
The coddled method
Troublesome HB eggs and
    what to do about them
Ways to use HB eggs—stuffed,
    to serve cold; sliced and stuffed,
    to serve hot

Poached eggs

The free-form poach and
    the perforated poacher
Ways to serve poached eggs, hot and cold
Les oeufs en gelée—poached eggs in aspic

Omelettes

L'omelette nature—plain French omelette
Filled omelettes
Le gâteau omni-omelette—many-layered
    omelette with multiple fillings

Soufflés and roulades

Soufflé au fromage—master recipe for
    soufflés; trouble-shooting
Roulade au fromage; soufflé au fromage
    roulé—cheese soufflé roll
Other soufflé mixtures and
    roulade fillings

*O*ne soft spring morning Ruthie Lockwood, our television producer, joined Paul and me for a jaunt into the countryside to see a cooking demonstration by James Beard. We arrived to great excitement and bustle, ladies of all ages, a sprinkling of men, everyone with notebooks and earnestly happy faces. It was a beautiful day to be in a theater-in-the-round. Just a roof covered the stage and the audience, while fresh breezes blew through from the open sides, wafting cooking suggestions from the central preparations to our nostrils. As we were settling in our seats a young woman grabbed me.

"Oh, Mrs. Child," she fixed me with anguished eyes. "I just have to talk to someone and I know I'll never get to Mr. Beard with all this crowd. I'm having the most terrible trouble with hard-boiled eggs. I just can't peel them and I have several dozen to do for a picnic supper tonight, but they just won't peel. And here I've all these eggs, and what am I going to do?"

We discussed cracking the shells gently and plunging the eggs into cold water immediately they were cooked, and peeling them under a stream of cold water. We talked of egg salad if the worst happened. Before we could get to the dark line problem between yolk and white, the demonstration began, and we were caught up in the fun and fascination of watching a great performer at work.

On the way home, however, our "HB Egg" program was born—we'd been planning our new series of shows and this fitted in perfectly. But I had never realized until I started our research on the subject that so very many people, not only private individuals but people in the food business, have real problems with the hard-boiling and peeling of eggs.

Since doing the program I have gathered even more facts, from viewers, and from people in the egg business such as the Georgia Egg Commission, and from the American Egg Board. Therefore, in this first section of the chapter I have tried to bring up all the hard-boiling problems and answer all the questions that have so far come my way. But I am sure, as in all things culinary, there is more to know. And surely that is one of the many reasons cooking is such a fascinating art: you can never know it all because new facts, products, and processes are continually appearing.

Hard-boiled are not the only eggs in this chapter, of course. You will also find a short discussion of poaching, and an illustrated section on omelettes, including a high-rise *gâteau* of multi-omelette layers. Following that is what I hope will be forevermore (at least at far as I am concerned) the recipe to end them all on how to make a magnificent cheese soufflé. Then, using these easily acquired characteristics, you are equipped to turn the same mixture into a *roulade,* a flat jelly-roll shape of a soufflé that you can roll up with a marvelous filling of mushrooms or crab or broccoli and serve at a luncheon party.

Hard-boiled eggs— the whys and hows

FRESHNESS OF EGGS

Grandmother always said that if an egg was too fresh you couldn't peel it; she was right but she never knew why, because it was not until the late 1950's that scientists began to discover the reason. A new-laid egg is more acid than alkaline, they found (its pH factor, as researchers would say, is too low) . After a few days, if the egg follows its natural course, the relationship changes, and when it swings over to the alkaline side (to pH 8.7 if you want the exact figure) your troubles are over. Then you can peel an egg with ease. Various factors influence the transformation, including storage temperature and the air that enters the microscopic pores in the eggshell. To maintain quality, many packers not only keep eggs well chilled, but also spray the shells with a fine mist of tasteless mineral oil, which retards not only air penetration but alkalization. That's where our egg-peeling difficulties lie: the sprayed egg won't get stale, which brings us to our first principle.

EGGS THAT ARE TOO FRESH. *Rule I.* When perfectly peeled hard-boiled eggs are important and you know yours are either very fresh or have been sprayed (eggs from out of state are often sprayed), scrub them rapidly in warm water to remove possible spray from shells, and leave them out at room temperature, uncovered, overnight before cooking them. (In hot weather, leave eggs uncovered for a day or two in the refrigerator.)

STALENESS OF EGGS. On the other hand, if your eggs are stale but still edible you are not likely to produce perfectly shaped hard-boiled eggs with perfectly centered yolks—again, if that is of any importance to you. Why? Because the air pocket at the large end of the shell has become enlarged, and you will have a lop-ended boiled egg; at the same time the white will have relaxed, and the yolk will hang off center. You can do nothing about filling the air pocket, but some people do believe that if you stir the eggs about as they cook you may re-center the yolk.

Rule II. Know your eggs. You can always cook one or two from a batch, as a test.

EGGS THAT LEAK

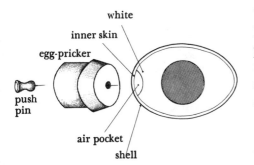

white
inner skin
egg-pricker
push pin
air pocket
shell

You should never ever have a leaking egg if you always pierce a pinhole in the large end, going right down through about ⅜ inch so as to pierce the membrane also. There is even an egg-pricker gadget available, illustrated on the left, but a pin will do as well.

Then, even if the egg is cracked, the air from that pocket will escape as it expands in the hot water and this releases pressure from the crack area. If there's no pinhole and the egg is cracked, the air from the pocket will travel around to the crack and burst out through the membrane at that point, drawing with it some of the egg white. Try this out yourself and you will see the miracle with your own eyes: lightly crack the shells of 2 raw eggs, pierce the large end of one and not of the other, then lower them both into simmering water. The non-pierced cracked egg will leak, but the pierced cracked egg should simmer cleanly throughout its allotted time.

Rule III. Always pierce your eggs before you cook them. Use an egg pricker designed for the purpose, or a push pin, or just a plain straight pin.

THAT DARK LINE BETWEEN YOLK AND WHITE

This is a chemical reaction between yolk and white that is accentuated by an excess of heat. In other words, if you really boil a hard-boiled egg you may get that ugly dark line around the yolk, especially if your egg is not very fresh. Our experiments showed, too, that the longer the yolk and white of a cooked egg remain in contact—several days, for instance—the more likely you are to get that line; again, this has to do with too much cooking heat and with the chemical climate of the particular egg in question.

Rule IV. Never boil a hard-boiled egg.

DOES SALT HELP?

I have read some scientific experiments to the effect that salt in the cooking water may have a slightly beneficial influence on peelability . . . sodium chloride and alkalinity, in other words. Whether or not it is helpful it can do no harm, and I now always add 1½ teaspoons of salt to every quart of egg-cooking water.

CONCLUSION

Forewarned is forearmed, as the good books say, and here are two methods for arriving at *les oeufs durs,* or hard eggs as the French call them, thereby skillfully avoiding the hard-cooked versus hard-boiled controversy. Which cooking method do I prefer? I do them either way, depending on how I feel at the moment of cooking. Certainly the first is faster, but the second produces a more tender egg white.

The straight simmer method for hard-boiled eggs

Cooking the eggs. Pierce the large end of each egg with a pricker or pin, going down ⅜ inch through the shell. Either put the eggs into a salad basket and lower them into enough boiling water to cover them by at least an inch, or very gently lower them into the pan by twos or threes with a slotted spoon or skimmer. Add 1½ teaspoons salt per quart of water, and as soon as water comes back to the boil again, begin timing the eggs, and regulate heat so that water is very slowly but very definitely at the merest bubble.

Timing. Time the eggs according to their size as follows for eggs taken directly from the refrigerator (subtract 1 minute for room-temperature eggs) :

U.S. Graded eggs:	*Small* and *Medium*	11 minutes
	Large	12 minutes
	Extra Large	13 minutes
	Jumbo	14 minutes

Cooling. Immediately the time is up, drain the eggs, crack each gently by tapping 2 or 3 places very lightly with the back of a spoon, and run cold water into the pan; or transfer eggs to a sinkful of cold water. (Cracking of shell allows cold water to penetrate and, hopefully, to shrink egg from membrane, while quick cooling minimizes yolk discoloration.)

Peeling. When your eggs are easy peelers, they shell perfectly even if still warm. Otherwise you are wise to refrigerate the eggs in their pan of cold water an hour or more to firm the egg white. To remove the shell, tap each egg gently all over its surface, breaking the shell into tiny fragments. Then hold the egg under a thin stream of water and start peeling membrane along with shell from the large end which, because of the air pocket, should start you off easily. (Another system for well-chilled easy peelers was suggested by one of our viewers: roll the egg back and forth on your counter under the palm of your hand to crack the shell all around its girth; hold under the cold water and peel around the circumference crack, then pull the two halves of shell off from both ends of the egg.)

Storing hard-boiled eggs. I find the best method for storing peeled eggs is to submerge them in a bowl of cold water and to refrigerate them uncovered; they keep perfectly for several days. But if you plan to do a large amount of stuffed eggs and are boiling them in advance, I suggest that you halve them as soon as you have peeled them, and separate whites from yolks to avoid discoloration. Then submerge the whites in lightly salted water, mash the yolks and place them in a covered dish, even mixing in a little seasoning and mayonnaise or cream; they will thus keep a good 2 days under refrigeration.

The coddled method for hard-boiled eggs

The 17-minute sit-in

Coddling produces eggs with a marvelously tender white and almost guarantees no yolk discoloration if the eggs are reasonably fresh, but it does take a little more time than the previous simmer. If you have eggs that are questionable peelers, however, I find the whites are so tender that peeling becomes even more difficult, although a thorough chill before peeling does help. In this system, which is favored by the Georgia Egg Commission, by the way, eggs are brought to the boil in cold water, then removed from heat, covered, and allowed to sit 17 minutes. Shape of pan and proportion of water to eggs are important, of course, since a dozen eggs would never cook properly in a skillet-shaped pan with a quart of water, for instance.

My water rules for coddled eggs. The water must cover the eggs by at least 1 inch, and you need a minimum of 6 cups of water whether you are cooking 1 or 4 eggs, with at least an additional cup of water for each additional egg.

For example: 6 eggs (6 cups plus 2) need 8 cups of water, or 2 quarts

12 eggs (6 cups plus 8) need 14 cups of water, or 3½ quarts

Prick the large end of each egg, going down ⅜ inch through the shell, and place in saucepan. Pour in the water, add 1½ teaspoons of salt per quart, and set over moderately high heat. Keep your eye on the water. When it reaches the boil, remove pan from heat, cover it, and set timer for 17 minutes. Immediately the time is up, drain the eggs, tap very gently with the back of a spoon to crack shells in several places, and run cold water into the pan, or transfer eggs to a sink of cold water. Peel and store as described on page 81—but if you have any trouble peeling, chill the eggs thoroughly and try again.

This system works for all sizes of eggs from small to jumbo, and whether the eggs are chilled or unchilled.

TROUBLESOME HB EGGS
AND WHAT TO DO ABOUT THEM

NON-PEELERS. There is not much you can do to remedy non-peeling cooked eggs. If you had planned to serve them whole and are faced with a ragged group, you will have to change gears and come up with a new idea. Salad or sandwiches using chopped eggs are obvious alternatives, or you can serve halved eggs yolk-side up and disguise the exterior with mayonnaise. Sometimes ragged eggs look acceptable when sliced crosswise.

OFF-CENTERED YOLKS. Try and halve them so the off center is least obvious, such as on a slant from top to bottom, even if one half is thicker than the other. There is no way to slice them crosswise properly; serve them quartered or chopped.

LOP-ENDED EGGS. For halved eggs, lop the end off cleanly, as though you meant them to be that way.

DISCOLORED YOLKS. This means the dark line between yolk and white. If the eggs are fresh, they are perfectly edible but you cannot remedy the situation; you can only disguise it by deciding to have stuffed eggs. Halve them and separate yolks from whites; wash the whites to remove the dark residue of yolk. Then mash the yolks with mayonnaise and so forth, perhaps adding a little heavy cream to lighten their color. Minced green herbs and items of color like pimiento or minced mushrooms are also helpful.

WAYS TO USE HB EGGS

I spent so much time in our program, just as I have here, on how to HB an egg that there was little left in that short half hour of television to show anything else. Two recipes were all I could manage. Now I shall add a few more for hot as well as cold dishes, since eggs are among the cheapest of our nutrient- and protein-rich foods. Treated with a bit of style they make splendid luncheon and supper dishes, even for the most elegant occasions.

Oeufs durs, mayonnaise

———◆———

HARD-BOILED EGGS
AND MAYONNAISE
IN DECORATIVE
POSES

Narcissa and Samuel Chamberlain, who died recently at the age of seventy-nine, (of *Bouquet de France* fame) had a daughter who married into a French family. She was expected to live and cook the French way right from the start. "One of the most difficult things for me at first," she said to her father, "was to find that *petite quelque chose pour commencer.*" That little something with which to begin the meal—but one always has it in France, even though it be very simple indeed. I like it, too, whenever we are having guests; it makes for more of a party, however informal the party or the little beginning may be. I've noticed, for instance, that our dinner guests never fail to enjoy eggs, some greenery, a few slices of ripe tomato or cherry tomatoes, plus a dollop or two of homemade mayonnaise. Accompanied by a light white wine like a Riesling and a chunk of homemade French bread, this makes a happy beginning to any meal. You don't really need a recipe, but here is one anyway.

<table>
<tr><td>Per serving—on individual plates, or on a platter</td><td>

1 hard-boiled egg

A small handful of watercress or shredded lettuce

2 tablespoons excellent mayonnaise (page 439)

Decorations for eggs: Parsley sprigs, tarragon leaves, strips of red pimiento, anchovies, sliced olives, capers, sliced artichoke hearts, or and so forth

Optional accompaniments in addition to the above: Thin slices of boiled ham, prosciutto, or salami; sardines or flakes of tuna; tomatoes, asparagus tips, sliced raw mushrooms; shrimp, lobster, crab, or and so forth
</td></tr>
</table>

Halve the egg lengthwise, using a sharp stainless-steel knife dipped in cold water. Place the egg halves yolk side down on watercress or lettuce. Just before serving, spoon a coating of mayonnaise over them. Decorate each egg with herbs, strips of pimiento, crossed anchovies and/or sliced olives, capers, artichoke hearts, or whatever appeals to you. Arrange attractively around the eggs whatever else you may have chosen, such as ham rolled into cornucopia shapes, or sardines or tuna, or vegetables, and serve.

Stuffed HB eggs, to serve cold

Serve stuffed eggs simply on a bed of watercress or shredded lettuce, or make them part of a cold combination such as sliced chicken or turkey, ham or cold vegetables. Here are just a few ideas to get you started.

Oeufs durs farcis aux asperges vertes

HB EGGS STUFFED
WITH ASPARAGUS
PURÉE

For 12 eggs,
serving 8 to 12

12 hard-boiled eggs
6 to 8 cooked fresh green asparagus spears,
    medium size
1 tsp very finely minced shallot or scallion,
    or chives
3 to 4 Tb excellent mayonnaise, heavy cream,
    crème fraîche, sour cream, and/or soft butter
Salt and pepper to taste

Equipment: A small food mill with fine disk to
    sieve egg yolks and asparagus, or a sieve and
    wooden spoon; a pastry bag with a cannulated
    ⅜-inch tube opening is easy and makes the
    most professional looking stuffed eggs, but
    you can use a spoon.

Using a stainless-steel knife dipped in water for each cut, slice the eggs in half lengthwise; shave a thin strip off bottom of each half so that it will not rock about on its dish. Sieve the yolks into a mixing bowl. Cut the tips off 6 of the asparagus (½ inch or so), slice in half lengthwise, and reserve for later. Cut off the tender part of the stalk, and purée through food mill or sieve, then twist in the corner of a towel to extract juice.

(*The use of towels in La Grande Cuisine.* You'll be sorry if you don't squeeze the purée in a towel here, since it is the only professional way to get rid of excess liquid. If the purée is damp it will so loosen the sieved yolks there will be no room for cream or mayonnaise, meaning you will have a disappointing texture and flavor. Don't worry about losing any purée—it scrapes easily off the towel. Don't worry about the green stain, either—soak the towel corner in a bowl of cold water and detergent immediately after the squeezing episode, and when you wash it later, it will come clean.)

Blend purée into yolks along with the shallot, scallion, or chives, and just enough of the mayonnaise, cream, and/or butter to soften and smooth the yolk mixture. Season carefully with salt and pepper. Either with a pastry bag or a spoon, fill the egg white halves, and decorate with the reserved asparagus tips. Cover with plastic wrap or a bowl, and refrigerate until ready to serve.

OTHER FILLINGS FOR COLD STUFFED HB EGGS

Use exactly the same system as described for the preceding hard-boiled eggs stuffed with asparagus purée, substituting one of the following for the asparagus. Proportions are flexible here; the important consideration is flavor.

Farce à la purée d'artichauts (*Artichoke filling*). For 12 eggs 1 large boiled artichoke should be sufficient, plus, for color, a handful of fresh spinach or chard boiled several minutes until limp. With a spoon scrape all tender flesh from inside large ends of artichoke leaves and sieve the flesh into a bowl along with the de-choked and chopped artichoke bottom, and the blanched green leaves. Scrape into the corner of a clean towel and twist into a ball to extract as much juice as possible.

(In case you have a towel hangup, see preceding page.) Scrape purée into bowl, blend with the sieved yolks, and proceed as for the asparagus; decorate with parsley or capers.

Farce au saumon fumé (*Smoked salmon filling*). Purée 2 to 3 tablespoons smoked salmon with the egg yolks and flavorings, adding a little Dijon mustard or lemon juice. Decorate with slivers of smoked salmon and capers.

Farce aux crevettes (*Shrimp filling*). You could use canned shrimp for this. Drain a 6- to 8-ounce can of small shrimp and soak 5 minutes or more in cold water to remove salt and preservatives. Drain again; and reserve half for decoration. Purée the other half into the egg yolks and flavorings, and beat in a pinch of tomato paste for color. You might like to add finely minced dill, parsley, chives, tarragon, or chervil, also for color. Decorate with shrimps halved lengthwise, and capers.

Farce à la tapénade

OLIVE, CAPER, AND ANCHOVY FILLING FROM PROVENCE

For a dozen eggs you will not need much of this pungent mixture, but any you have left over will keep a week or more in the refrigerator, and you can use it as a spread for toast or crackers, or toss it with your next dish of steaming pasta. Here is a minimum amount, that you may wish to double or triple.

½ *a small clove of garlic, puréed*
2 *anchovies* (*packed-in-olive-oil type*) ; *or*
  1 *Tb or so anchovy paste*
2 *Tb capers, squeezed dry in the corner of a towel*
1 *to* 2 *Tb canned tuna*
About 6 *Greek-type dry-cured black olives, pitted*

The yolks of the 12 eggs
Pinches each of pulverized imported bay leaf
and thyme
Drops of Cognac and lemon juice to taste
Black pepper, and Cayenne or hot pepper sauce
to taste
The 12 egg-white halves
2 Tb minced parsley

In a small bowl or mortar, pound the garlic and 1 of the anchovies with a pestle or the end of a wooden spoon to make a very fine paste. The rest of the ingredients are now to be puréed—the capers, tuna, and olives, along with the remaining anchovy; use a food-processor-super-blender, a regular electric blender, or mortar and pestle. Then sieve the egg yolks, blend into them the garlic-anchovy paste, and add as much of the olive mixture as suits your taste, along with a little oil from the tuna and anchovy cans if mixture is too stiff. Season carefully with bay, thyme, Cognac, lemon, and the peppers. Stuff the eggs, and garnish with the parsley.

Sliced and stuffed HB eggs, to serve hot

We never had time for any hot dishes on our program featuring hard-boiled eggs. That is a pity, since they are prime luncheon dishes and you can do all the cooking ahead. Just to have something made and ready to pop onto the stove or to slip into the oven is such a relief. Here are a few ideas on how to put your cooking vocabulary to work.

Oeufs à la tripe

SLICED HB EGGS
WITH ONION SAUCE

No one seems to know why this dish is called *à la tripe,* including the dictionary of the Académie des Gastronomes and the usually omniscient question-and-answer service of the French gastronomical magazine *Cuisine et Vins de France.* Probably, as some authorities suggest, a cook from Lyon ran out of the principal ingredient for his tripe and onion fricassee, and substituted hard-boiled eggs, since sliced onions are, by tradition, the trademark of that gastronomically famed city in central France. Whatever its origin, this is the kind of idea you can play around with and vary as you will; it is sliced onions cooked in butter, then incorporated into a cream sauce, and combined with sliced hard-boiled eggs. Classically it is served in a very attractive dish, and is garnished with carefully constructed and arranged toast points. The following is the traditional version for *Oeufs à la Tripe*, making a pleasant light luncheon, in which you might include a salad of sliced avocado and watercress or tomatoes, a white wine like a Chablis, and then finish with cheese and fruit.

For 6 people	*3 Tb butter; more if needed*
	About 4 cups thinly sliced onions (4 to 5
	medium-sized, 1 lb. or so)
	½ tsp salt; more if needed
	4 Tb flour
	2 cups milk brought to simmer in a small saucepan
	⅓ to ½ cup heavy cream
	Drops of fresh lemon juice
	White pepper
	8 to 10 hard-boiled eggs
	12 croutons (triangles of crustless white bread
	either sautéed in clarified butter or
	toasted and buttered)

The onion sauce. Melt the butter in a heavy-bottomed medium-sized saucepan, stir in onions and salt, cover, and cook slowly, stirring occasionally, for about 10 minutes, or until tender and translucent but not browned. Then blend in the flour, and cook, stirring, for 3 minutes more, adding a little more butter if the flour does not absorb easily. Remove from heat; gradually blend in the hot milk, stirring thoroughly with a wooden spoon to be sure flour and milk are perfectly blended. Simmer, stirring for several minutes until you are sure onions are thoroughly cooked. Stir in several spoonfuls of cream, simmering, and adding more by dribbles, but do not thin out sauce too much; it should coat a spoon fairly heavily. Carefully correct seasoning with more salt, drops of lemon juice, and white pepper to taste.

✪ If done in advance, clean sauce off sides of pan with a rubber spatula, and float a thin film of cream on top to prevent a skin from forming.

Assembling and serving. While sauce is simmering, slice the eggs crosswise into rounds about ⅜ inch thick, sieve the yolk of one onto a saucer or bit of wax paper, and reserve for decoration later. Warm and butter an attractive serving dish. Just before serving, very gently fold the sliced eggs into the hot sauce, let warm over low heat for a moment or two, then turn the eggs onto the dish. Strew the reserved yolk on top, surround the eggs with croutons, and serve at once.

VARIATIONS

When you want a readymade dish to heat up in the oven at the last minute, serve *Oeufs à la Tripe* as a gratin: butter a 6-cup baking dish such as a round one 8 inches in diameter and 2½ inches deep. Spread a third of the sauce in the bottom, strew the sliced eggs on top, cover with the rest of the sauce, and spread over it a quarter cup of fresh white bread crumbs or grated Swiss cheese, and dribble over that 2 tablespoons of melted butter. Or you might use the same system but lay a bed of chopped creamed spinach or broccoli in the bottom of the dish, or you could combine the eggs with sliced cooked mushrooms, potatoes, ham, or sautéed chicken livers. To serve any of these, set 5 to 6 inches below a low broiler for 10 minutes or so, to heat thoroughly and brown the top nicely; but do watch that the eggs are not overheated or they will toughen.

Oeufs à la Chimay

HB EGGS STUFFED WITH MUSHROOMS, GRATINÉED IN CHEESE SAUCE

This is my favorite of all the hot dishes using hard-boiled eggs. If you happen to have a little mushroom *duxelles* on hand—minced mushrooms sautéed with shallots and butter (and it freezes for months) —you can make this whole affair in a flash. Even if you do not have the *duxelles,* it is fast. While the eggs are cooking you sauté the mushrooms and make a good old white sauce. Then you mix the mushrooms with the sieved yolks, flavor them nicely with fresh green herbs, fill the eggs, add cream and cheese to the sauce, and arrange eggs and sauce in a baking dish. You can do this today, and 15 to 20 minutes before serving tomorrow, in it goes to bake and brown. You can be simple about the rest of the meal. Follow the eggs with an endive and beet salad for instance, and end with fruit or a sherbet. Homemade French bread would be good indeed with eggs and endive, as would a bottle of Pouilly Fuissé or Pinot Blanc. Some oenophiles frown on wine with eggs; if you happen to have invited one of these set a carafe of chilled Château la Pompe (plain water—"from the pump"—a French joke) by his glass, and there will be more Pouilly for you.

For 6 people

The mushroom duxelles (for about ½ cup)
About 6 ounces (2 cups) fresh mushrooms
1½ Tb butter
1½ Tb minced shallots or scallions
Salt and pepper

Sauce Mornay (béchamel with cheese)
3 Tb butter
4 Tb flour
About 2½ cups milk heated in a small saucepan
(or 2 cups hot milk, and ⅓ to ½ cup cream)
Salt and white pepper
2 ounces (about ½ cup lightly pressed) coarsely
grated Swiss cheese—some of this to be saved
for top of dish, later

The eggs and other ingredients
9 hard-boiled eggs
About 3 Tb minced fresh green herbs such as
parsley, tarragon, chervil, and chives,
or just parsley and a big pinch or two of
dried tarragon
Additional butter, cream, salt, and pepper as needed

The mushroom duxelles. While the eggs are cooking, trim and wash the mushrooms, mince them, and, a handful at a time, twist them in the corner of a towel to extract their juices (or use a potato ricer to juice them). Heat butter to bubbling in a medium-size frying pan, add mushrooms and shallots or scallions, and sauté over moderately high heat, stirring frequently until pieces begin to separate from each other (5 to 6 minutes). Season lightly with salt and pepper, and set aside.

The sauce Mornay. While eggs and mushrooms cook, make a white *roux:* melt 3 tablespoons butter in a heavy-bottomed medium-size saucepan, blend in the 4 tablespoons flour, and stir slowly over moderate heat until butter and flour foam together for 2 minutes without coloring more than a buttery yellow. Remove from heat and let cool a moment, until *roux* stops bubbling. Then, beating vigorously with your wire whip, pour in half the hot milk; when blended, set over moderately high heat, beating, until sauce comes to the boil. It will be very thick. Stir about ¼ cup into the mushrooms, then complete the sauce by simmering and adding dollops of milk and/or cream until sauce thins out gradually, but coats a spoon thickly enough to show it will coat the eggs, later. Beat in salt and pepper to taste. Clean off sides of pan with a rubber scraper, and float a thin film of cream on top to prevent skin from forming.

Assembling. Choose a shallow baking and serving dish that will just hold 18 egg halves comfortably, such as an oval one 9 by 12 inches; smear inside with butter. Using a stainless-steel knife dipped in cold water for each cut, halve the eggs lengthwise. Shave a strip of egg white off bottom of each so they will not rock about in the dish. Sieve the egg yolks into a medium-size mixing bowl, beat in the mushrooms and their ¼ cup of thick sauce, and the herbs. Season carefully with salt and pepper; if the yolks seem rather stiff, stir in a spoonful or so of heavy cream or soft butter. Divide the filling into sixths, so you will not run out; fill the eggs using a tablespoon, and heap filling into a dome. If you have filling left over, add it to the sauce, then stir sauce over heat just enough to decongeal; stir in two thirds of the grated cheese. Spread a ⅛-inch layer of sauce on the bottom of dish, arrange the eggs over it, filled side up. Eggs should be quite close together, but not crowded out of shape. Spoon a coating of sauce over each egg, sprinkle on the remaining cheese, and dot top of each egg with a speck of butter.

✵ May be completed as much as a day in advance; cover and refrigerate.

Baking and serving. About 20 minutes before serving, bake in upper-middle level of a preheated 425-degree oven, just until sauce is bubbling hot and top has browned nicely. Do not overheat or eggs will harden. If you are not serving at once, keep warm in turned-off oven, door ajar; but the sooner you serve the eggs, the more tender and delicious they will be.

OTHER FILLINGS

In all of the following the egg yolk mixture should be light, but still firm enough to hold its shape. If it is too stiff, beat in a little cream or *béchamel*. On the other hand, if it seems too soft, beat in a tablespoon or more of very fine fresh white bread crumbs. (These will absorb excess moisture, and are always useful to have in the freezer when things get loosely out of hand.) Count on 2 to 3 tablespoons of covering sauce for each egg half.

Farce au naturel (*Plain filling*). Beat 4 tablespoons of thick *béchamel* sauce, cream and/or soft butter into the sieved egg yolks, along with salt and pepper to taste. Bake the eggs in the preceding cheese sauce, or arrange them on a bed of creamed spinach before saucing them.

Farce aux fines herbes (*Herb filling*). Beat 3 to 4 tablespoons minced fresh green herbs into the preceding plain filling; use a combination such as parsley, chives, and chervil, or parsley, a good pinch of dried tarragon, and very finely minced shallot or scallion warmed briefly in butter. Bake as in preceding recipe.

Farce aux artichauts ou aux asperges (*Artichoke or asparagus filling*). Scrape flesh from leaves of a boiled artichoke or two, and purée along with the scraped bottom; or purée several cooked fresh green asparagus spears. Twist in the corner of a towel to extract juice; you should have a scant ½ cup of purée. Blend into the sieved yolks along with a tablespoon of finely minced shallot or scallion warmed in butter, and several tablespoons of heavy cream and/or softened butter, salt and pepper. Then proceed as usual.

Other ideas. Use the same general system for purées of poultry, ham, chicken livers, liver paste, *foie gras,* shellfish, or finely minced clams, tuna, salmon, and so forth.

Poached eggs

Since poached eggs appear in this book, and since, anyway, they are to my mind the purest and loveliest of ways to cook eggs, here is a rather detailed description of how to poach eggs in case you are not already a master of them. As is typical in cooking, I have found out much more about egg poaching during the years since my first description of them, and this gives me an opportunity to set down the additional information I have picked up. The method here is for the free-form oval shape and for the perforated oval metal egg poacher illustrated at the end of the free-form recipe.

Too often we consign poached eggs to buttered toast and breakfast, but they lend themselves to marvelous innovations as first course and luncheon dishes, both hot and cold and in aspic. A few ideas for these are included here, as well as two ways to do eggs in aspic.

Les oeufs pochés

POACHED EGGS

For 4 to 6 poached eggs

Poach 4 to 6 eggs only, at one time, and only 4 if this is your first experience.

4 to 6 fresh eggs (for free-form poaching, the white should cling closely to the yolk; if not, you will get a messy egg, and should resort to the metal egg poacher, page 94, or to the 6-minute egg on page 96)
2 quarts boiling water in a saucepan about 8 inches in diameter (depth of water should be 2½ inches)
⅓ cup white vinegar (2½ Tb per quart)

Equipment: A pin or an egg pricker; a perforated spoon; a kitchen timer; for eggs to be served hot and soon, a bowl of hot water (120 degrees) and a clean folded dish towel; for eggs to be served later or for eggs to be chilled, a bowl of cold water.

Preparing the eggs for poaching. Pierce a pinhole ⅜ inch deep in the large end of each egg, to let air out of egg and prevent shell from cracking. Lower the whole unbroken eggs into the slowly boiling water and time them exactly 10 seconds—count "one thousand, two thousand, three thousand, etc." not too fast, to time them. Remove immediately. This 10-second boil in the shell helps coagulate the loose-flowing white inside the egg, and gently sets the oval shape—if the egg is reasonably fresh.

Preparing the poaching water. Pour the vinegar into the boiling water, and reduce heat so water is just at the simmer—quietly bubbling. Vinegar quickly coagulates the white when the naked egg enters the water, and this in turn helps preserve its oval shape—again, if the egg is reasonably fresh. (*Note:* Whether or not to use vinegar, and how much, depends on the freshness of your eggs and on the quality of your local water. Use it in the proportions indicated for your first experience, then cut down on it until you have reached the right amount for your usual local conditions. Vinegar does alter the texture of the outside white to a slight degree, and the less you can use the more natural your egg.)

Breaking the eggs into the water. One at a time and rapidly, crack an egg sharply on the edge of the saucepan to break one side of the shell cleanly. Then, holding egg as close over the water as you dare—with your fingers almost in the water—swing the shells open fast and wide to let the egg slide with one movement into the simmering water. Set timer for 4 minutes. Rapidly continue with the 3 other eggs, adding them clockwise around edge of pan.

Finishing the eggs. Regulate heat so poaching water remains at hardly a bubble, and when 4 minutes are up, carefully remove first egg with perforated spoon and slide it into the bowl of hot water, to wash off the vinegar. Estimating how much time you took for each additional egg— 15 seconds at most when you are used to the movements—remove the other eggs in turn. (The eggs should be cooked just long enough so white is set but yolk remains liquid; if white is not coagulated throughout it tends to crack open and the unset liquid dribbles out onto your toast, or into your aspic, or whatever. I have found 4 minutes to be just right for me for large and extra-large eggs.)

☼ The eggs will keep warm as long as the water remains warm, and they cannot overcook if water is not hotter than 120 degrees; if your wait is a bit long, pour a little boiling water into the bowl from time to time.

The perforated oval metal egg poacher

For eggs not quite fresh enough to hold their shape by themselves, the oval egg poacher works remarkably well, and gives a very natural shape to the egg. Unless you have several of them, you can, of course, poach only one egg at a time.

Use the same preliminary 10-second boil-in-the-shell described above, and the same proportions of 2½ tablespoons vinegar per quart of water. Before dropping the egg into the poacher, dip the poacher in the water for several seconds to prevent the egg from sticking to it. Then, with the poacher standing in the simmering water, open the shell just above it, so the naked egg falls in one movement into the poacher. Poach 4 minutes, as usual, then slide the egg from the poacher into a bowl of fresh water, hot or cold, depending on your intentions. (To prevent the egg from sticking to the metal, some directions suggest that you butter the poacher, but I've found that useless, since the butter melts off in the water; the simmering of the empty poacher has worked perfectly for me.)

To serve poached eggs hot and soon

Take them one at a time out of the hot water with a perforated spoon; holding a folded towel in free hand, roll egg around against it to drain off all moisture. Then proceed as you wish, such as laying it on a piece of buttered toast, and sprinkling the egg with salt, pepper, droplets of melted butter, and perhaps a pinch of fresh minced herbs. Creamed spinach could be on the toast, and you could top the egg with a hollandaise sauce. Or use a bed of hot creamed broccoli, or of mushroom *duxelles,* or of chopped sautéed ham. Or dispense with the toast altogether: lay the egg in a hot baked potato that you have flavored with salt, pepper, cream, and minced chives. Or rest it in a buttered artichoke bottom or a giant broiled mushroom cap. Or be more elaborate: line a tartlet shell with creamed mushrooms or shellfish, lay in the egg, top with hollandaise or béarnaise sauce, or with a Mornay (cheese *béchamel*) sauce; in this final case you could sprinkle the top of the sauce with ½ teaspoon of cheese and run the dish very briefly under a hot broiler to brown. These make marvelous luncheon or supper dishes, and I only toss up these few ideas to give you a start.

To poach eggs in advance and reheat them

Dip the eggs as they are done into a bowl of cold water, to stop the cooking. To reheat, bring a saucepan of salted water to the simmer, remove from heat, slip the eggs into the water, and let warm through—usually 1 minute will do unless the eggs have been chilled, then add 10 to 15 seconds more.

To poach eggs in advance and to store them in the refrigerator

Submerge the eggs in a bowl of cold water and refrigerate uncovered. They will keep perfectly for 2 to 3 days.

To serve poached eggs cold

Cold poached eggs are lovely in cold vegetable combinations, especially with tomatoes and green beans, or artichoke bottoms, or with a French potato salad. I love them, too, coated with homemade mayonnaise and topped with the fat home-cured capers on page 437, plus a bit of salami or prosciutto and watercress; that makes a delicious light lunch or cold snack.

L'oeuf mollet

THE 6-MINUTE
BOILED EGG, AN
ALTERNATIVE TO
POACHED EGGS

When your eggs are impossible from a poaching point of view, you can always resort to the 6-minute egg cooked in its shell, following all the directions for hard-boiled eggs on page 80, "The Straight Simmer," timing them 6 minutes for large and extra-large eggs. The whites will be set through, and the yolks liquid, and you peel them as usual— but (and when is there not a but?) if your eggs are non-peelers, see the discussion on page 79. I have often resorted to the 6-minute simmer where we live in southern France, and where it is often impossible to find a poachable egg; we have no hen, and the markets carefully place their open flats of eggs on top of the refrigerator rather than in it. The *Oeuf Mollet* nicely replaces the poached egg in any circumstances.

Les oeufs en gelée

POACHED EGGS
IN ASPIC

Take chilled poached eggs embedded in a wine-flavored aspic, rest them on a fresh shredding of lettuce leaves, surround them with thin slices of cucumber and halved cherry tomatoes, accompany them with a bowl of homemade mayonnaise, a bottle of white Riesling wine, your own French bread, and you have a perfect first course or luncheon dish. Here are two methods for eggs in aspic, the first giving the conventional method of molding the eggs individually, and unmolding them just before serving. The second is a fast and unorthodox system in which a sheet of aspic is cut into pieces upon which each egg sits, and the egg is then decorated with chopped aspic and other attractions. The following are only brief descriptions to give you the general idea; I have not gone into decorative possibilities since they are all described for the trout in aspic on page 448.

Preliminaries. Either use your own homemade aspic as described on page 447, or canned consommé with wine and gelatin added (1 package or 1 tablespoon plain unflavored gelatin softened in 3 tablespoons Port or Madeira, and dissolved in 2 cups consommé for the molded eggs, in 1½ cups consommé for the eggs *on* aspic, second recipe). If your poached eggs have not been refrigerated, chill quickly by putting ice cubes in the bowl with them.

To serve the eggs in individual molds

Oval metal molds 3½ by 2½ inches top diameter, holding ⅔ cup, are ideal for "large" and "extra-large" eggs; but use anything of about this size and capacity, round or oval, though preferably of metal, since the eggs unmold more easily. Pyrex custard cups or muffin tins will do, however, if you have nothing else. (You will need almost as much aspic as the total capacity of your molds: for 6 molds ⅔ cup capacity each, almost 4 cups of aspic to be safe.) Set the molds on a tray, pour in ¼ inch of aspic, and refrigerate until set—20 minutes or so. Over the aspic, lay a thin slice of cooked ham, or of *foie gras,* or chopped chicken liver, diced shellfish, or whatever else you think appropriate. One by one, drain the chilled eggs, roll each against a folded towel, cut off any trailing white, and set the egg in a mold, yolk side down. When all the molds have their eggs, pour some aspic in a metal bowl and stir over ice until chilled and syrupy (if aspic isn't chilled it will melt the set aspic in the bottom of the molds); rapidly pour ⅓ to ½ inch of chilled aspic around the eggs. Chill 10 minutes, to anchor the eggs in the molds; chill more aspic, and fill the molds. Chill at least 30 minutes. To unmold, dip in very hot water for 3 to 4 seconds, then reverse the eggs over whatever bed you have prepared to receive them. Refrigerate if not served at once.

Eggs on aspic—a rapid alternative

Pour a ⅜ inch layer of aspic into a roasting pan lined with wax paper— a 9- by 12-inch pan for 6 eggs—and you need a fairly thick layer of aspic or it will break later, when handled. Chill until set (it will set faster in the refrigerator if you sink the pan in a larger one containing cracked ice, water, and a tablespoon or so of salt). Unmold the chilled aspic onto a cutting board, peel off the wax paper, and cut enough ovals, circles, or rectangles out of the aspic to hold the eggs—3 inches across should be about right. Arrange a *chiffonade* of lettuce (finely shredded leaves) on individual plates or a serving platter, place the aspic pieces over it, and center a chilled, dried, nicely trimmed egg on each. Cut 4-inch strips ⅜ inch or so wide from remaining aspic and lay a pair crisscrossed over each egg. Decorate interstices with bits of canned pimiento, sliced stuffed olives, or whatever else pleases you. Chop remaining aspic and spoon it around the eggs. (If for some reason your

aspic breaks, chopped aspic will hide your troubles.) Refrigerate if not
served at once.

Omelettes

There are fluffy omelettes, soufflé omelettes, Mère Poularde omelettes
made of whole eggs beaten to a froth, and there is the traditional 2-egg
meal-in-a-jiffy plain French flat omelette, which we are concerned about
here. I shall never forget my first one. It was in our rooftop kitchen in
Paris on the rue de l'Université, during the very early days of our cooking school, L'École des Trois Gourmandes. To give our students a treat,
and also to learn more ourselves, Louisette and Simca and I had asked
our wonderful *maître,* Chef Bugnard, to teach classes for us once in a
while. He was delighted. He had retired from active daily instruction,
but he occasionally presided over luncheons for Le Cercle des Gourmettes, the ladies' gastronomical club, and he occasionally cooked for
private parties. He lived with his married daughter and family on the
outskirts of Paris, where he did all the cooking for the household, but he
loved an excuse to come into Paris, and he loved teaching.

On the day of the omelettes we had our class of six students, Chef
Bugnard, and the three of us. Minette Pussy, perched on a rung under
the kitchen table, was ready to pounce on anything that fell her way.
Our main dish was an elaborate *chaud-froid* of boned chicken filled
with a truffled mousse, and while we were letting various elements chill,
Chef decided to show us the professional way with omelettes.

He took a long-handled black iron skillet from its hook on the wall,
heated it briefly, reached into the salt box for a small handful, and
sprinkled it in the pan. He rubbed the pan briskly with the towel tucked
at his belt—salt keeps the pan from sticking, he said. He cracked 2 eggs
into a bowl, added salt and pepper, and gave them some 20 deft whips
of the fork. He turned the gas flame high, set the pan over it, and plopped
in a fat lump of butter.

As it sizzled, he rapidly swirled it over the bottom of the pan and around the sides. Then he held the pan flat over the hot flame as the butter foamed up. Pointing to the butter all the while, he ordered us to look at it carefully, and that's where I learned to judge the heat of the pan by looking at the butter. When its foam had almost disappeared, it was hot enough: he quickly poured in the eggs. They hissed softly as they hit the hot pan. He held it still for a moment— to coagulate a layer of eggs on the bottom, he told us. Then, with a few flip-flips of the pan, the omelette magically formed itself.

"*Voilà, Mesdames!*" He turned the perfectly shaped, gently swelling oval onto a plate, speared a bit of butter with a fork, rubbed it on top, and handed the omelette to Simca. We all stood there gasping. He hadn't touched the eggs at all. He had just shaken the pan, the omelette forming itself as he did so, and it had taken but a few seconds.

"Now, Madame Child," he motioned me to the skillet, "you saw how I did it. Now you."

"No, Chef." I backed away rapidly. "Do it again, please."

He made half a dozen more, and we ate them rapturously as he showed us again and again, explaining how he jerked the pan toward him, forcing the omelette to form itself as it turned over and over against the far edge of the pan. I don't remember that any of us dared try in front of him, but as soon as school was over and I was alone in the kitchen I tried one. It worked. We had omelettes for supper, for breakfast, for lunch; I had acquired the feel of it, which will last me forever I hope.

Like most skills, it does take some practice to learn the omelette technique. If you are determined to master it, however, and are willing to make half a dozen, one right after the other with a devil-may-care attitude for those that may fall into the stove or onto the floor—you will succeed. The omelette will then be part of your life, too, forever more.

The omelette pan

To make a French omelette in the professional manner described here you want a frying pan with a long handle for easy manipulation, a bottom diameter of 7 to 7½ inches that is just right for 2 or 3 eggs, and outward-sloping sides 2 inches high that permit you to toss the omelette about without having it spill out onto the stove. You also need a surface that the eggs will not stick to. The one I've used in the illustrations farther on is of medium-weight Teflon-coated aluminum; I've had it for well over five years, and use it every day for general cooking. As you see in the photographs, the eggs stick a little bit to it now, since it is showing its age, but it works perfectly well. I see no reason to pay a large price for a fancy omelette pan; furthermore, a number of the ones I've seen are far too shallow.

However, if you do succumb, be sure the measurements are as stated above; if it is of plain aluminum, the interior should be highly polished, and you should use this type of pan only for omelettes. The French heavy-gauge iron pan should also be reserved only for omelettes: before using it, heat to warm, scrub thoroughly with scouring powder and steel wool, and dry it; heat again until it is warm to your hand, rub with olive oil, let sit overnight, heat again, rub with salt, wipe clean, and the pan is ready to use. With both plain aluminum and iron pans, never scour after use; simply wipe clean with an oiled paper towel—if it is necessary to wash them, however, do so in warm water only, then heat, dry, and rub with oil.

L'omelette nature

PLAIN FRENCH
OMELETTE

The best omelettes are single servings made from 2 or 3 eggs, since tenderness depends on the speed with which you make them. You will find the scrambled omelette-making technique (shaking the pan in one hand and stirring the eggs with the back of a fork in the other hand) both in Volume I of *Mastering* and in *The French Chef Cookbook*. The following no-hands technique forces the omelette to form itself by the manner in which you toss and shake the omelette pan. The whole process takes but a few seconds.

For each omelette

2 eggs (or 3 eggs, but start first with 2 "large" eggs until you are expert)
Salt and pepper
Optional: 1 Tb water
2 Tb butter

Equipment: A beating bowl and a table fork; a nonsticking frying pan 7 to 7½ inches bottom diameter; a warm dinner plate beside you.

Break the eggs into the bowl, add a pinch of salt and pepper, the optional water (to make a more perfect blending) and beat vigorously about 30 strokes of the fork to mix yolks and whites. Set the omelette pan over highest heat, add 1½ tablespoons of the butter; tilt pan in all directions to film bottom and sides. When melted, the butter will foam; when foam begins to subside and butter is on the point of browning, pour in the beaten eggs. They should sizzle as they hit the pan, indicating pan is hot enough.

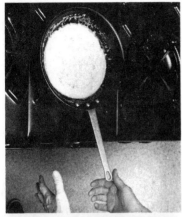

Wait 4 or 5 seconds for a film of coagulated egg to form in the bottom of the pan.

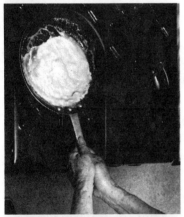

Grasp pan by its handle and swish it about right and left to distribute the eggs for several seconds.

Then jerk pan roughly toward you several times, throwing egg mass against far edge of pan, and forcing it to roll over upon itself; continue the movement, lifting handle slightly up as you do so.

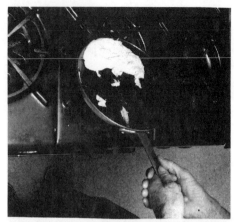

When omelette is nicely formed—
in a matter of several seconds and
4 or 5 tossing movements—
let it rest over heat in the
edge of the pan 5 seconds or so,
and unmold as follows.

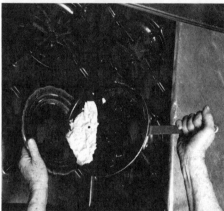

Immediately grasp pan handle
with your right hand, palm
underneath, fingers on top, and
hold warm plate in left hand.
Tilt plate and far edge of pan
together.

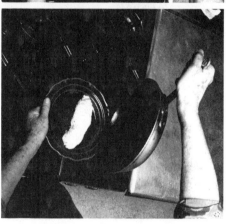

Quickly turn pan over upside
down onto plate, to unmold
the omelette.

Push omelette into shape with fork, if necessary, brush a bit of the
remaining butter over the top to glaze it, and serve immediately. The
omelette should be soft inside, the eggs barely set. The outside has hardly
a hint of brown; it is golden yellow. (The late great Dione Lucas, by the

way, was firm about not browning the omelette at all; however, the equally famous *doyenne* of omelettes, Madame Romaine de Lyon, lets her butter brown very lightly and produces a more golden omelette, while the omelette king, Rudy Stanish, follows the Lucas school.)

FILLED OMELETTES

Omelettes with cheese, potatoes, chicken livers, or other fillings make a whole quick main course, or are amusing for informal omelette parties. As an example, suppose you have a big bowl of seasoned and beaten eggs beside you, and a myriad of different fillings all ready in separate bowls on an electric warming tray. If one omelette takes less than 20 seconds to make, you can produce 3 omelettes a minute. Then suppose there are five of you tossing and serving omelettes together. The five of you could make 15 omelettes a minute, meaning you could easily serve a party of 300 people in 20 minutes! It works out on paper, anyway, and here are a few filling suggestions.

Omelettes aux fines herbes. Beat a tablespoon of fresh minced herbs into the eggs before making the omelette—parsley, chives, tarragon, chervil for instance.

Omelette au cresson. Chop a small handful of watercress leaves and tender stems, and beat into the eggs before making the omelette.

Omelette au fromage. Have a bowl of coarsely grated Swiss cheese at your side. When eggs have settled in pan, and you have swished them once or twice, rapidly sprinkle on 2 to 3 tablespoons of the cheese; finish the omelette.

Omelette au lard et aux pommes de terre. Cut chunk bacon into half-inch dice, sauté to brown lightly, then add diced boiled potatoes and sauté together to brown; season to taste and keep warm. Proceed as for the cheese omelette.

Creamed mushrooms, creamed lobster or crab, chicken livers, etc. Have these warm at your side—3 to 4 tablespoons per omelette. Either proceed as above, or slit top of finished omelette, and spoon in the filling, letting it also act as a decorative top to the omelette.

OTHER SUGGESTIONS

Among various books on eggs, there are two I like devoted only to omelettes and all the various fillings and trimmings that can go with them. Whether or not they are still in print, here are the names:

The Omelette Book, Narcissa Chamberlain (New York: Alfred A. Knopf, Inc., 1956)

The Art of Cooking Omelettes, Madame Romaine de Lyon (New York: Doubleday, 1963)

The Dione Lucas Book of French Cooking, Dione Lucas and Marion Gorman (Boston: Little, Brown and Co., 1973) gives a long and detailed section on Mrs. Lucas's very special techniques. And, finally, Rudy Stanish, who was one of her first pupils, has a little booklet on his special way with omelettes, The Man and His Pan, published by Club Aluminum, Cleveland, Ohio 44102.

Le gâteau omni-omelette

MANY-LAYERED OMELETTE WITH MULTIPLE FILLINGS

The following attractive dish is made of flat omelettes layered one upon the other in a baking dish with fillings in between; it is surrounded with a circle of cream, sprinkled with cheese and melted butter, and browned rapidly in the oven. Proportions and number of layers are up to you. Here is a suggestion for serving 4 people.

> 1½ to 2 cups creamed mushrooms (sautéed mushrooms folded into a thick well-seasoned béchamel enriched with cream, page 617)
> About 1½ cups pipérade (sautéed onions, green peppers, and fresh tomato pulp seasoned with garlic and herbs, page 427)
> 7 or 8 eggs, plus seasonings and sufficient butter for making omelettes
> About ½ cup heavy cream
> About ½ cup coarsely grated Swiss cheese
> 2 Tb melted butter
>
> Equipment: The usual for making omelettes, and a buttered 9-inch round shallow baking and serving dish

When your fillings are ready proceed as follows. Beat the eggs with seasonings. Heat omelette pan with the butter, and pour in about ⅓ cup egg mixture; let settle, swish about, and when eggs are coagulated and still flat in the pan, dislodge the circular disk of egg onto the buttered dish. Spread with part of one of the fillings. Continue, making 5 or even 6 thin omelette disks in all, alternating fillings; end with a *pipérade* topping. Pour the cream around, sprinkle omelette mass with the cheese and melted butter. A few minutes before serving, heat and brown lightly in upper middle of a preheated 400-degree oven.

Soufflés and roulades

A soufflé, in sooth, is mostly hot air—a thick sauce or purée into which you fold stiffly beaten egg whites. It automatically puffs in the oven because the air bubbles in the egg whites expand as they bake, pushing everything up. Why, then, are so many people afraid of soufflés? It is the timing, I'm sure. But you can control the timing. Although you cannot delay more than a few minutes at the serving end, you may assemble your soufflé as much as 2 hours in advance, and put it in the oven whenever it suits your schedule. A few minutes more or less fortunately make little difference, once your guests know what they are waiting for.

Another reason for fear is lack of experience. One has not beaten enough egg whites into stiff peaks, nor folded them rapidly, delicately, and often enough into a base so that they retain their maximum puff. But when you've done cakes, you can do soufflés, and there is nothing truer than the old adage of "where there's a will there's a way." If you are still timid, make the decision to conquer your fears, and you will be master of the soufflé.

To master it then, here follows a recipe giving every detail I can think of and, since all soufflés follow this general pattern, one set of rules should launch you for life. (As usual, I have soufflés in every book, but, as usual in this book, I am giving you a different view.)

Soufflé au fromage

CHEESE SOUFFLÉ

Cheese soufflé is the classic one, and because it is the lightest it rises to the greatest heights. It is also a classic luncheon dish, since you accompany it with only a salad, or something like artichokes or asparagus vinaigrette, an arrangement of cold vegetables or sliced ripe tomatoes and watercress, or vegetables _à la grecque_. Dessert cannot, of course, have anything to do with eggs, but could be a beautiful fruit tart, pears or peaches poached in wine, a bowl of muscat grapes, fresh pineapple, or fresh berries in season. Serve a white wine with the soufflé, such as a Chablis or one of the Pouillys.

A note on cheese. Real imported Swiss Gruyère—the Swiss with the small holes—has a strong, fine nutty flavor, and gives this soufflé the proper French taste. Others in the same category are Fribourg, and Spalen or Sbrinz. Imported real Swiss Emmenthal—the large-holed Swiss—and its foreign and domestic imitations are milder in flavor, so much so that you may want to combine them with grated real imported fresh Parmesan to give your soufflé a cheesier character. Sharp cheddar makes a fine soufflé with excellent flavor, but it is a strictly American taste. What to use is really up to you, and after making a few you will develop your own favorite cheese formula, but don't expect to get a strong flavor out of a weak cheese.

For an 8-cup
soufflé dish,
serving 4 to 6 people

Baking time:
About 45 minutes

_An 8-cup soufflé dish, such as a charlotte mold,
or any flameproof dish about 4 inches deep
and 6 inches in diameter_
_1 tsp soft butter for the dish, and 2 Tb
grated Swiss cheese_

The soufflé sauce base
3½ Tb butter
4½ Tb flour
1½ cups hot milk
½ tsp salt
⅛ tsp pepper
Cayenne pepper or hot pepper sauce
Pinch of nutmeg
6 "large" eggs

The egg whites and cheese
2 additional egg whites (¼ to ⅓ cup)

Scant ½ tsp cream of tartar
A pinch of salt
4 ounces (1 cup fairly firmly pressed down)
*   coarsely grated Swiss Gruyère cheese,*
*   see cheese notes preceding recipe*

Equipment: A heavy-bottomed 3-quart pan,
*   a wooden spoon, and a wire whip for the*
*   sauce base; a very clean, dry beating bowl*
*   and an electric beater or balloon wire whip*
*   for the egg whites, pages 635-37; a double*
*   thickness of aluminum foil, one side*
*   buttered, and 2 pins, to make a collar*
*   for the soufflé dish*

Preliminaries. Preheat oven to 400 degrees, if you are baking the soufflé immediately. Smear the inside of the soufflé dish with the soft butter, and roll the grated cheese around in it to coat interior. Assemble all the ingredients and equipment called for.

The soufflé sauce base. Melt the butter in the saucepan, blend in the flour with the wooden spoon, and stir over moderate heat until butter and flour foam and froth together 2 minutes without turning more than a deep golden yellow. Remove pan from heat, and let cool a moment. Using the wire whip, blend in all the hot milk at once, beating vigorously. Add the salt, pepper, and seasonings, and return over moderately high heat. Stirring with wire whip, bring to the boil, and boil 1 minute. Sauce will be very thick.

Remove from heat. Immediately start separating the eggs, dropping the whites into the beating bowl, and whipping the yolks one by one into the hot sauce.

☼ You may prepare the sauce ahead; clean off sides of pan with a rubber spatula and film top with melted butter to prevent a skin from forming. Before proceeding, reliquefy sauce by beating over low heat, just to warm it slightly but not to cook the egg yolks.

The egg whites and cheese. Add the 2 additional egg whites to the 6 already in the beating bowl; if egg whites are chilled, set bowl in hot water, stirring for a minute or so until you can feel with your finger that the chill is off—cold egg whites do not mount properly. Start beating rather slowly until egg whites are foaming, then beat in the cream of tartar and salt; gradually increase speed to fast, and continue beating until they are smooth, satiny, and form shining peaks when a bit is lifted with beater or a rubber spatula. Do not overbeat; egg whites must remain shiny, smooth, and velvety.

Immediately stir ¼ of them into the warm sauce base with a rubber spatula, to lighten the mixture. Scoop the rest of the egg whites on top of the sauce—or pour the sauce down the inside side of the egg white bowl if your saucepan is too small for easy folding. Combine the egg whites and sauce by plunging your rubber spatula down into the center bottom of the pan, rapidly draw it to the side of the pan as you turn it and lift it out: you are thus bringing a little of the sauce base up over the egg whites as you fold. Continue rapidly, rotating the pan slightly after each fold; sprinkle in several spoonfuls of the cheese from now on, with each fold of the spatula—reserve 2 Tb cheese for later. (Adding the cheese with the egg whites makes for a lighter soufflé than had you stirred it into the sauce base earlier.) Your object is to deflate the egg whites as little as possible, and the whole folding operation should not take more than a minute.

Into the soufflé dish. Scoop the soufflé mixture into the prepared dish, which should be about ¾ filled. Arrange the buttered foil around the outside of the dish, making a collar that sticks 3 inches above its rim; pin in place (see illustration, page 521).

Delayed action. If you are not ready to bake the soufflé turn a large bowl or kettle upside down over it; the soufflé may safely sit for 2 hours.

Baking and serving. Oven has been preheated to 400 degrees. Set the soufflé for 10 to 15 seconds over high heat on top of the stove, to give it an initial push. Immediately place it on the lower rack of the oven, and turn oven down to 375 degrees. Do not open oven door for 35 minutes. Then take a quick peek—soufflé should have risen about 2 inches over the rim of the dish, and top will be browned. Rapidly sprinkle on the 2 tablespoons reserved cheese, and bake 7 to 10 minutes more. It is done when a skewer, plunged through the side of the puff, comes out almost clean—meaning that when you remove the collar, the puff will hold. Remove the collar. (Although you may hold the soufflé for 3 to 4 minutes in the oven, it is best to bring it to the table as soon as possible.)

To serve, hold a large spoon and fork back to back and plunge them vertically into the soufflé, tearing the top of the puff for each portion.

TROUBLE-SHOOTING

Why did it collapse so soon when I took it from the oven? It was not cooked quite long enough. Although some people do like a soufflé with a soft, rather runny interior, that is the kind that sinks down very quickly when you take it from the oven. If you want it to stay up a few minutes longer for serving, give it the skewer test as described at the end of the recipe.

How about a non-collapsible soufflé? See the cheese soufflé either in *The French Chef Cookbook,* Number 86, or in Volume I of *Mastering,* page 171.

My soufflé didn't rise! Did you beat the egg whites into shining velvety peaks as described in the recipe? Was the sauce base cold and congealed rather than smooth, tepid, and the consistency of a heavy mayonnaise, and did you stir ¼ of the egg whites into this sauce to liquefy it more, so the rest of the egg whites could be folded in easily? Did you fold the egg whites rapidly into the sauce, deflating them as little as possible? Did you overcook the soufflé? Too long in the oven, and those air bubbles burst. Did you use a wide soufflé dish rather than the 6-inch diameter specified? Too wide a dish makes too large an area to be held up dramatically by a puff of air bubbles. It is true that you can bake a soufflé on a platter, as described in *Mastering* and in *The French Chef Cookbook,* and it does rise, but not to the dramatic height it puffs in a baking dish of the right dimensions. (You can also bake a soufflé in a jelly-roll pan, where it rises hardly at all; use it like a jelly roll in the following recipe.)

Roulade au fromage; soufflé au fromage roulé

———

CHEESE SOUFFLÉ
ROLL

A *roulade* is a flat soufflé baked in a rectangular shape, then rolled up with a filling like creamed mushrooms, spinach, broccoli, shellfish, chicken livers, or whatever other attractive item comes to mind.

You cut it crosswise, like a sausage, to make servings of soufflé layers alternating and contrasting with the filling. The recipe here is the classic cheese formula minus the two extra egg whites needed for puffing up a soufflé in a baking dish. I am repeating the formula again, so you won't have to turn back to it. Serve a *roulade* with cocktails, as the first course for a dinner, or the main course for a luncheon or supper with the same menu suggestions as for the cheese soufflé on page 106.

When a *roulade* calls for a creamed filling, make double the amount of sauce base you will need for your soufflé recipe, and you will then have enough for your filling, too.

The béchamel sauce base

For an 11- by 16-inch pan, and a roulade serving 4 to 6

¼ lb. *(1 stick) butter*
⅔ *cup all-purpose flour*
3 *cups milk, heated in a saucepan*
    (more if needed)
½ *tsp salt*
¼ *tsp pepper (10 grinds, approximately)*
A *big pinch of nutmeg*

For the soufflé-roulade

½ *the preceding béchamel sauce (or one with 4 Tb*
    butter, 4½ Tb flour, 1½ cups milk)
6 *"large" eggs*
¼ *tsp cream of tartar and ⅛ tsp salt for*
    the egg whites
4 *ounces (1 cup lightly pressed) coarsely grated*
    Swiss cheese; or Swiss plus a tablespoon
    or so of Parmesan
½ *cup toasted and buttered fresh*
    white bread crumbs

For the filling

4 *Tb butter*
3 *to 4 Tb minced shallots or scallions*
3 *to 4 cups cooked broccoli, spinach, mushrooms,*
    shellfish, or ham, for instance, chopped or
    diced; or a pipérade (cooked onions, peppers,
    tomatoes, and herbs, page 427)
Salt and pepper
The remaining béchamel sauce
Milk and/or cream to thin the sauce
About ¼ cup coarsely grated Swiss cheese

Optional accompaniment

1½ *cups hollandaise, tomato sauce, or*
    pipérade

Equipment: A jelly-roll pan about 11 by 17 inches,
    or a large-baking sheet about 16 by 20 inches;

egg-white beating equipment (pages 635-37);
extra wax paper and a tray or baking sheet
for unmolding; a serving platter or board
with inner surface about 8 by 20 inches;
the usual saucepans, whips, rubber spatulas,
and spoons

The béchamel sauce base. Make a white *roux:* melt the butter in a 2½-to 3-quart heavy-bottomed saucepan, blend in the flour with a wooden spoon, and cook over moderate heat until butter and flour foam and froth together for 2 minutes without coloring more than a deep yellow. Remove from heat, and when *roux* stops bubbling, pour in 3 cups of hot milk, beating vigorously with the wire whip to blend. Return over moderately high heat and bring to the boil, stirring; boil and stir 2 minutes. Sauce will be very thick. Beat in the seasonings, and transfer half of sauce to a 3-quart bowl or pan; this is for the soufflé. Clean off sides of pan with a rubber spatula, smooth top of sauce, and float a thin film of milk on top to prevent a skin from forming; this is for your filling, later.

Preliminaries to assembling and baking the roulade. Preheat oven to 425 degrees and place rack in middle level. If you are using a jelly-roll pan, butter it, line it with a piece of wax paper, leaving a 2-inch overhang of paper at each end; then butter the paper, roll flour over it, and knock out excess. Or if you are using a large baking sheet, butter it, spread a sheet of wax paper over it, then butter and flour the paper. Assemble all your ingredients and utensils.

The soufflé-roulade mixture. If necessary, reheat the half portion of *béchamel* reserved for the soufflé, beating to liquefy and smooth it. Break an egg; drop white into clean beating bowl, and whisk the yolk into the *béchamel* with a wire whip. Continue with the rest of the eggs. You are now ready for the egg whites; if eggs came from the refrigerator, set bowl in hot water, stir about for a moment and test with your finger until the chill is off—chilled whites do not mount properly. Then beat at moderate speed until they have begun to foam and froth; beat in the cream of tartar and salt, and increase speed gradually to fast. Continue beating until egg whites are smooth, satiny, and form little peaks when a bit is lifted in the beater. Immediately fold ¼ of them into the *béchamel* to lighten it. Pile on the rest, and fold them into the sauce, cutting down from top to bottom of mixture with the side of your rubber spatula, bringing it toward you to the side of the pan, then up and out. You are thus drawing a bit of the sauce up over the egg whites; repeat rapidly, rotating pan slightly as you go; sprinkle in several spoonfuls of the cheese from now on with each fold of the spatula. The whole operation should not take more than 30 seconds or so.

☼ You can pause here if necessary; cover pan with an upturned bowl or kettle, and it will hold for an hour.

Into the pan or onto the baking sheet. For a jelly-roll pan, turn the soufflé mixture into the paper-lined pan and smooth with a rubber spatula to distribute it as evenly as possible. For a baking sheet, spread the soufflé mixture on the buttered and floured paper, making a rectangular shape about 12 by 17 inches—you will trim the edges after baking; smooth the surface with a flexible-blade spatula to make thickness as even as possible.

Baking: 12 to 15 minutes. Set immediately in middle level of preheated 425-degree oven and bake just until soufflé has puffed and top feels lightly springy. In a jelly-roll pan, top will usually crack and soufflé should just begin to show the slightest line of shrinkage from edges of pan. On pastry sheet, edges will begin to brown very lightly. Do not overcook, or soufflé will crack when you roll it later—it must be definitely set so that it holds together but isn't dried out.

Cooling and unmolding. Remove soufflé from oven, sprinkle surface with ¾ of the bread crumbs (save the rest for later), and lay wax paper on top, allowing an inch of paper to overhang each end. Turn a tray or baking sheet upside down over the soufflé, and reverse the two, thus unmolding the soufflé. Leave it for 5 minutes to set and firm up, then lift off the baking pan. Carefully peel the baking paper off sides and surface of the soufflé, a little residue of which will probably adhere to the paper. (If by any chance the paper will not peel off, the soufflé is not sufficiently cooked—remold it for baking, and set it in the oven for several minutes more.) Brittle edges of soufflé will crack when you roll it; trim them off with a knife all around—you will probably have to take off a good quarter inch if you formed it on a baking sheet.

Keeping warm or reheating. For serving within about 30 minutes, cover the soufflé with a pan or tray and set over simmering water. Or you may cover airtight and refrigerate or freeze it, then reheat it, covered, in a 300-degree oven, being careful not to leave it too long or it will become dry and brittle.

Filling and serving the roulade. If your filling is something like cooked chopped broccoli or spinach, or cooked or canned shrimp or lobster, or diced boiled ham, melt the butter to bubbling in a medium-sized frying pan. Stir in the shallots or scallions and cook a moment, then stir in the filling, and salt and pepper to taste; toss and turn over moderate heat for several minutes so that butter and flavorings will absorb. Fold in just enough of the reserved *béchamel* sauce plus driblets of cream or milk to enrobe the filling. It should be a spreadable mass, but if you make it too soft you will have trouble rolling the *roulade*. Taste very carefully for seasonings, and fold in the cheese.

✿ May be prepared ahead. Set aside, top filmed with a little cream, and reheat before continuing.

Just before serving, spread the hot filling over the warm soufflé. Roll up from one of the long sides, using the wax paper to help you. Slide the *roulade* seam side down onto the serving platter or board, and sprinkle reserved buttered crumbs on top. Serve immediately, accompanied by optional sauce.

OTHER SOUFFLÉ MIXTURES
AND ROULADE FILLINGS

I have run into *roulade* formulas that do not have a *béchamel* base; flour has lost its chic, if it ever had any. But I find them lacking in texture; they seem a bit dry to me. I therefore always prefer the cream-sauce base, and any of the creamed fillings in the preceding recipe can become a soufflé. Simply stir in egg yolks and fold in beaten egg whites. A delicious example is the creamed spinach with onions in the turnover recipe on page 67; beat 3 egg yolks into it, fold in 4 stiffly beaten egg whites, and proceed to bake the soufflé as previously described. Fill it with ham or mushrooms, or a combination of the two. In other words, here is definitely where you can put your cooking vocabulary to work and come up with your own brand of *roulades maison.*

The fish course

The buying and keeping of fish
Filleting your own fish

Brochettes, kebabs, and skewers
Scallops two ways, and skewered fish fillets

Trout and other small whole fish
Meunière, fancy filleting, poaching
    in wine, and a number of sauces

Fillets of sole in white wine
Bonne femme, Dugléré, au beurre
    d'amandes, and variations

Fish steaks and thick fillets
Broiled fish and fish·baked en Chartreuse

Whole fish—baking and braising
Flamed in fennel, braised in wine,
    and the microwave alternative

Fish mousses

Shrimp sauté

Oysters
Opening oysters, on the half shell,
    broiled, baked, scalloped,
    and oyster stew

Lobsters
Boiling or steaming, serving and eating
    whole boiled lobsters,
    lobster mayonnaise

Salt cod
De-salting and poaching, brandade,
    and a hearty gratin

*D*uring my California youth, and indeed on up to the time we went
to France, my experience with fish was limited indeed. My mother, who
had been brought up in western Massachusetts, gave us codfish balls with
egg sauce on those Sunday mornings we didn't have waffles or pancakes.
We had broiled fish for Friday dinners, pan-fried trout when we camped
in the high Sierras, and boiled salmon the Fourth of July. That was it.

When my husband and I landed in France in the fall of 1948 and drove
from Le Havre to Paris in our old blue Buick, we stopped for lunch at
La Couronne in Rouen—my first meal in France. Paul, in his beautiful
French, ordered us *Sole Meunière*. Presently, after oysters and Chablis,
in came our fish on a large oval platter, a whole big flat sole for the two
of us. It was handsomely browned and still sputteringly hot under its
coating of chopped parsley, and around it swirled a goodly amount of
golden Normandy butter. It was heaven to eat, the flesh so very fresh, with
its delicate yet definite texture and taste that blended marvelously with
the browned butter sauce. I was quite overwhelmed.

A few days later in Paris I had my first fancy fish, a *Sole Normande*, at
La Truite, a cosy restaurant just off the Faubourg Saint-Honoré, back of
the American Embassy. In those days it was run by Chef Marcel Dorin,
a distinguished member of the old school; his tall son, now the proprietor,
assisted him. (Some months later, by the way, we learned that our restaurant in Rouen, the Couronne, was run by another branch of the same
Dorin family, and that is where, some twenty years later, we filmed our
pressed duck described on page 245.) La Truite's *Sole Normande* was
a poem of carefully poached and flavored fillets surrounded by oysters
and mussels, napped with a winy creamy buttery sauce that tasted subtly

of the sole, with hints of the garnishing shellfish, and of the fluted mush-rooms that topped it. I had simply never seen nor eaten anything like that before, and neither did I imagine fish could be taken so seriously and sauced so voluptuously.

Such were the beginnings of my *éducation piscivore,* and I have con-tinued to find the subject endlessly fascinating, since it calls upon all one's talents. You can be simple with a fish fry, or a broil, or a bake, but when you really want to do something, you have poachings in wine, and a vast gamut of saucings and garnishings. You have mousse work, *que-nelles,* chowders, and so on and so forth, but always the big problem in this country—even for many who live near the sea—is how to get really fresh fish.

THE BUYING AND KEEPING OF FISH

Of all foods that I can think of, fish is the most perishable and suffers most from maltreatment. Fresh fish should have no fishy smell at all, only a pleasantly edible odor. To retain this fresh, sweet quality, as though the fish had just swum in from the sea, it must be kept on ice.

Fresh whole fish have bright bulging eyes, bright red gills, and moist, glossy skin. Fresh fish fillets and steaks have a glossy look too; the meat holds closely together, and is springy to the touch. Frozen fish is hard to judge; certainly it must have no fishy smell, and no evidence at all, such as frozen driblets of water or juices around it, to indicate its having been partially or fully thawed and then refrozen.

To enjoy the best fish you must find a market that takes it seriously, and with fast modern transportation methods and modern packing, fresh fish is possible anywhere. Supermarkets, unfortunately, often use the fish counter as a training or a dumping ground for their personnel, and a look at their dreary dried-out fish fillets tells you immediately what to expect. A serious fish market packs ice around its whole fish, lays its fillets on wax paper or plastic over ice, covers them, and packs ice on top. If you cannot smell the fish at the market, pay for it, then open the package there in the store, and give a careful sniff; if it is not perfectly fresh, take it to the manager and complain. Luckily still, in this country, the customer is always right! I've had some ridiculous experiences in Europe where the customer is always wrong; if you bought it, it's your fault and that's that.

When you buy fresh fish, then, either pick it out just before coming home, or bring a thermal container with ice to pack it in. When you get home, unwrap the fish and place it immediately in a plastic bag, then in a pan, surround it with ice, and refrigerate it; drain out accumulated water and renew ice as necessary, usually twice a day. Kept this way, very fresh fish will retain its quality 2 to 3 days. For example, I've kept very fresh sole fillets, as a test, 5 days; on that fifth day they were still good, only just beginning to go downhill.

FROZEN FISH. Keep frozen fish solidly frozen at minus 5 degrees or colder (always keep a thermometer in your freezer) until you are ready to cook it. If the temperature has gone up to 20 degrees, for instance, the fish will still feel hard as a rock, but it has suffered a trauma from which it will never recover—plan to cook it within a few days—and that is why you must buy frozen fish from a serious market. Frozen fillets need not be completely thawed, just enough so that you can separate them from each other, and do to them those preliminaries you wish to do before cooking. Whole small fish like half-pound trout may be treated the same way. With larger fish you have the problem, in cooking, that if they are solidly frozen you will cook the outside before heat penetrates the inside; with large fish, then, you are probably wise to let them thaw almost completely. Thaw frozen fish slowly in the refrigerator if possible—overnight for fillets, a day or even two for a 5-pound salmon. The best alternative to the refrigerator is a large basin of cold water; place the fish in a plastic bag, and submerge it for an hour or more—a 5-pound fish will take 4 to 5 hours.

FILLETING YOUR OWN FISH

Welcome the fisherman who brings his own fresh fish, cleaned and filleted, to the cook. And you, yourself, should welcome the opportunity to fillet your own fish, since that teaches you the bone structure, and you then need have no qualms about eating a whole sole or trout *meunière* in public, or about serving one, either. Except for horror structures like those in shad, pike, and herring, most fish are easy to do, and they divide themselves into the flat family like flounder and the oval-shaped family like trout and salmon.

Fish and children. I think that children should learn to eat a whole fish and to bone their own at an early age. It is something they can take pride in, which all children need. Too often a squeamish parent, scared himself because he was never taught, will permanently traumatize a child about getting fish bones caught in his throat.

FILLETING FLAT FISH. Resting on the bones at either side of the spine are the two top fillets, from the dark side of the fish. Under the bones lie the two bottom fillets.

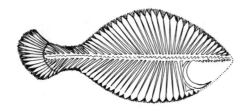

Sole and flounder are the easiest fish to fillet—meaning to remove flesh from bone—because the bones lie as flat as the fish and consist of a central spinal column from which they fan out horizontally.

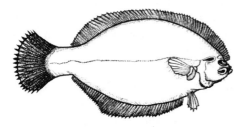

When you look at either side of a flat fish, like flounder, you will see a central line in the skin that runs from tail end to head end; it exactly traces the lines of the spinal column under the skin.

With a sturdy sharp-pointed knife, cut down through skin to bone, tracing this line first on the top and then on the bottom of the fish; you have now outlined the length of the fillets. Free them at the head end by cutting through skin to bone under mouth, gills, and back of head. Finally, to remove fillets from bone, start either at tail end or head end, whichever seems easier to you, and with a very sharp flexible-blade knife, scrape flesh from bone on one side of spinal column out toward edge of fish. Near the edge you will run into a line of small bones, indicating the limit of usable fillet meat; cut along the length of this line of bones with knife or scissors, thus freeing fillet from fish. Repeat with the 3 remaining fillets.

Unless fish is of the flimsy-fleshed variety, plan to remove the skin as follows: Place fillet skin side down on your cutting board, tail end (small end) facing you. One fillet at a time, scrape ⅛ inch of flesh from tail and, holding tail skin in one hand (in a towel if slippery), pull it toward you in a slow back-and-forth movement parallel to your work surface while you slide a knife almost parallel between skin and flesh in the other direction, thus scraping flesh from skin. To prevent fillets from curling while they cook, lightly score the skin side (milky side) with your knife, making crosshatch marks ½ inch apart and going less than 1/16 inch deep.

If you are not using the fillets immediately, wrap and refrigerate. Save the bones and head (fish frame), and the skin, for making stock to use in fish soups and sauces.

FILLETING OVAL-SHAPED FISH

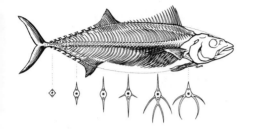

Fish like trout, bass, and salmon have a central spinal column running from head to tail, and fan bones that are vertical rather than horizontal.

The upper half of the fan runs from spine to back in a single line, but the lower half divides in two to enclose the viscera; in addition there is a line of small horizontal bones in the upper third of the body (which can be ignored in small fish).

To fillet, lay fish on board, its head away from you. Cut a line from head to tail on one side of back fin, letting point of knife scrape flesh off upper fan bones until you reach the spinal cord; then outline large end of fillet at gill and head end, cutting through skin to bone. Repeat on the other side. Finally, on the first side, scrape down along tail part of bone to release meat up to abdominal cavity; scrape along bones enclosing cavity on this side, and release the fillet from the fish. Repeat on the other side. Skin the fillet as described for sole and flounder fillets. You may wish to remove the small side bones from center top of fillets with tweezers.

A NOTE ON FISH HEADS. In France, when fish are cooked whole the heads are always left on, the idea being you then know who the fish is. Once on the S.S. *France* sailing to France, the whole dining room had been upset by a group of Irish Bostonians who were horrified to be served their trout *meunière* complete with heads: "Oh, those fish eyes staring at me!" And so forth. Should the *France* remove the heads to please the foreigners, or should they maintain French tradition? I hope they chose the latter solution, but I never did hear the outcome for the Bostonians on the return voyage.

Brochettes, kebabs, and skewers

A *brochette* is a small French skewer, a *shashlik* is Russian for *shish kebab,* while a *shish,* it appears, is a Middle Eastern *brochette,* and a *kebab* is a grill. I shall usually call everything skewers in our language and *brochettes* in French, and start out this fish chapter with them because they are so easy to do. But before getting started, do look at the illustrated skewer talk on page 293.

Coquilles Saint-Jacques en brochettes

SKEWERED SCALLOPS WITH BAY LEAVES

For 4 people

These make an attractive first course, or the main course for a light lunch or supper along with a risotto, a tossed salad or cold vegetables, and a dry white wine such as Chablis, Pouilly Fuissé, or Pinot Blanc.

1½ to 2 lbs. scallops
Salt and pepper
About ½ cup flour
4 to 6 imported bay leaves
About ½ cup melted butter
About 1 cup fresh crumbs from nonsweet white
  bread (such as French or Italian; make the
  crumbs in an electric blender)

Equipment: Paper towels and wax paper, a large
  sieve or a colander, skewer setup and
  drip pan, a pastry brush \

Wash the scallops, looking over each one carefully to remove any sand. Drain and dry on paper towels. Just before cooking, spread them on a sheet of wax paper. Toss with salt and pepper, and the flour; finally toss in sieve or colander to shake off excess flour. String the scallops on skewers, alternating each 2 scallops with a piece of bay leaf. Paint with butter, roll in crumbs, and dribble on more droplets of butter. Broil or barbecue 2 to 3 minutes on each side, just until scallops are springy rather than squashy to the touch. Serve immediately.

Coquilles Saint-Jacques en brochettes, Mornay

SKEWERED
SCALLOPS
BROILED IN
CHEESE SAUCE

For 4 people

Here is a more elaborate presentation, where the scallops are coated with a cheese sauce, then crumbed and broiled. You could serve these as a main course on a bed of risotto or spinach surrounded by baked cherry tomatoes; a fairly full white Burgundy would go well, or a white Châteauneuf, or Pinot Chardonnay. (You can prepare the scallops well ahead of time, refrigerate them, and cook them whenever you are ready to.)

The scallops
1½ to 2 lbs. scallops
Salt and white pepper
About ½ cup flour

The cheese sauce (bouillie sauce with cheese)
1 cup milk (more if needed)
½ cup flour in a heavy-bottomed 2-quart saucepan
2 Tb butter
¼ cup dry white Vermouth
1 whole egg and 1 egg yolk
Salt and white pepper
Drops of Worcestershire or Tabasco sauce
⅓ cup freshly grated Parmesan cheese

*About 2 cups fresh crumbs from nonsweet
    white bread (such as French or Italian;
    make the crumbs in an electric blender)*
4 Tb melted butter

*Equipment: Same as in preceding recipe,
    but the scallops will cook in a jelly-roll pan
    or on a baking sheet. For the sauce: a wire
    whip, spoon, and spatula.*

The scallops. Wash rapidly, drain, and dry on paper towels. Spread on wax paper, and just before covering them with the following sauce, toss with salt, pepper, and flour, then shake in a sieve to remove excess flour.

The cheese sauce. Stirring vigorously with a wire whip, gradually beat the milk into the flour, add the butter, and stir over moderate heat, beating thoroughly when sauce thickens and comes to the boil. Beat in the

Vermouth, and simmer, stirring, 2 to 3 minutes to cook the flour. Sauce should be very thick and hold its shape in a spoon; if too stiff, thin with droplets of milk. Remove from heat and at once break in the egg, beating to blend, then beat in the yolk. Season carefully with ¼ teaspoon or so of salt, several grinds of white pepper, and drops of Worcestershire or Tabasco; then blend in the grated Parmesan.

Assembling the scallops on skewers. String the seasoned and floured scallops on skewers, and set on a piece of wax paper. Spread ¾ of the sauce over tops and sides of scallops, brush on a light coating of crumbs, and rotate the skewers a quarter turn. Coat and crumb remaining side. Refrigerate the scallops 20 minutes or longer, to set sauce and crumbs.

Cooking: about 15 minutes. Preheat oven to 450 degrees. Set scallops on a buttered jelly-roll pan or baking sheet, and dribble the melted butter over them. Bake 8 minutes (for large sea scallops) in lower-third level of oven to cook the scallops partially and brown the bottom part, then set for 4 to 5 minutes under a very low broiler to brown the top lightly—keeping watch not to burn the crumbs. Serve at once.

Filets de poissons en brochettes, aux fines herbes

◆

SKEWERED SOLE,
FLOUNDER, OR
OTHER FISH
FILLETS WITH HERB
BUTTER

For 4 people

Even the most uninteresting fish will benefit from an herbal dressing, a roll in fresh bread crumbs, and a butter-basted broil. The following is for sole or flounder fillets, but you can adapt it to any kind of fish; if the fillets are thick, split them in half or cut them in chunks and slit a pocket in each to be filled with herb butter. Prepare these at least 30 minutes before cooking, to set the crumbs. For a light luncheon, you could accompany these with French bread, a salad of cooked green beans and sliced tomatoes, and a white Riesling wine.

*8 sole or flounder fillets about 8 by 2 inches,
and ¼ inch thick*
Salt and white pepper

The herb butter
8 Tb (1 stick) butter
2 Tb very finely minced shallot or scallion

½ tsp dried tarragon
1 Tb finely minced parsley
Optional, depending on the fish you use: other
    herbs, garlic, other flavorings, etc.
1 Tb lemon juice
Salt and white pepper

The bread crumb coating à l'Anglaise
About ⅔ cup flour in a pie plate
2 eggs beaten with 2 tsp oil and 2 Tb water
    in a pie plate
About 2 cups fresh white bread crumbs (made
    from homemade-type French or Italian
    bread; do them in an electric blender) spread
    on wax paper

For the cooking
About 4 Tb melted butter

Preparing the fillets. Score the skin side of each fillet—the milky side—making crosshatch knife cuts less than ¹⁄₁₆ inch deep and ½ inch apart; this prevents them from twisting out of shape as they cook. Sprinkle each side lightly with salt and pepper, and cut the fillets in half lengthwise, making 16 long strips. Lay on wax paper, milky side up.

The herb butter. If butter is hard, cut into pieces and beat over warm water to soften (then over cold water if you have softened it too much—it should be creamy). Beat in the shallots or scallions and herbs, then by droplets the lemon juice, and salt and pepper to taste.

Skewering and crumbing the fish. Divide the butter into eighths, so you will not run out, then spread a portion on each strip of fish. Roll the fillets up starting at one of the small ends, and thread 4 to a skewer. One by one, roll each in flour and shake off excess; roll in the beaten egg, covering all exposed parts of each fillet and shaking off excess; finally roll in the bread crumbs, patting them in place. Arrange on wax paper on a tray, and refrigerate for at least 30 minutes to set the crumbs.

Cooking: 8 to 10 minutes. Arrange on a buttered baking sheet, baste top side of each skewer with droplets of melted butter, and set under a low broiler about 4 minutes, watching that you don't burn the crumbs. Turn, baste other side with butter, and broil 3 to 4 minutes more. Fish is done when lightly springy rather than squashy to the touch. Serve at once.

Trout and other small whole fish

The trout is lean and delicate in taste, and although cultivated trout have not quite the allure of those caught wild in a mountain stream, they can be delicious and, what's more, you can buy them fresh in most good fish markets. At ours they come in by air from Idaho every Thursday morning, and I love them as an elegant change of pace. Whole trout sautéed in butter, *meunière,* makes a delightful lunch or light supper dish. Then it's fun to do a fancy French filleting job and bake them with buttered crumbs, or to poach them in wine and serve them in a wickedly rich and creamy sauce. Although these recipes are for half-pound trout you can treat other small fish in the same way, like fresh perch or rockfish.

Truites meunière

WHOLE TROUT
SAUTÉED IN BUTTER

This is the simplest way of cooking whole trout about half a pound each; success is only a matter of using clarified butter, and watching that the fish don't brown too much before they are cooked through. For the home cook 4 to 8 fish are probably all you can take care of, since 1 large frying pan 9 to 10 inches in diameter at the bottom will just hold 4 half-pound trout, and you could manage 2 pans at once, but the fish must be served immediately they are cooked. These could be a first course or a main-course luncheon dish. I suggest you serve them alone, however, accompanied only by French bread and a bottle of Riesling or Traminer, followed by whatever else you wish.

For 4 people   *4 half-pound trout cleaned, heads on*
Salt and pepper
Flour
½ to ⅔ cup clarified butter (butter melted,
    skimmed, clear liquid poured off
    milky residue)
A frying pan large enough to hold fish comfortably
The juice of ½ lemon
¼ cup chopped parsley
Optional: Melted butter and lemon wedges
    to serve with the trout

Just before cooking them, sprinkle trout inside and out with salt and pepper, and dust both sides with flour. Pour ⅛ inch of butter into pan, heat to bubbling hot, and arrange trout in pan. Maintain heat so butter is always very hot but not browning, and so that the trout aren't browning too much on bottom. In 5 to 6 minutes, turn trout and sauté 5 to 6 minutes on other side. Trout are done when you gently lift belly flaps, peer inside, and see there is no trace of reddish raw color inside at backbone; another indication is to slit one from outside along the back—flesh should lift from bone. Meat should be just cooked through and juicy— if it flakes easily, the fish are overcooked.

Remove to hot platter or plates, squeeze lemon juice over the fish, and sprinkle with chopped parsley. If butter has browned and burned, discard it and add ¼ cup fresh butter; heat to bubbling and pour over the fish— butter will sizzle as it goes on. Serve immediately, passing additional butter and wedges of lemon if you wish.

Truites aux amandes *(Whole trout sautéed in butter with almonds)*. Follow the preceding recipe for *Truites Meunière*. When trout are done and on the platter with their parsley and lemon, sauté ½ cup of shaved almonds (cut into very thin slices) in the butter as it browns, and strew it over the fish just before serving.

TWO FANCY FRENCH TROUT FILLETINGS

For 4 people   *4 half-pound trout, heads on (see cleaning*
    notes following)
⅓ to ½ cup melted butter
Salt and white pepper
About ½ cup flour
About 1 cup fresh bread crumbs
Parsley sprigs and lemon wedges

Truites en lorgnette (*Trout in the form of lorgnettes*). Here the back-bone of the trout is removed but the fillets remain attached to the head, and are rolled up on either side of it to form a lorgnette or ram's head shape.

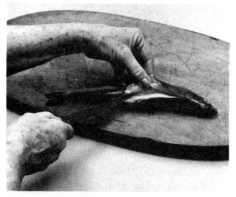

To bone the fish, lay it on its side, and cut on the upper side of the back fin, scraping flesh from bone on one side; release flesh from tail end but keep it attached to head end of trout.

To release flesh from other side of bone, scrape under bone starting at tail end.

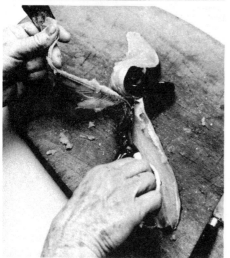

With scissors, cut off bone where it joins the head. Pull out any feather bones you may see in flesh at chest area, using tweezers.

Paint both sides of fillets with melted butter, season with salt and pepper, dust lightly with flour. Then, starting at small end of each, roll it up, flesh side out, to frame the head on each side, as pictured.

Arrange the rolled fish in a buttered baking and serving dish, sprinkle with fresh bread crumbs, and baste with droplets of melted butter. Bake in upper third of a preheated oven for 15 minutes, basting 2 or 3 times with droplets of butter. Serve at once, garnished with parsley and lemon.

Truites en colère (*Trout biting its own tail in anger*). Here the backbone is removed, but head and tail are intact, and the fish is turned inside out so the tail comes out the mouth. Ideally you need whole uncleaned trout with belly intact, but I've given directions for ready-cleaned fish with belly slit, since that's what most of us find in our markets. Starting at the back fin, as for the preceding recipe, scrape flesh from bone on either side, but leave fillets attached to both tail and head.

With scissors, snip off bone at tail end.

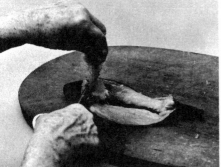

Then snip off bone at head end.

Paint skin and flesh sides of fish with melted butter, sprinkle with salt and pepper, and a dusting of flour. Then bring tail down around under, and push it through the mouth of the trout.

Arrange in a buttered baking dish, sprinkle with fresh crumbs, and bake as in the preceding recipe.

Note: For trout stuffed with a fish mousse, this is the way to fillet, by removing the backbone, although you will have a better result using whole fish with belly intact; in this case, remove viscera and gills when backbone is out.

Trout poached in wine

Trout and other small fish are easy to poach in wine: you arrange them in a baking dish, pour wine and water over them, add aromatic flavorings, and the cooking takes a mere 10 minutes. Serve them hot very simply with melted butter and lemon, or be elaborate with one of the great French fish sauces. On the other hand, let them cool in their poaching liquid, and their delicate flesh will reabsorb its own juices plus the flavor of the wine and seasonings. Then serve them forth cold, with a sour cream dressing or a homemade mayonnaise, or, for total elegance, dress them in aspic for a beautiful cool summer's meal. Too few of us take advantage of cold cooked fish, and we should, since it makes an easy first course or a delightful main-course luncheon dish.

Truites pochées au vin blanc

—————◆—————

TROUT POACHED
IN WHITE WINE

4 half-pound fresh trout, cleaned, heads on
2 cups dry white wine, like Chablis or Mâcon
  (be sure it is not thin and sour) ; or
1½ cups dry white French Vermouth
  (always safer than a doubtful white wine)
1 cup or so fish stock, bottled clam juice,
  or clear chicken broth
2 imported bay leaves
About 2 Tb finely minced shallots or scallions
6 peppercorns
Salt

Preheat oven to 350 degrees. Choose a flameproof oval or rectangular baking dish just large enough to hold the trout easily in one slightly over-lapping layer. Sprinkle insides of trout lightly with salt, and arrange them in the dish. Pour the wine around them, and just enough stock or broth barely to cover them. Add the bay leaves, shallots or scallions, peppercorns, and ½ teaspoon salt. Bring just to the simmer on top of the stove, cover with wax paper, and set in lower level of preheated oven. Trout should barely simmer and should be done in about 10 minutes; to check, gently lift open belly flaps and peer inside—there should be no trace of rosy color; all will be white. Do not overcook.

To serve cold. Remove from oven, cover, and let steep in cooking liquid 30 to 40 minutes, to pick up its flavor. Remove the trout gently, one by one, drain, and if you are not to serve them or arrange them for serving now, wrap each separately in lightly oiled plastic—trout that cool together stick together. To serve, simply peel off top body skin but leave heads and tails intact. Cover flesh with thinly sliced lemon or cucumber, garnish with parsley or watercress; accompany with mayonnaise or sour-cream sauce, and sliced tomatoes. For a glittering presentation in aspic, see *Truites en Gelée* on page 447. (Reserve cooking liquid to use again for fish poaching, or to turn into fish *fumet* for elegant fish sauces, or to turn into an aspic; strain into a container, cover, and freeze it.)

To serve the trout hot. Remove ⅔ of the cooking liquid to a stainless or enameled saucepan and reduce over high heat to about a cup of liquid. Meanwhile, set trout in their baking dish over a pan of barely simmering water. Neatly and rapidly peel skin from top of trout bodies, leaving heads and tails intact; remove also the dorsal fins and little bones attached along back. (Toss these trimmings into the boiling cooking liquid, to give added flavor; strain liquid when reduced.) Cover the peeled trout again with wax paper, then with a cover of some sort, and keep warm over pan of almost simmering water, while making one of the following sauces.

A NOTE ON POACHING LIQUID
AND SAUCE MAKING

In any of the following suggestions, make the sauce as quickly as you can since the fish is at its best the sooner you can serve it. In other words, these are not ahead-of-time dishes. Taste the cooking liquid carefully as it reduces. If you happen to have used an acid wine to poach the fish, you'll remember not to again because it will only get more acid and sour as it boils down and concentrates—add some clam juice, a bit of dry white Vermouth, or even a little Port; perhaps some herbs will help, and the addition of cream will soften the bite. On the other hand, if the sauce seems somewhat sweetish and heavy, particularly after the cream has gone in, droplets of fresh lemon juice will usually be all it needs. Finally, the enrichment butter added at the end gives the sauce a suave and sophisticated finish, comparable to nothing else; 1 or 2 tablespoons gives a fine effect, but you may add several more, as your conscience permits.

Truites
à la crème et
à l'estragon

POACHED TROUT
IN TARRAGON
CREAM SAUCE

The following is a particularly rich and succulent way to serve your trout, in a cream and egg yolk sauce enriched with butter. As an alternate sauce, use the system outlined for *Sole Bonne Femme* on page 135. All these methods are interchangeable, in fact, including the sauce for the braised salmon on page 150. Although you could accompany the trout with tiny boiled potatoes and peas, or with risotto, I do think it is best served alone, with French bread and a fine Burgundy wine. If this were an elaborate dinner, trout could be the first course, followed by a roast. Or it could be a luncheon dish, followed by artichokes or fresh asparagus, or salad and cheese.

For 4 people

The preceding poached trout, hot
The trout-poaching liquid
1 branch fresh tarragon, or
      ½ tsp fragrant dried tarragon
Salt and white pepper
⅔ cup heavy cream, more or less

> *1 egg yolk in a small bowl*
> *1 or more Tb butter*
> *1 Tb or so of fresh minced tarragon or parsley*

Add a branch of fresh tarragon or ½ teaspoon dried tarragon to the poaching liquid as you reduce it in a saucepan over high heat, and taste very carefully for seasoning (see notes preceding this recipe). When you have 1 cup, strain it, and return it to pan. Stir in ½ cup of cream, and continue to boil several minutes over moderate heat as liquid lightly thickens. Remove from heat, beat several spoonfuls of cream into the egg yolk, then beat in ½ cup of the hot liquid by driblets. Gradually beat egg yolk mixture back into hot liquid; stir over moderate heat, allowing liquid to thicken more, but do not let it come to the simmer or it will curdle. Correct seasoning again, and keep warm for a moment while you arrange the fish on a hot platter. Then remove sauce from heat, beat in butter by half tablespoons, adding more as each bit is absorbed. Stir in the herbs, spoon the sauce over the body of the fish, leaving tails and heads exposed. Place a pinch of parsley (or a caper) in each eye, and serve immediately.

VARIATIONS

Truites
à la crème,
bonne femme

WITH MUSHROOMS

Ingredients for the Truites à la Crème,
*   preceding recipe*
2 cups (5 to 6 ounces) fresh mushrooms
1 tsp minced shallot or scallion
1 tsp lemon juice
¼ tsp salt

While the 4 trout are poaching, trim, wash, and slice the mushrooms; toss in a bowl with the shallot or scallion, lemon juice, and salt. Add them to the reduced fish-cooking liquid along with the ½ cup of cream in the preceding recipe. Continue as directed in the recipe, spooning the sauce with mushrooms over the trout at the end.

Truites
à la crème,
Dugléré

WITH TOMATOES

Ingredients for the Truites à la Crème, page 132
1½ cups fresh tomato pulp (tomatoes peeled,
*   seeded, juiced, chopped)*
1 Tb minced shallot or scallion
1 Tb butter
Salt and pepper to taste

While the 4 trout are poaching, prepare the tomato pulp and shallots or scallions, then sauté in a small pan with the butter, at first covering the pan for a few minutes to allow juices to exude. Then sauté over high heat, uncovered, for a few minutes, to let almost all juices evaporate—this is important, so the tomatoes will not thin out your sauce. Season to taste. After the trout-cooking liquid has been reduced and thickened with the ½ cup of cream, fold in the tomatoes and simmer a moment, reducing if necessary. Complete the sauce with the egg yolk, herbs, butter and so forth, and spoon over the trout.

Fillets of sole in white wine

Like the poaching of whole small trout in white wine, the poaching of sole fillets is easy indeed. Lay them in a buttered dish, pour wine or fish stock and seasonings around them, cover with buttered paper, and they cook in 6 to 8 minutes. Then you have the lovely poaching liquid to play with for a sauce, and you have literally hundreds of ways in which to serve the fish. Listed in your Escoffier you will see dozens, and the French *Répertoire de la Cuisine* lists some 200 titles and descriptions starting with the elaborate *Filets de Sole Adrienne* (fold and poach the fillets, nap with a truffled and mushroomed white wine sauce, garnish with poached fish roe, tartlets filled with creamed *écrevisses*, and puff pastry *fleurons*). It ends with the relatively simple *Filets de Sole Yvette,* and its garnishing of tomatoes filled with fish mousse. The typical sauce can be the one used with the trout, on page 132—a reduction of the poaching liquid with cream, a light thickening with egg yolk, and a butter enrichment. Or it can be the *velouté* with cream, or its *beurre manié* variation described here, or the white wine sauce thickened with cornstarch and enriched with cream and egg yolks served with the braised salmon on page 150. Finally, you have a hollandaise type of sauce—the fish poaching liquid reduced down to an essence and then mounted with egg yolks and butter, page 140. The first and the last are the most elegant and delectable, but each has its place, and with these five versions you have the whole fish sauce story.

FISH TALK

Real sole does not grow in American waters, although the true sole of Europe is sometimes imported. What we call sole is flounder or lemon sole, dab or gray sole, with Monterey and Petrale sole available on the West Coast.

Count on 3 fillets 8 to 9 inches long, about 2 inches across, and ¼ inch thick per person, or around 2½ pounds of skinless and boneless fillets for 6 people.

To prepare them for cooking, cut the fillets in half lengthwise if they are whole (meaning that the pair from each side of the fish has not been cut down its central line). The milky side was the side next to the skin; score it to prevent the fillets from curling (meaning to cut very shallow crosshatch lines in the flesh, on the bias, ¼ inch apart). The fillets are now ready for cooking.

Until the moment of cooking, keep the fish covered and refrigerated to preserve its freshness; see also the notes, page 118, on how to store fish.

Filets de sole bonne femme

———

SOLE FILLETS
POACHED WITH
WHITE WINE AND
MUSHROOMS

Just as *Coq au Vin* is one of the most popular chicken dishes, *Sole Bonne Femme* is equally loved, since mushrooms, sole, and white wine sauce are a delicious combination—probably because mushrooms are a natural source of monosodium glutamate, the taste enhancer. Again, like *Coq au Vin,* which you may have seen as a twin dish with Chicken Fricassee on television, *Sole Bonne Femme* paired up perfectly in another program with *Sole Dugléré;* where the one uses mushrooms, the other has tomatoes, but both are assembled, cooked, and sauced like the twins they actually are. You will note that the following is a different version from the recipes for *Bonne Femme* in Volume

I of *Mastering* and in *The French Chef Cookbook;* this one is simpler and more direct, and equally as good, I think.

Timing note: Although you can prepare the fish for the oven well in advance, it is at its most delicious when sauced and served at once. This is because cooked sole fillets continue to exude their vital juices as they sit and wait; if you were working in a restaurant you could, of course, have your sauces made in advance, and there would be no juice-losing pause once the fillets came from the oven. As a home chef, you just have to hustle.

Serving notes: You can serve a sauced sole dish like this as a separate course, as is so often done in France, accompanied only by French bread and possibly tiny boiled potatoes or rice, or you can be less formal and add buttered peas or asparagus tips, or cucumbers cooked in butter, or a spinach or green bean purée. This kind of dish gives you an opportunity to serve your very best white Burgundy, or one of those most difficult-to-find great white Graves. Whatever wine you choose, it should be full, smooth, suave, and dry.

For poaching the fish

For 4 people

12 skinless and boneless sole fillets, each about 9 by 2 by ¼ inches in size
Salt and white pepper
About ¼ lb. (1½ cups) fresh mushrooms
2½ Tb minced shallots or scallions
2 Tb minced fresh parsley
1 Tb or so soft butter
½ cup dry white wine or dry white French Vermouth
About ½ cup fish stock or bottled clam juice

For the sauce velouté (white-wine fish sauce)
2 Tb butter
2½ Tb flour
½ cup or so heavy cream
Either: 2 or more Tb butter and drops of lemon juice
Or: 3 or 4 Tb leftover hollandaise or béarnaise sauce (which can come from the freezer), and lemon

Equipment: A flameproof baking and serving dish such as an oval one 9 by 12 inches and 2 inches deep; wax paper; a cover for draining juices out of the baking dish; the usual sauce-making paraphernalia

Preparing the dish for the oven. Prepare the fillets as described on page 135, salt and pepper them lightly on the scored milky side, and, if you wish, fold them in half end to end, milky side inside. Trim the mushrooms, wash them rapidly, drain, and either cut into very thin slices (1/16 inch thick), or mince them. Toss in a bowl with 2 tablespoons of the shallots or scallions, the parsley, 1/4 tsp of salt, and a big pinch of pepper. Smear half a tablespoon of butter in the baking dish, and spread in the mushrooms. Arrange the fillets, slightly overlapping, on top of the mushrooms (if fillets have not been folded, place them milky side down). Lightly salt and pepper top of fish, and sprinkle on the remaining shallots or scallions. Pour on the wine or Vermouth, and enough fish stock or clam juice almost to cover the fish. Smear butter on one side of the wax paper, and lay it buttered side down on the fillets.

☼ Refrigerate if you are not yet ready to cook the fish.

Baking, saucing, and serving: *20 to 30 minutes in all; oven at 350 degrees.* About 30 minutes before you are ready to serve, bring just to the simmer on top of the stove; set in lower middle of preheated oven for 8 to 10 minutes. Fish is done when springy rather than squashy to the touch, and when it has turned from translucent to milky white—do not overcook or fish will flake and lose its juices. Remove from oven, place a cover over dish, and drain cooking liquid into a stainless or enameled 3-quart saucepan.

(While making sauce, leave wax paper and cover on fish; place in turned-off oven leaving door ajar, or over a pan of simmering water.)

Rapidly boil down cooking liquid until a bit less than a cup remains; drain fish again during this period, adding liquid to pan. Meanwhile, in another saucepan, make a white *roux* with 2 tablespoons of butter and 2½ tablespoons of flour (stir butter and flour together over moderate heat until they foam and froth for 2 minutes without turning more than a buttery yellow; remove from heat). Whip the hot cooking juices into the warm *roux* to blend smoothly; bring to the boil, stirring, and boil 2 minutes. Sauce should be thick; drain fish again into sauce, then thin out sauce with spoonfuls of cream. It should now just be thick enough to coat fish nicely; correct seasoning carefully. Off heat and just before serving, beat in the butter or hollandaise by spoonfuls, adding drops of lemon juice if needed. Spoon the sauce over the fish, decorate with parsley if you wish, and serve immediately.

Alternate serving notes. If your fish fillets are the kind that hold their shape after cooking, you may wish to transfer them to a hot platter, and distribute some of the mushrooms on top before saucing the fish. On the other hand, if you wish to glaze the fish, and have used the hollandaise sauce enrichment, set fish so surface is as close as possible under a red-hot broiler to brown top of sauce lightly, about 2 minutes.

VARIATIONS

Filets de sole Dugléré

WITH WHITE WINE SAUCE AND TOMATOES

This is done exactly like *Sole Bonne Femme* except that you substitute tomatoes for mushrooms, making a lovely rose-colored sauce speckled with green herbs. The slight acidity of the tomatoes blends deliciously with the flavors of fresh fish, cream, and wine.

For 4 people

Ingredients for the preceding Sole Bonne Femme, but omit the mushrooms
Either 4 medium-sized tomatoes, or 2 to 3 out-of-season tomatoes plus several canned Italian plum tomatoes, as described below

Drop the fresh tomatoes in boiling water for 10 seconds, cut out the stems, then peel the tomatoes and cut them in half crosswise. Half a tomato at a time, gently squeeze out juice and seeds, cut the pulp into half-inch dice, and place in a mixing bowl. (If you are adding canned Italian plum tomatoes, cut them in half and drain well, then push through a sieve to remove seeds.) You should have about 1½ cups of tomato pulp; toss it with 2 tablespoons each of minced shallots and parsley, ¼ teaspoon salt, and a few grinds of fresh white pepper. Spread the tomatoes in the bottom of your buttered baking dish, arrange the seasoned fillets on top, season again, and sprinkle on the remaining shallots. Pour on the wine and fish stock or clam juice almost to cover, top with buttered paper, and continue exactly as in the preceding recipe.

Filets de sole au beurre d'amandes

WITH WHITE WINE AND ALMOND BUTTER

Here the fillets are folded over an almond butter, poached as usual, and the sauce is enriched with toasted shaved almonds and additional almond butter. Nothing wrong with that combination! Although you can use the same *velouté* sauce described for the *Bonne Femme,* here is a slightly different sauce method, using a *beurre manié,* for a change.

The almond flavoring

For 4 people

*½ cup almond flakes (almonds shaved thin;
     can be bought in packages)*
2 Tb minced shallots or scallions
6 Tb (¾ stick) soft butter
*½ cup ground almonds (whole blanched
     almonds pulverized; do in an electric blender)*
Salt and white pepper
Drops of lemon juice

The rest of the ingredients

*12 skinless and boneless sole fillets, each about
     9 by 2 by ¼ inches in size*
1 additional Tb minced shallots or scallions
*½ cup dry white wine or dry white
     French Vermouth*
½ cup fish stock or bottled clam juice
2 Tb flour
1½ Tb soft butter
½ cup heavy cream, more if needed
Sprigs of fresh parsley for decoration

The almond flavoring. Spread the almond flakes on a cookie sheet and bake in upper-middle level of a 350-degree oven for about 10 minutes, tossing several times until very lightly browned. Remove and reserve for final step, when they will be folded into the sauce. Cook the shallots or scallions in 2 tablespoons of the butter in a small saucepan for a moment or two, to soften; remove from heat, and beat in the ground almonds and the remaining 4 tablespoons of butter. Season to taste with salt, pepper, and drops of lemon juice.

Preparing the fish for the oven. Trim and score the fish fillets for cooking as described on page 135. Season milky side lightly with salt and pepper, and spread on it a teaspoon of the almond butter; fold in two end-to-end to enclose the butter. Reserve remaining almond butter for the sauce, later. Arrange the fillets slightly overlapping in a heavily buttered baking and serving dish, such as a 9- by 12-inch oval about 2 inches deep. Sprinkle with the additional minced shallots or scallions, and a dusting of salt and pepper. Pour the wine or Vermouth around the fish and enough fish stock or clam juice almost to cover. Top with heavily buttered wax paper.

☼ Refrigerate if you are not yet ready to cook the fish.

Baking, saucing, and serving: *20 to 30 minutes in all; oven at 350 degrees.*
Bring liquid in baking dish to simmer on top of the stove, then bake in
lower middle of preheated oven for 8 to 10 minutes, until fish is just
springy rather than squashy to the touch. Remove from oven, place a
cover over dish, and drain cooking liquid into a stainless or enameled
saucepan. Leave paper and cover on fish, and keep warm while finishing
sauce. Rapidly boil down cooking liquid to ½ cup; drain fish again,
pouring juices into cooking liquid. Then blend the flour and butter in a
small bowl with a rubber spatula, to make a soft paste, a *beurre manié*.
Remove cooking liquid from heat, and beat the *beurre manié* into it
with a wire whip. When thoroughly blended, bring to the boil, stirring;
thin out with spoonfuls of cream—it should be just thick enough to coat
a spoon. Season carefully with salt, pepper, and drops of lemon juice;
fold in the toasted almond flakes. Remove sauce from heat and, by half
tablespoons, fold in the remaining almond butter. Drain fish again if
necessary (but not into sauce, unless the sauce seems too thick), and
spoon sauce over fish. Decorate with sprigs of parsley, and serve immediately.

Sauce vin blanc

EGG YOLK AND
BUTTER SAUCE
FOR FISH

For 4 people

This is an alternate sauce, like a hollandaise, rich
and lovely, very *haute cuisine,* and it is one you
can use with any sole-in-white-wine dish. The recipe
is in its short form since full details on hollandaise,
if you want more, are on page 622.

Ingredients for any of the preceding sole dishes,
but omit sauce-making items and
substitute the following:
¼ to ½ cup heavy cream
3 egg yolks
8 to 12 Tb (1 to 1½ sticks) soft butter
Salt, pepper, and lemon juice

After the fish has poached, drain cooking liquid into a stainless or
enameled pan, and reduce it rapidly to ¼ cup or less, until it is almost
syrupy. Stir over cold water to cool for a moment, then add ¼ cup of
heavy cream, and vigorously beat in the 3 egg yolks with a wire whip.
Set over moderately low heat and stir rather slowly with whip, reaching
all over bottom of pan, for several minutes until mixture sends up a
faint whiff of steam, then thickens enough to coat wires of whip with a
creamy layer—be careful it doesn't come near the simmer and scramble

the yolks, but dare to heat it to the point where it thickens. Remove from heat and immediately beat in a spoonful of butter to stop the cooking. Rapidly beat in the rest of the butter by spoonfuls, adding a new bit when the last has almost absorbed—use as much of the butter amount as you wish, finishing off with dollops of cream, again, if you wish. Season very carefully with salt, pepper, and drops of lemon juice. Fold whatever garnish you wish into the sauce—almonds, almond butter, or mushrooms, or cooked tomato pulp—spoon it over the fish, and serve at once.

OTHER IDEAS

I really think that with these several recipes and sauces, you can do practically any sole dish described to you. *Sole Marguery,* for instance, is poached in the usual way, garnished with cooked shrimps and mussels, napped with the typical white wine sauce but with a difference—the sauce has been enriched with several spoonfuls of hollandaise before the dish is slipped a moment under a hot broiler to glaze. *Sole Sylvia* has artichokes and fish mousse. *Argenteuil* is garnished with asparagus tips, *Choiseul* has white truffles, *Chivry* has green herbs, and so it goes. Here is a splendid idea I shall just describe, leaving the execution of it to you.

Les filets de sole en surprise de Mme. Aimée Cassiot (*Sole in white wine with mushroom duxelles and lobster*) . Madame Cassiot, able chef-teacher for Le Cercle des Gourmettes' Paris luncheons in the 1960's and early 70's, produced the following one day I was there. She filleted a turbot (or one could use a large sole) and poached it in the usual white wine along with its carefully preserved whole head piece and tail piece. She then re-formed the fish on her serving platter with a creamed mushroom *duxelles* between the 2 sets of fillets, put the head and tail in their normal places, and decorated her fish with scallops of lobster meat cooked in butter, wine, and herbs. She napped the ensemble with the delicious *Sauce Vin Blanc* just described, and it was a charming presentation. Nothing impossible about that, and if you are cooking with friends, it's the kind of dish that's great fun to do.

Fish steaks and thick fillets

Tranches de poisson grillées

BROILED FISH
STEAKS AND THICK
FILLETS

I am not going into any elaboration about broiling fish, but do want to pass on a tip from George Berkowitz, who runs a most successful fish and chips restaurant in connection with his fresh fish market in Cambridge, Mass. That is, you don't need to turn the fish when you broil it, since who sees the other side anyway? The trick is to put a little liquid in the dish to keep the fish moist and to steam the bottom; then you concentrate on browning the top to a beautiful color. A thickness of ¾ inch is about right, I have found; thinner than that the fish often doesn't have time to brown —unless you sprinkle it with foreign matter like bread crumbs or paprika to hasten the process. Thicker than ¾ inch the fish tends to dry out on top before the bottom is done, unless you do a combination of broiling and either baking or microwaving—which, incidentally, works wonderfully well. Here is an example of the plain broil.

Serving suggestions. Sautéed or fried potatoes are delicious with broiled fish, or the mixed vegetable ragout on page 357, the baked zucchini on page 426, or one of the eggplant dishes starting on page 398. You will want a strong dry white wine, like a white Châteauneuf, Côtes du Rhône, or Pinot Blanc.

For 4 people

*About 2 pounds of swordfish steak ¾ inch thick,
    skinned and boned (or halibut, bluefish,
    pollack, or cod)*
Salt and pepper
Soft butter
*½ cup, more or less, dry white wine, dry white
    French Vermouth, or water*
*Lemon, fresh parsley, and, if you wish, a
    minced shallot or scallion, for garnish*

Dry the fish thoroughly on paper towels and season both sides with salt and pepper. Choose a shallow flameproof baking dish just big enough to hold fish comfortably in one layer. Smear inside of dish with butter, and arrange the fish in it. Dry top of fish again, and smear with butter. Pour liquid around fish to come about half way up.

Broil under moderately high heat 6 to 8 minutes, brushing top of fish with butter once or twice, and if liquid evaporates before fish is cooked, add a little more. Fish is done when its own juices just begin to exude into the dish; it will feel springy rather than squashy, and if you have any doubts, cut into it. It should not be flaky and dry, however, but moist.

Either serve the fish directly from the dish, accompanied with lemon wedges and sprigs of parsley, or arrange the fish on a hot serving platter, add a little more wine and a tablespoon of lemon juice to the baking dish, and boil down rapidly with the minced shallot or scallion. When liquid is syrupy, remove from heat and swirl in, a half spoonful at a time, several tablespoons of soft butter; swish in a tablespoon of minced parsley, pour over the fish, and serve at once.

Thon en Chartreuse; tranches de poisson en Chartreuse

FISH IN MONK'S CLOTHING: STEAKS OR THICK FILLETS BRAISED WITH LETTUCE, HERBS, AND WINE

The vegetarian monks of La Grande Chartreuse, who nourished themselves on roots and greens while making their famous liqueur, gave their name to a number of nineteenth-century dishes that were far from meatless. The great chef, Carême, for example, delighted in making elaborately constructed molded creations of presumably monkish vegetables to which he added forcemeats, shellfish, and truffles, and he served them glamorously during Lent and on meatless Fridays. Following Carême's splendid example, pheasant or partridge too old for roasting was braised in cabbage and root vegetables, molded decoratively, and presented as *Faisan en Chartreuse.* This tradition must have come down to the Mediterranean, because the colorful Provençal fish recipe described here is also *en Chartreuse,* but it is only the greens, onions, and carrots that remind us of the good monks and their simple roots, for the rest of the dish is accented with anchovies and black olives, and surrounded by a sea of fresh tomato sauce.

All of the originals of the Provençal recipes call for fresh red tuna, and although I experimented with it a number of times while preparing this dish for our television show, I just don't like fresh red tuna, cooked. I tried various marinades of salt, of lemon, of wine, and I just don't like it. Swordfish is infinitely superior, to my mind. Of course, shortly after its first showing over the air, the mercury scare hit this country, and swordfish disappeared. Now it is back, thank heaven. However, minus swordfish, you can substitute halibut, bluefish, cod, or even fresh tuna.

Serving suggestions. With its elaborate garnish, you need only boiled potatoes or rice, or simply French bread to complete the main course, and a strong dry white wine like a Hermitage, Pouilly Fuissé, or Pinot Blanc.

For 6 to 8 people	*About 3 pounds of swordfish steak 2 inches thick, skinned and boned (or halibut, bluefish, cod, or pollack, or—tuna)*
	Cold water to cover the fish, and 1½ tsp salt plus 1 Tb lemon juice per quart
	2 cups sliced onions
	½ cup thinly sliced carrots
	About ½ cup olive oil
	Enough greenery to make 6 packed cups (very green romaine or other lettuce leaves, plus spinach leaves and, if you have it, some young fresh sorrel)
	2 or 3 large cloves garlic, minced or puréed
	¼ tsp fennel seeds
	½ tsp salt
	Pepper
	1 cup dry white wine, or ⅔ cup dry white Vermouth
	Either: 2 cups fresh tomato pulp (4 or 5 tomatoes peeled, seeded, juiced, and chopped)
	Or: 3 fresh tomatoes and ¼ to ⅓ cup canned tomato (Italian plum tomatoes halved, drained, and sieved)
	About 12 flat fillets of anchovies packed in olive oil and drained (or your own, page 437)
	About 12 pitted black olives

*Equipment: A flameproof baking and serving
dish large enough to hold fish comfortably,
and a cover; a heavy frying pan for browning
fish; aluminum foil oiled on 1 side,
to cover fish in oven*

Freshening the fish. This applies to swordfish, bluefish, and tuna only. Wash fish and place in a flat enameled or glass dish. Cover with cold water, adding the specified amount of salt and lemon juice per quart. Let steep for 30 minutes (or longer in the refrigerator, if you wish) ; this will remove a little excess oiliness.

The braising base. Stir the onions, carrots, and ¼ cup of the oil into the baking dish, cover, and cook slowly, stirring occasionally, for 10 to 15 minutes, or until vegetables are tender and translucent but not browned. Meanwhile, wash the greens, shake dry, and cut by handfuls into *chiffonade* (⅛-inch strips) ; fold into the onions and carrots along with the garlic, fennel, salt, and pepper, blending greens and vegetables together. Cover, and cook slowly, stirring occasionally, for about 20 minutes. Correct seasoning.

Browning and braising the fish. Preheat oven to 350 degrees. Drain the fish and pat dry on paper towels. Film frying pan with $\frac{1}{16}$-inch layer of oil, heat to very hot but not smoking, and brown the fish lightly for 2 to 3 minutes on each side. Push braising vegetables to sides of their dish, lay in the fish, and cover with the vegetables. Pour on the wine, Vermouth, or other liquid. Lay the oiled foil over the fish, place cover on dish, and set in middle level of preheated oven. Regulate heat so fish simmers very slowly for 1¼ hours—this is a long simmer so the fish will absorb the flavor of the braising ingredients; basting is not necessary.

Sauce and serving. When done, drain cooking juices out of the dish into a frying pan, add tomatoes to the juices, and boil down rapidly. Meanwhile, arrange the vegetables over the fish, and top with a crisscrossing of anchovies interspersed with black olives. When tomato mixture is thick, correct seasoning, pour around the fish, and serve. (You may cover the dish and keep it warm for half an hour or so; in this case, do not make the anchovy decorations until just before serving, and do not let the fish overcook.)

Whole fish—baking and braising

One of the great fishy treats along the French Riviera, when you go to a good restaurant and sit looking out over the Mediterranean, is *Loup Grillé, Flambé au Fenouil*—a whole fresh bass grilled, then turned over flaming fennel stalks right at your table. The following recipe describes both the Mediterranean barbecue and flaming techniques for those who have stalks and grills, and an alternative using an oven and fennel seeds. However, with or without fennel and flames, this is a deliciously simple way to cook whole fish, especially when you serve it with the lemon butter described at the end of the recipe. The only other accompaniments you need are boiled potatoes, French bread, and a dry white wine like Muscadet, Pouilly Fumé, or Riesling.

Loup (or *loup de mer* and *bar*) are French for European sea bass, a handsome gray, salmon-shaped fish with lean, white, tender, rather flaky flesh, and delicate texture and taste. Atlantic and Pacific bass are worthy substitutes, while trout, salmon, whitefish, weakfish, and even fish of the mackerel type are delicious cooked and served this way.

Fennel belongs to the umbellifer group of plants, meaning that each flower head is a cluster of buds on long stems connected at the base, like an upturned umbrella. Some varieties of fennel are cultivated for their seeds, some for their bulbs, and some for their stalks. The fennel used in the south of France for *loup flambé* is the long stalky kind that grows wild along the coast. The stalks are harvested, folded into bundles 6 to 8 inches long and 3 inches in diameter, and left to dry until crackly and ready to flame a fish. Fennel grows wild also in America, but don't go gathering it unless you really know what you are about because many members of the look-alike umbellifers are among the most poisonous known to man. According to my source, Nelson Coon's *Using Wayside Plants* (New York: Hearthside Press, 1960), these include water hemlock and poison hemlock; the latter, presumably the one used in Socrates' lethal and final drink, produces an almost immediate total paralysis and death. Well, and here I had been gathering what appeared to be wild fennel or anise or caraway all these years until a botanist friend pointed out the danger. Anyway, the smoke from French fennel twigs is really more for drama than flavor, and you can forget this part of the recipe.

Fennel seeds, on the other hand, have the perfume of wild anise. Sprinkled inside the fish, they give out their subtle flavor as it cooks, and will make you think of Provence. Thus with the seeds alone—and most of the well-known spice houses bottle them—you can produce a fish with the right taste, and you can even flame fennel seeds in brandy to pour over it before serving.

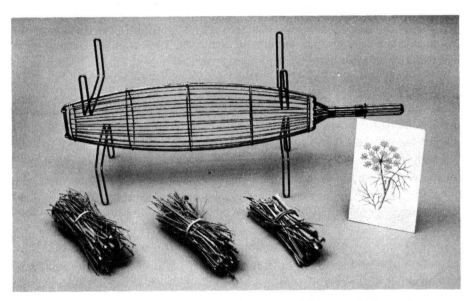

Equipment for Loup Flambé au Fenouil: the fish-flaming basket and the bundles of dried fennel, along with a portrait of fennel in flower.

Loup grillé ou rôti, flambé au fenouil

———————

GRILLED OR
ROASTED
WHOLE FISH,
FLAMED
IN FENNEL

For a 3½- to
4-pound fish,
serving 4 people

A whole 3½- to 4-lb. fresh sea bass (see also preceding alternatives), cleaned but with head on, and scales too, if you are barbecuing or flaming in a fish basket—scales give more strength to skin

½ tsp salt

5 or 6 grinds of fresh pepper

1 tsp fennel seeds

Optional: 3 or 4 dried fennel stalks

2 Tb olive oil or salad oil

Preparing the fish for cooking. Dry the fish thoroughly inside and out. Sprinkle the salt, pepper, and fennel seeds inside the cavity, and thrust in the fennel stalks also, if you have them. Paint whole outside of fish with oil.

If you are barbecuing the fish

A long-handled double rack, hinged at the large end, is recommended here, for ease in turning the fish. (A fish-shaped, hinged wire basket, such as the one shown in the illustration, is useful only if all joints are welded; most models are only soldered together, and are designed for the final flaming, not the initial cooking.) When barbecue heat is ready for cooking, oil the rack, place the seasoned and oiled fish in it, and barbecue over moderate heat about 15 minutes on each side. Basting is not necessary unless skin breaks—then baste with oil several times.

Fish is done: when it feels springy to the touch rather than squashy; when the juices begin to exude and splutter into the heat; when you look into the cavity and see no trace of rosy or reddish color; when you slit the skin along the back, and can just lift the flesh from the bone. The flesh must remain juicy; when it flakes easily and no extra juice exudes, you have overcooked the fish—too bad, and pay close attention to these points next time.

If you are roasting the fish in the oven

Preheat oven to 400 degrees, and set rack in upper-middle level. Place the seasoned and oiled fish on a large baking sheet (rather than roasting pan, so you can slide fish off easily when done). Enclose end of tail in oiled aluminum foil; tuck a piece under head if head sticks over edge. Roast 30 to 40 minutes, until juices just begin to exude—see preceding paragraph for details. No basting is necessary.

If you are to flame the fish in fennel stalks

For barbecued fish, strew 2 bundles of very dry fennel stalks over the hot coals, and when it catches fire, hold the fish over the smoke, turning from side to side for a minute or so. For roasted fish, plan to flame it in the dining room; slide fish into a basket or onto a rack; strew fennel stalks in the bottom of a large roasting pan. Have a chafing-dish flaming device at the table, a saucepan, a bottle of Armagnac, Cognac, or bourbon at hand, and matches. Heat about ⅓ cup of liquor to bubbling, pour it over the fennel stalks, and set over flaming device. Light the stalks, and turn the fish over the smoke for several minutes, then slide fish onto platter, and extinguish flames by setting a cover or tray over them.

If you have no fennel stalks but want to flame the fish anyway

Transfer the cooked fish onto a serving platter, and bring to the table. Heat 1 teaspoon of fennel seeds and ¼ to ⅓ cup Armagnac or Cognac in a small pan; when bubbling, set aflame with a lighted match, spoon up for drama, then slowly ladle the flaming liquid over the fish. Serve immediately.

If you do not wish to flame the fish

A perfectly cooked fish needs no flaming at all; serve it as it is. But you cannot, of course, call it a *loup flambé*.

Beurre françoise

BUTTER CREAMED
WITH LEMON:
FOR ALL KINDS
OF FISH, AND
FOR VEGETABLES

This lovely light sauce melts quickly when spread over a hot serving of fish or vegetables. It was introduced, by the way, to Le Cercle des Gourmettes by Françoise Régnier. You will find another version of it in *Simca's Cuisine,* and one in *Escoffier* called *Sauce Mousseuse* (for which, in my American edition at least, the butter has been mistranslated as being a *beurre manié,* when in the original it is a butter *déjà manié,* already worked and softened).

For 4 servings

4 ounces (1 stick) soft butter
The grated rind of 1 lemon
The juice of ½ lemon
3 Tb heavy cream
About ⅓ cup tepid liquid—fish stock, or
  cooking juices, or vegetable cooking juices
¼ tsp salt
4 grinds of pepper
2 to 3 Tb minced parsley

Beat butter in a small bowl until soft and fluffy (you may wish to use a portable electric beater). Beat in the lemon rind and then, by droplets, the lemon juice and the cream. Finally, by droplets again, beat in the tepid liquid. (Keep on beating if the liquids refuse to homogenize with the butter; they will eventually. If butter softens too much, beat over cold water.) Season to taste, stir in the parsley, and scrape into a serving bowl. Serve at room temperature.

Poisson entier braisé au Porto

WHOLE LARGE
SALMON, BASS,
TROUT, OR OTHER
LARGE FISH OR
FILLETS
BRAISED IN WINE
AND AROMATICS;
PORT WINE AND
MUSHROOM SAUCE

Braising a large fish or large piece of fish and serving it in a Port wine sauce with mushrooms is not nearly the *tour de force* that it sounds. You sauté your aromatic vegetables in butter so they will render their essences, lay them under and around the fish, add enough wine to the pot so the fish will steam while it bakes in the oven, you baste it a few times, and in about an hour, a 10-pound fish is done. There you have this most delectable of fish, all juicy, tender, and subtly flavored, and the most heavenly cooking juices imaginable. These you can serve just as they are, or turn into a creamy sauce with mushrooms and wine as suggested here, or follow any of the four other sauce systems outlined in the fillet of sole section, pages 134 to 141.

Menu suggestions. To give examples from this book, you might start out your dinner with something chic but already cooked, like the cold liver *pâté* on page 368, and have a ready prepared dessert such as the glittering pear tart on page 501 or the grapefruit sherbet on page 539. A handsome platter of sliced ripe tomatoes, cucumbers, and watercress would go nicely with the fish, plus steamed rice if you wanted it, or only French bread. An excellent white Burgundy, one of the greats, would be the wine.

Note: The recipe here is for a large center cut of salmon, but you may cook a whole salmon or whole or large pieces of other fish the same way, and the microwave oven does a beautiful job too, as described at the end of the recipe.

Preparing the fish for braising

For 10 to 12 people

6 Tb butter in a 2- to 3-quart saucepan
2 cups thinly sliced onions
1 cup each thinly sliced carrots and celery stalks
The following tied in washed cheesecloth:
> *6 to 8 parsley sprigs, 2 imported bay leaves,*
> *½ tsp tarragon*
8 to 9 lbs. fresh salmon, center cut, and in two
> *pieces if you wish (washed and scaled)*
Salad oil
Salt and pepper

*Braising liquid: 5 to 6 cups white wine fish stock;
or 1 bottle dry white wine and 1 cup
bottled clam juice*

*Equipment: A large piece of cheesecloth, washed
and wrung out; a covered roaster with rack
or a rack, pan, and aluminum foil; the
usual sauce equipment*

Melt the butter, stir in the sliced vegetables, add the herb packet, cover the pan, and cook slowly, stirring occasionally, until vegetables are tender but not browned—10 minutes or so. Meanwhile, wash and dry the fish, brush outside with salad oil, and sprinkle inside with ½ teaspoon of salt and several grinds of pepper. Place cheesecloth under rack in roaster (or roasting pan), and lay fish on rack. Sprinkle with ½ teaspoon of salt. When vegetables are tender, season with salt and pepper, and spread half of them over the fish. Fold cheesecloth over top of fish, and place rest of vegetables and the herb packet around inside edges of roaster. Pour in the braising liquid—you should have enough to cover bottom of roaster to a depth of about ½ inch.

☼ If you are not ready to cook the fish, cover and refrigerate.

Braising the fish: *About 1 hour, and fish can wait another hour before being served; oven at 350 degrees.* Set roaster over moderately high heat on top of the stove, and bring liquid barely to the simmer. Cover the roaster (using foil if you have no conventional cover), and set in lower-middle level of oven. Regulate heat so liquid barely simmers throughout the cooking—this is to prevent the fish from bursting its skin and from flaking. Baste several times, using liquid in roaster. Fish is done at a meat thermometer reading of around 165 degrees, or when there is no raw-red tinge of color inside cavity near backbone, or when you cut into flesh from edge of back, it comes easily off the bone. Do not overcook; fish should remain intact and juicy.

You may serve the fish just as it is, with no sauce, just the juices and braising vegetables, but the following makes a delicious accompaniment.

Port wine sauce

For about 3½ cups   *¼ cup or more dry Port wine
3 Tb cornstarch in a 4- to 6-cup bowl
3 egg yolks*

½ cup or more heavy cream
Optional: 1½ cups thinly sliced fresh mushrooms
sautéed in 2 Tb butter
2 Tb finely minced parsley
Optional: 4 or more Tb soft butter

Spoon or drain most of liquid and vegetables out of the roaster into a saucepan; boil down, if necessary, to about 3 cups. Stir ¼ cup of Port wine into the cornstarch. Remove braising liquid from heat and beat into it the cornstarch-Port mixture; when blended, bring to the simmer for 2 to 3 minutes to cook the starch. Place the egg yolks in the starch bowl, and blend in ½ cup of the cream. Remove braising liquid again from the heat, and beat 1 cup of it by driblets into the egg yolks, then beat the egg yolk mixture back into the braising liquid. Set again over heat and stir, reaching all over bottom and sides of pan while sauce comes to the simmer; simmer 1 minute, stirring slowly. Blend in the optional mushrooms and their juices, and simmer a moment. Sauce should be thick enough to coat the fish nicely but not too heavily; thin out, if necessary, with more juices from the roasting pan or with more cream. Carefully taste for seasoning and flavor; add more salt, pepper, or Port wine if you feel them needed—sauce can have a final addition of butter just before serving, to smooth and enrich it. Clean off sides of pan and film top of sauce with a spoonful of cream until you are ready to serve.

Serving. Provide yourself with a lightly buttered hot serving platter, a warmed serving bowl for the sauce, parsley for decorations, and steamed rice hot and ready to go, or whatever you have chosen to go with the fish.

Brush vegetables off top of fish; lift fish out of roaster (using rack to help you) and slide it onto serving platter. Peel skin off top side of fish, and scrape off any brownish bits of flesh. Pull remains of fins out of back ridge, along with any small bones. Bring sauce again to simmer and remove from heat. Stir in the parsley, then, by spoonfuls, the optional enrichment butter, adding a new piece as the last is absorbed. Spoon a coating of sauce and vegetables over the fish. Pour rest of sauce into warmed bowl. If there is room on the platter, arrange the rice or other accompaniments around the fish. Serve immediately.

☼ You may keep the fish warm, but unpeeled and unsauced, for 30 minutes or so on its platter, covered with foil in a slow oven (120 degrees) , over simmering water, or on an electric warming tray. Peel and sauce it just before serving.

Fish braised in a microwave oven. This works beautifully, and the process is almost identical to braising in a standard oven, except that it takes a third the time. Use a ceramic cooking and serving dish, and a 5- to 6-lb. piece of salmon. Arrange as described but pour in only enough braising liquid to make ½ inch. Spread cooked vegetables over and around fish, add the herb bouquet, and cover fish closely with wax paper. Braise 10 minutes, turn the fish on its other side, and braise 10 minutes more. Let the fish sit, covered, for 10 minutes to finish cooking by itself. To make more braising juices for your sauce, drain juices out of dish, measure, and add wine and clam juice to make 3½ cups—boil down to about 3 cups to evaporate alcohol, then proceed with the sauce as described.

Fish mousses

Before electricity entered the culinary arena, anything like a mousse, meaning puréed fish or meat beaten into a soft and delicate mass with eggs and cream, was a horrifying chore. When our class of eight made one with our *maître,* Chef Bugnard, in the old days before any electrical appliances graced French kitchens, we filleted our fish—a pike, with all its bones—and puréed it by pounding in a mortar, a black marble affair that looked like a large funeral urn and sat on a sturdy wooden pedestal. The pounding instrument was a very heavy dumbbell-shaped pestle 2 feet long, made of boxwood. We hand-pounded that fish 30 minutes at least, taking turns, until Chef said it was reduced to a fine enough paste. Then we pounded it another 20 minutes with *pâte à choux* flour paste, Chef continually testing it, until it was good and sticky and ready for the pounding in, bit by bit, of eggs. At last it was fine and smooth enough to be turned out onto a special type of puréeing sieve, a *tamis,* its taut wire mesh stretched across a wooden hoop; it looked like the top of a drum. Now the thick sticky purée had to be hand-rubbed through that drum sieve with a wooden pusher, called a *champignon* because it resembled a giant upside-down mushroom. This was the worst of it, the heavy sticky purée sliding away from the head of the *champignon* as we rubbed and pushed, again by turns. Chef would stop us every 5 minutes or so, and scrape the emerging mousse mix from the other side of the *tamis,* using a *corne,* a smallish oval scraping disk made of genuine horn.

At last all that would go through the sieve got through, and a little mess of crushed bones and gristle remained on top. We put the purée into a metal bowl, set it over ice, and beat in cream, bit by bit, by bit, Chef testing continually. It took us half the morning to make that mousse, and by the time we were through we had just a little bowl of it, about a quart. Smooth as silk it was, and it cooked up into the most delectable *quenelles* and a beautiful mousse interlaced with fillets of sole, baked in a loaf pan, a *pain de poisson,* which was served with one of Chef's velvety rosy shellfish sauces. He was delighted with the results and so were we, but we agreed among ourselves it wouldn't be fun to be faced with a mousse all alone in one's kitchen.

Now that grinders, blenders, mixers, and other electrical aids can take over the dog work, however, these formerly infinitely arduous dishes of the *haute cuisine* are available to all of us who love to cook. Mousses, and forcemeats in general, take literally minutes rather than hours, and if you have one of the electric super-blender-food-processors pictured here, those minutes are reduced to seconds. That is why we are seeing more and more *mousses chaudes de poisson, terrines* of salmon, fish *pâtés,* and *quenelles* in the fancy restaurants, as well as on the tables of the best cooks in town. Here are two formulas to start you off.

Note: I am suggesting blenders and mixers for the manufacture of the following recipes, but again the electric super-blender-food-processor is far easier. And I am not going into *quenelles*—those sausage-shaped small mousses you poach in flavored liquid, and bake with a luscious sauce; use any of these general ideas for them, but follow the directions for *quenelles* either in Volume I of *Mastering* or in *The French Chef Cookbook.*

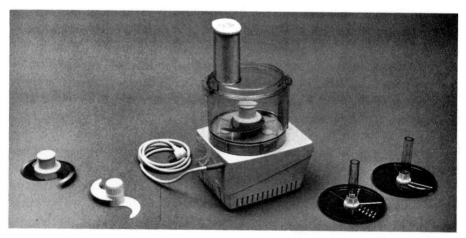

THE ELECTRIC SUPER-BLENDER-FOOD-PROCESSOR. So far, at the date of this writing, at least, only one manufacturer has come out with a heavy-duty home model of what in restaurant language is called a vertical cutter. The one pictured opposite is imported from France and you'll see it in many a mail-order catalogue and import cookware shop. The container-jar is of heavy plastic, with a sleeve that holds either blades or disks. The double-bladed metal knife at left is for general chopping and puréeing while the plastic one next to it is for mixing mayonnaises and liquids (I, personally, never use the plastic blade, only the metal one). To the right is a grater that does cheese or vegetables so rapidly you can't believe it, and next to the grater, a slicing disk for potatoes, carrots, salami, and so forth.

Mousse chaude de crevettes; pain de crevettes

SHRIMP MOUSSE
GARNISHED WITH
SOLE AND
ASPARAGUS

Timing note: You may assemble the mousse and make the sauce hours in advance, and refrigerate them. Baking takes about 1 hour in a long thin loaf pan, longer in a fat one, but you might allow an extra half hour and be safe, since the mousse may be kept warm if you are not ready to serve when it is done.

Raw shrimp have a naturally gelatinous quality that makes the flesh mass up when ground, allows it to accept a goodly amount of cream, and to hold its shape like a soft custard when cooked. Shrimp is therefore a natural for quenelles and mousses. Here it both lines a loaf pan and makes alternate layers in the pan with sole and diced asparagus. Then when you unmold it after baking you have slices of a creamy pink patterned with white and green.

When you shell your own raw shrimp, you can make a fish stock out of the shells, and a delicious sauce out of that stock to serve with the mousse. Here it is a *Sauce Parisienne,* a fish *velouté* with cream and egg yolks, from the same family of *sauces vin blanc* described in the fillet of sole section starting on page 134; or pick another version from that group if you wish. On the other hand, if you lack the wherewithal for one of these, you might settle for the light butter sauce, *Beurre Françoise,* on page 149, or a *Hollandaise Mousse-line,* page 623.

Menu suggestions. As so often with important fish creations like this, I would prefer it as a separate course. Begin a dinner party with the mousse for instance, follow it with an elegant something simply cooked, like a roast of beef or saddle of lamb, and a fancy but non-rich dessert, such as a beautifully arranged fruit tart, or a mixture of fresh berries in a wine-flavored fruit syrup, and walnut wafers. Again, for an important luncheon or supper, the mousse makes a perfect main course, followed by a composed salad or a vegetable course, and cheese and fruit. One of the great white Burgundies is the wine to serve, or a full and fine Pinot Chardonnay.

For the shrimp mousse

For a 2-quart mold, such as a 12 x 3 inch loaf pan, serving 8 as a first course, 4 to 6 as a main course

2¼ lbs. fresh or frozen uncooked shrimp of impeccably fresh-smelling quality (see notes, page 162) and in the shell if you want to make the sauce described here
2 to 2½ cups chilled heavy cream or crème fraîche
¾ to 1 tsp salt
White pepper and nutmeg

For the garniture

About 1¼ lbs. skinless and boneless sole or flounder fillets
2 Tb Cognac
Salt and white pepper
1 Tb very finely minced shallots or scallions
1 to 1½ cups cooked fresh asparagus tips (or tiny peeled cooked fresh broccoli flowerets) warmed in 1½ Tb butter and salt and pepper, then chilled

For the fish stock, if you are making one

½ cup each sliced carrots and onions
2 Tb butter
The shrimp shells, and any sole or flounder trimmings; plus ½ cup or so bottled clam juice if you have no fish trimmings
1 cup strong dry white wine (not sour), or ¾ cup dry white French Vermouth
1 cup water, more or less
1 bay leaf
About 12 parsley stems (not the leaves)
¼ tsp thyme

For the sauce parisienne, if you are making it

3 Tb butter
4 Tb flour

2 egg yolks
½ cup, more or less, heavy cream
Drops of lemon juice, and salt and white pepper
2 or more Tb soft butter

Equipment: If you have the electric super-blender-
food-processor shown on page 154, make the
mousse in that; otherwise use a meat grinder
to purée the shrimp, and beat it in a
metal bowl over ice, using a portable
electric mixer as described here. You will
want an 8-cup container, a loaf pan, or a baking
dish of any shape you wish, bottom lined with
wax paper, and inside thoroughly buttered.

The shrimp mousse. Thaw and peel the shrimp as described on page 162; reserve the shells and, if shrimp are whole, the heads too. Reserve and refrigerate 8 whole peeled shrimp for final decoration (and just before using them, sauté in hot butter and seasonings). Put remaining shrimp through the finest blade of the meat grinder into a mixing bowl. Set over ice (a tray of ice cubes and water to cover them, plus a tablespoon of salt). Start beating the shrimp with the electric mixer and pour in several tablespoons of cream; beat 2 minutes, add more cream, and continue beating and adding cream as long as mixture retains enough body to hold its shape softly when lifted in a spoon; 2¼ to 2½ cups of shrimp purée should be able to absorb 2 to 2½ cups of heavy cream. Beat in salt, pepper, and nutmeg to taste. Keep refrigerated and over ice until ready to use. (For the super-blender-food-processor, purée the shrimp in the machine, then, with machine still on, dribble in the cream.)

Assembling the mousse. (Directions here are for a loaf pan; adapt them to whatever other shape you may be using.) Split the raw fish fillets in half if they are attached in the middle (from the whole top or bottom of the fish, in other words), and lay them in a dish with sprinklings of Cognac, seasonings, and shallots; let macerate in the refrigerator if you are not ready to use them. To assemble, spread a third of the mousse in bottom of pan, and reserve ¼ of remaining mousse for top of pan later. Then arrange a layer of fish fillets in bottom of pan, and spread a very thin layer of mousse over them. For easy serving later, it is best to dice the cooked asparagus (or broccoli), spread half of it into the pan, cover with mousse, then with a layer of fish, another layer of mousse and asparagus, and a final layer of mousse and fish fillets. Spread reserved mousse over top of the fish, and cover with buttered wax paper.

☼ May be assembled in advance; cover and refrigerate.

Baking the loaf. Preheat oven to 350 degrees 20 minutes before you wish to bake. Pour an inch of water into a pan large enough to hold loaf pan, and set in oven. When oven is heated, place loaf pan in the water. Bake for 40 to 60 minutes depending on shape of pan, and regulate oven heat so water in pan is barely simmering. Mousse is done when top feels springy, and when it has shrunk slightly from sides of pan. Save all cooking juices; they will go into the sauce.

White-wine fish stock. While mousse is cooking, or at any convenient time beforehand, sauté the carrots and onions briefly in the butter to soften them, then add the shrimp shells and sauté over moderately high heat, turning and tossing for several minutes until shells turn pink. Pour in the fish trimmings or clam juice, the wine, water to cover, and add the bay, parsley, and thyme. Simmer 30 to 40 minutes, strain, and set aside.

Sauce parisienne. When the stock is done, melt the 3 tablespoons butter in the saucepan, stir in the flour, and cook slowly without browning at all for 2 minutes. Remove from heat, and pour in a cup or so of the fish stock; beat vigorously to blend. Set over moderately high heat, stirring, and boil 2 minutes. If mousse is not yet done, float a tablespoon or so of fish stock on top of sauce, and set aside. As soon as mousse is ready, set a cover over the loaf pan, and drain all juices into the sauce; you will have at least a cup of juices. Beat to blend, then boil down rapidly, stirring until sauce is thick enough to coat a spoon quite heavily. Blend the egg yolks and ⅓ cup of cream in a bowl with a wire whip, then dribble in a cup of the hot sauce, beating. Gradually beat the egg yolk mixture back into the saucepan, set over moderate heat; beat slowly, reaching all over bottom and sides of pan, and let boil gently for 2 minutes. Thin out as needed, with spoonfuls of cream. Taste carefully, adding drops of lemon juice, salt, and pepper to taste. Just before serving, remove from heat and beat in as much enrichment butter, by spoonfuls, as you wish.

☼ If made in advance, clean off sides of pan, float a film of stock or cream on top of sauce, and refrigerate.

Serving. Again drain juices, remove the wax paper, and unmold mousse onto hot serving platter. Decorate top with sautéed shrimps, spoon a little of the sauce around the loaf, and pour the rest into a warm sauce bowl. Serve immediately.

Mousse chaude de poisson; pain de poisson

MOUSSE OF SOLE
OR FLOUNDER
GARNISHED WITH
SALMON OR
SHELLFISH;
FANCY FISH LOAF

When fish like sole, halibut, or conger eel have enough natural gelatin, you can make a mousse by just adding egg whites and cream. However, although I appreciate its delicate quality, it does exude an inordinate amount of cooking juice during its baking and afterward. I usually prefer the old-fashioned use of a *panade,* meaning a *pâte à choux* (thick flour-based sauce) that is combined with the ground raw fish. Less juice exudes, and the *panade* gives, I think, a pleasant texture and body. This one can be baked in a ring mold lined with sole fillets, as described in the final recipe of *The French Chef Cookbook,* or use the loaf pan system described here, where the recipe is much the same as the preceding shrimp mousse except for the addition of the *panade* to the ground fish. It is useful for you to have both versions.

For the garnish

For a 6-cup mold or
loaf pan serving 6
as a first course,
4 as a main course

1 Tb tasteless salad oil
3 Tb Cognac
2 Tb lemon juice
1 Tb very finely minced shallots or scallions
Salt and white pepper
Optional: 1 small truffle and its juice
1 lb. fresh raw salmon fillets, or shelled raw
   shrimp, or cooked fresh crab or lobster meat

For the fish mousse

Pâte à choux ingredients: ½ cup water, 3 Tb
   butter, ½ tsp salt, 6 Tb all-purpose flour
   measured into a cup, and 2 "large" eggs
½ lb. (1 cup) finely ground raw sole,
   flounder, or halibut
½ cup, more or less, heavy cream or
   crème fraîche

Salt, white pepper, and nutmeg as needed
Optional, to decorate top of cooked mousse:
     truffles, cooked shellfish meat, fluted
     mushrooms, for instance, or simply sauce
About 2 cups sauce to serve with the mousse:
     either the Sauce Parisienne or its equivalent
     described in the preceding recipe, or a
     Hollandaise Mousseline, page 623

Preparing the garnish. Beat the oil, Cognac, lemon juice, shallots or scallions, ¼ teaspoon salt, and several grinds of white pepper in a stainless or porcelain bowl large enough to hold the fish, adding the truffle juice if you are using it. For salmon, slice the fillets into scallops about ⅛ inch thick and as long and as wide as you easily can—it is their thinness that matters here. Place the salmon or shellfish in the bowl, turn and baste with the marinade, and refrigerate while preparing the rest of the dish; turn and baste occasionally.

The pâte à choux and fish mousse. To make the *pâte à choux* (full details are on page 549), bring water to boil in a 2-quart saucepan with the butter cut into ½-inch pieces, and the salt. As soon as butter has melted, remove pan from heat and pour in all the flour at once. Beat vigorously with a portable beater or wooden spoon. When blended, stir with wooden spoon over moderate heat, and beat 2 to 3 minutes to cook flour and evaporate excess moisture. Remove from heat, make a well in the center of the hot paste, break in an egg, and beat it in vigorously. When absorbed, beat in the second egg. Stir over ice several minutes, until cool. (Makes about 1 cup, proportions are about 1 cup *choux* pastry to 1 cup fish.)

Beat the ground fish in a metal bowl over ice for several minutes, until chilled and massed together. Beat in the cold *choux* pastry, then by spoonfuls the cream, beating vigorously after each addition; continue adding cream as long as the mixture continues to have enough body to hold its shape softly when lifted in a spoon. Beat in salt, white pepper, and a pinch of nutmeg, to taste . . . meaning taste a bit, really, to see how it is.

Assembling the mousse in its pan. Drain the fish or shellfish garniture; add marinade liquid to mousse, and beat it in. Spread ⅓ of the mousse in the bottom of the buttered loaf pan, arrange over it half the marinated salmon or shellfish, and cover with half the remaining mousse. Finish with the rest of the salmon or shellfish, and cover with the last of the mousse.

(Mixture should fill pan to within about ¼ inch; if fuller, surround pan with a collar of buttered aluminum foil.) Lay a piece of heavily buttered wax paper on top of mousse.

✲ May be prepared several hours ahead to this point; cover and re-frigerate.

Baking and serving. Bake, unmold, decorate, and serve as described in preceding recipe, page 158.

OTHER IDEAS

These two recipes give you the usual mousse-making methods. As noted, you can bake them in any shape of dish, mold, or pan, and you may serve them from the dish, or unmold them as described here. Analyze other mousses you may sample when you go out, and you will probably be able to figure out what went into them and how they are made.

Leftover shrimp or fish mousse. To reheat. You may reheat either mousse; cover with buttered wax paper and a cover, and set in a pan of boiling water in a 350-degree oven until hot through.

To serve cold. Either mousse is delicious neatly sliced and served cold; if you have any leftover sauce, beat into it a little lemon juice, fresh homemade mayonnaise, and a good pinch of fresh parsley or other fresh herbs like dill, tarragon, or chervil—or make a new sauce of mayonnaise, sour cream, lemon, and herbs. Cold mousse makes a fine lunch or supper, or the first course for a dinner.

Frozen leftover mousse. Slice or dice it, and reheat in a cream sauce, or dice it and include it as a garniture for leek and potato or watercress soup, or with a fish chowder.

Shrimp

Big frozen shrimp can be very good indeed when you buy them with care, shopping with your nose as well as your mind and heart, and when you add plenty of extra flavor in cooking them. In the preceding pages they are used in a splendid mousse, and here are two other ideas, one a simmer *à la grecque,* and the other a sauté with Provençal overtones. First here are notes on buying and defrosting frozen shrimp.

BUYING AND DEFROSTING SHRIMP. Frozen raw shrimp in the shell are usually the best in quality, says my fish dealer, simply because they are usually frozen quickly, before they have a chance to sit around and take on that unpleasant ammonia taste that comes with age. And you should buy them solidly frozen, since they age rapidly as soon as they are thawed. If your market will not let you smell them—and it is the rare market that will—pay for them, and then open them just outside the cashier's counter; if you aren't satisfied, complain immediately and rather loudly. Keep them solidly frozen until you are ready to cook them, then thaw in a sinkful of cold water; start detaching and peeling them in a few minutes, as soon as the ones on the outside begin to work their way loose. I do not bother to remove the dark vein at the curve of the back unless it is unusually black and ugly. Cook the shrimp immediately, even if some are partially frozen.

SHRIMP SIZES. Shrimp are classified in this country according to how many headless shrimp in the shell make up a pound, going from "small" (41 to 60 per pound), through "medium," "large medium," "large," "jumbo," and "extra jumbo," which weigh in at under 15 per pound. I usually get "large medium" at 26 to 30 per pound, and count on 4 to 6 per serving. Stretched out, these measure 3 inches from large end to the beginning of the tail piece, and are 2¼ inches in diameter when curled up.

Crevettes à la grecque

————◆————

SHRIMP SIMMERED
WITH ONIONS, OIL,
LEMON, AND HERBS

For about 1 pound
of shrimp, serving
5 to 6 as a first course

Serve these cold as a first course, with a garniture of tomatoes and watercress. Or make them a fish course, with rice, and perhaps some broiled tomatoes and fresh green peas. Or spear them, cold, on toothpicks and pass them around at cocktail time.

30 "large medium" raw shrimp, fresh or frozen
1 cup thinly sliced onions
1 medium clove garlic, finely minced or puréed
¼ cup olive oil
The zest (yellow part only) of ½ lemon, minced
2 Tb fresh lemon juice, more if needed
½ cup dry white French Vermouth
½ cup water
½ tsp salt
¼ tsp each: crushed peppercorns and cardamom
  seeds (or a big pinch of mace)
1 imported bay leaf
½ tsp thyme or oregano
¼ cup chopped fresh parsley

Thaw the shrimp, if frozen, and peel, as directed in paragraphs preceding this recipe.

Meanwhile prepare the *court bouillon à la grecque* as follows: In a heavy-bottomed stainless or enameled saucepan, blend the onions, garlic, olive oil, and lemon zest, cover, and cook slowly, stirring occasionally, for 8 to 10 minutes, until the onions are tender and translucent but not browned. Then add the lemon juice, Vermouth, water, salt, and all the herbs except the parsley, and simmer 10 minutes, covered.

Add the peeled raw shrimp, frozen or not, to the simmering *court bouillon* and toss with the liquid and seasonings—liquid will not cover shrimp. Cover and boil slowly, tossing frequently, until the shrimp curl and are just lightly springy to the squeeze; this will take only several minutes, and do not overcook them. Remove pan from heat, and let the shrimp steep in the liquid for 10 minutes, tossing and turning them occasionally, so they will absorb the flavor of the *court bouillon*.

Then dip the shrimp out to a serving dish, using a slotted spoon. Rapidly reduce the *court bouillon* (boil down over high heat until syrupy), taste carefully for seasoning, and add more salt and pepper and drops of lemon juice if you think them needed. Pour the *court bouillon* and its vegetables over the shrimp, basting several times.

Serve warm or cold and, just beforehand, baste several times again, the last time with the chopped parsley included.

☼ Will keep 2 days or so in the refrigerator.

Crevettes sautées au citron

This sauté is a distant cousin of the preceding simmer, and less elaborate. Serve it hot or cold, and as part of a meal or as an appetizer as suggested at the end of the recipe.

SHRIMP SAUTÉED
WITH LEMON,
GARLIC, AND HERBS

For about 1 pound
of shrimp, serving
5 to 6 as a first course

30 "large medium" raw shrimp, fresh or frozen,
*   and peeled (see notes, page 162)*
About 5 Tb excellent olive oil (3 for the sauté,
*   and 2 for later) or olive oil plus a few drops*
*   of dark sesame oil*
1 or more cloves of garlic, minced or puréed
The zest (yellow part of peel only) of
*   ½ lemon, minced*
2 Tb fresh lemon juice, more if needed
Drops of soy sauce, salt, and freshly ground
*   white pepper*
2 or more Tb fresh minced parsley and fresh dill
*   (or ¼ tsp dried dill weed mixed with*
*   the parsley)*

Dry the shrimp in paper towels. Heat 3 tablespoons of the oil in a large no-stick frying pan, add the garlic and lemon zest, and toss several seconds. Then add the shrimp and toss (swirling pan by handle) over high heat for 2 to 3 minutes only, just until shrimp have curled and feel springy to the touch. Remove from heat and toss with the lemon juice, drops of soy sauce, and salt and pepper to taste. Then toss with the 2 tablespoons of fresh olive oil and the herbs.

To serve hot. Serve them just as they are, speared with toothpicks; or arrange them around a bed of rice, and accompany them with a green vegetable or a salad. Or pile the shrimp into individual baking shells, sprinkle with fresh bread crumbs and droplets of oil; just before serving, brown under a moderately hot broiler to heat through and color the crumbs.

To serve cold. Let cool, basting several times with liquid in pan; serve on toothpicks. Or include the shrimp as part of a first course or salad, with cucumbers, tomatoes, and other appropriate trimmings.

Oysters

Oysters are having a comeback in this country, thank heaven. Pollution controls are strictly enforced in most oyster-raising regions, new oyster farming methods are producing bumper crops, scientific packing keeps them from spilling their juices, and fast refrigerated transportation can deliver them fresh and fine to any part of the country. But how do you open them? I envy the professionals, who hold an oyster in the palm of one hand, slip a knife effortlessly between the shells near the front, and open it just like that. For those of us lacking that touch of genius, it takes longer but it can be learned and, like the happy occupation of learning about wines through drinking them, you learn about oysters through opening and eating them.

If you are doing a recipe for cooked oysters the solution is simple: set the oysters curved side down either right on an electric burner or on a metal simmer plaque over a gas burner—in a minute or so you can see the shells begin to part, and opening is easy.

To open oysters by hand is, of course, a different matter. You will need a long-bladed oyster knife (see illustrations next page), and a heavy pot-holder to protect your hand. Then look carefully at the oyster. Of its two shells one is fairly rounded, forming a basin to hold the meat—that is the bottom shell. Look at the hinge at the small end; the bottom shell overlaps the small end of the top shell slightly. Follow the lines along the upper edge of the top shell and you will see that they are slightly recessed, that the rim of the bottom shell protrudes ever so slightly. Thus, when you seek to open the shells you do not try to penetrate them from the outside edge because they do not meet at the edge—they meet just a line or two in from the outside edge of the top shell. Once this fact becomes apparent, you will make progress—I made none, myself, until I put on my glasses and really got my eye down into that area.

Hold the oyster in the potholder in your left hand, curved side of shell down and hinge pointing away from you. Rest your hand on your work table, if you wish.

Insert knife point one or two lines in from edge, about halfway from hinge to lip as indicated by the arrow on the oyster on the lower left; as you press you will usually see oyster juices seeping out, indicating where the shells join.

Pry into the oyster with your knife, then sweep it back and forth inside, against the top shell, to cut the muscles of the oyster loose; swing the top shell up and off, bending it back toward the hinge. (If you can't enter the shell from that side, turn the oyster the other way around, hinge toward you, and try again. If you still don't succeed—but do not give up easily— try prying the shell open from the hinge end [see arrow on oyster at the right], using the stubby knife illustrated, or a screwdriver. The last resort, but an ignominious one, is to knock a quarter inch of shell off one side of the lip with a hammer, and enter the oyster from that point with your knife.)

When the oyster is open, cut under the meat where it is attached to the bottom shell and, if you wish, turn the oyster meat over to present a smoother side. Always serve raw oysters in their bottom shell halves, to retain all their delicious juices.

BUYING AND STORING OYSTERS. Once you know how to open them, you will have no hesitation in buying fresh oysters. Be sure, however, you know exactly where they come from and that you have complete confidence in your source of supply. Most states that grow and ship oysters have strict regulations about their purity; ask to see the container they came in as well as the official inspection and certification tags.

Oysters should feel heavy, sound full when tapped, and contain not only the oyster, but also its juices; if they are dry, they are not fresh. Discard any oyster with a partially opened shell, any dry oyster, any oyster with other than a fresh and sweet smell. It is a good idea before refrigerating or opening oysters to hold them one at a time under a thin stream of cold water and to scrub them rapidly clean with a vegetable brush; this will rid them of dirt, foreign matter, and of anything on the shell that might breed or transmit bacteria. (This does not harm the oyster; it will clench its shell shut when you touch it and no water penetrates.)

According to the U.S. Bureau of Fisheries, very fresh oysters will keep perfectly well for 2 to 3 weeks in the refrigerator at around 37°: scrub them clean, pack them curved side down (to prevent juice leakage) on a rack in a pan or a bowl, and cover loosely with a damp towel, then with foil. Rock weed (seaweed) on top or between layers is always a help, if you happen to have any available. (The keeping of oysters reminds me of the stories my father used to tell about life during the 1880's in rural Illinois: my grandmother not only had a French cook, it seems, but she always kept a barrel of oysters in the cellar during the winter months.)

Already shucked very fresh oysters, packed in their natural juices in a sealed container, set in ice, and then refrigerated, keep about 1 week.

TO SERVE AND EAT RAW OYSTERS ON THE HALF SHELL. An attractive way to serve raw oysters on the half shell is to arrange them, at the last moment, curved side down in a big platter of crushed ice, which prevents them from tipping and spilling their juices. Or steady them on a bed of rock salt, or a crumpled napkin or large piece of foil, using either a big communal platter or individual dinner plates. Special plates with built-in depressions to hold each oyster shell do exist, and should be in the home of any oyster buff with plenty of storage space.

To eat a raw oyster, you need either a small oyster fork with sharp prongs and flat rather thick tines, or a teaspoon. Dig the oyster out of its shell, pop it whole into your mouth, chew the soft flesh, and savor its juices as the oyster slides down into oblivion. Then lift the shell to your lips and drink the oyster juices.

My husband, Paul, likes three oysters for breakfast, and he eats them with a spoon just as they come, with no condiments. I like either spoon or fork, but I must have halved or quartered lemons with mine; I squeeze a few drops over the oyster, watch it cringe so I know it is alive and well, then in it goes. Some people grind a bit of pepper over their oysters, and others like drops of wine vinegar that has been steeped in pepper and minced shallots.

What to serve with raw oysters? If you like to dunk yours in spicy tomato cocktail sauce, you had better stick to beer. Otherwise serve a dry white wine like Chablis, Pouilly Fumé or Fuissé, Sancerre, Muscadet, Riesling, or Pinot Blanc. The only other accompaniment can be very thin slices of buttered whole wheat or light rye bread.

Huitres gratinées en coquilles

OYSTERS BROILED ON THE HALF SHELL

For 4 people as a first course

For a first course, you need serve only 3 or 4 oysters per person or, if the oysters are shucked, 3 or 4 arranged in individual baking shells or ramequins. This is a plain and pure recipe and, I think, perfectly delicious. A chilled Riesling or Chablis would be a good choice of wine.

12 large fresh oysters in the shell (or 12 or more shucked oysters, and buttered ovenproof shell-shaped individual dishes to hold 3 or 4 oysters)
3 to 4 Tb butter in a small saucepan
1 Tb finely minced shallots or scallions
The strained juice of ½ lemon
Salt and pepper
About ½ cup fine crumbs from homemade-type fresh white bread

Equipment: A baking dish, pizza pan, or baking sheet; and rock salt or crumpled foil to line it and hold the oysters in place

Open the oysters, keeping meat and juices in curved half of the shell; arrange on the foil in the baking dish, bedding them solidly to prevent tipping. Melt butter, add shallots or scallions, and stir over moderate heat for 2 minutes without browning. Remove from heat, and stir in the lemon juice, a big pinch of salt, and a grind or two of pepper. Spread ½ tablespoon of crumbs over each oyster, and top with ½ teaspoon of the butter mixture.

☼ May be prepared an hour or so in advance; cover and refrigerate.

At serving time, set under a moderately hot broiler for 2 minutes or so, watching carefully, to brown crumbs lightly and heat the oysters through. Serve immediately.

Huitres gratinées, sauce vin blanc

OYSTERS ON THE
HALF SHELL,
GRATINÉED WITH
WINE, EGG YOLK,
AND BUTTER
SAUCE

For 12 large oysters

Here is a more elaborate presentation than the simple bread-crumb coating in the previous recipe. For a first course 3 or 4 large oysters are sufficient, and 6 would serve for the main course of a luncheon or supper.

12 large fresh oysters in their shells (or 12 or
   more shucked oysters, and buttered ovenproof
   shell-shaped individual dishes to hold
   3 or 4 oysters)
⅓ cup dry white wine or dry white
   French Vermouth
1 Tb finely minced shallots or green onions
½ cup crème fraîche or heavy cream
2 egg yolks
6 to 8 Tb soft butter
Drops of fresh lemon juice
Pepper
Salt as needed

Equipment: A baking dish, pizza pan, or baking
   sheet; and rock salt or crumpled foil to line it
   and hold the oysters in place

Open the oysters, drain the meat and juices in a sieve set over a bowl, then return meat to curved side of shells. Pour juices into a stainless saucepan, leaving any grit behind, add the wine and shallots or onions, and boil down rapidly until liquid has reduced to 3 tablespoons. Add ⅓ cup of the cream and boil down again, to thicken the cream. Set pan in cold water and stir for a moment until cool, then whip in the egg yolks. Stir over moderate heat to cook and thicken the egg yolks, as for making a hollandaise, but do not let the liquid boil or the egg yolks will curdle. When thick as mayonnaise, remove from heat and rapidly beat in the butter, a half teaspoon at a time, adding more as each previous piece is almost absorbed. Beat in more cream by dribbles to thin sauce slightly, but it should be thick enough to enrobe a spoon with a quite thick creamy layer. Taste very carefully for seasoning, adding drops of lemon juice if you think it necessary, also pepper, and a little salt if needed. Spoon the sauce over the oysters.

✻ May be prepared ahead to this point. Cover and refrigerate (remove oysters from bed of salt, if so, since chilled salt would take too long to warm up later).

Preheat oven to 450 degrees. Seven to 8 minutes before you are ready to serve, set arrangement of oysters in upper-middle level (or arrange individual dishes of them on a baking sheet and place in oven). Bake until bubbling and lightly browned. Serve immediately, either from baking dish or onto individual plates.

Scalloped oysters

As far as I can reconstruct it, this was my grandmother's way of doing scalloped oysters, when she dug them out of her barrel in the cellar and took over from her French cook way back before the turn of the century. She used to serve them to us this way for Sunday night supper, in later years. There should be just one layer of oysters here, and 6 to 8 per person, baked either in a big shallow pan, or, in small baking dishes, one for each serving, which I prefer.

Per serving of 6 to 8 large oysters

2 Tb butter
1½ Tb minced shallots or green onions
½ cup, lightly pressed down, fresh
 white bread crumbs
Salt and freshly ground pepper
1½ Tb minced fresh parsley
6 to 8 large oysters
Additional butter if you wish

In a saucepan, melt the butter and sauté the shallots or onions for a minute or two to soften without browning. Add the bread crumbs, stir about to coat with the butter, and cook several minutes, stirring, to brown very lightly. Season to taste with salt and pepper, and fold in the parsley. Drain the oysters in a sieve set over a bowl (decant oyster liquor and freeze for soups or fish sauces). Spread half the crumbs in a small baking dish, arrange the oysters on top, and cover with the rest of the crumbs. Add dots or dribbles more butter if you wish—but more is not imperative.

✿ May be prepared in advance to this point; cover and refrigerate.

Preheat oven to 450 degrees. Eight to 10 minutes before serving, set oysters in upper-middle level and bake until bubbling hot and crumbs have browned lightly on top. Serve at once.

Grand Central oyster stew, vintage 1937

For each serving of 6 to 8 large oysters

One of the in-group places to go for a supper or a snack in the New York of the 1930's was Grand Central Station's Oyster Bar. You sat up on a stool and peered over the counter into a series of steam bowls, where they made their famous oyster stew. It was so good I took notes on how the old chefs made it, and this is my version.

3 or more Tb butter
¼ tsp Worcestershire sauce
¼ tsp celery salt
6 to 8 large oysters, drained, and the
*   juices reserved*
1½ cups light cream (or half milk and
*   half heavy cream)*
Salt and white pepper
Paprika
Oyster crackers, or "common" crackers,
*   or ship's biscuits*

Melt 3 tablespoons of butter to bubbling in a saucepan, add the Worcestershire and celery salt, then the oysters. Cook, swirling pan, for 2 minutes, or until the oysters' edges begin to curl. Add the oyster juices and cream, and bring just to the simmer. Season to taste with salt and pepper, and turn into a soup bowl. Float a spoonful of butter on top, sprinkle over it a good dash of paprika, and serve at once, accompanied by the crackers.

Lobsters

Lobsters were a dollar a dozen in great-great-grandmother's fish market, if she lived near the New England coast. Nowadays, although lobsters are unfortunately priced in the luxury category, you can buy live lobsters from the north Atlantic coast even in Europe, because they are shipped by air all over the world. Thus it is part of one's gastronomical baggage to know not only how to buy and cook them, but also how to eat whole lobsters.

BUYING LOBSTERS. Unless you are buying already boiled lobsters, which you should do only from a most reliable source, any lobster you purchase should be alive; dead raw lobsters, like dead raw shrimp, spoil very quickly. A live lobster should look thoroughly lively: he should arch his back, flap his tail against his underside, and wave his big claws. Once you have bought them, you can keep live lobsters safely for a day or two in a brown paper bag pierced with a dozen pencil holes in the bottom of your refrigerator, at a temperature of around 37 degrees. Several handfuls of native rock weed, often used to pack lobsters for shipment, will help keep them lively a day or so longer.

LOBSTER TERMS AND WEIGHTS. The smallest legal size for New England lobsters is 1 pound, but there is no limit on largeness. Years ago lobsters 5 and 6 feet long were reported along coastal waters, but now the largest ones come from the deep-sea fisheries, and are fast disappearing. Large lobsters are just as good eating as small ones, except sometimes for the last half inch or so at the very end of the big claws of a 20-pound behemoth, and large ones are a good buy for salads because you get more meat per pound for your money. Lobstermen have names for the various sizes, as follows:

> 1- and 1¼-lb. lobsters, "chickens" and "quarters" respectively, are for single servings.
> 1½- to 2½-lb. lobsters, "selects," are the most popular restaurant sizes, and the most expensive per pound. Use them for single servings, and for stuffed lobsters where you can give half a lobster to each person.
> 2½- to 3½-lb. lobsters, "jumbos," are less

expensive than the preceding sizes, and are
recommended for stuffed lobsters and
cooked lobster meat.

4 pounds and over are nameless monsters, and
the least expensive. Use them, if you can
find them, to make stuffed lobsters for a
crowd, or for cooked lobster meat and salads.

HOW TO BE A HUMANITARIAN. "Julia Child," begins a typical letter every
time our old black-and-white "Lobster à l'Américaine" is rerun, "I saw
your show where you were cooking a lobster and I couldn't believe your
cruelty when you cut it up alive and struggling. Don't be so cruel to an
animal, and don't tell me that he died within a few seconds so what does
it matter? It matters *plenty!* I could never do something so cruel and you
are no exception." Now, when we know that old show is scheduled, we
run off several dozen of our form letter titled: LOBSTERS, *Information
about cutting up, boiling, killing, etc.* "That was not a live lobster," I
repeat for the hundredth time. "We knew there would be a reaction, so
we killed him 2 hours before the show, but his muscle reactions still
went on," and so on and so forth. When a letter is particularly passionate,
I usually conclude: "The only alternative to killing animals for food is
to be a complete vegetarian; just because one has not personally par-
ticipated in the assassination of a steer for one's beefsteak does not mean
one is free of guilt. And now it appears that even plants have feelings."

Then, of course, there is another
alternative. I have had this
George Price cartoon tacked over
my desk since it came out in
The New Yorker, and am
delighted that we were
given permission to print it here.

Finally, in preparation for a new program, "The Lobster Show," in living color and telling all about the boiling and steaming of live lobsters and no shillying around the murder aspects, I talked to the U.S. Bureau of Fisheries, and the head marine biologist at the Massachusetts State Lobster Hatchery, as well as to other marine biologists and people in the business. The lobster's blood, or life fluid, flows almost randomly through the body spaces, I learned. Any large incision made in the shell allows the fluid to drain out (it forms a pale blue clot); the lobster then slowly suffocates because the main function of this fluid is to transport oxygen around to the body tissues. Thus, plunging a knife between the eyes is slow suffocation, as is plunging a knife in the back where tail joins chest. This last is not only slow suffocation, but, worse, it severs the intestine, dumping its contents over the tail meat. The only knife work that can be effective is plunging it in ½ inch across the underside, close to the chest; this severs the spinal cord and kills the lobster, as well as draining out its life fluid.

Many humanitarians, including for a while the International Society for the Protection of Animals, have been under the delusion that setting lobsters in cold water and bringing them slowly to the boil was the kindest treatment. No! This, again, is slow suffocation—plus death by drowning.

The most humane way to deal with live lobsters is to plunge them head first and upside down into boiling water. Since their circulatory functions are centered at the back of the head, they die within a few seconds. Then, if you are to cut up the lobsters before proceeding to the cooking, remove them in about a minute, when limp. Otherwise continue to boil them for the amount of time specified in the recipe.

WHETHER TO BOIL OR STEAM WHOLE LOBSTERS. This depends, I think, on your equipment and the number of lobsters you want to cook at once. When you are in the business and have a tremendous cauldron of boiling sea water or a professional steamer, your problem is only one of timing. For the home cook, boiling or steaming more than 4 lobsters means decision making. If you want to boil a number of them by complete submersion, for instance, you need either a huge kettle 18 inches in diameter and a powerful heat source, or a wash boiler (used only for cooking, of course) that you can set over 2 burners; otherwise the water takes too long to come back to the boil again after the lobsters are in, and timing is difficult. On the other hand, and in my experience, if you try to steam more than 1 layer of lobsters in a kettle or roaster you may overcook the ones on the bottom and undercook those on top. I suggest, therefore, that you be sure you have the right equipment before offering whole hot boiled lobsters to a crowd; instead, serve them something like *Lobster Thermidor, Lobster à l'Américaine, Lobster Gratinéed with Cheese,* in its shell—all in *The French Chef Cookbook*—or the cold lobster with mayonnaise described here.

Whole boiled or steamed lobsters

———

TO SERVE HOT
OR COLD

Either: A very large kettle or wash boiler of rapidly boiling sea water, or tap water with 1½ tsp salt for each quart of water

Or: A large kettle or wash boiler fitted with a rack with surface 1½ to 2 inches above bottom of kettle and 1½ inches rapidly boiling sea water or salted water

A cover (or tray) for the kettle plus, if needed, a weight of some sort to make a tight fit

Live lobsters (1- to 2-pounders for single servings)

If you are boiling by complete submersion. Plunge live lobsters head-first and upside down into boiling water, cover kettle and weight down if necessary. As soon as water comes back to the boil, remove cover, reduce heat so lobsters boil slowly but steadily, and begin timing.

If you are steaming. Place lobsters on rack, cover kettle, weight down if necessary, and as soon as steam begins to escape, start timing.

Timing: from moment water boils again or steam escapes

1- to 1¼-lb. lobsters	10–12 min.
1½- to 2-lb. lobsters	15–18 min.
2½- to 5-lb. lobsters	20–25 min.
6- to 10-lb. lobsters	25–35 min.*
10- to 15-lb. lobsters	35–40 min.*
15- to 20-lb. lobsters	40–45 min.*

* Add 5 minutes more if shells are very thick

When is the lobster done? Here are several ways to check. Some clever people are able to tell by looking at and feeling the underside of the tail section, which should be opaque and springy; I have had no success with this system. I do pull off one of the little legs close to the body, and break it open; the meat should come easily away from the shell. Or gently pull the shell up from the chest section and peer inside at the green matter, which should be just set, not liquid. Finally, you can take the lobster's temperature immediately you remove him from the pot; use a small instant-type pocket thermometer and insert it through the vent hole at the end of the tail, an inch into the center of the meat—165 degrees is done.

Drain the lobsters. After boiling or steaming, it is a good idea to drain the water out of the lobsters if you're going to serve them whole in their shells. Plunge a knife into the front of the head, between the eyes, to split the shell. Hold the lobster up by its tail and let the water drain out the head; then you might hold it up by its claws to drain them, and again hold it by its tail in case more water is still to come.

Serving and eating whole hot boiled lobsters. The most satisfying way to enjoy whole boiled lobsters is for each to have his own, served as a separate course with bowls of melted butter for each person, French bread, halved or quartered lemons, salt and pepper, finger bowls, and a large stack of paper napkins. Provide a plate for each lobster, and a communal bowl or individual ones for shell scraps. If you don't have lobster shears for everyone, have several sharp-pointed kitchen shears for the group, or nutpicks and nut crackers. Oyster forks, or some such small instruments, are useful as well. Serve a dry white wine like Riesling, Pouilly Fuissé, Muscadet, or Pinot Blanc, and you will not need much after the lobsters except perhaps a green salad or coleslaw, and a dessert of fresh berries or a fruit tart.

One way of attacking a whole boiled lobster is first to break off all the little legs. While the lobster cools, eat them one at a time, twisting them apart at the joints, and drawing the pieces through your teeth to squeeze

out the meat. Then break off the big claws and claw joints; cut or crack the joints to break the shell and get at the meat, lifting it out with nutpick or fork, and dipping it into melted butter for each mouthful. For the claws, bend small end downward to break it away and draw its cartilage out of the main claw; dig meat out with nutpick. Cut or crack open the main claws to get their meat. Twist tail from chest, then break off end flaps from tail and push meat out of shell with your forefinger, from that end. For the chest meat, pull body out of chest shell; pull off and discard feathery gills on outside of chest. Scoop green matter onto plate and reserve for the finish. Pull out and discard stomach sack in head. Break chest in half lengthwise, and dig out tender meat between cartilages with pick or fork. All coagulated white matter inside chest shell is edible, as is all green matter and pink roe; eat with fork or spoon, or spread it on your French bread.

Note: Even after all is eaten, the cook can still chop the discarded shells and boil them with a few chopped onions, carrots, and celery to make a fine fish stock. Thus, although lobsters are a luxury, nothing need be wasted.

Homard froid à la mayonnaise

———————

COLD HALVED
LOBSTER WITH
HERB MAYONNAISE

For 2 people

A 2-lb. cold boiled lobster
1 sieved hard-boiled egg
4 Tb minced parsley
½ cup thick homemade mayonnaise, page 439
1 Tb minced chives
1 Tb capers, squeezed dry and minced
Additional flavorings: Dijon-type prepared
    mustard, lemon, salt, pepper

Split lobster in half lengthwise, discard stomach sack in head and intestinal vein running down through the center of tail meat. Rub green matter (tomalley) and pink roe (if any) through a sieve into a mixing bowl. Beat in half the sieved egg, 3 tablespoons of the parsley, the mayonnaise, chives, and capers; season carefully to taste with mustard, lemon, salt, and pepper. Mound into chest cavities of the 2 lobster halves and arrange them on a platter or plates. Toss rest of sieved egg with the remaining parsley, and salt and pepper; spread over the tail meat. Decorate platter or plates with parsley or watercress and lemon wedges.

For lobster salad, follow the directions for the chicken salad, page 443.

Salt cod

Salt cod, that homely item, was formerly the only kind of ocean fish available if one lived away from the sea. Now it is something of an exotic because of its special taste and texture. It is always a useful staple to have on hand because a package of salt cod will preserve itself indefinitely in a back corner of your refrigerator, and recipes for salt cod abound in both American and European cookery, including not only main course dishes, but also salads, soups, and chowders, like the one in this book on page 36. Here are two excellent ways of serving cod, one an unusual purée, called a *brandade,* and the other a hearty casserole of cod, onions, and potatoes that is great to serve at an informal brunch or a supper. But whatever the dish, you must first soak the preserving salt out of the fish as follows:

THE SOAKING (DE-SALTING) OF SALT COD. Salt cod fillets bought in pound packages take 24 hours or more of soaking; a whole fish with skin on (*bacalhau,* or stockfish) takes 2 to 3 days depending on how dry and hard it was to begin with; chopped or shredded salt cod takes only a few hours. To soak the cod, wash under cold running water, cut it into half-inch pieces if you wish, and place in a large bowl of cold water—in the refrigerator, because as soon as the preserving salt is out the cod will be just as perishable as fresh fish. Change water several times, and soak until cod has softened and feels almost like fresh fish—when you taste it there should be no trace of salt. (If for some reason you cannot cook the de-salted fish within 24 hours, drain, package, and freeze it.)

PRELIMINARY COOKING: POACHING

The only trick to cooking salt cod is never to let it simmer or boil because that toughens it. Poach it, as described here, and it will be just right, always a little chewy—since that is its character—and subtly flavored with the onion, pepper, cloves, and bay in its cooking water.

For 1 pound of cod, de-salted	*1 cup water in a 2½- to 3-quart pan*
	1 medium onion, grated
	4 peppercorns
	3 whole cloves
	2 imported bay leaves
	1½ tsp salt
	4 more cups cold water
	1 lb. salt cod fillets, thoroughly de-salted

Bring water to boil with the onion, peppercorns, cloves, bay, and salt; cover and simmer 10 minutes. Add the 4 cups additional cold water and the soaked cod. Set over moderate heat and watch until scum begins to rise and water is making slow movements but is not at the simmer (190 degrees). Remove from heat, cover the pan, and let steep 10 minutes (or longer if you are not ready to continue). Finally remove the fish with a skimmer or slotted spoon, pick it over to remove any bones, skin, or dark bits, and the cod is ready to use. Save liquid for codfish chowder, or for boiling the potatoes in the casserole recipe.

Brandade de morue

PURÉE OF SALT COD WITH POTATOES, OLIVE OIL, AND GARLIC

This marvelous Provençal mixture has been known to drive people mad with desire for more and more of it, once tasted. If you haven't had it before, your first impression is of a wonderfully flavored mashed potato dish that, somehow, is not mashed potatoes; it has overtones of garlic, a deliciously creamy quality, a taste of olives, and of what else? It couldn't be codfish, but it is.

In the old days a *brandade* was pounded vigorously in a marble mortar, then beaten at length in a heavy pan while oil and milk were dribbled in —the name comes from the Provençal *brandado*, meaning stirred. The first recipe I ran into using an electric mixer was from Craig Claiborne, and we can all be grateful to him for making the *brandade* so very easy to do.

For about 1 quart

1 lb. salt cod, soaked, poached, and drained
¼ cup excellent olive oil
1 large warm baked potato, skinned (about 1½ cups)
2 or more large cloves of garlic, puréed
About ½ cup more of olive oil, warmed
½ to 1 cup cream (or milk), warmed
Salt and pepper
Drops of lemon juice

Break up the cod into a heavy 3-quart saucepan, add the olive oil, and stir vigorously over moderate heat for several minutes to shred and warm it. Then turn it into a large mixing bowl, or the large bowl of an electric mixer, add the potato and garlic, and beat at moderately fast speed, adding alternate dollops of warm oil and cream until mixture is the consistency of fluffy mashed potatoes—amounts of each are up to you. Season to taste with salt, pepper, and drops of lemon juice.

☼ If you wish to make the *brandade* in advance, save out some of the oil and cream; just before serving beat the *brandade* over heat to warm it, then add the final oil and cream.

To serve as a dip, place in a bowl and surround with crackers or potato chips.

To serve as an hors d'oeuvre or as part of a brunch buffet, turn the *brandade* out onto a warm platter, surround it with croutons (triangles of white bread sautéed in olive oil), and decorate with parsley sprigs and small black olives.

Leftovers—turn them into codfish balls or cakes, following your favorite system.

Gratin de morue à la lyonnaise

CASSEROLE OF COD
WITH POTATOES
AND ONIONS

For 8 to 10 servings

This rib-sticking dish can be the main course of a supper or informal Sunday lunch, or part of a brunch buffet. If it is the main course, it needs only coleslaw or a salad to accompany it and beer or a strong white wine such as a Mâcon or Pinot Blanc.

1 cup (4 ounces) diced lean salt pork
1 Tb olive oil or butter
4 cups sliced onions
⅓ cup (5½ Tb) flour
3½ cups light cream, or milk and cream, heated
Salt and pepper
2 or 3 large boiled potatoes, sliced ⅜ inch
*   thick (3 cups)*
1 cup (4 ounces) coarsely grated Swiss cheese
1 lb. salt cod fillets, poached and flaked
2 to 3 Tb fresh white bread crumbs

Blanch the salt pork (simmer 5 minutes in 2 quarts water, drain, dry). Brown the pork lightly in a saucepan with the oil or butter; add onions and cook slowly until tender, then brown lightly. Pour into a sieve set over a bowl, to drain out fat. Return onions and pork to pan, and blend in flour, if necessary adding dribbles of pork fat to moisten flour. Stir over moderate heat 2 minutes, remove from heat, and beat in 3 cups of the cream. Simmer, stirring occasionally, 15 to 20 minutes; thin out with milk or cod-cooking liquid if necessary, but sauce should be moderately thick. Season to taste. Remove one third of the sauce and reserve. Spoon a thin layer of remaining sauce in the bottom of a shallow buttered 6-cup baking dish (such as an oval one 9 by 13 inches), and fill with alternating layers of potatoes, cheese, codfish, and sauce, ending with potatoes and cheese. Beat remaining cream into reserved sauce, pour over final layer, and sprinkle on bread crumbs; drizzle over a spoonful of pork fat or melted butter.

☼ Refrigerate until ready to cook.

About 30 minutes before serving, bake in upper-middle level of a preheated 375-degree oven just until bubbling and top has browned lightly. Serve now or, if you are having a buffet, set on an electric warming tray and let guests help themselves.

Poultry

Chicken

Poulet sauté à brun, croustillant—the crisp
  brown sauté—sauces and variations
Poulet poêlé—brown covered sauté
  of chicken; with herbs; variations
  including additions of cream,
  mushrooms, potatoes, salt pork, onions,
  plus poulet sauté au vinaigre, and
  poulet sauté Marengo

Coq au vin versus chicken fricassee
A barbecue and a rabbit ragout

All about chicken breasts, illustrated
Suprêmes de volaille en goujons, meunière
  and other quick-cooking ideas for
  slivered, skewered, whole, and
  sauced breasts
Chicken Kiev, and other stuffed
  breast fantasies

Roast chicken
Trussing a chicken, illustrated
Poularde à la broche—spit-roasted chicken
Poularde rôtie au four—oven-roasted
  chicken—roasting timetable

Stewed chickens and boiled fowls
To disjoint a chicken, illustrated
Poule au gros sel, and other ideas

Turkey

General information, buying, defrosting,
  stuffing talk, turkey stock
Roasting timetable
Dinde rôtie au four—roast turkey

Frozen turkey breasts
Poitrine de dinde farcie et braisée—turkey
  breast stuffed and braised

Duck

Canard à la rouennaise; canard à la
  presse; canard au sang; and canard en
  salmis—pressed duck and salmis of duck
Frittons; grattons—cracklings

Goose

Ragoût d'oie au chou—cut-up goose
  braised with cabbage

We never seem to tire of chicken in our house, even though I have fed my husband upon it for weeks, even months at a time when I've been immersed in "The Poultry Chapter" of some book or other. It is said that if one were sentenced to devour a quail a day for a year or, in the words of the great English comedienne Bea Lillie, "to eat caviar and grouse in an overheated house," or duck, turkey, or goose, one couldn't force down a bite of it after a few weeks. But not chicken. At least, not for me: I can go on eating chicken forever. A good reason, I am sure, is that you can do so many things with it and present it each time in a very different guise. Who cannot adore a big roaster, turning slowly on an electric spit, its aroma of ever-browning skin filling the room? How lovely are the leftovers of that roast chicken, served cold with homemade mayonnaise and a cucumber salad. Then there is the sauté Marengo, with its fresh tomatoes, its mushrooms, and its French fried eggs; Chicken Kiev with its spurt of herbal butter; chicken salad; homemade chicken soup; and on and on almost endlessly.

Fortunately chicken and turkey are among the most reasonably priced of our high-protein foods, and they also contain the least fat—except for fish. Fortunately, too, if you shop around for quality rather than price per pound, I hope you find, as I do, that our mass-produced chickens have improved immensely in flavor during the last number of years. And how lucky we are that we can buy chicken in parts—breasts only, thighs only, gizzards and hearts and livers. And when the purse is flat we can feast on the tender finger-food meat in the necks and wings.

The major portion of this chapter, then, deals with chicken, from a crisp brown sauté that finishes in the oven, to *Coq au Vin* done in a new way, and spit roasting, the stewing of hens, and a full rundown on chicken breasts. You will even find a rabbit among these chickens—a rabbit ragout with lemon and herbs. I put this in to remind you that rabbit can substitute for chicken in almost any recipe, and raising one's own rabbits is certainly an easy way to beat the price squeeze.

To round out the chapter, turkey, our great national bird, comes in for a roasting session, with timetables and a marvelous Provençal stuffing; and, in case you do not want to cook a whole turkey, there's the frozen breast that you can slice, stuff, and braise in wine and herbs. We travel to Rouen, Joan of Arc's city, for the famous pressed duck of the region, and end with an unusual recipe for goose—a ragout in red wine with cabbage.

TO WASH OR NOT TO WASH CHICKEN. Still, in France, when you buy whole chicken, it may well not have been eviscerated, and this means that its cavity is hermetically closed to entering bacteria. With modern cleaning and packing methods, however, the eviscerated chickens frequently sit all together in a common bath of ice and water; one infected bird can spread salmonella or other sick-making bacteria through the whole lot. I am therefore in favor of washing chicken just before I cook it; I even go so far as to hold it under the warm water faucet, and I rinse it rapidly all over and inside and out. I make sure the chicken and its wrapping have not touched any working surface, and I then dry the chicken thoroughly with paper towels. I certainly have found no loss of flavor nor change in texture—its flesh is not porous, after all, and even one case of bacteria poisoning is too miserably much to risk. (I now wash French chickens, too.)

Chicken: the crisp brown sauté

**Poulet sauté
à brun,
croustillant**

———◆———

CRISP BROWN
SAUTÉED CHICKEN:
HOT OR COLD

This simple and straightforward chicken sauté with its combination of browning and baking is the French answer to American fried chicken—it's crisp and beautifully brown on the outside, while the flesh is moist and tender inside. Accompany it with grilled or stuffed tomatoes and a fresh vegetable like broccoli or spinach—home French fries would go beautifully too. Or try one of the eggplant dishes on page 397, or the garlicky potatoes with herbs on page 416, and a salad of raw vegetables. Serve a not too heavy red wine like Beaujolais, Côtes du Rhône, Bordeaux Supérieur, Gamay, or Zinfandel. (When you want to take cold chicken on a picnic, by the way, the crisp brown sauté is the recipe to use.)

For 4 people

For the chicken
*2½ lbs. ready-cut frying chicken (a selection
of parts, or all of one kind)
About 1 cup milk in a bowl
Salt and pepper
About ½ cup flour
Butter and olive oil or cooking oil, or oil only
(enough for browning the chicken, for
basting it in the oven, and, if you wish,
2 to 3 tablespoons of butter to enrich
the sauce)*

For a brown deglazing sauce
*1 Tb minced shallots or green onions
¼ cup dry white wine or dry
white French Vermouth
1 cup chicken stock or bouillon
The optional 2 to 3 tablespoons enrichment
butter*

Equipment: A large piece of wax paper; a heavy iron frying pan with short iron handle to brown and bake the chicken in, or a frying pan to brown the chicken and a shallow roasting pan for baking; tongs or a wooden spoon and fork for turning the chicken without piercing its flesh

Browning the chicken: *8 to 10 minutes, and may be done ahead.* Just before you brown the chicken, dip each piece in the milk, shake off excess, and arrange chicken on wax paper. Sprinkle lightly with salt and pepper. Shake the flour over the chicken, and turn it about to coat completely. Pat in the flour with your hands, then shake each piece to remove excess flour. Immediately set frying pan over moderately high heat, adding 2 tablespoons butter and 1 of oil (or oil only), or enough to film bottom of pan by almost ⅛ inch. When butter foams up and foam then almost subsides (or oil is very hot but not smoking), arrange as many chicken pieces in the pan as will fit easily without crowding, skin side down. Brown several minutes on each side, adding a little more oil if needed; as one piece is done remove it and add another. At end of browning, pour out the fat. Either return all chicken to pan, if it is ovenproof, or transfer the chicken to a shallow roasting pan. Preheat oven to 375 degrees in time for next step.

☼ Chicken may be browned in advance; if done several hours or a day in advance, let cool, then cover and refrigerate.

Final baking of the chicken: *20 to 30 minutes, oven at 375 degrees.* If you have a mixture of dark and light meat, remove the light meat (wings and breasts); it will be added later, since it takes less time to cook. Melt 2 tablespoons of butter and 1 of oil (or use oil only), and baste the chicken in the pan with droplets, reserving rest for later basting. If skillet has cooled off or roasting pan is heavy, heat on top of stove until chicken is sizzling, then set in upper-middle level of preheated oven. In 5 minutes, or when chicken has begun to sizzle in the oven, baste quickly again. (Use accumulated fat in roasting pan when butter and oil are used up.) In 4 to 5 minutes, turn the chicken, add the white meat, and baste again.

☼ At this point, you may set chicken aside uncovered, at room temperature, and continue later; it will take 15 minutes or more to finish since it will have cooled off.

In 5 minutes, turn and baste the chicken; repeat in 5 minutes, and check on doneness. Juices beginning to emerge in the pan are a sure sign that the time is near. Drumsticks and thighs should feel tender when pressed. Pierce the meat with a fork: the juices should run clear yellow with no rosy traces. Check carefully, since while underdone chicken is inedible, overdone chicken with dried out, juiceless flesh is a shame.

Brown deglazing sauce, and serving. When done, arrange the chicken on a hot serving platter and keep warm in hot turned-off oven with its door ajar. Pour excess fat out of pan, add the minced shallots or onions, and stir for 1 minute over moderate heat on top of the stove. Add the wine and stock, scraping up into it all coagulated roasting juices, and boil down rapidly until liquid is slightly syrupy. Taste for seasoning. Just before serving, remove from heat and add optional enrichment butter, swishing pan to melt butter into the sauce; pour sauce into a warm bowl —you will have just enough for a small spoonful of concentrated essence to surround each serving. Decorate chicken platter with sprigs of parsley or watercress, or whatever vegetables you wish, and serve as soon as possible.

OTHER SAUCES, FOLLOWING THE SYSTEM

Deglazing sauce with cream. After removing excess fat from pan, add a tablespoon of minced shallot or scallion and sauté a moment, then stir in ¼ cup wine or Vermouth and ¼ cup stock and boil down rapidly. When syrupy, stir in 1 cup of heavy cream or *crème fraîche,* and boil a moment or two until lightly thickened. Off heat, swish in 2 to 3 table-spoons fresh butter, if you wish, and a spoonful of fresh minced herbs (chives, parsley, tarragon, or parsley only) .

Mustard sauce. Make the preceding sauce with cream as described, but blend 2 tablespoons of strong Dijon-type prepared mustard in a small bowl with ¼ cup of the cream. Stir it into the pan along with the rest of the cream, and continue as directed. Mustard gives a subtle bite to the sauce, as well as a light thickening.

Fresh tomato fondue. This makes a pretty as well as delectable accompani-ment, particularly in tomato season. Peel, seed, and dice several tomatoes, to give you 2 cups of pulp. After removing excess fat from the pan, and sautéing 1 to 2 tablespoons of minced shallot or scallion for a moment, stir in ¼ cup each of white wine or Vermouth and chicken stock. Boil down rapidly until syrupy, then stir in the tomato, a clove of puréed garlic if you wish, and a teaspoon of fresh tarragon or basil, or a big pinch of dried tarragon, thyme, or oregano. Sauté, stirring and folding, for 2 to 3 minutes, to cook the tomatoes; taste for seasoning, fold in a spoonful or two of fresh parsley, and turn into a warm bowl. You will have about 2 spoonfuls to accompany each serving.

Chicken parmigiano (*Crisp brown sauté of chicken with Parmesan cheese*). This is not an Italian recipe. I just happen to like the name, and it doesn't need formal directions at all. Follow the main recipe for the Crisp Brown Sauté on page 187. When the chicken is almost done, and has 5 minutes or so to go, arrange it skin side up in its pan. Paint top sides with a thin coating of strong Dijon-type prepared mustard, spread on a fairly thick coating of freshly grated Parmesan cheese—⅛ inch or so—and baste with the juices of the pan. Finish the cooking and serve with the plain brown deglazing sauce outlined in the recipe.

Poulet poêlé: brown covered sauté of chicken

When you want a tenderer and juicier chicken than the crisp brown sauté, you brown it, then cover-cook it so it steams in its own juices and whatever other ingredients and flavorings you may wish to add to it, such as herbs, potatoes, onions, and so forth. The French culinary term for this type of sauté is *poêlé*. In the old days before covered casseroles you browned the chicken in one frying pan or *poêle,* and covered it with another *poêle* to finish cooking. Nowadays, however, the distinction rarely appears in the title of a dish. I suppose you could call it smothered chicken, but I have always translated *poulet poêlé* as a covered sauté because I think that is a more accurate description.

Poulet poêlé aux herbes; poulet sauté aux herbes

Here is the plain herbal version, to serve with a fresh green vegetable like peas, beans, asparagus, or broccoli, or one of the zucchini dishes suggested on page 426. Your own French fries or a potato sauté could also be part of the garniture, and you will want a rather light red wine, like a Beaujolais, Bordeaux, or Cabernet Sauvignon.

CHICKEN SAUTÉED
WITH HERBS

For 4 people

2½ lbs. cut-up frying chicken (a mixture
    of parts, or all of one kind)
Butter and olive oil or cooking oil
    (or oil only)
Salt and pepper
2 Tb fresh minced herbs such as thyme,
    tarragon, basil; or ½ Tb dried herbs
Optional: Several cloves garlic, unpeeled

Optional deglazing sauce
1 Tb minced shallots or scallions
¼ cup dry white wine or dry white
    French Vermouth
1 cup chicken stock or bouillon
Optional: 2 to 3 Tb butter for enrichment
1 or 2 Tb fresh minced herbs used above, or
    fresh minced parsley only

Equipment: A large heavy frying pan with a
    cover, or a covered casserole, or an electric
    skillet; tongs or a wooden spoon and fork for
    turning chicken without piercing flesh

Browning the chicken: *8 to 10 minutes.* Dry the chicken thoroughly. Set frying pan or casserole over moderately high heat (or use 360 degrees for an electric skillet). Add 2 tablespoons of butter and 1 of oil (or 3 tablespoons of oil only), enough to film bottom of pan by almost ⅛ inch. Heat to very hot but not smoking or burning, and brown the chicken as for the Crisp Sauté on page 187. At end of browning, pour the fat out of the pan.

✿ You may brown the chicken hours or even a day in advance of final cooking. Let cool uncovered and if wait is more than an hour, cover and refrigerate.

Finishing the cooking: *20 to 30 minutes.* Add a tablespoon or so fresh butter or oil to the pan, season dark meat lightly with salt and pepper, and return to pan—white meat will be added later since it takes less time to cook. Sprinkle with half the herbs (or all, if you are using dark meat only), add the optional garlic cloves, and heat to sizzling. Then cover pan and either set in a 350-degree oven, reducing heat to 325 degrees in 5 minutes or so, or set over moderately low heat (300 degrees for an electric skillet). After about 8 minutes, turn the dark meat over in the pan, season the white meat and add it to the pan; baste all the chicken with accumulated pan juices, and sprinkle the remaining herbs over the white meat. Cover and cook slowly, turning and basting once or twice more, for another 12 to 15 minutes. Start testing for doneness when juices begin exuding into the pan: the chicken is done when the thickest part of drumstick or thigh feels tender and when juices run clear yellow if meat is pierced with a fork.

☼ If you are not ready to serve, set cover slightly askew and place chicken over almost simmering water, or on an electric warming device, or in a warming oven at 120 degrees. Half an hour will not hurt flavor and texture, but too long a wait will drain the flesh of its juices.

Optional sauce, and serving. You need no sauce at all with the chicken; simply skim off excess fat, and spoon a little of the pan juices over each serving. However, if you wish a sauce, arrange the chicken on a hot platter along with whatever garnish you may have chosen, and keep warm for the few minutes it takes for the sauce. Remove excess fat from the pan. Add the shallots or scallions and stir over moderate heat for 1 minute, then add the wine and chicken stock and boil rapidly, scraping into the liquid all coagulated cooking juices. When liquid has boiled down to the lightly syrupy consistency, correct seasoning, swish in optional butter by spoonfuls, blend in the herbs, pour the sauce over the chicken, and serve.

OTHER SAUCES AND ADDITIONS
TO THE COVERED SAUTE

Use the preceding master recipe as a springboard for infinite alterations, additions, and improvisations. ·Here are just a few brief ideas to give you a start.

Poulet sauté à la crème et aux champignons (*Chicken sautéed with cream and mushrooms*). Cream and mushrooms are classically French with almost anything, from veal to shrimp to scallops to fish fillets, and certainly with chicken. After browning the chicken, remove it from the pan and sauté ⅓ to ½ pound of quartered fresh mushrooms. Remove them and set aside. When the chicken is done, remove it, sauté 2 table-spoons of shallots or scallions for a moment, then add ¼ cup each of dry white wine or Vermouth and chicken stock. Boil down until almost syrupy, then stir in 1 cup thick cream or *crème fraîche* and the mush-rooms. Boil several minutes to reduce slightly, carefully correct season-ing, and return the chicken to the pan. Simmer a minute or two, basting with the sauce, and serve. (Tarragon is a lovely herb to use here.)

Poulet sauté grand'mère (*Chicken sautéed with potatoes, salt pork, and mushrooms*). Here is a main course in a single dish, needing just a green vegetable or salad to complete the picture. I love this combination: the potatoes pick up a wonderful flavor, the salt pork adds its special charac-ter, and everything simmering together makes for very good eating in-deed. Cut a 4- to 5-ounce chunk of salt pork into *lardons* (sticks about 1½ inches long and ⅜ inch to a side), and blanch them (simmer 5 min-utes in 1 quart of water and drain). Brown them lightly in a tablespoon of butter or oil, remove them, then brown the chicken. Meanwhile peel 3 or 4 "boiling" potatoes, cut into ½-inch dice, blanch 2 minutes in boil-ing salted water, and drain. When chicken is browned, remove it and brown the potatoes lightly. Remove them and brown ¼ pound or so of quartered fresh mushrooms; remove them. Return pork, dark meat of chicken, and potatoes to pan, sprinkle with herbs, and cook 10 minutes, then add the white meat, being sure to baste potatoes as well as chicken occasionally with the pan juices. Add the mushrooms 5 minutes before the end of the cooking—which will take 30 minutes or so in all. You will not need any special sauce since the pan juices suffice.

Poulet sauté bonne femme (*Chicken sautéed with potatoes, salt pork, and onions*). This is just another version of our preceding *grand'mère*, substituting onions for mushrooms. Use the small pearl onions, little white onions not more than an inch in diameter, or small whole frozen onions. If fresh, drop them for 1 minute in boiling water, drain, and peel, piercing a cross in root end about ¼ inch deep to discourage their burst-ing during cooking. Brown them lightly after you have browned the potatoes, then add to the chicken along with the potatoes and salt pork at the beginning of the covered cooking.

Other additions. Add other vegetables to the chicken in time for them to finish off their cooking in good company, such as fresh green peas boiled until almost tender, or carrots, either one with a handful of sautéed mushrooms; or a sauté of diced zucchini or eggplant with the fresh tomato *fondue* described for the Crisp Sauté on page 187.

Poulet sauté au vinaigre; fricassée au vinaigre

CHICKEN SAUTÉED WITH WINE, WINE VINEGAR, AND HERBS

Whether or not the great Fernand Point, who died in 1955, originated this chicken idea, he at least featured it in his restaurant under the name *Poulet au Feu d'Enfer*—Hell's Fire Chicken. The three-star restaurant group in France, most of whom apprenticed *chez* Point at La Pyramide in Vienne at some moment in their careers, revived it in the early 1970's as *Poulet au Vinaigre.* Its popularity has undoubtedly been due to the vast increase in French battery-raised chickens, some quite lacking in flavor, and a strong vinegar sauce helps disguise the weak flesh. Although I don't find it one of the world's great dishes, it makes an interesting change of taste. The original Point recipe is a sauté of chicken with a deglazing of vinegar, and you can duplicate it by following the master recipe on page 191. After browning the chicken, however, pour in ¼ to ⅓ cup of wine vinegar—the amount will depend on the strength of your vinegar, and you can always add more at the end if need be. Reduce the vinegar to nothing (boil down rapidly to a syrupy state). Then add ⅓ cup dry white wine or dry white French Vermouth and let that in turn rapidly reduce to nothing. Continue with the recipe, adding the herbs, garlic, and seasonings, and finish the dish, completing the sauce; taste it, and if you feel it needs a little more authority, add droplets of wine vinegar to reduce with the rest of the ingredients. (Some versions have a lightly thickened and more copious sauce. For this, follow the *Coq au Vin* recipe on page 199, retaining or omitting the *lardons,* onions, and mushrooms, but substituting wine vinegar for Cognac after browning the chicken; reduce it to nothing before continuing with the recipe. In this case, you will be making a *Fricassée de Poulet au Vinaigre.*)

Note. A memorial book to the renowned chef contains many interesting ideas, most of them merely sketched out: *Fernand Point, Ma Gastronomie* (French-language edition by Flammarion, Paris, 1969; English-language edition with translation by Frank and Patricia Kulla, Lyceum Books, Wilton, Conn., 1974). Another book on famous French restaurants and their special recipes is Louisette Bertholle's *Secrets of the Great French Restaurants* (New York: Macmillan, 1974).

Poulet sauté Marengo

——————

NAPOLEON'S
CHICKEN,
GARNISHED WITH
TOMATOES,
MUSHROOMS,
CRAYFISH OR
SHRIMP, HERBS,
BLACK OLIVES,
CROUTONS, AND
FRENCH FRIED EGGS

After Napoleon's famous battle at Marengo, where he amazingly, after an apparent debacle, turned around and defeated the Austrian forces of Baron Melas and sent them packing out of Italy, he was served a chicken dinner that has become legendary. It was cooked on the battlefield, they tell us, with whatever was to be had in the neighboring Italian countryside. What that "whatever" was, besides chicken and tomatoes, no one can really say, since the recipe was never formally catalogued. Thus, of course, there are many stories and as many recipes, and any cook can pick any version of that much-told tale. My favorite is that Napoleon's chef was able to find only some garlic, olives and olive oil, tomatoes and mushrooms, a few eggs, a bit of bread, a handful of crayfish, and a chicken—which he slashed into pieces with his terrible swift sword. (What a glorious picture, that of the battle-scarred chef complete with saber. And apron and chef's hat, too, one wonders? Yes! Or we would not know who he was in the scene.) Out of these found ingredients our noble chef constructed his masterpiece that today is far more renowned than the battle. All of this took place, it should be noted, on June 14, 1800, while Napoleon was still First Consul, not Emperor. You probably will not find Marengo on any but a most detailed map; it lies in the pre-Alpine mountains some seventy miles north and west of Genoa, near Alessandria.

French versions of the recipe vary more than the Italian, but those Italian books I have consulted, such as Ada Boni's *Il Talismano* and Anna Gossetti della Salda's *Ricette Regionali,* give the same basic ingredients I have listed, crediting Napoleon's chef with the recipe. Amusingly enough—or I might even better say, with a chauvinistic bravado uniquely his own—Francesco Ghedini, in his *Northern Italian Cooking* (New York: Hawthorn Books, 1973), proclaims the dish to be entirely of Italian origin, and not at all the invention of some foreign French chef.

Whatever and however the origins and the authenticity of ingredients, the recipe given here is a marvelous combination of elements, and although the garniture is somewhat time consuming, you can get it all done ahead with no loss of glory. The eggs I particularly like; combining with and flowing into the olive oil–browned croutons, and the tomatoes, and the various other elements, they give Napoleon's chicken a very special character.

Serving suggestions. Accompaniments should be of the simplest and best, I think: tiny fresh green peas tossed in butter, if you want greenery, and either a fine red Bordeaux wine or one of the greatest of the great white Burgundies, Corton Charlemagne.

Sautéing the chicken

For 4 people

About 2½ lbs. cut-up frying chicken
   (I like the leg-thigh combination here,
   despite Napoleonic tradition)
Olive oil
Optional: ¼ cup Cognac
½ cup minced onions
Salt and freshly ground pepper
About ½ tsp mixed herbs, such as Italian
   seasoning, or thyme, oregano, and bay

The garniture

12 large fine fresh mushrooms
4 slices white sandwich bread cut into 8
   crustless triangles
12 large peeled raw shrimp, fresh or frozen
   (or whole fresh-water crayfish)
1½ to 2 cups fresh tomato pulp (3 to 4 tomatoes
   peeled, seeded, juiced, and roughly chopped
   —add 2 Tb tomato paste if tomatoes are
   out of season)
2 large cloves garlic, puréed or finely minced
¼ tsp Italian seasoning, or thyme and oregano
4 very fresh eggs
8 to 12 small black olives
2 Tb chopped fresh parsley

Other ingredients

Additional olive oil, a little butter, salt and pepper,
   ½ cup or so of dry white wine or dry
   white French Vermouth

Equipment: A large, heavy frying pan, casserole, or
   electric skillet with cover for cooking the
   chicken; tongs, wooden spoon, and fork; a small

*stainless covered saucepan for mushrooms;
a medium frying pan for croutons; a 5-inch
saucepan for eggs*

Sautéing the chicken. Dry chicken thoroughly in paper towels. Film pan
with ¹⁄₁₆ inch of olive oil, heat to very hot but not smoking, and add the
chicken, skin side down. When chicken is golden brown on one side, in
4 to 5 minutes, turn and brown on other side, taking 8 to 10 minutes
in all.

Pour in the optional Cognac and, averting your face, ignite it with a
match; shaking pan by handle, let flames rise for a minute, then extinguish with cover. Mix the onions into the liquid in the pan, season
chicken with salt, pepper, and herbs, cover pan again, and cook at a
slow simmer for 10 to 12 minutes. Turn chicken, baste with pan liquid,
cover, and cook 10 to 12 minutes longer, or until meat is tender when
pressed, and juices, when thickest parts of meat are pricked deeply with
a fork, run clear yellow with no trace of rose. While chicken is cooking,
or at any convenient time beforehand, prepare the garniture as follows:

The mushrooms. Break stems from caps of mushrooms; wash both rapidly,
and pat dry in paper towels. Mince stems and set aside. Flute the caps, if
you wish, adding peelings to the minced stems. Place caps in small stainless pan with 3 to 4 tablespoons of the wine or Vermouth, ¼ teaspoon
salt, and a tablespoon of butter; bring to simmer, cover, and simmer
slowly for 5 minutes; set aside.

The croutons. Pour a ⅛-inch layer of oil into the frying pan, and set over
moderately high heat; when oil is hot but not smoking, sauté bread triangles 1 minute or so on each side, until lightly browned. Drain on a
plate lined with paper toweling.

The shrimp. In the same frying pan, adding more oil if needed, sauté
the shrimp, shaking and swirling pan by its handle for a minute or two
until they begin to stiffen. Season rapidly with salt and pepper, and pour
in 2 to 3 tablespoons of wine or Vermouth. Swirl a moment more over
heat, and transfer with their juices to a bowl. (Cook crayfish—*écrevisses*—
like shrimp, but if alive, first pull out intestinal tube attached to central
tail flap.)

The tomato and mushroom sauce. Add another tablespoon or so of oil to the frying pan, stir in the minced mushroom stems, tomatoes, garlic, herbs, and salt and pepper to taste. Cover pan and simmer 5 minutes until tomatoes exude their juices, then uncover pan and cook over moderately high heat (add liquid from shrimp and mushroom caps at this point) until juices have almost evaporated.

The French fried eggs. Pour about 1 inch of olive oil into the second small saucepan and heat to very hot but not smoking. One at a time, break an egg into a small bowl or a ladle and tip into the hot oil. Immediately roll egg against side of pan with spoon to give it an attractive oval egg shape. Let cook about 1 minute, then remove to drain on plate with croutons. Continue with the 3 other eggs.

Final assembly and serving. Preheat oven to 400 degrees. When chicken is tender, remove it to a side dish, and spoon excess fat out of pan. Pour in tomato sauce, return chicken to pan, baste it, and simmer for a moment to blend flavors. Correct seasoning.

✿ If you are not yet ready to serve, cover loosely and keep warm for half an hour or so, but do not let chicken continue to cook or it will lose its fresh texture and flavor.

Just before serving, reheat croutons and eggs in hot oven for a moment, reheat shrimp and mushrooms together in mushroom pan, and turn chicken out onto a hot platter. Arrange the croutons around the edge of the platter, topping them alternately with an egg or 3 shrimp. Arrange the mushroom caps over the chicken, and the olives. Sprinkle parsley over the eggs, and bring the *Poulet Sauté Marengo* to the table, displaying the platter so that your guests may admire the arrangement before you serve them.

Coq au vin versus chicken fricassee

Chicken, onions, and mushrooms—simmer them in red wine for *Coq au Vin,* served brown and hearty; in white wine for old-fashioned chicken fricassee, all suave and creamy. Except for small details, the two recipes are parallel in technique yet so different in taste you would never dream they were sisters under the sauce, and to illustrate their twinship, I've combined them together into a single recipe. (You may notice the procedure is slightly different here than for either recipe in our other books.) Both dishes are useful cook-in-advance ones for parties since they lose none of their special qualities when cooked, refrigerated, and then reheated a day later. Serve the *Coq au Vin* with rice, noodles, or boiled potatoes; the fricassee with rice. You need no other vegetable accompaniment, although fresh buttered peas or broccoli flowerets make a nice touch of green. The red wine to serve with *Coq au Vin* can be either the same used in the cooking, or one of the regional Burgundies or Côtes du Rhône, or domestic Pinot Noir. Serve either a red Bordeaux or a white Burgundy or Pinot Blanc with the fricassée.

Coq au vin	*Chicken fricassee*
CHICKEN IN RED WINE	CHICKEN IN WHITE WINE

For 4 to 6 people

For both coq au vin and chicken fricassee

*2½ lbs. ready-cut frying chicken (a selection of parts, or
    all one kind), thoroughly dried*
Salt and pepper
*16 to 20 small white onions, peeled (or double the amount
    if you want to use tiny frozen peeled raw onions)*
3 Tb flour
*1 quart (¾ lb.) fresh mushrooms, trimmed, washed,
    and quartered*
Optional enrichment: 2 to 3 Tb butter

For coq au vin only

Optional: ½ *cup lardons (fresh
    fat-and-lean pork strips,
    ¼ by 1½ inches)*
2 or more Tb olive oil or cooking oil
Optional: ¼ *cup Cognac or Armagnac*
1 imported bay leaf and ¼ tsp thyme
*2 cups red wine (Burgundy, Côtes
    du Rhône, or Pinot Noir)*
*About 2 cups brown chicken stock
    or beef bouillon*
*1 or 2 cloves of garlic, mashed
    or minced*
About 1 Tb tomato paste

For fricassee only

3 to 4 Tb butter
½ tsp tarragon
*2 cups dry white wine or 1½ cups
    dry white French Vermouth*
About 2 cups chicken bouillon
About ½ cup heavy cream
Drops of fresh lemon juice

*Equipment for both: A large heavy frying pan, casserole,
or electric skillet; tongs; wooden spoon and fork*

Coq au vin. If you are using *lardons,* sauté several minutes in 2 tablespoons oil until lightly browned; remove *lardons* to a side dish and leave fat in pan. (Otherwise, film pan with ⅛ inch of oil.) Heat fat or oil in pan to moderately hot, add chicken, not crowding pan; turn frequently to brown nicely on all sides. Pour in the optional Cognac, shake pan a few seconds until bubbling hot, then ignite Cognac with a match. Let flame a minute, swirling pan by its handle to burn off alcohol; extinguish with pan cover.

Chicken fricassee. Over moderate heat cook butter in pan until foaming. Add chicken pieces and turn frequently in the butter for several minutes, regulating heat so chicken does not brown. Meat should stiffen slightly in contrast to its squashy raw state, and become a golden yellow.

For both. Then season chicken pieces with salt and pepper; add bay leaf and thyme to *Coq au Vin,* tarragon to Chicken Fricassee. Place the onions around the chicken. Cover and cook slowly 10 minutes, turning once. Uncover pan, sprinkle on the flour, turning chicken and onions so flour is absorbed; cook 3 to 4 minutes more, turning once or twice. Remove from heat, gradually stir and swirl in the wine and enough stock or bouillon almost to cover the chicken. (Add the browned *lardons,* garlic, and tomato paste to the *Coq au Vin.*) Cover pan and simmer slowly 25 to 30 minutes, then test chicken; remove those pieces that are tender, and continue cooking the rest a few minutes longer. If onions are not quite tender, continue cooking them; then

return all chicken to pan, add mushrooms, and simmer 4
to 5 minutes. Taste carefully, and correct seasoning.

oq au vin. Sauce should be just thick
hough to coat chicken and vegetables
ghtly. If too thin, boil down rapidly to
oncentrate; if too thick, thin out with
oonfuls of bouillon.

Chicken fricassee. Add ½ cup of cream,
and bring to the simmer, thinning out if
necessary with spoonfuls of more cream
until sauce coats chicken and vegetables
lightly. Correct seasoning again, adding
drops of lemon juice to taste.

Serving and holding notes for both. For immediate serving,
arrange the chicken and vegetables on a platter, surrounded
by the rice or whatever else you are including; swirl the optional butter enrichment by tablespoons into the sauce,
and spoon sauce over chicken. For later serving, baste
chicken with its sauce, and let cool, uncovered, to room
temperature; then cover and refrigerate. To reheat, simmer slowly, covered; baste and turn chicken every 2 minutes until thoroughly warmed through (6 to 8 minutes),
but do not overcook.

A barbecued or broiled chicken

Chicken bar-b-q à la chinoiserie

BROILED OR
BARBECUED
CHICKEN WITH
ORIENTAL
OVERTONES

We have a Chinese-Japanese fancy grocery store
in our neighborhood, and I find some of their condiments delicious with chicken. Here is an example of utterly mixed up genealogy that we have
found particularly successful, either as a barbecue
or as a broil.

*4 quarters of frying chicken (we like the leg-
thigh sections rather than the breast)*
2 lemons

2 or 3 slices ginger pickled in sweet vinegar (or
    fresh ginger, shaved thin)
For 4 people   2 Tb soy sauce
4 Tb olive oil
1 tsp dark sesame oil (for its particularly
    pungent flavor)
½ tsp thyme, oregano, or Italian seasoning
2 to 4 large cloves of garlic, puréed or finely minced
¼ tsp cracked peppercorns

Marinating the chicken. Dry off the chicken in paper towels. With a vegetable peeler, shave off the yellow part of the peel of 1 lemon, and cut into julienne (matchsticks $\frac{1}{16}$ inch wide). Cut the ginger also into julienne. Place both in an enameled or Pyrex casserole or baking dish, along with the strained juice of the peeled lemon, the soy, oils, herbs, garlic, and pepper. Beat to blend, then add the chicken and baste with the marinade. Marinate for 2 hours (or longer) in the refrigerator, turning and basting the chicken several times. Just before cooking, scrape the marinade off the chicken and back into the casserole; pat chicken dry in paper towels. Cut remaining lemon into very thin slices, and set aside.

To broil. Arrange the chicken skin side down in shallow broiling pan, and set under a moderately hot broiler. Broil 10 to 12 minutes on one side, basting several times with oil from marinade, until chicken is lightly brown; turn and broil 10 minutes on the other side (skin side up). Transfer to the upper-middle level of a 375-degree oven, baste with the remaining marinade, and cover with the reserved slices of lemon. Bake 8 to 10 minutes, basting 2 or 3 times with remains of marinade, or with accumulated pan juices.

To barbecue. Barbecue the chicken for about 30 minutes, turning it frequently and brushing it with a little oil from the marinade, until just done. Then return it to the casserole, scrape over it the remaining marinade, and cover with the lemon slices. Cover the casserole. Set over a moderately hot spot on the barbecue, and let steep slowly 8 to 10 minutes, basting 2 or 3 times with accumulated juices in casserole.

Rabbit ragout

What's a rabbit doing in here with all these chickens? Well, you can cook them in the same way, using the same recipes, but unless rabbit is small, young, and delicate, it takes a little longer because the flesh is not as tender. And the chicken with lemon reminded me of a very good rabbit with lemon that I want to pass on to you. Around where we live, a number of the markets carry an excellent quality of packaged frozen rabbit raised in California, and our Italian markets have fresh rabbit. The frozen rabbit comes ready cut up, and our Italian butchers will cut fresh rabbit to order.

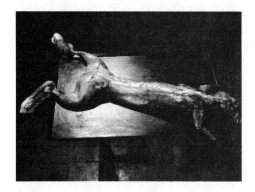

The whole rabbit is always sold with its hind feet on, in foreign markets, so you will know it really is rabbit.

When you have a whole rabbit and are cutting it yourself, you can simmer the tail and the head along with the rest of the meat, the way cooks do in France and Italy, but you will not find these appendages in cut-up packaged rabbit. You won't find, either, the lungs, kidneys, heart, and liver, which you may use like chicken parts.

The usual package will contain, starting at the tail end, the leg-thigh sections, which you separate into two; the loin or *rable,* the choicest morsel, which you chop into 2 or 3 pieces crosswise; the rib section, which you halve crosswise; and the 2 front legs, which you leave whole.

Ragoût de lapin; lapin sauté au citron

RABBIT STEW WITH
LEMON

This rabbit is marinated for a day or two in lemon and herbs before it simmers in an aromatic broth. For a change of pace, try serving it with the lentils described on page 336, and a salad of fresh green beans briefly cooked and cooled in the French manner, and tossed with oil and lemon, seasonings, parsley, and thin rounds of sliced raw red onion. A more conventional accompaniment would be steamed rice and fresh green peas, beans, or broccoli. I like a strong dry white wine with my rabbit, a Pouilly Fuissé, a white Châteauneuf, or a Pinot Blanc; however, I would not refuse a fresh young red Beaujolais or its equivalent.

For the marinade

For 4 to 6 people

A 3- to 3½-lb. frying rabbit, cut up
4 to 8 cloves garlic, peeled and
*   quartered lengthwise*
3 medium onions, sliced thin
2 medium carrots, sliced thin
⅓ cup olive oil
1 lemon, the zest (yellow part of peel) minced,
*   and the juice strained*
2 imported bay leaves
½ tsp rosemary or thyme
⅛ tsp fennel seeds
½ tsp salt

For browning and simmering

Optional: 4 to 6 ounces lean salt pork
Olive oil or cooking oil
About ½ cup flour
Optional: 2 strips dried orange peel, about
*   4 inches by 1 inch each*
1 lemon, cut into thin crosswise slices
*   just before using*
2 or more cups veal stock, or chicken stock
*   or bouillon*
Salt and pepper
Optional: Parsley or watercress for decoration

*Equipment: A stainless, glass, or porcelain bowl
large enough to hold the rabbit for its
marinade; wax paper; a large frying pan or
electric skillet to brown the rabbit in; tongs
or a wooden fork and spoon; and a covered
electric skillet or casserole for the simmering*

Marinating the rabbit. Dry off the rabbit pieces in paper towels. Stir all the marinade ingredients into the marinade bowl, then add the pieces of rabbit, basting and turning them to cover with the marinade. Cover and refrigerate, turning and basting several times a day for, if possible, 2 days—or 3 days. Before you are ready to cook the rabbit, scrape the marinade off each piece and back into the bowl. Pat pieces of rabbit fairly dry with paper towels, and arrange on a long sheet of wax paper.

Browning the rabbit. If using the salt pork, cut into *lardons* (sticks 1½ inches long and ¼ inch across) and blanch them (simmer 5 minutes in 1 quart of water, and drain). Sauté with a tablespoon of oil in the frying pan or skillet until lightly browned, then remove to a side dish. You can use the rendered fat to brown the rabbit, or film pan with about ⅛ inch of cooking oil. Sprinkle the flour over the rabbit pieces, roll them in it to cover completely, and shake off excess. Heat fat or oil to very hot but not smoking, and brown the rabbit all over, turning with tongs or a wooden fork and spoon. Remove to a side dish. Strain liquid out of marinade vegetables (but reserve liquid); brown the vegetables very lightly in the hot fat. Turn them into a sieve set over a bowl to drain out excess fat, and return to pan or to a casserole, along with the rabbit. Add the marinade liquid, the optional orange peel, and the optional browned pork.

✷ May be prepared in advance to this point; when cool, cover and refrigerate, where rabbit can remain until the next day.

Simmering the rabbit. Cover rabbit with the slices of lemon. Pour into the pan or casserole enough veal stock, or chicken stock or bouillon, barely to cover the meat. Bring to the simmer; taste for seasoning, adding a little salt if needed. Cover, and simmer either on top of the stove or in the oven—at 375 degrees until casserole is bubbling, then at around 325 degrees. Regulate heat so liquid is bubbling quietly; turn and baste occasionally, just to check on it. Rabbit should take 1 to 1½ hours of simmering, depending on its youth and tenderness; it is done when a sharp fork pierces the flesh easily, but do not let it overcook or flesh will fall from bone.

Finishing the dish. When rabbit is tender, carefully skim all accumulated fat off surface of sauce—remove meat to a side dish, if necessary. You should have almost 2 cups of sauce just thick enough to coat the rabbit lightly. If too thick, thin out with a little chicken stock. If too thin, remove from heat, and make a *beurre manié* (1 tablespoon of flour worked into a smooth paste with 1 tablespoon of butter); blend it into the sauce, and bring to the simmer, basting rabbit with sauce until it thickens—a minute or two. Very carefully correct seasoning, adding salt and pepper as you see fit. To serve, arrange rabbit on a platter and spread over it the lemon slices from the simmering, or rearrange attractively in a cooking dish. Decorate, if you wish, with sprigs of parsley or watercress.

☼ May be cooked a day or two in advance; when cold, cover and refrigerate. To serve, reheat slowly basting with sauce, then cover and keep at the barest simmer 5 minutes or so. You may have to thin out the sauce with a little bouillon; retaste for seasoning.

Chicken breasts

We are all so used to buying chicken breasts it's hard to remember what a luxury they used to be when Great-grandmother, and even Grandmother, had to buy the whole bird just to get those two tender morsels. Boned breasts are so fast to cook they are a boon when you are pressed for time, and if your market doesn't package them boned, you'll find them quick to do yourself. Boned breasts are called *suprêmes*—the supreme delicacy the chicken has to offer (unless, of course, you are a dark-meat-only type).

TO BONE A CHICKEN BREAST

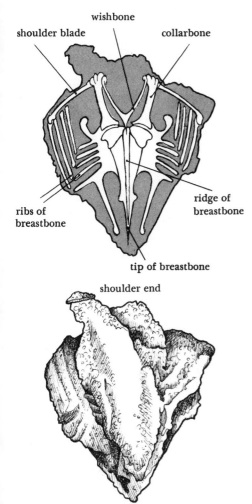

shoulder blade

wishbone

collarbone

ribs of
breastbone

ridge of
breastbone

tip of breastbone

shoulder end

vent end

When you buy chicken breasts you may find them whole, as illustrated, or split in half the length of the breastbone. Once in a while the wings will be on, and sometimes the breastbone will have been snapped out, leaving just the cartilage at the tip. The whole breast pictured here is the easiest to bone because you can see what you are doing. However, in whatever form you have bought them, boning is a simple matter following the general procedures outlined: remember the cardinal rule of cutting and scraping against the bones wherever you find them, and you will make out, ending up with the boned breast and its two flaps of meat, shown in the final drawing of this series.

WINGS. If the wings have been left on, locate the ball joint attaching wing to shoulder by wiggling the wing back and forth and feeling for the joint with your finger; cut through the joint from the shoulder side, and you will detach the wing from the breast.

SKIN. Rip the skin off the meat, grasping it in a towel to get a firm hold.

WISHBONE. Locate the wishbone buried in the flesh, feeling it with your finger. Cut flesh from around each fork, cut through attachments at end of each fork, then around top of wishbone, and twist it out. (If you have a half breast, don't bother.)

Now you are ready to go. Cut down one side of breastbone, from hump along ridge toward tip, scraping meat from bone as you go. Always aim knife against bone, not against flesh, and use a sideways scraping motion as you cut. At the same time, pull flesh away from bone with your fingers, so you can see what you are doing.

Continue cutting and scraping meat from bone down side of breastbone and to end of rib cage. Finally, cut meat loose from bone at shoulder end.

On the underside of the meat, where it was attached to the shoulder end, you will see a white tendon. If left in, this will shrink up and twist meat out of shape. To remove it, hold the end of it with a towel and, scraping against it with your knife, pull the tendon slowly out.

You now have the skinless and boneless breast half of a chicken, known as a *suprême*. It is ready for sautéing, for poaching in butter, or for stuffing. If you are not ready to cook your *suprêmes,* wrap and re-frigerate them, or wrap each individually and freeze them.

Plain chicken stock (*Made from bones, skin, and scraps*) . Chop up bones and skin, and place in a saucepan. Cover with cold water, add a little salt, bring to the simmer, skim off scum for a few minutes, then simmer partially covered for an hour. Strain, chill, degrease, and you have a delicious plain chicken stock to use in sauces and soups.

Bouillon vs. stock vs. broth. These three terms are really interchangeable, but I use stock when I am referring to a fresh brew rather than a canned one. Brown chicken stock simply means that the ingredients were sautéed before the simmering began, to give the stock an attractive brown color, as for the brown turkey stock on page 234.

Suprêmes de volaille en goujons, meunière

SLICED CHICKEN BREASTS SAUTÉED

The very quickest way to cook boned chicken breasts is to slice them into strips, season and dredge in flour, and sauté them. In 2 or 3 minutes they're done and delicious. Accompany them simply with a salad and French bread, or be more elaborate with a fresh green vegetable, or artichoke hearts and mushrooms, or stuffed tomatoes Provençale, sautéed potatoes, or a rice concoction. Serve a light red wine of the Bordeaux or Cabernet Sauvignon type, or a dry white like a Pouilly or a Pinot, or even a *rosé. Goujons,* by the way, are tiny fish, like whitebait, and when fillet of sole is cut into strips and fried for a garnish, it is called *en goujons;* thus it follows that anything cut into small slices can be described as *en goujons.*

For 4 people

4 to 6 suprêmes (boned and skinned breast halves from a frying chicken)
3 or 4 Tb clarified butter (butter melted, clear liquid skimmed off milky residue) ; or olive oil
Salt and pepper
About ½ cup flour on a large piece of wax paper
Parsley sprigs and lemon wedges

Equipment: A large frying pan or an electric skillet, and a pancake turner

Separate top from the bottom flap of each *suprême,* and cut the meat into slices about 2 inches long and ⅜ inch wide. Clarify your butter, if you are using it. Just before sautéing, spread sliced chicken meat on wax paper, and season both sides with salt and pepper. Toss in the flour to cover completely, then toss the pieces in a sieve to shake off excess flour. Film pan with ⅛ inch of butter or oil; set over highest heat until very hot but not brown or smoking. Add the chicken pieces, toss and turn for 15 seconds, and keep tossing and turning frequently for 2 to 3 minutes. Meat is done when it is springy rather than squashy to the touch of your finger. Turn out onto a hot platter and serve immediately, decorated with the parsley sprigs and accompanied by the wedges of lemon.

OTHER IDEAS

Persillade. Chop fine a handful of parsley with 2 or 3 cloves of peeled garlic. When the chicken pieces are done, toss in the pan with the parsley and garlic for several seconds, then serve as before.

Suprêmes de volaille Henri IV. This and the next suggestion are from Gringoire and Saulnier's chef's guide. Pile each serving of sautéed sliced *suprêmes* onto and around a hot artichoke bottom lined with an excellent and heavily buttered *demi-glace* sauce and accompany with *sauce béarnaise.* What a marvelous main course for a chic little luncheon, and all the elements are right here in this book.

Suprêmes de volaille Marie-Louise. Fill artichoke bottoms with a purée of mushrooms and onions, pile the sautéed strips of *suprême* around and on top, and accompany with a browned butter sauce. Or you could use the creamed mushroom *duxelles* described for our artichoke bottoms on page 387, and a *sauce béarnaise* rather than browned butter—but then you would have to invent another name, like Marie-France, who does not appear to have been used before with chicken breasts.

Suprêmes de volaille en goujons, à la crème et aux champignons. There they are again, mushrooms and cream, but this version is when you want a sauced dish to serve with rice or with rice and onion *soubise,* page 348. Cut about a half pound of trimmed and washed fresh mushrooms into slices, and sauté along with the chicken, adding 2 tablespoons of chopped shallots or scallions. When barely done, pour in a cup of chicken bouillon, boil rapidly to thicken, then add a half cup of heavy cream and boil again rapidly until lightly thickened, taking but a minute or two, so as not to overcook the chicken. Toss in some chopped parsley, and serve.

☼ This will take to reheating, if you want something you can do ahead.

Crumbed chicken breast strips. When you want a crustier texture, season and flour the strips of meat, then roll in beaten egg, shake off excess, and roll in fresh bread crumbs, following the Chicken Kiev system on page 214. (For added interest, use a mixture of half grated Parmesan and half crumbs.) Either sauté the strips in clarified butter or olive oil, or deep fry in fresh peanut oil. Serve them as they are, or as in any of the previous suggestions.

Marinated chicken breasts. For a different flavor, you might like to marinate the chicken breasts before cutting them into strips. Use the herb and lemon marinade on page 294, leaving the meat to steep 30 minutes at least; scrape it off and dry the meat in paper towels before slicing and proceeding with any of the previous suggestions.

P.S. After numerous adventures with sliced chicken breasts, my preferred method is to marinate them, then to coat them with a combination of fresh bread crumbs and grated Parmesan cheese, and sauté them in olive oil. A garnish of sautéed artichoke hearts with tomato *fondue* and herbs goes nicely, for instance.

Chicken shish kebabs

SKEWERED CHICKEN
BREASTS WITH
CHICKEN LIVERS,
MUSHROOMS, AND
SAUSAGE

As with all things cooked on skewers, every item in this attractive combo must take the same time on the spit; thus the mushrooms and sausages are precooked before they are assembled with the livers and chicken. Serve shish kebabs with rice or noodles, and peas, sautéed asparagus tips, or a mixed vegetable salad. A red Bordeaux or Cabernet Sauvignon would be a good choice in wine. (See notes and illustrations on the kind of skewers to use, page 293.)

For 4 people

12 to 16 fresh mushroom caps about 1¼
    inches in diameter
¼ cup water
1 Tb butter
¼ tsp salt
4 to 6 mild Italian sausages or plain
    pork breakfast sausages

> *4 suprêmes (skinned and boned breast halves*
> *from frying chicken)*
> *4 or more chicken livers*
> *Salt and pepper*
> *¼ cup melted butter*

Rapidly wash and drain mushroom caps and place in a small saucepan with the water, butter, and salt. Cover and simmer 3 to 4 minutes, barely to soften. Cut sausages into ½-inch lengths, and sauté 3 to 4 minutes, just to cook through and to brown very lightly—they are to retain enough fat to baste the chicken later. Bone and skin the chicken breasts, and cut into skewer-sized pieces. Cut the livers in half. Sprinkle chicken and livers with salt and pepper. String all on skewers, starting and ending with pieces of sausage; paint with melted butter.

☼ May be prepared ahead to this point.

Broil or barbecue 5 to 6 minutes on each side, basting once or twice with melted butter. Serve immediately.

Suprêmes de volaille sautées, andalouse

———◆———

WHOLE SUPRÊMES
SAUTÉED, WHITE
WINE SAUCE
WITH TOMATO
FONDUE AND
TARRAGON

For 6 to 8 people

Here is another chicken breast dish for those times you want to get the cooking done ahead, and rather than mushrooms and cream, which you could use, we have a fresh tomato fondue. Serve this on a bed of steamed rice, and accompany with a green vegetable or follow with a salad. Even one of the great white Burgundies could go with this dish, or a Pinot Chardonnay. (Note that there are a number of other ideas for whole *suprêmes* sautéed, in Volume I of *Mastering* as well as in *The French Chef Cookbook*.)

> *8 suprêmes (skinless and boneless chicken-*
> *breast halves)*
> *Salt and pepper*
> *½ cup flour in a plate*
> *1 Tb light olive oil or salad oil*
> *4 to 5 Tb butter*

> *Optional: ⅓ cup Cognac*
> *1 Tb minced shallots or scallions*
> *About 1½ cups fresh tomato pulp (5 or 6*
> *tomatoes peeled, seeded, juiced, and*
> *cut into ½-inch pieces)*
> *1 tsp tarragon*
> *½ cup each: dry white wine or Vermouth,*
> *chicken stock, and heavy cream*
> *2 to 3 Tb chopped fresh parsley*

Just before you are ready to sauté them, season the *suprêmes* lightly on each side with salt and pepper, dredge in flour, and shake off excess.

Choose a large heavy frying pan or an electric skillet; add 1 tablespoon of oil and 2 of butter, and heat until butter foam begins to subside but is not browning. Add as many *suprêmes* as will fit easily in one layer, and sauté for a minute or two on one side, until lightly browned; turn and sauté on the other side only until the meat is lightly springy when you press it with your finger, as opposed to its squashy raw state. Remove the sautéed *suprêmes,* and continue with the rest, adding more oil and butter to keep pan filmed. If you wish to flame them in Cognac, return *suprêmes* to pan, pour in the Cognac, and, when bubbling, avert your face and ignite the liquid with a lighted match; shake pan for several seconds, then pour contents into a side dish.

Add another tablespoon or so of butter, stir in the minced shallots or scallions and cook for a moment; then add the tomatoes and tarragon, and cook over high heat for 2 to 3 minutes more. Then pour in the wine, stock, and cream; boil hard for several minutes until liquids have reduced and sauce has thickened lightly. Taste, and correct seasoning. Return *suprêmes* to pan, and baste with the sauce.

✲ Set aside until you are ready to serve—a half hour wait at room temperature will not harm the *suprêmes.*

Cover and reheat for 2 to 3 minutes at below the simmer, to warm the meat through without overcooking it; arrange the *suprêmes* on a hot platter, swish the parsley into the sauce, and spoon it over the meat. Serve immediately.

Chicken Kiev

———

CHICKEN BREASTS
STUFFED WITH
HERB BUTTER AND
DEEP FRIED

When you want to stuff chicken breasts, you not only skin and bone them, you also enlarge and flatten them so that you can fold the meat around a stuffing; then you give them a bread crumb coating, *panure à l'anglaise*. Certainly one of the favorite fillings is the stick of flavorful herb butter that goes into Chicken Kiev; sometimes it even spurts out at you when you cut into the browned piece of chicken—drama!

Here, following the recipe for the Kiev filling, are illustrated directions for stuffing and crumbing the chicken breasts. Do this well ahead of cooking, to be sure the crumbs are set—allow at least an hour, or do them the night before. You may even freeze them and let thaw overnight before cooking.

Menu suggestion. Jellied consommé, eggs in aspic, or *Salade Niçoise* to begin with, and a purée of peas or green beans and watercress, or braised spinach, plus rice or fresh homemade mashed potatoes to serve with the chicken. For dessert, either a sherbet or ice cream, or a selection of fresh fruits and cheeses. Serve a red Bordeaux wine or Cabernet Sauvignon, or a fine white Burgundy.

Butter stuffing, beurre maître d'hôtel

For 8 suprêmes
(skinned and boned
breast halves from
frying chicken)

1½ sticks (6 ounces) soft butter
2 tsp lemon juice
2 Tb finely minced fresh parsley
½ tsp tarragon
1 Tb very finely minced shallots or
*   scallions, or chives*
½ to 1 tsp salt, or to taste
Several grinds of the peppermill

Beat the butter in a bowl (warm the bowl if butter is chilled, then beat over cold water if butter gets too soft). When creamy, beat in the rest of the ingredients. Form into a rectangle 4 inches long and 3 inches wide on wax paper, and chill. Cut into 8 sticks 3 inches long when firm, and keep chilled (set over cracked ice while you stuff each *suprême*).

Flattening and stuffing the suprêmes

Turn each *suprême* on its underside, from where you removed the tendon, and you will see that it consists of 2 flaps. Lift the underflap and fold it back, to the outside, thus enlarging the breast meat area.

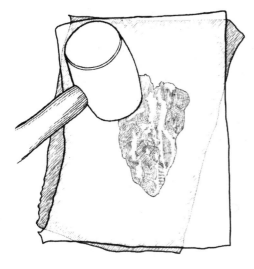

Lay the breast between 2 sheets of wax paper and beat it firmly but not too roughly to flatten it and also to enlarge it more. Use a pestle, a rolling pin, a plumber's hammer, or the side of a bottle, working up and down and back and forth until meat is about ¼ inch thick and almost double in width. Do not worry if the 2 flaps separate; you can press them together with your fingers.

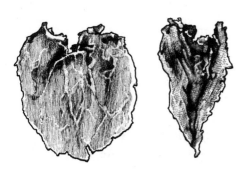

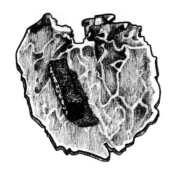

Place a prepared stick of flavored butter on the large side of the meat.

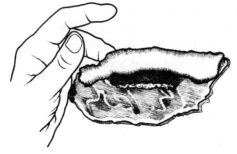

Fold the small side over the butter.
Then fold down the 2 ends, and
finally the remaining side. Press
meat together on all sides to
enclose stuffing completely.

Crumbing the suprêmes

Line up 3 plates, 1 with flour,
1 with beaten eggs (2 eggs, salt
and pepper, 2 tsp water, and
1 tsp oil), and the third plate
with 3 cups of fairly fine fresh
white bread crumbs. Season the
suprêmes lightly with salt and
pepper. One by one, roll first
in the flour (A).

Then roll in the beaten egg,
being sure the egg coats it
completely so the crumbs
will adhere (B).

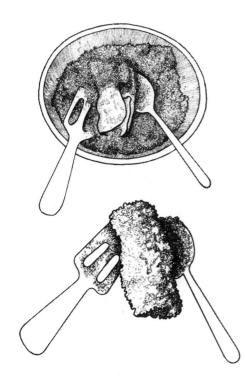

Finally lay the *suprême* in the plate of crumbs, toss them over the top and sides, and pat them in firmly all over (C). The crumbs must cover the entire surface.

Place on a rack over a tray, and refrigerate an hour at least to set the crumbs. (Or freeze, but thaw before cooking.)

Deep fry in fresh new peanut oil at 375°, 4 at a time, for 5 minutes. Drain on a plate covered with paper towels, and place in a 200° oven while continuing with the rest. You may keep them in the oven up to 30 minutes before serving, but a longer wait in the oven may cause the butter filling to leak out.

Butter spurting note. When the chicken is deep fried and waits for a certain length of time, I have found, the butter is partially absorbed into the meat, giving it a lovely flavor, but there's no dramatic spurt as you cut into the Kiev. Evidently you can't have it both ways.

OTHER STUFFINGS FOR SUPRÊMES

Suprêmes de volaille farcies au foie gras. Use only ¾ stick of butter rather than the 1½ called for in the Kiev stuffing, and replace with 3 ounces of *foie gras, mousse de foie,* or excellent liver paste, and proceed as for the Chicken Kiev.

Suprêmes de volaille Cordon Bleu. Make a pile ½ inch thick of very thin layers of boiled ham and sliced Swiss or Mozzarella cheese. Press firmly together, and cut into sticks 3 inches long and ½ inch wide, paint sides and top with a thin coating of strong Dijon-type prepared mustard, and proceed as for the Chicken Kiev.

Suprêmes de
volaille
farcies,
duxelles

MUSHROOM
STUFFING

½ cup finely minced onion
3 Tb butter
1 cup (lightly pressed) finely diced fresh
    mushrooms (4 ounces whole) squeezed
    dry in a towel
2 Tb flour
3 to 4 Tb heavy cream
½ tsp dried tarragon
2 to 3 Tb finely minced prosciutto or boiled ham
3 Tb Port or Madeira wine
Salt, pepper, and nutmeg
6 to 8 Tb soft butter

Cook the minced onion and butter in a small saucepan until onion is tender and translucent, then stir in the mushrooms and cook over moderately high heat for several minutes until pieces begin to separate. Stir in the flour and cook 2 minutes, then blend in the cream, tarragon, ham, and wine. Simmer 2 minutes or so, until thickened. Season carefully to taste, remove from heat, and beat in the butter by spoonfuls. Refrigerate, or stir over cracked ice, until cold and very thick. Divide into 8 portions, form into sticks 3 inches long and ½ inch across, and proceed as for Chicken Kiev.

Roast chicken

From that marvelous aroma of roasting that fills the air to the first plunge of the knife down through its brown skin, the juices pearling at the break in the second joint as the carving begins, and finally that first mouthful, roast chicken has always been one of life's greatest pleasures. With twice the flavor of broilers and fryers, large roasters are almost twice as expensive, since they need a good 6 months of cosseting and feeding before they reach the desirable roasting weight of 5 to 6 pounds. Roasters of this size and quality are not everyday birds; you may have to order yours in advance. While you can certainly oven roast in the usual way, as described at the end of the recipe, you will find chicken particularly delectable done on a revolving spit either in the oven or on a portable rotisserie; the fact of its turning constantly seems to make the meat juicier and tenderer, and the wrapping of pork fat means you need give it no basting except at the very end.

Accompany roast chicken with roast, mashed, sautéed, or scalloped potatoes or creamed onions, a fresh green vegetable such as peas, broccoli, or asparagus tips, and a fine red Bordeaux wine. Attractive alternatives would be either the baked halved Eggplant Provençale on page 401, or the zucchini *pipérade* on page 427, along with a fresh loaf of your own French bread, and either a white Côtes du Rhône or a *rosé* wine.

PREPARING THE CHICKEN

Remove the package of giblets (neck, heart, liver) from inside the chicken's cavity, and pull out all loose fat from around the vent opening (usually adhering to flesh just inside opening). You may wish to roast the liver inside the chicken; reserve the rest of the giblets for the stock pot. Render the fat, which you can use for basting the chicken (directions are on page 230). Carefully look over the entire chicken, tweezing out any feather follicles lodged in the skin and inspecting back of tail piece to be sure fat glands have been completely removed—these are yellow-orange lozenge-shaped deposits lodged in the flesh at either side of the bone. If the neck protrudes beyond the point where wings join shoulders, cut it off, and add to giblets. Cut off the little nubbins attached to the outside of the wing elbows. Finally, run warm water inside and outside the chicken, dry thoroughly inside and out with paper towels, and chicken is ready for trussing.

STUFFING. More often than not, French chickens have only a flavoring rather than a stuffing inside their cavities. With no stuffing to bother about, then, you can get the chicken ready for the oven well in advance, and not only is the cooking quicker, but also the breast meat is juicier, since it isn't overcooked. If you want to stuff your chicken, however, remember to add 20 to 30 minutes more to your over-all roasting estimates.

TRUSSING. Trussing the legs and wings to its body gives the chicken an attractive shape after roasting and, in addition, prevents these appendages from falling off during cooking. Use any system that appeals to you, such as metal skewers and string, or fancy looping about the bird with string alone, or use the French needle and string system described here. You will need white kitchen string (butchers use corned-beef twine) and a regular trussing needle, a sailmaker's needle, a mattress needle, or a knitting needle with a hole bored in one end.

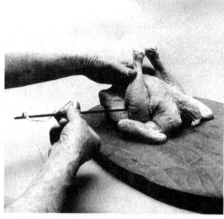

Make the first trussing tie by pushing your needle through the second joints at the hip, going in through the body on one side and out the other.

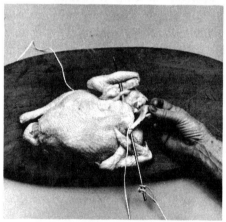

Then bring needle around this side to secure one wing through its elbow to the backbone, catching neck skin at the same time. With a second plunge, if need be, go into the backbone again and come out the elbow of the opposite wing.

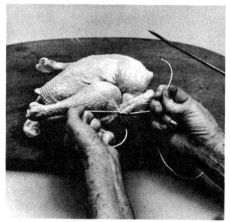

You are now on the side of the chicken you went in at the beginning; tie tightly and both wings and knee joints are secured to the body.

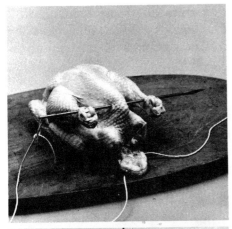

For the second tie, go under the tail piece, up and through top of one drumstick; catch tip of breastbone, then go through top of other drumstick, coming out the same side you went in.

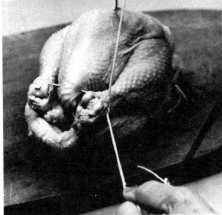

Tie, and you are also closing the vent.

Here is your neatly trussed chicken ready for roasting, spit roasting, poaching, or stewing.

Massage a tablespoon of soft butter or rendered chicken fat into the skin of the chicken all over. To provide automatic basting, useful for oven roasting and essential for spit roasting, use strips of fresh pork fat or of blanched bacon (5 or 6 strips of thick-sliced bacon simmered 10 minutes in 2 quarts of water). Lay them over the breast and thighs, and tie in place with loops of white string. The chicken is now ready to roast.

Poularde à la broche

SPIT-ROASTED
CHICKEN

For a 5½- to 6½-pound roaster, serving 6 to 8 people

Estimated roasting time: 1¾ to 2 hours plus 20 minutes rest before carving (see page 225 for the timing of other sizes)

The roasting chicken, prepared as
described above
For inside the chicken: 1 Tb soft butter, ½ tsp
salt, ½ tsp tarragon, 1 Tb finely minced
shallots or scallions, several parsley sprigs,
and, if you wish, the chicken's liver
White kitchen string
Salt

Spitting the chicken. Smear butter inside cavity, sprinkle in the salt, tarragon, and shallots or scallions, add the parsley, and tuck in the optional liver. Truss the chicken, rub with butter, and tie on the blanched bacon, as described. For whatever type of rotisserie you have, measure where chicken should fit on length of spit, then tightly fasten the prong nearest the spit handle. Push point of spit through chicken starting at the neck end, and do your best to balance chicken evenly—if it is top- or bottom-heavy, the spit will revolve with difficulty. Push neck end of chicken well into prong, then insert second prong onto spit and push firmly into bones at other end of chicken; screw tightly in place. As an extra precaution, wind a double loop of string around length of chicken at both sides of prong; tie securely.

Here is a chicken ready for the rotisserie. It is trussed, smeared with butter, barded with strips of fat, and tied securely onto the spit with white string.

✻ May be prepared in advance and refrigerated; for accurate timing, remove an hour or so before roasting.

Roasting the chicken. Two and a half hours before you expect to serve, set the chicken to roast. For most oven rotisseries, heat should be moderate and oven door is left ajar; you need a pan under the chicken to catch juices. Most closed portable rotisseries follow the same pattern, with moderate heat and a drip pan. For open rotisseries where heat is underneath, set chicken so that it rotates as close as possible to heat element without touching it. In order to brown the breast, remove chicken about 15 minutes before end of estimated roasting time, take off the strips of bacon (which you may set aside, to serve with the chicken) . Sprinkle salt over chicken, and return to finish cooking; baste several times with fat drippings or butter.

How to tell when chicken is done. When drumsticks are tender if pressed, when they move easily in their sockets, and when the last juices to drain from vent are clear yellow with no trace of rosy color, chicken is done. Shut off heat element, and let chicken turn on rotisserie for 15 to 20 minutes before carving, allowing juices to retreat back into flesh. Chicken will stay warm for half an hour at least; if wait is longer, turn heat on low for several minutes every 10 or 15 minutes.

Presentation, carving, and serving. When ready to serve, remove chicken from spit to a hot platter; cut and discard trussing strings, and decorate platter with watercress or parsley. Present the chicken to your guests, so they may admire its glory. (If you are new to carving, you may then prefer the solitude of the kitchen; remove chicken to a carving board.) Carve one side at a time as follows.

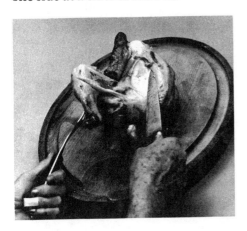

Place the chicken on its back, vent-end facing you. Slit skin of left side of lower breast to expose knee of drumstick. Secure outside of knee with your fork, and bend it at right angles down to the cutting surface, thus breaking open the second joint at the small of the back.

Cut through joint to detach whole leg assembly, then cut through knee joint to separate drumstick from second joint (thigh). If you wish, cut a fat lengthwise strip of meat off second joint to give you an extra serving of dark meat.

Now turn chicken so wings face you and, on same side from which you removed the leg, you are to remove the wing along with a strip of breast meat—to make an attractive serving: To do so, cut a strip from lower third of breast, starting at small of back and reaching up to shoulder joint; cut through joint to release the wing and strip of breast meat.

Slice the breast meat off this side of the chicken, to give you two or three attractive pieces.

From this side of the chicken you have carved six pieces, reading up from lower right: 2 slices of breast, the wing with breast strip attached, the drumstick, and the second joint. Carve the other side in the same manner.

Poularde rôtie au four

OVEN-ROASTED
CHICKEN

Timing: 1¾ to 2
hours for a 6-pound
bird, plus 20 minutes
rest (see following table
for the timing of
other sizes)

Prepare and truss the chicken as described on page 219; rub all over with soft butter, and tie the blanched bacon strips in place—if you don't use them, you will have to baste at least every 10 minutes to make up for it. Choose a shallow roasting pan or oval gratin dish that will just hold the chicken comfortably.

Two and a half hours before serving, place chicken breast up in middle level of a preheated 425-degree oven. In 5 minutes turn chicken on its side, and baste rapidly with a tablespoon of melted butter; turn on the other side in 5 minutes, and baste again. At the 15-minute mark, turn oven down to 350°, and add a chopped onion and carrot to the roasting pan. Baste the chicken every 20 minutes or so, using fat accumulated in pan. After 30 minutes, turn the chicken on its other side. And for the last 15 minutes, turn the chicken breast up. Remove bacon strips. Baste again, and salt the chicken lightly. Chicken is done when drumsticks are tender and move easily in their sockets, and when last juices drained from vent are clear yellow with no trace of rosy color.

Set chicken on a hot platter or on a carving board, and let rest 15 to 20 minutes before carving. Meanwhile, spoon excess fat out of roasting pan, pour in a cup or so of chicken stock, and boil rapidly over high heat, mashing the chopped carrot and onion into the liquid and scraping up all coagulated roasting juices. Strain into a warm bowl, and you will have just enough of these deglazing juices to moisten each serving. (Carving notes are in preceding recipe.)

✿ After making deglazing juices, you can return chicken to roasting pan, and set in turned-off oven, door ajar; or keep in a 120-degree warming oven. But plan to serve it within three quarters of an hour to enjoy the full, fine juiciness of a freshly roasted chicken.

HOW TO TIME THE ROAST

That old rule of 20 minutes a pound for chicken is not accurate, since a large bird takes proportionally less time to roast than a small one. Here's the rule I've used with success.

45 minutes plus 7 minutes per pound

That means an initial 45 minutes for any size, then multiply the pounds the chicken weighs by 7, and you have the approximate roasting time. However, I think it safe to add on the following appendages:

—A buffer of 10 to 30 minutes, depending on the size of the bird
—A 10- to 20-minute rest after roasting, to let the meat juices retreat back into the meat before carving
—10 to 30 minutes more if the chicken has a stuffing, depending on size
—A few minutes more, in all, if the chicken came from the refrigerator, although the buffer should take care of this.

Here are some examples of unstuffed chickens:

A 1-lb. squab chicken: 45 minutes plus 7 minutes   52 to 60 minutes
                        (1 lb. × 7 minutes = 7)
                        Plus resting period   10 minutes
                        Total   _____
                                                           70 minutes

A 3½-lb. fryer: 45 minutes plus 24.5 minutes   70 to 85 minutes
                        (3.5 lbs. × 7 minutes = 24.5)
                        Plus resting period   10 minutes
                        Total   _____
                                                           95 minutes

A 7-lb. capon: 45 minutes plus 49 minutes   94 to 120 minutes
                        (7 lbs. × 7 minutes = 49)
                        Plus resting period   20 minutes
                        Total (2½ to 2¾ hrs)   _____
                                                           140 minutes

Keep a record of your own experiences. Ovens and cooking techniques differ, and you want to know how things work for you.

Stewed chickens and boiled fowls

For boiled dinners, chicken salad, and sandwiches

Boiled fowl, anyone? Way back in the springtime of the early 1950's we were driving north of London in the countryside. Around dinner time we stopped at a charming Tudor inn by a stream and a rude bridge. Its rear garden, filled with roses, bordered the water, and the dining room beside it was presided over by a resplendent major-domo with striped waistcoat and pendulous gold watch. After a glass of sherry in the wood-paneled bar, we entered his domain and he ceremoniously ushered us to a table by the windows. Would we have roast joint on the dinner menu, or boiled fowl? Paul took the one, and I the other. After a suitable wait following a nameless soup, his slice of joint arrived, flanked by generous helpings of well-boiled cabbage, carrots, and potatoes. My fowl, on a very large, very white plate, was a leg and thigh combination, rather bony, and partially covered with a stark pale blanket of what turned out to be the famous English white sauce, through which poked a good half dozen long brown chicken hairs. We were both delighted with my fowl; it somehow represented what we had always heard about English cooking but had never quite believed before. It looked so perfectly what it was, a thoroughly boiled, quite elderly hen, and a sauce that was literally only flour and water with barely a pinch of salt to flavor it. (I should really apologize for mentioning this splendid exception to the very good fare we have almost always been offered in England, and I hasten to say that among the very best private cooks I know, a goodly proportion are English.) Remembering that fowl as I write this, I have just looked up the inn, Bridge House, in my current *Good Food Guide*. Not listed. And I have looked up the village, Catterick-on-Swale, in the index of my old *Bartholomew's Road Atlas*. Not listed. But if you get your eye right down into the map in the North Riding of Yorkshire, there is Catterick. I'd rather like to go back, and I'd order that very same meal all over again, for old times' sake if not for gastronomic delight.

But a stewing chicken is perfectly delicious when you have got yourself a chicken meant for stewing and for eating, and when you follow the French method described here.

STEWING CHICKEN TALK
AND COOKING PREPARATIONS

A large preamble to a short recipe, since there is nothing much to stewing a chicken. A fine young stewing hen, properly cooked, produces not only good eating meat with full flavor, but a delicious broth as well. Pick a chicken that looks plump and handsome—a scrawny tough old hen is useful only for soup stock, and you want a chicken you can eat. It will be labeled "stewing fowl" or "stewing hen," and will usually weigh 4 to 5 pounds. You can stew it whole, as in the *Potée Normande* recipe in Volume I of *Mastering*, or you can add a whole trussed stewing chicken to the *Pot-au-feu* here, on page 273, and come up with a *Poule-au-pot*. But it is easier to stew when cut up; it cooks more quickly and evenly, takes less of a pot, and is easier to handle in every way. Have it cut up as follows—or, better, do it yourself, since it is good practice to know how a chicken is put together and comes apart.

TO DISJOINT A CHICKEN, OR ANY OTHER BIRD

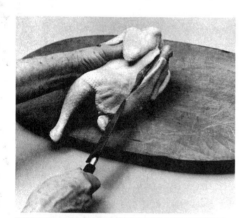

With a sharp knife, slit the chicken down the back bone, from neck to tail, to free skin from carcass.

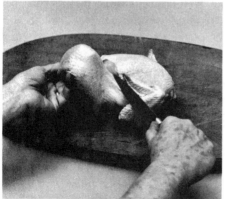

Slit the skin around the drumstick knee with a sharp knife, going from small of back around to vent, thus exposing drumstick-thigh assembly.

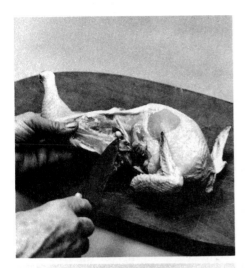

Bend knee back at right angles to body, to break open the thigh joint at the small of the back. Then cut all around joint to remove oysters (nuggets) of meat lodged in small of back and from joint to tail; these should remain attached to thigh. (You may muff this at first, and no matter: you'll get them next time.) Remove the thigh-drumstick assembly, and cut through joint at knee, to separate drumstick from second joint.

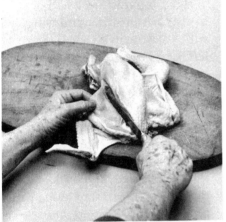

On same side of chicken from which you remove the leg, you are now to remove the wing with a piece of breast meat attached, to make a good serving. To do so, cut a strip from lower third of breast starting at small of back and reaching up to shoulder joint. Cut through shoulder joint, and scrape meat from carcass at lower portion of breast.

You now have an attractive serving from the wing. Carve the leg and wing portions off the other side in the same way, and you have only the breast remaining on the carcass.

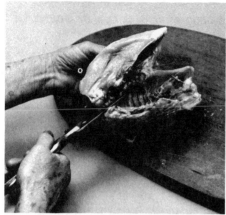

Using poultry shears, cut through rib cage and end of shoulder at each side, to free whole breast from carcass. Chop breast in two, crosswise.

You now have 8 pieces of chicken to serve, reading from left to right, top row: neck half of breast, 2 drumsticks, and wing with breast-strip attached. From left to right, bottom, are the tip half of the breast, the 2 second joints (which may be halved after cooking) , and the second wing-breast piece. Thus the chicken will serve 5 to 6 people, depending on your menu, and you also have the neck, giblets, and back of carcass which will stew along with the chicken.

Chicken fat, to render. Pull off all excess fat, chop it up, and simmer with a little water in a covered saucepan for 10 minutes or so, until fat has rendered and residue has lightly browned. Strain the clear yellow liquid into a jar, pressing fat out of residue. Use rendered chicken fat for basting, for sauce making, and in general cooking to replace butter.

Poule au gros sel

PLAIN STEWED CHICKEN (BOILED FOWL!)

Plain boiled chicken is fine to serve when you are on a diet, or when the fleshpots have become too rich for your blood. *Gros sel* means just a sprinkling of coarse salt and a spoonful or two of the cooking liquid to go with it. Garnish with wedges of steamed cabbage, boiled carrots and onions, and boiled potatoes, all nicely sprinkled with fresh parsley; you might like to follow the *Pot-au-feu* system on page 275 for those vegetables. A simple red wine like a young Beaujolais, Chianti, or Gamay would go nicely, or a *rosé*. When the chicken is to be served cold, let it cool in its liquid so that the flesh will be juicy. Use it for salads or sandwiches.

For 4 to 6 people, served hot as a main course	*A fine-looking, well-formed stewing chicken, 4½ to 5 lbs., with its giblets*
	1 cup each: sliced carrots, onions, celery
Cooking time: 2 to 3 hours	*Cold water*
	Salt
	A medium herb bouquet (4 to 5 parsley sprigs, 1 imported bay leaf, 1 teaspoon thyme, all tied together in washed cheesecloth)

Cut up the chicken as described in the preceding recipe. Wash all pieces, bones, and scraps briefly in warm running water. Chop the carcass (backbone and neck) into 2-inch pieces. Choose a heavy saucepan or flameproof casserole just large enough to hold all the chicken pieces easily. In the bottom of it place the carcass and scraps, heart, gizzard, and drumsticks of chicken. Strew over them half the sliced vegetables. Arrange the rest of the pieces on top and strew over them the remaining vegetables. (Reserve liver for another purpose, or add it the last 15 minutes of cooking.) Measure in enough water to cover ingredients by 3 inches, and add 1 teaspoon salt per quart of water.

Bring to the simmer, skim off scum for several minutes, and add the herb bouquet. Cover partially, and simmer 2 to 3 hours (depending on age of chicken), until meat is tender when pierced with a small sharp knife.

To serve hot. Leave chicken in pot until you are ready to serve, or reheat. Arrange on platter with whatever vegetables you have chosen, and decorate with parsley or watercress. Skim fat off surface, taste liquid for seasoning, ladle a little over chicken and vegetables, and pass a bowl of it with the chicken. Have coarse salt and a pepper grinder on the table and, if you wish, a dish of pickles, such as the sour French *cornichons*.

To serve cold. Let chicken cool an hour in the stock; the meat will be juicier. Remove chicken, strip off skin, and cut and pull flesh from bone, then cut meat into sizes you need for salad or sandwiches.

Chicken stock. Return skin and bones to pot and simmer another hour; strain, chill, and degrease. This will give you a delicious chicken stock for soups, sauces, aspics, and another meal.

OTHER IDEAS FOR SERVING
STEWED CHICKEN

Poule au riz (*Stewed chicken and rice*). About 25 minutes before you think the chicken will be tender, in the preceding recipe, skim fat off surface of cooking liquid, remove herb bouquet, carcass bones, neck, and so forth, and correct seasoning. Stir in 1¼ cups plain raw long-grain Carolina rice (to give you 3¾ cups cooked rice). Bring to the simmer, cover, and continue simmering for 20 minutes or until rice is just tender. If liquid is absorbed before rice is done, add a little boiling water. Serve the chicken from the pot, if you wish, or transfer to a serving casserole, and ladle chicken and rice into deep dinner plates. (This is the simplest way of doing the dish, giving you more or less liquid, and vegetables mixed in with rice. To be more formal, drain the chicken and return to a casserole; degrease the liquid and measure exactly twice the amount of liquid you have of rice, then proceed.)

Poule à l'ivoire (*Stewed chicken with rice and a creamy ivory-colored sauce*). Stew the chicken as in the main recipe, peel off the skin, and keep the chicken warm; cook the rice separately. Make 3 cups of cream sauce with some of the cooking liquid (a *roux* of 4 to 5 Tb butter and 6 Tb flour cooked together, moistened with 2½ cups degreased cooking stock, then ½ cup heavy cream, seasonings, drops of lemon juice—*Sauce Velouté*, page 617). Mound the rice in the middle of a serving platter, and arrange the chicken around it, spooning a little sauce over each piece. Decorate with parsley or whatever vegetables you are serving—like fresh peas or broccoli—and pass the rest of the sauce in a bowl.

------◆------

To roast a turkey

Turkeys are so easy to roast, and so easy to keep warm for an hour or more if you treat them right, that they are the big answer at any time of the year to that problem of what to serve a large crowd of people. Turkeys are reasonably priced, too, when you buy them frozen and out of season. I admit I used to despise and loathe frozen turkeys, but that was some years ago, when we were stationed in Germany in a military housing project. During every holiday season the local PX market was piled with surplus frozen turkeys garnered from heaven knows where, and soon the hallways of every building on the project were steeped in the odor of roasting rancid turkey fat. It took me a while to stomach any turkey at all after that trauma, and I was delighted to find when we did our television show—and had 5 frozen turkeys to roast—that they were delicious. But I do think you must buy carefully from a market that takes turkey seriously, and if the price is ridiculously low you may be getting last year's frozen bird reduced for clearance. In that case, ask the manager of the meat department or of the market itself, and find out what's going on in the turkey bin.

How much to buy? Count on ½ pound of whole turkey per serving, and that means about 1 pound per person if you want second helpings. Thus a 16-pound turkey will feed 16 to 20. But if you want leftovers, buy a 20-pounder, which is a good size for taste and tenderness.

How long does it take a frozen turkey to defrost? A 20-pound bird, I have found, takes 3 to 4 days to defrost in the refrigerator, or about 12 hours in a sinkful of water. In either case, leave the turkey in its original plastic wrapper until it seems thawed. Then unwrap as soon as possible, and pull out the package of giblets from inside the turkey. Often these are still frozen, indicating, too, that the inside of the turkey is also still frozen. Finish thawing either at room temperature or, if you're not in a hurry, in the refrigerator. Keep thawed turkey under refrigeration, since it spoils more rapidly than fresh turkey, and plan to roast it within a day or at most two days of thawing.

TO STUFF OR NOT TO STUFF,
AND TURKEY ACCOMPANIMENTS

An unstuffed turkey is easy to prepare for roasting, and with no stuffing spoilage to worry about, you can get the turkey ready for the oven the day before roasting. The bird will cook faster, the breast will be juicier because it is less likely to overcook, and a handful of aromatic vegetables trussed inside the cavity will flavor the meat very nicely indeed. So I'm against stuffing in the bird, but I do like stuffing made separately and baked for an hour in a covered casserole in a pan of water, along with the turkey if there's room. Given several bastings with turkey roasting juices as it cooks, the stuffing then tastes even better, I think, than if it is sewn up inside the turkey. (A delicious and unusual stuffing with olives and mushrooms is at the end of the roasting recipe, on page 238.)

If you have a stuffing, you will not need any starchy vegetables. If you don't, you could serve one of the potato dishes from Volumes I or II of *Mastering,* like the garlic mashed potatoes, potatoes Anna, the gratin with endives, or try the potatoes sautéed with onions and peppers *à la catalane* here on page 416, or the rice and onion *Soubise* with cream and cheese on page 348. Brussels sprouts, broccoli flowerets, or buttered fresh peas are attractive for greenery, and baked whole small tomatoes will add color unless you are having the traditional cranberries. An excellent choice in wines would be either a red Bordeaux Saint-Émilion or a Cabernet Sauvignon.

Brown turkey stock and turkey gravy

For about 3 cups

You can make your turkey gravy base way ahead of time, which will save you that much fussing at the last minute. This is a strong white-wine turkey stock thickened at the end with cornstarch. When the turkey is done and the roaster degreased, blend the gravy base into the roasting juices.

The turkey giblets (neck, heart, gizzard—
　　save the liver and either add to your stuffing
　　or keep it for another purpose)
4 Tb cooking oil
2 cups each chopped onions and carrots (remove
　　half after sautéing, and save for flavoring
　　turkey cavity later)
1 cup dry white wine or ⅔ cup
　　dry white French Vermouth
2 cups chicken stock or canned broth
Water as needed
Salt
1 imported bay leaf
½ tsp thyme or sage
3 Tb cornstarch blended with ¼ cup
　　Port wine or cold chicken broth

Chop neck into 2-inch pieces, quarter gizzard, and halve the heart. Dry in paper towels. Heat oil in a heavy 2½- to 3-quart saucepan, stir in the giblets, and brown them rapidly on all sides, regulating heat so oil is not burning. Remove giblets and stir the vegetables into the pan; cover and cook slowly 5 to 8 minutes until tender. Then uncover, raise heat, and brown lightly for several minutes. Remove half the vegetables and reserve for flavoring turkey cavity later. Return giblets to pan, add the wine, stock, and enough water to cover ingredients by an inch. Salt lightly, add herbs, and simmer partially covered for 2½ to 3 hours; strain, degrease, and return stock to pan. You should have about 3 cups. Beat in the cornstarch mixture, simmer 2 to 3 minutes, and correct seasoning. Liquid will be lightly thickened. When cool, cover and refrigerate until turkey is done. Directions for using the gravy base are in the last paragraph of the following roasting recipe.

TURKEY TIMING

It takes a 25-pound roast turkey 2½ hours to cool down from oven temperature to 120 degrees on a meat thermometer; I timed one, just to see. Thus you are much better off estimating on the longer rather than the shorter side of any timetable, since it is awful if the turkey isn't done on time, and it's not only embarrassing but also possibly dangerous to serve an underdone turkey. Don't be taken in by theories that you can partially cook a turkey in the evening, finish it off in the morning, or that it will cook properly in a 225° oven all night and all morning, and be done by lunchtime. These two suggestions are definitely dangerous, since both partial precooking and very low temperature cooking can allow bacteria to develop in the bird—because the heat does not reach the interior for hours—and then goodbye happy holidays.

Turkey timetables vary enormously, and every one I have seen gives different times. I suppose a good reason for variants is that turkeys do come in different shapes, from average mesomorph to the extreme pectoral endomorphy of some modern birds; a chunky, chesty turkey with its thicker meat layer will take longer to cook than a more elongated type. I have used the following timings with success, and I do think every cook should keep notes on his or her own experience. That is the way to develop not only confidence but also your own special way of doing things.

Roasting timetable: *for unstuffed moderately chilled turkeys*

Pounds	Hours roasting at 325°	Buffer	Rest before carving	Estimated safe total
6 to 8 lbs.	2¾–3½ hrs.	20 min.	20 min.	4¼ hrs.
8 to 12 lbs.	3¼–4 hrs.	20 min.	20 min.	4½–4¾ hrs.
12 to 16 lbs.	3½–4½ hrs.	30 min.	30 min.	5½ hrs.
16 to 20 lbs.	4–6 hrs.	30 min.	30 min.	5½–7 hrs.
20 to 26 lbs.	5½–7½ hrs.	30 min.	30 min.	7–8½ hrs.

TURKEY IS DONE WHEN: Meat thermometer in thickest portion of thigh, next to body, reads 180 to 185 degrees; the legs can be wiggled in their sockets; the thickest portion of the drumsticks feels tender when pressed. There will be a cup or more brown turkey juices in the pan; if there is no juice, but only fat, the turkey is definitely not done.

STUFFING. Allow ½ to ¾ cup—or less if you wish—of stuffing per pound of turkey, but it is impossible to be accurate in estimates because a heavy, chesty bird sometimes has less room inside. The cavity does not need to be filled completely, and certainly must not be packed tight, since stuffing tends to swell during cooking. Add 20 to 30 minutes additional roasting time to the preceding estimates for turkeys up to 12 pounds. Over that weight, the stuffing does not affect the over-all timing unless it is a very compact sausage type of mixture.

Dinde rôtie au four

ROAST TURKEY

Timing: 4½ to 6 hours for roasting, ½ hour rest before carving, ½ hour safety buffer—5½ to 7 hours (see preceding timetable for other sizes)

An 18- to 22-pound turkey, thawed if bought frozen, and ready to roast
Salt
The 1 cup each cooked carrots and onions reserved from turkey stock preliminaries (page 234)
½ tsp each thyme and sage
A handful each of celery tops and parsley sprigs
2 Tb soft butter
A pan of cooking oil or melted lard, for basting
An additional 2 cups each of chopped carrots and onions

Equipment: Skewers, white string, or a trussing needle and string; a roasting pan with rack; a large double thickness of washed cheesecloth to cover turkey; a basting brush, spoon, or bulb; a meat thermometer is useful

Preheat oven to 325 degrees. Remove any loose fat from inside cavity. Cut knobs off wing elbows; add knobs to turkey stock. Remove any feather follicles or pinfeathers in skin. If neck protrudes beyond shoulders, cut it off and add to stock. Dry turkey inside and out with paper towels. Sprinkle 2 tsp salt in cavity; salt the cooked vegetables lightly, blend in the herbs, and strew inside turkey with the celery and parsley. Skewer, tie, or truss turkey to close neck and vent, and to hold legs and wings in place. Rub skin all over with soft butter. Place turkey breast up on rack in roasting pan. Dip cheesecloth in oil or lard and drape over turkey. (May be prepared for roasting a day in advance because there is no stuffing to spoil inside the bird. Cover and refrigerate.)

Roast in preheated 325-degree oven, lifting cheesecloth and basting the turkey every 30 minutes or so, first with oil or fat in pan, then with the accumulated drippings in pan. About 1½ hours before end of estimated roasting time, strew the remaining carrots and onions in the pan, to flavor roasting juices.

Indications that turkey is nearly done. (I am purposely repeating these directions so you won't have to turn back to the timetable.) Juices are exuding from the turkey into the pan; you will have a cup or more when turkey is done. Thickest part of drumstick feels tender when pressed, and drumstick moves fairly easily in its socket. Lower part of thigh, when pricked deeply with a fork, exudes clear yellow juices. (Meat thermometer reading in thigh should be 180 to 185 degrees.) Do not let turkey overcook or meat will dry out.

When turkey is done. Remove to a platter, and discard skewers or strings. Turkey should sit half an hour before carving, for juices to retreat back into meat tissues. If you will not be ready to serve for some time, turn off oven and open door to cool it. In 20 to 30 minutes, reset thermostat to 140 degrees, and return turkey to oven, where it may sit for an hour or more. (Or return turkey to oven, and heat it to 250 degrees every half hour, then turn it off.)

Finishing the sauce or gravy. Spoon excess fat out of roasting pan, pour in the thickened turkey stock, and stir over moderately high heat for several minutes, scraping bottom of pan with a wooden spoon to gather coagulated juices into sauce. Strain into a saucepan, pressing juices out of vegetables. Degrease again, and carefully correct seasoning. Reheat just before serving, and pour into a warm sauce bowl.

Farce à la tapénade

MUSHROOM AND
OLIVE STUFFING
FROM PROVENCE

I used this mixture for my last turkey, while writing
this chapter, and we loved it. With sausage, onion,
herbs, and toasted croutons to lighten the mixture,
and the subtle taste of anchovies and capers—
tapéno is Provençal for caper—the mushrooms and
olives are in good company, as is the turkey. Use
this either as a regular stuffing, or bake it separately
in a covered casserole set in a pan of boiling water,
basting occasionally with turkey roasting juices.

For about 2 quarts,
enough for a 16- to
20-pound turkey

1 lb. (2 cups) fresh sausage meat
(your own, preferably, page 363)
1 cup minced onions
The turkey liver, minced
1 lb. fresh mushrooms, trimmed, washed,
and diced
1 cup pitted black olives, diced
2 anchovies (flat strips of anchovy
packed in oil), diced
2 Tb capers, squeezed dry, and minced
2 "large" eggs, lightly beaten
1 small clove garlic, puréed through a press
½ tsp thyme
½ imported bay leaf, pulverized
4 cups croutons (homemade-type white bread
cut in ½-inch dice and dried out in oven)
Salt and pepper to taste

Break up sausage meat and sauté slowly in a frying pan until lightly
browned; remove to a big mixing bowl, and pour sausage fat into another bowl. Return 2 tablespoons fat to pan, and sauté the onions 6 to 8
minutes, until tender and very lightly browned; add minced liver and
sauté with onion for a minute or two, just to stiffen. Scrape with onions
into mixing bowl. A handful at a time, twist mushrooms in the corner
of a towel or squeeze through a potato ricer (add juices to your turkey
stock) ; sauté in 2 tablespoons of fat in pan until pieces begin to separate
from each other, then scrape into mixing bowl. Beat in the olives, anchovies, capers, eggs, garlic, and herbs. Fold in the croutons, add salt
and pepper to taste.

☼ If you make the stuffing in advance, omit the croutons and fold them
in at the last moment; stuffing will keep 2 days or so in the refrigerator,

or may be frozen. Chilled stuffing, however, will slow up your roasting schedule, so warm it to tepid before filling the turkey.

Frozen turkey breasts

When you want a small turkey dinner with stuffing and gravy and all the fixings, frozen turkey breast is your meat all year around. Buy them in midsummer, when the price is low, and if 10-pounders are selling at a bargain, have them cut in half lengthwise along the ridge of the breast-bone, rewrap airtight, and store them in your freezer. With the savory meat stuffing suggested here, there will be no clamorings for dark meat, just for second helpings.

A 10-pound breast, boned, can be cut into 14 to 16 serving slices and, with a meat stuffing, it will feed 12 people amply, while a 5-pound breast will serve 6 to 8. For this recipe the breast need be defrosted only enough so that you can remove the meat from the bone; to do so leave it at room temperature for several hours, or in the refrigerator overnight.

To prepare the breast for stuffing, I suggest you peel off and discard the skin and all fat, since both are liable to be a little off in flavor. You are now to remove the two large pieces of meat from the breastbone on each side as follows. The ridge of the breastbone runs down the length of the breast, separating the two halves; cut down vertically against the ridge on each side. Then, with knife and fingers follow the outward curve of the bone down one side, freeing the meat in one piece. Repeat on the other side. On the inside of the meat you will see a tough white tendon; grasp one end in a towel, and scraping meat from tendon, pull out and discard tendon. Repeat for second breast half. Cutting on the bias, divide the meat into slices ½ to ¾ inch thick and as equal in size as you can make them—several too-small slices may be grouped together, if necessary, when you re-form the roast later. Trim remaining lumps of meat off breastbone structure, and reserve for stuffing. With cleaver and hammer, chop carcass into 2- to 3-inch pieces, and reserve.

A NOTE ON TOUGH TURKEY BREASTS. Once in a while you will run into tough breast meat even though it comes from a young roasting turkey and you can see a good half inch of the breastbone tip is cartilage—a proof of youth. Why is it tough? It was probably frozen too fast, before the turkey meat had relaxed and cooled after slaughter. This is enraging, and you can do nothing about it but bring whatever remains of it back to your market, give the manager a chew, and get your money refunded. If we don't complain, how is he to know what's wrong? And he wants satisfied customers, if he runs a serious market.

Poitrine de dinde farcie et braisée

TURKEY BREAST
STUFFED AND
BRAISED

For a 5-pound breast
serving 6 to 8

Once you get this dish ready for the oven, you can hold off for a day before cooking, and once cooked—which takes 1¼ hours—you need be in no tearing hurry to serve it. In addition, it is a first-class dish you can count on for any dinner party. The usual turkey accompaniments go beautifully with it, like mashed potatoes and buttered Brussels sprouts, or you could have glazed carrots and onions with mushrooms, or braised endive and sautéed potatoes, or fresh buttered peas and baked tomatoes. A great red Bordeaux would be a fine choice in wines, or a Cabernet Sauvignon.

For marinating the turkey slices
The boned and sliced turkey breast meat
¼ cup Cognac
¼ tsp salt
Big pinch white pepper
2 Tb minced shallots or scallions
½ tsp tarragon

The braising base
½ cup each sliced carrots and celery
1 cup sliced onions
2 Tb butter
The turkey carcass bones, chopped

**For the stuffing, and remaining
    braising ingredients**
The marinated turkey slices

About 2 cups turkey stuffing, your favorite,
*   or the pork and veal mixture on page 373*
Olive oil or cooking oil
1½ cups dry white wine or 1 cup
*   dry white French Vermouth*
2 cups chicken broth
Salt
1 tsp tarragon
1 imported bay leaf

Equipment: A 3-quart stainless or porcelain bowl
*   for marinade; a heavy covered casserole or*
*   roaster about 9 by 12 inches across, and 5 inches*
*   deep; a large square of damp well-washed*
*   cheesecloth about 18 inches to a side; white*
*   kitchen string; a large heavy frying pan*

Marinating the turkey meat. Arrange the turkey slices in the stainless or porcelain bowl, interspersing them with drops of Cognac and the seasonings and herbs. Cover and let marinate while assembling the rest of the ingredients; or prepare a day ahead and refrigerate.

The braising base. Meanwhile stir the vegetables and butter into the casserole, add the chopped carcass, cover, and cook over moderately low heat while you assemble the turkey in the next step. Stir occasionally; let vegetables cook till tender, and brown very lightly.

Forming the roast. Preheat oven to 350 degrees. Beat turkey marinade liquid into stuffing. Building them into a loaf-shaped roast on the cheese-cloth, arrange turkey slices upright with stuffing in between. Fold cheese-cloth over length of roast to enclose it completely; twist one of the ends, and tie with string. Twist opposite end, pushing turkey slices into shape, and tie. Wind a spiral of string around circumference of roast from one end to the other and back again, thus holding it in a sausage shape. Cut off excess cheesecloth at the two ends.

Browning. Film frying pan with ⅛ inch of oil and heat to very hot but not smoking; brown the roast on all sides. Then, pushing vegetables and carcass bones to the sides, arrange roast in casserole. Pour in the wine and chicken broth, salt lightly to taste, and add the herbs.

☼ May be prepared a day in advance to this point; let roast cool in the liquid, then cover and refrigerate.

Roasting. Bring casserole to the simmer on top of the stove. Cover, and set in middle level of preheated oven. Check in about 20 minutes, and regulate heat so turkey simmers quietly throughout its cooking. It is done at a meat temperature reading of 170 degrees. A 5-pound breast, unchilled, will take about 1¼ hours—as will any loaf-shaped roast that is 4½ to 5 inches in diameter, whatever its length.

Preparations for serving. As soon as roast is done, remove from casserole and let rest 20 minutes. (Prepare sauce, next step, during this period.) Then cut off string, carefully peel off cheesecloth, and transfer roast to a warm serving platter. If you are not ready to serve, spoon a little sauce over roast to keep it moist, cover with foil, and set in warming oven or turned-off oven at a temperature of no more than 140 degrees.

The sauce. Skim off fat, and strain roasting liquid into a saucepan, pressing juices out of ingredients. Continue skimming off fat as you bring liquid to the simmer. Taste carefully for seasoning, adding salt and pepper as you think necessary. You should have about 2 cups. Blend 1½ tablespoons cornstarch or arrowroot to a paste with 2 tablespoons cold wine or stock; off heat, blend into the liquid with a whip. Simmer 2 minutes. To serve, simmer again, remove from heat, and beat in a tablespoon or two of butter to enrich the sauce. Spoon some over the turkey to glaze it, and pour the rest into a warm bowl.

Serving suggestions. Decorate platter with watercress or parsley, or with whatever vegetables you have room for. To serve, remove a slice of turkey with its stuffing from one of the ends of the roast, using a large spoon and fork; pour a spoonful of sauce around the meat, and surround with the vegetables.

OTHER IDEAS FOR TURKEY BREASTS

Although turkey breasts are a little drier and firmer than chicken breasts and veal scallops, you can use sliced turkey breast in place of either one in any recipe. They are also delicious seasoned, floured, and rolled in beaten egg, and in fresh bread crumbs, as described for the Chicken Kiev on page 214; sautéed in butter, and served on a bed of braised spinach or of creamed mushroom *duxelles,* they make an elegant dish.

To press a duck

Along with its magnificent cathedral, its medieval half-timbered houses, and Joan of Arc, Rouen is also renowned for its pressed duck, *Canard à la Rouennaise*. Rouen has even developed its own special ducks for this celebrated recipe; they stem from domestic females crossed with wild males, producing a handsome dark-feathered bird that is full-breasted and toothsome. When we were filming in France for our television programs, this dish was high on our list because of its visual splendor—involving, as it does, a large silver-plated machine designed only for the pressing of ducks. However, you don't have to have a duck press, as you will see, to produce an excellent alternative, a *salmis*. Thus to Rouen we went.

On the historic Place Jeanne d'Arc, where that heroine met her fiery finish, stands the Restaurant La Couronne, originally built in 1345. The brothers Dorin, who own and run it, turned out to be most engagingly enthusiastic when we approached them about filming their famous *Canard à la Rouennaise*. They asked us to come for dinner, and to see the whole process. And, when the guests had left, they would do it over again for our camera.

That meant we would start filming at around eleven o'clock, calculated the brother Dorin who managed the dining room. He would stay up all night with us and on into the next morning if necessary, he said, but we'd have to finish before noon, when they opened for lunch.

On the evening of the filming, Paul and Ruthie and I, with Dave Atwood, our director, arrived at the half-timbered Norman-style restaurant around 8:30, and descended into the comfortably old-fashioned brown dining room. At the far end was an enormous fireplace with rotary spit, and we were shown to a table not far from it. After a *kir*, we decided to begin with the cold mousse of sole, presented in a long porcelain tureen— sole, with pieces of lobster and strips of green asparagus embedded in it. Served with a creamy pale-green lightly herbal mayonnaise and a spoonful of marinated cucumber slices, it was delightful, and is, by the way, the inspiration for the fish mousse with asparagus here, on page 153.

Then the great silver duck press was wheeled up to our table, and Monsieur Dorin, who, while the spit was turning, had been basting our duck, brought it forth, all brown and mouth-watering. He gravely sharpened his knife on the back of a dinner plate, speared the duck onto a board, and deftly carved off the legs. Then he very carefully peeled all the skin off the breast of the duck. It must be roasted very rare, he told us, only 20 minutes. The breast is hardly cooked, and is poached with the juices from the press later. And the carcass must be full of juices, for the press.

The captain, hovering near, handed him a buttered platter; on it he strewed a small sprinkling of coarse salt and exactly 40 grinds of the peppermill. Then he carved the breast into very thin slices, arranged them on the platter, and sprinkled over them a very small dusting of finely minced shallot. He removed the wings of the duck, rolled both wings and legs in mustard, and in crumbs, and handed them on a platter to the captain, who bore them off. They were barely cooked, he showed us, and now they were to be grilled in the kitchen. With that he peeled the remaining skin off the duck, cut up the carcass, and into the canister of the press it went.

He was to press the juices out of the carcass, he explained, and later they would go over the breast meat to make a sauce. He turned the big handle, the pressing plate descended slowly into the canister, and we could hear the crackling of bones. Almost immediately a dribbling stream of red juices trickled out of the spout into a copper saucepan. He tilted it toward us; it contained the duck's liver, raw, puréed with butter; it would enrich and thicken the juices, later.

He added a dollop of red Burgundy wine to the press, turned the crank again, more juices emerged, he released pressure, added a little more wine, turned the crank again, and continued until finally the carcass had rendered its all.

Well, I shall not go on, since it is fully described in the recipe. But we marveled over his every move, then over every mouthful. First there were the tender slices of duck breast poached in their juices over his chafing dish flame, only duck with a little wine and delicate seasoning to point up its own deep natural flavor, then the grilled legs and wings with their crisply crumbed exterior as contrast. By the time we had finished our pears and our cheese, the restaurant was all but emptied of guests, and our crew had arrived. We started filming at eleven and finished at five in the morning, Monsieur Dorin always patient and endlessly cooperative, as Peter Hoving, our talented cameraman, followed each ritualized step, and Willie Morton caught each crackle of bone and drip of juice on his sound apparatus.

"Be sure to let me know when it goes on in America," Monsieur Dorin called to us as we left in the dawn's faint light. "I shall tell my friends there to watch." He is a ham radio operator in his spare time.

Unfortunately, few restaurants even in France have the staff or the time to prepare pressed duck at the tables of their clients anymore, but a little sweet talk and discreet tipping could make it possible. You can always do it yourself, though, according to the following directions, and if you've not the several hundred dollars needed for a duck press, have the *salmis* instead.

Canard à la rouennaise; canard à la presse; canard au sang; and canard en salmis

———◆———

PRESSED DUCK AND
SALMIS OF DUCK

Pressed duck and *salmis* of duck start out the same way, with a very rare roasted duck. Its legs and wings are removed and are baked or grilled with a crumb and mustard coating; the breast meat is carved into thin strips, and the carcass is peeled and chopped. At this point the two recipes briefly part company. For the pressed duck, the carcass is then squeezed dry in a press, and the juices are collected. For the *salmis*, the chopped carcass is sautéed briefly, then simmered, to extract its essences of flavor. The two recipes now come together for the finish. The juices or essences are blended with the puréed duck's liver and are poured over the rose-red breast meat, which is poached slowly in a chafing dish (or on top of the stove) , and you are ready to serve.

Timing. As you see from the description, all of the preliminary work can be completed in advance—the roasting, the carving, the juice or essence making; it is only the poaching of the breast meat and the grilling of the crumbed legs and wings that are done at the last minute. This ease

of final cooking is one reason you will see so many *Canard au Sang* and
Aiguillettes de Canard dishes on the menus of the fancy restaurants; it can
all be done way ahead, and a token duck press in operation on a dais or in
the corner of the room gives you the illusion that your own particular duck
is being worked upon. (*Aiguillettes* are thin slices of breast meat.)

Menu suggestions. The duck should be served as a separate course, with
home-fried shoestring potatoes or your own make of potato chips if you
wish them, and a garnish of fresh watercress for the grilled legs and wings.
French bread and a fine red Burgundy wine would be the only other requirements. You could start the dinner with a cold fish mousse or a soup,
follow the duck with fresh asparagus or a combination salad, and finish
with a fruit dessert, such as fresh berries, fruits poached in wine, or a
fruit tart or sherbet.

Preliminaries

For two 5-pound
ducks, serving 6 to 8

Two 5-pound roaster ducklings, thawed if frozen
1 tsp salt
4 Tb soft butter

For roasting and carving the ducks

¼ tsp coarse (Kosher) salt
A large oval platter, about 14 inches long,
*   smeared with 1 Tb soft butter*
A full peppermill
½ cup Dijon-type prepared mustard, in a dish
1 cup fairly fine fresh white bread crumbs,
*   in a plate*
4 Tb melted butter
An excellent young red wine, Burgundy type:
*   2 cups for pressed duck; about 3 cups*
*   for salmis*

Sauce and serving

1 Tb very finely minced shallots or scallions
Salt, and grinds from a peppermill
Best-quality French Cognac (you will need about
*   ⅓ cup, and a small saucepan for flaming*
*   it at the table)*

Preliminaries. Remove package of giblets from ducks, pull excess fat out of cavities, cut off extra neck skin, and chop off wings at elbows. Dry the ducks inside and out with paper towels, and sprinkle cavity of each with ½ teaspoon salt. Trussing is not necessary unless you are using a rotisserie. Chop the livers and push through a sieve with the 4 tablespoons of soft butter, using a wooden spoon; scrape into a 6-cup saucepan and refrigerate, covered, until later.

Roasting the ducks. Preheat the oven to 450 degrees, and place ducks on their sides in a shallow roasting pan. Set in middle level of oven for 20 to 25 minutes. Turn them on their other sides halfway through. Cook just long enough to stiffen the flesh of the breasts very slightly—they will just begin to feel springy rather than squashy, meaning you will be able to carve the meat easily; but the meat is blood rare, and the legs and wings are barely cooked.

Carving the ducks. Duck by duck, first carve off the drumstick and second-joint assemblies, being sure to include with the second joints the oysters of meat at the small of the back and the one from joint to tail. In strips, remove skin from breast and back of duck, and scrape any fat from flesh. (Reserve skin for making cracklings, at end of recipe.)

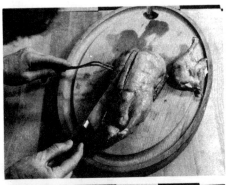

Set duck on its back, and cut down vertically through flesh on each side of breastbone to outline it. Then make very thin, long, slices from each side of the breast, cutting parallel to your work surface, and including the meat from the tops of the wings at the shoulders; you should get 4 and perhaps 5 slices per breast side. Carve second duck.

Sprinkle the ¼ teaspoon of coarse salt on the bottom of the buttered platter, and add a generous grinding of pepper. Arrange the slices neatly on top, and cover with plastic wrap.

Remove the wings from the carcass. Separate drumsticks from second joints, and cut off any fatty skin pieces from them and from wings. Roll legs and wings first in mustard and then in bread crumbs; arrange on a baking and serving dish. Sprinkle with the melted butter, and set aside or cover and refrigerate until serving time. Discard fatty tailpiece from carcass, and cut or chop carcass into 2-inch pieces; reserve. (Reserve all bits of fat and skin for cracklings, described at end of recipe.)

You are now ready to turn the ducks either into Pressed Duck, or *Salmis* of Duck as follows, taking each method separately from now on to avoid confusion.

For pressed duck

Set the small saucepan with sieved liver and butter under the spout of the press. Put the still warm carcass pieces in the press, squeeze until juices run, and add progressive driblets of wine to press, releasing then increasing pressure to extract as much juice and flavor as you think possible.

☼ Pressed duck may be prepared even a day in advance to this point; cover and refrigerate juices, breast slices, and crumbed appendages.

Finishing the ducks and serving. (I am assuming you will complete the sauce and poach the breast meat at the table; otherwise adapt the following directions to your kitchen.) About 30 minutes before serving, set the crumbed legs and wings in the upper-middle level of a preheated 375-degree oven, to bake until just tender and nicely browned. Have all the ingredients for serving in appropriate containers—salt, peppermill, minced shallots, the saucepan of sieved duck liver, the juices from the pressed duck, the platter of sliced breast of duck, the Cognac and its pan, long-handled fork and spoon, hot plates, and so forth.

Set pan of duck juices and sieved livers over chafing dish flame and, stirring continuously, warm slowly just to poach the liver, but do not let it come near the simmer or it will curdle—it just warms and lightly thickens. Remove from heat. Sprinkle breast slices lightly with salt and pepper, and strew the minced shallots or scallions over them. Pour the Cognac into the small pan, heat it, flame it, and dribble over the meat. Spoon the warmed liver and juices over the duck slices, and set platter over flame, turning and basting the meat as it slowly warms through; do not let the sauce come to the simmer—3 to 4 minutes should be sufficient. Serve onto very hot plates, and pass the crumbed legs and wings now, or serve on separate plates when the breast meat has been consumed.

Additional ingredients for salmis only
1 cup each diced carrots and onions
4 Tb cooking oil
The duck giblets, minus the livers
4 cups chicken stock or bouillon,
   plus necessary water
2 imported bay leaves
½ tsp thyme
2 Tb arrowroot, or potato starch, or
   cornstarch (for later)

While the ducks are roasting, sauté the sliced carrots and onions in the oil in a heavy-bottomed saucepan, with the chopped-off wing ends of the ducks, and the necks, hearts, and gizzards chopped into pieces. When lightly browned, add the chicken stock, water to cover ingredients, and bring to simmer; skim several minutes, then add the herbs. Simmer an hour, strain, degrease, and boil down to 1 cup. Reserve, to simmer with the chopped carcass when the time comes.

After carving the ducks, sauté the chopped carcass in a little oil, to brown lightly; add the 3 cups of red wine and the cup of duck stock; simmer 30 minutes. Strain, skim fat off surface, return stock to pan, and reduce rapidly to about 2 cups. Blend the arrowroot or starch in a small bowl with a spoonful of wine or water, stir into the stock, and simmer 2 to 3 minutes. Correct seasoning.

☼ *Salmis* of duck can be prepared even a day in advance to this point; cover and refrigerate all elements.

Finishing the salmis and serving. Follow the two paragraphs of directions for the Pressed Duck under *Finishing the ducks and serving,* including the roasting of the crumbed legs and wings, and the arrangements for table-top cookery if you are doing it that way. The only difference in method is that you substitute the *salmis* sauce for the duck-press juices. In other words, the sauce goes into the pan of sieved liver and butter, is poached over the chafing dish flame, and is then spooned over the duck breast slices on the platter, to heat and finish cooking exactly as in those preceding directions.

Frittons; grattons

CRACKLINGS,
RENDERED FROM
THE SKIN AND
FATTY PIECES
OF DUCK, GOOSE,
CHICKEN, PORK

Cracklings are an old-fashioned specialty familiar to anyone who has worked on a farm that raises pigs, geese, and other animals for family consumption. When you have rendered their fat, you have a lovely brown residue of crisp bits in the pot that make very good eating. Here you will have all that duck skin to play with, and in the next recipe all that goose skin. Cut the skin into strips about 1½ inches long and ⅜ inch wide, and chop the fat. Put it all into a large baking dish and set for 35 to 45 minutes in a 375-degree oven, stirring about once in a while to check on the cooking. The liquid the fat has rendered should remain clear yellow throughout the cooking—if it darkens your oven is too hot—while the bits of skin will slowly turn crisp and brown. Strain, toss the browned bits on paper towels, then toss with a sprinkling of salt and pepper, and a pinch of allspice. Serve with cocktails, sprinkle into salads, or crumble into stews, chowders, or curries. (If you are creating this with goose, chicken, or pork bits, save the rendered fat for general cooking; duck fat is not considered culinarily desirable.)

P.S. I tried this in the microwave oven, and while the fat rendered nicely, the skin turned tougher than leather.

Ragoût de canard (*Ragoût of duck; duck stew*). For a change, and for easy serving, try a duck ragout. You cut it up, peel the skin off each piece—removing all that fat—then stew the duck in wine. Follow the goose recipe on page 252, but duck will need only 45 minutes or so of simmering. Use either red or white wine for the cooking, and you might also like to garnish the stew with sautéed mushrooms and small white onions, *à la bourguignonne*, like the beef on page 263.

To ragout a goose

Supposing you've got a goose, and you don't want to roast it or braise it—you've done that. What else can you do? What's new? Well, how about a *Ragoût d'Oie*—a goose stew? You cut up your goose, pull all the skin and fat off it, brown the goose pieces, and simmer them in a deliciously winey broth laced with onions. There's no goose grease to skim, no complicated carving to execute in front of an audience, nothing but the rich brown meat of that bird and its cooking liquor. Geese by the piece, all cut up, are available in France during the *foie gras* season, around Christmas, when those enormous pinky-ivory goose livers can be bought fresh in the markets. Here you would usually be buying frozen goose, and if you don't want to cook all of it, ask your butcher to cut it in half lengthwise with his buzz saw. Repackage one frozen half, thaw and cut up the other half. A whole 9- to 10-pound ready-to-cook goose makes 12 serving pieces, enough for 8 to 10 people.

TO CUT UP A RAW GOOSE. If goose is frozen, leave in original wrapper and either thaw for 2 days in the refrigerator, or overnight in a sinkful of water. Remove wrapping, drain liquid out of vent (tail end), and pull out all loose fat from around inside of vent. Remove giblet package and save for goose stock. Chop off wings at elbows, leaving just the upper arm attached to the goose; chop up removed parts of wing and add to stock pot.

Then proceed to cut up the goose exactly the same way as described for the stewing chicken on page 228; they are built the same way, although the goose is much bigger and the bones are tougher. When you get to the breast, however, you may want to chop it in two lengthwise, and then each lengthwise piece in two crosswise. You can also divide the thighs (second joints) in two, lengthwise along one side of the bone. This will give you 12 serving pieces in all.

Since you are to make a ragout, you will want to remove the skin; do so by pulling and cutting it from the flesh of the legs, wings, breast, and from the carcass. The pieces of goose are now ready for the ragout, but you still have some valuable parts of the goose to use:

GOOSE STOCK. Chop the carcass into convenient pieces and simmer them to make a goose stock for soups and sauces, using the turkey stock recipe on page 234 (but omit the cornstarch thickening at the end).

GOOSE FAT AND CRACKLINGS. Goose fat is much prized in European cookery for sautéing potatoes, for flavoring simple dishes like steamed cabbage, and for general basting and browning jobs. Chop all the fat into ½-inch pieces, and cut the skin into strips 1½ inches long and ½ inch wide; render them like the chicken fat on page 230, or like the duck skin and fat on page 250. Rendered goose fat will keep for months in a covered jar in the refrigerator. The brown bits of fat and skin left over from the rendering are called cracklings, and make a delicious cocktail snack.

Ragoût d'oie au chou

CUT-UP GOOSE
BRAISED WITH
CABBAGE

Serves 8 to 10

Goose and cabbage are an old-world combination delighting those with hearty appetites. A fitting accompaniment would be mashed potatoes or noodles, and a robust red wine like Burgundy, Châteauneuf-du-Pape, Pinot Noir, or Gamay. (*Note:* Although the title suggests a communal simmer, I find you get a better sauce and fresher cabbage when you do them separately.)

For the goose
A 9- to 10-lb. young roasting goose, cut up
    (preceding directions)
Salt and pepper
About 1 cup flour
Rendered goose fat, or pork fat, or oil
About 1 cup (4 ounces) diced lean salt pork,
    blanched (simmered 5 minutes)
5 to 6 cups sliced onions
2 to 3 large cloves garlic, minced
2 imported bay leaves
1 tsp each caraway seeds and thyme
1½ cups dry white wine, or dry white
    French Vermouth
2 or more cups goose stock or beef bouillon

For the cabbage
A hard-head cabbage about 6 inches across
    (8 cups, sliced)
½ cup stock or bouillon
¼ tsp salt

⅛ tsp pepper
3 Tb goose fat, or pork fat, or butter

Equipment: Large frying pan; a casserole or heavy covered roaster just large enough to hold goose pieces; covered saucepan for the cabbage

Cooking the goose. Preheat oven to 350 degrees. Spread pieces of goose on wax paper, season with salt and pepper, and roll in flour; shake off excess. Immediately set frying pan over moderately high heat, film with 1/16 inch of fat or cooking oil; when very hot but not smoking, brown as many pieces of goose as will fit into pan easily, turning to color on all sides. Remove to a side dish and continue until all pieces are nicely browned. Meanwhile, brown the salt pork lightly in a spoonful of fat or oil in the casserole, then add the onions and sauté until tender and beginning to color slightly. Add the browned goose, the garlic, bay, caraway, thyme, and wine or Vermouth, plus enough stock or bouillon to come two thirds the way up the goose. Bring to simmer on top of the stove, lay a piece of wax paper or foil over the goose, cover the casserole, and set in lower-middle level of preheated oven. Regulate heat so that goose simmers slowly for 1½ to 2 hours, or until tender when pierced with a fork; turn and baste several times during this period. While goose is cooking, prepare cabbage as follows.

Six-minute cabbage. Quarter the cabbage from top to bottom, core out stem from each quarter, then shred cabbage into pieces about ¼ inch wide. Place in a covered saucepan with the stock or bouillon, salt, pepper, and fat or butter. Cover, bring to the boil, and boil hard 5 to 6 minutes, tossing several times, until barely tender. Uncover and set aside.

Serving. If goose is done before you are ready to serve, set casserole cover askew and keep warm in turned-off oven, over simmering water, or on an electric warming plate. Skim any fat off surface of cooking liquid, which should be lightly thickened; if too thin, drain out and boil down rapidly to concentrate it, then pour back over goose. Carefully correct seasoning.

☼ May be prepared ahead to this point, and reheated.

At serving time, arrange goose pieces over a bed of buttered noodles or mashed potatoes. Toss cabbage to heat with a tablespoon or two of goose-cooking sauce, then arrange cabbage around goose. Spoon a little sauce over each piece of goose, decorate platter with parsley sprigs, and serve rest of sauce, with its onions and pork bits, in a warm bowl.

The meat course

BEEF

Beef stews

Ragoût de boeuf tout simple—
plain brown beef stew
Additions and variations, including
boeuf bourguignon

Braised beef—pot roast

Boeuf à la mode; boeuf en daube—
whole piece of beef braised in red wine
Additions and variations, including
stuffed flank steak and braised tongues,
hearts, livers

Boiled beef

Pot-au-feu—French-style boiled beef and
vegetable dinner
Sauce crème à la moutarde—cream and
mustard sauce for boiled beef
Additions and variations, including
boiled beef tongue, corned beef,
New England boiled dinner

Beef tenderloin, filet de boeuf, beef fillet

Filet de boeuf rôti, sauce périgueux—
roast tenderloin of beef, brown
Madeira sauce with truffles
Sauce semi demi-glace

Sautés and brochettes of beef tenderloin

LAMB

To roast and carve a leg of lamb
Gigot d'agneau rôti—roast leg of lamb
Lamb on brochettes, kebabs, and skewers
Curry dinner
A fast moussaka—ground lamb and
eggplant gratin
Other ideas for leftover lamb
Barley soup; Scotch mutton broth—
the last of the leg

PORK AND HAM

Médaillons de porc—medallions of pork
loin sautéed and sauced
Ragoût de porc, chasseur—braised
cubed pork

Ham and smoked shoulder of pork, whole and sliced

Braisé au Madère—braised in wine
Gratiné, duxelles—gratinéed
with mushrooms
Saupiquet à la nivernaise—ham slices
sautéed and sauced

HAMBURGERS, VEAL-BURGERS, OTHERBURGERS

Bifteck haché, sauté nature—sautéed
hamburgers with wine, cream,
and tomato sauce
Other flavorings, other sauces
Fricadelles de veau—vealburgers
en papillote
Otherburgers—lamb, pork, turkey, chicken

STUFFED BREASTS, FLANKS, AND CABBAGES

To prepare a breast of veal for stuffing
Poitrine de veau farcie—boned stuffed
breast of veal braised in wine
To stuff a cabbage
Chou farci—stuffed whole cabbage,
braised and sauced
Tripes à la mode—tripe cooked in wine
and aromatic vegetables
Tripes à la niçoise and à la florentine—
with tomatoes and herbs

Beef

*E*very bit as important as how to stew, braise, or roast beef is how to pick the right cut for the dish you plan to make. This means knowing meat cuts, and the more you know, the more meat you will get for your money, since often a less expensive cut from the unfashionable chuck will do better than the more modish round when you are doing a stew or a braise. I wish I could suggest an easy way to learn meat, for those of us who are not in the butchering business. Certainly you can't learn it all at once: you start in with the big general areas from which the smaller cuts come—the rib section, the loin, the flank, the brisket, the round (hind leg section), and the chuck (shoulder). Then you take them up one at a time and learn the cuts in each of those areas. You should also relate all of these to your own body; that makes it not only easier for you to visualize them, but helps you to describe the cut of meat you want when you have trouble communicating with your butcher. After all, every one of us has the same general structure, from squab to lamb, from turkey to beef, and from pork to butcher to you yourself. The late Adelle Davis, in *Let's Cook It Right,* gives an amusing and useful lesson on how to pretend you are a cud-chewing animal in order to learn where all the muscles are, and which get the most exercise. An active part of the beast—shoulder chuck, for instance—makes a tough muscle that needs stewing or braising, while the pampered inner muscle at the small of the back, the tenderloin, produces those most luxurious and expensive of steaks, the *Châteaubriands*.

For years the greatest block to the self-teaching of meat cuts, particularly beef, has been the fanciful nomenclature used by markets in various parts of the country. A tip roast from the round may be called a bell of knuckle in one town, a ball tip in another, and a veiny or crescent roast in still another area. A pot roast from the bottom round can be a silverside or gooseneck, while the sirloin can be a rump steak, a hip, or a bottom butt, and a boneless cut from the chuck blade is a medallion in some regions, a chuck tender, a Jewish tender, or a fish muscle elsewhere, depending on where you live and your butcher's whim.

Finally, in 1973, to put a stop to this ridiculous, confusing, and frequently deceptive state of affairs, the National Live Stock and Meat Board in cooperation with a number of the big meat packers and grocery chains agreed on a uniform terminology for meat cuts and labeling. By 1974 a number of states adopted these recommendations, including my own Massachusetts—glory be! Whether or not your state has fallen into line, you should insist that your butcher follow these recommendations to the letter. It is only through public pressure that we can finally install this uniform system throughout the country. When we do, every piece of meat in the display counter will be labeled as to:

The kind of meat it is: Beef, pork, lamb, or whatever

The primal or wholesale cut from which the piece comes: chuck, rib, loin, etc.

The retail cut, or name of each particular piece of meat: chop, pot roast, steak, etc.

The suggested cooking method: roast, pan-fry, braise (cook in liquid)

This last category—how to cook it—is one many markets skip over. The other day my supermarket had some gorgeous 2-inch squares of well-trimmed, nicely marbled meat all beautifully packaged in see-through containers. A big red extra label, not the weight and price label, announced loudly: *Barbecue. Brochettes.* In a hurry, I grabbed up a package, rushed home, skewered it, basted it, broiled it, and was it ever tough! Blind faith in my market had made me careless. When I fished the wrapping out of the trash, later, I read: *Beef Round. Bottom Round Steak.* Bottom round is a braising cut, not a steak cut, and I know that. I discussed this with the meat manager a few days later, complimenting him on using the new system, but wishing he had carried it that one step further, and used the recommended cooking method on the label. Next week the same enticing package appeared in the meat counter, with a new red label: *Barbecue. Brochettes. Marinate in wine before cooking.*

But wine wouldn't help, though it would make a tastier stew, which is what that meat was really meant for—a de luxe *Boeuf Bourguignon*. This only goes to show that we, the customers, must know what we are about. And if we can persuade our markets to cooperate, then, when we are looking about for a big piece of beef to simmer in wine for our *Boeuf à la Mode,* we shall find among other choices, the following:

Beef chuck, Shoulder Pot Roast Boneless (Braise, Cook in Liquid)

Beef brisket, Middle Cut Boneless (Braise, Cook in Liquid)

Beef round, Bottom Round Roast (Braise, Cook in Liquid)

The official guide for identifying meat cuts is now available to anyone who wants it, and while it may tell a little more than you want to know since it is designed for those in the business, I do think you will find it marvelously useful. It is clearly illustrated, earnestly worked out, and gives not only the agreed-upon official name of each cut, but all aliases. A better way to document yourself for adventures in meat cuts would be hard to imagine. For information and price, send a self-addressed stamped envelope along with your query about *Uniform Retail Meat Identity Standards* (manual with binder), to: Director of Merchandising, National Live Stock and Meat Board, 36 S. Wabash Avenue, Chicago, Illinois 60603.

In the meantime, there is a meat chart here in this book, on page 647, giving not only recommended and frowned-upon names for cuts, but cooking methods as well as French equivalents.

Beef stews

While the joys of roast ribs of beef, filet mignons, and T-bone steaks are undeniable, the soul-warming appeal of a beef stew is eternal, and certainly the most famous of the French beef stews is *Boeuf Bourguignon*. Although it may sound difficult, fancy, and expensive just because it has a foreign name, it is only a basic brown meat stew, and all brown meat stews, whether of lamb, pork, veal, or beef, are almost identical in method. Generous chunks of meat are browned, then simmered in liquid and aromatic seasonings—carrots, onions, garlic, herbs. That's all there is to a stew. What makes a beef stew a *Bourguignon* is that the simmering liquid is red wine, and the final garnishing is little onions and mushrooms. If you leave out the wine and use stock instead, you still have a delicious stew; if you leave out the garnish, throw in several sliced onions, go heavy on the garlic and herbs, again you have a marvelous dish. Thus let us start with a plain brown stew, and serve up the *Bourguignon* as a small variation coming at the end of the main theme. Whether or not you may have it both in *Mastering*, Volume I, and *The French Chef Cookbook*, I have to include it here too because we did *Boeuf Bourguignon* on color television, and this book contains every one of those dishes. It's useful, anyway, to see slightly different versions of the same thing as an illustration that recipes of this type are not graven on slabs of marble, immutable forevermore.

BEEF CUTS FOR STEWING. Here you would look for cuts marked "braise; cook in liquid," and I recommend you buy a whole roast and cut it up yourself following the natural seams and muscle separations in the meat. Then you know exactly what you have, you can cut nice big pieces, and you can trim them the way you want. I am partial to the beef chuck for stews because of its good flavor and reasonable price—compared to other parts of the animal. Look for an arm pot roast, the cross rib, the shoulder, neck, or cuts from the blade. Other suggestions are listed in the beef chart on page 650.

Ragoût de boeuf tout simple

———

PLAIN BROWN
BEEF STEW

Perfectly plain, so easy to do, and always delicious, this beef stew can be started a day or two in advance of serving: brown the meat any spare moment you have, let it simmer when it suits your schedule, and serve it a day or two later if you wish. Although steamed potatoes are in the French tradition, I prefer rice or noodles with my stew, and a decoration of fresh green vegetables, like broccoli, or steamed green cabbage, or spinach. Include French bread, if you wish, and serve an honest red wine, either the one you used for the stew itself, or a Burgundy, a Beaujolais, a Côtes du Rhône, or one of the various domestic wines like Gamay or Barbera.

For 6 to 8 people

Simmering time:
2 to 4 hours
depending on
quality of meat

Optional, but recommended for flavor:
    a 5- to 6-ounce chunk of fat-and-lean
    fresh side pork, or pork shoulder blade;
    or salt pork, or bacon chunk
Olive oil or peanut oil
3 to 4 lbs. beef stew meat cut into either

2-inch squares or 3- by 1½-inch pieces
(see remarks on beef cuts preceding
this recipe)
If you are making a plain stew with no
trimmings: 1 sliced carrot and 2 cups
sliced onions
Optional: 3 cups strong young red wine, such as
Mâcon, Mountain Red, Gamay; or dry
white wine, or 2 cups dry white
French Vermouth
2 or more cups excellent homemade beef stock;
or canned beef bouillon plus any available
beef bones and scraps
1 imported bay leaf
1 tsp thyme
A 2-inch piece of dried orange peel, or
⅓ tsp bottled dried peel
1 moderately large tomato, and
1 Tb tomato paste
2 or more cloves garlic
Salt as needed, and pepper
Beurre manié for the final sauce: 3 Tb flour
blended with 2½ Tb soft butter

Equipment: A large, heavy frying pan for
browning the meat; a heavy 4- to 5-quart
casserole with cover for stewing, or an
electric frying pan

Browning the beef. Cut the optional pork into *lardons* (sticks ¼ inch across and 1 to 1½ inches long), and if you are using salt pork or bacon blanch it (simmer 10 minutes in 2 quarts water to remove salt and/or smoky taste); sauté slowly in a tablespoon of oil in the frying pan for 5 minutes or until lightly browned, then remove the *lardons* and set aside. Heat the fat they have rendered, or enough oil to film pan by ¹⁄₁₆ inch, to very hot but not smoking. Meanwhile dry beef with paper towels, and add as many pieces to pan as will fit in 1 layer easily without crowding (they must have room or they will steam rather than brown). Brown nicely on all sides, regulating heat so fat is always very hot but not smoking. Add more oil if needed, and when one piece of meat is browned, transfer it to casserole and add another piece of beef until all are browned. Stir in the optional sliced carrot and onions, and brown briefly, then transfer with a slotted spoon to casserole. Pour browning fat out of frying pan and discard; pour a cup of wine or stock into pan, bring to simmer, scraping up coagulated browning juices, and pour this liquid over the beef.

☼ Recipe may be completed a day or two in advance to this point; or you may add the wine to it now, as well as the stock and seasonings from the next step; then set it aside, or cover and refrigerate. The wine tenderizes the meat, and the other ingredients will also flavor it as it marinates.

Stewing the beef. Set casserole over heat; add the optional wine, and enough stock (or bouillon and bones and scraps) barely to cover the meat. Add the browned *lardons,* the bay, thyme, and orange peel; wash the tomato, chop it roughly, and add it to the beef along with the tomato paste and the unpeeled garlic cut in half. Bring to the simmer, taste, and salt lightly if necessary. Cover and cook at a slow simmer either on top of the stove or in the oven—for oven cooking, start at 350 degrees, then lower heat in 20 to 30 minutes to 325 or even 300 degrees.

Timing. Choice or prime cuts of chuck or round may take only 2 hours, while shank and heel may take up to 4 hours. If you have top-quality meat, therefore, check every 15 minutes or so after 1½ hours of simmering; the beef must not overcook and fall apart when served, but it must be tender enough for a pleasant chew.

Finishing the stew. When beef is tender, set a large colander over a saucepan and pour contents of casserole into colander. Wash out casserole, and return the meat to it. Press juices out of remains in colander, and discard residue. Skim fat off cooking liquid in saucepan, and taste liquid very carefully for strength and seasoning. You should have about 3 cups of delicious meaty rich stock. Boil down rapidly if weak, to concentrate flavor, adding a bit more stock or bouillon or wine, herbs, garlic, or tomato paste if you feel them necessary. Remove from heat, blend the *beurre manié* into the liquid with a wire whisk. Bring to the boil, stirring, as it thickens into a light sauce, check seasoning, and pour the sauce over the meat. Simmer slowly for 2 to 3 minutes, basting meat with sauce, and you are ready to serve.

☼ Stew may be prepared a day or two in advance to this point; let cool uncovered, then cover and refrigerate. Reheat slowly at below the simmer for 20 minutes or so, to let meat warm through and soften before serving.

Serving. Serve from casserole, if you wish; or turn the stew out onto a large warm platter and surround with rice or noodles, whatever vegetables you have chosen, and sprigs of fresh parsley or a sprinkling of chopped parsley for decoration.

ADDITIONS AND VARIATIONS

You may add numerous things either to finish their cooking with your beef stew, or to warm up with it after the sauce has been made. I personally prefer to cook most things separately, and add them at the end—such as sautéed fresh mushrooms, or carrots or turnips browned in a frying pan and steamed in their own juices, or a cup or so of fresh peas blanched in salted water until almost tender. Dried beans cooked and drained or even canned and drained are especially good when you are a little short on meat. Other additions might be a handful of tiny Mediterranean-type black olives or the larger canned and pitted supermarket black olives, simmered a few minutes in a quart of water to remove excess salt; or diced sautéed eggplant or zucchini, or cherry tomatoes simmered with the beef in the final sauce just enough to warm them through. Now here is that all-time favorite, *Boeuf Bourguignon*, with its garniture of onions and mushrooms.

Boeuf *bourguignon* BROWN BEEF STEW IN RED WINE For 6 to 8 people	*The ingredients listed for the Plain Brown* *Beef Stew, page 260, including the pork and* *the red wine but omitting (if you wish)* *the sliced carrot and onions* *Plus: 18 to 24 (or more) small white onions about* *1 inch in diameter; ½ lb. (more or less)* *fresh mushrooms*

Cooking the beef. Brown and simmer the beef exactly as described in the preceding master recipe, but save out the browned pork bits. While beef is simmering prepare the onions and mushrooms as follows:

The onions. To peel them easily, drop onions into a saucepan of boiling water, bring rapidly back to the boil, and boil 1 minute; drain, and run cold water over the onions. Shave off 2 ends of each onion, slip off the skins, and pierce a cross ⅜ inch deep in root ends to prevent them from bursting during cooking. Place in a heavy saucepan, add ½ inch of water, a pinch of salt, and the browned pork *lardons*. Cover and simmer slowly, tossing occasionally, for about 30 minutes, or until onions are just tender when pierced with a knife. Set aside.

The mushrooms. Trim off dry or sandy stem ends, wash the mushrooms thoroughly but rapidly, and dry in a towel. Leave whole if ¾ inch across or less; halve or quarter lengthwise if larger. Film a frying pan with ¹⁄₁₆ inch oil, heat to very hot but not smoking, and add enough mushrooms to cover bottom of pan; toss (shake pan by handle) over high heat for 2 to 3 minutes until mushrooms are lightly browned. Add them to the cooked onions, and proceed with the rest of the mushrooms (if any) in the same manner.

Finishing the stew. After you have made the sauce as directed in the master recipe, arrange the onions, mushrooms, and *lardons* over the beef in the casserole along with any onion-cooking juices. Pour on the sauce, and simmer 5 to 6 minutes, basting meat and vegetables with the sauce to blend flavors. Stew is now ready to serve, or may be set aside and re-heated.

The pressure cooker and beef stews. The pressure cooker comes in very handy when you need a stew in a hurry, since it will cook the meat in a third the time. To use the cooker, brown the meat and whatever aromatic vegetables are to simmer with it, add enough liquid almost to cover the ingredients—but do not fill the cooker pan beyond two thirds of its capacity. Cook at full pressure a bit less than a third the time you would estimate ordinarily, then release pressure. Finish simmering partially covered, to reduce the cooking liquid and let the meat and sauce pick up their full flavor.

Braised beef—pot roast

The only difference between beef stew and braised beef or pot roast is that you use small pieces of meat for a stew and a whole big piece for a pot roast. In both cases the meat is browned, then simmered in an aromatic liquid that serves to make its sauce. The French versions, *Boeuf à la Mode* or *Boeuf en Daube,* include wine, the American pot roast does not. *Daube,* by the way, comes from *daubière,* or "braising pot"; *à la Mode*—in the latest fashion—probably meant that it's a big surprise to have a simple pot roast so nicely dressed up. There is also another name for the same process, *Estouffade de Boeuf,* meaning stifled, or cooked slowly in a covered pot. Anyway, a whole piece of beef braised in wine— or in stock *à l'Américaine*—is a particularly good party dish because the actual cooking requires a minimum of attention, and you need hardly worry about overcooking. The preliminaries to braising, which include browning the meat and the aromatic vegetables and the flour that thickens the sauce, are exacting; however, since you can do them well in advance, you can give them the time they need. *Boeuf à la Mode,* of course, appears in all our books, but, again, as with *Boeuf Bourguignon,* it was on color TV, so it belongs here too. Besides, I did it a little differently from before, on this occasion, to give you another version.

This was a difference with a purpose, since few cooks, once they have mastered a recipe, want to do it exactly the same way twice—that's a pedestrian and boring way to cook. You want to try a new flavor like chopped green peppers, or you want to simmer the meat in white wine instead of red, or to try out a vinegar marinade and no wine at all. In other words, the main theme of the recipe is in your memory bank, and you can begin to have some fun with variations of your own. Now you are really cooking. Some combinations will be only so-so, but that is how you learn what not to do, while others may have that touch of genius that will make your reputation as an imaginative and creative cook.

BEEF CUTS FOR BRAISING. To make an attractive roast you want a quite solid piece of meat with no or few muscle separations; then it will slice neatly. Thus you will be spending more money for a braising piece than for stewing meat. *Top round* and *bottom round* are ideal choices, and the most expensive. Good and a bit cheaper is a boneless *chuck shoulder pot roast.* The boneless *chuck eye roast* is another possibility, and has, in contrast to the previous suggestions, a bit of fat larded into its lean. The *tip roast* from the round has good flavor, but is more expensive than chuck and has more muscle separations than the top or the bottom round. The *eye of the round* is a handsome piece, as is a boneless middle cut of *brisket,* but both tend to be fibrous and must be sliced on the bias to make attractive servings. See also the chart on page 650 for other suggestions.

MANUFACTURING NOTES. The following recipe suggests that you marinate the meat for 2 days or more in red wine and aromatic flavorings, and if you've not the 2 days to give, do not bother with a marinade; simply add all the listed ingredients to the beef in *Preliminaries to braising,* in the recipe. Some people do not like the slightly gamey taste of marinated meat, so be prepared for a change if you've never marinated before. The recipe also suggests that you lard the meat by pushing strips of pork fat through its interior with a special larding instrument. Larding fattens up very lean, tough meat, is rather fun to do anyway, and the pattern of white cubes is attractive when you slice the meat. Omit the larding if you wish, and you won't need it at all if you have a lean-and-fat chuck or brisket. (I must confess that when very young, and dining at the Plaza in New York, I was confronted with my first slice of larded roast. I thought those imbedded little pieces of white were fat white worms. Too shy to make a remark, I ate them anyway, since I concluded they would be harmless cooked, and they were unexpectedly rather good, for worms, served as they were in a rich winey sauce.)

FAT-FREE BRAISED BEEF. See page 270.

TIMING. A 7- to 8-pound piece of beef 5½ inches in diameter will take 3 to 4 hours of braising, or even longer, depending on the initial tenderness and quality of the meat. (I, personally, like to leave a good 5 hours, therefore, from the time the meat goes into the oven to the time I hope to serve it.) You will note that you may get the meat all ready for cooking even a day in advance, that you can keep it warm when it is done, and that you may even carve and sauce it, and reheat it later.

SERVING SUGGESTIONS. Attractive with the beef is a *garniture forestière*, fresh onions and carrots tossed with sautéed fresh mushrooms. Noodles or rice go beautifully, as would *Pommes Anna*, that marvelously fattening cake of sliced potatoes baked in butter, crisp and brown on the outside, tender and buttery inside; the recipe is both in *Mastering*, Volume II, and in *The French Chef Cookbook*. You will want a full-bodied red wine, like a Burgundy, Châteauneuf, or Pinot Noir.

Boeuf à la mode; boeuf en daube

———◆———

WHOLE PIECE OF
BEEF BRAISED
IN RED WINE

For 8 to 10 people

Larding and marinating the beef

*A 7- to 8-lb. piece of trimmed and boneless braising
    beef, as evenly shaped a rectangle or cylinder
    as possible, around 5½ inches in diameter
    (see beef-cut suggestions preceding recipe)*
*Optional: A sheet of larding fat about 4 by 8 inches
    and ¼-inch thick (fresh pork fatback,
    pork loin-roast fat, or fat salt pork blanched
    5 minutes, or beef suet)*
¼ cup olive oil or peanut oil
*1 bottle (about 1 quart) full-bodied young
    red wine (Mâcon, Beaujolais, Mountain Red)*
4 to 6 large cloves garlic, unpeeled, chopped

1 cup each sliced onions and sliced carrots
1 Tb salt
Tied in washed cheesecloth: 2 imported bay
leaves, 4 whole cloves, 6 peppercorns,
½ tsp each of fennel seeds, thyme, dried
orange peel

For braising the beef
Olive oil or peanut oil
4 ounces lardons (fresh fat-and-lean pork
shoulder cut into 1-inch strips ¼ inch across;
or salt pork, blanched 5 minutes in
simmering water)
⅓ cup flour
For additional flavor: 1 quart or about 2 lbs. sawed
beef and veal bones browned in a hot oven;
a 6-inch square pork rind, blanched
5 minutes
Useful: barding fat (an additional sheet, or strips,
of fat to tie over the beef and baste the meat
as it cooks)
3 or 4 medium-sized tomatoes, washed,
unpeeled, chopped
2 or more cups beef stock or bouillon

Larding and marinating the beef: *2 to 6 days.*

If you have a choice of larding needles, buy the one with the longest blade, such as in the left-hand illustration, where it is 12 inches. Needle at center has a hinged point and removable handle; you push it through the meat, and then pull it out using hinged point as a handle. Always cut fat into strips just the size to make a snug fit into the metal trough of the *lardoir*—French name for larding needle.

Always lard a roast going in the direction of the grain, because you will be slicing across the grain and want a pattern in each slice. Using a gentle clockwise and counter-clockwise rotating movement to hold fat in place, push needle through meat from one end to the other. If fat was a snug fit, it will remain in the trough of the needle.

Loosen fat strip from point of needle on far side of meat.

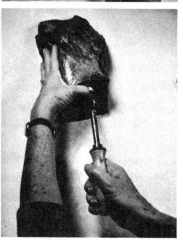

Loosen fat from handle end of needle also, then hold fat in place with your thumb as you slowly draw the needle out, rotating it slowly back and forth to hold fat in meat. For a roast 4½ to 5 inches in diameter, 3 or 4 larding strips are all you need—or can manage.

Lay the raw roast in an enameled, porcelain, or stainless container (an oval casserole is perfect here), pour over it the oil and the wine, and strew over and around it the garlic and vegetables. Sprinkle on the salt, and bury the herb packet in the surrounding liquid. Cover and re-frigerate, turning and basting several times a day for 2 to 3 days, or up to 5 or 6 days. Before proceeding to next step, drain the meat and dry thoroughly in paper towels, then with white kitchen string, tie the roast, forcing it into as cylindrical a shape as possible. Strain the marinade, re-serving both solids and liquid. Wash and dry the casserole (if you used one).

Preliminaries to braising. Preheat the broiler. Choose a heavy casserole or covered roaster just large enough to hold the meat comfortably; film it with ⅛ inch of oil, stir in the *lardons,* and sauté until lightly browned. Then add the vegetables and the herbs (in their cheesecloth) from the marinade—or fresh vegetables, if you have not marinated the meat—and sauté to brown lightly. Meanwhile, place the meat on the rack of a broiler pan, baste with oil, and brown slowly under the broiler, turning and basting every 4 to 5 minutes—about 15–20 minutes until meat is nicely browned all over. When vegetables in casserole are lightly browned, blend in the flour and stir over moderately low heat fairly continuously (but keep your eye on meat under broiler as well, and remove it when evenly browned). Cook the flour slowly to an even dark walnut-brown, 10 minutes or so, then remove from heat. Beat in the marinade liquid by driblets to blend smoothly; bring to the simmer, stirring; remove again from heat. When meat has browned, and as soon as you can handle it, tie the barding fat around it with white string. Lay it in the casserole and sur-round it with the optional browned bones and pork rind. Add the toma-toes, and pour around enough stock or bouillon to come three quarters the way up the meat.

✿ May be prepared a day in advance to this point; when cool, cover and refrigerate.

Braising the beef: *3 to 4 hours.* Preheat oven to 350 degrees. Bring casse-role to the simmer on top of the stove, drape a sheet of aluminum foil over the meat, cover the casserole, and set it in lower-middle level of pre-heated oven. In about 30 minutes baste the meat with the cooking liquid, and regulate oven so liquid is very slowly simmering, and remains so throughout cooking. Baste and turn the meat several times during this period. Beef is done when a fork pierces it quite easily: it should be tender but hold its shape nicely for slicing.

Finishing the beef. When the meat is done, remove to a platter and dis-card trussing strings and barding fat. Drain contents of casserole through a colander or sieve into a saucepan, pressing juices out of residue. Skim surface fat off braising sauce as you bring it to the simmer. Carefully correct seasoning. Sauce should be thick enough to coat a spoon nicely— boil down rapidly if too thin; add a little beef stock if too thick.

☼ If you are not ready to serve, return meat and sauce to casserole, set cover askew, and keep warm over simmering water or on an electric warming device. (Or you may slice the meat, arrange in an ovenproof platter, spoon the sauce over, cover and refrigerate; reheat slowly, basting, when you are ready to serve.)

To serve. Either arrange the meat on a platter, glaze with a bit of the sauce, garnish with whatever vegetables you have chosen, and have it carved in front of your guests; or carve it in the kitchen, arrange on a platter with a little glazing of sauce, and a decoration of parsley sprigs or vegetables. Pass the rest of the sauce in a warm bowl.

ADDITIONS AND VARIATIONS

Sauce and fat-free talk. The preceding *Boeuf à la Mode* is a fairly standard version of the dish, but, as with a beef stew, you can approach it in many moods. Here you browned flour along with the aromatic braising vegetables, giving you a ready-made sauce at the end of the cooking; except for skimming and final flavoring, you have nothing more to do with it. However, you may prefer the sauce for the beef stew, on page 260, where the simmering liquid does not become a sauce until after cooking; in this method you can be sure of removing every trace of fat before thickening the liquid with *beurre manié* (flour-butter paste). Or stir 3 to 4 tablespoons of cornstarch or potato starch to a paste with wine or stock, beat into the braising liquid, then simmer several minutes until cooked and thickened, and you have no fat at all.

Vegetable additions. You may wish a vegetable garnish to finish cooking with the meat; in this case see the suggestions at the end of the beef stew recipe on page 263.

For cold braised beef. Omit the flour thickening altogether, braising the beef simply in liquids and aromatic vegetables; turn cooking stock into an aspic, following the directions on page 447. You can then make an elegant dish with a layer of aspic on the bottom of your platter, carefully sliced pieces of beef, separately decorated and glazed, laid upon it, a decoration of vegetables equally glazed, and chopped aspic all around.

Braised stuffed flank steak. Get yourself a 2-pound trimmed flank steak, slit a pocket in one side, and fill it with a stuffing. Skewer the pocket closed, and proceed to brown and then braise the flank steak according to the directions for braised beef (but using probably only half the braising ingredients called for). The last stuffed flank I did took about 2 hours to braise, served 6 people nicely, and I used the following stuffing:

> *For 2 cups: ½ lb. (1 cup) lean ground beef; ¼ cup*
> *each—minced boiled ham, chopped black olives,*
> *pine nuts, freshly grated Parmesan or Swiss*
> *cheese; 1 egg; ½ tsp thyme or mixed herbs;*
> *2 cloves garlic, puréed; ½ tsp salt and*
> *a big pinch of pepper.*

Braised beef tongue, braised beef heart, braised beef liver. Follow the same general system for all of these. For tongue, boil it an hour or so first, so that you can peel it, then proceed to the braising. Whole beef heart wants stuffing, I think; use the preceding ground beef mixture, substituting veal for beef if you wish, or, if you have leftover roast meat or poultry, see the mixture for the stuffed cabbage on page 324; other suggestions are listed in the index under Stuffings. Whole beef liver needs no stuffing, but it should be larded like the beef pot roast, page 267, and tied in strips of fat for cooking.

Boiled beef—pot-au-feu

Every culture has its boiled meat dinner, from New England to Vienna, from Russian borsch to Mexican and Spanish *pucheros,* Irish stew, Italian *bollito misto,* and the French *pot-au-feu.* After all, it is the way the world of cooking began as soon as pots were invented to hang over the fire. The advantage of all these national recipes is that they are easy to do, they use the cheapest cuts of meat, and you end up literally with a whole dinner in your pot. There is the rich and beautiful bouillon from the boiling that you may begin the meal with or save for other soups and for the concoction of the best kind of brown sauces. Your main course is a platter of tender meat surrounded by as large a variety of vegetables as your heart desires. Not the least of your joys is the wonderfully appetizing aroma of that boiled dinner filling your kitchen.

BEEF CUTS FOR BOILING. A boiled dinner is not boiled, of course; this is a culinary poesy. It is cooked at a slow bubble, a quiet simmer, and you will get much the best results all around with a beef stock boiled up in advance. If you've no stock you simmer your beef in water, and why do that when a stock is so very simple to make?

The beef itself should have some veins of fat with the lean, and a bit of gristle; these give character to boiled meat as well as body and texture to the bouillon. Here are some suggestions, and others are on the chart, page 650.

Heel of the round, short ribs, and center cuts from the *foreshank* are all fine for boiling, and Jewish butchers are particularly adept at providing excellent cuts from the chuck, including *neck pot roast* and *flanken* (chuck ribs). Supermarket-packaged *boneless chuck* pot roast and *blade* pot roasts are other possibilities. Boiled *brisket* of beef is a favorite of many; single brisket with 1 layer of meat should be rolled and tied; double brisket with 2 layers should also be tied, but separate the layers before slicing because their grains run in opposite directions. (My favorite cuts of the moment are neck, short ribs, and brisket.)

TIMING. Please remember that this is long, slow, almost effortless cooking; you go on about your other business, and the *Pot-au-feu* will take care of itself. The beef will take from 2 to 4 hours to cook, depending on the cut and the grade of beef. Unless you know from your own experience, it is wise to allow the full 4 hours, since you can stop the cooking when the meat is done, it will stay warm for 30 to 40 minutes at least, and it can be kept warm if need be. The vegetables take 30 to 40 minutes at least, and can be done somewhat ahead. The beef stock to begin with, which I most highly recommend to you, takes around 5 hours or more, but it can be done the day before—or weeks before and kept in the freezer.

THE VEGETABLE GARNISH. Although it is traditional and easy to cook the vegetables along with the beef, adding them at appropriate times according to how long each takes, I do think this system too often produces a miserable crop of faded inedibles. I like my vegetables fresh and fine, just cooked to a turn, a pleasure to look at, and a delight to eat. I therefore suggest that they be done separately, and that their juices then be combined with a bit of the bouillon just before serving.

SERVING SUGGESTIONS. The recipe here suggests turnips, parsnips, small onions, carrots, cabbage, and potatoes. These are the usual accompaniments, but there is no reason you could not include a tomato *fondue,* for instance (cooked fresh tomato pulp with herbs), or beets, or broccoli, or fresh green peas, leeks, celery, or, in fact, anything you like. You might also want coarse salt and sour French pickles, or horseradish sauce, or the mustard and cream sauce suggested at the end of this recipe. Serve a good loaf of French bread, and a simple red wine such as a Beaujolais, Chianti, or friendly jug. As for the entire menu, if you don't precede the *Pot-au-feu* with its bouillon, you could start with oysters, clams, or a crab or lobster tidbit in mayonnaise, and you could end with a fruit tart, ice cream, sherbet, a great chocolate dessert, or that delectable puff pastry creation, *Le Pithiviers*.

Pot-au-feu

FRENCH-STYLE
BOILED BEEF AND
VEGETABLE DINNER

For 8 people

For the beef stock

2 or more quarts or about 2 lbs. sawed beef bones including knuckles and some bones with bits of raw meat attached (you may also include veal and poultry bones and scraps, raw or cooked)
3 large carrots, scrubbed and roughly sliced
3 large onions, roughly sliced
Sufficient cold water to cover ingredients by 4 inches
1 large washed leek (or another onion)
3 celery ribs with leaves, washed
1 Tb coarse salt (or table salt)
1 large herb bouquet tied in cheesecloth:
8 parsley sprigs, 1 large imported bay leaf, 1 tsp thyme, 4 whole cloves or allspice berries, and 3 large cloves of garlic unpeeled but roughly chopped

The beef

About 5 lbs. boneless meat (or sufficient bone-in meat) either in 1 piece or several different cuts, from the suggestions preceding the recipe
White kitchen string

The vegetable garnish

Young white turnips, parsnips, and fresh young carrots, peeled and quartered
Small fresh white onions, peeled, and a ⅜-inch cross pierced in each root end

1 head of cabbage, the crinkle-leafed Savoy suggested
Potatoes, peeled and boiled or steamed in time for serving
Chopped fresh parsley

Simple brown beef stock: *about 5 hours.* The first step here is to brown the bones and vegetables so that they, in turn, will brown the stock. To do so, preheat oven to 450 degrees. Spread the sawed bones and scraps (except poultry bones and scraps) in a roasting pan, strew around them half of the sliced carrots and onions, and set in upper-middle level of oven. Turn and baste several times with accumulated fat in pan until nicely browned—30 to 40 minutes. Transfer the bones and vegetables to a large soup kettle, leaving fat in pan. Discard fat, and deglaze roasting pan (add a cup of water to it, set over heat, scrape up coagulated browning juices), and pour into kettle. Add rest of water to kettle along with the remaining onions and carrots, the leek, celery, salt, and herb packet and optional poultry bones. Bring to the simmer, skim off gray scum that will continue to rise for 5 minutes or so. Then cover partially, and let simmer slowly 4 to 5 hours. Add more water if liquid evaporates to expose ingredients; then, if you are continuing with the recipe, simply add the beef to the pot in the next step.

☼ If you are making the stock in advance, however, strain it into a large bowl, refrigerate, and remove congealed fat from surface when stock has chilled; you may then bottle the stock and freeze it. Bring to the simmer in a kettle before proceeding.

Simmering the beef. When you are ready to cook the beef, tie it securely with white string so it will keep its shape, and plunge it into the simmering stock. Let simmer, covered with liquid (add water if need be) until meat is tender when pierced with a fork—2 to 4 hours, depending on grade and cut of meat. Cut off a little piece if you're not sure, and eat it: the meat should be pleasantly tender and chewable, yet hold its shape. When cooking several cuts, like short ribs, shank, and shoulder, some may be done before others; remove these to a bowl or pan, cover with a bit of stock from the pot, and return to reheat with the rest for serving.

☼ If you are not ready to serve, let meat keep warm in the pot, reheating gently if necessary. As long as the stock is at around 120 degrees the meat cannot overcook. (*Warning:* Unless it is actually cooking, never cover a warm pot airtight. Always set cover askew for air circulation or the contents will sour and begin to ferment; cover only when cold.)

The vegetable garnish. (Prepare these while the beef is simmering.) The turnips and parsnips cook together: simmer them in a covered saucepan with ½ inch of bouillon from the *Pot-au-feu* about 15 minutes, or until just tender; set aside, and reheat just before serving. Cook the carrots and onions together in a covered saucepan, using the same system; they will take about 30 minutes. Cut the cabbage into wedges, remove core, and place wedges curved side down in a vegetable steamer, colander, or sieve set over a saucepan with 1½ inches of bouillon from the pot; baste the cabbage with more bouillon, season with salt and pepper, cover tightly and steam about 15 minutes, only until just tender; reheat just before serving.

Serving the Pot-au-feu. If the beef has just finished cooking, let it rest in the pot 10 to 15 minutes to make carving easier; if you have kept it warm you may carve immediately. Remove strings, and slice the meat into attractive pieces; often a bias cut will make handsomer slices; arrange them on a hot platter. Place the hot vegetables around the meat, using an extra platter if you are crowding things. Meanwhile combine the vegetable cooking juices into one pan, add degreased cooking stock to make about 4 cups, heat to the simmer; finally spoon half a cup or so over meat and vegetables. Pour the rest of the stock into a warm bowl, decorate platter with parsley, and serve.

Sauce crème à la moutarde

———◆———

CREAM AND
MUSTARD
SAUCE FOR
BOILED BEEF

For about 2 cups,
serving 6 to 8

2 cups bouillon from the Pot-au-feu, page 273, thoroughly degreased
2 Tb strong Dijon-type prepared mustard
1½ cups heavy cream
1½ Tb potato starch or cornstarch blended with ¼ cup dry white French Vermouth
Salt, pepper, and a tablespoon or so fresh minced parsley or mixed green herbs

Boil the bouillon rapidly in a saucepan until reduced by half. Meanwhile blend the mustard with a bit of the cream, then all of it, and stir into the reduced stock. Boil slowly to reduce by about a third; remove from heat and blend in starch mixture; simmer for 2 to 3 minutes. Sauce should be lightly thickened. Taste carefully for seasoning, adding salt and pepper as needed. Set aside, and reheat just before serving; then blend in the herbs, and pour into a warm sauce bowl.

ADDITIONS AND VARIATIONS

Beef is, of course, not the only meat for a boiled dinner. Using the same general method, you can boil a whole stewing hen, trussed and stuffed, thus making the French *Poule-au-pot,* so beloved of King Henry IV that he vowed during his reign that every Frenchman should have a chicken in his pot. (I wonder how far he succeeded in this worthy project, and was it to be only 1 chicken once, or 1 chicken once a week?) Shoulder of pork, boned and rolled shoulder of veal, homemade or store-bought French or Italian or Polish cooking-type sausages can all go into the pot along with the beef and/or chicken, making a *Potée,* or mixed bag. We did this in the old black-and-white television days and called it "Dinner in a Pot," and the recipe appears as well in *Mastering,* Volume I. However, you don't really need more of a recipe than the preceding *Pot-au-feu* to make up your own combinations.

Beef tongue boiled dinner. Use the same system for fresh or smoked beef tongue. With either one, blanch it first—10 minutes of simmering in water to cover; rinse and wash in cold water. Then into the *Pot-au-feu,* following the master recipe. I recently did a smoked tongue weighing 4 pounds, and it took about 2 hours to cook tender. I then peeled and trimmed it, and kept it warm in the pot until I was ready to serve. It was delicious accompanied by lentils and a dish of fresh broccoli flowerets blanched 2 minutes, then sautéed in olive oil and garlic. (Everything you need to know about preparing fresh beef tongue, incidentally, is in both *Mastering,* Volume II, and *The French Chef Cookbook.*)

Corned brisket of beef in Pot-au-feu. Corned beef, with its special flavor, can be substituted for fresh beef in the *Pot-au-feu* recipe. However, I like to give store-bought corned brisket a 4- to 5-hour soak in several changes of cold water, just to be sure it won't be too salty; soaking removes none of the flavor, just excess salt. The mustard and cream sauce on page 275 is delicious with corned beef, and you might stir into it a spoonful of prepared horseradish and a few capers, along with the green herbs. (As this book was going to press, I began seeing "mild cured" corned beef at our supermarkets, and I tried some. It needs no presoaking, in fact it needs no boiling at all; you can cover-roast it. Although it cooks up nicely in a *Pot-au-feu,* I don't think it has nearly the interesting taste of the old-fashioned salty cure.)

New England boiled dinner. This is made like a *Pot-au-feu* either with corned beef or with fresh beef (often the shin), and tradition calls for boiled beets on the side. No sauce is also traditional, which seems a pity. For those serious about this classic recipe, I recommend John J. Pullen's hilariously pseudo-scholarly treatise, *The Transcendental Boiled Dinner* (New York: Lippincott, 1972).

Beef tenderloin, filet de boeuf, beef fillet

Whatever you call it, including *filet de boeuf,* the beef tenderloin is the tenderest and most luxurious part of the animal. And whether or not you can afford one at the moment, when that great day arrives you will want to know exactly what to do with it. Although we have braised and stuffed tenderloin in Volume I of *Mastering,* one version of Beef Wellington in *The French Chef Cookbook* and another in Volume II of *Mastering,* we have never roasted one. This is the easiest of all: just a simple roast tenderloin, rare and rosy, cut into rather thick slices, and accompanied with a truffled brown Madeira sauce.

Although it is the most expensive cut of beef, tenderloin has the least flavor since it is an inside muscle from the small of the back. Therefore, if you've the time, I think a marinade in wine and aromatic ingredients does a great deal for it; even 2 hours will help, although 24 are more effective. (Since it is tender meat, the marinade acts more quickly than with braising cuts.) The marinade then serves to deglaze the roasting pan and goes into the accompanying sauce. Again, if you have time, a long-simmered brown sauce is delicious with the beef, garnished, if you are feeling flush, with diced truffles, or, if not, with a little mushroom *duxelles.* You'll find the sauce at the end of the beef recipe.

NOTES ON TIMING FOR BEEF TENDERLOIN. A trimmed tenderloin of beef, whatever its weight and length, always has about the same diameter, and always takes 35 to 45 minutes of roasting to reach an internal temperature of around 125 degrees; it then needs 15 to 20 minutes out of the oven for the meat tissues to reabsorb their juices before carving. You can therefore and with perfect confidence put the meat into an accurately controlled 400-degree oven 45 minutes before you plan to serve dinner, check again after 35 minutes, then take it out of the oven as you bring in your first course, and it is ready to carve and serve on schedule. On the other hand, and again if you have a reliable oven (or controlled warming oven), you may roast it somewhat ahead, let it cool 20 minutes while you turn off the roasting oven and open its door, then return meat to oven and set the thermostat at 120 degrees. The beef cannot overcook because your tested and reliable oven is thermostatically sure and cannot go over 120 degrees. This system applies to all roasts, and I think most of them are tenderer anyway when they are allowed to sit and commune for half an hour or more with their own inner juices.

BUYING AND TRIMMING A TENDERLOIN. Some years ago I got a letter from a woman who said she was so disappointed in our *Filet de Boeuf, Prince Albert*. She was doing it for a big party, and it was inedible; it was tough, she said. Then she wrote down all the prices she had paid for things—looking at them now they seem so reasonable! She had more than doubled the recipe, she said, and had bought a ready-to-roast 8-pound tenderloin that cost her $12.52. It was immediately clear, of course, what had happened. No trimmed tenderloin weighs as much as 8 pounds, and even if it did—and even in those days—it would have cost her close to $30.00. The poor dear had obviously bought herself an eye of the round, which is stylishly shaped like a tenderloin, but is a tough braising cut. *Caveat emptor*, in other words; know your meat and know your butcher.

Actually, you can save money and garner yourself some useful extra meat if you trim the whole tenderloin yourself. A whole one is about 23 inches long, weighs 8 to 9 pounds untrimmed, and 4½ to 5 pounds fully trimmed. It includes the tail, or *filet mignon*, which rests against the thirteenth rib and constitutes the tenderloin part of a T-bone steak; it also includes the heart of the tenderloin, which, if cut into steaks, would be the tenderest round of meat on one side of the lofty Porterhouse. Finally there is the butt end, which rests against the hip bone, and, again, if cut into steaks, would be part of the sirloin. Some markets do not include the butt end, only the heart and tail, and don't even know what you're talking about when you speak of the butt. Anyway, whether it is whole or not, remove loose surface fat on one side and the membrane covering that lies underneath it; leave on the side strap of meat that runs the length of the tenderloin and is attached to it by a line of fat. After you cut a roast about 10 inches long from the central portion of a whole tenderloin, you will get a steak or two from the butt end, and, from the tail, delicious beef for brochettes or a sauté, as described on page 284. If you want to roast a whole tenderloin, fold about 4 inches of the tail back against the meat to make a roast of even circumference, and tie in place with loops of white string.

SERVING SUGGESTIONS. You will want something colorful to arrange around a platter of roast tenderloin, such as braised lettuce or celery hearts, fresh green beans or peas, nicely trimmed fresh potatoes sautéed in butter, or rosettes of potatoes Duchesse, and baked or stuffed tomatoes. A fine red Bordeaux from the Médoc or Graves districts, or an exceptionally good Cabernet Sauvignon, could be your choice in wine. You might precede the roast with stuffed artichoke hearts topped with a *Sauce Béarnaise,* as we did on our television "Sit-down Dinner Party," and you could follow with the meringue and ice cream dessert colorfully decorated with glazed fruits poached in wine on page 512.

Filet de boeuf rôti, sauce périgueux

————◆————

ROAST TENDERLOIN
OF BEEF, BROWN
MADEIRA SAUCE
WITH TRUFFLES

For 6 to 8 people

For the marinade
A 3-lb. tenderloin of beef (fully trimmed weight)
1 cup excellent dry white wine, such as Mâcon or
*   Pinot Blanc, or ⅔ cup dry white*
*   French Vermouth*
¼ cup Cognac or Armagnac
Either: A 1-ounce can of truffles or truffle
*   pieces, and the juice from the can (Sauce*
*   Périgueux must have truffles)*
Or: 4 to 6 fresh mushrooms for later use
2 Tb light olive oil or fresh peanut oil
1 tsp salt
6 peppercorns
1 small clove of garlic, minced
1 imported bay leaf
¼ tsp thyme and/or basil
2 Tb minced shallots or scallions

For roasting the beef and making the final sauce
About 6 Tb soft butter (some for rubbing on
*   roast; some for final sauce)*
Sufficient strips of fresh pork fat or beef suet
*   to tie around beef (fat from a roast of pork*
*   or beef; or strips of top-quality salt pork*
*   blanched 5 minutes in simmering water)*
1 each: roughly sliced carrot and onion
¼ cup dry (Sercial) Madeira
2 cups excellent brown sauce (see recipe following)
Salt and pepper

Marinating the beef: *2 to 24 hours.* Place the beef in a stainless or enameled bowl or casserole (an oval enameled iron casserole is perfect for this). Add all the marinade ingredients, baste the meat well, cover, and refrigerate. Turn and baste the meat several times, until you are ready to prepare the beef for roasting. (An extra day or two of marinating will not harm the meat.)

Preparing meat for roasting. Preheat oven to 400 degrees 15 to 20 minutes before you plan to roast. Drain the meat, reserving the marinade, and dry thoroughly in paper towels, then rub with 2 tablespoons of the soft butter. Lay fat strips lengthwise over the beef (they do not have to cover it completely), and tie in place with loops of white string—these will also hold the beef in shape during its roasting. Set the meat in a shallow oval or rectangular roasting dish just large enough to hold it easily, and strew the sliced onion and carrot around it.

✿ Beef may be prepared for roasting several hours in advance; cover and refrigerate. Leave at room temperature an hour before roasting unless kitchen is very hot: chilled meat will take a little longer to roast than room-temperature meat.

Roasting: *35 to 45 minutes at 400 degrees. The roasted tenderloin also needs 15 to 20 minutes of rest after it is done.* Roast in upper-middle level of preheated oven, turning and basting the beef 2 or 3 times with the fat that accumulates in the pan. The tenderloin is done at an internal meat thermometer reading of 125 degrees, for rosy rare; immediately remove from oven when this degree is reached. (If you have no thermometer, the meat will be just slightly resistant to the pressure of your finger, in contrast to its squashy raw feel; for most tastes, it is better to serve a tenderloin slightly too rare than slightly overcooked.)

The sauce. While the meat is roasting or beforehand, remove truffles from marinade, if you have used them, dice into ⅛-inch pieces, and place in a small covered jar with the Madeira (if you are not using truffles, set Madeira aside; mince and sauté 4 to 6 medium-sized mushrooms and stir into sauce during its final simmering). Boil down the marinade rapidly until you have barely ¼ cup, and reserve. When beef is done, skim fat out of roasting dish and deglaze with marinade (pour it in, scrape up coagulated roasting juices into liquid) and strain back into marinade pan, pressing juices out of carrots and onions. Add 1½ to 2 cups of the brown sauce (see end of recipe), and the Madeira, and either the truffles or the sautéed minced mushrooms. Simmer a moment; carefully correct seasoning, and set aside. Bring to the simmer just before serving, remove from heat, and stir in several spoonfuls of the soft butter, a tablespoon at a time.

Serving. After meat has rested 15 to 20 minutes, it is ready to be carved either at the table or in the kitchen; remove trussing strings and covering fat. If it is to be carved at the table, glaze with a spoonful or so of the sauce, and decorate hot platter with vegetables, watercress, or parsley. For carving in the kitchen, have a lightly buttered warm platter, and spoon a little of the sauce down the middle. Rapidly cut the beef into slightly bias slices (slanting from top to bottom, so they will look bigger), making them ¾ to 1 inch thick. Place the slices slightly overlapping each other over the ribbon of sauce. Arrange the garnishing vegetables attractively around the meat, and if you have braised celery or lettuce, glaze with a little of the sauce. Serve immediately, accompanied by the rest of the sauce in a warm bowl.

☼ See *Notes on timing* preceding the recipe, page 277, for ahead-of-time suggestions.

Brown sauce

In the old days of *la grande cuisine* no great house or restaurant was without its brown sauces in various stages of preparation, from the *Pot-au-feu* providing the rich brown meat stock that went into the preliminary *Sauce Espagnole* to the final and perfect basic brown sauce, the *Demi-Glace,* that culminated several days of simmering. You must go through every motion if it is to be called a *Demi-Glace,* and no fudging; this is all so carefully described by Escoffier that it would be foolish for any other mortal to attempt a duplication. So what are the alternatives? A number of contemporary chefs in France, who profess to scorn brown *roux* (flour and butter) and other starchy sauce thickeners, have taken to blending a strongly reduced and concentrated meat stock into the deglazing liquid of their roasts, and then thickening it with a liaison of butter. When made for a roast chicken or a sauté, where the sauce is light and the amount a bare spoonful per serving, this is delicious and desirable, but for larger amounts a strong reduction of basic stock can become so powerful and heavy that it drowns out whatever accompanies it. Far better, to my mind, when you need a large amount of sauce for a big roast or a braise, is to make either the rapid *Jus Lié* (deglazing or braising liquid thickened with starch or arrowroot) or the following brown sauce. This is a mock *Demi-Glace*, and it can be very good indeed when you give it the simmering time and hovering-over attention it needs. However, all of these remarks are for you, chef, to ponder, since your own opinions and experiences should be your guide.

Semi demi-glace; sauce brune

This sauce can be used for roasts of meat and poultry, sautés and steaks, braised meats, and braised vegetables. It is a splendid sauce to have on hand, and it freezes perfectly—but you must simmer it a long time before it develops its full flavor.

MOCK DEMI-GLACE; BASIC BROWN SAUCE

For about 4 cups

Cooking time: 4 to 6 hours or more

4 ounces (1 stick) butter, clarified (melted butter; clear yellow liquid poured off milky residue)

4 Tb flour

Ingredients for a mirepoix (⅓ cup each: finely diced carrot, onion, and celery and 3 Tb finely diced boiled ham)

8 or more cups hot beef stock or bouillon (preferably of your own make, like the bouillon from a Pot-au-feu, page 273)

2 medium-sized ripe red tomatoes, or 2 Tb tomato paste

A medium herb bouquet (3 or 4 parsley sprigs, ½ imported bay leaf, and ¼ tsp thyme, tied together in washed cheesecloth)

Make a brown *roux* as follows: blend 4 tablespoons of the clarified butter with the 4 tablespoons of flour in a heavy-bottomed 2-quart saucepan, and stir fairly continuously with a wooden spatula or spoon over moderately low heat for 8 to 10 minutes or more, until flour slowly turns an even dark walnut brown. Meanwhile, cook the *mirepoix* ingredients in 2 to 3 tablespoons of the clarified butter in a separate pan, until tender and lightly browned. (For this sauce I have found it better to cook the flour and the vegetables separately: it is very important that the flour be slowly and evenly browned, which it does best by itself.) When the flour is browned, remove pan from heat, let cool a moment or two, and beat in 6 cups of stock with a wire whip. If you are using fresh tomatoes, simply slice roughly and add, as is, to the pan; for tomato paste, whip it into the stock. Scrape in the *mirepoix,* deglazing pan with a bit of stock, add the herb bouquet, and bring to the simmer.

Simmer very slowly, partially covered, for 4 hours or more. Skim off scum at first, then fat, and finally the fatty skin that will collect on top of the sauce after an hour or so of simmering. Add more liquid if sauce reduces and thickens too much—it should be the consistency of a light cream soup; if taste is getting too strong, thin with water rather than stock. How long to simmer? Until it has a lovely smooth velvety-rich taste, and that final judgment is yours alone.

Finally strain the sauce, pressing juices out of ingredients, degrease it, and let it cool. Chill, remove coagulated fat from surface, and sauce is ready to use.

☼ May be bottled and frozen.

How to use semi demi-glace. After you have roasted your meat, as in the preceding tenderloin recipe, or sautéed or pan-fried chicken, steak, or veal scallops for instance, spoon excess fat out of meat-cooking pan. If there are no other flavorings in the pan (like roasted sliced carrots and onions), add 1 or 2 minced shallots or scallions, cook a moment, then deglaze the pan with dry white wine, or dry Madeira or Port (pour in the wine, scrape into it all the coagulated cooking juices), boil down rapidly until syrupy. Then pour in as much *Semi Demi-Glace* brown sauce as you think you need (for a roast of beef or pork serving 8 people, you will want 1½ to 2 cups; for a sauté of chicken or steak serving 4 people, ½ to ⅔ cup). Then strain into a saucepan, and add whatever else your recipe calls for, such as minced truffles, sautéed mushrooms, little braised onions, or whatever. Simmer a moment to blend flavors, and set aside. Reheat before serving; remove from heat and gradually beat in a spoonful or more of soft butter to smooth and enrich the sauce.

Semi demi-glace with heavy cream. In the preceding recipe, use half brown sauce and half heavy cream, simmering enough to thicken the sauce lightly. This goes nicely with pork, turkey, and veal.

Sautés and brochettes of beef tenderloin

When you are trimming your own whole tenderloin, as described on page 278, you will have some marvelous bits of meat left over that you can save for another meal. There will be the side strip, that chain of

meat that ran the length of the tenderloin, and which you may have removed; there will also be pieces of tail and of butt. Cut these into 1- to
1½-inch cubes for brochettes, or into larger pieces for a sauté. Save any
small scraps for the making of a fine brown sauce, like the preceding
Semi Demi-Glace (add them to brown with the *mirepoix* vegetables and
they will simmer with the sauce, giving it even better flavor). If you are
not to cook the meat now, wrap and freeze it.

Mignons de filet de boeuf, sautés Madère

CUBED TENDERLOIN
SAUTÉED IN
BUTTER,
BROWN MADEIRA
SAUCE

One reason for the elevated prices in all the luxury
beef cuts is that you can cook them so quickly and
luxuriously, and with such little fuss. Here is the
basic recipe, with variations at the end.

Since you will usually reserve your tenderloin
for a quick but elegant meal, you will want to
serve it with an easy accompaniment such as rice
or noodles, fresh green beans or peas or broccoli,
and perhaps broiled or baked tomatoes. Any of
the fine red Bordeaux wines would be appropriate,
or one of the lighter Burgundies, or a Cabernet
Sauvignon.

For 4 people

*1 to 1½ lbs. (2 to 3 cups) trimmed tenderloin cut
    into 1½- to 2-inch pieces
2 Tb butter and 1 Tb olive oil
2 Tb minced shallots or scallions
½ cup dry white wine, or ⅓ cup dry white
    French Vermouth
Either: ½ cup excellent beef bouillon and 1 to
    1½ cups Semi Demi-Glace brown sauce
    (preceding recipe)
Or: 1½ cups excellent beef bouillon and 2 Tb
    cornstarch dissolved in ¼ cup additional
    bouillon
Flavor additions as needed: a pinch of thyme,
    an imported bay leaf, 2 Tb minced mushroom
    stems or 1 to 2 tsp mushroom duxelles or
    mirepoix vegetables (you may have some in*

*your freezer) , 1 tsp or so tomato paste or
leftover fresh tomato sauce*
⅓ cup dry (Sercial) Madeira
Salt and pepper
2 Tb soft butter

Dry the meat on paper towels. Heat butter and oil in a heavy frying pan (I like a heavy-duty no-stick pan for this kind of cooking) large enough to hold all the meat easily in 1 layer. If you are sautéing a large quantity use 2 pans or sauté in several batches. When butter foam has subsided, add the meat. Let sizzle undisturbed for 30 seconds, then toss it (swirling and shaking pan by its handle), and continue for several minutes until meat is nicely browned on all sides and, when you press it, it has just changed from its squashy raw feel to a very slight springiness —meaning it is rare. Transfer to a side dish and spoon all but a tablespoon of fat out of frying pan. Add the minced shallots or scallions and sauté for a minute; add the wine or Vermouth and reduce to almost nothing. Sauce in either of the following ways:

Either, use your own brown sauce. Add the bouillon and brown sauce. Simmer, stirring and scraping into it all coagulated sauté juices from pan; taste, stir in flavor additions if needed, simmering to incorporate them. Then stir the Madeira into the sauce. Salt and pepper the sautéed beef, and return it to the pan.

Or, use bouillon and cornstarch. Simmer the bouillon in the pan, scraping into it all coagulated sauté juices. Taste, and stir in flavor additions as needed, simmering several minutes in order to incorporate them into the bouillon. Remove from heat and, when bubbling has ceased, blend in the dissolved cornstarch mixture; return over heat, stirring, and simmer 2 minutes. Then stir the Madeira into the sauce. Salt and pepper the sautéed beef, and return it to the pan.

☼ May be done in advance to this point.

Just before serving, bring sauce and meat to under the simmer; fold meat and sauce together for several minutes, only enough to warm it through but not to overcook it—it should remain rare and rosy inside. Fold the butter into the sauce, turn the meat out onto a hot platter, decorate with whatever you have chosen, and serve immediately.

VARIATIONS

Add sautéed mushrooms to the beef: wash and dry them, quarter them, sauté them separately, and add them to the finished sauce to warm up with the meat. Small braised white onions (done as for the *Boeuf Bourguignon* but you may want to omit the pork *lardons,* page 263) are another attractive addition, along with the mushrooms.

OTHER SAUCE IDEAS

After sautéing the beef and removing it, and sautéing the shallots and deglazing with the wine, swish in and reduce to nothing ½ cup of beef bouillon and continue with one of the following:

Cream and mustard. Stir in 1½ cups of *crème fraîche* or heavy cream into which you have blended a tablespoon of Dijon-type prepared mustard. Simmer a moment to blend flavors, then season the beef, and add it to the sauce, and finish as in the master directions.

À la provençale. Stir in 2 cups of fresh tomato pulp (tomatoes peeled, seeded, juiced, and chopped), a small clove of puréed garlic, and a few leaves of fresh chopped basil or a pinch of dried thyme. Fold over heat for several minutes to cook the tomato, then add the beef and finish as in the master directions.

À la bordelaise. Add 2 cups of strong healthy red wine, such as a Mâcon or a Gamay, include an additional ½ cup of beef bouillon, an imported bay leaf, ¼ teaspoon thyme, and a teaspoon of tomato paste; simmer to reduce by half. Correct seasoning and thicken the sauce with a *beurre manié* (1½ teaspoons each flour and butter blended to a paste, beaten into the liquid off heat, then brought to the simmer for ½ minute) Season the beef, fold into the sauce, and warm together just before serving. Instead of butter, fold in, if you have it, a quarter cup or so of poached beef marrow (split raw beef marrow bones and remove marrow; dice or slice with a knife dipped in hot water; bring 2 cups salted water to a boil, remove from heat, drop in marrow and poach 3 minutes or until soft, remove with a slotted spoon and add to sauce). Also fold in 2 tablespoons of fresh chopped parsley. (Sautéed mushrooms and braised onions could also be included here, if you wished.)

Brochettes de filet de boeuf

CUBED TENDERLOIN
ON BROCHETTES

Cubes of beef tenderloin are perfect for skewering either on a barbecue or under the broiler. All remarks on lamb brochettes, including type of skewers, method of broiling, and so on and so forth, apply to beef (see page 293). You can simply season the beef with salt and pepper, baste it with melted butter, and cook it, or you could give it a marinade in herbs, oil, and Cognac—for about 1 pound of cubed beef, ¼ cup of Cognac, 2 tablespoons olive oil, ½ teaspoon of tarragon, and 1 tablespoon of finely minced shallot or scallion, plus salt and pepper. Toss and turn the meat and leave for 30 minutes (or longer), tossing several times. Skewer the meat, baste with melted butter, and then baste with remains of the marinade as it cooks. Serve with rice or risotto, or sautéed potatoes, or your own home-fried or souffléed potatoes, plus a green vegetable like fresh peas or broccoli and perhaps some baked tomatoes Provençal.

Lamb

Roast lamb cooked pinkly rare, the way not only the French like theirs but also a growing number of Americans, makes wonderfully juicy and satisfying eating for all lovers of roast red meat. The saddle, that precious loin area at the small of the back, is easy elegance for a small roast, lamb chops are heavenly, and wonders can be made with the shoulder in the way of braised meat and a variety of stews. In addition, lamb leftovers have much more flavor and interest than cold beef for the making of moussakas, curries, meat loaf, and stuffed eggplant. Yet in some parts of our country, notably in the South and the Middle West, there are those who won't touch lamb at all. Is it because they scorn their old-world beginnings and consider lamb to be peasant food? Is it because they grew up on old gray roasts with thick gravy and mint sauce, or heavy stews reeking of mutton fat? I was fed on gray legs and heavy stews myself, and lamb to me, like fish, was of no great interest until I went to France in the late 1940's. Then I was introduced to my first *gigot d'agneau rôti à point,* and the world changed for me. Those in your family who will have nothing but beef might well begin to change their minds, too, after their first bite of your leg of lamb roasted medium rare; it's a whole new meat, really, and heaven knows we all need variety in our menus. The two volumes of *Mastering,* and *The French Chef Cookbook* abound in lamb recipes; here I shall concern us solely with the easiest way to roast and carve a leg of lamb, some good ideas for leftovers, an excellent recipe for skewered chunks, and a Scotch barley soup for the bones.

TO ROAST AND CARVE A LEG OF LAMB
"Waiting for Gigot"

It was on a flowered terrace at a comfortable and informal restaurant near Saint-Paul-de-Vence that we saw, Paul and I, our first *gigot à la ficelle,* a large leg of lamb hung by a string tied to its shank, slowly revolving in front of a banked-up wood fire. Every once in a while a waiter, going by, would give it a twist to keep it revolving, until it was finally brown and crisp and ready to carve. If you ordered lamb, and few diners could refuse its temptation, Alex, the headwaiter, would bring the whole leg to your table.

He held his *gigot* by the shank, and with his very sharp, long, thin knife, he would begin to carve it into long, wide, thin slices. He cut it lengthwise, starting at the large end, first on the right of the main leg bone, then on the left, and when he had finished one side he turned the leg over and repeated his maneuvers on the other. Watching him, as he moved from table to table, we saw that he carved every scrap of meat off that leg, digging the final unsliceable nuggets out of the hip bone at the end. Having always been taught at home that one must only carve crosswise to the grain, I was shocked in a way, until I tasted the meat; it was deliciously tender and juicy. "Another old wives' tale bites the dust," laughed Paul. He signaled for a second helping, and suggested we ourselves have a leg of lamb the very next time we had anyone for dinner.

Three days later, we had our own *gigot,* but, not having an outdoor set-up like the restaurant, we would oven-roast it. The carving of the lamb particularly interested us, as well as the initial preparation. For years I had fussed around, taking hours with a leg of lamb, either cutting out the hip bone, or boning it entirely except for the shank bone—all to make carving across the grain easier. This time I just cut off extra fat, rubbed the leg all over with oil and a little soy sauce, and popped it into the oven. It was so blissfully easy. Then, after its preliminary browning, I added chopped carrots, onions, and a few garlic cloves to make an aromatic base for my *petit jus de rôti*. Paul carved like a master, to the applause of his guests, and we have never returned to the slow old ways again. If you saw our television show "Waiting for Gigot" that was the very same Alex, who gave us our first lesson in carving on that same flowered terrace at that same restaurant.

CHOOSING THE LAMB. Lamb is a young sheep, less than a year old. Top quality has the purple certificate of grade stamped right on the fat covering the meat—*USDA Choice* or *USDA Prime*. The leg should have a well-rounded, well-muscled look, and the fat should be a firm creamy white; the ankle bones (break joint) should be pink at the tips (with age the ends of the bones turn white). Because of modern raising and feeding methods, a choice fall or winter 7½-pound leg should be just as tender as the 5-pound "genuine spring lamb" that appears around the end of March.

BONE STRUCTURE WHOLE LEG OF LAMB

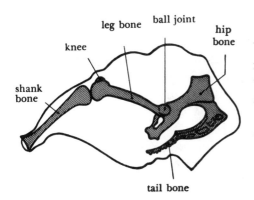

You will need a whole leg of lamb for this recipe, meaning that it will include the hip bone and tail at the large end, the main leg bone (hip to knee), and the lower leg or shank bone (knee to ankle).

Except for removing excess fat and the hock (ankle and foot), the leg is to be left alone: the knee joint is not to be broken open and bent back, in other words, because you want the drama of the whole leg, and you also want the stylish maneuverability of holding onto the shank with one hand while you carve with the other.

TIMING NOTES. To be absolutely safe, put the lamb into the oven 2½ hours before you plan to serve: it will take around 1¼ hours to roast, and it must have a 20-minute rest so that the juices will be reabsorbed into the tissues before carving. A longer wait in the warming oven at 120 degrees seems to make the meat even more delectable, and you can keep it perfectly at that temperature for 2 hours or more with no fear of over-cooking.

SERVING SUGGESTIONS. You might garnish the platter with watercress or parsley and baked tomatoes, and accompany it with *haricots panachés*, fresh green beans tossed in butter surrounding white beans tossed with parsley and butter. A fairly full red wine goes well with lamb, like a Côtes du Rhône, Saint-Émilion, Cabernet Sauvignon.

RARE VERSUS WELL DONE. Lamb roasted to an internal temperature reading of 125 to 130 degrees is pinkly rare; if you have never had pink lamb before, you may wish, as a trial, to roast it to 140 degrees, medium rare. At either stage, again if this is your first time, it will seem like a delicious new kind of meat—if you love rare beef, you will love pink lamb.

Gigot d'agneau rôti

———◆———

ROAST LEG OF
LAMB

A 6½- to 7½-pound
leg serves 10 to 12;
a 5-pound leg, 8

A 5- to 7½-pound leg of lamb (for accurate timing, leave at room temperature at least an hour before roasting)
Optional: 1 or 2 cloves garlic
⅓ cup olive oil or cooking oil
Optional: Soy sauce
Vegetables for roasting pan: ½ cup each chopped onions and carrots; 3 cloves garlic, unpeeled
½ cup dry white wine or dry white French Vermouth
1½ to 2 cups lamb stock or beef bouillon

Preparations for roasting. Preheat oven to 450 degrees. Shave off all but a 1/16-inch layer of fat from top (rounded side) of leg, and sides; dig extra fat out of tail assembly, and shave excess fat off bottom side. For optional garlic flavor, cut cloves into slivers; make small incisions all over lamb with the point of a knife and insert a sliver into each slit.

Massage oil all over surface of lamb. To help it brown, and to give a subtle extra flavor, rub all over with optional soy sauce. Place topside up on rack in pan. If ends overhang, make extensions under them with double folds of aluminum foil. If you are using a thermometer that remains in the meat, insert it so that the point reaches the center of thickest side of solid meat.

✿ May be readied for the oven hours in advance of roasting; refrigerate if wait is longer than an hour or if kitchen is hot.

Roasting. Set lamb in middle level of preheated oven and roast for 15 minutes. Baste with oil, turn oven thermostat down to 350 degrees, and strew the chopped vegetables and garlic in the pan. Whether you have a 5- or a 7½-pound leg, it will take about 1¼ hours, in all, to reach a meat thermometer reading of 125 to 130 degrees—10 minutes or so longer to reach 140 degrees. (If you have no thermometer, a sure indication that you have reached medium rare is when the first meat juices begin to appear in the pan: if you prick the meat, the juices run light pink, and if they run clear yellow, the lamb is well done.)

Finishing and holding the lamb: the sauce. As soon as lamb is done, remove to a board or platter; turn off oven and open oven door. Skim fat out of roasting pan and deglaze pan with the wine (pour it in, set over heat, and scrape coagulated roasting juices into it with a wooden spoon). Transfer ingredients to a saucepan, add stock, and simmer slowly for 20 minutes. Just before serving, reheat, correct seasoning, and strain into a warm sauce bowl, pressing juices out of vegetables; there will be just enough sauce, *jus de rôti,* to moisten each serving of meat.
When lamb has rested 20 minutes it is ready to serve.

✿ Or you may then return it to the roasting pan and set again in the oven; reset thermostat to 120 degrees (or regulate heat by turning oven on to 250 degrees, then off, every 20 minutes or so). Meat will keep perfectly for several hours, as long as its internal temperature never goes over 120 degrees. (Before serving, pour any accumulation of juices into sauce.)

Carving. Furnish yourself with a very sharp long knife, the type used for slicing Virginia ham and smoked salmon. If you like, use a clean towel or napkin, hold the leg by its shank, the large end of the lamb away from you.

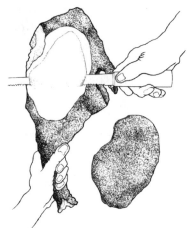

Start the first slice midway between shank and large end, cutting toward you, and holding knife almost parallel to surface of lamb. Cut a long, thin, flat slice, lift it off, arrange on a hot platter, and start the next slice ⅜ inch farther toward the large end.

Continue thus, angling knife to the right side of the lamb as you come down to the large leg bone, and then to the left side. When you come to complications at the hip assembly at the large end, leave that until later. Turn the leg over, and carve the underside in the same manner. Dig out nuggets of meat at large end for second servings, using the tip of your knife.

Lamb on brochettes, kebabs, and skewers

The most delicious lamb brochettes I have ever eaten were at Aïssa Bernard's couscous restaurant near Denfert-Rochereau in Paris, some years ago. The main reason for their delectability was the lamb itself, from the center cut of the leg. Luxurious, yes, but why bother otherwise? Far better to braise in wine and herbs than to skewer tough shoulder and shank pieces, say I. In fact, I find it very useful indeed to have brochette meat on hand in the freezer, and when legs of lamb are on special, I'll buy one. I bone it out, cut several steaks from the big pieces, cut others into 1½-inch brochette size, grind the remainders for burgers or stuffed eggplant, and save the bones for barley soup. Neatly packaged and clearly labeled, they are ready for almost instant defrosting in the microwave oven if I have a quick dinner to get.

You will note that the following skewers contain no onions, cherry tomatoes, or green peppers; although these make a very pretty magazine-cover coffee-table-book type of brochette, they don't work. The lamb needs only a few minutes to cook, onions want half an hour, tomatoes can't take the heat, and peppers remain raw. In other words, everything on the skewer must take the same time, and if you want good eating, use lamb only with a little blanched bacon to baste it as it broils; this makes the best brochette. But first, a word about the skewers themselves.

Skewering Equipment. Directions for skewered meats always sound so easy: "Broil 2 minutes on one side, baste, turn, and broil the other side." Try turning the skewer, however, and unless you have been warned, the skewer turns all right, but the meat stays right where it was: the skewer simply twists around in the hole it has made.

The solutions are several: use flat rather than round skewers—but that means a flat blade about ½ inch wide to be successful and it's a rare skewer that is so shaped. The 2-pronged skewer, lower middle in the illustration, solves the problem; or use 2 skewers. Or place your skewered meat in a hinged double-sided broiler rack, as illustrated on the left, and turn the rack over when the time comes to broil on the other side.

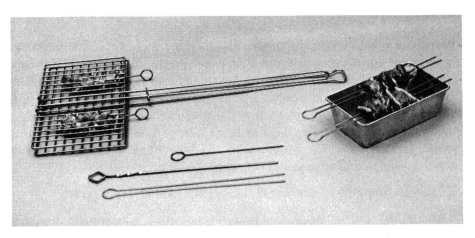

However you solve the problem, have a drip pan with bottom surface far enough from broiler heat—5 inches or more—so that cooking juices exuding from the food do not burn; you want to preserve all that delicious liquid for saucing the meat as you serve it. When you are skewering for only two, a bread pan does nicely, as shown at the right of the illustration.

Brochettes d'agneau

LAMB SHASHLIKS;
LAMB KEBABS;
LAMB SKEWERED
WITH BACON,
HERBS, AND
LEMON

For 4 people

Serve these with risotto, a mixed vegetable salad, and a good young red wine like a Beaujolais.

4 or 5 slices bacon ¼ inch thick
2 lbs. fully trimmed center-cut leg of lamb

Herb and lemon marinade
1 lemon
1 tsp salt and ⅛ tsp pepper
½ tsp rosemary or thyme
1 or 2 large cloves garlic put through a press
¼ cup olive oil

Preparing the brochettes. Cut the bacon into 1-inch squares and blanch it (simmer 10 minutes in 1 quart of water, drain, and dry). Meanwhile cut lamb into cubes about 1½ inches across and place in a stainless or glass mixing bowl. Remove the lemon zest (yellow part of peel) with a vegetable peeler, and mince. Strew the peel over the lamb along with a tablespoon of lemon juice. Toss with the salt, pepper, rosemary or thyme, garlic, and oil; let marinate 20 to 30 minutes. Then string the lamb on skewers, alternating with pieces of bacon.

✿ May be prepared in advance to this point; cover and refrigerate.

Cooking. Broil or barbecue 5 to 6 minutes on each side, basting the meat once or twice with the marinade. Lamb should still be rosy inside, and is done when it just begins to exude its juices—or to feel gently springy rather than squashy to your finger. Immediately remove from heat. If you are broiling, pour remaining marinade into drip pan (or add a little white wine, stock, or water), set over heat, and boil rapidly, scraping up coagulated juices into liquid; when syrupy, pour over each serving.

Serving. You may wish to arrange the brochettes on a hot platter, or over a bed of risotto; then let each guest take his own and, holding the brochette up by one end, dislodge the meat with a fork from the other. Or the host may act as *maître d'hôtel*, removing the meat from each brochette as he serves it.

Kebabs sans brochettes (*Non-skewered lamb*). When in a hurry, I often forego brochettes altogether, as well as the blanched bacon. After marinating the lamb, I arrange the pieces on a hinged broiler rack (I have a small one to fit my oven), broil it on one side, turn the rack, and broil the meat on the other side. I heap it in a ring of risotto, deglaze the drip pan, pour that over the meat, stick on a few sprigs of parsley, and serve.

Curry dinner

Surrounded with puffed-up poppadums and bowls of spiced lentils, chopped eggs, chutney, fresh coconut, sautéed pine nuts, diced bananas, crisp Bombay ducks, steamed rice, and a fragrant curry sauce, yesterday's roast becomes the basis for a curry dinner party. As anyone who is at all familiar with India knows, curry is not an Indian word and curry powder is something manufactured only for Anglo-Saxons (meaning British and Americans and other foreigners). Thus it is obvious that this dinner has nothing whatsoever to do with Indian cookery and any resemblance is purely coincidental, blending itself with English suggestions, Yankee ingenuity, and a bit of French know-how. It is an illustration—and a rather good one if I do say so—of how we ordinary beings can have fun in the exotic foods section of the supermarket. By the way, when you want to do the real thing, an excellent book on the subject is Madhur Jaffrey's *An Invitation to Indian Cooking* (New York: Alfred A. Knopf, 1973).

Curry dinner à la French Chef

———————

CURRIED MEAT
WITH COCONUT,
SAFFRON RICE,
POPPADUMS,
BOMBAY DUCK,
AND VARIOUS
CONDIMENTS

For 6 to 8 people

Use roast lamb, beef, turkey, duck, or pork for the meat here, or omit meat altogether, since all the other ingredients served with the rice make a deliciously nourishing main course. What of the whole menu? I don't really think one needs a first course with this kind of dinner, and dessert could well be fresh fruit, a fruit compote with a delicious cake on the side, or ice cream or sherbet. Probably beer is best when the curry taste is strong, but if it is mild you might have a strong white wine like a Côtes du Rhône or Pinot Blanc, or a *rosé*; or have wine and a pitcher each of beer and of lemonade, and let guests take their choice.

The main dish: curried lamb, beef, pork, duck, or turkey

2 cups sliced onions
Olive oil or peanut oil
2 to 4 Tb fragrant curry powder

3 Tb flour
3 cups excellent meat stock (or canned bouillon)
    brought to the simmer in a small pan
½ cup red wine or dry white wine, or
    dry white French Vermouth
2 or 3 cloves garlic, minced or puréed
⅓ cup small seedless raisins or currants
1 smallish sour apple peeled, seeded, chopped
½ tsp thyme
1 imported bay leaf
Salt and pepper to taste
1 cup coconut milk (see recipe following)
About 6 cups roast lamb, beef, turkey, duck, or
    pork, cut into 1½-inch cubes or
    bite-sized pieces

Cook the onions slowly in 3 tablespoons of the oil in a large covered casserole, frying pan, or electric skillet for 10 minutes or so, until tender and translucent but not browned. Stir in the curry powder, cook slowly 3 minutes more, then blend in the flour, and a little more oil if needed, to make a malleable paste; stir over low heat again for 3 minutes. Remove from heat; when bubbling has stopped, pour in all the hot meat stock at once and blend vigorously with a wire whip. Return over heat; blend in the wine, garlic, raisins or currants, apple, herbs, and salt and pepper to taste. Simmer slowly for 30 minutes, adding coconut milk to thin the sauce as necessary. Correct seasoning.

☼ May be done in advance; refrigerate or freeze. Bring to simmer before proceeding.

When you are ready to continue, film a large frying pan with ¹⁄₁₆ inch of oil, heat to very hot but not smoking, add the meat, and sauté rapidly, tossing and turning to brown briefly and lightly. Toss with a sprinkling of salt and pepper, then scrape the meat into the simmering sauce. Bring almost back to the simmer and maintain at below the simmer for 20 to 30 minutes, allowing the meat to heat through slowly and to soften, but do not let it overcook, particularly if you have rare roast lamb or beef. Carefully correct seasoning—and add more coconut milk if sauce thickens too much.

☼ If you are not serving immediately, keep warm at not over 120 degrees, where meat will stay perfectly for a good half hour or more.

Fresh grated coconut meat, fresh coconut milk

If you cannot find fresh coconuts, omit coconut altogether, since, in my opinion, the dried, grated variety is no substitute for the fresh. Grated coconut is simply the white meat of the coconut, minus the brown skin, shredded either on a grater or in a blender. Coconut milk is not the liquid sloshing about in the nut; it is the juice obtained from grated coconut meat when you steep it in a little boiling water and then squeeze it dry—out comes a milky white juice, coconut milk. Coconut cream is the fat that rises to the surface of coconut milk when you let it settle; coconut butter is the cream that you have chilled until it congeals; use it like butter in sauces, soups, and cake frostings. (Coconut milk, alas, contains over 250 calories per cup; the cream and grated fresh meat over 340. But how delicious they are.) First, here is how to open your coconut.

To open a coconut. Preheat oven to 400 degrees. With hammer and ice pick, pierce the 3 small depressions in the top of the nut and drain out the water. Place the coconut in the oven, middle level, and in about 20 minutes the shell will crack open. Remove the coconut, wrap it in a big kitchen towel, and smash it hard in several places with a hammer—the towel prevents shell fragments from flying about the kitchen. Remove and discard shell, and shave the brown skin off the white meat with a vegetable peeler. Wash and drain the meat to remove shell particles.

Grated coconut and coconut milk. Cut the meat into ½-inch pieces. Grate half of it, ½ cup at a time, in an electric blender (or on the rough side of a grater—much more difficult), and set aside for the curry condiment tray. Add remaining meat to blender along with just enough boiling water to cover; purée until smooth. Pour into a potato ricer set over a bowl (or into the corner of a heavy dish towel set over a bowl), and squeeze milky liquid out of coconut meat. Blend the fibrous residue again with boiling water if you wish, but if you squeezed hard in the beginning you will not get much more of value after that first good pressing.

✿ If you aren't going to use the grated coconut meat and milk immediately, cover and refrigerate; if you are doing it a day or more ahead, freeze it, since it turns rancid rather rapidly.

Saffron rice

For about 4½ cups cooked rice

1½ cups raw untreated white rice
3 cups water
2 Tb butter
2 tsp salt
Big pinch saffron threads

Bring rice and water to the boil in a heavy-bottomed 2½- to 3-quart saucepan, adding the butter, salt, and saffron. Stir up once when the boil is reached, reduce heat to the simmer, cover, and let simmer undisturbed over moderately low heat for 15 minutes, or until liquid has been absorbed. Do not stir rice during the cooking, but, to check on liquid, tilt pan and lift rice with a fork from the bottom. When liquid has been absorbed, set pan aside, covered, for 10 minutes to let the rice finish cooking. Fluff the rice with a fork, taste, and correct seasoning.

☼ If you are serving the rice within half an hour, set pan uncovered in a large pan of simmering water. If you are doing it ahead, set pan aside uncovered until cool; to reheat, cover and set over a larger pan of simmering water, fluffing rice gently with a fork every 4 to 5 minutes, just until it's heated through.

Poppadums and Bombay duck

Poppadums are paper-thin brown wafers usually 3 inches in diameter that come neatly packed in a round container; they are made of lentil flour, and when you deep-fry them they puff up and swell out. Bombay duck are sun-dried salted fish fillets about 5 inches long that are also deep-fried before serving. (A color photograph of the actual fish is in Time-Life's *The Cooking of India*.) They are rather strong and fishy, not to everyone's taste, and you may substitute crisp bacon for Bombay duck if you wish; by the way, some boxes of Bombay duck tell you to soak them in water first, but these directions are obviously for the squeamish foreign trade, since soaking takes out all the taste and *raison d'être,* in my opinion.

To cook poppadums and Bombay duck. Heat about 3 inches of fresh peanut oil to 400 degrees in an electric fryer or electric skillet. Slip one poppadum at a time into the hot oil, press into the oil with a slotted pancake turner as the poppadum rapidly swells out; turn it over in the oil, and in no more than a few seconds it is brown, crisp, and done. Drain on paper towels, and continue, making 2 or 3 per person. Then, 3 or 4 at a time, fry the Bombay duck for 5 or 6 seconds, until crisp and brown; drain on paper towels, counting on 1 per person.

☼ These should be done almost at the last minute, so they will be crisp and fresh.

The condiment tray

Besides the fresh grated coconut, poppadums, and Bombay duck or crisp bacon, you will want other fanciful items to sprinkle over your meat and to mix with your rice. Here are some suggestions, all of which can be done in advance (except for cutting up the bananas), put into small separate serving bowls, and covered until you are ready for them.

> Cucumbers, peeled, halved lengthwise, the seeds
> scooped out and discarded, then the flesh diced
> and tossed with diced green pepper, minced
> shallots or scallions, and salt and pepper
> Chutney
> 1 cup or so of pine-nut meats, sautéed lightly
> in oil and seasoned
> Chopped peanuts
> 1 or 2 diced bananas
> Cooked lentils tossed with oil, minced onions,
> parsley, and seasonings

Serving the curry dinner

When you are ready to serve, heap the rice around the edge of a large platter, spoon the curried meat in the center, and decorate with parsley. Place the condiments on a large lazy Susan in the middle of the table, or simply arrange them in a circle for easy passing around. Each guest helps himself to curry and rice, and the various condiments, crumbling the Bombay duck or bacon over the steaming curry at the end.

A fast moussaka

GROUND LAMB AND EGGPLANT GRATIN

Here is a lamb and eggplant main course that is quick to do and very good, too. Use either your own ground raw lamb, or cooked lamb, ground. The full-dress French type of moussaka in Volume I of Mastering is a long affair, perfectly beautiful with its tower of purple eggplant skins surrounding an inner and savory core of spiced lamb. The recipe here is far more informal, but has the same enticing flavor, and it is just as attractive to eat cold as it is hot. A green salad, French bread, and a good young red wine are all you need to serve with this.

For about 6 people, depending on your menu

A rather large eggplant, or several smaller ones (1½ to 2 lbs.)
Olive oil or peanut oil
1 cup minced onions
About 2 cups ground lamb, raw or cooked
1 or 2 cloves garlic, minced or puréed
Herbs, such as rosemary and thyme, or a Provençal or Italian mixture
Salt and pepper
About 1 cup tomato sauce (this can be bottled spaghetti sauce, if need be; a peeled, seeded, juiced, and chopped fresh tomato would help in this case)
About ½ cup Mozzarella cheese, diced
⅓ cup freshly grated Parmesan cheese

Discard the green top, but do not peel the eggplant. Cut eggplant into lengthwise slices about ⅜ inch thick, and halve the slices if necessary, to make them about 3 inches long. If you are not in a hurry, bake the slices as described for the eggplant pizza on page 398 (macerate in salt, dry, bake in a covered pan with oil and herbs). If you are rushed, blanch the slices 3 or 4 minutes in boiling salted water, until barely tender, drain, and dry on paper towels.

Reserve those eggplant slices with skin covering one side; these are to cover the moussaka. Brush a shallow baking dish, such as a 9- by 12-inch oval, with oil, and arrange half the remaining eggplant slices in the bottom of the dish.

Meanwhile or beforehand, you will have sautéed the minced onions in a little oil until tender and translucent. If the ground lamb is raw, add it and sauté, stirring, for several minutes until it turns from red to gray. If cooked, stir the lamb into the onions to heat through. Blend in the garlic, herbs, and salt and pepper to taste—flavor should be delicious, fragrant, and hearty.

Spread half the lamb mixture over the first layer of eggplant, spread on one quarter of the tomato sauce and one third of the two cheeses. Spread rest of non-reserved eggplant in the dish, then the rest of the lamb, and one third of the remaining sauce and cheese. Cover with the reserved eggplant, skin side up, and sprinkle with a little oil. (Reserve remaining sauce and cheese.)

☼ May be prepared a day in advance to this point; cover and refrigerate.

Final cooking. Preheat oven to 375 degrees. Cover the baking dish with oiled aluminum foil and set in upper-middle level of oven. In 25 to 30 minutes, or when contents are bubbling, remove foil. Spread on the remaining tomato sauce, then the cheese, and return to oven for about 15 minutes, or until top is nicely browned. Serve right from the baking dish.

☼ If you are not ready to serve, keep warm in turned-off oven, door ajar; or over barely simmering water; or on an electric warming device.

OTHER IDEAS FOR LEFTOVER LAMB

Using the flavorings suggested for the preceding *moussaka*, turn ground raw or cooked lamb into lambburgers or meat loaf, or use it as a stuffing for onions, peppers, or tomatoes. It can go into the lasagne recipe on page 351, or the braised stuffed cabbage on page 324. I often, too, mix ground lamb with ground beef, pork, or chicken if I have a collection begging for employment; the flavor of lamb, of course, usually takes over. Incidentally, I do think that for raw ground lamb you are better off making your own, since you never know what old scraps of gristle and fat go into the store-bought variety; it is much like making your own pork breakfast sausages, which are always so surprisingly better than anything you can buy simply because you have put good fresh meat into them.

Barley soup;
Scotch
mutton broth

———

THE LAST OF THE
LEG OF LAMB

You will find versions of this on the back of most boxes of barley, in all the old cookbooks, and even in *Larousse Gastronomique* under foreign soups, *Potage mutton-broth (Cuisine anglaise)* . The following recipe is even simpler, and a fine peasanty soup it is for a Sunday supper. Although a few scraps of lamb and some lamb broth or gravy are desirable in addition to your bones, you can instead add a can of beef bouillon at the end if you feel your broth lacks flavor.

For 2 quarts or
more of soup,
serving 6 to 8

Bones from the leg of lamb, chopped into 2-inch
pieces, plus any extra bones or scraps of
meat from lamb or beef or poultry
About 6 cups in all: combined chopped carrots,
onions, and celery
2 quarts water, more if needed

> *If available: 1 leek (white and tender green*
> *part), sliced*
> *2 imported bay leaves*
> *½ tsp rosemary or thyme*
> *2 large cloves of garlic, peeled and chopped*
> *½ cup barley*
> *1 tsp salt, more as needed*
> *Leftover lamb gravy and/or either 2 cups*
> *strong lamb or beef stock, or 1 can of*
> *beef bouillon*
> *Minced fresh parsley*

Brown the lamb bones and chopped vegetables in a shallow roasting pan in the upper-middle level of a 400-degree oven, turning and basting with accumulated fat, if any, for 30 minutes or so. Transfer to a soup kettle, discard fat in pan, and deglaze with hot water (pour in a cup of water, set over heat, and scrape coagulated juices into liquid with a wooden spoon), pour into kettle, and add the rest of the water. Bring to the simmer, and skim off scum that will continue to rise for 5 minutes or so. Then add the optional leek, the herbs, garlic, barley, and salt. If meat bits are raw or gristly, add them now. Bring kettle again to the simmer, cover partially, and simmer 1½ to 2 hours, until barley is tender, skimming occasionally, and adding more liquid if barley has absorbed the original amount.

Finally, pour contents of kettle through a colander set over a saucepan; remove all bones, and the bay leaves. Skim any fat off liquid in pan, then return the lamb, vegetables, and barley to pan. Bring again to the simmer, adding any available gravy, and then cut with stock or bouillon to your taste, along with any attractive roast lamb bits, neatly cut. Carefully correct seasoning, simmering a few moments more, and the soup is done. Stir in the minced fresh parsley, and serve in soup cups or wide soup plates.

☼ May be cooked in advance: let cool uncovered, then cover and refrigerate or freeze.

Additions to the soup. This kind of soup takes well to other tasty leftovers, like braised or boiled beef, tripe, chopped breakfast sausages, cooked dried beans or lentils, cabbage, turnips, spinach, onions, carrots, mashed potatoes, pasta, and so forth.

Pork and ham

Pork can be an elegant dish, which some of us forget, associating pork as we so often do with thick chops, great roasts, and sauerkraut. But when you do a pork sauté and sauce it like veal, you have a delicious dish that you can serve to the most VIP guests. Again, with ham, we too often picture it only as a large roast leg, sitting solemnly on the buffet table and lasting endlessly in the refrigerator. But braise ham in wine and it becomes a new dish. Then sauce and bake it with mushrooms and you have an even newer dish. You don't have to confine yourself to large and expensive legs, either, since the more comfortably priced smoked shoulder has just the same flavor. Here, then, are a handful of ideas for both pork and ham.

Médaillons de porc sautés à la crème

MEDALLIONS OF
PORK LOIN
SAUTÉED WITH
HERBS AND CREAM

"Medallions" mean smallish rounds of meat, medal-shaped, and they always come from the loin strip or the tenderloin. Medallions are sometimes called *noisettes*, meaning the round, fleshy part of a chop —we would call it the eye. Thus, being actually boneless chops, these tender morsels cook quickly, and after a brief sauté they are sauced with a reduction of wine, cream, and herbs made right in the cooking pan. Serve them on a bed of homemade mashed potatoes, braised spinach, puréed dried or green beans, rice, or noodles; surround them with fresh broccoli flowerets or baked tomatoes, and accompany them with one of your best white Burgundies or a Pinot Chardonnay.

THE PORK MEDALLIONS. Although you can use a tenderloin strip for this, I prefer the top loin strip (large side of loin chop or eye of rib chop) because of its more generous size. Use a boned pork top loin or rib roast, then cut into ½-inch crosswise slices; or buy pork rib chops. Keeping just the triangular-shaped eye of solid meat, remove all surrounding meat, fat, and any bone. Save all fat and meat trimmings for homemade sausages or meat stuffings; you can grind, package, and freeze it. Add bones to your collection for future meat stock, and these you can also freeze.

For 4 to 6 people, depending on the rest of your menu

12 medallions of pork (see directions above)
2 or more Tb rendered pork fat or peanut oil
Salt and pepper
Big pinches each allspice and thyme
¼ cup minced shallots or scallions
1 small clove of garlic, puréed
1 cup dry white wine, or ¾ cup dry
white French Vermouth
1 cup heavy cream
Minced fresh parsley

Sautéing the pork. Dry pork thoroughly in paper towels. Heat fat or oil in pan until very hot but not smoking, and add as many pieces of pork as will fit in one layer without crowding pan. Brown for about 2 minutes on each side; remove as done, and brown the rest. Season each side of each medallion with salt, pepper, and spices, and return all meat to pan with the shallots or scallions and garlic. Cover pan, and cook slowly for 5 to 6 minutes until when you prick meat with a sharp-tined fork the juices run clear yellow with no trace of rosy color. Remove pork to a side dish.

Sauce and serving. Pour the wine or Vermouth into the pan and boil down rapidly to reduce by half, then pour in the cream and boil rapidly a minute or two to thicken lightly. Return pork to pan and baste with the sauce.

✿ Dish may be completed to this point in advance; set aside uncovered. (It is better not to refrigerate, and not to let meat cool off completely, or its texture will firm up and it then will taste like reheated rather than freshly cooked meat.)

Several minutes before serving, reheat to simmer, cover, and simmer slowly until meat is well heated through. Taste sauce carefully, and correct seasoning. Arrange on a hot platter with whatever accompaniments you have chosen, spoon the sauce over the medallions, sprinkle with parsley, and serve.

ADDITIONS AND VARIATIONS

You could certainly add small braised onions and sautéed mushrooms to the pork, cooking them separately and simmering them a few minutes in the sauce before adding the sautéed pork at the end. If you wanted a tomato sauce rather than a cream sauce, omit the cream and, after the wine has reduced, stir in 2 cups or so of fresh tomato pulp (tomatoes peeled, seeded, juiced, and chopped), boil slowly to cook the tomato, then return the sautéed pork to the pan. Sautéed mushrooms could also go here along with the tomato.

Ragoût de porc, chasseur

———◆———

BRAISED CUBED
PORK WITH
TOMATOES, HERBS,
AND MUSHROOMS

"It's not beef, it's not veal, it's not lamb or duck or turkey or chicken. So what is this tender meat with its subtle taste?" asks an imaginary guest. It's a pork ragout and it's delicious. More family-style cooking than the preceding sauté, the ragout could well be part of an informal buffet, and pork is far more reasonable in price than beef or lamb. I like to use fresh pork shoulder for this, or the blade end of the loin, buying a whole boneless roast and cutting the meat myself. Following the natural separations of the muscles, I can then get some good solid pieces for my ragout, and save scrappy morsels and fat for sausage meat or *pâtés*.

Since pork is an invitation to serve some of the fragrant earthy vegetables, you might accompany the ragout with a turnip and potato purée, a purée of potatoes and celeriac, or braised turnips or rutabaga. Cooked dried beans or lentils are another attractive accompaniment, or you could be more conventional with rice, noodles, or mashed potatoes. You don't really need another vegetable, although you could have braised onions or broccoli flowerets, or simply follow the ragout with a salad of mixed greens. As for wine, a light red of the Beaujolais or Gamay type would go nicely, or a white Riesling, or a *rosé*.

The recipe here suggests a short dry marinade in herbs, spices, and garlic; if you have a day or two to spare, a longer sojourn will give an even more interesting flavor to the pork.

For 6 people

2½ lbs. lean boneless shoulder of pork or blade end of loin, cut into cubes approximately 1½ inches across

For the dry marinade: 2 *tsp salt,* ⅛ *tsp allspice,*
½ tsp thyme or mixed herbs such as Italian
or Provençal seasoning, and 2 or 3 large
cloves of garlic, puréed
2 *or more Tb rendered pork fat, or*
olive oil or peanut oil
1½ *to* 2 *cups thinly sliced onions*
½ cup dry white wine or dry
white French Vermouth
3 *or 4 ripe red tomatoes, peeled, seeded, juiced,*
and chopped; or a mixture of some fresh
tomato pulp and some canned Italian plum
tomatoes, drained, seeded, and chopped
2 *cups (1 pint), more or less, fresh mushrooms*
1 *tsp lemon juice and 1 Tb butter for*
simmering the mushrooms
Salt and pepper as needed
To thicken the sauce: 1 to 2 Tb cornstarch or
potato starch blended with 2 Tb wine
¼ cup or more heavy cream or créme frâiche
Fresh minced parsley

Marinating the pork. This takes 20 minutes, while you are assembling the rest of the ingredients, or 1 to 2 days, if you wish. Place the pork in an enameled or stainless mixing bowl, add the marinade ingredients, and stir about vigorously with a rubber spatula to be sure all pieces are well covered. Let stand, turning occasionally (or cover and refrigerate), until you are ready to begin cooking.

Browning the pork. If pork has exuded its juices during the marinade, dry in paper towels (reserve juices). Film a large frying pan or electric skillet with 1⁄16 inch of rendered fat or of oil, heat to very hot but not smoking, add as many pieces of pork as will fit comfortably in one layer, and brown lightly on all sides; remove browned pieces and add fresh until all is browned. Tilt pan and spoon out browning fat. Stir in the sliced onions and toss with the pork for several minutes to brown lightly. (You may now wish to transfer meat and onions to a casserole to finish cooking. In this case, deglaze the frying pan with the wine—meaning, pour in wine and scrape into it all coagulated brown pan juices, and pour this now into the casserole.)

Braising the pork: *1 to 1½ hours.* Stir the tomatoes into the pork and onions, as well as any marinade juices, turning and tossing the meat to blend ingredients. Bring to the simmer, cover, and simmer slowly either in a 325-degree oven or on top of the stove. Meat will exude juices as it cooks; turn and baste every 15 minutes or so. It will take 1 to 1½ hours, depending on the cut and its initial tenderness, and it is done when a fork pierces it fairly easily; do not overcook.

Stewed mushrooms. While pork is cooking, trim and wash mushrooms, quarter them, and place in a small saucepan with the lemon juice, butter, and a pinch of salt. Add ¼ cup of water, cover pan, and simmer 3 minutes. Pour the juices into the simmering pork, and reserve the mushrooms for later.

Finishing the ragout. Skim any fat off accumulated cooking juices, and you will probably want to thicken them unless they have reduced and thickened naturally. To do so, blend some of the hot juices into the starch and wine mixture, then pour this back into the ragout. Add the mushrooms, set over moderate heat and simmer, basting meat with juices, for several minutes until sauce thickens and starch cooks. Taste very carefully for seasoning and then, still simmering, add the cream; this will not noticeably lighten the color of the sauce, it will simply enrich it nicely. You may omit it if you wish.

✪ May be cooked ahead and slowly reheated for 5 minutes or so before serving.

Serve either on a hot platter or from a casserole, and decorate with parsley.

Ham and smoked shoulder of pork, whole and sliced

Rather than boiling or baking a ham or a smoked pork shoulder, braise it with wine and spices, and you will think it is an entirely new kind of meat. On our television program "Ham Transformation," I used a smoked shoulder and I shall also suggest it here with the understanding that you may substitute a whole ham for shoulder any time—just double all the containers, ingredients, and timing. Ham refers only to the smoked hind leg of pork, I was firmly admonished after the program, since I kept referring to "my shoulder of ham." It is not ham, it is smoked shoulder, although it tastes like ham. Shoulder is always much more reasonably priced, however, and is easy to carve because you have just the upper arm with its one bone to steer around. The shoulder is also called a "picnic," for some reason, and the shoulder-blade portion, or Boston butt, is usually boned and rolled into a cylindrical shape; it is then officially known as "smoked pork shoulder roll." This, too, may be braised as in the following recipe, but it would take much less time to cook.

HAM TALK. Almost all modern ready-to-cook hams in the markets today are actually what they say they are—ready to cook, meaning they need no presoaking and simmering, as was the case years ago when the curing processes were longer and saltier. In buying an unlabeled and unfamiliar brand, however, ask the head of the meat department for cooking advice. If you are still doubtful, cut a slice ⅜ inch thick from the bottom of the ham, sauté it slowly to cook through, and taste it. If the ham seems overly salty, soak it 6 hours or overnight in a basin of cold water before cooking. ("Country" hams and "old Virginia" hams are not being considered in these recipes.)

Jambon braisé au Madère ou au Porto

HAM OR SMOKED
SHOULDER BRAISED
IN WINE

A 6-pound shoulder
will serve 12 to 16
people

This is a delicious way to cook ham or smoked shoulder, whether you serve it as is, hot or cold, or have other plans. Accompany it with spinach braised in butter or cream and a purée of chestnuts, lentils, or mashed potatoes; a smooth red Burgundy or Côtes du Rhône would go nicely, or a fine strong white Burgundy such as a Meursault.

A 5½- to 6-pound smoked shoulder of pork,
    ready to cook
⅔ cup each: sliced carrots, onions, and celery
If available, 1 small sliced leek
2 imported bay leaves
6 allspice berries or cloves
6 peppercorns
1½ cups dry white wine or dry
    white French Vermouth
½ cup dry (Sercial) Madeira, or dry Port
1½ cups chicken stock, fresh or canned
Fresh white bread crumbs

Equipment: A covered casserole just big enough
to hold shoulder comfortably, a rack for the
casserole, a meat thermometer

Preheat oven to 350 degrees. Shave off inspection marks, etc., place meat fat side up on rack in roaster, and strew the sliced vegetables, leek, bay, and spices around it; pour on the wines and chicken stock. Drape with foil, and bring to simmer on top of the stove. Cover, and place in lower-middle level of preheated oven. In 30 minutes, turn thermostat down to 325 degrees. Braise 2¼ to 2½ hours, or to a meat thermometer reading of 160 degrees, basting several times during cooking, and regulating oven heat so that liquid in casserole simmers very slowly.

When done, remove meat from casserole. If you are to serve it as is, slice off rind and all but ⅛ inch of covering fat. Place meat in a shallow roasting pan, sprinkle top with a layer of fresh bread crumbs, and baste with its own fat or with melted butter. Brown 15 minutes in upper third of a preheated 425-degree oven. Meanwhile, strain braising juices, pressing liquid out of vegetables. Degrease the juices (almost 2 cups, and delicious) ; pour into a warm sauceboat to accompany the meat.

☼ Meat will stay warm for a good half hour; or return it to casserole with its juices, set cover askew, and place over barely simmering water or on an electric warming device, being sure meat is only kept warm and is not overcooking.

Carving. I like the French system, which is easy and makes attractive slices. The shoulder is lying lengthwise, and the arm bone runs down the middle, lengthwise, a bit to one side. Cut long slices lengthwise parallel to bone on the right, then on the left, alternating; turn the meat over when bone is fully exposed, and continue the same system on the other side.

Jambon braisé et gratiné, duxelles

BRAISED HAM OR
SMOKED SHOULDER
SLICED, RE-FORMED
WITH MUSHROOM
STUFFING, AND
GRATINÉED

Here the preceding recipe is given a full-dress finale, a luxury treatment to which few shoulders are accustomed. As before, you may of course use ham rather than shoulder; just double all ingredients.

The preceding braised smoked shoulder
with its juices
¾ lb. fresh mushrooms
About 4 ounces (1 stick) butter

For 8 to 10 people

2 Tb minced shallots or scallions
7 tablespoons flour
About ½ cup heavy cream
4 Tb fresh minced parsley
Pepper
1 to 1½ cups milk, heated in a small saucepan
¼ cup grated Swiss cheese

The mushroom stuffing. While meat is braising, or at any other convenient time beforehand, trim, wash, and finely dice the mushrooms. To extract their juices, either twist by handfuls in the corner of a towel or squeeze in a potato ricer; add these juices to the braising liquid. Heat 2 tablespoons of the butter in a medium-sized frying pan, stir in the mushrooms and shallots or scallions, and sauté over moderately high heat, stirring, for several minutes until mushroom pieces begin to separate from one another. Lower heat to moderate, blend in 2 tablespoons of the flour, and cook 2 minutes, stirring. Gradually blend in about ¼ cup of the braising juices with equal amounts of cream; simmer until mushroom mixture is very thick. Stir in the parsley and pepper, but no salt, since meat is salty enough.

Slicing, stuffing, and re-forming the meat. Slice rind and fat off top of meat, then cut serving slices going parallel to bone; make 2 or 3 per person, but leave a good layer of meat on the bottom around the bone, to act as support for the re-formed structure. Place bone structure in a buttered baking and serving dish, and pile the slices, with mushroom stuffing in between each, on and around to make an attractive arrangement in which an end of the bone peeks out to indicate what this is all about.

The glazing sauce: *about 2½ cups.* Make a blond *roux* as follows: heat 5 tablespoons of butter to bubbling in a heavy-bottomed 2-quart saucepan, blend in 5 tablespoons of flour, and cook slowly, stirring, for 3 minutes without browning the flour. Remove *roux* from heat, let cool a moment, then blend in 1 cup of the hot milk, beating vigorously with a wire whip. Return over heat, bring to simmer, and thin out with alternate tablespoons of meat-braising juices and cream. Sauce should be thick enough to coat a spoon, meaning it will coat the meat nicely. Carefully correct seasoning, and spoon the sauce over the meat to mask it completely except for the protruding bone. Sprinkle on the cheese, and over it a tablespoon or so of melted butter.

Final baking and serving. Set in middle or upper-third level of a pre-heated 425-degree oven for 25 to 30 minutes, to reheat and to brown nicely. Serve from baking dish, accompanied by the remaining juices in a warm bowl.

☼ Although the meat is at its juiciest and best when cooked, sliced, re-formed, baked, and served without too much delay, you may prepare the dish somewhat ahead. Again it is juicier if not refrigerated before baking, but if you must prepare it the day before serving, remove the assembled structure from the refrigerator an hour before baking; start it in a 325-degree oven in the lower third for half an hour, then place in upper third and increase heat to 375 degrees, allowing about 1 hour in all for the ham to reheat through and for the sauce to brown nicely.

Saupiquet de jambon à la nivernaise

HAM SLICES IN
HEAVENLY SAUCE

For 6 people

I adapted this recipe from an old French cookbook when I was doing newspaper articles on ham some years ago; since it is quick and delicious, and we are on ready-to-cook ham and smoked shoulders, it fits in. Serve with braised spinach and noodles or rice, and accompany with a white Burgundy, Côtes du Rhône, or Pinot Chardonnay.

2 lbs. ready-to-cook ham cut into ¼-inch serving slices (use either the supermarket packaged center-cut ham slices, or slices from ham, bone-in smoked shoulder, or boneless shoulder roll)
Rendered ham fat, olive oil, or peanut oil
1 cup sliced onions
2 Tb flour
1 cup ham-braising juices, beef stock, or canned beef bouillon, heated
1 ripe red tomato, peeled, seeded, juiced, and chopped, or 2 Tb tomato paste
½ cup dry white French Vermouth
1 Tb tarragon
¼ cup wine vinegar

6 peppercorns
4 juniper berries
About ¼ cup crème fraîche or heavy cream
Salt and pepper
Minced fresh parsley

Trim off extra fat from ham, and save all small ham pieces and trimmings. Sauté the ham in a frying pan in hot fat or oil, browning each side, then arrange in a fireproof serving dish. Adding a little more oil to frying pan if needed, sauté the ham trimmings to brown very lightly along with the 1 cup onions. Lower heat, blend in the flour, and cook slowly for 2 minutes. Remove from heat, let cool a moment, then blend in the ham juices, stock, or bouillon, the tomato, Vermouth, and tarragon. Simmer slowly, partially covered, 20 minutes, adding a bit more liquid if sauce becomes thicker than a light cream soup.

Meanwhile, simmer the vinegar, peppercorns, and juniper berries in a small saucepan, letting liquid reduce to 1 tablespoon; scrape into the previous sauce. Beat in the cream, simmering to reduce it slightly. Season carefully with salt and pepper, then strain the sauce over the sautéed ham.

☼ May be completed in advance to this point.

About 5 minutes before serving, cover and warm slowly until ham is well heated through, basting several times with the sauce. Decorate with parsley, and serve.

Hamburgers, vealburgers, and otherburgers

According to my butcher, the glory of a meat market rests largely on the quality of its hamburger, so popular is ground beef in the American diet. Who but the butcher knows what goes into those packages labeled hamburger, chopped sirloin, ground round, and ground chuck? Anything near the sirloin rates that name and that special price, even though it be the skirts and trimmings from steak tails. Ground round is frequently the gristly portion at the knee end of the various muscles in that area, but it gets a higher price than ground chuck just because it can be called ground round. A package labeled simply "hamburger" can be anything from anywhere on the beast, a catch-all for scraps. What is the proportion of fat to lean? That depends on the laws of your community. Most hamburger buffs recommend 8 to 10 percent, or 1¼ to 1½ ounces of fat per pound. James Beard, who knows and loves his hamburger, uses lean meat and often beats in a tablespoon or so of heavy cream per pound of beef; or one could beat in butter.

Unless you are really up on what goes on behind the meat display, therefore, I suggest you buy stew meat or a whole piece of beef and grind your own hamburgers. It's easy in an electric grinder. You'll find, besides, that stew meat is about the same price as ground beef, yet has been trimmed of fat, so you are getting more meat for your money. In addition, you will be using your own clean equipment; unfortunately some markets are not careful about their machines, so bacteria builds up in them and you can get a nice case of food poisoning, particularly if you like your burgers rare.

As to choice of cuts, I prefer the chuck for hamburger, either the neck pot roast or chuck stew meat, which is usually neck, or a combination of neck, arm, and blade.

STORING AND FREEZING. Ground meat loses its freshness much more quickly than whole pieces, and if you cannot use your hamburger within a day or at most two days, it is best to form the meat into patties, package, and freeze. It keeps perfectly well for several weeks. Then, when you come to cook it, let defrost just enough so that it bends a little but is not leaking out any juice; now cook immediately to sear in those juices.

Bifteck haché, sauté nature

SAUTÉED
HAMBURGERS WITH
WINE, CREAM,
AND TOMATO
SAUCE

Hamburgers can certainly appear at dinner parties, in fact they can take the place of *filet mignon* when served and sauced with elegance. Here they are simply sautéed, but sauced with a deglazing of shallots and wine, and then perked up with cream, tomato, and herbs. Suggestions for flavoring the meat itself, and for other sauces, are at the end of the recipe. And if this is indeed to be a banquet, you might like to follow the menu for our TV show, "Hamburger Dinner," and start out with oysters gratinéed on the half shell—only 3 per serving so not too expensive—and a chilled white Riesling wine. Serve the hamburgers on a delicious bed of rice and onion *Soubise,* with a stout red Côtes du Rhône, Beaujolais, or Mountain Red, plus a green vegetable or tossed salad. Finish with flaming apricot-flavored *Crêpes Sainte Claire,* and a Champagne or sparkling Vouvray. (All the recipes are, of course, right here in this book—page 167 for the oysters, page 348 for the *Soubise,* page 537 for the *Crêpes.*)

For 2 lbs. of beef
serving 4 people, or
6, depending on
your menu

2 lbs. freshly ground lean beef chuck
½ tsp salt
⅛ tsp freshly ground pepper
Optional James Beard enrichment: 2 to 4 Tb
    crème fraîche or heavy cream or butter
Olive oil or peanut oil

For the sauce
2 Tb minced shallots or scallions
¼ cup red wine, white wine, or dry
    white French Vermouth
½ cup crème fraîche or heavy cream
1 Tb tomato paste
2 to 3 Tb minced fresh basil or parsley

Toss the beef with a fork to blend in the salt, pepper, and optional cream. Form into 4 cakes about 5 inches in diameter and 1 inch thick.

✲ Wrap and refrigerate or freeze if done in advance (see notes on storing, preceding recipe).

Film a large heavy frying pan (or electric skillet) with $\frac{1}{16}$ inch oil and heat to very hot but not smoking; sauté the hamburgers 3 to 4 minutes on each side, depending on how rare you like them: for pinky rare, they will feel slightly springy when pressed, and a pearling of red juice will appear on the surface. Immediately remove hamburgers to a hot platter, or arrange on a bed of rice and onion *soubise*. Spoon all but a tablespoon of cooking fat out of pan, add the shallots or scallions, and sauté a moment; deglaze with the wine (pour in the wine, and boil rapidly, scraping sauté pan juices into it with a wooden spoon). Add the cream and the tomato, and boil rapidly to thicken lightly. Swish in the herbs, pour the sauce over the hamburgers, and serve.

OTHER FLAVORINGS, OTHER SAUCES

Flavoring the meat itself. For a change, you might mix puréed garlic into the ground beef, and/or a half teaspoon of thyme or an herbal mixture such as Italian seasoning, or a half cup of minced sautéed onions. To turn them into more of a meatball type of dish, beat in a whole raw egg, and when you have formed the meat into patties, dredge lightly in flour just before sautéing.

Fresh tomato sauce. Peel, seed, juice, and chop 2 or 3 tomatoes and mince up a tablespoon or so of shallots or scallions; set aside. When the hamburgers are done and the fat is out of the pan, deglaze it with ¼ cup of wine or beef bouillon, then stir in the tomatoes and shallots and cook rapidly 2 to 3 minutes until reduced and thickened. Toss in a spoonful of fresh minced herbs, correct seasoning, and spoon over the hamburgers.

Mustard and herb sauce. While the hamburgers are sautéing, blend 2 tablespoons of strong Dijon-type prepared mustard with ½ cup of beef bouillon, ¼ teaspoon thyme or mixed herbs, and a clove of puréed garlic. When the beef and fat are out of the pan, deglaze with ¼ cup of white wine or Vermouth, then stir in the mustard mixture. Boil rapidly to thicken lightly, remove from heat, and swish in a tablespoon or two of soft butter; pour over the hamburgers.

Fricadelles de veau Champvallon, en papillote

———

GROUND VEAL
PATTIES BAKED IN
FOIL PACKAGES
WITH SLICED
POTATOES AND
HERBS

Tired of the ubiquitous hamburgers? Try veal for a change, and you will like the way it lends itself to flavoring ideas and sauces; veal is far more interesting to play around with than beef. Here the ground veal is seasoned, formed into patties, browned briefly, then each portion is wrapped in foil with potatoes, herbs, onion, and chopped olives. It is the kind of dish you prepare ahead for serving at home, or take on a picnic or barbecue, and finish off on the grill. A salad of sliced tomatoes and cucumbers would be all you'd need here, and either a red, or a white, or a *rosé* wine. (By the way, why Champvallon? It indicates to those in the know that there must be some sliced potatoes in there because of the classic old recipe of shoulder lamb chops Champvallon, baked with potato slices.)

The veal patties

For 6 people

*1½ lbs. (about 3 cups) ground lean shoulder
     of veal, or ground veal stew meat
1 medium-sized onion, peeled (you will
     need a second one, later)
¾ tsp salt; pepper to taste
½ tsp mixed herbs such as thyme, oregano,
     and sage; or Italian seasoning
Either: 4 Tb soft butter
Or: 2 ounces cream cheese
Either: ⅓ cup boiled rice
Or: ⅔ cup, lightly
     pressed down, fresh white bread crumbs
     moistened with 3 Tb milk
1 egg
Flour for dredging
Olive oil or peanut oil*

The rest of the ingredients

*3 or 4 medium-sized all-purpose potatoes
1 medium-sized onion, peeled
2 Tb butter
Salt and pepper*

> *About 1 cup fresh tomato pulp (tomatoes peeled,*
> *seeded, juiced, chopped) ; or canned and*
> *drained sliced tomatoes*
> *¼ tsp mixed herbs, same as used in the veal*
> *½ cup chopped black olives*
> *¼ cup chopped fresh parsley*
> *⅓ cup diced Swiss cheese*

Forming the patties. Place the ground veal in a big mixing bowl or in the bowl of a heavy-duty electric mixer. Rub the onion through the large holes of a grater and into the veal, then add the salt, pepper, herbs, and butter or cream cheese. Either purée the rice or soaked bread crumbs with the egg in an electric blender, or force together through a vegetable mill or coarse sieve. Add to the meat, and beat all together vigorously using a wooden spoon or the flat beater of your mixer, until meat looks almost fluffy. Divide in half, then divide each half into thirds, to make 6 equal lumps. Spread a large piece of wax paper on your work table. Dip your hands in cold water, roll each lump into a ball, and flatten with your palms to make an oval patty about ½ inch thick; set on the wax paper.

☼ May be done in advance; cover and refrigerate.

Browning the patties. Just before cooking, dredge patties in flour. Shake off excess flour. Meanwhile film a large frying pan or electric skillet with a $\frac{1}{16}$-inch layer of oil, heat to very hot but not smoking, and lay in as many patties as will fit easily in one layer. Brown a minute or so on each side, remove to a side dish, and brown the remainder. Discard browning oil, rinse out pan, and set aside.

The potatoes. Bring a quart of water to the boil in a saucepan with 1½ teaspoons of salt. Meanwhile, peel the potatoes, halve lengthwise, and cut into crosswise slices ⅜ inch thick; drop into the boiling water, bring rapidly back to the boil, and boil 1 minute. Drain, and shake the potatoes dry. Grate the onion onto a piece of wax paper and reserve. Set the pan in which you browned the veal over moderately high heat with the 2 tablespoons of butter, add the potatoes and toss about, shaking pan by its handle. Add a sprinkling of salt and pepper, the reserved grated onion, the tomatoes, herbs, and olives, and continue to toss over heat for several minutes until ingredients are well mixed together. Remove from heat, and toss with the parsley and cheese.

Packaging the patties. Provide yourself with six 12-inch squares of aluminum foil. Divide the potato mixture into 12, and place 1 portion in the center of each square, set a browned pattie on top, and cover with the remaining portions of potatoes. Bring up two opposite sides of foil and roll them together over the meat, then roll up each end to make a sealed package. Arrange in one layer on a baking sheet or pizza tray.

☼ If done in advance, be sure potatoes and meat have cooled before they are sealed in packages, otherwise potatoes can develop a "smothered" taste. (Most hot foods should never be closed tight unless they are actually cooking.)

Baking and serving. Some 30 minutes before you wish to serve, bake in middle level of a preheated 375-degree oven until foil is puffed with cooking steam. Let each guest open his own. (For a barbecue, double wrap the patties, so you can grill on each side without juice drippage— about 20 minutes per side.)

Otherburgers. Ground lamb, pork, turkey, chicken, either cooked or raw, can be flavored like the veal or the hamburger described in this section, and you can substitute beef for veal in the preceding recipe. See also the lamb mixture for moussaka on page 299. Often, with cooked meat, a little fresh pork sausage fattens and flavors it up nicely, but soaked bread crumbs and cream cheese have much the same effect too. The important consideration is flavor and texture; sauté a bit of your mixture in a frying pan, taste carefully, and run ideas over your tongue. Would a little chopped ham help things? Some leftover meat gravy? More herbs? Butter? Ground leftover pâté or liver paste? Keep note of discoveries, too, since it is easy to forget even the greatest ideas when six weeks have passed.

Stuffed breasts, flanks, and cabbages

European, and especially French, cookery is famous for its *cuisine mijotée*, those delicious stews and braises that simmer away in wine and aromatic ingredients, filling the kitchen with heady aromas. Braised beef, beef stews, and *pot-au-feu* are typical, but so are stuffed breasts, stuffed flanks and hearts, and stuffed vegetables; these are a savory way to make use of the lesser cuts of meat and leftovers. Here, then, is a stuffed breast of veal and a stuffed cabbage. Stuffed beef flank, by the way, is not in this section at all but appears as variation of the braised beef recipe, on page 270; I liked the sound of it in the title here, but it seemed to fit more naturally where it is.

Stuffed breast of veal

Breast of veal takes to stuffing and braising better than anything else in this category, it seems to me. The meat is mild in taste and does not intrude upon its surrounding flavors, yet it holds together, slices well, and the only difficulty we have in our country is finding it in the first place, unless we live in an area catering to European cooking tastes. Anyway, ask your butcher what he can do for you, and if he can order you a fine, big half side of a prime breast of veal weighing around 7 pounds. Then you will be all set to do this recipe, except you may have to do the boning of the breast yourself. But the more practice you have in home butchering the better.

BUYING AND PREPARING A VEAL BREAST FOR STUFFING. An American breast of veal is one half side of the whole chest, from the breastbone through the lower parts of the 13 ribs; if it were beef, this would be the brisket from the tip of the breast through the 5th rib, and the plate, from ribs 6 through 13. Locate it on yourself: feel your breastbone where it joins your collarbone, run your finger straight down to where your breastbone ends, and you will feel your 13th rib curving up from your backbone to join it. Top-quality prime veal will be pale pink rather than pale red, and will weigh 7 to 7½ pounds untrimmed. This is ideal, but if you can find only smaller breasts of 4 pounds or so, bone them out, and sew or skewer them together; then adapt them to this recipe, using your own marvelous ingenuity—it is not a difficult business, and the actual final shape of the stuffed meat isn't very important.

The first operation is to separate the breast into 2 parts; cut between ribs 5 and 6, and set the brisket with its breastbone rib side up, in front of you. This is the part of the breast you are going to stuff, but it needs to be boned. To do so, outline the ribs with the point of a boning knife, cutting right down through the flesh against each side of the rib bones. Then, starting at the exposed rib ends, scrape under each bone to detach flesh; when you come to the white cartilage attaching a rib to the breast-bone (which runs the length of the 5 ribs), bend rib up at right angles and snap it loose. With all the 5 ribs removed, turn the breast over and cut along the side of the breastbone to remove it from the meat, then trim off excess fat from surface of meat. The boned brisket will be triangular in shape; the small pointed end is the top, and the bottom of the triangle opposite it is to be the opening of the pocket into which you will place the stuffing. Lay meat flat, non-rib side up, and with a long sharp knife slit the pocket in the bottom end, continuing inside the meat almost up to the point and to within ½ inch of the 2 sides. Try not to pierce the outside of the meat, but if you do make a hole don't worry since you can patch it later.

The plate section, containing ribs 6 through 13, will furnish meat for the stuffing. Bone it, cutting and pulling off flaps of meat, and scraping meat from membranes and bones. Grind the meat and reserve.

Save all bones and scraps to make a veal stock in which to braise the breast, browning the bones with aromatic vegetables in a 425-degree oven, then simmering in water for several hours. (This is the same system as for the meat stock in the *Pot-au-feu,* page 273.)

Poitrine de veau farcie

———◆———

BONED STUFFED
BREAST OF VEAL
BRAISED IN WINE
AND AROMATIC
VEGETABLES

Stuffed breast of veal is just as good cold as it is hot, and looks very much like a *galantine.* Served hot, accompany it with a green vegetable, such as a sauté of grated zucchini and onions, something colorful like baked cherry tomatoes, your own marvelous French bread, and a not too heavy red wine such as a Bordeaux or Cabernet Sauvignon.

NOTE: Because fine veal breasts are rare in our markets, pick up one when you see it, bone it as described, and freeze it, until you feel the urge to make this recipe.

Ground meat and mushroom stuffing, for 4 cups

For 8 people

½ cup (pressed down) fresh white crumbs from non-sweet French or Italian type bread

1 cup milk

3 cups meat stuffing mixture as follows: fresh raw lean pork; either raw veal or boned raw chicken breast; fresh raw pork fat (see notes on fat, page 362)

½ cup minced onions sautéed in butter

2 eggs

2 tsp salt

⅛ tsp freshly ground pepper

⅛ tsp allspice

Big pinch nutmeg

½ cup mushroom duxelles (1 quart fresh mushrooms diced fine, squeezed dry, sautéed in butter)

The boned brisket of veal

For braising the veal

Olive oil or peanut oil

½ cup each sliced carrots and onions

1 cup dry white wine or dry white French Vermouth

About 2 cups veal stock (or 1 cup each chicken broth and beef bouillon)

1 bay leaf

For the sauce

1½ to 2 Tb cornstarch

¼ cup white wine or Vermouth

Optional: 2 to 3 Tb mushroom duxelles

Salt and pepper

Equipment: Wooden or metal skewers or a trussing needle and white string; a heavy covered casserole just large enough to hold veal comfortably; aluminum foil

Stuffing the veal. Stir bread crumbs and milk in a saucepan over moderate heat, and boil several minutes until very thick; turn into a large mixing bowl. Vigorously beat in the meat mixture, onions, eggs, salt, pepper, spices, and *duxelles*. Check seasoning by sautéing a spoonful until cooked through; taste, and add more salt, pepper, or spices if you feel them necessary—the flavor of the stuffing should not overpower the veal, however. Lightly salt inside of veal pocket, and pack in the stuffing, but do not overfill the pocket. Skewer or truss the pocket closed; fold triangular top tip of meat against rib side of pocket, and skewer in place. This gives you a rectangular cushion shape. Skewer or truss closed any holes you may have made in surface of meat. (Leftover stuffing may be baked separately, or use it like hamburger for another meal.)

Browning and braising. Preheat oven to 350 degrees. Film bottom of casserole with ⅛ inch of oil. Heat to very hot but not smoking, and brown veal on both sides, adding the carrots and onions as you brown the second side. Salt lightly, pour in the wine or Vermouth, and enough stock to come two thirds the way up the veal. Add bay leaf, bring casserole to simmer on top of stove, lay foil over the veal, cover casserole, and set in middle level of oven. Baste several times during cooking, turn the meat once, and regulate oven so that liquid in casserole remains at a very slow simmer. Braising time 2½ to 3½ hours, until meat is tender when pierced with a fork.

Sauce and serving. When meat is done, remove it to a hot platter and degrease braising juices. Blend cornstarch and wine in a saucepan, pour in the juices, and simmer 3 to 4 minutes until thickened. Stir in optional *duxelles,* and carefully correct seasoning.

☼ If you are not ready to serve, return meat and sauce to casserole, cover loosely, and set in warming oven or on an electric warming device; the stuffed breast may be kept warm for a good hour at around 120 degrees.

When ready to serve, spoon a little sauce over the meat to glaze it, and pass the rest of the sauce in a warm bowl. To serve, cut the meat crosswise, like a sausage, but slightly on the slant from top to bottom, to make large attractive slices.

Other stuffings for breast of veal. Although I am inclined to a raw meat stuffing for veal, you could most certainly use leftover cooked meat such as poultry, pork, or even beef. A favorite Provençal mixture combines a cup of cooked chopped green chard or spinach leaves with the raw veal and other ingredients, and also adds half a cup each of mild-cured ham and of Parmesan cheese; the green makes attractive slices.

Stuffed vegetables: to stuff a cabbage

Stuffed vegetables. That usually brings to my mind, unfortunately, battalions of drearily filled green peppers drying out as they sit hour after miserable hour in a big pan on the steam table of the local cafeteria. But how about *moussaka?* That's stuffed eggplant with onions, herbs, garlic, and ground roast leg of lamb, delicious hot or cold, and you'll find it on page 299. Volume II of *Mastering* has stuffed onions, zucchini, and cabbage and here is a slightly different version of that whole cabbage. It comes in steaming on a platter, and inside is a marvelous meaty stuffing. It is a colorful way of making a little look like a lot, since just the flavor of a relatively small amount of meat does a great deal to give the effect of a fully meaty dish.

NOTES ON PEELING AND COOKING. A properly stuffed cabbage has a deliciously flavored mixture spread on the inside of each leaf. It is re-formed into its original shape, and then simmered 2 to 3 hours in an aromatic liquid. How do you get the leaves off the cabbage without breaking them? If crinkle-leaf Savoy cabbage is in season, you just peel them off the raw cabbage and boil them a few minutes to soften. Hard-headed cabbage won't peel, so the old-fashioned method is to drop the whole cabbage in boiling water and remove the leaves one by one, as they loosen. After I did this on television, two kind viewers from New York State suggested a bright modern idea: core the cabbage, freeze it for a day or two, thaw in a basin of hot water and the leaves peel right off. My New York correspondents don't blanch the leaves after this since they are soft enough to manipulate; I do, but that small item of procedure is up to each individual chef.

How do you cook the cabbage so it remains whole and handsome? You can tie it with string, but I think that a bit risky. You can wrap it in a clean towel or in cheesecloth and simmer it in the kettle that is boiling up a meat stock, but I find that hard to unpackage afterward. In Grasse, perfume capital of the Mediterranean, at the edge of the Alpes Maritimes, old recipes call for the cabbage to be formed in a *fassumier,* a string bag designed especially for stuffed cabbage. The traditional *farce grassoise,* incidentally, includes rice, minced salt pork, onions, garlic, bread crumbs, herbs, and either a handful of fresh green peas or of minced dark green chard, whichever is in season. Rather than wrapping and tying, however, I like to form the cabbage in a fairly round-bottomed bowl lined with salt pork, and to baste with bouillon; it is then a simple matter to drain out the cooking liquid and unmold the cabbage for serving.

Chou farci

———

STUFFED WHOLE
CABBAGE, BRAISED
AND SAUCED

For 8 to 10 people

Stuffed cabbage is definitely a complete main course, since you have your meat and vegetables all rolled into one fragrant package. You'll need no starchy vegetable, unless you'd like plain boiled potatoes. Big chunks of good French bread would be welcome, as would a simple red wine, like a Beaujolais, or a Mountain Red out of the jug. Then you could continue with the red wine for a cheese course, followed by fresh fruit. If you are having a first course, make it something light, like an arrangement of tomatoes and cucumbers in a fresh oil and wine-vinegar dressing, plus, if you wish, a decoration of anchovies and small black olives, or of baby sardines dressed in lemon, oregano, and a sprinkling of freshly ground pepper.

Preliminaries

A 2½- to 3-lb. cabbage (either crinkly-leafed
Savoy or smooth-leafed type)
2 tomatoes if out of season; 4 if in season
About 6 ounces lean salt pork
2 cups finely minced onions
Butter and olive oil or cooking oil
1 each thinly sliced carrot and onion

For stuffing and assembling the cabbage

4 cups ground cooked meat or poultry (this
may include a cup or more of boiled rice if
you need an extender)
1½ cups (12 ounces) fat-and-lean fresh pork
or sausage meat
2 eggs
2 or more cloves garlic, puréed
½ tsp salt
⅛ tsp freshly ground pepper
¾ tsp thyme or sage
¼ tsp allspice or cloves
¾ of the cooked minced onions
2 to 3 cups beef stock or bouillon

For the tomato sauce

The remaining cooked minced onions

> *2 cups tomato pulp (from the fresh tomatoes,*
> *peeled, seeded, juiced, and chopped; plus*
> *additional pulp from drained, strained,*
> *canned Italian plum tomatoes)*
> *Salt and pepper*
>
> *Equipment: A large kettle of boiling water, a large*
> *tray, a long-handled spoon, and tongs for*
> *blanching cabbage and cabbage leaves; a 2½- to*
> *3-quart round-bottomed bowl or baking*
> *dish in which to mold the cabbage*
> *for braising*

Preliminaries. (See also alternate suggestion for freezing rather than blanching cabbage leaves preceding recipe.) For crinkly-leafed cabbage, peel off leaves whole until you come to the heart; leave heart whole. Drop heart and leaves into boiling water and boil leaves several minutes, removing them to the tray when limp, and letting heart boil 5 minutes. For hard-headed cabbage, cut out stem, going about 2 inches deep. Drop whole cabbage into kettle and start nudging outside leaves off head with 2 spoons; remove them to the tray, and continue boiling and removing leaves until you come to heart; leave heart in to boil 5 minutes, and return leaves, removing them to tray when limp. While cabbage is boiling, to save time blanch the tomatoes in the cabbage kettle for 10 seconds, peel, and set aside. Then slice rind off salt pork, cut pork into 12 neat slices about ¼ inch thick and 2 to 4 inches in diameter; place slices and rind in a sieve and blanch 2 to 3 minutes with the cabbage, then rinse in cold water and dry.

During or after the cabbage boiling, mince the onions, and sauté until tender in 2 tablespoons of butter or oil, using a 2-quart saucepan which will later contain the tomato sauce; remove ¾ of the onions to a large mixing bowl, where they will be combined with the stuffing ingredients, and reserve the rest in the saucepan. While the minced onions are cooking, brown the sliced carrot and onion lightly in a tablespoon of oil, in a small frying pan; these are to line the cabbage cooking bowl.

The stuffing: *6 cups.* Vigorously beat the cooked meat, pork, eggs, and seasonings in the mixing bowl with the sautéed onions, adding a few tablespoons of the stock or bouillon to lighten the mixture and make for fairly easy spreading. Sauté a small spoonful until cooked through, and taste. Correct seasoning as necessary, exaggerating a bit, since flavoring disperses somewhat when cabbage braises.

Assembling the cabbage. Line bottom of bowl with half the blanched salt pork strips; strew on half the cooked carrot and onion slices. Bowl will be turned upside down to unmold cabbage when cooked—the bottom will become the top. Chop cooked cabbage heart and mix into the stuffing, and you are ready to begin.

Choose the largest, greenest, and finest of the cabbage leaves; these are to line the inside of the bowl, large ends down and stem ends up.

After lining bottom and sides of bowl with largest leaves, spread in a layer of stuffing about ½ inch thick.

Continue, pressing smaller cabbage leaves on top of stuffing, and spreading on more stuffing. Occasionally slip a large green leaf down sides of bowl to be sure all is well covered.

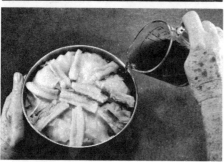

Fill bowl to within ½ inch of top, cover with a final layer of leaves, the rest of the salt pork and sliced vegetables, then pour in enough stock or bouillon around edge of cabbage to come within 1 inch of bowl's rim.

☼ May be prepared in advance; cover and refrigerate.

Braising: *2 to 2½ hours; longer if cabbage has been refrigerated.* Preheat oven to 400 degrees. Lay a piece of foil over top of bowl, bring contents slowly to the simmer on top of the stove (if bowl is flameproof), set a cover over the bowl, and place in lower-middle level of oven. Set a drip-pan on a rack just under the cabbage. In about 30 minutes, or when cabbage is slowly simmering, turn heat down to 350 or 325 degrees, and regulate during entire cooking so liquid very slowly simmers. Add more bouillon as necessary, and prepare tomato sauce base (next step). Cabbage is done at a meat thermometer reading of around 165 degrees (or, when top is pressed, no rosy-colored meat juices exude).

Sauce and serving. Stir the tomato pulp into the reserved minced onions, cover, and simmer 10 to 15 minutes. When cabbage is done, drain cooking liquid (or a cup or so of stock or bouillon) into tomatoes, and simmer while arranging cabbage. Remove salt pork from top of cabbage and set aside; turn a hot serving dish upside down over bowl, and reverse the two to unmold the cabbage. Remove rest of pork strips from cabbage if you wish, and brown all of them in a frying pan; either serve separately or arrange over cabbage. Correct seasoning of tomato sauce, pour around cabbage, and serve.

☼ If you are not yet ready to serve, unmold the cabbage, finish the sauce, and sauté the pork. Turn a bowl upside down over cabbage, and set in warming oven, over simmering water, or on an electric hot tray, where it will keep for a good half hour.

Other stuffings, and stuffed cabbage leaves. You can use any type of stuffing you wish for cabbage, including any of the ideas from the preceding pages. Another and easier presentation, when you haven't the time or the will for a whole cabbage, or when you have just a few people to serve, is to stuff single leaves. Choose big ones, blanch them to soften, and roll up around several spoonfuls of stuffing, making sausage-shaped or cushion-shaped individual packages. Arrange closely together in a baking dish, pour on a little bouillon, lay strips of blanched salt pork or bacon on top, cover, and bake an hour or so. Serve with the same tomato sauce.

Tripes à la mode

Two of the most sophisticated cuisines of the world, the French and the Chinese, are marvels at turning the humblest ingredients into the most savory dishes. Centuries of wars, famines, and struggle, along with centuries of civilized living, have taught both of them to use anything edible the land or the beast can offer, from wild herbs to pigs' ears, calves' heads, cows' udders, sheep's trotters, and tripe, which is the lining of a beef's stomach. Sautéed with onions it is *Tripes à la lyonnaise;* sprinkled with chopped egg and browned bread crumbs it is *à la polonaise;* tomatoes and herbs characterize tripe *à la portuguaise, à la créole,* and *à la niçoise.* You'll find a résumé of *Tripes à la niçoise* at the end of this section, and its delectable variation, *Tripes à la florentine,* where it is taken one further stage and gratinéed with a generous spreading of Parmesan cheese.

The most famous recipe of all, however, is *Tripes à la Mode de Caen,* a homegrown version of which this recipe brings you. When we did it for the television we had an audience in the studio. Among them were a group of middle-aged types from a club, and 15 young high schoolers with their Home Ec. teacher. After the taping we were having a question-and-answer session and it appeared that few in the audience had ever tasted tripe, so I passed among them to give everyone a bite. The oldsters, almost to a man, drew back: "No, I just couldn't taste it. No!" They were rather apologetically but incurably squeamish. All of the young people, boys and girls and their teacher, tried it with interest and asked for more, proving, if proof there need be, that in our youth there lies the hope of the country.

BUYING FRESH TRIPE AND PREPARING IT

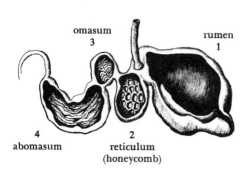

omasum
3

rumen
1

4
abomasum

2
reticulum
(honeycomb)

You may have to search around for tripe if you live in a neighborhood catering only to the steak, chop, and hamburger crowd. Most markets that do carry it usually have only honeycomb tripe, which is the reticulum, second stomach, or *bonnet.* Fortunately, this is considered the choicest.

It looks like a thick whitish honeycombed bathing cap, and will usually be in a plastic pouch in the refrigerated packaged meat section. Be sure it is labeled "Fresh Tripe," not "Pickled Tripe." Tripe is perishable; keep it refrigerated, and plan to cook it almost immediately.

To prepare any fresh tripe for cooking, cut it with heavy shears into several large pieces. Wash it under cold running water, then set in a pan of cold water to cover and blanch it (bring to the boil, and boil 5 minutes). Drain, rinse in cold water, and smell it: tripe has its own special smell, as does liver, or beefsteak, or lamb, and you should familiarize yourself with all of them as part of your culinary training. Tripe should have a fresh and healthy but typically tripe-type odor—some like it stronger than others, and if this is your first experience, give it 3 or even 4 blanchings, and it is then ready for cooking.

TIMING. Tripe is far from being a fast-food operation. It needs soaking, and simmering, and the long slow cooking—5 to 7 hours or more, depending on your recipe—in which it gradually absorbs the flavors of the wine, onions, spices, and any other ingredients you have put with it, and all the while it is developing a marvelously savory taste. I don't know why people shy away from a 3-hour dough rise, a 5-hour simmer, or a 12-hour oven session. You are not sitting there, eyes glued to the pot. No! You are out at the movies, or you are writing your novel, or you are playing tennis, and you return to your tripe when its time is due. This is, really, the easiest kind of cooking, where, once you've put it all together, it does the rest of the work for you.

Tripes à la mode

TRIPE COOKED IN WINE AND AROMATIC VEGETABLES

This is the idea of *Tripes à la Mode de Caen,* using dry white wine instead of the traditional dry cider of Normandy, and pig's trotters rather than the skinned beef feet recommended by Escoffier. If you are able to get the 4 kinds of tripe in the previous illustration, so much the better because of the interesting differences in texture, but just the honeycomb does beautifully. Although you may serve tripe as a main course, it is particularly agreeable in an informal Sunday luncheon or supper, accompanied by boiled potatoes and good

French bread. Drink a dry white wine or fresh cider, and follow the tripe with salad, cheese, and fresh fruit or a fruit tart.

Timing note. For this dish the tripe must cook very slowly indeed, and needs no watching once in the oven. Put it in when you go to bed, and it will be done after breakfast. It makes a wonderful-smelling kitchen to come into.

For 4 to 6 people

Cooking time:
10 hours at 275
degrees

2 whole ready-to-cook fresh (not pickled)
honeycomb tripe (or 3½ to 4 lbs. tripe)
3 ready-to-cook pig's feet, split in half lengthwise
(or 2 to 3 lbs. veal knucklebones sawed into
pieces and a 6-inch square of fresh or
salt pork rind)
2 cups sliced carrots
Either: 3 cups sliced white of leek and 3 cups
sliced onions
Or: 6 cups sliced onions only
2 or 3 large cloves of garlic, unpeeled and sliced
10 each: peppercorns and allspice berries
2 large bay leaves
1 Tb salt
Sufficient strips of fresh beef fat or pork fat
(from loin or rib roasts) , ⅜ inch thick, to
cover ingredients in casserole
1 bottle dry white wine (such as Mâcon,
Chablis, Pinot Blanc)
Optional: ⅓ cup Calvados, Eau de Vie,
or Cognac
If needed: chicken stock or water
Optional: dough cover made of 2 parts all-purpose
flour and 1 part cake flour plus water
(see directions in recipe)

Equipment: A flameproof 6- to 8-quart covered
casserole, such as a small-mouthed pot
for baked beans

Preparing the tripe for the oven. Prepare the tripe for cooking as described in *Buying fresh tripe and preparing it,* blanching the pig's feet (or knucklebones and rind) once with the tripe—these will give the cooking juices their characteristically gelatinous quality. Cut the blanched and drained tripe into 3-inch squares. Toss the vegetables and seasonings in a bowl.

Cover bottom of casserole with a layer of vegetables, half of the pig's feet or rind and bones, then with layers of tripe and vegetables; finish with remaining pig's feet or rind and bones, and cover with strips of beef fat or pork fat—these are to protect the tripe during its leisurely baking, and to keep it from browning. Pour in the wine and the optional Calvados or other liquor; if needed, add sufficient chicken stock or water barely to cover ingredients.

✿ May be prepared in advance to this point; cover and refrigerate, but bake within 24 hours.

Baking the tripe. Bring contents of casserole just to the simmer on top of the stove, and preheat oven to 275 degrees. For an old-fashioned touch, and also for added protection to the tripe, mix enough of the two flours and water into a sufficient quantity of soft dough to cover ingredients with a ½-inch layer; roll or stretch it out, and press it on top of ingredients, then well against the insides of the casserole. When contents of casserole have just reached the simmer, set uncovered in lower middle of oven. In an hour or more, when dough has crusted over, put a cover on the casserole. (If you are not using the dough, lay a sheet of wax paper over fat layers in casserole. Drape aluminum foil over mouth of casserole, pressing it down the sides; put on the casserole cover. Set in lower middle of oven.)

Bake 10 to 12 hours in all; 2 or 3 hours longer will not harm the tripe. Liquid should remain at the barest simmer—275 degrees is right for most ovens.

Finishing the tripe. When you feel the tripe is done, remove casserole from oven; lift off and discard dough and layer of beef fat. Skim off as much surface fat as you easily can, then pour contents of casserole into a colander set over a large bowl. Remove the pieces of tripe and return them either to the cooking casserole or to a clean one. Add also, if you wish, the boneless remains of the pig's feet, cutting them first into strips or squares. Skim remaining fat off cooking liquid in bowl, correct seasoning, and pour liquid back over tripe.

✿ If you are not serving immediately, let tripe cool to room temperature, then cover and refrigerate.

To serve. Reheat to bubbling hot, and dish out into very hot shallow soup plates, decorating each serving with small boiled potatoes.

OTHER WAYS WITH TRIPE

Tripes à la niçoise. Tripe baked with lots of onions, tomatoes, and herbs is the typical Mediterranean way of doing things. After you have washed and blanched about 4 pounds of tripe as described on page 329, along with the pig's feet or a calf's foot, or a veal knucklebone sawed into quarters, you are ready to begin. Cut the tripe into 3-inch squares, or into strips 4 inches long and less than 3/16 inch wide. Cook all of these very slowly in a heavy covered casserole with 4 cups of sliced onions and ½ cup of olive oil for 2½ hours either in a 300- to 325-degree oven, or on top of the stove. Bone the pig's or calf's feet, if you are using them, cut meat into strips, and return both meat and bones to casserole. Fold in 2 cups of fresh tomato pulp (tomatoes peeled, seeded, juiced, and chopped), 1 cup of white wine, several cloves of chopped garlic, salt, and the usual herbs—bay, thyme, fennel seeds, dried orange peel. Cover and cook very slowly 2 or 3 hours more, adding a little meat stock or bouillon from time to time if tripe needs moistening, but the tomatoes should provide sufficient sauce. When the tripe is finally tender to your tooth, remove any bones and other extraneous items, and serve the tripe with boiled rice, boiled potatoes, or just French bread. (This recipe takes nicely to precooking and reheating, and any leftovers are good indeed in a bean or lentil soup.)

Tripes à la florentine. This marvelous Italian-inspired concoction is nothing more or less than *Tripes à la niçoise* gratinéed with Parmesan cheese. Be sure to cut the tripe into long thin strips before you begin, and then proceed as described above. About 20 minutes before you are ready to serve, having preheated your oven to 425 degrees, use a slotted spoon to dip the tripe from its casserole to a gratin dish 1½ inches deep. Moisten with several spoonfuls of its cooking liquid, enough to enrobe each strip. Spread ⅔ to 1 cup freshly grated best-quality imported real Parmesan cheese over the tripe, and fold it in. Spread over it another ½ to ⅔ cup of Parmesan—you need much more cheese here than you would think. Dribble on a spoonful or two of good olive oil, and bake in the upper third of the oven for 15 to 20 minutes, to brown the cheese nicely. You should get the effect, almost, that each strip of tripe has its own individual coating of browned cheese. Serve immediately.

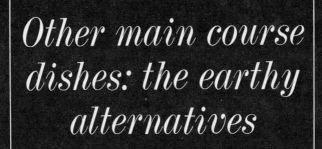

Other main course dishes: the earthy alternatives

Lentils

Maître d'hôtel
Garnies—en cassoulet
The pressure cooker—lentil purée

Dried beans, shell beans, chick peas

Pressure cooking—and quick soaking
With butter and herbs; with cream;
    provençal; with roast or braised meats
    and stews; en purée
Fresh shell beans and chick peas
    pressure cooked
Black beans with pork and sauerkraut
    à l'alsacienne

Rice and risotto

Plain boiled rice
Risotto garni, a main course
Soubise—braised rice and onions

Pasta à la French Chef

Lasagne à la française
Spaghetti Marco Polo, a main course
Acini de pepe and other small sizes
Books on Italian cooking in English
    and Italian

A provençal ragout

Main course vegetable sauté with giblets

*W*hen lentils, beans, rice, or pasta are on the menu, a little meat goes a long way, and it can sometimes even be left out altogether. Beans and lentils have the most protein in the group, pasta comes next, and while rice has only half the protein of spaghetti, it has less than half the calorie count of the same amount of braised beef. Why did I get into this? Not being a nutritionist, I shall pursue it no further except to note that calorie-count booklets are available in every dime store, and if you are serious about the whole subject I recommend to you the U.S. Department of Agriculture's Handbook Number 8, *The Composition of Foods,* 190 large pages of close print listing every calorie, protein, vitamin, and mineral in 2,483 kinds of food, from abalone to zwieback, plus tables on fatty acids, cholesterol, magnesium, and everything else the mighty modern nutritionist should know. For sale by the Superintendent of Documents, Washington, D.C. 20402. [Alice B. Toklas was once quoted as saying, "But I don't want nutrition. I want food!"]

These earthy alternatives really are food, with their robust tastes, and with all the good things you can put with them—the onions, and garlic, and tomatoes, the bits of pork, the browned sausages, the healthy sprinklings of cheese, the fragrant herbs. Now that we shall all be using more legumes and pastas and trying out new ways of combining them, we shall realize how hearty and satisfying a meal they make. This is peasant food in the best sense of the word, the kind of food that has nourished generations before us, and to which we are now returning with good appetites.

Lentils

The biblical Jacob would have had Esau's birthright in one-quarter time had his pottage been made with the modern lentil. In those days as well as in our grandmother's and even our mother's youth, the lentil needed a lengthy presoaking and a long slow boil of 2 to 3 hours. Today's lentil, smaller and thinner-skinned, needs no soaking and should not be boiled at all unless it is going into lentil soup. Curiously, many package labels have not caught up with progress, but I have yet to find a contemporary lentil here or in France that needed either soaking or long cooking. Here are lentils as a vegetable accompaniment both whole and puréed, lentils as the base for a fulsome main-course casserole, and some aspects of lentils under pressure.

Lentilles maître d'hotel

BUTTERED WHOLE LENTILS

For about 3 cups, serving 4 to 6

For this recipe, the lentils must remain whole throughout their cooking, and are tossed with seasonings just before serving. They are particularly attractive with lamb dishes, pork, sausages, turkey, and game.

1 cup washed lentils
3 to 4 cups water
Salt
Pepper
2 to 4 Tb melted butter
1 to 2 Tb finely minced shallots or scallions
2 to 3 Tb minced fresh parsley

Place the washed lentils in a 2½- to 3-quart saucepan, add 3 cups of water—no salt yet—and bring to just below the simmer. Maintain at just below the simmer for 35 to 45 minutes, adding a little boiling water if necessary, until lentils are as tender as you wish them to be; test by eating a few. Just before serving, drain them, and toss over moderate heat in a frying pan to dry off as much moisture as possible. Then toss with salt

and pepper to taste, butter, and shallots or scallions, to heat thoroughly
—2 minutes or so. Toss with parsley, turn into vegetable dish, and serve.

Lentilles garnies; lentilles en cassoulet

Given a preliminary blanching, a simmering with wine and seasonings, then a topping of pork or sausages, lentils make a wonderful main dish. Serve with French bread, a green salad, and a strong young red wine such as Beaujolais, Côtes du Rhône, or Mountain Red.

GRATIN OF LENTILS
WITH MEAT

For 6 people

2 cups washed lentils
6 cups water
2½ to 3 lbs. meat cut into serving chunks:
  homemade or Italian or Polish sausages
  and/or pork shoulder butt, ham, country
  spareribs, or lamb shoulder
About ⅔ cup mirepoix (½ cup each finely diced
  carrot, onion, and celery cooked until
  tender in 3 Tb butter or oil) , in a
  medium saucepan
3 Tb flour
½ cup red or white wine, or
  dry white French Vermouth
1½ cups ham stock, meat stock, or
  canned beef bouillon
1 bay leaf
¼ tsp thyme or oregano
Salt and pepper
3 Tb minced shallots or scallions
3 Tb minced parsley
¼ cup fresh white bread crumbs

Preliminaries. Preheat oven to 450 degrees. Cook the lentils very slowly in water as described in the previous recipe, but only for about 30 minutes, until barely tender. Drain. Meanwhile, dry the chunks of meat in paper towels, spread in a roasting pan, and brown in the upper-middle level of preheated oven for 25 to 30 minutes, turning the meat and basting occasionally with accumulated fat and juices in the pan. Prepare the *mirepoix* also, and when done, blend in the flour, cook slowly, stirring, for 2 minutes, and remove from heat; beat in the wine, then the stock, and simmer 5 minutes, add the herbs to this sauce, and correct seasoning.

Assembling the casserole. Choose a baking dish such as a 9- by 12-inch oval 2 inches deep, and butter it lightly. Fold the lentils and sauce together, and spread in the baking dish. Arrange the browned meat on top, pushing the pieces into the lentils. Pour fat from roasting pan into a small bowl, and deglaze pan with a little wine or bouillon (pour in the liquid, set over heat, and scrape coagulated meat juices into liquid with a wooden spoon, boiling rapidly until liquid is syrupy); pour over the meat. Season meat lightly with salt and pepper; sprinkle the shallots or scallions, parsley, and bread crumbs over all. Baste with 2 spoonfuls of fat reserved from the roasting pan.

✵ May be prepared a day in advance to this point; when cool, cover and refrigerate.

Baking and serving. Preheat oven to 375 degrees. About 40 minutes before serving, set in upper-middle level of oven, until sauce is thick and bubbling hot, and crumbs are nicely browned.

✵ May be kept warm on an electric heating device, but do not let the casserole overcook, drying out the lentils and the meat.

LENTILS AND THE PRESSURE COOKER

When you want a purée of lentils, or lentil soup, the pressure cooker works very nicely. When you want them to remain whole, however, pressure-cooking is risky; sometimes it works, sometimes not, and I've not been successful at all lately—I've had to turn my pressure-cooked lentils into a purée. There's nothing wrong with a purée, of course, unless you had hoped for whole lentils in a salad.

For lentils as a purée, or for lentil soup

1 cup lentils
3 cups water
½ teaspoon salt
1 Tb butter or minced salt pork or bacon
Optional for flavor: ¼ cup each of roughly chopped celery, carrot, onion, and turnip

Wash the lentils but do not presoak them. Add to the pressure-cooker pan with the ingredients listed and cook at full pressure 3 minutes. Remove pan from heat and let pressure go down by itself—about 20 minutes. Uncover, and the lentils are ready to use either as a purée in the following recipe or in the lentil soup on page 12.

*Purée de
lentilles*

PURÉED LENTILS

Drain cooked lentils and purée through the finest disk of a vegetable mill (or in a blender or food processor, and then push through a sieve to get rid of any skins). Place in a saucepan and set in another and larger saucepan of simmering water. Beat in salt and pepper to taste, a little of the cooking liquid if purée is too thick, and as much soft butter as your conscience will allow.

*Dried beans, shell beans,
chick peas*

Again, since grandmother's day, great strides have been made in the cooking of legumes, and we can thank our U.S. Department of Agriculture for their work on the subject. The first breakthrough was their discovery of the quick soak, making it unnecessary to give dried beans an overnight sojourn in water to soften them for the morrow's meal. The quick soak cuts all that down to a little over an hour. Now, to make bean cookery even easier, the USDA people are working on a quick-cooking bean that needs no soaking at all and, furthermore, produces no flatulent aftereffects (no rooti-ti-toot!); at this writing, alas, that marvel has not yet made its public debut. In the meantime I suggest we all turn to the pressure cooker, since with the quick-soak and the pressure cook, you can have dried beans on the table in 1½ hours, from start to finish. Actually, since you can accomplish the preliminary cooking ahead, I think it a fine idea to do just that: some night, for instance, give them their quick soak while you are having dinner, and their short pressure cook as you clean up afterward. The cooked beans will then keep nicely for 2 to 3 days in the refrigerator, ready and waiting to be turned at once into an accompanying vegetable, a minor *cassoulet,* a soup, or a salad. Here is how to go about things, beginning first with some useful measuring facts.

Measurements for all dried beans (1 cup raw beans
 makes approximately 3 cups cooked beans)
 2 lbs dried beans: 4½ to 5 cups
 2 lbs. dried beans, soaked: 7 cups
 2 lbs dried beans, cooked: 14 cups, or 3½ quarts

Dried beans pressure cooked

FOR PEA BEANS, NAVY BEANS, GREAT NORTHERN BEANS, BLACK BEANS, SOY BEANS, ETC., BUT NOT FOR FLAGEOLETS

For pressure-cooked beans, I put only salt and a little olive oil with them for the initial cooking—oil or fat reduces foam that could clog the pressure valve. This gives me plain beans, and I can add whatever other flavorings I want later. But if you wish onions, garlic, herbs, and so forth to pressure cook with the beans, remember to let them sit a good 20 minutes after their cooking so they will absorb the flavors of these ingredients. This is true with anything cooked under pressure—taste it just when the pressure has been released, then after a wait, and you will be surprised at the difference.

Note: I have not found pressure cooking satisfactory for the delicious pale green French flageolet bean; although it takes to quick soaking, it tends to disintegrate under pressure.

For 3 cups of cooked beans, serving 4 to 6 people

1 cup dried beans
3 cups water
¾ tsp salt
1 to 2 Tb olive oil or butter

Equipment: A 4-quart pressure cooker

The quick soak. This is not done under pressure. Turn the beans into a sieve, pick over and remove any foreign matter; run cold water over the beans. Bring 3 cups of water to the boil in your pressure pan, drop in the beans; bring to the boil again, uncovered, and boil exactly 2 minutes. Remove from heat, set the cover loosely on the pan, and let sit for 1 hour.

Finishing the cooking. Then add the salt and olive oil or butter, cover pan, and bring to full pressure. Cook exactly 3 minutes, remove from heat, and let pressure go down by itself—15 to 20 minutes. Taste a bean, and if not quite tender, simmer slowly partially covered for 5 to 10 minutes, adding a little boiling water if necessary. (Extra simmering is rarely necessary, but you never know for sure.) Beans are now ready for any further treatment you choose to give them; heat them in their cooking liquid if they are cold, drain them, and proceed in one of the following manners:

Haricots secs à la maître d'hôtel. Melt 2 or 3 tablespoons of butter in a frying pan, stir in a tablespoon of minced shallots or scallions, or a large clove of minced garlic, cook a moment, then add the cooked beans. Toss about, shaking pan by its handle to throw the beans and flavoring together, adding salt and pepper to taste, drops of lemon juice, and finally 2 to 3 tablespoons of fresh minced parsley and basil or tarragon. (Out of herb season, use parsley and dried tarragon or Italian seasoning.) Serve these with roast pork, pork chops, roast lamb, sausages, rabbit stew.

Haricots secs à la crème et au fromage. Proceed as for the *Maître d'Hôtel* above, but after seasoning with salt and pepper, simmer the beans with half a cup or so of *crème fraîche* or heavy cream, letting it soak into and enrobe the beans. Then, if you wish, fold in ⅓ to ½ cup freshly grated imported real Parmesan cheese, and finally the herbs. Wickedly good, especially with white beans or flageolets. Serve these with steak or roast chicken.

Haricots secs à la provençale. Sauté a cup of minced onions in 3 table-spoons of olive oil and when tender fold in a clove or so of minced garlic and a cup or more of fresh tomato pulp (tomatoes peeled, seeded, juiced, and chopped) plus, if out of season, a little strained canned Italian plum tomato. Cook for several minutes, then fold in the cooked beans, salt and pepper to taste, and minced fresh herbs (parsley, basil, or tarragon; or parsley and dried tarragon, oregano, thyme, or Italian seasoning).

Heat through thoroughly, correct seasoning, and serve. Good with pork, ham, sausages, or fried eggs.

With roast or braised meats and stews. Just before serving, let the cooked beans simmer for a moment or two with the braising or roasting or stewing juices of lamb or pork, or with a rabbit stew or simple chicken sauté.

Purée de haricots secs. Use the same system suggested for the purée of lentils on page 339. A purée of white beans can be blended with a purée of cooked celeriac, white turnips, or mashed potatoes to give a change of flavor.

Brandade à la soissonnaise

PURÉE OF WHITE BEANS WITH GARLIC AND HERBS

Some of the best dried beans in France come from the town of Soissons, so anything *à la soissonnaise* of a culinary type would be dried-bean oriented. And a *brandade,* though usually associated with a purée of codfish liberally doused with garlic and olive oil, is actually just a Provençal word describing something that has been stirred vigorously. Thus, combining the two ideas, we arrive at the *Brandade à la soissonnaise,* a purée of white beans with garlic and olive oil plus a secret ingredient the ordinary *brandade* never knew existed—sesame paste. This *brandade,* once you have cooked or canned white beans, makes a very quick cocktail spread, or part of a rapid hors d'oeuvre arrangement that could also include hard-boiled eggs, olives, and sliced tomatoes.

For about 2 cups,
serving 8 or more

*1 ¾ cups drained cooked or canned white beans
   (or you could use black beans or chick peas)
1 Tb or more fresh lemon juice
¼ cup sesame seed paste
1 or 2 large cloves garlic, puréed
   through a press
Salt and pepper
8 or more fresh basil leaves; or dried herbs to taste,
   such as oregano, thyme, or a mixture
2 or more Tb good olive oil
Optional: Chopped fresh parsley*

Put the beans through the fine blade of a vegetable mill (or place them in a super-blender-food-processor, which goes very quickly indeed). Beat in the lemon juice, sesame seed paste, garlic, seasonings, and herbs. Then beat in enough olive oil to loosen the mixture to a consistency that will hold its shape in a spoon. Carefully correct seasoning. If you are to serve it in a bowl or mound it onto a serving dish, sprinkle heavily with chopped parsley. (Habit forming, and horrifyingly fattening.)

Fresh shell beans in the pressure cooker. These are the beans in their fresh state before they have been dried. Shell the beans, and for each cup add 3 cups of water, ¾ teaspoon salt, and 1 to 2 tablespoons olive oil or butter. No presoaking is necessary. Cook at full pressure exactly 10 minutes; release pressure immediately. If not quite tender, simmer partially covered a few minutes more. Serve in any of the preceding ways.

Dried chick peas, garbanzos. These do especially well in the pressure cooker, while sometimes you can get nowhere at all with them in an open pot. Use the quick soak described for dried beans on page 341, and 3 cups of water per cup of chick peas plus ¾ teaspoon salt and 2 tablespoons olive oil. Cook at full pressure 30 minutes; release pressure immediately. Serve in any of the preceding ways, or like the lentil *cassoulet* on page 337.

Haricots secs garnis à l'alsacienne

BLACK BEANS WITH BRAISED PORK AND SAUERKRAUT

Serving 4 to 6 people

I don't think this is Alsatian at all, but if the Alsatians were blessed with black beans they would surely use them in this hearty combination that you can get ready bit by bit, as your schedule allows. It is a one-dish main course, and you should really serve an Alsatian Riesling with it, but a strong dry white wine like a Côtes du Rhône would do, or a *rosé*, or even a big pitcher of beer.

The sauerkraut
2 lbs. fresh sauerkraut
2 ounces salt pork
1 Tb olive oil
1 each: medium-sized onion and carrot, sliced

1½ cups chicken stock
¾ cup dry white French Vermouth
1 cup, more or less, water
1 imported bay leaf
6 peppercorns
6 juniper berries
1½ Tb cornstarch or potato starch

The pork
Either: 4 to 6 pork chops, browned on each side
Or: 2 to 3 lbs., more or less, pork shoulder
    butt, country spareribs, or homemade or
    Italian or Polish sausage, cut into 2-inch
    chunks and browned in a frying pan

3 cups cooked black beans, page 340,
and their cooking liquid

Braising the sauerkraut. Drain and rinse the sauerkraut, and soak in several changes of cold water for 20 minutes. Drain, and squeeze dry by handfuls, then fluff up in a colander. Meanwhile slice the salt pork into strips ¼ inch thick and blanch them (drop in a quart of cold water, bring to simmer, and simmer 10 minutes, rinse in cold water, drain, and dry on paper towels) . Choose a heavy flameproof casserole, 2½- to 3-quart size, and in it brown the salt pork lightly with the olive oil. Then stir in the sliced onion and carrot, cover, and cook slowly 5 minutes until almost tender. Stir in the sauerkraut, mixing thoroughly with the salt pork and vegetables, cover and cook slowly, stirring up once, for 5 minutes. Add the chicken stock, wine, and enough water almost to cover the sauerkraut. Add the bay leaf, peppercorns, and juniper berries, and bring to the simmer on top of the stove. Lay a piece of wax paper over the sauerkraut, and set the cover on the casserole. Either bake slowly in a 325-degree oven, or simmer slowly on top of the stove.

Adding the pork. After the sauerkraut has cooked about 1¼ hours, salt lightly, and bury the browned pork or sausages in it. Bring again to the simmer, and continue cooking another 45 minutes, or until the sauerkraut is just tender but still slightly crunchy when you chew it.

Finishing the casserole. Drain all the liquid out of the sauerkraut into a 4-cup measure. Add enough bean-cooking juices to the measure to make

2 cups of liquid. Place the starch in a small saucepan, beat in the combined juices, and simmer 3 to 4 minutes to thicken the liquid into a sauce as well as to cook the starch. Carefully correct seasoning. Fold the cooked beans and the sauce into the casserole with the sauerkraut and pork.

☼ May be completed in advance a day ahead of serving; when cool, cover and refrigerate.

Simmer slowly, basting contents with sauce, for 5 to 10 minutes before serving, and either bring the casserole to the table, or transfer to a hot platter and decorate with parsley.

Rice and risotto

Rice is so easy to cook when you know how, and to know how is certainly far from difficult. You can cook it ahead, it keeps several days in the refrigerator and warms up beautifully, it makes a delicious salad, and mixed with other ingredients it can be a whole main course. When we were with the OSS in Ceylon during World War II this very main course was featured daily by a Chinese restaurant we frequented in Kandy, near the Temple of the Tooth; it was called by all, customers and waiters alike, "Flied Lice with Mix." In France it is usually billed as a risotto. "But it is not a risotto, it is a type of pilaf," Marcella Hazan, my mentor in all things Italian, remonstrates in her excellent *The Classic Italian Cook Book* (New York: Harper's Magazine Press, 1973). When you want a real Italian risotto you buy Italian Arborio rice—thicker, stubbier, and chewier than our usual rice—and you cook it her way. Here we have rice and risotto the French and French Chef ways, and you'll find other ways with rice in *The French Chef Cookbook* and in *Mastering*, Volume I, where it is boiled, braised, buttered, molded *en couronne*, and steamed.

Plain boiled rice

Rice is so painlessly and successfully cooked this way, with all grains dry and separate, that it is now my basic recipe whenever I want plain rice on hand. The same system but with saffron, you may have noticed, is on page 297 in the Curry Dinner, but the master recipe is here, where it belongs.

For about 4½ cups cooked rice (1 cup raw rice makes 3 cups cooked rice)

1½ cups raw untreated plain white rice—
Carolina long-grain type
3 cups water
2 Tb butter or olive oil (which you may
omit if you wish)
2 tsp salt
Pepper

Choose a heavy-bottomed 2- to 2½-quart saucepan with a cover. In it bring the rice and water to a rolling boil with the butter or oil and the salt. Stir up once, reduce heat to a simmer, cover the pan, and let the rice simmer undisturbed over moderately low heat for 15 minutes. Do not stir the rice at all during this period, but be sure liquid is actually simmering—not boiling hard, but simmering. At the end of 15 minutes there will be little steam holes going down through the surface of the rice and all liquid should be absorbed; tilt pan and lift rice from lower bottom of pan with a fork to check. Simmer 2 to 3 minutes more if necessary. Then set pan aside off heat, still covered, for 10 minutes; this allows the rice to finish its cooking. Uncover, fluff the rice lightly with a fork (never with a spoon or you may break the grains). Correct seasoning, adding more salt if necessary, a little freshly ground pepper, and more butter if you wish and if you are serving immediately.

✿ If you are serving in half an hour, set rice uncovered in a larger pan of simmering water until you are ready; fluff lightly again. If you are doing it way ahead, or are reheating chilled rice, cover the pan and set over simmering water fluffing and tossing every 4 or 5 minutes until heated through; you may need to add a sprinkling of hot water if rice seems dry. Do not overcook it, however, or the grains will swell out of shape—splayed ends rather than rounded ones mean the rice is overdone.

P.S. I ran into a chap the other day who said his wife just couldn't seem to cook rice properly. I showed him this recipe and he said, "What does that mean, fluff with a fork?" "It's in Webster's Collegiate," I said, "fluff, a verb." "I don't think you should use words like that," said he. "Well," said I, quite defeated—and I am still as I remember it, "if neither you nor your wife can find out how to fluff with a fork, you'll never be able to cook rice." The only reason for this foolish recital is that I now feel better having recounted it and, besides, I cannot come up with a fluff substitute.

Risotto garni

FRIED RICE WITH
MIX, A MAIN
COURSE

The classic example is, of course, a curry dinner, where you may or may not have a meat in sauce, but you have all the condiments to stir into the rice, from chopped peppers and onions to peanuts, hard-boiled eggs, crumbled bacon or Bombay duck, and so on and so forth as described on page 295. Here are some other combinations, starting with a formal recipe. A green salad and cheese could follow it, or a fruit dessert. Our family, by the way, likes to eat this dish with chopsticks.

For 6 people

6 to 8 to 10 fresh pork breakfast sausages
1 to 2 cups diced onions
1 or 2 diced green bell peppers
About 4½ cups cooked rice (the preceding recipe)
⅓ to ½ cup chopped seedless raisins
1 or 2 diced bananas
½ cup or so chopped almonds, walnuts, pine
  nuts, peanuts, or whatever else in the
  way of nuts you have
Salt and pepper
2 or 3 hard-boiled eggs, chopped, in a bowl
2 or 3 Tb fresh minced parsley, or a mixture
  of fresh green herbs such as parsley and
  chives and/or tarragon or basil

Choose a large frying pan or electric skillet. In it brown the sausages, remove and chop them, and leave about 3 tablespoons of their rendered fat in the pan: or add oil or butter instead, if you prefer. Stir in the diced onions; cover and cook slowly until the onions are tender and translucent —10 minutes or so. Add the peppers, and sauté a few minutes to soften, then add the rice and fluff with a fork to coat with the seasonings. Fluff in the raisins, bananas, and nuts; taste carefully for seasoning. (Turn onto a hot platter, if you wish.) Toss the chopped eggs with salt, pepper, and herbs; spread them over the top of the risotto, and serve.

ADDITIONS AND VARIATIONS

Additions and variations are endless, and the risotto is a prime repository for leftovers, although they should never, of course, be suspected as such. Rather than sausages, for instance, dice some cooked ham, sauté it lightly in butter and oil, then remove it while you cook your onions, and continue with the preceding recipe. Mushrooms are always attractive additions to a mixture such as this, either a handful of fresh mushrooms sautéed, or a spoonful or two of mushroom *duxelles*—very finely diced cooked mushrooms that you may have stored in your freezer. There is nothing wrong with shrimp, lobster, or crab, either, and any of these could first be sautéed in butter with a sprinkling of chopped shallots and seasonings, then folded into the risotto in addition to other meats, giving a *paëlla*-like effect. Just a little meat or fish, only something like 2 tablespoons per person, can give an impression of abundance when the rest of your ingredients and your seasonings are carefully considered. Finally, some cooked greenery is eye-appealing—fresh peas, diced fresh green beans, broccoli flowerets, and I shall not go on since the rest is up to your own imagination.

Soubise

BRAISED RICE AND
ONIONS

You can cook a *soubise* in any number of ways, as we have in our various books, but this is the easiest. It is a lovely mixture you can make even more attractive by adding heavy cream and grated cheese at the end. Plain or cheesed, it makes a savory bed for hamburgers, pork chops, sautéed chicken, sausages, turkey, veal, fish, poached eggs, or other vegetables.

Serving 4 to 6 people

2 *cups minced onions*
2 *Tb olive oil or butter*
¾ *cup plain raw white untreated rice,*
   such as long-grain Carolina
¼ *cup dry white French Vermouth,*
   dry white wine, or chicken broth
1⅓ *cups hot water*
½ *tsp salt*
½ *imported bay leaf*
Optional: ½ *cup crème fraîche or heavy cream;*
   ⅓ *to* ½ *cup freshly grated imported*
   real Parmesan cheese

Select a heavy-bottomed 2-quart saucepan with cover. In it cook the onions in the oil or butter, covering the pan, but stirring occasionally for about 20 minutes, until onions are thoroughly tender but not browned. Pour in the rice and stir for 3 to 4 minutes over moderate heat until rice has turned from milky to translucent and back to milky again—this cooks the starch coating, and prevents rice grains from sticking to one another later. Pour in the wine or broth and hot water, add the salt and the half bay leaf, and bring to the simmer. Stir up once. Cover and let cook at a moderate simmer, without stirring at all, for 15 to 18 minutes, until liquid has evaporated and rice is just tender. Discard bay leaf. Fluff with a fork, and correct seasoning.

☼ If done ahead, keep warm or reheat as described for plain boiled rice, page 346. Just before serving, if you wish, fluff in the cream, simmering a moment, and then add the cheese.

Pasta à la French chef

Lasagne, spaghetti, acini de pepe, and various unorthodox suggestions concerning them

Whenever I step out, over the television air, into any extra foreign activity, such as doing a curry dinner, a *paëlla,* or anything else not considered classically French, I get slapped down by angry nationalistic chauvinists. In the case of our program called "Lasagne à la Française" I was almost lynched by the Italian anti-defamation league. I should give a public apology over the air, one viewer from Boston said; I was an insult, a hedonist, an ignoramus. "What do you mean, using our national dish, lasagne, for leftovers. The very idea made me ill!" shrieked one letter from New Jersey. Anyway, I am always very careful indeed at the beginning of such a program. In this case, I announced that it was not an Italian version of lasagne, that I was not an Italian cook, that this was *à la française*, as the title clearly stated. But there's blood in their eye and fury in their ears on these occasions, and the message is not sometimes received. However, I did notice in reading the printed transcript of the show afterward that I was a bit carried away, made a few Italianesque cracks, and even ended up with *"buon appetito,"* which I shouldn't have done. But the title, "Lasagne à la Française," came up loud and clear on the screen at the end, if there were any doubts.

In addition to a transcript of every gasp, hiccup, and word uttered over the air for each program, we have a form letter book in our French Chef office. The one on lasagne, written with great enjoyment by me, tells enraged viewers that the whole idea of learning how to cook is so that one can grab any idea from anywhere and put it to good use. Here, it is the idea of lasagne that is "freed from ethnic restrictions and limitations," and is ready for improvisation. "This happens to be a delicious recipe using lasagne," the letter concludes, "I enclose it for you to try." And to enrage them further, the final touch, "We should be thankful to the Italians for having invented lasagne-shaped pasta, and to the French for their fine cooking methods that make such a splendid dish possible." Strangely—or should I say, thankfully—I have never had any reply whatsoever to this masterful rebuttal.

In truth, Mediterranean France abounds in pasta of every sort. Some of it is cooked in the Italian manner, but the French, in typical fashion, cook anything they take over in any way that appeals to them, and so should we all when it is a matter of improvisation. Certainly, for an attractive way to serve the remains of a turkey, poached or roast chicken, or roast veal or pork, a great dish of baked lasagne is a handsome solution. The lasagne, those wide strips of pasta about 12 inches long, are boiled until just done, then are arranged in layers in a baking dish alternating with layers of an inner sauce—an onion-flavored white-wine *béchamel*, cheese, a vegetable or two, and the diced meat. More white-wine onion sauce goes on top, a little tomato flavoring, and a final topping of cheese. All of this can be prepared even a day ahead of time, and baking takes only 30 to 40 minutes. The vegetables in this dish may be anything you choose, like cooked eggplant, asparagus, green peas, broccoli, or the always attractive and typically French combination of spinach and mushrooms. Since the vegetables must be precooked anyway, plan to do double the amount you need; serve them hot at one meal and save the remainder for your lasagne. Proportions, as in all recipes of this sort, are utterly flexible; it is the general idea that counts.

Lasagne à la française

Although you could start out with a soup or appetizer, this is the kind of meal that needs no first course. Serve French bread and a hearty red wine, such as a Mountain Red or Beaujolais, with the lasagne, and a tossed salad accompanying or following it. A dessert of fresh fruit—ripe pears for instance, would be attractive, or a fruit compote, sliced pineapple, or grapefruit sherbet; in any case, it should be a light finish to the meal, nothing starchy or rich.

I am listing the steps in the recipe the way I did them on the television show, but you may complete the two sauces, prepare the vegetables and meat, and sauté the optional mushrooms at any convenient time. Boil the lasagne only at the last minute, however, since it dries out if it hangs about any length of time.

An excellent tomato sauce, for about 2½ cups

For 8 people

1 cup minced onions (after cooking, ½ are for the second sauce)

2 Tb olive oil

2 large tomatoes, peeled, seeded, juiced, and chopped

A No. 1 can (2 cups) Italian plum tomatoes

½ tsp Italian seasoning (or ¼ tsp thyme and ½ bay leaf)

1 or 2 large cloves garlic, puréed

Big pinch saffron threads

¼ tsp dried orange peel

Salt and pepper

The lasagne

10 to 12 curly lasagne about 2 by 12 inches (made from best quality No. 1 semolina; read the label)

A large kettle containing 8 to 10 quarts of boiling water

1½ tsp salt per quart of water

2 Tb olive oil

For the white-wine onion sauce (béchamel ou velouté aux oignons), about 4 cups

(*Note:* I am giving more sauce here than in the original TV recipe; too much is better than too little!)

½ *the cooked onions from the tomato sauce*
6 *Tb butter*
8 *level Tb (or ½ cup scooped and leveled) flour*
3 *to 3½ cups hot liquid (milk plus chicken stock and/or mushroom juices)*
⅓ *cup dry white wine or dry white French Vermouth*
Salt and pepper to taste

For assembling the lasagne

An oiled baking dish, such as an oval one 9 by 12 by 1½ to 2 inches deep
The cooked lasagne
The white-wine onion sauce
About 2 cups well-seasoned cooked chopped green vegetables (such as broccoli, asparagus, or spinach)
About 1 cup grated cheese (a mixture of Parmesan, Swiss, and Provolone, for instance)
2 to 3 cups cooked diced chicken, turkey, veal, or pork
Optional: About 2 cups diced mushrooms, fresh or canned, sautéed in butter and seasoned
Optional: ½ to 1 cup ricotta cheese or cottage cheese
The tomato sauce

The tomato sauce. Cook the onions and oil in a 2-quart covered saucepan, stirring occasionally, until tender but not browned—6 to 8 minutes. (Remove half the onions and reserve for later.) Stir in the fresh tomatoes, cover, and cook slowly several minutes. Drain the canned tomatoes, and sieve about 1 cup of the pulp into the fresh tomatoes. Stir in the herbs, garlic, saffron, orange peel, and salt and pepper to taste. Simmer slowly, partially covered, for 30 minutes at least, adding a little juice from the canned tomatoes if sauce becomes too thick. While sauce is simmering, prepare the rest of the ingredients.

Boiling the lasagne. Drop lasagne into boiling water, add salt and olive oil, and boil slowly, uncovered, for 13 to 15 minutes or until lasagne is just tender but still has a slight texture, chewiness, or *al dente,* when you cut off a sliver and bite into it. Drain immediately, rinse rapidly in cold water, and hang piece by piece over the edge of a colander. While lasagne is cooking, continue with other parts of the recipe.

The white-wine onion sauce. Blend the onions with the butter in a heavy-bottomed 2-quart saucepan over moderate heat. When butter is bubbling, blend in the flour and cook, stirring with a wooden spoon, for 2 minutes without browning the flour at all. Remove from heat. When mixture has stopped bubbling, pour in two thirds of the hot liquid all at once, blending vigorously with a wire whip. Blend in more, leaving about ½ cup for later. Beat in the wine, and set over moderately high heat, stirring, until sauce comes to the boil. Thin out, if necessary, with the remaining liquid; sauce should be thick enough to coat a spoon fairly heavily. Boil, stirring frequently with a wooden spoon, for 4 to 5 minutes; beat in salt and pepper to taste. (If not used immediately, keep over a pan of simmering water, stirring occasionally. If done in advance, clean sauce off sides of pan with a rubber spatula, and float a film of milk over surface to keep a skin from forming; beat over heat to liquefy before using, and thin out with droplets of milk if sauce seems too thick.)

Assembling the lasagne. Line bottom of oiled baking dish with a layer of lasagne. Being sure to reserve 1 cup for top of lasagne later, spread 2 to 3 spoonfuls of white-wine onion sauce over the lasagne. Spread on half the green vegetables, sprinkle on 3 tablespoons of the grated cheese, half the diced meat, and half the optional mushrooms. Spread over this a few tablespoons of the white sauce. Cover with another layer of lasagne, and spread over it the rest of the green vegetables, more cheese, the remaining meat and optional mushrooms. Spread on a final layer of white sauce, cover this with optional ricotta or cottage cheese, and finish with a covering of lasagne. Trim off protruding ends of lasagne, and tuck it all down into the edges of the dish. Mask top of lasagne with remaining white sauce, covering as much as you can. Spoon the tomato sauce unevenly over the surface, leaving no lasagne exposed. Sprinkle grated cheese over all, using ⅓ to ½ cup.

✿ If not baked immediately, cover and refrigerate.

Baking and serving. Bake in upper third of a preheated 400-degree oven for about 30 minutes (40 if chilled), until dish is bubbling hot and top of cheese has browned nicely. Serve as soon as possible, to preserve the fresh green of the vegetables and the texture of the meat.

Spaghetti Marco Polo

————◆————

AN UNORTHODOX
MAIN-COURSE
SPAGHETTI DISH
TO BE EATEN
WITH CHOPSTICKS

Be adventurous with spaghetti. Get out of the old tomato and meatball syndrome. Here is a delicious combination to give you some new ideas; it happens to be meatless, but that doesn't mean you couldn't toss in some chopped sautéed ham, or diced browned sausages, or even a handful of shrimp. This was part of our program "Spaghetti Dinner Flambé," which suggested scallops *en brochette* or stuffed eggs to begin the meal, and finished with wine-baked apples flamed in Bourbon whiskey. Of course you don't have to eat the spaghetti with chopsticks, but that was in memory of Marco Polo's journeys in China, from whence, some say, he returned with a saddlebag full of pasta, and that's where spaghetti began in the western world. It's more fun with chopsticks, and they truly eat spaghetti that way in China; I've seen them do it.

For 4 people

*½ lb. spaghetti made from No. 1 semolina
    (read the label)
⅔ cup chopped walnuts
½ cup chopped black olives
½ cup chopped canned red pimiento (sweet
    peeled red pimiento not packed in vinegar)
⅓ cup chopped fresh parsley
8 to 10 large leaves fresh basil, chopped, or
    1 tsp fragrant dried basil
Salt and pepper
About 4 Tb best-quality olive oil
2 or 3 cloves garlic, peeled and very finely
    minced or put through a press
2 cups or so freshly grated best-quality imported
    Parmesan cheese in a serving bowl*

About 10 minutes before serving, cook the spaghetti in a large kettle of rapidly boiling salted water; test by eating a bite now and then until just done and very slightly crunchy *al dente*. (It's inedible if not cooked enough, but sad when mushy—bite with an alert tooth, therefore.) Meanwhile, mix the nuts, olives, pimiento, parsley, and basil in a bowl with salt and pepper to taste. When spaghetti is done, drain immediately into a large colander. Pour the olive oil into the hot empty kettle, set over moderate heat, and add the garlic. Stir a moment to cook briefly

without browning, then return the spaghetti. Toss about to coat with
the oil and garlic, season very carefully with salt and pepper, and turn
the spaghetti out onto a hot serving platter. Scoop the nut and herb
mixture on top, and bring to the table at once.

With dramatic gestures and a large serving spoon and fork, lift the
spaghetti high to blend with the flavorings before serving it. Each guest
adds his own Parmesan cheese.

THOUGHTS ON OTHER PASTA SHAPES

Acini di pepe and other small sizes. When you want a quick and easy
starchy something to go with broiled meats, roasts, hamburgers, and the
like, try some of the very small pasta shapes. I am particularly fond of
those tiny dots, *acini di pepe,* peppercorns, sometimes called "soup mac,"
and the rice-shaped pasta usually labeled *orzo.* They take but a few
minutes to boil in salted water, and after draining them, I toss them in
butter and good olive oil, season them, simmer a few moments in as
much heavy cream as I think decent for our weight at the time, and finish
them off with a toss in freshly grated (imported, real!) Parmesan. If we
are making a main course of pasta, I fold in some sautéed mushrooms
or sautéed chicken livers, ham, or shrimp as I add the cream, and a
sprinkling of fresh chopped parsley at the end.

BOOKS ON ITALIAN COOKING

For authentic information on pasta there is, of course, Jack Denton
Scott's *The Complete Book of Pasta* (Bantam Books No. NE5347), and
numerous recipes in the aforementioned *Classic Italian Cook Book* by
Marcella Hazan. There is pasta also in *The Romagnolis' Table* (Boston:
Atlantic, Little Brown, 1975), by Franco and Margaret Romagnoli,
whose televised program on Italian cooking comes over the Public Broad-
casting network. If you read Italian, Ada Boni's 1,188-page *Il Talismano
della Felicità* (Carlo Colombo, Rome) is the classic; Mme. Boni died
at the age of ninety-two, by the way, in May of 1973. Another marvelous
tome is Anna Gosetti della Salda's *Le Ricette Regionali Italiane* (Casa
Editrice "La Cucina Italiana," Milan), which gives a vast selection of
dishes, including pastas, region by region.

A provençal ragout

In the midst of the great 1972 meat boycott, my husband and I happened
to be on a cooking business trip covering a dozen cities in the eastern
part of the country, from Pittsburgh down to Miami and back through
Chicago, Philadelphia, Rochester, and Boston. Talking was easy. The
subject was inevitably meat versus meatlessness and I fitted nicely into
talk shows, interviews, and demonstrations by sheer chance because my
standard program for the trip was "Entertaining with Eggs." It had to be
some kind of table-top cookery that I could whisk up on my portable
two-burner stove and borrowed electric skillets. I did a fancy dish of
scrambled eggs layered between beds of creamed mushrooms and cheese;
there were closed and open-faced omelettes with various fillings; and to
top it all, a flaming *frittata* banana finish.

Although a number of people we talked to felt they just had to have
their daily slab of meat or they weren't being fed properly, we could see
that the stream of publicity was making people think. I remember one
television interviewer in Birmingham who said, "You know, since prices
went up so high, my wife has really begun to cook. She's loving it. We
used to stick a steak or a couple of chops under the broiler and that was
it. I didn't really care what I ate, but it was getting awfully expensive.
Now she's reading cookbooks and snooping around the markets for
special things, and it smells wonderful when I come in the house. We
have stews, or stuffed cabbage, or braised lamb shanks, or an Oriental rice
dish, and all sorts of fresh vegetables I never thought I'd eat. You know,
I'm enjoying it, too. I never know what she'll come up with next, but
I'm loving it. Maybe I'm getting to be a gourmet!"

Certainly the road to gourmetude is not paved with steaks and chops,
nor with mountains of *foie gras* and truffles, nor even with great wads
of cash, though there is nothing wrong with any of these, particularly the
cash. Wonders can be done with the simplest of ingredients, and indeed
the genius shows forth his true quality when faced with humble means.
Along these chaste lines, we mounted a television show called "A Two-
dollar Banquet," featuring the eggplant pizza on page 398 as a first
course and the following Provençal ragout for the *pièce de résistance*.
At the time it did all come to about two dollars, and a very simple dessert
like a homemade sherbet or caramel custard would have fitted into the
budget, but no wine. For that you needed to depend on the generosity
of your guests.

The point of it is that you poke around in your market. See what's on sale, what's on special, and what are the seasonal products in great supply at the lowest price. An open mind and a willingness to experiment are usually the mothers of creation.

Ragoût provençale des quatre saisons

———

PROVENÇAL
VEGETABLE SAUTÉ
WITH GIBLETS,
A ONE-DISH
MAIN COURSE

You can make this dish out of anything in season, as I learned from Richard Olney, the talented American cook, author, and painter, when he served it to us in the south of France. If it is to be Provençal, you must of course start out with onions, garlic, and olive oil. Otherwise any vegetable goes as long as it is fresh, and the more variety you have the more interesting your final dish. You need only one or two of each item, such as potatoes, zucchini, turnips, a trimmed artichoke bottom, a carrot and parsnip, for instance, a handful of cooked chick peas or navy beans. Find something bright to add at the end for decoration, such as fresh peas, beans, snow peas, or broccoli flowerets. The whole dish may be nothing but vegetables, or you can include bits of ham, sausage, chicken liver, or giblets. Proportions are of little importance; freshness is, and here is a sample combination.

For 4 people

Optional: 1 lb. or so chicken hearts and gizzards,
    plus salt, pepper, and flour
¼ cup or so olive oil and, if you wish,
    2 to 3 Tb butter
2 or 3 large onions, sliced
4 or more large cloves garlic, peeled
Optional: 1 or 2 trimmed fresh artichoke
    bottoms, cut into quarters or eighths
Salt and pepper
2 or 3 turnips or part of a rutabaga,
    peeled and diced
2 or 3 parsnips, peeled and diced
2 or 3 carrots, peeled and diced
2 or 3 potatoes, peeled and diced

½ tsp each fennel seeds and tarragon
1 imported bay leaf
2 or 3 ribs of celery and/or part of a
*   fennel bulb, sliced*
2 or 3 zucchini, diced
1 head of broccoli and/or a handful of
*   fresh peas or diced fresh green beans*
Optional: A handful of black olives

The chicken giblets. If you are using chicken giblets, wash them, cut hearts lengthwise, and slice meaty part of gizzards from their thick underskins. Place the skin in a small pan with lightly salted water to cover, and simmer 30–40 minutes to make a light chicken stock. Salt and pepper the prepared hearts and gizzards, toss in flour, then brown in 1 tablespoon oil in a small skillet. Cover, and cook very slowly for 30 minutes; strain in the gizzard-skin stock, and simmer 30 minutes more, or until meat is just tender. Set aside.

Cooking the vegetables. For the vegetable ragout itself, film a chicken fryer or electric skillet with ¹⁄₁₆ inch olive oil, and add the onions. Cook over low heat, stirring occasionally, while you prepare the rest of the vegetables and drop them into the pan, starting with the garlic, which you may want to quarter lengthwise, then the artichoke bottoms, a little salt and pepper, and follow down the list through the zucchini. Toss occasionally, and add more oil or, by this time, 2 or 3 tablespoons of butter. Cover the pan, and let cook very slowly until vegetables are tender. Meanwhile, cut broccoli into flowerets, if you are using it; peel and dice central stalk and add to ragout, then peel stems of flowerets and set aside. Prepare the peas and beans and join to broccoli. Blanch these vegetables in a large saucepan of boiling salted water, for 4 or 5 minutes, or until just tender; drain immediately, refresh in cold water, and set aside. When ragout vegetables are tender, uncover and set them aside too.

✲ May be completed in advance to this point; set pan aside uncovered. Cover and toss over moderate heat to warm through thoroughly before proceeding.

Serving. Just before serving, add the giblets and any juices to ragout vegetables, cover, and heat through for several minutes, tossing frequently. Add the blanched green vegetables, toss to cover with juices, and to heat through again. Taste for seasoning. Either turn out onto a warm platter or serve from cooking dish. Decorate with the optional olives.

Charcuterie maison

Sausages

Pork and pork fat for sausages
Books on sausage making and charcuterie
Chair à saucisse—pure pork sausage meat
Nitrites, nitrates, and saltpeter
Saucisson de ménage—large home-cured
   fresh sausage to simmer in bouillon and
   serve with potatoes, beans, or
   sauerkraut, or to bake in pastry
Forming sausages, in natural casings
   or in cheesecloth

Terrines and pâtés

Pâté de campagne—pork and liver pâté
   with veal or chicken
Terrine de canard; pâté de canard—
   pâté of duck in its own container
Terrine de ris de veau—terrine of pork
   and veal with sweetbreads
Pâté en croûte, pâté pantin—free-form
   meat pâté baked in a crust

*F*resh sausages hanging in the window, delicious-smelling earthenware terrines full of rich meat mixtures on the counter, a *pâté en croûte* being sliced before your eyes—these are only some of the everyday delights a French *charcuterie* shop has to offer. Although *charcuterie* is still going on there in France, and we've a bit of it in New York and in a few of our other big cities, *charcuterie* on the small-shop artisan scale, where it always seems to be at its best, is gradually disappearing everywhere. It is a trade that takes time and training and hand work, all of which cost money when you are running a shop. But when you are making your own sausages at home, or your own *terrine de campagne,* or your great *pâté pantin* in its beautiful brown crust, you have only the raw ingredients to pay for. Speaking of ingredients, the sausage business was invented, one must remember, to take care of scraps in as succulent a manner as possible. But at home you don't have to use scraps of uncertain vintage; you can use fresh meat, and what a difference in taste that makes. You will simply be amazed when you sit down to Sunday breakfast with your own first homemade pork sausage; it tastes like some marvelous new food, yet it is nothing but fresh ground meat and seasonings. In fact all of these exotic-sounding creations are but fresh ground meat of one type or another, plus seasonings; it is the packaging—the presentation—that gives each item its special character. We shall start, then, with the simplest—fresh sausage meat.

Note. Because I did them on television, this chapter inevitably repeats some material already covered in Volume II of *Mastering,* such as sausage meat, stuffing, hanging, and the liver *pâté.* They are illustrated here, however, with photographs rather than drawings, and there are 3 fine new *pâtés,* one of duck in its skin, another with sweetbreads, and a final beauty—a free-form *pâté en croûte.*

Sausages

PORK AND PORK FAT FOR SAUSAGES. In all sausages and *pâté* mixtures the proportion of fat to lean should be between a third and a half, and while most of the fat renders out during cooking, its action during cooking, as well as its residue, makes the lean meat tender, gives it flavor, and prevents it from turning into a hard, stiff mass. I do not know why this is, but I do know that if I skimp on fat because of some misplaced scruple, I produce a poor, rather tough sausage. If you are on a fat-free diet, then, don't get into this chapter at all. But it is the fresh pork fat that is the most difficult ingredient to find here—thin sheets of it to line *terrines,* and fat to grind with the lean. Those who live on farms, raise their own hogs, do their own butchering, salting, curing, and so forth, have plenty of fresh fat from back and belly, and plenty of fresh lean meat trimmings for any sausage making that it pleases them to do. And if you live in a neighborhood that goes in for foreign butchering or has a pork-loving clientele you can usually find exactly what you want; if not, you have to scrounge around. I, for instance, make little collections in the freezer of fresh pork chop tails, raw fat shavings from a pork loin roast, and whenever I see a fresh fat-and-lean pork shoulder butt or meaty and fatty country-style pork ribs, I grab them for sausage meat. Thus the only difficulty about homemade *charcuterie* in our country, really, is getting the right ingredients easily. But where there is a will to make it, and a greed for it, there's always a way.

BOOKS ON SAUSAGE MAKING AND CHARCUTERIE. We've a large chapter on salting and curing meats and making *charcuterie* in Volume II of *Master-*

ing, but if you are interested in the subject I most earnestly recommend *The Art of Charcuterie* by Jane Grigson (New York: Alfred A. Knopf, 1968). It is one of the best books I know of that is in English and for the home cook.

Chair à saucisse

————◆————

PURE PORK
SAUSAGE MEAT
FOR BREAKFAST
PATTIES AND LINKS,
AND FOR USE IN
MEAT STUFFINGS,
PÂTÉS, AND
TERRINES

For 4½ cups,
about 2 pounds

The pork

Either: 1½ lbs. (3 cups) lean fresh pork
such as fresh ham, shoulder, or loin
and ¾ lb. (1½ cups) fresh pork fat such
as fatback, side pork (belly), fat trimmed
from a loin roast, or leaf (kidney) fat
Or: Fat-and-lean fresh shoulder, spareribs,
or whatever mixture you feel will give
you about 2 parts lean for 1 part fat
¾ Tb salt
¾ tsp mixed ground herbs and spices (such as
allspice, bay, paprika, sage, and thyme)
¼ tsp freshly ground pepper

Put meat and fat through coarse, then fine blade of meat grinder into a large bowl or the bowl of a heavy-duty mixer. Beat in the salt and other seasonings. If you are to make sausage links, add a few spoonfuls of cold water by droplets, beating, to soften the mixture, for easy encasing. Sauté a spoonful to cook through completely, and taste to check seasoning. Cover and refrigerate for 12 to 24 hours; this will allow full flavor to develop. Form into sausage cakes, or form into links as described later, on page 365.

NITRITES, NITRATES, AND SALTPETER

Nitrites and nitrates have, for generations, been added to cured meat products to give them color, to act as a preservative, and, it appears, to protect against botulism. Excessive amounts, however, have been shown to be dangerous to human health. Before the general furor about nitrites arose in the press in 1972, we had already taped our program "To Stuff a Sausage." I immediately wrote to the U.S. Department of Agriculture for information, and paraphrase their reply as follows:

A lethal dose of sodium nitrite is about 2 grams, meaning you must eat that amount all at once. The legal amount of sodium nitrite that may be added to meat is ¼ ounce (7.5 grams) per 100 pounds; during the processing of sausages about ¾ of this amount disappears, leaving some 35 parts per million, considerably less than the legal permissible residual limit of 200 parts per million. To reach the lethal dose of 2 grams, then, one would have to eat 120 pounds of frankfurters all at one time. Even if you wanted to achieve the maximum permissible dose, you would have to eat 20 pounds of franks at one sitting.

Saltpeter, an optional ingredient in our home-cured sausages that follow, is potassium nitrate, which slowly converts into nitrite salt as a result of bacterial activity. This is a slow process in which only low levels of nitrite are formed. The amount of saltpeter recommended in the sausage recipe is in compliance with government regulations. It is entirely up to you whether or not you wish to use the saltpeter, and it will make little difference in the finished product if you omit it.

Saucisson de ménage

—————

LARGE HOME-CURED
FRESH SAUSAGE
TO SIMMER IN
BOUILLON AND
SERVE WITH
POTATOES, BEANS,
OR SAUERKRAUT,
OR TO BAKE IN
PASTRY

For about 6 cups,
making a dozen
5-inch sausages, or
2 fat 12-inch
sausages

4 cups (2 lbs.) lean fresh pork and 2 cups (1 lb.) fresh pork fat (see notes on pork and pork fat on page 362)

¾ tsp white pepper

½ tsp cracked black peppercorns

½ tsp ground mixed herbs and spices (allspice, bay, paprika, sage, and thyme, for example)

Optional: ¼ tsp saltpeter (potassium nitrate, obtainable in a pharmacy, and see discussion of nitrates preceding this recipe)

¾ tsp sugar

1½ Tb salt

1 clove garlic, puréed

Optional: ¼ cup chopped pistachios

¼ cup Cognac

Put the pork and fat through coarse blade of grinder into a large mixing bowl. Blend vigorously with the rest of the ingredients. Sauté a small spoonful to check seasoning. Form the sausages as described below, and hang for 3 days in the dry airy part of your kitchen or anywhere else that temperature remains between 70 and 80 degrees. Then the sausages are ready for cooking.

☼ You may refrigerate them for a week after hanging, or freeze for several weeks before cooking.

Cooking whole. If sausages are in natural casings, prick with the sharp tines of a 2-pronged kitchen fork in 6 to 8 places, to let fat escape during cooking. Simmer slowly in bouillon and wine, in salted water, or with sauerkraut or cabbage for about 40 minutes. Sausage is done when juices run clear yellow when pricked, or at a meat thermometer reading of 165 to 170 degrees. Or you can do them in slices:

Sautéing in slices. After poaching, cut in thick slices and brown slowly in a frying pan. Serve with potatoes, beans, cabbage, with sauerkraut, or with egg dishes.

Forming sausages, in natural casings or in cheesecloth

Natural casing. Small hog casings and sheep casings are the easiest to procure. If your butcher cannot supply you with a few lengths, ask him where to buy them, or look up under "sausages" in the Yellow Pages. Wash a 6-foot length of small casing, and soak for about 1 hour in a large bowl of cold water. Cut into 2-foot lengths.

Wet sausage stuffing horn or metal tube of a pastry bag, fit end of a piece of casing onto small end of horn and hold large end under slowly running cold water faucet. Gradually ease casing onto end of horn, and fit remaining pieces onto horn in same manner; leave a 3-inch piece of empty casing dangling.

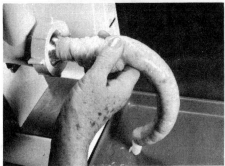

Fill casing with sausage mixture, using whatever mechanism you have chosen (illustrated is the attachment to the electric meat grinder).

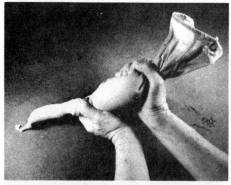

Here is an alternate method using a pastry bag.

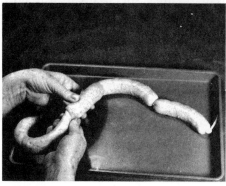

Tie sausages into links or lengths.

Cheesecloth casing. Wash cheesecloth and wring dry. For each sausage, large or small, cut cloth 3 inches wider and at least twice the circumference of the sausage you plan to make.

Have a saucepan of melted lard at hand, then dip cheesecloth into the lard and spread out on a tray. Form the sausage meat near one edge of the cheesecloth and roll it up to enclose the sausage meat completely.

Twist one end and tie with string, then twist the other, pushing meat to pack it tight; tie. For large sausages, wrap a spiral of string around the circumference from one end to the other; paint again with lard, and the sausages are ready for hanging. (The cheesecloth is removed after the sausages have been cooked, and before serving.)

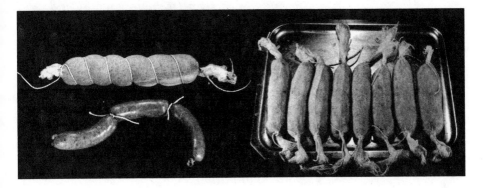

Terrines and pâtés

A combination of fresh ground meats mixed with wine and spices, baked in a comfortable dish, and served cold in thick, fragrant slices makes a marvelous first course and is luxurious on a picnic, or for lunch with tossed greens and a bottle of wine. That's the French *terrine* or *pâté;* if you can make a meat loaf you can make a *pâté*. It's as simple as that.

The traditional base is lean pork and pork fat, usually cooked onions, plus raw eggs, Cognac, herbs, and spices. Special additions to this base mixture, like strips of ham or veal, or game, rabbit, or hare determine the name of the final dish. Here the additions are veal or chicken and liver for *Pâté de Campagne,* and duck for *Terrine de Canard.*

NOTES ON NAMES. *Pâté* comes from pastry, because originally it was meat baked in a pastry crust; it has now come to mean the meat mixture itself. If served in a crust it is *pâté en croûte,* if served in a baking dish it is usually called a *terrine* but may still be known as a *pâté*. *Terra* is earth, and *terrine* means simply an earthenware dish.

Pâté de campagne

———————

PORK AND LIVER
PÂTÉ WITH VEAL
OR CHICKEN

For a 6-cup terrine,
16 servings

*8 ounces (1 cup) each of the following, finely
ground: lean raw pork, fresh pork fat, and
raw veal or chicken (see notes on pork and
pork fat, page 362)*
1 Tb salt
½ tsp pepper
⅛ tsp allspice
½ tsp thyme
1 clove garlic, puréed
2 to 3 Tb Cognac
2 "large" eggs
*½ cup finely minced onions sautéed in 2 Tb
pork fat or butter*
*About 12 ounces (1½ cups) pork, beef, or
calf's liver cut into ½-inch dice*
*Sheets of fresh pork fat ⅛ inch thick (fatback,
fat from a pork loin roast, or blanched
fat salt pork) to line terrine and to cover meat*
1 imported bay leaf

*Equipment: A 6-cup terrine, baking dish, or
bread pan; aluminum foil; a pan of boiling
water to hold terrine*

Forming the pâté. Beat the ground meats and fat, seasonings, herbs, garlic, Cognac, eggs, and onions (not liver) vigorously together to blend thoroughly. Sauté a small spoonful to cook through, taste, and add more seasonings if you feel them necessary—you should overseason slightly because the *pâté* will be served cold, and some of the flavors then become muted. Fold in the diced liver. Cut sheets of pork fat to line bottom and sides of *terrine,* and press them in place. Turn the meat mixture into the *terrine,* smooth top with wet hands or a spatula, and place bay leaf on top. Cover with a final sheet of pork fat, and press aluminum foil over and around the edges of the *terrine* to enclose meat completely.

✿ May be prepared in advance to this point; refrigerate for a day or two, or freeze for a month.

Baking. Preheat oven to 350 degrees. Place a cover on the *terrine,* weighting it down if necessary, and set in pan of boiling water in lower-middle level of oven. Bake 1½ to 2 hours, depending on shape of *terrine.* *Pâté* is done when it has begun to shrink from sides of *terrine* and the surrounding fat is clear yellow with no trace of rosy color—press top of meat with the back of a spoon to verify color of escaping liquid. A meat thermometer reading would be 170 to 175 degrees.

Cooling. Remove *terrine* from pan, discard water, and return *terrine* to pan. *Pâté* must now be weighted down as it cools, to squeeze out rendered fat, and to press the meat together so that it will slice attractively. Choose another pan, dish, or a piece of wood that will just fit into *terrine,* and press it down with a 5-pound weight of some sort, like a brick, canned goods, or pieces of a meat grinder. When cool, refrigerate the *terrine,* still with weights on.

Serving. *Pâté* may be served as soon as it has chilled, but its flavor will improve after 2 or 3 days of refrigeration. If you wish to serve from the *terrine,* remove first slice in the kitchen, then cut and serve the rest at the table. To serve the *pâté* unmolded, which can be attractive when you have used neat sheets of fresh pork fat to line the dish, set over a hot burner on the stove for several seconds to loosen bottom, run a knife around sides of *terrine,* and turn upside down on a serving board or platter. Scrape off coagulated cooking juices and reserve them for sauce or soup; smooth sides and top of *pâté* with a spatula dipped in hot water, and cut off a first slice in the kitchen to get rid of excess fat.

Storing. A *pâté* will keep a week to 10 days under refrigeration. It is the coagulated cooking juices that will go off first; for slightly longer storage unmold the *pâté,* and scrape and wipe them off. Then wrap in foil or plastic. Although you may freeze a cooked *pâté,* it will never have its same fresh taste and texture again.

OTHER IDEAS FOR TERRINES AND PÂTÉS

Terrine de canard; pâté de canard

PÂTÉ OF DUCK IN ITS OWN CONTAINER

For this attractive *pâté,* you bone the duck and remove the meat, then you line the *terrine* with the duck skin rather than pork fat; you arrange your basic ground meat mixture in layers interspersed with layers of duck breast cut into strips, plus truffles if you are feeling flush. After baking, unmold the *pâté,* to show off the cleverness of your idea, and when you cut serving slices they are nicely patterned with those strips of duck breast and, perhaps, truffles as well. Here is as good an excuse as any for learning how to bone poultry, since a few skin slits here and there make no difference—you can tuck the skin together to hide them —and there is nothing crucial about how the meat becomes available, whether in chunks, bits, or slices; thus plow in fearlessly, and you will find there's not much of a trick to boning.

For a 7- to 8-cup terrine, baking dish, or bread pan, providing about 16 slices

A 5- to 6-lb. roaster duckling

For marinating the duck breast strips
3 Tb Cognac
Salt and pepper
Optional: A 1-ounce (or smaller) can of truffles
  —peelings and pieces are the most reasonable
  in price—and the can juices

8 ounces (1 cup) each: lean raw pork and fresh
  raw pork fat ground together (see notes
  on page 362)
1 Tb salt
½ tsp each freshly ground pepper and thyme
⅛ tsp allspice
1 clove garlic, puréed through a press
2 "large" eggs
½ cup finely minced onions sautéed until soft
  in 2 Tb pork fat or butter
1 imported bay leaf

Boning the duck. If you have never boned poultry before, start right in with a short, very sharp knife, and just remember to cut and scrape against the bone; that will prevent you from cutting holes in the skin, and even if you do cut the skin, you can patch it. Now, starting at the back of the duck, slit the skin down to the backbone from tail to neck. Scrape meat from carcass first down one side, detaching wing joint at shoulder when you come to it, and thigh joint at small of back; stop just at the ridge of the breastbone. Repeat on the other side. Then lift up the carcass to disengage it, and very carefully scrape against top of breastbone to remove covering skin. Chop off the ball joint of each drumstick, then scrape meat from thigh and leg bones, drawing skin inside out as you do so. Chop off wings above elbows, scrape meat from upper arm bones, again drawing skin inside out. You now have just the skin of the duck, with all the meat attached. Carefully scraping against meat rather than skin, remove as much of the breast meat, thigh meat, and leg meat as you easily can. (Chop the carcass bones and use for duck stock, cooking it like the turkey stock on page 234, and then you can turn it into an aspic, if you wish, following directions on page 447; the aspic could then decorate the finished *pâté*.)

Marinating the duck breast strips. Cut the breast meat into ¼-inch strips and place in a small bowl with the Cognac, and a sprinkling of salt and pepper. If you are using truffles, mince them and add to the marinade along with the juices from the can. (Marinate 5–10 minutes or overnight.)

The basic ground-meat mixture. Grind the remaining duck meat with the pork and pork fat; beat vigorously in a bowl with the seasonings, herbs, garlic, eggs, and onions. Beat in the liquid from the duck-breast marinade. Sauté a small spoonful of the meat mixture, taste, and add more seasoning if needed.

Forming the pâté in the terrine. Line the *terrine* with the duck skin, skin side against walls of *terrine,* letting excess drape over sides. Spread a third of the meat mixture in the bottom of the lined *terrine,* cover with half the strips of duck breast meat, laying them lengthwise and interspersing them with the optional truffles. Spread on half the remaining meat mixture, cover with the rest of the duck strips and truffles, and top with the last of the meat mixture. Place bay leaf on top, then draw overhanging duck skin back to cover the meat (lay on a double thickness of wax paper if skin leaves a gap). Lay a sheet of aluminum foil (or wax paper) on top, and place a cover on the *terrine.*

Baking, cooling, and serving. Follow exactly the instructions for the *Pâté de Campagne,* page 368.

Terrine de ris de veau

TERRINE OF PORK AND VEAL WITH SWEETBREADS

Sweetbreads make an interesting change, and the unwary would never know what that soft pale delicacy was, buried between layers of fragrant meat. For this you can use the same basic mixture as in the *Pâté de Campagne,* page 368, or the slightly more delicate combination here.

For a 2-quart terrine, about 20 servings

1 lb. sweetbreads
1 lb. fresh lean pork (see notes on pork and pork fat, page 362)
1 lb. lean veal

1½ cups fresh pork fat
¼ cup Cognac
¼ cup dry white French Vermouth
2 "large" eggs
2½ tsp salt
¼ tsp white pepper
¾ tsp mixed herbs and spices, such as allspice,
        nutmeg, thyme, sage, crumpled bay leaf
Optional: A 1-ounce can of truffle peelings or
        pieces, and their juices

Equipment: An 8-cup terrine or baking pan lined
        with strips of fresh pork fat

Six hours or the night before you plan to bake the *terrine,* soak the sweetbreads in several changes of water, peel and trim them, then blanch 3 minutes in salted water; refresh in cold water, and cut in half. (Full treatment on sweetbreads is in both Volume I of *Mastering* and *The French Chef Cookbook.*)

While sweetbreads are soaking, put the meats and fat through the coarse and then the finest blade of your grinder, and beat in a large bowl with the rest of the ingredients. Sauté a bit, taste, and correct seasoning, then cover and refrigerate.

When the sweetbreads are ready, pack a third of the meat mixture in the *terrine,* arrange half the sweetbreads on top, salt and pepper them, cover with half the remaining meat mixture, the rest of the sweetbreads, salt and pepper, and the remaining meat. Cover with a strip of pork fat, aluminum foil, and a cover; and bake, cool, and serve as for the *Pâté de Campagne,* page 368.

Pâté en croûte; pâté pantin

FREE-FORM MEAT
PÂTÉ BAKED IN
A CRUST

There are few creations more glorious to behold on the buffet table than a *pâté en croûte,* its brown crust handsomely decorated with pastry cutouts, and each patterned slice of it smelling of carefully spiced meats. Wonderful for a party, it is also the perfect luncheon or supper dish, needing only a salad and a bottle of red or *rosé* wine to make the main course memorable. This free-form version can be made as large as you like, and in any shape from round to the giant rectangle suggested here, 18 to 20 inches long, 6 inches wide, and 3 to 4 inches high, serving 25 to 30 people.

For the pastry dough
7 cups (2 lbs.) all-purpose flour (scoop
dry-measure cup into flour and level
off with a knife)
½ lb. (2 sticks) chilled butter
6 ounces (¾ cup) chilled lard or shortening
1½ Tb salt
2 cups liquid as follows: 4 egg yolks
plus necessary iced water

For 8 cups all-purpose pork and veal stuffing
2¾ cups lean ground raw veal
2¾ cups lean ground raw pork (or
raw goose or duck meat)
2½ cups ground fresh raw pork fat (or
1¾ cups goose or chicken fat
ground with 1¼ cups fresh white bread
crumbs moistened with 3 to 4 Tb milk)
4 eggs
1½ Tb salt
1 or 2 cloves garlic, puréed
1 tsp thyme
Optional: ¼ tsp ground bay leaf
¼ tsp allspice
¼ tsp pepper
⅓ cup Cognac or Armagnac
1 cup finely minced onions cooked tender
in 2 Tb butter

For the garniture
Either: 2 half-pound loaf tins of truffled foie gras,
chilled and quartered lengthwise
Or: All of the following:
½ lb. veal scallops ¼ inch thick
Optional: 1 or 2 canned truffles
Salt and pepper
1 Tb minced shallot or scallion
3 Tb Cognac or Armagnac
½ lb. ready-cooked ham slice
about ¼ inch thick

Other items
*Egg glaze (1 egg beaten in a cup with
1 tsp water)
Optional: 3 cups wine-flavored aspic
(see end of recipe)*

The pastry dough (pâte à pâté). Measure the flour into a large mixing bowl or bowl of electric mixer; cut butter and lard or shortening into ¼-inch pieces and add to flour along with the salt. Blend fat and flour rapidly together with electric beater or pastry blender until mixture resembles coarse meal. Rapidly blend in the liquid, massing dough together; turn onto a board, press firmly into a ball, wrap airtight, and chill until pastry is hard and firm—2 hours or overnight. (Dough may be frozen.)

The ground-meat mixture (farce fine pour pâtés). Beat all the listed in-gredients together until light and fluffy. To check seasoning, sauté a spoonful until cooked through, let cool briefly, then taste; add more salt, spices, or whatever you think necessary. If not to be used immediately, cover and refrigerate. (May be frozen for several weeks, but too long in the freezer will diminish the spice flavors.)

The garniture. If you are using the alternative to *foie gras*, cut the veal into ¼-inch dice. Cut the optional truffle into ⅛-inch dice, and toss with the veal in a bowl, adding a sprinkling of salt and pepper, the shallot or scallion, Cognac or Armagnac, and the truffle juices. Cut the ham into ¼-inch dice and keep separately. Set both aside until ready to use.

Forming the pâté. Preheat oven to 425 degrees for next step. Choose the largest rimmed baking sheet or jelly roll pan that will fit into your oven, and dust with flour. To make as long a rectangular *pâté* as possible, you place it diagonally across the pan, from near corner to far corner. Al-though you may enclose the *pâté* in a single large rectangle of dough and transfer it upside down to the baking sheet, an easier alternative for such a large *pâté* is to form it right on the sheet.

First roll out half the dough ³⁄₁₆ inch thick and 6 to 8 inches longer and wider than you wish the *pâté* to be; roll dough up on your pin, and un-roll it diagonally across the pan. Prick with a fork at ½-inch intervals.

If you are using truffled *foie gras,* spread half the ground meat in a loaf shape down the middle of the dough, center the *foie gras* pieces in a line on top, the length of the meat, and cover with the rest of the ground meat. On the other hand, if you are using the veal and ham garniture, beat the liquid from the veal into the ground meat, fold in both the veal and ham garniture and the optional truffles, and form into a loaf shape down the central length of the dough.

Cut a square corner out of each of the four ends, and fold the dough up against the sides of the meat; paint sides of dough with cold water. Roll rest of dough into a rectangle ¼ inch thick, and long enough and wide enough to drape over the top and sides of *pâté,* plus an extra 3 inches of width to use for decorations. Trim off these 3 inches and reserve. Paint the dough already surrounding meat with cold water. Then roll dough rectangle up on pin and unroll over *pâté,* pressing it in place with your fingers. Prick deeply all over surface at ½-inch intervals with a sharp-tined fork or skewer.

If you are not to bake it immediately, paint surface of dough with cold water; otherwise paint with egg glaze. From the reserved strip of dough, cut decorations for the top of *pâté,* such as a long branch and big leaves; press them onto the surface of the *pâté* dough. Just before baking, paint entire surface of dough with egg glaze. Pierce three ¼-inch steam holes at intervals down top of *pâté,* and insert funnels, such as the metal ends of a pastry bag, or pieces of aluminum foil formed into cone shapes around a pencil end; paint surface of dough again with egg glaze. Draw the tines of a fork over glaze to make decorative cross-hatch marks. If you wish, insert a meat thermometer through central steam hole.

Baking: *1¾ to 2 hours.* Bake in middle level of preheated 425-degree oven for 30 minutes, or until pastry has begun to brown nicely. Turn oven down to 350 degrees, and when juices begin bubbling up, reduce oven to 325 or even 300 degrees to minimize crust cracks—these frequently occur anyway, and do not worry if they do. *Pâté* is done at a meat thermometer reading of around 165 degrees, or when juices in funnel holes are clear yellow with no trace of rosy color. Remove from oven, rest an edge of baking sheet on a spoon or a plate to let juices drain away; spoon them into a container, and save for next step. Let *pâté* cool to room temperature, then chill for 12 hours at least. (If crust has cracked, push gently in place several times as *pâté* cools.)

Optional aspic filling. Because the meat mixture shrinks from the surrounding crust as the *pâté* cools, you may wish to fill the void with aspic—clear sparkling meat stock that would include the baking juices drained off in the last step, or consommé, with gelatin added. (The proportions are 2 packages or 2 tablespoons of plain unflavored gelatin softened in ¼ cup of Port wine or Madeira, and dissolved in 3 cups of consommé. Directions for clarification of stock, and so forth, are on page 447.) Stir half the aspic in a saucepan over cracked ice until cold and almost syrupy;

pour through a funnel into the steam holes of the chilled *pâté*. Chill the *pâté* again for 20 to 30 minutes, and repeat the process until crust appears filled. (If crust has cracked, pour slowly, and the chilled *pâté* will congeal the aspic, clogging the cracks.) Chill again for at least half an hour.

Serving. Cut the *pâté* into slices ⅜ inch thick, like a loaf of bread; an inch or so at the ends will have no meat in them, and are not served.

Fresh from the garden

*T*his should really be called a continuation of vegetables, since it takes up from where the two *Masterings* and *The French Chef Cookbook* left off, loops back to pick up some old favorites, and diverges on its own tangents. I am very much of a fresh vegetable buff, and we use few convenience vegetables in our family simply because we think so many of them lose their flavor when canned or frozen. There are exceptions, of course. We love canned beets and canned corn, for instance; I am a pushover for frozen Fordhook lima beans, and I have recently discovered the tiny frozen white onion. Frozen beans, asparagus, and broccoli I find unduly limp and lacking in flavor, and frozen spinach, while useful on occasion, is mostly stem rather than leaf. But I keep trying, since (who knows?) the frozen string beans I found so dolefully disappointing yesterday might go through a revolutionary new process that would delight me tomorrow, and the same could be true of asparagus. (I think they'd do much better with that vegetable, though, if they peeled it first.) Thus my mind and taste buds remain dutifully and hopefully open.

Those of us who love fresh produce, however, should do everything we can to encourage the good people who run the fresh fruit and vegetable sections of our local markets. So much is now known about how to handle fresh produce that there is no excuse for not having perfect tomatoes, firm and shiny eggplants, pears and plums that will ripen. Wonderful work on the subject has been done not only by our U.S. Department of Agriculture, but also by the United Fresh Fruit and Vegetable Association (1019 19th St., N.W., Washington, D.C. 20036) through their monthly newsletters and their "Facts and Pointers" studies on each item of produce. If your market is inept, urge them to subscribe to the service; the cost is minimal, and the benefits to all concerned will repay them many times over.

PLASTIC WRAPPING. Plastic wrapping on vegetables helps keep them fresh since it seals in humidity, which most of them need, and wither without. However, you should have no hesitation, if you are a serious customer, in removing it to inspect the vegetables you are going to buy. If the store objects, then open the package after you have gone through the check-out counter and howl if you are deceived. The store manager, after all, wants satisfied customers and a small public scene can be useful.

Artichokes

Artichokes have always been a luxury vegetable from the time of the Romans, through Catherine de Medici, on up to the present day, and what a pleasure to have something at hand that is both a vegetable and a luxury. Then you can feature it on important occasions as a beginning, or display it as a special vegetable course all by itself, or even serve artichokes as the main attraction. Their special nutty, meaty flavor makes them good for dieting, since you need no sauce to enjoy them, but they are also a beautiful reason for pots of melted butter or hollandaise sauce. Boiling and steaming are the usual cooking methods, but braising in wine gives them added character, as does a sauté with herbs and olive oil. But first, here is what to look for when you are buying artichokes, and how to preserve their freshness when you get home.

BUYING AND STORING ARTICHOKES

Artichokes are in season all year long, but they are most plentiful in March, April, and May, when they are also, of course, most reasonable in price. Look at each one carefully when you are buying them. Select only those that feel heavy, that have crisp, fresh, fleshy, handsome leaves.

A few darkish spots or frost blisters are permissible as long as the leaves feel fresh and full. If you are not going to cook the artichokes almost at once, wrap them in a damp towel and store them in a plastic bag in the refrigerator; I have kept very fresh artichokes perfectly this way for a week.

HOW TO PREPARE ARTICHOKES FOR COOKING

THE SIMPLE WAY. If you are going to boil or steam artichokes you need do nothing at all to prepare them except hold each head under the cold water faucet, spreading leaves gently apart, to give them a thorough washing. Then slice off a half inch at the bottom of the stem, and pull off any small or withered leaves at the base. Cook them, now, as is. (There is usually a bit of edible meat in the stem, inside, particularly near the base of the artichoke.)

THE MORE ELABORATE WAY. On the other hand, you can be more elaborate as follows: Provide yourself with a lemon cut in half, a heavy knife, and a pair of kitchen shears. If you are to boil the artichokes, have your kettle bubbling; if you are to steam or braise them, have your contraption ready to go. Prepare the artichokes rapidly one at a time; begin by cutting off stem of artichoke even with base, then bend down and break off small leaves at base.

With heavy knife, slice off top inch of cone of leaves. Then, with scissors, cut off top half inch of each remaining leaf to remove the prickly points.

Trim the base of the artichoke, if necessary, so that it sits solidly upright. Run cold water into artichoke, spreading leaves apart. To minimize discoloration, rub all cut parts with lemon (or drop prepared artichoke into acidulated water—1 tablespoon lemon juice or vinegar per quart of cold water) .

Artichauts entiers, bouillis

WHOLE BOILED
ARTICHOKES, HOT
OR COLD

You may serve whole boiled artichokes hot, warm, or cold—and how convenient that is to the cook. Make them a first course, or a vegetable course in place of a salad, or the mainstay of a luncheon or supper along with hollandaise or mayonnaise and perhaps some stuffed eggs, cold meats or fish, and a selection of cheeses. Cold artichokes are delightful on a picnic, by the way, and I even know of one young couple who eat theirs in the bleachers while they watch the baseball game. What about wine with artichokes? Some spoilsports insist that artichokes ruin the taste of wine, or that artichokes make wine taste sweet. Since I have fortunately never experienced these phenomena, I recommend white wine with artichokes, such as a bottle of Alsatian Riesling or a Traminer.

For boiling 6 to 8
large artichokes,
1 per serving

You will need a large kettle of rapidly boiling water, enough to cover the artichokes by an inch or more, and 1½ teaspoons salt per quart of water. You will also want some device to keep the water over the artichokes since they float up; the usual system is a double thickness of washed cheesecloth draped over them, and it acts like a wick, drawing the water up. I have lately been successful laying a cake rack or a vegetable steamer in the kettle over the artichokes, and weighting that down with a well-washed stainless steel pan or bowl containing a brick or a 2-pound can of beans. Finally you will need tongs to remove the artichokes, and a large colander in which to drain them when done.

Whatever system you have chosen, drop the prepared artichokes into the rapidly boiling water, drape or weight them as described above, and boil slowly, uncovered, until bases of artichokes are tender when you pierce them with a knife, and when flesh at bottom half of a leaf is tender when you scrape it between your teeth. This will take 30 to 45 minutes, depending on the size and freshness of your artichokes.

Immediately they are done, lift the artichokes out of the kettle and drain upside down in the colander. If you are serving them cold, let them cool to room temperature, then place in a covered bowl and refrigerate.

Artichauts entiers à la vapeur

————◆————

WHOLE STEAMED
ARTICHOKES,
AN ALTERNATIVE
TO BOILING

Steaming is preferred to boiling by some artichoke enthusiasts, and we have one viewer who insists the only way to do so is bottoms up. Then, he says, the flavor remains in the edible parts, and a greater proportion of each leaf is cooked tender. I alternate between boiling and steaming, myself, and do not have any strong commitments, either, about the cooking method or which end is up. But since I usually like to pour a spoonful of olive oil into each specimen when I am steaming, here they are bottoms down.

For any number
of artichokes

*Optional: A teaspoon of good olive oil per
    artichoke*

*Equipment: A vegetable steamer, colander, or
    sieve set over a pan of boiling water, and a
    tight-fitting cover; or a covered roaster with
    rack and ½ inch of water. If needed, a clean
    towel or a double thickness of washed
    cheesecloth*

Make the artichokes ready for cooking as on page 381, *The more elaborate way.* Then cut the stems of the artichokes even with the base, so the vegetables will sit upright. Arrange them close together in one layer, bottoms down, in the steaming contraption. If you wish, pour over each a teaspoon of olive oil, letting it seep down into the leaves. Cover steamer tightly, bring to the boil on top of the stove and, if necessary, insert a towel or cheesecloth where a loose fit allows steam to escape. Maintain at the slow boil, checking once in a while to be sure water has not evaporated. Steaming will take 30 to 40 minutes or longer, until bases of artichokes are tender when pierced, and bottom half of a leaf is tender when eaten.

Serving. See suggestions for the boiled artichokes, preceding recipe.

Artichauts braisés, mirepoix; artichauts à la barigoule

WHOLE
ARTICHOKES
BRAISED IN WINE
AND AROMATIC
VEGETABLES

For 4 people

I love artichokes done this way; they take on a quite new flavor and, if you fill them with a meat stuffing, they can be a light main course. Unstuffed, they are particularly good cold, as a first course.

*Ingredients for a mirepoix: ¼ cup each finely
    diced carrots, onions, and celery*
2 Tb olive oil or butter
4 large fine artichokes
Lemon juice, salt, and pepper
*For inside each artichoke: Either 1 tsp butter, or
    2 to 3 Tb mushroom filling (page 287),
    or fresh sausage meat, or any appropriate
    meat stuffing like that on page 373*
*½ cup dry white wine or dry
    white French Vermouth*
½ cup chicken broth or beef stock or bouillon
1 imported bay leaf
4 tsp olive oil
*Final flavoring: Lemon juice, butter or oil,
    minced parsley*

*Equipment: A covered casserole or saucepan wide
    and deep enough to hold the 4 artichokes
    upright; a bulb baster and tea strainer are
    useful for basting*

Cook the diced vegetables in oil or butter in the casserole about 10 minutes, until tender and barely beginning to brown. Meanwhile, prepare artichokes for cooking as described, page 381, *The more elaborate way.* Then pull the central cone of leaves apart with your fingers to expose the choke; dig out choke with a teaspoon to expose flesh of artichoke bottom. Season with lemon juice, salt, and with either a teaspoon of butter per artichoke or a lump of stuffing; press cone of leaves closed. Arrange the artichokes bottom down over the cooked *mirepoix*, and pour around them the wine and broth. Add the bay leaf to the pan, and pour a teaspoon of olive oil over each artichoke. Cover pan, and simmer very slowly over moderately low heat for 30 to 40 minutes or longer, basting with the liquids in the pan 2 or 3 times; to prevent vegetables from falling into artichokes, baste over a strainer. (Add a little more bouillon or some water, if liquid evaporates.) Artichokes are done when bases are tender if pierced, and bottom half of a leaf is tender when eaten.

Serve hot, warm, or cold. If hot or warm, season juices with lemon, butter, and parsley; pour juices and diced vegetables into little pots for each serving. If you are serving the artichokes cold, season the juices with lemon, oil, and parsley.

Artichoke bottoms

The last time we were in Venice, in mid-May, we wandered down to the Rialto markets one early morning, and it was the height of the artichoke season. At almost every vegetable stand one member of the family was sitting with a large pile of them rapidly slicing off the cone of leaves to expose the artichoke bottoms, which were then plopped into a bucket of acidulated water. "Oh, terrible," said our New England friends, "think of the waste!" Indeed the Western world resounds to the wails of Americans bemoaning the waste of artichokes when bottoms are on the menu. To disprove them while we did our television program, "First Course: Sit-down Dinner," that featured *Fonds d'Artichauts Farcis, Béarnaise,* I showed how little waste there was when raw artichoke bottoms are prepared in the professional manner: I had a collection of leaves trimmed from an artichoke bottom, I boiled them, then scraped the edible portion off with a spoon, and from a whole large artichoke garnered hardly a teaspoon of flesh. Please do try it yourself if you doubt me. But the Italian method, in mid-season when artichokes are cheap, is necessarily more wasteful because it must be rapid.

To trim and cook artichoke bottoms

8 large fine fresh artichokes, 4 to 4½ inches at largest diameter
1 or 2 lemons, halved
A bowl of acidulated water (1 quart water and 2 Tb lemon juice)
¼ cup flour in a 3-quart saucepan
1 quart cold water (for cooking)
2 Tb lemon juice
1½ tsp salt

Preparing the artichoke bottoms for cooking. The professional way to prepare artichoke bottoms is to trim them raw, then cook them in a *blanc* to prevent discoloration—floured and lemoned liquid. Prepare the artichokes for cooking one at a time as follows: Break stem off base of artichoke.

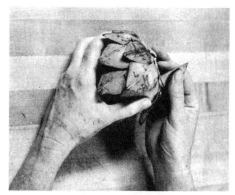

Then, holding artichoke bottom up, bend a lower leaf back on itself until it snaps; peel it off toward base leaving meat at bottom of leaf attached to bottom of artichoke.

Proceed all around until you have gone beyond the curve where leaves fold inward over top of artichoke bottom; cut off remaining cone of leaves just above this curve, as illustrated.

Rub cuts with lemon to prevent discoloration, and trim all bits of green off bottom to expose whitish tender flesh, frequently rubbing with lemon as you do so.

Drop prepared bottom into bowl of acidulated water, and continue with the other artichokes. The chokes will be removed after cooking.

Cooking. Gradually beat 1 cup of cold water into the flour and bring to the boil; pour in 3 cups more water and simmer a moment, stirring, to be sure liquid is smooth and lump free. Add the lemon juice and salt, the prepared artichoke bottoms, and a little more water if they are not completely covered with liquid. Simmer 30 to 40 minutes, until artichokes are tender when pierced with a knife. Let cool in liquid, and refrigerate until needed. They will keep perfectly for 2 or 3 days in their cooking liquid.

Just before using, wash under cold water, and scoop out choke with a teaspoon; trim off any tough leaf ends. Reheat as indicated in your recipe.

Fonds d'artichauts farcis, béarnaise

———◆———

ARTICHOKE
BOTTOMS
STUFFED WITH
MUSHROOMS AND
POACHED EGGS,
TOPPED WITH
BÉARNAISE SAUCE

For 8 people

All parts of this dish may be cooked in advance, then reheated and assembled at the last minute. This was the first course for our televised sit-down dinner party, followed by a roast tenderloin of beef with fresh vegetables, and a pretty dessert, a pear and meringue fantasy. The artichoke combination is equally good as the main course for a smart luncheon and you could, of course, omit the poached eggs in either case, though their soft yolks blending with sauce, mushrooms, and artichokes are a luscious experience. Serve a chilled dry white wine here, one with some body, like a Pouilly Fumé, Pouilly Fuissé, or Chablis—again, there are some who declare wine goes with neither eggs nor artichokes and again I say to you, serve such old harpies plain water and there will be more wine for your glass.

The mushroom duxelles filling
½ lb. fresh mushrooms, washed and
    finely minced (2 cups)
3 Tb butter in a no-stick medium-sized frying pan
2 Tb minced shallots or scallions
Salt and pepper
¼ tsp dried tarragon
2 Tb flour
¼ cup dry Port wine
½ cup heavy cream

For the sauce béarnaise, about 1 cup
A small saucepan containing ¼ cup each
    excellent wine vinegar and dry white Vermouth

1 Tb minced shallots or scallions
½ tsp dried tarragon
¼ tsp salt and ⅛ tsp pepper
3 egg yolks in jar of blender
6 ounces (1½ sticks) butter heated to bubbling
*   in a small pan—reuse the vinegar*
*   pan if you wish*
Salt and pepper as needed
Optional: 2 Tb minced fresh tarragon and parsley,
*   or parsley only*

Other ingredients
Melted butter, for reheating the artichoke hearts
8 poached eggs in a bowl of cold water, page 93
Salt and pepper
8 croutons (rounds of white bread
*   sautéed in clarified butter)*
Fresh minced parsley

Equipment: The usual frying pans and saucepans,
*   plus a towel or potato ricer for squeezing*
*   mushrooms, an electric blender, a funnel, a*
*   casserole or electric skillet for reheating*
*   artichokes, and a hot serving platter*

The mushrooms. A handful at a time, twist mushrooms into a ball in the corner of a towel to extract their juice (or squeeze in a potato ricer). Heat butter to foaming, add shallots or scallions and cook a moment, then stir in the mushrooms; cook over moderately high heat for several minutes, stirring, until mushroom pieces begin to separate from each other. Season with salt, pepper, and tarragon; blend in the flour and stir over moderate heat for 2 minutes. Blend in the wine, simmer a moment, then the cream. Boil to reduce cream and thicken the *duxelles;* carefully correct seasoning, and set aside.

Blender béarnaise sauce. Boil the vinegar, wine, shallots, tarragon, and seasonings rather slowly until liquid has reduced to about 2 tablespoons —may be done in advance. Cover blender and whiz the yolks several seconds at high speed. Still blending, pour vinegar mixture by driblets through funnel (to prevent spattering) onto egg yolks; blend several seconds. Finally, again by driblets through funnel, pour bubbling butter into blender; mixture will gradually become so thick blender will clog.

Blend in more seasoning if needed. Set jar in warm, not hot, water until ready to use sauce, then stir in the optional herbs. (*Note:* If sauce is too thick, stir in droplets of warm water.)

Serving. About ½ hour before serving, trim bottoms of artichokes to be sure they will stand upright. Fill with *duxelles,* making a trough for the egg on top. Arrange in casserole, cover, and heat through in a 300-degree oven, or in covered skillet. Just before serving, drain cold water off eggs, sprinkle eggs with salt, and pour on about a quart of boiling water; let steep 2 or 3 minutes to warm through. Remove one by one with a slotted spoon, drain over a folded towel, and place on top of artichokes. Set each artichoke on a crouton and top with 2 tablespoons of béarnaise sauce and a sprinkling of parsley; serve at once.

Petits artichauts ou fonds d'artichauts sautés à la provençale

———————

BABY WHOLE ARTICHOKES OR ARTICHOKE BOTTOMS SAUTÉED WITH ONIONS, GARLIC, AND HERBS

For 4 to 6 servings

Here is the kind of idea you can play about with as you will, adding other things to it like eggplant or fresh tomato, a bit of sausage or ham, leftover roast pork or a stew or ragout of pork, beef, or lamb cut into cubes. In full season, when artichokes are small, young, and tender, you can halve or quarter them, remove any tough outside leaves, and sauté them without further trimming. For older models either trim them down to the tender heart, or go all the way, with bottoms only. If you have added meat, this can be a main course; if not, serve them with chops, steaks, broiled fish or chicken, a roast of red meat, or with omelettes or fried eggs.

Artichokes or artichoke bottoms, the equivalent
*   of a 3-inch bottom per person*
Optional: ½ cup salt pork lardons, blanched
*   (strips 1 inch long and ⅜ inch across,*
*   simmered 5 minutes in 1 quart of water,*
*   drained, and dried)*
2 Tb olive oil, more if needed
1 cup sliced onions
2 cloves garlic, minced

> Salt and pepper
> ¼ to ½ tsp mixed herbs, such as Italian or
>   Provençal seasoning, or thyme and oregano,
>   or rosemary and thyme
> 2 Tb wine vinegar
> Fresh minced parsley

If using whole artichokes, cut and trim them as suggested in the paragraph above; for artichoke bottoms, prepare for cooking as described on page 385, and cut into quarters. In either case, drop them into boiling salted water and blanch (simmer) 5 minutes. Drain. Meanwhile, sauté the optional pork *lardons* in 2 tablespoons of olive oil, and when very lightly browned, add the onions and garlic (and ¼ cup olive oil in all if you did not use *lardons*). Sauté 4 to 5 minutes, until almost tender but not browned. Then add the artichokes, salt and pepper lightly, sprinkle on the herbs, and toss, shaking pan by handle, to blend all ingredients. Sauté, tossing, for several minutes, then pour in the vinegar and let it boil away, tossing several times. Finally, cover the pan and cook very slowly 20 to 30 minutes, tossing several times, until artichokes are tender.

☼ May be done in advance.

Serve hot, warm, or cold, tossed with fresh minced parsley.

Asparagus

The best asparagus is peeled asparagus, and I don't know why it is often so difficult to convince beginning cooks of that obvious fact. You only need to cook an unpeeled spear versus a peeled spear and the difference is immediate: the peeled spear cooks in 5 to 8 minutes, remains green and beautiful, has a fresh lovely taste, and can be eaten all the way down to the butt. The unpeeled spear takes twice as long to cook, can be eaten only part way down, and the strings from the butt end get caught in your teeth. I can only say, try it both ways and you will see. Although we've had asparagus in other books, I want to go over it again informally, since there is always more to say and more to learn.

CHOOSING AND STORING ASPARAGUS. Fresh asparagus should have heads tightly closed at the tip, and the whole length of the stalk should be fresh, moist-looking, and firm—no withering at the butt. If your market knows its business, the bunches of asparagus will be standing upright either in a shallow pan of water or on damp paper toweling. However, for convenience, some markets package it in cardboard flats; look at it carefully in this case, and be sure the stalks are firm and fresh all the way to the butt. (Think of asparagus stalks as flowers: they need coolness and moisture.) When you get the asparagus home, cut off half an inch at the butt ends, and stand the stalks upright in a saucepan, in an inch of water; cover with a plastic bag, and refrigerate, where the asparagus will keep perfectly for 2 or 3 days. (The New Jersey asparagus people, by the way, recommend that you soak the asparagus in a sinkful of warmish water for half an hour before refrigerating. I follow this advice if I think my asparagus is not as fresh as it might be: warm water penetrates the stalks more effectively than cold water.)

PEELING ASPARAGUS. I always use a small sharp knife for peeling, since I love wielding knives. My husband prefers a Norwegian triangular-bladed cheese scraper, and my friend Rosie uses the blade part (without the handle) of a vegetable peeler that she carries in her purse during asparagus season. Whatever your instrument, start at the butt end and peel to about 2 inches of the tip, your object being to remove more peel at the butt portion to expose the tender flesh. If you are not to cook them immediately, wrap the peeled spears in a damp towel and refrigerate.

BOILING ASPARAGUS. When you have peeled asparagus, the butt ends are almost as tender as the tips, and the whole spear cooks at the same time. You do not, therefore, want to cook them upright, boiling the butts and steaming the tips; you lay them down flat in the boiling water. Unless I'm doing a lot, I boil them loose in a large oval casserole; but if I am doing a large quantity, I tie them with white kitchen string into bundles of about 10 spears, one tie near the tip and another near the butt. Thus, for 32 to 40 fat spears, I use a 9- by 12-inch casserole about 5 inches deep, fill to within 2 inches of the top with hot water, and bring to the rapid boil. This makes about 5 quarts of water, and it needs salting, in the proportion of 1½ teaspoons per quart. In go 3½ tablespoons of coarse salt. Then, in goes the asparagus, flat, and the water comes as fast as possible back to the boil—I cover the casserole until the boil is reached to make it go faster, then immediately remove the cover. I set the time for 5 minutes, then keep my eye on things; as soon as the spears begin to bend slightly, they are done—sample the end of one to be sure. With two metal spatulas, one a super wide one, out comes the asparagus onto a clean folded towel set on a tray, or onto a double damask napkin folded on a platter. That is all there is to it, and you have beautiful long, green, perfect asparagus every time.

Asperges étuvées à la crème

————◆————

ASPARAGUS SPEARS
SIMMERED IN
CREAM

For 4 people

This makes a lovely vegetable accompaniment for roast chicken, veal scallops, poached eggs. What is useful here, too, is that you can get it done ahead.

About 24 fresh, fat, peeled asparagus spears, boiled until barely tender (see discussion above)
2 Tb minced shallots or scallions
2 to 3 Tb butter
Salt and pepper
½ to 1 cup crème fraîche or heavy cream
Drops of lemon juice if needed
Fresh minced parsley

Leave the asparagus spears whole, or cut them into ¾-inch lengths, whichever works out best with your menu and equipment. Choose a frying pan that will hold the asparagus easily, and in it cook the shallots or scallions in butter for 2 minutes without browning, then add the asparagus; salt and pepper lightly, and turn or toss in the butter and seasonings. Then add the cream and simmer slowly, basting the asparagus frequently, until the cream has reduced and thickened—8 to 10 minutes. Taste carefully for seasoning, adding drops of lemon juice if you think they are necessary.

☆ If done in advance, simmer only a few minutes with the cream, and finish just before serving.

Fold the minced parsley into the sauce, baste the asparagus to enrobe it, and turn out onto a hot platter.

VARIATION

Asparagus gratinéed with Parmesan cheese. After the asparagus in the preceding recipe has simmered down with the cream, fold in about ⅓ cup freshly grated imported real Parmesan cheese and turn it into a buttered gratin dish. Spread over it another ⅓ cup or so of cheese, dribble on a tablespoon of melted butter, and brown under the broiler—or set aside and bake in the upper-middle level of a preheated 425-degree oven just until bubbling and cheese has browned.

Asperges marinées à la niçoise

ASPARAGUS
SIMMERED
IN ONIONS, GARLIC,
LEMON, AND HERBS

This recipe was inspired by Jacques Médecin in his fine little book *La Cuisine du Comté de Nice* (Paris: Julliard, 1972). He gives it for wild asparagus, "as thin as little pencils, that grow in the crooked feet of the olive trees in the month of April, and whose taste is absolutely inimitable." I have had that wild asparagus in the Midi, gathered by Jeanne, the charming *guardienne* of the property where we live. She sautés it and folds it into omelettes. But I have looked and looked in the hills, and the bushes, and the crooks of the olive trees, and I've never found one wild asparagus spear. Perhaps it is like four-leaf clovers; I have never found one of those, either, but my sister-in-law picks them up wherever she walks. Anyway, I love this method for our own green asparagus, to serve hot, warm, or cold as a first course.

For 4 people

About 24 fat fresh asparagus spears, or an appropriate number of thin asparagus spears, peeled, but not boiled

For the marinade ingredients
1 cup thinly sliced onions
About ⅓ cup excellent olive oil
2 to 4 large cloves garlic, peeled, and thinly sliced lengthwise
The zest (yellow part of peel only) of 1 lemon cut into julienne matchsticks

½ tsp thyme, or an herb mixture such as
     Italian or Provençal seasoning
1 imported bay leaf
½ tsp peppercorns
½ cup dry white wine or dry
     white French Vermouth
¼ cup fresh lemon juice
About 2 cups water
½ tsp salt
Fresh minced parsley

Before you start peeling the asparagus, set the marinade mixture to cook as follows: In a heavy saucepan, cook the onions slowly in the olive oil along with the garlic, julienne of lemon, herbs, and bay leaf. When tender, in about 10 minutes, add the peppercorns, wine, lemon juice, water, and salt, cover and simmer very slowly 20 minutes.

Lay the peeled asparagus spears in a flameproof oval casserole, pour the marinade over them, adding a little more water if needed, so asparagus is just covered with liquid. Bring to the boil, cover, and simmer very slowly about 20 minutes, until the asparagus is tender. Remove the asparagus, and arrange on a platter. Rapidly boil down the cooking liquid until lightly syrupy, carefully taste and correct seasoning; spoon it over the asparagus along with the herbs, lemon peel, and vegetables; sprinkle with fresh minced parsley. Serve warm or cold.

Cabbage

We have a six-minute cabbage in our goose recipe, page 253, and steamed cabbage wedges in the *Pot-au-feu* recipe on page 275. Now here is a sweet and sour ten-minute red cabbage recipe that I love with pork, sausages, or ham.

When you buy red cabbage, by the way, the head should feel heavy, and the leaves should be fresh and crisp, both indications that the natural moisture of a fresh head of cabbage is still in there. Use a stainless steel knife to shred or cut the cabbage, since its juices rapidly tarnish ordinary steel and that, in turn, discolors the cabbage. Another note about red vegetables in general is that they must cook with something acid or their color fades; that's why you find wine and vinegar with beets and red cabbage, and apples, too. The acid counteracts the alkalinity of the water and of the salt. Conversely, one sprinkles salt on the table-cloth when a glass of red wine tips over—because salt fades the red color.

Sweet and sour red cabbage

For 4 people

1 medium-sized red onion, thinly sliced
    (or a white or yellow onion)
3 Tb rendered pork fat, or goose fat, or butter
2 large cloves garlic, minced or puréed
About 4 cups thinly shredded red cabbage
½ tsp salt
1½ tsp caraway seeds
1 imported bay leaf
Several grinds of fresh pepper
3 Tb red wine vinegar (or ½ cup red wine)
Optional: 1 medium apple, peeled and
    roughly grated
1 Tb sugar
½ cup water
Fresh minced parsley

In a large heavy-bottomed saucepan, sauté the onion slowly in fat or butter along with the garlic. Meanwhile shred the cabbage, and when onion is tender, add the cabbage and all the other ingredients except the parsley. Toss and turn to mix, then cover pan and boil rather hard for about 10 minutes, tossing occasionally and adding a little more water if all has boiled away before cabbage is just tender. On the other hand, if liquid has not evaporated entirely, boil hard uncovered for a few minutes. Taste and correct seasoning.

✿ If cooked in advance, set aside uncovered; cover and heat through, tossing, when ready to serve.

Toss with the fresh parsley, and turn out onto a hot vegetable dish.

Cauliflower and broccoli

In the old black-and-white days, we had a television program named "Lest We Forget Broccoli," one of our better titles, I think, though not quite on a par with "Waiting for Gigot," one of my favorites. On that program I had placed the broccoli in a wire salad basket, then in a big pot of boiling water. It was done. The close-up camera swooped down into the pot as I began lifting the basket out of the boiling water with two forks. Up it came, caught on the handle of the pot, tipped over, and spilled all the broccoli onto the floor. We had to stop taping. Had it fallen on the stove I could have gathered it up and continued, but not from the floor. Not in public, anyway. That meant an hour's delay until we could pick up where we left off; finally the camera again swooped down into the pot, and that same broccoli, washed off after its lowly experience, rose safely to the surface and we finished the show without further incident.

I shall not, in this brief section, go into great detail about broccoli and cauliflower, other than to say they cook infinitely faster, fresher, and better when you cut them into flowerets, peel their stems, then cut and peel the main stem too. Peeling broccoli, like peeling asparagus, simply makes all the difference between a stringy vegetable and a tender fast-cooking one. Please try it both ways, as a comparison; I know you will find the peeling worth it. By the way, if you cook cauliflower whole, one of our viewers sent in a splendid suggestion that works: cut out the stem of the cauliflower, going way up into the head with a grapefruit knife; it then cooks much faster and remains much fresher tasting.

I am not giving full-scale treatment here, merely quick ideas on how to serve these fresh vegetables easily.

Cauliflower sautéed with oil and garlic. Break the cauliflower into flowerets, peel the stems, and blanch 2 to 3 minutes (simmer in salted water), until almost but not quite tender. Drain and, just before serving, toss in a frying pan with olive oil, minced garlic, salt and pepper, and, if you wish, a sprinkling of thyme or Italian seasoning. Toss with fresh minced parsley, and serve.

Cauliflower Ortensia. This is a delectable and unusual suggestion from one of our viewers, who named it after her mother. Sauté the peeled and blanched cauliflower briefly with oil, garlic, and seasonings, as in the preceding recipe. Then pour in half a cup or so of red wine and boil slowly, tossing and folding the cauliflower, until the wine is absorbed and evaporated. Toss with fresh minced parsley and serve.

Cauliflower sauté à la provençale. Sauté the peeled and blanched cauliflower briefly with oil, garlic, and seasonings as in the preceding recipe, then fold in 1½ to 2 cups fresh tomato pulp (tomatoes peeled, seeded, juiced, and chopped). Fold and toss over high heat for 5 minutes or so to cook the tomato and evaporate its juice. Toss with fresh parsley, and serve.

Broccoli. Sauté peeled and blanched broccoli flowerets with oil, garlic, and seasonings as with the cauliflower. Then, if you wish, turn it into an oiled baking dish, fold in ⅓ cup or so freshly grated real imported Parmesan cheese, sprinkle on another ⅓ cup or so, dribble on a little olive oil, and bake in the upper third of a 425-degree oven to brown the cheese.

Broccoli or cauliflower étuvéed à la crème. After sautéing either peeled and blanched broccoli or cauliflower briefly in oil, garlic, and seasonings, pour in a cup of *crème fraîche* or heavy cream, and boil slowly, basting, until the cream has been absorbed and has thickened. Fold in some fresh minced parsley, if you are doing cauliflower, and with either one you could also fold in ⅓ to ½ cup freshly grated (imported, real) Parmesan cheese. Delicious.

Eggplant

Eggplant is a marvelous vegetable, to my mind. Not only is it beautiful, but it is also amenable, suggestible, and transformable, as a vegetable, as a meat partner, as a purée, as a carrier of other flavors. Baked with ground lamb, as in our fast *Moussaka* on page 299, it is just as good cold as it is hot, and we've a lengthy eggplant section in Volume II of *Master-*

ing, including sautés, soufflés, *persillades.* Here are some ideas for egg-plant in slices, and for whole baked eggplant, but first how to choose eggplant.

HOW TO CHOOSE THE RIGHT EGGPLANT. Eggplants must be very fresh and firm all over, with bright shining purple skin. Soft, dull, or blemished eggplants will have a bitter taste you can do nothing to dispel. Eggplants are perishable, and do not keep more than a few days under refrigeration; buy them firm and use them soon, therefore. My Italian groceryman, by the way, told me that long, thin, female eggplants are the best, and you can tell the female because it has a smooth bottom; the male has a depression. I confidently gave this bit of lore over the air, and was roundly scolded by letter afterward. There is no such thing as sex in fruit, it appears. When I faced my Italian mentor with this he said, "Well, maybe so. But the long, thin eggplants with the smooth bottoms are still the best. We call them females." So there!

Tranches d'aubergine à l'italienne

❖

EGGPLANT PIZZAS,
A FIRST COURSE,
OR TO SERVE WITH
ROASTS, STEAKS,
BROILED FISH

Ingredients for 4
people, as a first
course

Rather than making a pizza base of dough, use slices of baked eggplant. Top them with tomato sauce and cheese, which you can do ahead of time, then slip them under the broiler to brown for a moment or two just before serving.

1 shiny, firm, fresh eggplant, long and thin
    if possible, about 9 by 3¼ to 4 inches
½ tsp salt
Olive oil or salad oil
Oregano, thyme, or rosemary
About ½ cup excellent tomato sauce,
    homemade if possible
About ½ cup coarsely grated cheese, such as a
    mixture of Mozzarella, cheddar, Swiss,
    Parmesan

Shave off cap and bud ends of eggplant but do not peel; if eggplant is fat rather than long, cut it in half lengthwise. Slice into pieces about ½ inch thick and 2 by 3 inches across. To remove excess moisture and puckery quality, sprinkle both sides of each slice with salt and arrange on a double thickness of paper toweling. Let drain 20 to 30 minutes, and when you are ready to continue, preheat oven to 375 degrees. Pat the slices dry, and arrange in one layer on an oiled ovenproof serving platter or baking sheet. Paint tops with oil, sprinkle with a dusting of herbs, and cover with a large lid or with aluminum foil. Bake in lower-middle level of oven 15 to 20 minutes, just until soft when pierced with a knife, but not so long that the slices become mushy and lose their shape. Spread each with a spoonful of tomato sauce, a sprinkling of cheese, and a dribble of oil.

☼ Set aside until shortly before serving.

Then place under a moderately hot broiler to brown 2 to 3 minutes. Serve.

EGGPLANT COOKED WHOLE

Bake the eggplant whole in the oven or steam it on top of the stove, and it is ready to use in a number of simple ways. Be sure to choose firm, shiny examples; before cooking them cut off the green caps.

To bake eggplants. Pierce them in 2 or 3 places with a sharp knife on one side and on the other. Place in an oiled baking dish in the middle level of a preheated 425-degree oven and bake 25 to 35 minutes, until thoroughly soft to the touch. (I have baked eggplant in the microwave oven, turning it several times, but have concluded the regular oven produces a more even and trouble-free result.)

To steam eggplants. Place them in a vegetable rack or a sieve, and set in a pan of boiling water, not letting the water touch the eggplants; cover tightly, and steam 15 to 20 minutes or longer, depending on size. Watch that you don't overcook them. (I have only lately tried steaming them, since it seemed a shame to light a whole oven just to cook 2 eggplants; I find it works very well, and the eggplants cook evenly from one end to the other. *Note:* I have had no luck with the pressure cooker, though I thought it surely would be ideal. The eggplant bursts its skin before it gets soft, and you can't time it since size makes a difference, and you can't see what's going on. Too bad.)

Here are some suggestions for serving baked or steamed eggplants, and I notice that every one of them contains garlic.

Purée d'aubergine à l'ail

EGGPLANT SAUTÉED
WITH OIL AND
GARLIC

For 4 servings

This is so easy to do, and goes with steaks, chops, hamburgers, broiled chicken, broiled fish.

1 firm, fine, shiny medium-sized eggplant
   (about 1 pound)
3 Tb olive oil
1 or 2 cloves garlic, puréed
Salt and pepper
The juice of ½ lemon, more or less
2 Tb fresh minced parsley

Bake or steam the eggplant as described above; when soft all over, cut in half lengthwise and scrape flesh from skin. Heat the olive oil in a frying pan, add the garlic, and cook slowly a minute, then add the eggplant. Beat and stir with a wooden spoon for several minutes to break the eggplant meat into a purée. Beat in salt and pepper to taste, then drops of lemon juice.

☼ May be cooked in advance.

Just before serving, reheat, fold in the parsley, and turn into a hot vegetable dish.

Caviar d'aubergine

EGGPLANT CAVIAR:
A PURÉE WITH
GARLIC, SESAME,
AND LEMON

For about 2 cups

There are many versions of this delicious concoction, one of which is the eggplant and ground walnuts, in Volume II of *Mastering,* a specialty of Simone Beck's. This is another way, with sesame seed paste. Use eggplant caviar as a hot vegetable, as a cocktail dip, or as part of a cold hors d'oeuvre platter to go with hard-boiled eggs, anchovies, tuna fish, sliced tomatoes, olives, and the like.

Ingredients for the Purée d'Aubergine à l'Ail, above
¼ cup sesame seed paste
More olive oil if needed

Bake or steam the eggplant as described on page 399; scrape out the flesh, and sauté with the olive oil and garlic to evaporate excess moisture. Either put through the finest blade of a vegetable mill into a mixing bowl, or, which is very fast, put into the jar of an electric super-blender-food-processor. Beat in the sesame seed paste, salt, pepper, and drops of lemon juice to taste, and add a little more olive oil if paste is too thick. Fold in chopped parsley, and serve either warm or cold.

P.S. I have also done this leaving the skins on the eggplants, giving a purplish speckling, and, although the taste seems the same, I am sure the result is more nourishing—aren't skins supposed to have more nutrients than flesh?

Aubergines au four, à la provençale

EGGPLANT HALVES
GARNISHED WITH
FRESH TOMATO
AND HERBS

For 4 servings

These make an attractive first course or cold vegetable; the baked or steamed eggplants are halved, flavored with oil and herbs while still warm, then topped with a layer of chopped fresh tomatoes. Choose long, thin eggplants, if possible, so that one half will do for one serving; a long, fat one, however, can be cut into quarters if you don't find anything smaller.

*2 fine, fresh, firm, shiny eggplants about 8
     inches long and 2 inches in diameter*

The basting sauce
1 medium-to-large clove garlic
½ tsp salt
2 Tb fresh lemon juice
⅓ cup good olive oil
Freshly ground pepper

The tomato garnish
3 firm, ripe, red tomatoes
¼ tsp salt
3 Tb fresh minced parsley
*Other herbs: 1 Tb fresh minced basil, or a
     sprinkling of dried herbs such as
     oregano or Italian seasoning*
More salt and pepper as needed

Bake or steam the eggplants as directed on page 399, and while they are cooking make both the basting sauce and the tomato garnish.

The basting sauce. Mash the garlic and salt to a paste in a small mortar or heavy bowl, using a pestle or the end of a wooden spoon. Beat in the lemon juice and olive oil, and pepper to taste. Immediately the eggplants are soft, cut them in half lengthwise, and score the flesh deeply at ½-inch intervals with a knife, not piercing the skin. Baste with half the oil and lemon sauce, and reserve rest of sauce for later.

☼ If you are not ready to continue with the recipe, cover the eggplants and finish them later—you may reheat them, if you want to serve them warm.

The tomato garnish. An hour or so before serving, so the garnish will be fresh, peel, seed, juice, and chop the tomatoes and place in a sieve set over a bowl; toss with the ¼ teaspoon of salt and let drain 10 minutes, tossing gently 2 or 3 times. Turn them into another bowl, fold in half the remaining oil and lemon sauce, and the herbs; taste, and fold in salt and pepper as needed.

Finishing the eggplants. Spoon the tomato garnish over the eggplants, and baste with the remaining oil and lemon sauce. Serve warm, tepid, or chilled.

Green beans

It was the daring young chef Michel Guérard who started the green-bean salad craze, by reviving an idea of Fernand Point's. That was in the early 1970's, at Guérard's little restaurant, Le Pot-au-feu, at Asnières. Although it was in one of the grubbier Paris suburbs, *le tout Paris* crowded his tiny dining room and exclaimed in chic rapture over those baby-thin freshly cooked green beans arranged upright around the delicate heart of an immature frizzy lettuce. It was the decoration of truffles and *foie gras,* quite lavishly interspersed with the beans, that gave the touch of genius—truffles and *foie gras,* indeed. Soon everyone began copying him, and at this writing even the most humdrum establishment has changed over from the usual *Salade Niçoise* to *"Notre petite salade maison, spe-cialité."* "And what is that?" you ask. It's green beans, and the once bright thought is rapidly going down the drain, with frozen beans rather than fresh, with liver paste rather than *foie gras,* and bottled dressing—certainly the ultimate in degradation. It is still a delicious idea, however, and all you need is perfectly cooked beans. That means fresh fine green snappy string beans done the French way: we have illustrated it before, and I shall remind you of the process again. They are so simple to cook, and even if our markets do not supply the very thin baby beans one finds in France, any very fresh fine American bean will do.

NUTRITIONAL NOTES ON GREEN BEANS. A great many people, having been scared by nutritionists, never dare to believe in the great French bean system. They have been told they must not cook beans in "a lot of water," and they have not made the distinction between "a lot of water" and the immense amount of rapidly boiling water called for here. The very quantity is the key to the process, since the more boiling water you have, the faster it comes back to the boil again when the beans go in; it is this that seals in their color, flavor, and texture. As an example, I ran into a quite nutty woman the other day who accosted me, appropriately enough, in the fruitcake section of our local supermarket. "You know, I love the way you cook your green beans," said she, pawing over the glacéed cherries. "But I only do it your way on weekends." Why would that be? "Well, of course, the rest of the week I use the way (name deleted) says because I want to be sure of getting all my vitamins." When I got home I looked up the way (name deleted) says, and there was a lot of talk about nutrients, vitamins, minerals, excess water. I boiled up my beans the way (name deleted) said. They were to take 15 minutes to cook in ¼ cup of water, and the directions didn't tell me whether or not to cover the saucepan, so I did half and half. And what did I end up with? Gray, color-bleached, taste-leached, miserable beans, and you can't tell me a cooked green vegetable that looks and tastes like those beans has any but the most minimal nutritional value. Anyone, name deleted or not, who cons the public into acceptance of such culinary balderdash deserves to be disposed of, bit by bit, in an electric super-blender-food-processor.

Haricots verts frais à la française

———◆———

BOILED FRESH
GREEN BEANS

Set a very large soup kettle of water on the stove—10 quarts of water at least for 2 pounds of beans. While the water is coming to the boil, snap the 2 ends off each bean, and put the beans into a large colander. You will need salt to the tune of 1½ teaspoons per quart of water (1½ tsp × 10 qts. = 15 tsp; divided by 3 = 5) ; add 5 tablespoons of coarse salt to the boiling kettle. Run cold tap water over the beans to wash them, and immediately drop them into the kettle. Cover, so boil will be reached again rapidly, then uncover at once.

Set kitchen timer for 5 minutes, and then begin testing by eating a bean or two—chopsticks are great bean retrievers, by the way. The beans should be just tender, with the slightest crunch, and a beautiful bright green. Immediately drain the boiling water out of the kettle (tilt kettle into sink, holding colander curved side down in kettle to prevent beans from escaping) . With colander still in place, refresh the beans (run cold water into kettle for several minutes to cool off the beans rapidly) . Drain, and dry in a very clean fresh towel. The beans are now ready to be served either hot or cold.

✿ May be cooked and refreshed in advance. If not to be served shortly, place in a covered bowl or plastic bag and refrigerate, where the beans will stay green and fresh and fine for a day. (In my experience, the drying off of the beans is very important when you are doing them in advance; I do not know why, but I do know that they retain their fresh-cooked taste more effectively. Obviously, there must not be the slightest hint that they were cooked in advance, for even the smell of stale blanched beans is immediately recognizable.)

WAYS TO SERVE GREEN BEANS

Perfectly cooked fresh green beans are so delicious in themselves that often the simplest serving methods are the most successful, such as tossing them the moment before serving in a dry frying pan for a few minutes (shaking pan by handle to make them jump and turn about) to evaporate excess moisture, then tossing with butter, salt, and pepper, a few drops of lemon juice, and a sprinkling of fresh parsley. When you are serving them cold in a salad, toss them just before serving with a little good olive oil, salt and pepper, minced scallions or shallots if you like, and again, with drops of lemon juice and a sprinkling of fresh parsley;

arranged in a wide bowl, and surrounded with sliced ripe tomatoes in season, or cherry tomatoes out of season, they are a most appetizing and delightful accompaniment to roast or broiled meat; they can also be served simply by themselves as a salad or a first course. More ideas for beans in salads are on page 438, and here are two recipes for hot green beans.

Haricots verts frais à l'ail

GREEN BEANS
SAUTÉED WITH OIL,
GARLIC, AND FRESH
BREAD CRUMBS

For 4 people

Here is another idea suggested by Jacques Médecin's *La Cuisine du Comté de Nice* (Paris: Julliard, 1972). I say "suggested" because I changed things around to fit my requirements, but the idea is all his—easy, unusual, and delicious.

1½ lbs. fresh green beans
3 Tb good olive oil (or butter)
*1 large clove of garlic, puréed or
    very finely minced*
Salt and pepper
1 cup fresh white bread crumbs

Boil the beans as directed on preceding page but only 5 minutes, until almost but not quite tender. Refresh in cold water, drain, dry, and cut into 1-inch lengths. Just before serving, heat the oil or butter in a large frying pan, add the garlic and cook a moment; add the beans and toss with the oil and garlic, then with salt and pepper to taste. Cover and cook slowly for 2 to 3 minutes, until just tender. Then uncover, raise heat, and toss with the bread crumbs to brown and crust the crumbs very lightly, adding a little more oil or butter if you wish. Serve immediately.

Haricots verts frais à la provençale

GREEN BEANS WITH
TOMATOES AND
HERBS

For 4 people

I don't find sauce and fresh green beans always successful since one must be super careful not to overcook the beans, yet if they do not absorb the flavor of the sauce it is a waste of time. Here the blanched beans are simmered briefly in the flavorings, then allowed to steep a bit before being resimmered and served.

1½ lbs. fresh green beans
1 large clove of garlic, puréed or
*   very finely minced*
About ⅔ cup sliced onions
3 Tb good olive oil (or butter)
2 cups fresh tomato pulp (tomatoes peeled,
*   seeded, juiced, and chopped), or a mixture*
*   of fresh tomato and strained plum tomatoes*
*   from a can*
Salt and pepper
Fresh minced basil, or oregano, or an herb
*   mixture such as Italian seasoning*
About ⅓ cup freshly grated imported
*   real Parmesan cheese*
Fresh minced parsley

Boil the beans as directed on page 404, but for only 4 to 5 minutes, until almost but not quite tender; refresh in cold water, drain, dry, and, if you wish, cut into 1-inch lengths. Meanwhile, in a large frying pan, cook the garlic and onions slowly in the olive oil for 8 to 10 minutes or until tender but not browned. Add the tomato pulp, salt and pepper to taste, and the herbs. Simmer 2 to 3 minutes, and fold the beans into the sauce; cover, and simmer 2 to 3 minutes or until beans are just tender. Correct seasoning, and set aside uncovered.

☼ May be done in advance to this point.

Just before serving, reheat slowly to the simmer, fold in the cheese and parsley, turn into a hot dish, and serve.

Mushrooms and vegetables à la grecque

Mushrooms weave themselves in and out of French recipes with astounding frequency, and here, for example, they are minced fine, squeezed dry, and sautéed for mushroom *duxelles* to act as a bed for poached eggs nestled in artichoke bottoms; they appear again as *duxelles* in a ham gratiné; they are sautéed to go with a spinach turnover; simmered for a chicken fricassee; and so on. Since in each case the method is described in the recipe itself, I shall content myself here with a new version of mushrooms *à la grecque,* a dish to serve cold as an hors d'oeuvre, or with cold meats or chicken, or on a picnic. We had a batch of them with a special flavor in a little restaurant near Les Halles in Paris, and after numerous combinations, I have settled on the following as a reasonable facsimile.

Champignons à la grecque

MUSHROOMS
SIMMERED WITH
LEMON, ONIONS,
AND HERBS,
TO BE SERVED WARM
OR COLD

For about ½ pound
fresh mushrooms,
serving 4 people

½ cup thinly sliced onions
3 Tb good olive oil
The zest (yellow part of peel only) of 1 lemon,
    cut into julienne matchsticks
⅛ teaspoon each mustard seeds and
    ground cardamom
¼ tsp each thyme, cracked peppercorns,
    and coriander seeds
¾ cup water
2 Tb fresh lemon juice
1 Tb minced parsley stems
¼ tsp salt, and more as needed
About ½ lb. (3 cups) fresh mushrooms,
    trimmed, washed, and quartered
2 Tb fresh minced parsley leaves

Choose a heavy-bottomed stainless or enameled saucepan, and in it cook the onions slowly in the olive oil with the lemon zest, covering the pan and stirring several times, until onions are tender and translucent but not brown—8 to 10 minutes. Add the rest of the ingredients except for the mushrooms and parsley leaves, and simmer 5 minutes. Then add the mushrooms, toss to blend with the liquid, cover, and boil slowly 3 minutes, tossing several times.

With a slotted spoon, remove mushrooms to serving dish, then reduce liquid until syrupy (boil it down rapidly). Taste, correct seasoning, and pour the contents of the saucepan over the mushrooms. Spoon it up over them now several times and again before serving, this time with the minced parsley.

✿ May be done a day or two in advance; when cool, cover and refrigerate. Leave out of the refrigerator for 15 minutes or so before serving, basting several times, since the chilled oil may congeal and needs time to liquefy.

VARIATIONS À LA GRECQUE

Once you get the idea of the flavored cooking liquid that is boiled down to act as a sauce, you will come up with other combinations that appeal to you. Here are 2 more examples.

Petits oignons à la grecque

LITTLE WHITE ONIONS

2 cups small fresh white raw onions
Water
3 Tb olive oil
The zest (yellow part of peel) of
   ½ lemon, minced
½ tsp salt
½ tsp each fennel seeds and oregano
1 Tb fresh lemon juice
2 Tb currants

Drop the onions into a saucepan of boiling water, bring to the boil for ½ minute, drain, and run cold water over the onions. Slip off the skins, and pierce a cross ¾ inch deep in the root ends to discourage them from bursting later. Arrange in 1 layer in a heavy-bottomed saucepan and pour in enough water to come halfway up the onions. Add the rest of the ingredients, bring to the simmer, cover, and simmer very slowly (to keep the onions from bursting) 20 to 30 minutes, or until onions are tender but still hold their shape. Dip out with a slotted spoon, arrange in a serving dish, and rapidly reduce the liquid (boil down until syrupy); correct seasoning, and pour over the onions, basting them several times. Serve hot, warm, tepid, or cold. They go nicely with roast turkey, pork, and cold meats.

Céleri en branches à la grecque

CELERY HEARTS SIMMERED WITH OIL, LEMON, AND HERBS

For each celery heart about 2 inches in diameter and 8 inches long (1 heart serves 2 people)

Celery heart
Water
½ imported bay leaf
4 allspice berries
½ tsp mustard seeds
3 Tb olive oil
¼ tsp thyme
½ tsp salt
The zest (yellow part of peel only) of ½ lemon, minced
½ Tb fresh lemon juice
2 Tb fresh minced parsley

Preheat oven to 350 degrees. Trim the celery heart or hearts, and quarter them lengthwise. Lay them closely together in a flameproof baking dish, slightly overlapping if you have several hearts. Pour in enough water to come halfway up, add the rest of the ingredients except for the parsley, and bring to the simmer on top of the stove. Cover and bake in the lower-middle level of the oven, basting with cooking liquid several times, for 30 to 40 minutes, or until the celery is tender. Arrange the celery in a serving dish. Reduce liquid rapidly (boil down until syrupy), correct seasoning, and pour over the celery, basting several times. Serve warm or cold, and sprinkle on fresh minced parsley if you wish.

Potatoes

Deep-fried potatoes

Souffléed potatoes, homemade potato chips,
French fries, potato nests

You will find French fries on all the menus from Paris and Prague to Peru, Indiana, but none will be as brown, as crisp, and as fresh as those you make yourself at home. It is the freshness of the frying oil that makes all the difference.

FRYING FATS AND OILS. In our French-fry sprees, my husband and I found that we could use a frying oil twice, but that the third time, in every case, the oil began showing signs of age: it had developed an off taste and odor. It began, in other words, to take on the honky-tonk greasy spoon characteristics that are so offensive, and that give deep-fat frying a very bad name. In fact, in all frying, I use an oil or fat only twice, which does indeed make deep-fat frying a luxurious way to cook. But it is not only freshness that counts in an oil; quality is important too. I've tried out all the oils on the market, and always come back to fresh pure peanut oil as the one that has the least odor when heated and the most pleasant taste. I also like a combination of half-rendered beef suet (fresh fat from around the beef kidney; render it like chicken fat, page 230), and half commercially packaged fresh pork-leaf lard; it is more trouble to fix, but makes a beautiful frying medium and gives a fine flavor to the foods that cook in it. For convenience, however, I shall always refer to the frying medium as "fresh new peanut oil."

Pommes soufflées

SOUFFLÉED
POTATOES,
TO SERVE WITH
FILET MIGNONS,
CHÂTEAUBRIANDS,
SMALL ROAST BIRDS,
AND OTHER LUXURY
MEATS AND FOWLS

Drama is hardly a word one associates with ordinary French fried potatoes, but it does indeed apply to the extraordinary *Pomme Soufflée,* which puffs itself up like a little pillow. When you want to show off, and have your ego soar on *ohs* and *ahs* of adulation, there is nothing like a presentation of souffléed potatoes. You can even go so far as to offer them in the individual potato nest baskets described farther on in this section. But in addition to drama, souffléed potatoes are delicious eating. Some of your guests, however, may never have had them before; they will wonder, when they bite with delight into this crisp brown airy smallish puffy rectangular object, what in the world it is. It tastes like the most ethereal of potatoes, but how could it be? How can a potato puff itself like that? Well, it does so because it has two fryings: the first one cooks the 3-inch rectangular slices of potato slowly through without browning them; the second frying, in very hot oil, seizes and browns the exterior while the moisture of the interior expands, puffing the potato slices into a pillow shape. Even the cooking of them is spectacular and magical.

That sounds easy, and it is easy when the potatoes act as you hope they will. Potatoes, however, are far more complex than they look and, although you may do them Wednesday exactly the same way you did them Tuesday, they may stubbornly refuse to puff. But don't let that discourage you at all, because if Tuesday's method fails, there is always another angle, and since you must fry in two stages anyway, and since the first one may be done several hours in advance of serving, allow yourself time to experiment. You need only 4 or 5 pieces, anyway, per person, or the equivalent of 1 medium-sized baking potato.

For 6 people

2 batches of fresh new peanut oil, about
    1½ quarts each
6 or 7 evenly oval-shaped baking potatoes 4 inches
    long and 2 inches in diameter
Salt

*Equipment: 2 electric deep-fat fryers, or electric
skillets, or deep saucepans and deep-fat frying
thermometers; a wire deep-fat frying
skimmer or a large slotted spoon; a tray
lined with several thicknesses of paper towel;
and, if possible, a slicing device like a
mandoline or its equivalent (see illustration)*

Heat the 2 batches of frying oil, the first to 285 degrees and the second to 400 degrees. You will be frying 1 potato as soon as you have sliced it, as a test case.

Slicing the potatoes. For souffléed potatoes, you want perfectly even, smooth rectangular slices about 3 by 1½ inches, exactly ⅛ inch thick. Very careful slicing and measuring are essential or your potatoes won't puff. Wash the potatoes and prepare them one at a time as follows.

Peel the potato and cut into an even, smooth, lengthwise rectangle; its widest pair of sides should be about 3 by 1½ inches, and this is the side you will slice. Blunt off the 4 corners, cutting a bias slice ¼ inch in from the point of each.

From one of the wide sides of the rectangle, cut the potato lengthwise into absolutely even perfectly smooth slices exactly ⅛ inch thick—this is where a slicing machine is wonderfully useful. (*Note:* You slice the potato lengthwise on the theory you are cutting with the grain and will get a better and easier puff!)

Dry the potato slices between a double thickness of paper towels, and soufflé this first batch as a test, before slicing the rest.

First frying. Slip the potato slices (never more than 6 to 8) into the first oil (285 degrees). They will sink to the bottom, and rise slowly in a minute or so. Gently turn them, or agitate the pan slowly by its handle, to be sure slices remain separated. They should not brown at all in this first frying, but in 6 to 8 minutes a slice or two should begin to develop big skin blisters, and you may observe around the circumference an ⅛-inch border that is opaque and milky. Transfer these slices one by one with a slotted spoon to the hot oil (400 degrees); if the potato is ready to do so, it will almost at once blow itself up into a small cushion. Turn it about for a few seconds, then transfer to a tray lined with paper towels; the puff will collapse. Continue with the rest of the slices, adding new ones to the first skillet to replace those you removed. A few slices always refuse to puff in the hot oil; set them aside if they don't react immediately, since they may decide to cooperate in the final frying later.

(If potatoes refuse to puff: Are you using real baking potatoes? Did you slice them smoothly, and exactly ⅛ inch thick? Is the temperature really at 285 degrees for the first frying? Did you really cook them long enough in this first frying, and turn them about in the oil? You may have to try another system: Slice them a shade thinner or thicker; or soak 10 minutes in cold water, or for 30 minutes to 2 hours in iced water, and try again.)

Final frying. A few minutes before you are ready to serve, drop a dozen of the precooked slices into the 400-degree oil. They will repuff; turn them about and brown on both sides for 2 to 3 minutes. You must cook them long enough to evaporate inner moisture or they will not remain crisp for serving. Remove to paper towels as they are done, and salt them. Serve as soon as possible.

Pommes chips

POTATO CHIPS

Heat 2 to 2½ quarts of oil to 375–400 degrees in a deep-fat fryer. Wash and peel baking potatoes, and cut into paper-thin crosswise or lengthwise slices—the slicing slot of a hand grater works nicely. Swish potatoes in cold water to remove surface starch (and to prevent them from sticking together when fried) ; dry in paper towels. Remove basket from fryer. Place a large handful of potatoes in basket and, holding it firmly by its handle, lower it into the hot oil; be ready to lift basket immediately if oil bubbles up; lower again, and repeat as necessary until potato moisture evaporates and bubbling quiets down. Then lower into oil. Stir potatoes with a slotted spoon to keep them circulating, and fry until nicely browned and crisp. Drain, turn potatoes out onto paper towels, salt them, and transfer to a serving basket or dish. Continue with the rest. The sooner you serve them, the more delicious they will be.

Pommes frites

FRENCH FRIED POTATOES

French fries need 2 fryings, one to soften them and the second to brown and crisp them; the second frying is just before you serve, but may take place several hours after the first. Heat 2½ quarts of oil to 330 degrees in a deep-fat fryer. Wash and peel baking potatoes, trim into even lengthwise rectangles, and cut into strips ⅜ inch wide. Swish in cold water to wash off surface starch, drain, and dry in paper towels. Remove basket from fryer, and place the equivalent of 2 cut potatoes in it; lower into hot oil and fry 2 to 3 minutes, until a potato is soft and cooked through, but not browned. Drain, spread on paper towels, and continue with the rest. Let cool at least 5 minutes, or for several hours.

Shortly before serving, heat oil to 375–400 degrees (depending on how brown you like the potatoes to be). Remove basket from fryer, place in it 2 handfuls of the precooked potatoes, lower into oil, and fry 3 to 5 minutes; bubbling should almost cease, indicating moisture inside potatoes has almost completely evaporated so they will remain crisp. Drain, turn out onto paper towels, and salt them lightly. Transfer to a serving basket or dish, and continue with the rest of the potatoes. The sooner you serve them, the better.

Nids de pommes de terre

POTATO NESTS OR BASKETS

Although you can use twin sieves to form these little baskets, the special imported bird's nest fryer with its long handle and double-nested wire basket 5½ inches across and 3 inches deep is far easier. Heat 3 to 3½ quarts of oil (4 inches) to 400 degrees in a deep-fat fryer. Grate baking potatoes (1 medium potato per basket) or raw leftovers from preceding recipes through the coarse side of a hand grater; swish the grated potato in cold water, squeeze out moisture, and pat dry on paper towels.

Dip the whole bird's nest basket in the hot oil first, to prevent potatoes from sticking to it later, then line the largest basket with a ⅜ inch layer of potatoes, and clamp on the insert.

(Remove fryer basket from deep-fat fryer: you will not need it.) Dip and turn potato nest in the hot oil until wild bubbling subsides, then submerge it, and fry about 3 minutes, until nest is nicely browned. Drain, knock off protruding potato bits from outside and inside baskets, and let cool 2 to 3 minutes. Carefully remove insert basket; unmold potato nest by turning upside down and knocking gently, or poking. Salt potato nest lightly, turn right side up, and it is ready to serve.

☼ If you are not to use them shortly, place the baskets on a baking sheet in a 120-degree oven. In my experience they are at their best eating when freshly cooked, and when kept warm.

Uses for potato baskets. Use them as individual containers for souffléed potatoes, or for French fries or home-fried chips. They are very attractive filled with small deep-fried foods such as croquettes, clams, sweetbreads, smelts, and the like. Another idea I am particularly fond of is spooning into the baskets, just before serving, creamed chicken and mushrooms, or sweetbreads, or shellfish; the crunchy fresh potatoes make a delicious contrast with the soft filling.

Garlicky sautéed potatoes and a pressure-cooked quickie

Pommes de terre sautées à la catalane

POTATOES SAUTÉED
WITH ONIONS,
PEPPERS, AND
HERBS

For 4 to 6 servings

Serve these with steaks, chops, hamburgers, broiled or sautéed chicken, or even fried eggs; you can leave out the salt pork if you wish, but I love the flavor it gives. Or you could substitute diced pork sausages or chunks of ham, browning them and then removing them to add at the end for final heating; this would then make a main-course potato dish.

4 to 6 medium-sized "boiling" or all-purpose potatoes
2 ounces (¼ cup) fat-and-lean best-quality salt pork
½ cup sliced onions
½ cup sliced green pepper
1 or 2 cloves finely minced garlic
2 Tb or so olive oil
Salt and pepper
¼ tsp thyme, rosemary, or an herb mixture such as Italian seasoning
Fresh minced parsley

Wash the potatoes but do not peel them, and set in a vegetable steamer or sieve over a saucepan of boiling water, cover closely, and steam 15 to 20 minutes, or until almost tender. Peel them, and cut into slices ⅜ inch thick.

Meanwhile, cut the salt pork into *lardons,* and blanch them (cut into matchsticks 1 inch long and ¼ inch across; drop them into a quart of cold water and simmer 5 minutes, drain, rinse in cold water, and dry). While the pork is blanching, slice the onions and pepper, and mince the garlic. When the pork *lardons* are done, sauté them slowly in 2 tablespoons of olive oil in a heavy medium-sized frying pan (no-stick recommended); when very lightly browned, add the onions, cover the pan, and cook slowly until onions are tender. Then fold in the garlic and peppers, a sprinkling of salt and pepper, and sauté several minutes until peppers are almost tender. Finally add the potatoes and toss them (shaking pan by handle to make potatoes jump and turn), adding the thyme or rosemary or mixed herbs, and another sprinkling of salt and pepper. Cover pan and cook over moderately low heat 10 to 15 minutes, tossing and turning several times to brown the potatoes lightly and finish their cooking.

☼ If done in advance, keep warm, uncovered, over low heat and an asbestos pad; if they cool off or sit about with a cover on, they will lose their fresh-cooked taste.

Just before serving, reheat, tossing; correct seasoning and toss again with the fresh parsley.

A Parmesan variation. Toss the potatoes with ⅓ cup freshly grated imported real Parmesan cheese, turn into an oiled baking dish, spread on another ¼ cup of cheese, a drizzle of olive oil, and brown under a hot broiler.

Pommes de terre sautées à l'ail

POTATOES SAUTÉED WITH GARLIC AND HERBS

For 4 to 6 servings

Here is a slightly different technique, where the potatoes are sautéed raw rather than being cooked first. It gives a subtly different taste and is, of course, a less involved method. There is no salt pork here, but you could put it in if you wished.

4 to 6 medium-sized "boiling" or all-purpose potatoes, all the same size and shape
Olive oil
8 to 12 largish cloves of garlic, whole, unpeeled
Salt and pepper
Big pinch thyme, sage, or rosemary

Wash and peel the potatoes, and cut into quarters lengthwise. Dry in a clean towel. Film a medium-sized heavy frying pan (no-stick recommended) with ¼ inch of olive oil and heat to very hot but not smoking. Add potatoes and let sit over moderately high heat for 2 minutes. Toss, shaking pan by handle to make them jump and turn, and let sit 2 minutes more—this sears the outside and helps prevent them from sticking to the pan. Continue sautéing, tossing fairly frequently for 7 to 8 minutes more, until the potatoes are lightly browned all over. Then add the unpeeled garlic cloves, and toss the potatoes with a sprinkling of salt and herbs.

Cover pan, and cook over moderately low heat, tossing occasionally, for 8 to 10 minutes more, until potatoes are tender. Correct seasoning.

✿ If not to be served immediately, keep warm over an asbestos mat or warming device, but do not cover the pan or the potatoes will lose their freshly cooked taste.

At serving time, raise heat and toss the potatoes again for a moment or two, and serve. Each guest crushes his garlic with a fork, and the soft savory flesh oozes out to mix with the potatoes.

Pommes de terre à la minute

———

FAST POTATOES
WITH ONIONS AND
HERBS, PRESSURE-
COOKED

When you are in a hurry for a potato garniture with character to go with your sautéed or roast chicken, or your roast or barbecued lamb, don't forget the pressure cooker. You can get these ready in no time, and let them sit on a warming device while you receive your guests and have your first course. These have the usual herbs and garlic, and I like the pork bits too, as well as onions. Although I have at times had success and delicious results when I've added no liquid to the cooker, I have also run into scorchy bottoms and conclude a little water is better than none.

For 4 to 6 servings

2 ounces fat-and-lean best-quality salt pork
4 to 6 medium-sized "boiling" or all-purpose
potatoes, all the same size
1 cup sliced onions
1 or 2 cloves minced garlic
2 Tb olive oil
¼ tsp salt
¼ tsp herbs, such as thyme, sage, rosemary, or a
mixture like Italian seasoning
⅓ cup water (or chicken broth or beef bouillon)
Fresh parsley, basil, or chives

Cut the salt pork into *lardons* and blanch them (cut into matchsticks 1 inch long and ¼ inch across, drop into 1 quart of cold water, simmer 5 minutes, drain, rinse in cold water, and dry). Meanwhile peel and wash the potatoes, and quarter them lengthwise; slice the onions and mince the garlic. When pork is done, sauté briefly with the oil in the bottom of your pressure-cooker pan, barely to brown. Stir in the onions and garlic and sauté a moment, then add the potatoes and toss with the salt and herbs. Add the liquid, bring to full pressure, and cook 3½ minutes. Immediately release pressure. Potatoes should be just tender; if not, cover (not under pressure) and simmer over low heat 5 minutes or so.

✿ Keep partially covered over an asbestos mat or warming device.

Rewarm and correct seasoning just before serving, tossing, if you wish, with fresh minced parsley, basil, or chives.

Pommes de terre à l'huile (*French potato salad*). See page 437.

Spinach

We have so many references to cooked chopped spinach in this book that I'd better have a quick recipe for it right here. Of course you can use frozen spinach for fresh, and when it is mixed with other things like ham, cheese, and so forth, it is acceptable. But just to show yourself what you are buying, unwrap a 10-ounce package of frozen leaf spinach and let it thaw completely in a bowl (that is not going to hurt the spinach; you can still use it). Lift it up by a stem and see what you have—usually a long branch with leaves attached, and about one third stem to two thirds leaves. Squeeze out the spinach over the bowl to catch all juices. Put the spinach in a measuring cup and see how much you have; then measure the juices, and calculate how much you have paid for a quite appallingly large quantity of greenish water. If truth in packaging were truly enforced, frozen spinach would be labeled "Branch Water & Leaves."

Cooked chopped spinach

———◆———

A PRELIMINARY TO
FURTHER COOKING

For about 1½ cups,
serving 4 to 6 people

*Three 10-ounce packages of either fresh spinach or
frozen plain leaf spinach*

For fresh spinach. Discard any wilted leaves, strip off and discard stems, and plunge spinach into a sinkful of cold water, pumping it up and down for several minutes to dislodge sand and dirt. (If you have garden spinach in bulk—not in plastic bags—lift into a large colander, and wash several times again in clean water.) Lift the spinach from the water into a large colander, leaving any sand behind. Have a large kettle of rapidly boiling salted water on the stove (7 to 8 quarts at least), and plunge the spinach into it. Cover, to bring water rapidly back to the boil again, and when boil is reached immediately uncover the kettle; boil 2 to 3 minutes, just until leaves are limp. Immediately set colander curved side down into kettle, drain out the boiling water, and with the colander still in the kettle, run cold water in for several minutes to stop the cooking and to set the green color and fresh texture. Lift the spinach out into the colander, leaving any final particles of sand behind.

For frozen spinach. Unwrap and thaw in a large basin of cold water; drain in a colander.

Finishing the spinach: squeezing and chopping. The two sets of spinach are now at the same stage, for cooking purposes. By handfuls, squeeze out as much water as you can (last squeeze has some flavor, and you can collect it in a bowl for soup or reserve it as a green refresher for the cook). Place the spinach on a board, and chop with a stainless steel knife into a fairly fine purée—1/16-inch pieces. Scrape into a bowl.

☼ If done in advance, cover and refrigerate, where the spinach will keep for 24 hours at least.

Serving. Stir the plain cooked chopped spinach in a heavy-bottomed saucepan over moderate heat to evaporate as much moisture as possible—until it begins to stick to the bottom of the pan. Then beat in 2 or more tablespoons of butter, salt and pepper to taste; cover and simmer slowly over moderately low heat for 5 minutes or so, stirring frequently, until the spinach is tender; serve. Or simmer the spinach with half a cup or so of *crème fraîche* or heavy cream, and salt and pepper; when tender, and just before serving, fold in a spoonful or so of butter. Or heat several tablespoons of olive oil in a pan with a clove of puréed garlic, stir in the spinach along with salt and pepper, cover and simmer, stirring, until the spinach is tender. Other recipes are in the two *Masterings* and in *The French Chef Cookbook,* and are also listed in the index here.

Tomatoes

There are so many tomatoes strewn about in this book that I must add a special word about them here, beginning with a fact known to every gardener: tomatoes begin to die below 40 degrees, and this injury is cumulative, according to the United Fresh Fruit and Vegetable Association. Later chilling during transportation and marketing increases the damage so that the tomatoes, although they may redden, will never develop the delicious flavor they are supposed to possess. But also, as every gardener knows, you can pick green tomatoes that have developed seeds and jelly in their interstices, set the tomatoes on top of the refrigerator at normal room temperature, and they will ripen beautifully in just a few days. These are officially known as "mature green tomatoes," and if you are so lucky as to have a cellar that remains at 57 to 60 degrees, you can hold them for 2 weeks or so, where they will ripen more slowly. Any temperature below 50 degrees, it appears, is dangerous for the tomato unless it is fully ripe. Then you can refrigerate it to preserve it, but I do think a refrigerated tomato never has quite the lovely taste of one that has never been chilled.

All of these facts make the marketing of tomatoes a difficult business, and it is no wonder we find good out-of-state tomatoes so hard to get out of tomato season. However, too few customers and storekeepers know the basic temperature facts about the tomato, and it is time we all began heckling our markets to inform themselves, to learn how to run their vegetable sections. Then we, at last, could get decent tomatoes that would ripen as they should, all year long.

In the meantime, keep your tomatoes at room temperature until they are ripe and red, and hope for the best.

Now, having gotten that off my mind, here are a few useful recipes that have appeared before but that I repeat again, so you won't have to plow through other books to get at them.

Tomates concassées

FRESH TOMATO PULP; TOMATOES PEELED, SEEDED, JUICED, AND CHOPPED

Fresh tomato pulp is an essential ingredient in any good cooking, particularly when it is French or Italian. The flavor is in the pulp, so you want to rid the tomato of its skin, of its seeds, which are hard when cooked, and of its juice, which would dilute whatever the tomato is joined to. To skin the tomato either spear it on a fork and turn it over a gas flame for several seconds until the skin splits and loosens, or drop it for exactly 10 seconds in a pan of boiling water; core out the stem, and peel the tomato from stem end. To rid the tomato of its juice and seeds, cut it in half crosswise (not through the stem) , then, holding a tomato half in the palm of your hand, gently squeeze to extract juice and seeds out from interstices, also poking at the seeds with a finger to dislodge them—you are not squeezing juices from the flesh, just from those inside jellylike seedy sections; the flesh remains intact. (Most novice American cooks hate to do this. "Losing the best part!" they wail, and by refusing to squeeze their tomatoes they end up with watery sauces full of seed speckles.) For a sauce or a stew the flesh, or pulp as we now call it, is roughly chopped, *concassée;* for a garniture, it is sliced or diced. And the juice, of course, is strained and is then either consumed by the cook or is used in sauces or other preparations; the seeds are discarded, but the skins may be added to the stock pot.

Tomato fondue. This is tomato pulp diced and sautéed for several minutes in butter or olive oil with minced shallots or garlic, herbs, and seasonings. Use it as is to garnish steaks, chops, broiled chicken or fish, egg dishes, or add it to the pan juices after roasting or sautéing meat or poultry, to make an attractive little sauce. A good example is in the chicken sauté on page 189.

Tomates au four

BAKED WHOLE
TOMATOES, EITHER
REGULAR SIZE OR
CHERRY TOMATOES

These are easy to do, delicious mixed with meat juices on one's plate, and make an attractive garnish to any meat or fish platter, or to egg dishes. Choose either medium-sized tomatoes about 2 inches in diameter, or cherry tomatoes. For the larger tomatoes, core out the stem end. Arrange the tomatoes in one layer in a baking dish, pour on a little olive oil and roll the tomatoes around to coat them; sprinkle on salt and pepper. If tomatoes have been cored, set them core end up. Bake 5 to 8 minutes at 425 degrees, just until the skins start to split, showing that the tomatoes are warmed through. (Or bake a longer time at a lower temperature if you are using the oven for other things as well.) Serve the tomatoes soon after baking; they wither and lose an excessive amount of juice if they sit around waiting for you.

Tomates farcies à la provençale

TOMATOES BAKED
WITH A TOPPING
OF HERBAL CRUMBS

This simple preparation is one of my favorites for tomatoes, but the bread crumbs must be fresh! I've been served them made with fine brown store-bought crumbs and the effect is brown, damp, store-bought, and dismally bready rather than light, crunchy, and herby the way baked tomatoes *à la provençale* should be. Serve them around broiled fish, meats, or chicken, or with roasts, or eggs. Any leftovers go nicely with cold meats, or as part of a cold hors d'oeuvre platter.

For 8 tomato halves,
2 per serving

4 firm, ripe, red tomatoes about 2½
inches in diameter
Salt
1 to 2 cloves garlic, finely minced or puréed
Optional: 1 or 2 anchovy fillets (canned, or
your own desalted brand, page 437)
2 Tb minced shallots or scallions
5 or 6 big leaves fresh basil, minced; or
¼ tsp thyme or oregano

3 to 4 Tb fresh minced parsley
½ cup, lightly pressed down, fresh, fairly fine,
white crumbs (use non-sweet homemade-
type bread, and an electric blender)
3 to 4 Tb olive oil
Freshly ground pepper

Cut the tomatoes in half crosswise (not through the stem), and gently squeeze out juice and seeds, poking around to clean them out from interstices. Salt lightly inside, and drain upside down on a rack while you prepare the filling.

Mash the garlic in a bowl with the optional anchovies and the shallots. Stir in the herbs and crumbs, and toss with 2 tablespoons of oil. Season to taste with salt and pepper. Fill the tomatoes with the mixture, and sprinkle about half a teaspoon of olive oil over each. Arrange in an oiled baking dish.

☼ May be prepared several hours in advance of cooking.

Bake for about 15 minutes in the upper-third level of a 400-degree oven—or for a longer time in a slower oven—until crumbs have browned nicely and tomatoes are soft. But do not overcook and let them collapse. They are best served quite promptly, since their juices exude and they wither when they sit around in a warming oven.

Zucchini

Zucchini, like broccoli and spinach, is one of the few green vegetables that is always with us, winter and summer. Easy to grow, as home gardeners know, it is also easy to cook. Your only gastronomical problem is to cope in some way with its natural moisture, or the zucchini will drown in its own juices. This is true of all the squash family, as well as of its cousin, the cucumber, and of eggplants. A standard method is to cut and salt them, letting the salt draw out the vegetable juices; another is to boil or bake them whole before cutting. The third, and most direct method for zucchini, is to grate it, let stand a few minutes with salt, then squeeze out the juices. You are then ready to turn it into any number of delicious concoctions, two of which are suggested here—zucchini baked with cheese, and a zucchini *pipérade*. In addition, for the horticulturist who has let his zucchini run wild, here is what to do with those end-of-the-season giants, and don't miss the unusual zucchini soup, *Pistou Verte*, on page 8.

BUYING AND STORING ZUCCHINI. Choose bright-green shiny zucchini that are firm to the touch all over, heavy for their size, and glossy-skinned. Acceptable lengths are anywhere from 4 to 10 or 11 inches; seeds, when you halve the zucchini, should be soft and immature, and the skin tender and edible. Store them in a plastic bag in the refrigerator, where, if perfectly fresh to begin with, they should remain firm and fine for a week to 10 days.

Grated zucchini sautéed with onions

1 lb. zucchini (3 zucchini, for instance, 8 inches long and about 1¾ inches at widest diameter)
½ tsp salt
1 to 1½ cups sliced onions
3 Tb butter or olive oil
Optional: 1 clove garlic, puréed

THE ALL-PURPOSE
PRELIMINARY

For about 1½ cups

Slice off stem, shave off other end, and scrub the zucchini under cold running water with a soft vegetable brush. Using the large holes (not the slicer) of a grater, grate the unpeeled zucchini into a colander set over a saucepan. Toss with the salt; let macerate (stand) while you set the onions to cook with the butter or oil in a covered frying pan for 8 to 10 minutes, until tender and translucent but not browned. (Add optional garlic at end of cooking.) Then pack the zucchini into a potato ricer (or twist by handfuls in the corner of a dish towel) and squeeze hard, letting juices fall into saucepan; reserve the juices. When onions are tender, stir in the zucchini and sauté over moderately high heat, tossing and turning zucchini for several minutes until fairly tender. If you wish to serve the zucchini as is, cover and cook a few minutes longer, season, and turn into a hot vegetable dish; or use it as a base for one of the following recipes.

Gratin de courgettes, Mornay

———————

ZUCCHINI BAKED
WITH CHEESE
SAUCE

For 4 people

Serve this with steaks, chops, broiled fish or chicken, or as a first course.

The preceding sautéed zucchini in its frying pan
2 to 4 Tb melted butter
3 Tb flour
The zucchini-squeezing juices, heated
⅓ to ½ cup milk and/or cream
Salt and pepper
About ½ cup grated Swiss cheese
2 to 3 Tb fresh white bread crumbs

Setting frying pan with onions and sautéed grated zucchini over moderate heat, add a tablespoon of melted butter, and stir in the flour; cook, stirring, for 2 minutes, and remove pan from heat. Mix in the hot zucchini juices, blending thoroughly with the vegetables and flour, and return over moderate heat. Bring to the simmer, thinning out with spoonfuls of milk and/or cream—mixture should be fairly thick but not stiff. Season to taste with salt and pepper, then stir in ⅓ cup of the cheese. Butter a shallow 4-cup baking dish, and turn the zucchini into it. Spread on a mixture of the remaining cheese and bread crumbs, and dribble on a half tablespoon of butter.

✻ May be completed to this point the day before; cover and refrigerate.

About 15 to 20 minutes before serving, set in upper third of a preheated 425-degree oven until bubbling and top has browned nicely.

Zucchini en pipérade

GRATED ZUCCHINI
WITH ONIONS,
PEPPERS, AND
HERBS

For about 4 cups

Serve this as a condiment to go with egg dishes, steaks, chops, or keep it on hand to dress up a dish of beans, a leftover beef stew. Serve it also as a cold hors d'oeuvre with hard-boiled eggs and olives, or mix into boiled rice for a salad. Proportions are not of much importance here; they depend on your resources at the moment. This is a useful mixture to have on hand, and a good way to use vegetables that won't last another day.

The cooked grated zucchini and onions in their
frying pan (see page 425)
2 or 3 sweet green peppers
1 or 2 sweet red peppers; or 1 to 2 cups fresh
tomato pulp (tomatoes peeled, seeded, juiced,
and sliced, plus some strained canned Italian
plum tomatoes if out of season)
Salt and pepper
¼ to ½ tsp thyme, oregano, or chopped fresh
basil, or an herb mixture like Italian
seasoning

While the zucchini and onions are cooking, cut the peppers into slices about ³⁄₁₆ inch wide. When zucchini is almost tender, add the peppers (and tomatoes), along with a sprinkling of salt and pepper and the herbs. Toss and fold to blend, cover pan and cook, folding several times, until the peppers are just tender. Uncover pan and boil rapidly to reduce cooking juices (especially if you used tomatoes) until they are syrupy. Correct seasoning. This is now ready to use; or, when cool, refrigerate or freeze it.

Courgette géante en barquette, belle-soeur

GIANT ZUCCHINI
VEGETABLE BOAT

Every September, when my sister-in-law leaves her flourishing garden in Maine and heads home, she brings us a giant zucchini or two. At first I kept them among the potted plants in the front hall, as an amusing decoration. Then one fall she happened through with her garden gifts shortly before we were to do our zucchini program, "A Vegetable for All Occasions," and she revealed to me her great solution for those end-of-season giants. Boil them up whole, she said, and use them as containers for salads or hot mixed vegetables, and when they have served you, peel them and grate the flesh for zucchini soup (page 8) . Of course, for a monster 18 to 20 inches long you have to find a big something to cook it in. She uses her lobster boiler, actually a big galvanized washtub called "The Happy Home Laundry," purchased at the local country store. I've seen that kind of rectangular tub 3 feet long and some 20 inches wide advertised in the Sears Roebuck catalogue. On our TV program I used a laundry boiler of tinned metal that I've had for years and keep for cooking hams, lobsters, and salmon. A fish poacher would also serve.

Now, having procured your zucchini and set your boiler to bubbling on the stove with salted water, cut a cover out of one of the long sides of the zucchini, and scrape the seeds out of the resulting boat-shaped bottom. Lower the zucchini into the water, and boil slowly for 30 minutes or longer, until its flesh is fairly tender but the boat still keeps its shape.

For hot vegetables. Drain zucchini. Brush inside boat with melted butter, sprinkle with salt and pepper, and fill with a mixture of hot vegetables such as diced boiled potatoes, carrots, turnips, and green beans, plus green peas and kernels of fresh corn—all turned in melted butter and seasonings. Or use the mixed vegetable ragout on page 357.

For salads. Remove the zucchini boat from the water and refresh it in a sinkful of cold water. Drain and pat dry, season it with oil and lemon dressing, and pile the salad into it—mixed vegetables, fish, chicken, lobster, or any combination that appeals to you.

Salads, aspics, and summer fare

Caesar salad
Musings
Recipe

Salades composées—
    mixed vegetable salads
Salade niçoise
Other ideas in mixed vegetables—
    green beans, tomatoes, cucumbers;
    white beans, black beans, kidney beans,
    lentils; and rice

Mayonnaise
Mayonnaise by hand, and in the electric
    super-blender-food-processor
Sour cream dressing, plain and
    with cucumbers
Cole slaw
Mayonnaise de volaille—chicken salad
Other summer salad combinations—
    turkey, lobster, crab, shrimp

Aspics
Truites en gelée—trout in wine aspic

Musings upon Caesar
and his salad

*O*ne of my early remembrances of restaurant life was going to Tijuana in 1925 or 1926 with my parents, who were wildly excited that they should finally lunch at Caesar's restaurant. Tijuana, just south of the Mexican border from San Diego, was flourishing then, in the prohibition era. People came down from the Los Angeles area in droves to eat in the restaurants; they drank forbidden beer and cocktails as they toured the bars of the town; they strolled in the flowered patio of Agua Caliente listening to the marimba band, and they gambled wickedly at the casino. Word spread about Tijuana and the good life, and about Caesar Cardini's restaurant, and about Caesar's salad.

My parents, of course, ordered the salad. Caesar himself rolled the big cart up to the table, tossed the romaine in a great wooden bowl, and I wish I could say I remember his every move, but I don't. The only thing I see again clearly is the eggs. I can see him break 2 eggs over that romaine and roll them in, the greens going all creamy as the eggs flowed over them. Two eggs in a salad? Two one-minute coddled eggs? And garlic-flavored croutons, and grated Parmesan cheese? It was a sensation of a salad from coast to coast, and there were even rumblings of its success in Europe.

How could a mere salad cause such emotion? But, one remembers, that was way back in 1924, when Caesar Cardini invented it, and it was only in the early twenties that refrigerated transcontinental transportation came into being. Before then, when produce was out of season in the rest of the country, there was no greenery to be had. Before then, too, salads were considered rather exotic, definitely foreign, probably Bolshevist, and, anyway, food only for sissies.

Almost 50 years later, when we decided upon Caesar Salad as one of the events for our program "Kids Want to Cook," I had, as usual, studied all the sources and found, as usual, there was no agreement among any of them. I evolved what most appealed to me but it lacked a certain authenticity, and it had no drama. Then my producer, Ruthie, suggested we try to locate someone from that era who knew Caesar and really knew that salad. Was there anyone? Indeed there was, Ruthie found. Rosa Cardini, his daughter, was living in the Los Angeles area, and was the head of a successful spice and salad dressing business. I had a long Boston-to-Los-Angeles telephone conversation with her, taking copious notes. She was born five years after her father created his masterpiece, she said, but she knew every detail because it had been so much discussed and remembered.

As we went over each move, the salad began to take on life for me. At first, she said, Caesar used only the tender inside leaves, the hearts, of romaine, and he served them whole, arranging each portion on a large chilled dinner plate, leaf by leaf; you picked up a leaf by its stem end, and you ate it in your fingers, leaf by leaf. What a great idea! What fun for television. But, she went on, since most Americans do not like plucking up sauced items with their fingers—witness the reaction to lobster à l'américaine served in the shell—he later changed to bite-sized pieces. Was there anything special in the way he manipulated the salad? Yes, he had a uniquely Caesar way of tossing the salad. In fact, he didn't toss it, he scooped under the leaves to make them turn like a large wave breaking toward him, to prevent those tender shoots of green from bruising. Again, drama, and a new twist for our show. How about anchovies, mustard, herbs, and so forth? No! No anchovies! Caesar never used anything but the best oil, fresh lemons, salt and pepper, a little Worcestershire—that's where those anchovies crept into so many of the recipes I had seen: Worcestershire does have a speck of anchovy. Caesar also insisted on the best and freshest Parmesan, and homemade croutons basted with oil in which fresh garlic had been steeped.

That is the way we did the salad on our television program, and I have always been delighted with it. It is a very simple salad, really, and its beauty rests entirely in the excellence of its ingredients—the best and freshest of everything, from romaine, to oil, eggs, lemons, croutons, garlic, and cheese.

Caesar salad

HEARTS OF
ROMAINE
LETTUCE WITH OIL
AND LEMON,
CODDLED
EGGS, PARMESAN
CHEESE, AND
GARLIC CROUTONS

Serve this as a first course, or it could be a main-course luncheon or supper dish followed or preceded by a *terrine* or *pâté* and sliced fresh tomatoes. On our television show I didn't have time to do the croutons Caesar's way, and you may want to follow Rosa's directions for them: cut homemade type unsweetened white bread into half-inch dice and dry out in the oven, basting them as they brown with olive oil in which you have steeped fresh crushed garlic for several days. Except for the croutons, the following recipe duplicates Rosa Cardini's instructions for her father's salad, as she repeated them to me.

For 4 to 6 people

2 large crisp heads romaine lettuce
2 large cloves garlic and a garlic press
Salt
¾ cup best-quality olive oil
2 cups best-quality plain unseasoned toasted croutons
1 lemon
2 eggs
¼ cup (1 ounce) genuine imported real Parmesan cheese, freshly grated
Peppercorns in a grinder
Worcestershire sauce

The romaine. You want 6 to 8 whole unblemished leaves of romaine, between 3 and 7 inches long, per person. Strip the leaves carefully from the stalks, refrigerate rejects in a plastic bag and reserve for another salad. Wash your Caesar leaves gently, to keep them from breaking, shake dry, and roll loosely in clean towels. Refrigerate until serving time.

The croutons. Purée the garlic into a small heavy bowl, and mash to a smooth paste with a pestle or spoon, adding ¼ teaspoon salt and dribbling in 3 tablespoons of the oil. Strain into a medium-sized frying pan and heat to just warm, add the croutons, toss for about a minute over moderate heat, and turn into a nice serving bowl.

Other preliminaries. Shortly before serving, squeeze the lemon into a pitcher, boil the eggs exactly 1 minute, grate the cheese into another nice little bowl, and arrange all of these on a tray along with the rest of the olive oil, the croutons, pepper grinder, salt, and Worcestershire. Have large dinner plates chilled, arrange the romaine in the largest salad bowl you can find, and you are ready to go.

Mixing the salad. Prepare to use large rather slow and dramatic gestures for everything you do, as though you were Caesar himself. First pour 4 tablespoons of oil over the romaine and give the leaves 2 rolling tosses—hold salad fork in one hand, spoon in the other, and scoop under the leaves at each side of the bowl, bringing the implements around the edge to meet each other opposite you, then scoop them up toward you in a slow roll, bringing the salad leaves over upon themselves like a large wave breaking toward you; this is to prevent them from bruising as you season them. Sprinkle on ¼ teaspoon of salt, 8 grinds of pepper, 2 more spoonfuls of oil, and give another toss. Pour on the lemon juice, 6 drops of Worcestershire, and break in the eggs. Toss twice, sprinkle on the cheese. Toss once, then sprinkle on the croutons and give 2 final tosses.

Serving. Arrange the salad rapidly but stylishly leaf by leaf on each large plate, stems facing outward, and a sprinkling of croutons at the side. Guests may eat the salad with their fingers, in the approved and original Caesar manner, or may use knives and forks—which they will need anyway for the croutons.

Salades composées— mixed vegetable salads

Certainly the most famous of the composed salads is the *Niçoise,* colorful and nourishing, with its eggs, potatoes, beans, anchovies, tuna, and other Provençal garnishings. Serve it as a main-course luncheon dish any time of the year, accompanied by plenty of fresh French bread and a dry white wine or a *rosé;* a little cheese and some fruit to finish, and you have a delightful meal. So we shall start with the *Niçoise,* since its various elements are useful for other salads and cold dishes as well. By the way, I was surprised to find a great disagreement about *"la véritable recette de la Salade*

Niçoise." Since I love cold green beans, potatoes, eggs, tomatoes, anchovies, and tuna, I have always followed the recipe of Escoffier, who was born and brought up, after all, at Villeneuve-Loubet on the outskirts of Nice.

But there are other versions, such as Escudier's in his *Wonderful Food of Provence,* ably translated by Peta Fuller (Boston: Houghton Mifflin, 1968): sliced tomatoes minus their seeds, says Escudier, arranged on a round serving dish with a cross-hatching of anchovies, bits of green pepper, and black olives, plus, if you wish, a border of sliced hard-boiled eggs. Then we have my oft-cited Jacques Médicin and his *La Cuisine du Comté de Nice.* Such terrible crimes, he says, are committed in the name of *Salade Niçoise:* the base is tomatoes and raw vegetables, no vinegar, no potatoes, no boiled green beans. On the other hand, the great English authority on French cuisine, Elizabeth David, takes a sensible approach, I think, in her *French Provincial Cooking* (Baltimore: Penguin Books, 1969): It depends on the season, says she: hard-boiled eggs, anchovies, olives, tomatoes, and garlic in the dressing are constant elements, with other additions of tuna, red peppers, artichoke hearts, and so forth. It also depends, she adds, on what comes next, after the salad. (The only disagreement I would have with Mrs. David here is on garlic in the dressing, which I have not universally found in every Mediterranean *Salade Niçoise* seen, sniffed, or sampled.) Obviously it is one of those recipes like Bouillabaisse and Chicken Marengo; you do pretty much what you want and declare emphatically, like any proper French cook, that yours is the one and only real authentic serious and veritable *Salade Niçoise.*

Salade niçoise

COMBINATION SALAD WITH POTATOES, TOMATOES, GREEN BEANS, ANCHOVIES, TUNA FISH, OLIVES, CAPERS, AND LETTUCE

All the elements of this salad may be prepared in advance, but it must not be dressed and arranged until just before serving. I deplore the system employed by many restaurants and even individuals—including some of my best friends—of making a beautiful arrangement in a salad bowl, then pouring on the dressing and mixing it all up. A horrid mess, and it is not right. No! Toss each individual item separately in a separate bowl with the dressing and seasonings, then make your beautiful arrangement, and it stays beautiful for serving.

(We have *Salade Niçoise* in *Mastering I,* and in *The French Chef Cookbook;* this is a slightly different version.)

Ingredients for
6 to 8 people

For the sauce vinaigrette—about ⅔ cup

1 clove garlic
Salt
About 1 Tb each lemon juice and wine vinegar
½ tsp dry mustard
½ to ⅔ cup best-quality olive oil
Freshly ground pepper
Fresh or dried herbs, such as basil

For the potato salad

3 or 4 medium-sized "boiling" or "all-purpose"
* potatoes*
1 Tb finely minced shallot or scallion
Salt and pepper
2 to 3 Tb each white wine or chicken stock, and
* water*

Other ingredients

5 anchovies packed in salt (or a 2-ounce tin of flat
* fillets in olive oil)*
2 to 3 Tb capers
1 large head Boston lettuce, washed, separated into
* leaves, and chilled*
4 ripe red tomatoes, quartered (or cherry tomatoes,
* halved)*
½ lb. fresh string beans, blanched and chilled,
* page 404*
2 or 3 hard-boiled eggs, peeled, and halved or
* quartered*
½ to ⅔ cup black olives, preferably the small
* brine-cured Mediterranean type*
A 7-ounce can of tuna fish
2 to 3 Tb chopped fresh parsley

Sauce vinaigrette. Purée the garlic through a press into a small mortar or bowl, add ¼ teaspoon salt, and mash vigorously with a pestle or wooden spoon to make a very smooth paste. Beat in a tablespoon each of lemon juice and wine vinegar, and the dry mustard. (Strain, if you wish, into another bowl or into a screw-topped jar.) Beat in gradually (or add all at once and shake to blend) ½ cup olive oil—5 to 6 parts of oil to one of vinegar and/or lemon juice is about right, because too tart a dressing will spoil the taste of any wine you are serving. Beat in a grind or two of pepper, a big pinch of herbs, taste carefully, and correct seasoning, beating in more oil, salt, pepper, or herbs as necessary.

Pommes à l'huile *(Potato salad)*. Scrub the potatoes under cold water. Place in a vegetable steamer or in a sieve or colander, set over a pan of boiling water, and cover closely. (If steam escapes from sides of steamer, insert a towel around the edges between steamer and pan, to hold in the vapor.) Potatoes should steam until just tender when pierced with a knife—about 20 minutes. Spear each with a fork; peel and cut in half lengthwise, then into slices ⅜-inch thick. Toss the warm potatoes gently in a large bowl with the minced shallot or scallion, sprinkling on ¼ teaspoon of salt and several grinds of pepper. Then toss with the wine or chicken stock and water. Let sit for 5 minutes or so, tossing twice more, and allowing potatoes to absorb as much liquid as they will. Then fold gently with ¼ cup of the dressing, taste, and correct seasoning. Cover and refrigerate until serving time.

Anchois au sel *(Salt-packed anchovies)*. In most Italian markets here, you can buy whole anchovies preserved in salt or in a salt brine. They have an excellent flavor, and keep for several years in a cool place as long as they are surrounded by the coarse (kosher-type) salt that preserves them. To prepare for use, first wash off the salt, then soak the anchovies in several changes of cold water until softened—40 minutes to 2 hours, depending on how long they have been salted. Test by boning one as follows: lay it on a board or on a piece of brown paper, and with 2 forks separate one side (top) from the central bone, then remove the bone from the second side or fillet; run fork along length of each fillet to remove any fins or extraneous matter. Taste a small piece; if still too salty, soak the anchovies (along with the filleted anchovy) in fresh water another 15 minutes or so. Arrange the fillets in a dish and cover with a spoonful of dressing, or with a little olive oil, pepper, oregano, and a spoonful of capers. Refrigerate if not to be used fairly soon, and do not prepare the anchovies more than 2 hours before serving. (To preserve their freshness, open oil-packed canned anchovies only a few minutes before serving, and use as is, or flavor with dressing or herbs as suggested above).

Câpres au sel *(Salt-packed capers)*. The very large capers available on the Mediterranean can often be found here in bulk, packed in salt, in Italian markets. To prepare them, wash off the preserving salt, and soak the capers in several changes of cold water for 40 minutes or longer, until the salt has worked itself out. Test by eating one. Drain, squeeze gently to remove excess water, and pack in a screw-top jar; cover with a mixture of wine vinegar and dry white wine or Vermouth. These are now pickled capers, and will keep for months; they need not be refrigerated. (Regular capers, bottled in vinegar, are drained and served as is, although you might improve their flavor when you buy them by pouring out half their vinegar and replacing it with dry white French Vermouth.)

Assembling the salad. Do this the moment before serving. Choose a deep round platter, or a wide bowl. Toss the lettuce with several spoonfuls of dressing, and arrange the leaves around the edge of the platter or bowl. Turn the potato salad into the middle. Arrange groups of tomatoes around the potatoes; sprinkle with salt and droplets of dressing. Toss the beans with a spoonful of dressing, plus a sprinkling of salt and pepper to taste; arrange in groups between the tomatoes. Distribute eggs, yellow side up, at decorative intervals, and place anchovies and capers over them. Ring the potatoes with a line of black olives; break up the tuna fish and arrange it in the center of the potatoes or at intervals around their edge. Spoon a little of the dressing over the tuna, and dribble the rest over the potatoes. Decorate the tuna with parsley, and the salad is ready to serve.

OTHER IDEAS IN MIXED VEGETABLES

Green beans, tomatoes, cucumbers. The green bean salad craze is hard to tire of when you have cooked the beans the French way, so they remain fresh, green, and slightly crunchy to the chew. I love them seasoned with French dressing, topped with rounds of thinly sliced red onion, and surrounded with sliced tomatoes dusted with salt and a little olive oil; a sprinkling of fresh minced basil or parsley completes the picture. Cucumbers and tomatoes garnished with fresh watercress is always a refreshing combination, and here is a cucumber system I very much recommend. Peel them, slice into thin rounds, and toss with salt, wine vinegar, and a small amount of sugar (for 2 cups of sliced cucumbers use ½ teaspoon salt, ¼ teaspoon sugar, and 2 teaspoons more or less of good wine vinegar) ; let stand 20 minutes, and you can use the juice they render as part of your salad dressing.

Raw vegetable mixtures. These are endless, depending on the season and your resources. One combination we like is celery stalks, green and red peppers, and red onions all thinly sliced, and tossed with grated carrots and dressing; it is attractive in a salad bowl lined with lettuce leaves and garnished with black olives and cherry tomato halves. Cucumber goes with this mixture too, but you might prefer it peeled, halved, seeded, and then sliced, and the salt–sugar–wine vinegar marinade described above goes nicely with the rest of the vegetable combination.

White bean, black bean, kidney bean, and lentil salads. These are delicious when you want a main-course salad, and you should season the beans while they are still warm—or reheat them if they have been chilled or come from the can. Toss them with the garlic dressing described for the *Salade Niçoise* on page 436, plus, if you wish, diced green peppers, minced shallots, and fresh herbs. Serve them like a *Niçoise*, with hard-boiled eggs, tomatoes, tuna fish, and olives, all arranged in a lettuce-lined bowl. The zucchini *pipérade* on page 427 is another idea to go with beans: either fold it into them, or mound the beans in a platter and arrange the *pipérade* around them.

Rice salads. Whenever you are boiling up some rice (the real raw un-treated kind) , make a cup or so extra and use it for salad. Mix it into the raw vegetable combination suggested above, or fold into it chopped hard-boiled eggs, diced canned red pimiento and chopped black olives, pine nuts, minced shallots, tuna fish or minced ham, and chopped fresh herbs; toss with olive oil, salt, and pepper. (I omit lemon juice and vinegar here, but you may wish it.) Pass homemade mayonnaise on the side, since not everyone likes salad too much fattened. Another idea is to use a spiced-up rice salad as a base for cold poached or broiled fish; arrange the fish over the rice, spoon over it a little mayonnaise, decorate with capers and herbs, surround with watercress, and you will ever after poach a little extra fish while you're at it, just to use in a salad. Speaking of mayonnaise, here it is:

Mayonnaise

Homemade mayonnaise, your own brand, with its wonderful taste of fresh eggs, fresh lemon, and the best oil is such an unexpected pleasure to those who have forgotten what mayonnaise should taste like—and such a revelation to those who have never en-joyed it before—that you find yourself thinking up every kind of excuse to use it. Savor it on your tongue and your thoughts will turn to mayonnaise and a simple hard-boiled egg decorated with 3 capers, or the delights of cold roast chicken, mayonnaise, and tomatoes. Then there is mayonnaise and cold lobster or crab, mayonnaise and a great chicken salad or a brim-ming bowl of fresh cole slaw. Mayonnaise is very easy to make, either in a table-model electric mixer, or with a hand-held portable mixer, or with a wire whip. Mayonnaise is also something every cook must confidently and rapidly whip up on command with nary a qualm, because it is one of the elemental cookery procedures.

Note: Mayonnaise is in all our books, but if you have had troubles, per-haps a slightly different turn of phrase will give you new insight. Blender mayonnaise is in *Mastering, Volume I,* and in *The French Chef Cookbook;* mayonnaise in the electric super-blender-food-processor follows here on the next page.

For about 2¼ cups

3 egg yolks
¼ tsp dry mustard
½ tsp salt
Fresh lemon juice and/or wine vinegar
2 cups best-quality olive oil or salad oil, or a
  combination of the two
Salt and white pepper

Equipment: A 2½- to 3-quart fairly round-bottomed
  bowl (cul de poule, as illustrated on page 635);
  a heavy saucepan set on a wet potholder, to
  hold the bowl if you are beating by portable
  mixer or by hand; an electric mixer or a large
  wire whip

Beat the egg yolks for 2 to 3 minutes, until pale, thick, and the texture of mayonnaise. Add the mustard, salt, and a teaspoon each of lemon juice and vinegar (or 2 of either one); beat for another minute. Then, by half-teaspoon driblets, begin beating in the oil; do not stop beating until about ½ cup has gone in and the sauce has thickened into a heavy mayonnaise— as soon as this initial emulsion has occurred, you may stop beating if you wish. Then begin adding the oil by tablespoon dollops, being sure to beat several seconds after each addition so that the sauce will absorb the oil. When the sauce becomes too thick and heavy for easy beating, thin out with droplets of lemon juice or vinegar, and continue with the rest of the oil. Taste for seasoning, beating in more salt, lemon juice or vinegar, and pepper as you feel necessary. Turn sauce into a smaller bowl or a jar, cover airtight to prevent a skin from forming over its surface. Refrigerate, if sauce is not to be used promptly. Mayonnaise will keep 5 to 6 days under refrigeration, but let it come to room temperature before stirring it up, or the chilled egg yolks may release the oil from the emulsion.

Notes: If you always beat the egg yolks to thicken them before you begin to add the oil, if you always add the oil very slowly at first until the sauce thickens and the emulsion process is established, and, finally, if you never exceed the proportions of 2 cups of oil for 3 egg yolks, you will never have any trouble with mayonnaise. However, if your hand or eyes have failed you, and the sauce turns—meaning it will not thicken, or if it thins out, or if it curdles—do not despair. Warm a mixing bowl in hot water, drain, and place 1 tablespoon of Dijon-type prepared mustard and 1 teaspoon of the turned sauce in the bowl. Beat for a moment until they thicken together, then beat in the turned sauce by half-teaspoon driblets until the emulsion and thickening begin again. Beat in the remainder of the turned sauce by tablespoon dollops.

Every time I do mayonnaise on the television I let it turn and bring it back. I start out normally, allowing the sauce to thicken as it should, then I pour in a big splash of oil and it immediately thins out, since egg yolks cannot digest too much oil at once. If the sauce sits a while it takes on a broken curd look—soft masses of yellow with little rivulets of separation between them—a dreadful sight that looks particularly fine in a close-up view on color television. Then the bringing back, and the contrast of those miserable curds side by side with the thick yellow reconstituted sauce coming into being beside it, is sheer drama. Try it, since there is nothing like mastery of mayonnaise to make you feel peerless, and hope some time a worried cook will come to you at a party, "Oh, I'm so upset, my mayonnaise has turned!" That has happened to me only once, but the memory still nourishes my ego.

Mayonnaise in the electric super-blender-food-processor

The marvelous machine illustrated on page 154 does a beautiful job on mayonnaise, far better than the old-fashioned electric blender because you can make more at once, and get a fine thick smooth yolky sauce.

For about 2¼ cups

1 whole egg
2 egg yolks
¼ tsp dry mustard
½ tsp salt
Fresh lemon juice and/or wine vinegar
2 cups best-quality olive oil, or salad oil, or a
  combination of the two
Salt and white pepper

Using either the metal or the plastic blade, whizz the egg, yolks, mustard, and salt in the machine for 1 minute. Then add a teaspoon of lemon juice or vinegar, and begin adding the oil in a thin stream of droplets. After a cup or so has gone in, you can stop the machine, check on thickness, add a little more lemon juice or vinegar, and continue with the oil until the sauce is as thick as you want it to be. Correct seasoning, and that is all there is to it—a matter of 5 minutes or less. (The use of a whole egg in the machine prevents the sauce from becoming too thick before you have added the allowed amount of oil.)

Sour cream dressing

❖

FOR COLD FISH,
LOBSTER, SHRIMP,
CHICKEN, EGGS, AND
COLD VEGETABLES

Sour cream dressing is not as rich as mayonnaise, and you can use it in just as many ways. My two systems for making it are so simple they need no formal recipes.

The easiest is to stir thick sour cream into mayonnaise, about half and half; correct seasoning, adding a little lemon juice or vinegar if needed, and fold in fresh minced parsley and other fresh green herbs such as dill, or chives, or basil.

For the other method, beat together a tablespoon of prepared Dijon-type mustard, ¼ teaspoon of salt, and several grindings of pepper along with a tablespoon of wine vinegar or fresh lemon juice; gradually beat in ⅔ cup, more or less, of sour cream, correct seasoning, and fold in fresh minced parsley, dill, chives, or basil. With either of these, you may want to add also a teaspoon or so of finely minced shallot or scallion, and minced capers.

Cucumber and sour cream dressing. Another addition could be cucumbers, giving a little more body to the dressing and a fresh crunch to the texture. For a cup or so of the dressing, use half a cucumber, peeled and halved lengthwise. Scrape out and discard the seeds, put the cucumber through the coarse side of a grater into a bowl, and steep 10 minutes with ¼ teaspoon each of salt, sugar, and wine vinegar to bring out the cucumber taste and to eliminate excess liquid. Drain the cucumber and fold into the sour cream dressing. (If you wish to beat the steeping-liquid into the sauce too then you can stir in more sour cream.)

Green mayonnaise and miscellaneous remarks are on page 620.

Cole slaw

❖

For about 1 quart,
serving 6 to 8

This should be called Son of Avis DeVoto's Cole Slaw, because I asked for and was kindly given her recipe years ago thinking it a particularly tasty mixture, but it has naturally taken on a few changes of my own since. Essentially, however, it is hers.

For the dressing

½ cup homemade mayonnaise, page 439, plus a little more if needed later

⅓ cup sour cream or crème fraîche (page 500)
½ tsp caraway seeds
¼ tsp ground imported bay leaf
1 tsp salt
1 tsp sugar
Freshly ground pepper
2 Tb wine vinegar
½ Tb Dijon-type prepared mustard

The rest of the ingredients
1 medium-sized cucumber, peeled, seeded, diced,
 then macerated 20 minutes in ½ tsp salt, ¼ tsp
 sugar, and 1 tsp wine vinegar
1 fine fresh cabbage weighing about 1½ lbs.
 (making about 4 cups sliced cabbage)
⅔ cup diced celery
½ cup grated carrot
¼ cup diced scallions
⅓ cup diced green pepper
1 small sour apple, peeled and grated
2 to 3 Tb fresh minced parsley

Mix the dressing ingredients in a large bowl. Prepare the cucumber and let it macerate while you are amassing the other ingredients. Quarter the cabbage, cut out the tough core, wash and drain the quarters, then shred very finely into the mixing bowl. Add the other ingredients and the drained cucumber. Toss, check seasoning, cover and chill at least 1 hour. If the salad has exuded an oversupply of liquid, drain it out. Toss the salad again and taste carefully for seasoning. If you want a creamier cole slaw, fold in more mayonnaise and/or cream. The salad is now ready to serve.

Mayonnaise de volaille

————◆————

CHICKEN SALAD

A handsomely decorated salad, such as this one, can be the center of attraction on a buffet table or the main course for a luncheon or supper. In this case you need only serve with it something simple like a platter of sliced tomatoes and cucumbers, French bread, and a chilled white wine, such as a dry Graves (if you can find one), Chablis, Pouilly Fuissé, Pinot Blanc, or Riesling.

Chicken Note. This is the perfect time to use a stewing chicken, full of flavor, usually reasonably priced, giving you more meat for your money than roasters, and giving you as well a delicious chicken broth that you can treasure in your freezer. The recipe is on page 230.

For about 1 quart of chicken meat, serving 10 to 12

About 1 quart diced cooked chicken meat and a dozen or more thin slices of cooked chicken
2 to 3 cups diced celery stalks (⅜-inch pieces)
½ cup finely minced scallions
⅓ cup (lightly pressed down) fresh chopped parsley
Salt and freshly ground pepper
Fresh lemon juice (½ to 1 lemon)
4 or more Tb olive oil or salad oil
Optional: ½ to 1 cup walnut meats
2 or more cups homemade mayonnaise, page 439
A platter lined with lettuce leaves; or a chiffonade (very thin strips) of romaine; or watercress

Decorative suggestions
½ cup each of chopped black olives, chopped parsley, and sieved hard-boiled eggs
Strips of canned red pimiento

Preliminary seasoning. Keep diced chicken and sliced chicken separate. Fold the celery, all but ½ tablespoon of the scallions and parsley, ½ teaspoon of salt, and several grinds of pepper into the diced chicken; toss with a tablespoon of lemon juice and 2 to 3 of oil. Correct seasoning, cover, and let steep for 20 to 30 minutes at least (or longer in the refrigerator). Season the sliced chicken in the same manner, cover, and refrigerate.

Assembling the salad. When you are ready to assemble, drain all the accumulated juices out of the diced chicken. Fold in the optional walnuts and ¾ cup or so of the mayonnaise—just enough to enrobe the chicken and other ingredients. Taste, and correct seasoning. Toss greenery on platter with a sprinkling of salt and pepper, and mound the salad attractively upon it. Arrange the slices of chicken over the mound, and mask with a coating of mayonnaise.

Decoration. An attractive decoration is a multicolored top—pie-shaped segments of black alternating with, for instance, green and yellow, each segment separated by a line of red pimiento. To keep the segments neat, provide yourself with several foot-long strips of wax paper; fold them in two lengthwise to make a V-shape. If you are making 6 segments, as an example, 2 of each color, set the V-shape with its point at the center of the salad mound to mark the limits of 1 pie-shaped segment. Sprinkle inside the V-area with half the chopped olives: reverse the V-shape in the opposite direction, and fill in the corresponding segment. Continue with the other colors, then outline each segment with red pimiento. Decorate center of mound with a curl of pimiento, a cherry tomato, or whatever appeals to your sense of color and symmetry.

✭ If you are not serving shortly, cover salad with an upside-down bowl and refrigerate.

Accompany the salad, if you wish, with a bowl of additional mayonnaise.

OTHER SUMMER SALAD COMBINATIONS

Turkey salad. Turkey is usually a very good buy in summer, and if you do not want a whole bird, use just the turkey breast. (Frozen turkey rolls, however, in my experience, should not be bothered with; at least when I've defrosted several to see what they were all about, I found turkey skin acting as a casing for chopped meat.) Cook the turkey like stewed chicken, on page 230, and treat it exactly like the chicken for the preceding salad.

Lobster salad. Use fresh boiled lobster, or best-quality frozen lobster meat (I have never found any canned lobster I could stomach) . Treat it exactly like the chicken salad, and I do think it is particularly important that the lobster have its preliminary seasoning before being folded into the mayonnaise.

Crab salad. You are lucky if you have fresh boiled crab. Frozen crab meat can be very good, but it is usually best to defrost it slowly in the refrigerator to prevent it from taking on a watery quality. (That was the advice given to me in Seattle with Alaska king crab, and it was true with some New England deep-sea crab we tried.) Canned crab must be drained, picked over to remove cartilage bits, then washed in cold water to remove the preserving brine. Treat the crab like the chicken.

Shrimp salad. If you are using raw shrimp, you might boil them as directed on page 163, *à la grecque,* and they will need no preliminary seasonings, just an arrangement with tomatoes and lettuce, and mayonnaise on the side. Or boil them in salted water and treat them like the chicken. For canned shrimp (which should, incidentally, always be bought from a large-turnover market, and stored in the refrigerator) , drain them and soak 10 minutes or more in cold water to remove the preserving salt; then proceed at will.

Aspics

A touch of aspic is a touch of magic. It can turn a plain poached egg into a glittering *Oeuf en Gelée,* a naked chicken into a *Poulet en Chaud-froid,* a pot roast of beef into *Boeuf à la Mode en Gelée,* and a modest poached fish into a glistening poem. The most elegant way to serve any of these is to glaze and decorate each serving piece before arranging it on a platter lined with aspic, and to decorate the platter with aspic cutouts. The effect is so dazzling you would think only a professional could execute it until you realize that the complex-looking whole is but an assembling of standard parts.

It is the look of high sophistication, I think, that scares most of us off aspics, but once you have tried one you will realize that a creation in aspic is almost entirely a question of time. It is the kind of time, however, that you can snatch at odd moments during the day. You have the aspic itself to make, of course, where you do stand over it while it clarifies into a sparkling glory. The rest of the time is in pieces, some of which you do not supervise, such as 20 minutes for the layer of aspic to set at the bottom of the serving platter. Other times require your presence, such as the few minutes it takes to liquefy a small saucepan of aspic, then to chill it over a bowl of ice before you spoon it onto your trout. Again a time for chilling: 20 minutes in the refrigerator, but it can sit unwatched until you are ready to coat the trout again with another layer. Thus an aspic is a labor of love, but not of difficulty. And you will be richly rewarded by the pleasure not only that your guests receive, but also that you yourself savor in presenting a beautiful piece of work that you have created entirely by yourself.

Include the trout as part of a cold buffet table, or serve them as a first course, or have them as the main course for a lunch or supper along with a bowl of homemade mayonnaise, a tossed salad, your own French bread, and a rather light dry white wine like Chablis or Riesling.

(The following recipe is for whole poached trout, 1 per serving, but exactly the same procedures hold for chicken poached in wine, for braised beef *à la Mode en Gelée,* and for whole poached salmon. If you have done one, in other words, all the rest follow the same general pattern.)

Truites en gelée

COLD DECORATED
TROUT IN WINE
ASPIC

For 4 half-pound
trout, serving
4 people

For the aspic

*4 chilled poached trout and 4 cups of their
    white-wine cooking stock, page 131*
*½ cup egg whites (1 egg white makes about
    2 tablespoons)*
*2 packages (2 Tb) plain unflavored gelatin (2½
    packages in very hot weather)*
*⅓ cup white Port wine, Cognac, or dry white
    French Vermouth*

For decorating the trout

*2 strips of leek green or several green scallion tops,
    blanched (boiled a minute or two until limp,
    rinsed in cold water, and dried)*
*1 hard-boiled egg yolk sieved into a bowl with ½ tsp
    mayonnaise or soft butter*
Fresh parsley sprigs

*Equipment: A very clean 2½-quart saucepan for
    making the aspic; a straining apparatus for the
    clarification of the aspic (washed cheesecloth,
    a sieve, a colander, a bowl, and a ladle); a
    serving plater, such as a round one 14 inches in
    diameter; a roasting pan 8 to 9 inches square
    in which to form an aspic sheet; a rack large
    enough to hold the trout, set over a tray (to
    catch aspic dribbles); a paper decorating
    cone, page 572*

The aspic. The first step is to clarify the cooking stock, meaning to render it clear and sparkling by heating it with raw egg whites; these draw to themselves all the particles suspended in the stock that make it cloudy.

Beat 1 cup cool stock into the egg whites to blend thoroughly. Heat rest of stock to the simmer; by driblets, whisk it into the egg white mixture. Set saucepan over moderate heat and, whisking slowly but reaching all over pan to keep egg whites and stock continuously blended, let liquid come just to the simmer. Immediately remove to side of heat and stop whisking. The egg white mass will slowly coagulate and rise to top of liquid, which should remain on the point of simmering; in 5 minutes rotate pan a quarter turn, and rotate again in 5 minutes, letting pan stay at the edge of the heat source 15 minutes in all.

Meanwhile prepare the straining contraption: set a large colander over a bowl, lay a sieve across the colander, and line the sieve with 4 thicknesses of washed cheesecloth. When stock is ready, very carefully dip ladlesful into sieve, disturbing egg whites as little as possible. Let stock drip through undisturbed; it should be perfectly clear and sparkling. (If not—because stock was not properly degreased, was not correctly heated with the egg whites, or was roughly strained—repeat the process.)

Pour the gelatin onto the wine; when softened, stir into the warm clarified stock, swishing cup about in stock to be sure all gelatin has gone in. If stock has cooled, then heat it to dissolve gelatin completely. This is now your aspic, and is ready to use.

Assembling and decorating the truites en gelée. Pour a ³⁄₁₆-inch layer of liquid aspic into platter, and a ⅜-inch layer into roasting pan; chill 20 minutes or until set.

Provide yourself with a small saucepan and a bowl with ice cubes and water to cover them; the small pan will hold a cup of liquid aspic, which you will chill over ice until it is cold and syrupy. With this you will glaze the trout, melting and chilling a small quantity after each operation.

With a sharp-pointed knife, trace a rectangular side window 4 inches long in the exposed skin of each trout, starting ½ inch from gills, top fin, and belly. Carefully strip skin from window, leaving flesh as smooth as possible. Scoop out the eyes. Spoon a layer of syrupy aspic over the whole trout, then another layer; chill 10 minutes, and repeat several times to build up a ¹⁄₁₆-inch layer. To make traditional mimosa-branch decorations, cut the blanched leek or scallion greens into strips ¹⁄₁₆ inch wide; lay several in graceful branching curves on the exposed flesh of each trout. Fill decorating cone with the egg mixture, and make yellow dots along the green, to simulate mimosa flowers. Glaze the fish with 2 or 3 more coats of aspic. Transfer fish to aspic-lined platter, arranging them tails together and heads fanning out, if platter is round.

Aspic sheet in roasting pan is for decorations, such as cutouts for edges of platter, and diced or chopped aspic to fill spaces, gill openings, and so forth. The simplest system is to cut down through half the aspic with a knife, making criss-cross lines 1½ inches apart. Lift out the resulting squares and arrange on platter. Turn remaining aspic out onto a board, and dice or chop fine; spoon into vent and gill spaces, or anywhere you feel a little decoration is needed. Insert fresh parsley leaves into eyes. Keep platter refrigerated until serving time.

French breads

*W*hen you want to produce an earthy, old-fashioned, great big loaf of bread, try the yeast starter method—yeast and flour mixed with enough water to make a thick liquid, like a batter. You let it sit for a couple of hours until the yeast cells have gobbled up all the starch in the flour, multiplying themselves mightily in the process and belching forth great gassy bubbles. Then, when there is nothing more to eat, they settle down quietly, waiting for the next offering. At this point, but you need be in no tearing hurry about it, you knead in the main body of your flour, be it rye, or whole wheat, or white, plus anything else you like, such as wheat germ, oat flakes, caraway seeds, beer, buttermilk, honey, molasses, and so forth. The dough then has a leisurely rise, and is ready for forming and baking.

I certainly never knew a thing about yeast and doughs until my colleague, Simca, and my husband, Paul, and I went through the 750 days of our great French bread spree, while we were working on Volume II of *Mastering the Art of French Cooking*. I had sometimes wondered, when I ordered a frankfurter and sauerkraut on a bun in one of those sausage snack bars, why the bun usually disintegrated into a slimy mass in the bottom of the plate. I also used to wonder about the soggy disappearance of the French bread crouton in the onion soup gratinée. I hadn't a clue until Simca arranged for the three of us to learn about French bread from Professor Raymond Calvel at the École Française de Meunerie in Paris.

It was Professor Calvel who pointed out that during the rise of any dough, while the yeast is munching away on its starch, a mysterious enzyme action can be taking place in the gluten—the elastic-protein part of the flour—provided you give it time. This enzyme action gradually changes your dough into something with a wheaty, grainy, elemental taste; it also develops the texture of the gluten, to give body to the bread. (If you rush things you get little or no enzyme activity, just hot air, and that does a lot to explain the slimy bun and the disappearing crouton.) Besides the precious gift of time, if you also go in for the yeast starter you will give the dough a certain built-in moisture that prevents your final loaf from going stale and dry too quickly, and you will produce a most attractively chewy eating quality.

By the greatest of good fortunes we have two television programs on French bread, where you can see films, taken in France, of Professor Calvel teaching the forming and baking of the familiar long loaves of bread, and big round loaves, and buns. A third bread show uses the yeast starter, and has in addition a ballet-like sequence in Pierre Poilane's famous bakery on the rue du Cherche-Midi in Paris, down in the bowels of the sub-cellar, where two bakers in shorts and espadrilles, naked to the waist, are slapping big balls of dough into great round country loaves, and sliding them into a wood-fired oven.

Although the first directions for forming bread in the following recipe involve bread pans, the second recipe is done in the French way because the ordinary French bread of France stands alone when it is baking; it is not sitting in a pan. Thus it must be formed in a special way, with various turns, and twists, and folds, to develop enough surface tension on the outside of the dough to hold it in shape. Surface tension sounds hideously technical, I know, but you can actually feel it develop when you begin manipulating the dough. It is as though there were a thin web of rubber on its outside that you were stretching with every move until it holds firm, like a girdle over a buttock. Big round bakery loaves, after forming, rise in round wicker baskets lined with heavy linen; long fat country loaves rise in long wide baskets. When risen, the loaves are unmolded onto a wooden paddle that has been sprinkled with cornmeal, the tops are slashed to make those typical designs, and the loaves are slid off the paddle onto the hot firebrick of the baker's oven. There they swell and brown, keeping their shape because the tension has held.

Few among us have linen-lined wicker bread baskets—they call them *bannetons*—so Paul had the bright thought of placing the formed long-loaf dough in a canvas sling, and suspending it by closing the two ends of the sling in the top of a drawer, or a door, or weighting them on the edge of a table and letting the sling hang over the edge. It works perfectly; the dough rises as it should, and you can bake it either on a pastry sheet or slide it onto hot tiles in your simulated baker's oven, as described on page 466. One enthusiastic bread baker writes, by the way, that he has invented his own sling system, where the two ends of the canvas are attached to rods, and the rods are then suspended from a cradle large enough to hold three or four slings of rising dough at once.

NOTES ON YEAST

Is cake yeast better than dry-active yeast? Does it have more flavor? Cake yeast often acts a little faster, but there are some brands of dry yeast that are very fast. I have not found any difference in flavor, because flavor in my opinion comes from the amount and length of the rise. How much yeast should one use? When you are doing the slow long rises that I recommend, use as little as possible because you want the dough to take its time. In general, take 1 package of yeast per pound (3½ cups) of flour unless you are using the yeast starter in the following recipe for 8 cups of flour, where ½ package goes into the starter and ½ into the final mixture. Weather, however, affects yeast action. The recipes here are based on a rising temperature of 75 degrees. Below 70 degrees you may want double the yeast, since cold slows down the action; at 80 degrees, halve them, since warmth increases activity. But do not worry too much about yeast proportions, since you can always speed up the action by warmth—set the dough bowl in a basin of 80-degree water, for instance. Or slow down the rise by setting it in cool water; or refrigerate it for 20 minutes or so.

WARNING ABOUT YEAST. Be sure your yeast is fully dissolved and liquid before you mix it into the flour, or it will not act. Be sure you do not kill the yeast by using hot water—100 to 105 degrees is warm enough to dissolve and activate it, but you can also dissolve it in cold water: cold does not kill yeast; it only slows it down.

PROVING YEAST. Unless you are worried that your dry yeast is beyond its prime, I can see no reason for proving it—that is, dissolving it in warm water with a little sugar, until it bubbles actively. Cake yeast is active when it is firm, unblemished, fresh looking, and fresh smelling.

NOTES ON BREAD PANS

A 9 x 5 x 2¾-inch loaf pan holds 8 cups, and so does a 9⅝ x 5½ x 2¾-inch pan. Such information is useless because it gives only the top measurement, and who knows how steeply the sides slant? A straight pan holds more than a slant-sided pan, in other words. All you want to know, when you have 3 cups of dough that are to rise up to almost triple, is the capacity of the pan: it should hold 8 cups, and no mistake. Small difference what the shape of the pan may be, from round to oval to loaf, and the depth may vary from 1½ to 4 inches. I shall base timing and descriptions, however, on the conventional steel or aluminum loaf pan about 2¾ inches deep and shall give the size in cups. I suggest that you mark the capacity of all your pans—fill them with water, then pour the contents into a quart measure—and scratch the number of cups contained on the bottom of each pan. Then you will never be caught with the wrong size.

Basic rye or whole grain bread

Pain de seigle

RYE BREAD, AND WHOLE WHEAT BREAD, WHITE BREAD, OR YOUR OWN MIXTURE

The following recipe is a generic one, meaning you can adapt it to any kind of bread you wish. It begins with a yeast starter, or batter, or *poulisch* as it is called in France, which is simply flour and water and yeast that is set to rise and bubble, then sink, and, while allowing the yeast cells to multiply, it also begins a certain enzyme action that gives moisture and texture as well as excellent flavor to your bread. I recommend making the starter the night before, and the next morning you can begin with the main rise, having gained 3 hours in the process.

Note: If you want to make less, just halve all the ingredients listed, but the timing remains the same.

For about 8 cups of flour, making 3 loaves baked in 2-quart pans of any shape, for example a loaf pan 9⅝ by 5½ inches top diameter, and 2¾ inches deep; or 1 large free-form oval loaf 20 inches long and 5 inches in diameter.

The yeast starter: 2½ to 3 hours, or make it the night before

½ *package (0.3 ounce) fresh cake yeast, or ½ package (1¼ tsp) dry-active yeast*
⅓ *cup tepid water (105 degrees) in a 1-cup measure*
2 *cups all-purpose flour (scoop dry-measure cup into flour and sweep off excess; sifting is not necessary)*
An 8-quart fairly straight-sided mixing bowl (or a pail)
1½ *cups tepid water*

The final dough mixture: 2½ to 3 hours, or more

The preceding yeast starter

½ package additional yeast, dissolved in ⅓ cup tepid water (or milk)

6 cups flour as follows: 4 cups rye flour and 2 cups all-purpose white stirred together, for a dough that is not too heavy and that will rise nicely (or a combination of rye and whole wheat and white; or whole wheat and white; or unbleached all-purpose white flour only)

1½ Tb salt

1¼ cups tepid water not over 105 degrees (or milk, or buttermilk, or a combination)

Additional water or flour if needed

Optional: Other ingredients as you wish, but try the plain version first

The yeast starter: *minimum of 2½ hours.* Stir the yeast into the tepid water and let dissolve completely—5 minutes or so for dry-active yeast. Measure the flour into the mixing bowl; gradually beat in the water with a wire whip. When yeast has dissolved—stir about to make sure—beat that in also. You will have a smooth liquid the consistency of heavy pancake batter. Cover with plastic wrap, and let rise at around 75 degrees, if possible, for a minimum of 2½ hours—longer if kitchen is cold. The whole mass should first double in volume and be filled with large bubbles, then it should sink down slightly, and the bubbles will remain in its surface.

If you are not ready to proceed in an hour or so, refrigerate the starter, where it can remain overnight. Let come to room temperature before continuing, or set in a basin of warm water and stir about to take off the chill (cold yeast is sluggish and will slow down the action in your next step).

The final dough mixture and kneading by hand. (See page 472 for machine kneading.) Beat the additional yeast and 4 cups of the flour into the starter along with the salt and tepid water or other liquid. Continue beating with a wooden spoon, adding sprinklings of flour until dough is too stiff to work; turn it out onto a work surface and let it rest. In 2 to 3 minutes, sprinkle onto it about ¼ cup of flour, and work it in with the heel of one hand, sprinkling on more until dough has some body but is still soft and pliable. Then, with a scraper or stiff spatula, scrape dough off work surface with one hand, turning it into your other hand as you do so; immediately slap it down hard, pushing it out with the heel of your hand as it hits the surface. Continue scraping it up, slamming it down, and pushing it out. Add a little more flour if you feel it is still too damp, but in 4 to 5 minutes of vigorous work it should feel smooth and pliable—it is not to be a stiff firm dough; it should become rather elastic, indicating the gluten molecules have fused together into an interconnecting web throughout the dough, and that is what kneading is all about. Let it rest 2 minutes while you wash out the mixing bowl. Give the dough another vigorous minute of kneading, and scoop it into the bowl.

Rising: *at least 3 hours.* Cover with plastic wrap, and let rise at around 75 degrees if possible, until dough has tripled in bulk; it will fill a 6-quart bowl. (If kitchen is warm, however, let dough double in bulk, then turn it out on work surface, flatten it with the palms of your hands, fold it in three, and return it to the bowl; let rise again, to almost double.) Rising time should be a minimum of 3 hours, but it will take longer if kitchen is cool; don't worry if it takes longer than 3 hours, since it is the amount of rise that is important in this case.

Note: Although you cannot speed up the rise or you will lose the benefits of enzyme action, you can slow it down by placing the bowl in the refrigerator, or even by freezing. Do not be afraid to experiment!

The dough is now ready for forming and for its final rise before it goes into the oven. Here is the complete story for baking the bread in bread pans; the free-form loaf follows.

Forming and baking the bread in bread pans

Forming the dough. Choose 3 two-quart bread pans (or smaller or larger pans, as you wish), and grease them with lard or shortening. Turn the risen dough out onto a lightly floured work surface, cut the dough into 3 pieces, and let rest 2 minutes. Then, one by one, form each piece as follows: Pat dough out, left and right, with the palms of your hands on a lightly floured board, flattening it into an oval several inches shorter than your bread pan. Flip it almost in half, lengthwise, from the bottom. Flatten again, and flip dough almost in half again, this time from the top. Flatten once more, about the length of your pan, and press a trench lengthwise across center of dough, using the side of your hand like a hatchet. Fold in two along trench and seal the two edges of dough together with the heel of your hand. Turn dough seal side down and press into pan—pan should be ½ full. (As soon as you are used to the forming system it takes but a few seconds, and is designed to make a well-shaped, evenly rising loaf.)

Rising: *1½ to 2 hours.* Let dough rise to fill the pans, at around 75 degrees. If kitchen is damp and humid, leave pans uncovered; if dry, cover them loosely. But check surface of dough occasionally: cover if crusting over, uncover if sweating and moist. It is the *amount of the rise, not the timing,* that is important here.

Baking: *about 1 hour in a 450-degree oven.* Be sure your oven is preheated to 450 degrees by the time the dough has risen to fill the pans. Provide yourself with a razor blade, and a large spray can or atomizer filled with water, or a pastry brush and water. Just before baking, take the razor blade and slash the top of the dough along its length, going ⅜ inch, almost parallel to the surface—to make a decorative mark, and also to allow the dough to rise more in the oven. At once spray or paint top of loaves with water, and immediately set in middle or lower-middle rack of oven, leaving space between pans for heat circulation. Spray or paint again with water in 3 minutes, and again after 3 minutes. (Water allows the yeast action to continue a little longer, and also coagulates the starch on the surface, to make a brown crust.) Bake 20 to 30 minutes, until bread has swollen and begun to brown nicely. Turn thermostat down to 350 degrees and bake about 20 minutes more, until bread shows a faint line of shrinkage from pan, and can be unmolded easily. Unmold it: the sides and bottom should be brown and lightly crusted; thump the loaf in several places with your fingers, and it should make a hollow thumping noise, not a dead thud. Turn the loaves out onto a baking sheet, on their sides; return to turned-off oven, leaving the door ajar, for 15–20 minutes, to dry out moisture inside bread and prevent crust from becoming soggy. Finally remove the loaves from the oven and cool on a rack.

Forming one long large loaf in a sling, and baking it

Forming the dough. Provide yourself with the largest baking sheet that will fit into your oven, and a canvas pastry cloth or a new heavy linen towel about 24 by 30 inches, plus a piece of plastic wrap or a plastic bag the same size as the canvas or towel.

Turn the risen dough out onto a lightly floured work surface; fold in half, and let rest 2 minutes. You are now to form a long fat loaf (with surface tension!) that will eventually fit diagonally across your baking sheet from near corner to far corner; take careful note of that size so you won't make too long a shape.

Patting the dough out left and right with the palms of your hands, flatten it into a fat oval about 12 inches long.

Flip it almost in half, lengthwise from the bottom. Flatten again, to about 14 inches, and flip dough almost in half again, this time from the top—be sure work surface is always lightly floured to prevent dough from sticking to it. Flatten again into an oval, about 16 inches long.

Press a trench lengthwise along center of dough, using the side of your hand like a hatchet.

Fold in two along trench, and seal the two edges together with the heel of your hand.

Turn dough seal side down and, rotating it back and forth under the palms of your hands as you slide them to the two ends, lengthen it, repeating the movement, to the size you wish. (If you've messed up this step, fold dough in two end over end, let rest 10 minutes covered with plastic, and fold it again.)

Rising in a canvas sling: *1½ to 2 hours.* Place the pastry cloth or linen towel over the sheet of plastic (plastic prevents dough from crusting as it rises) , and rub all-purpose flour onto cloth.

Arrange the formed dough, sealed side up, in the center. Hold ends of plastic and cloth and roll them over upon themselves several times so they will hold. (*Note:* Plastic is so transparent that it doesn't show in these photos.)

Then close in a drawer, or over the top of a door, or weight heavily and hang from the edge of a table—to suspend the dough as though in a sling. It can thus swell freely but will not spread out of shape. Let rise until almost triple in bulk; it should be puffed, light, and spongy. The rising temperature, if possible, should be at around 75 degrees.

Baking: *about 1 hour.* The oven should be preheated to 450 degrees, the rack in middle level. Provide yourself with 2 to 3 tablespoons of cornmeal, a sharp razor blade, and a large spray can or atomizer filled with cold water (or a pastry brush and bowl of water).

Spread a thin layer of cornmeal diagonally across your baking sheet, where loaf is to lie. Unmold dough upside down onto sheet very carefully so as not to deflate it. Immediately make 3 or 4 slightly diagonal lengthwise slashes about 4 inches long down the top of dough with razor blade, cutting almost parallel to surface and going in about ½ inch; at once spray or paint with water, and set dough in hot oven. In 3 minutes, rapidly spray or paint again, and repeat once more in 3 minutes—this helps the crust to brown. Bake 20 to 30 minutes, until bread has swollen and begun to brown nicely, then turn heat down to 350 degrees and bake about 20 minutes more. Turn off oven, open door ajar, and let bread stay an additional 20 minutes; this is to dry out interior moisture so it will not exude and soften the crust. Cool on a rack.

To store bread. When bread is thoroughly cold, wrap in a plastic bag and refrigerate where it will keep fresh for several days. Or wrap airtight and freeze, where it will keep a month or more.

Round loaves and rolls. See French Bread, page 467.

———————◆———————

French bread

A fine loaf of French bread has a crackly crust; the bread itself inside the loaf is full of holes yet has texture and body when you chew it; and, above all, good French bread has that wonderful taste of the grain, of nature itself, of bread the way you dream it should be. It is hard to buy the good old-fashioned kind of French bread now even in France, and you very rarely indeed find it here in this country. But you can make an excellent home version right in your own kitchen, and produce bread that is much better than anything you can usually buy. The method here is one adapted from the professional French bakery system, as we filmed it in France with Professor Calvel for our television programs.

MANUFACTURING NOTES. The previous recipe, for rye bread, gives the yeast batter system, while the recipe here is the so-called direct method, and the one I did for our television program as well as for Volume II of *Mastering*. The two methods are interchangeable, and it is useful to know both ways, but the yeast batter gives a slightly moister loaf.

TEMPERATURES AND TIMING. The ideal rising temperature is around 75 degrees; if the temperature is higher, the dough will rise too fast, will begin to ferment, and you won't get the enzyme action you want for flavor and texture. (On hot days, set your dough bowl in a larger bowl of cool water, for instance, to slow the action.) Although the actual time you spend on making the bread is less than half an hour, its long slow rises take a minimum of 7 hours from mixing bowl to bread-in-hand. That sounds horrendous to the non-cook—7 hours! Ye gods! But you're not standing around holding it by the hand all this time. No. You are out shopping, but remembering to come back on time; or you are teaching a course in croquet, or you are playing the flute—and the dough takes care of itself. While you cannot speed up the process, you can slow it down at any point by setting the dough in a cooler place, or by refrigerating it, or even by freezing it; then continue where you left off, when you are ready to do so. In other words, you are the boss of that dough, and when you have become familiar with yeast doughs, you will invent all kinds of systems of your own in addition to the suggestions you will find here.

Pain français

FRENCH BREAD

Ingredients for 3 loaves 16 to 18 inches long and 3 inches in diameter

The dough mixture
1 package dry-active yeast
⅓ cup tepid water (not over 105 degrees or you may kill the yeast)
3½ cups (1 pound) all-purpose flour, preferably unbleached (measure by dipping dry-measure cups into flour and sweeping off excess)
A fairly straight-sided mixing bowl, 3- to 4-quart capacity (if sides slant outward, dough spreads out too much and has difficulty in rising)
2¼ tsp salt

1¼ cups tepid water
A rubber spatula

Kneading
A wooden or plastic working surface about
*   2 feet square*
A pastry scraper or stiff spatula

Final rising of formed loaves
A canvas pastry cloth, available in any household
*   department; or a heavy linen towel*
A large baking sheet or tray, 20 by 24 inches
A floured towel

Baking
About ½ cup cornmeal
An unmolding board—a stiff piece of cardboard, a
*   shingle, a piece of plywood, or a baking sheet*
*   wrapped in a floured towel—18 inches long and*
*   at least 4 inches wide*
Your largest baking sheet
An atomizer of some sort, filled with cold water;
*   or a soft brush and a cup of cold water*

The dough mixture. Stir the yeast into the ⅓ cup of water and let dissolve; measure the flour into the mixing bowl, add the salt, and the rest of the water. Then stir yeast with spatula until granules have dissolved completely, pour into bowl, and mix vigorously with spatula. Turn out onto working surface, and let rest 3 to 4 minutes. Meanwhile wash out bowl, pour in 10½ cups tepid water, and mark level on outside to guide you later when the dough rises. Drain and dry the bowl.

Kneading. Dough should be quite soft and sticky.

Start kneading by flipping one side over onto the other with scraper or spatula; continue this movement rapidly for a number of seconds, until dough begins to have enough body so that you can push it with the heel of your hand after flipping.

Finally, sweep dough off work surface with scraper, and throw it roughly back; flip it over, sweep it up, slap it down, and continue thus, vigorously, until dough feels free of lumps and draws back when pushed out. Let rest again for 2 minutes. Knead again for a minute or two; dough should be soft, smooth, elastic, and pliable.

Scoop into clean bowl and cover with plastic wrap. (You now have approximately 3 cups of dough; kneading time is 8 to 10 minutes.)

First and second risings in bowl: *3½ hours minimum.* Let rise at room temperature of between 70 and 75 degrees, until dough reaches the 10½-cup level marked on the bowl—3 to 5 hours. Lightly flour working surface, and scoop dough onto it. Flatten (patting with the lightly floured palms of your hands) into a 10- to 12-inch circle. Flip near side over onto far side, then left side onto right, and finally flip near side completely over and just under far side. Clean out bowl, lift dough back into it, cover, and let rise again almost to the previous level, 1½ to 2½ hours at 70 to 75 degrees.

Forming long loaves, and final rise: *1½ hours minimum.* Scoop dough out onto lightly floured surface, and cut cleanly into 3 pieces. Flip near side of each over onto far side and let rest 4 to 5 minutes.

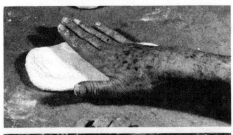

One at a time, flatten a piece of dough with lightly floured palms of hands, patting left and right into an oval 8 or more inches long.

Flip near side almost up to far side; flatten again. Always lightly dusting work surface with flour, flip far side almost down over near side. Flatten again. Then, with the heel or the side of your hand, press a trench lengthwise across center of dough.

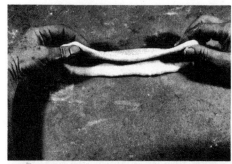

Fold in two by flipping far side down to cover near side.

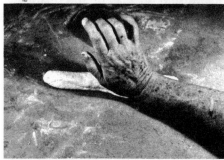

Seal the two edges with the heel of your hand.

You now have a fat sausage shape; lengthen it to fit the length of your baking sheet as follows: place your hands together, palms down, at the center of the sausage shape; rotating it back and forth under your palms, slide your hands toward the two ends.

Keeping the circumference as even as possible, repeat the movement several times as you roll the dough into as long a sausage as you wish.

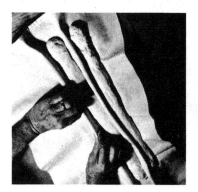

Rub flour into surface of pastry cloth, and place dough sealed side up (if you can still find the seal), at one side of cloth. Pinch a ridge in cloth to make a trough to divide the pieces of dough. Form the two other pieces and lay on cloth.

Cover loosely with a floured towel, and let rise to almost triple at 70 to 75 degrees; dough should look puffed and swollen. Time: 1½ to 2½ hours.

Baking: *30 to 40 minutes.* Preheat oven to 450 degrees. Sprinkle cornmeal over surface of baking sheet and along edge of unmolding board.

One at a time, flip formed dough from canvas to unmolding board, and arrange on baking sheet, soft underside of dough on top.

Immediately make three lengthwise slashes in the top of the dough with a razor, cutting almost parallel to surface, as follows: 1st, from one end down a third of the length, just left of center and off a little to the left; 2nd, from upper to lower third, at a slight angle from right to left across the middle; 3rd, from lower third to end of loaf, just right of center, slanting left.

At once, spray surface of loaves with a light film of water, and set in lowest level of oven. At minute 2, rapidly spray surface again; at minute 4, spray again. At minute 6, set in upper-middle level, and spray a final time.

Bake 20 to 25 minutes in all, until loaves are crusty and sound hollow when thumped. Turn off oven, and leave 5 to 10 minutes longer, to dry out interior, then remove, and place upright to let air circulate freely around the loaves until they cool.

THE SIMULATED BAKER'S OVEN

A baker's oven has a hot firebrick surface onto which the naked risen loaf of dough is slid from a wooden paddle; then a live steam jet whooshes a cloud of vapor into the oven for the first few minutes of baking. The hot surface crusts the bottom of the dough and gives an extra push to its final rise while the steam coagulates the surface of the dough, crisping and browning its crust. After working with Professor Calvel in Paris, we evolved the following system to simulate a baker's oven, and have found it produces a crustier and more authentic loaf than the conventional method. Also, for the home baker, it creates far more excitement and fun.

TO SIMULATE THE FIREBRICK BAKING SURFACE. You will need high-fired quarry tiles or ceramic tiles, or firebrick splits, enough to cover your oven rack. Look in the Yellow Pages for these; the tiles are 6 by 6 inches or 3 by 6 inches and ½ inch thick. Fit them closely together on a rack in the upper-middle level, and let them heat for about ½ hour at 450 degrees in the oven.

THE STEAM CONTRAPTION. To produce the steam, heat a metal object, such as an ax head, iron wedges, or an antique pressing iron—or a firebrick—on top of a burner until red hot. Shortly before baking, set a roasting pan (large enough to hold the hot object easily) with 1 inch of water on the bottom rack of an electric oven, or on the floor of a gas oven. Just before you are to slide your risen dough into the oven, you will grab the hot object with fire tongs or large stainless-steel spoons, plop it into the pan of water, close the door for 5 seconds so the oven fills with steam, then in goes the dough. (When you are baking several batches of rolls, you will run out of steam and so should have other hot objects to plop into the water just before each batch of rolls goes in.)

THE BAKER'S PADDLE OR SLIDING BOARD. Finally, to take the place of the baker's paddle, called peel in this country and *pelle* in French, you need a smooth sliding board of some kind, like the bottom of an old drawer, a thin piece of plywood, or a cedar shingle; it should be 20 to 24 inches long, and not quite the width of your oven rack. Then, for long loaves of French bread, you need a long thin board about 4 inches wide and 20 inches long for unmolding the risen dough from the canvas.

Now, here is how to bake 3 long loaves of French bread in a simulated baker's oven, and following that are directions for forming and baking round loaves and rolls.

French bread in a simulated baker's oven

Your oven has been preheated to 450 degrees, the tiles or firebricks are in place, the steam system is on the ready, you have your unmolding board, your sliding board, your razor for slashing, and your 3 long pieces of dough are fully risen.

Just before you are ready to bake, place the pan of water in the bottom of the oven. Sprinkle a dusting of cornmeal over the 2 boards. Flip 1 risen loaf upside down from the canvas onto the unmolding board, and slide it onto the far edge of the sliding board. One by one, rapidly unmold other loaves onto the board, spacing them 2 to 3 inches apart. Rapidly slash the loaves (page 465), and immediately activate the steam contraption: lift the heated object into the pan of water in the oven and close the door. In 5 seconds, quickly open oven door, set far edge of sliding board at far edge of hot tiles at back of oven and, with a quick pull toward you, dislodge the loaves onto the hot surface and close the oven door. (This is always a tense moment, at least for me, and I've found you just have to pull that board toward you with a smooth confidence and the dough will slide off neatly; once the dough is on the hot surface, you can't touch it for 5 minutes, until it has crusted and can be moved. You will probably mess up a loaf or two at first, but they will bake into bread anyway; serve them sliced and no one will know what happened.)

In 5 minutes, remove the steam contraption, and bake about 25 minutes in all, until the loaves are brown and crusty and the bread makes a hollow thump. To dry out interior of loaves, turn oven off, open door ajar, and leave bread in oven 5 to 10 minutes. Remove and cool upended, to allow for air circulation.

Rolls and round loaves

Although many of us link French bread only with the familiar long loaf, the very same dough makes neat rolls and hefty round country-style loaves. However, just as the long shapes have their special forming technique, so do the round loaves and rolls. If you want professional-looking bread, then, you will want to know the professional system for forming the dough, and this is the way Professor Calvel taught me at the École Française de Meunerie in Paris, when we filmed our television show with him.

Petits pains; galettes

———◆———

ROUND ROLLS

For 8 to 12

Forming. Cut the risen dough (master recipe for French bread, page 461) into 8 to 12 pieces. After letting it rest for 3 to 4 minutes, to relax it, form the rolls one at a time on a lightly floured surface as follows: Flatten dough with your fingers. Fold left side ⅔ the way over to right side with fingers, then push from right to left, and fold far side almost down over near side, pushing again. Rotate the dough a quarter turn clockwise, and continue the movement rapidly several more times, until underside of dough is a smooth cushion, then turn dough smooth side up. Rotate it clockwise under the palm of your hand, using thumb and little finger to push edges of dough under where they will meet at the middle on the bottom, forming a pucker. Turn smooth side down, and pinch puckered edges together with your fingers; lay pucker side up on floured canvas, and proceed with next piece.

Rising. Cover the balls of dough with floured towel and let rise to almost triple—1½ to 2½ hours at 70 to 75 degrees. (If dough is damp and room humid, flour the canvas very heavily before you place the formed dough upon it, and sprinkle flour on top of the dough balls; on the other hand, if room is hot and dry, cover dough loosely with a sheet of floured plastic rather than a towel, to prevent top of dough from crusting over.) Bake either in the conventional manner or in a simulated baker's oven, as follows:

To bake in the conventional manner. Preheat oven to 450 degrees before rise is complete. Sprinkle cornmeal over surface of baking sheet, with floured hands gently lift rolls one by one, and arrange smooth side up on baking sheet. At once rapidly slash tops of dough balls with a razor, either making one straight central cut almost parallel to the surface, or a cross, or a crescent around the circumference. Spray or paint surface with a thin film of water and set in lowest level of oven. In 2 minutes, rapidly spray or paint again, and again 2 minutes later. At minute 6, set in upper-middle level, and bake about 20 minutes in all, until rolls are crusty and sound hollow when thumped. Turn off oven and leave 5 minutes longer, to dry out interior of rolls, then remove and cool on a rack.

To bake in a simulated baker's oven. Provide yourself with the hot baking surface, steam contraption, and sliding board described on page 466, and preheat as directed. Sprinkle cornmeal on sliding board, place 3 rolls smooth side up at its far edge and rapidly slash as described in previous paragraph. Drop the hot object into the pan of water in the bottom of the oven, close oven door for 5 seconds, then slide the rolls onto the far side of the hot baking surface. Rapidly slash and slide in the rest of the rolls—and a second hot object to engender more steam could be useful here, to provide extra steam as your final batch of rolls go into the oven. Remove steam contraption in 5 minutes, and bake the rolls about 20 minutes in all, until crusty and hollow sounding when thumped. Turn off oven and leave 5 minutes longer; remove and cool on a rack.

Champignons

MUSHROOMS, OR
TOP-KNOTTED ROLLS

For 9

These are attractive and unusual, a round roll with a little flat hat on top, like a mortarboard. The topknot is a separate piece of dough stuck onto the first but kept from fusing with it by a buttered aluminum foil collar that you remove after baking. Here is how to proceed:

Cut the risen dough (master recipe for French Bread, page 461) into 12 pieces. Form 9 of them into round balls of dough as described in the preceding recipe. Cut each of the 3 remaining pieces of dough into 3, and form 9 tiny balls in the same manner. Let the dough rest while you form 9 aluminum collars as follows: cut 2-inch squares of foil, and make a scissor cut in each, from one corner to the center, then cut a circle ½ inch in diameter out of each center, and butter both sides of the collars—the scissor cut from corner to center allows you to pull the collar off after baking.

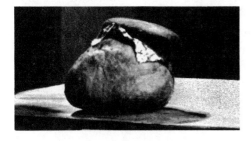

To form the rolls, flour one of the tiny balls and flatten it into a disk about 2 inches in diameter with the palm of your hand. Turn a large ball of dough smooth side up, place a collar on top, and the dough disk on top of that. Then plunge your index finger down through the dough disk, and the center hole in the collar, and through the large ball until your finger touches the work surface; turn it upside down so the disk is on the bottom, and place on floured canvas. When all 9 rolls have been formed, cover loosely with a floured towel, and let rise to almost triple. Reverse them so that disk is on top, bake as described in the preceding recipe, or as in the simulated baker's oven on page 467. (No slashing is necessary.) Remove aluminum collars after baking, and the disk will remain as a little topknot on the roll.

Boules; pains de campagne

LARGE ROUND LOAVES

For a single loaf

Flatten whole mass of dough (master recipe for French bread, page 461) into a 12-inch circle. Flip left side two thirds of the way over to the right; flip far side almost down over near side; flatten. Pick up dough and slap it down, same side up, but giving it a turn so the side that was nearest you is now the left side. Flip far side down almost to cover near side; flatten; pick up and slap down, same side up, this time giving a quarter turn so the side that was nearest you is again to your left. Flip left side almost over to right side, and turn the dough over. Smooth bottom side is up, on board. To create surface tension that will hold the ball of dough in shape, rotate it between palms of hands, tucking a bit of dough under the ball as you rotate it. In a dozen rapid turns, you should have a neat ball with a pucker underneath where edges have met. Place pucker side up on floured canvas, pinch pucker firmly with fingers to seal, and cover loosely with a floured towel. Let rise and bake as described for the rolls on page 468, making either a large cross or a slash in the top of the dough, or 4 slashes diagonally across the top crossed with 4 more slashes going in the opposite direction.

Note: After 10 minutes or so of baking, watch that your large loaf is not browning too much on top; you will probably have to move your oven rack down to the lower-middle level, and it will not harm the bread if you take it from the oven while you rapidly rearrange the rack and the tiles.

Sandwich bread

Unsliced French sandwich bread is *pain de mie,* meaning bread with a special crumb, as the professionals call the body or interior of bread as opposed to its crust. It is close-grained, rather firm for easy slicing, and has a natural body and moisture content that prevent it from drying out too quickly on the sandwich tray. Equally important, its quality is interesting enough by itself to make plain bread-and-butter sandwiches a treat. These delicious attributes of texture and taste—and why make homemade bread if it is not infinitely better than anything you can buy— are due to a long slow rise of the dough to begin with, a second rise to develop even more character and better keeping qualities, and a final rise in the pan. Slow rising takes time, but you may delay or stop the process at any step along the way either by chilling or by freezing, and thus make the process suit your convenience. There are no rules for this; you will make up your own as you go along. Since you may mix and knead the dough either by hand or by machine, the two methods are described simultaneously. Directions for turning the same dough into raisin bread are at the end of the recipe.

BREAD PANS. For sandwich bread, pick a rectangular pan with sides almost vertical. To force the dough into a symmetrical shape, you then cover the pan with a baking sheet and weight it down when it goes into the oven, as described here in the recipe. There are special French *pain de mie* pans with covers sometimes available in import shops.

Pain de mie

WHITE SANDWICH BREAD FOR CANAPÉS, FANCY SANDWICHES, TOAST, CROUTONS

3½ cups (1 lb.) all-purpose flour (measure by scooping dry-measure cups into flour and sweeping off excess)
2 tsp salt
1 package dry-active yeast dissolved in 3 Tb tepid water (105 degrees)
1⅓ cups tepid milk
2 ounces (½ stick) chilled butter

For about 3 cups of unrisen dough, enough to fill one 8-cup covered pan such as a loaf pan 9 x 5 x 2¾ inches, or two 4-cup covered pans, or one 6-cup open pan

Mixing and kneading the initial dough. Measure the flour and salt into a fairly straight-sided 4- to 5-quart mixing bowl (or bowl of heavy-duty electric mixer). Blend the dissolved yeast and the milk into the flour with a rubber spatula (or with dough hook of mixer). If you are mixing by hand, then turn dough out onto work surface, pressing it firmly together. In either case let the dough rest 2 minutes, in its just-massed-together state.

If you are mixing by hand, use a stiff scraper or spatula to flip near side of dough over onto far side, then right side onto left, left onto right; continue rapidly a dozen times or until dough has enough body so that you can sweep it off the kneading surface, slap it down hard, and push it with the heel of your hand as you continue to flip it. In 3 to 4 minutes, when dough begins to clean itself off work surface and draw back into shape, it is ready for the next step. (By machine, knead at moderate speed for a minute or two, until dough balls on hook and draws back upon itself.)

Kneading in the butter. Beat the cold butter with a rolling pin, then smear it out with the heel (not the palm) of your hand, to make it malleable but still cool. By tablespoon bits, rapidly fold and smear (or beat in mixer) the butter into the dough, working in new bits as each previous bit is absorbed. Dough will be ropy and sticky at first, but will become smooth with vigorous kneading. Let rest 2 minutes again, and if you are kneading by machine, remove dough to the work surface at this point. Meanwhile wash out mixing bowl, pour in 10½ cups tepid water, and make a mark on outside of bowl to indicate level of water—this will guide you in judging the first rise, next step. After its rest, knead the dough briefly with the heel of your hand; it is ready for rising when it cleans the butter off the work surface, and off your hand. It will remain quite soft and somewhat sticky, but will be smooth and elastic.

The first rise: *minimum of 3 hours.* Lift the dough into the bowl, cover with plastic wrap and a bath towel, and set on a wooden or plastic surface anywhere that the room temperature is around 72 to 75 degrees. Dough should take a minimum of 3 hours to reach the 10½-cup mark; refrigerate for brief periods if dough is rising too fast or room is too hot. (To delay the rise, start it at room temperature, then finish in the refrigerator overnight; risen dough may be frozen.)

The second rise: *minimum of 1½ hours.* Turn risen dough out onto lightly floured work surface and pat into a rough rectangle about 12

inches long. Flip right side over to middle, and left side over to cover it; pat again into a rectangle, and repeat the process. (This redistributes the yeast cells, and makes for a finer grain.) Return dough to bowl, cover, and let rise again, this time to slightly below the 10½-cup mark on the bowl. (You may complete this rise overnight in the refrigerator; set a plate and a weight on the dough to prevent it from over-rising. Risen dough may be frozen.)

Forming the loaf, and final rise in the pan: *1 to 1½ hours.* Grease inside of pan (or pans) with white vegetable shortening. Turn dough out onto work surface, and push it into a rectangle slightly longer than your bread pan. Fold dough in half long side to long side; seal edge with heel of hand. Roll dough forward, seal on top, and press a lengthwise trench down center with side of hand; fold in half along trench, seal again, and lay dough in pan seal side down. (If you are to bake in a covered pan, it should be only ⅓ to ⅔ filled with dough.) Let rise to slightly more than double, uncovered, at around 75 degrees. Preheat oven to 425 degrees in time for next step. (Risen dough may be frozen; thaw and let rise start again before baking.)

Baking. If you are using a covered pan, grease the shiny side of a piece of aluminum foil and lay it over the top of the pan, place pan in lower-middle level of oven, and cover with a baking sheet and a weight of some sort (a brick, stone, or flatiron, for instance). Bake for 35 minutes (checking once or twice to be sure dough has not dislodged baking sheet), then remove coverings. Bread is done when lightly browned, and when it comes easily out of the pan. If not quite done, return to pan, cover with foil, and bake several minutes longer. (For an open pan, bread will have risen over rim, forming the familiar humped loaf.) When done, unmold onto a rack and cool on its side.

Cooling and storing. When thoroughly cold, wrap airtight and refrigerate (or freeze). Flavor and texture improve after a wait of 24 hours, and you should wait 1½ to 2 days if you want very thin-sliced bread for fancy sandwiches.

Pain de mie aux raisins *(Raisin bread)*. Just as you are kneading in the last of the butter in the preceding recipe, knead in along with it 1½ cups seedless black currants (small black raisins), and proceed with the rising and forming as described. (Because of the sugar in the raisins, the dough tends to rise a little faster.) Form in an open 8-cup pan, and bake as described, but you may have to cover the loaf lightly with foil if top is browning too much.

Brioche dough, doughnuts, and coffee cake

Out of real French brioche dough, made with yeast and flour and butter and eggs, you can produce the most delicious raised doughnuts imaginable, as well as coffee cakes, Danish pastry, and crusts for such delicacies baked *en croûte* as sausages, coulibiacs, and Beef Wellingtons. Since we have taken up the forming of brioches in *The French Chef Cookbook* and in *Mastering*, Volume II, I shall concentrate here on a new way of making the dough itself; it is a marvelous one not only for any of the above-named purposes, but also for bread. This new dough system grew out of yeast-batter-starter experiments for the rye bread at the beginning of this chapter, and I find it particularly successful for the rich, otherwise very slow-moving mass that brioche dough is; using the starter you get not only a faster rise, but also a moister end result, plus excellent texture and taste. A faster rise, however, doesn't put this dough in the category of a fast-food operation; it is only faster in relation to the conventional system—you will still need a minimum of 4½ hours to produce the initial dough. But there are various stopping points along the way, and the finished raw dough will keep 2 to 3 days under refrigeration. As usual, in this book, final magnificence of the product takes precedence over speed. Following the dough recipe are directions for doughnuts and coffee cake, and if you want to turn the dough into lovely light bread, excellent for toast and tea, follow the rising and baking directions for the preceding white sandwich bread.

Pâte à brioche

For the batter, or
starter: rising time
about 1½ hours

1 package yeast (fresh or dry-active)
⅓ cup tepid milk (not over 105 degrees)
    in a 2-cup measure
2 Tb sugar
2 "large" eggs
1 cup all-purpose flour (scoop dry-measure cup
    into flour container and sweep off excess)

*Equipment: A 4- to 5-quart mixing and rising bowl
    with fairly vertical sides*

Sprinkle yeast into milk, add sugar, stir up, and let
stand 5 minutes or more, until yeast is completely
dissolved and mixture is foaming. Meanwhile, if
eggs are chilled, break into a metal bowl and stir
over hot water until tepid—chilled eggs will slow
yeast action. Combine eggs and dissolved yeast in a
mixing bowl, and beat in ¾ cup of flour with a
wooden spoon, continuing to sprinkle in more flour
until mixture is the consistency of a thick pancake
batter. (Reserve any unused flour for next step.)
Cover with plastic wrap and a bath towel, and let
rise at 70 to 75 degrees for 1½ to 2 hours; batter
should inflate to about triple, then sink into a bub-
bly wet mass.

☼ You may leave the risen starter for several hours in a cool place, or let
it rise overnight, if you wish. Stir over warm water until tepid before
proceeding.

Rising time: about
3 hours

For the final dough
2 "large" eggs
1 tsp salt
2 sticks (8 ounces) tepid melted butter
For doughnuts: ½ cup sugar and
    1 tsp mace or cinnamon
2½ cups additional all-purpose flour
    (measure as previously directed)

Again, if eggs are chilled, beat to tepid in a metal bowl over hot water,
then beat them into the batter along with the salt and the tepid melted

butter (beat butter first over cold water if too warm, since hot butter will kill the yeast). Then, for doughnuts, add also the sugar and spice. Sprinkle in any flour left over from previous step; gradually mix in 2 cups of the additional flour, reserving ½ cup for later.

If you are making the dough by hand, beat vigorously with a wooden spoon until too stiff to stir, then turn out onto your work surface. Let the dough rest 5 minutes or more; butter must firm up in the dough so that you can begin kneading it. After its rest, start kneading by scraping it up with a heavy spatula held in one hand, and slapping the dough roughly down onto your work surface with your other hand, adding sprinklings of the remaining flour. Lift and slap the dough vigorously for several minutes, also pushing it out in front of you with the heel (not the warm palm) of your hand until dough is perfectly smooth and elastic. (If dough softens and becomes oily, let it rest a few minutes, then continue —work fast and vigorously, however, and you will have no trouble.) Wash and dry the mixing bowl, and return the dough to it. (Dough will be soft and pliable.)

On the other hand, if you want to make the dough in a heavy-duty mixer with dough hook, start kneading the mixture, and gradually beat in the ½ cup of flour. When incorporated, let the dough rest 5 minutes or more, until butter has congealed. Knead until dough balls up on hook, then turn dough out onto your work surface and let it rest for a minute or two. Slap it about and push it out with the heel of your hand several times to be sure it is perfectly smooth and elastic, then wash out and dry the mixer bowl, and return the dough to it. (Dough will be soft and pliable.)

Rising: *about 3 hours.* Cover the dough again with plastic wrap and a bath towel and let it rise to almost triple, which will take about 3 hours at 75 degrees; or you may let it rise overnight in the refrigerator. Turn it out onto a lightly floured work surface, pat it out into an oval about 9 by 16 inches, fold into three as though folding a business letter; pat out again and fold again into three. (This is to redistribute the yeast in the dough, for its final rise, after it has been formed into whatever shape you wish.)

☼ If you are not to form and bake the dough now, chill it between sheets of waxed paper, covered by a board and a 5-pound weight; push it down if it starts to rise, but as soon as the butter has chilled and congealed in the dough, it will rise no more and you can safely keep it refrigerated for 2 to 3 days. I have not had much luck freezing brioche dough for more than several days, and therefore do not recommend it.

Beignets viennois

RAISED DOUGHNUTS

For about 3 dozen

The French do not make our type of doughnuts, but they do use brioche dough to form various deep-fried filled sweet pastries. For doughnuts, roll the dough ¼ inch thick and form the traditional doughnut shape either with a special cutter or with 2 round cutters, one 3 inches in diameter, and the other, for the hole, ¾ to 1 inch. Place both doughnuts and holes on lightly floured pastry cloth or wax paper, cover with floured wax paper, and let rise to slightly more than double, until swollen, puffy, and soft to the touch—1 to 1½ hours, at around 75 degrees. Heat 2½ to 3 inches of fresh new lard or peanut oil to 380 degrees in a deep-fat fryer or electric skillet. Dip a slotted pancake turner into the frying oil—to keep raw dough from sticking to it—then remove, and with it transfer 4 or 5 doughnuts and holes into the fryer. Turn them in 2 to 3 minutes, when brown on one side, and brown 2 to 3 minutes on the other side. Transfer the doughnuts to a rack lined with paper towels, and continue with the rest. While the next batch is frying, sift confectioners' sugar onto the last, while they are still warm. The sooner these are eaten, of course, the more delicious they will be.

☼ Wrap leftover doughnuts airtight and refrigerate or freeze; warm or thaw in a 350-degree oven, and dust, if desired, with fresh sugar.

Coffee ring; coffee cake

For 2 rings, 12 inches in diameter using brioche dough (page 475) or ready-mix

1½ cups chopped walnuts
1 cup dark brown sugar (packed down)
1 tsp cinnamon
½ tsp mace
2 cups currants
Egg glaze (1 egg beaten with 1 tsp water)

For homemade brioche dough. Mix the nuts, sugar, spices, and currants in a bowl and set it beside you. Roll half the recipe for chilled brioche dough into a rectangle 24 by 8 inches; roll up on pin and unroll over wax paper set on a no-stick baking sheet. Spread half the filling over the dough, pressing it in; work rapidly before dough softens too much. Using the wax paper to help you, roll dough longways like a jelly roll; keep roll fairly tight and finish with seam on bottom. Form dough into a ring, pressing ends together with your fingers. With scissors, cut 12 slanting gashes about ¾ inch apart; lift and turn gashes alternating outward and inward, to form a petal design. Form second ring in the same manner.

Cover with a floured towel or an upturned bowl, and let rise an hour or more at around 75 degrees, until swollen, puffy, and light. Preheat oven to 375 degrees, and just before baking, paint surface of rings with egg glaze. Bake in middle level of oven (switching pans halfway through if you use 2 levels) for 25 to 35 minutes, until puffed and nicely browned. Slide onto serving platters if you are serving immediately, or onto racks if serving cold.

✿ If you are baking ahead, wrap coffee cakes airtight and freeze them; thaw in a 350-degree oven shortly before serving.

For ready-mix hot rolls. Follow package directions, then proceed as for the homemade dough above.

For ready-made crescent-roll dough. Use 2 tubes, unroll them, and seal the dough with your fingers into one rectangle about 24 by 8 inches; then proceed as for homemade dough.

French croissants—crescent rolls

The perfect Continental breakfast to start the perfect day is fresh croissants and *café au lait*. To make these light, buttery crescent rolls, you start out as though you were doing bread dough but end up doing French puff pastry. The result is quite unlike any other pastry except Danish, and if you can make the one you can make the other. Equally, if you can make bread dough and puff pastry, you can make croissants and, conversely, if you can make croissants you can then make bread and *pâte feuilletée.* This is indeed an example of one thing learned leading to a host of others.

TIMING NOTES. The whole process takes 10 to 12 hours, but you may make croissants fit into your schedule by slowing them down or stopping them altogether at almost every step during the way, as indicated in the recipe.

BUTTER PROPORTIONS. On our television show and also in *Mastering,* Volume II, the proportions of flour to butter are 2 to 1; these are the usual ones, and certainly the recommended proportions for anyone new to pastry work. But as soon as you feel more expert, use equal weights of flour and butter, to make the flakiest, tenderest, most deliciously mouth-watering, and melting-on-tongue croissants imaginable. Some of the very best I know have come from *Chez Rohr* in Cannes; they are my touchstones. If what I produce can approach *les croissants de Chez Rohr,* I have won. The oil in the initial dough, by the way, is a tenderizing agent for American flour—it counts as butter; therefore the 7 ounces rather than 8 in the maximum proportions of butter that follow.

Croissants

————————

For one dozen 5½-inch crescent rolls

½ cake (about ⅓ ounce) fresh yeast or
1¼ tsp dry-active yeast
3 Tb tepid water (not over 105 degrees)
in a cup measure
2 tsp sugar
1¾ cups (½ lb.) all-purpose flour (measure by
scooping a dry-measure cup into flour and
leveling off with a knife)
1½ tsp salt
⅔ cup tepid milk
2 Tb tasteless salad oil
4 to 7 ounces (1 to 1¾ sticks) chilled unsalted
butter (see notes preceding recipe)
Egg glaze (1 egg beaten in a bowl with
1 tsp water)

Mixing and kneading the dough. Mix the yeast in the tepid water with the sugar, and let liquefy completely while measuring the flour into a fairly straight-sided 3-quart bowl, with the salt; also warm the milk to about 100 degrees. Then blend the milk, oil, and dissolved yeast into flour with a rubber spatula, cutting and pressing to be sure all elements are blended. Turn out onto kneading surface and let rest 2 to 3 minutes while you wash the bowl. Dough will be soft and sticky. Start kneading by lifting near edge, using scraper or spatula; flip it over onto the other side. Rapidly repeat the movement from one side to the other and end over end 8 to 10 times until dough feels smooth and just begins to draw back into shape when pushed out. Do not knead any more than this or you will overactivate the gluten and have difficulty rolling out the dough later.

Pour 7 cups tepid water into bowl, make a mark on the outside, empty out the water and dry the bowl. Scoop the dough into the bowl, cover with plastic wrap and towel, and place at a temperature of not more than 75 degrees.

The 2 risings. Dough is to have 2 long, slow, cool rises to develop its natural taste and texture. During the first it should more than triple in volume, reaching the 7-cup mark on the bowl, and should take a minimum of 3 hours—refrigerate once in a while if dough rises too fast in a warm room. After the first rise, turn dough out onto work surface, pat into a rectangle about 12 inches long, fold in three as though folding a business letter, and return to bowl. Cover and let rise again at around 75 degrees, this time to double its volume—1½ to 2 hours. Then turn out onto a floured plate, cover, and chill 30 minutes before proceeding.

☼ Delaying tactics. You may wish to complete the second rise in the refrigerator overnight, covering dough with a plate and a heavy weight to prevent over-rising. You may freeze the dough at the end of either rise.

Rolling the butter into the dough: the turns. Dough is now to be spread with butter, folded, rolled out, folded again 4 times in all to build up layers of butter between layers of dough, exactly as you would roll French puff pastry.

Beat the cold butter with rolling pin to soften; smear out with the heel of your hand, gather up, smear out again rapidly, until butter is easily spreadable but still cold. Place cold dough on a lightly floured surface; push and pat and lightly roll it out into a rectangle about 14 by 8 inches. Spread the butter as evenly as possible over ⅔ the length of the dough, leaving a ¼-inch unbuttered border all around. Fold the unbuttered third up to the middle, then fold the buttered remainder down over it, as though folding a business letter. This is the first turn.

For the second turn, lightly flour the dough, rotate it so top flap is to your right, as though it were a book, and rapidly roll it out into a rectangle about 10 by 16 inches. Fold into 3 as before, flour lightly, wrap in plastic, and refrigerate. Dough must now rest at least 45 minutes to de-activate the gluten and firm the butter. To prevent it from rising, weight it down with a plate or a cutting board topped with a weight—a large stone or can of food, for instance. (Dough may be refrigerated overnight at this point if well weighted down, or it may be frozen.)

For the third and fourth turns, if dough has been thoroughly chilled, beat back and forth and up and down with rolling pin to break up congealed butter. Roll again into a rectangle and fold in 3 for the third turn; repeat the process for the fourth and final turn. Wrap and chill 2 hours before forming the croissants.

✵ Or weight the dough down, in the refrigerator, where it will keep 2 to 3 days.

Forming the croissants. Roll chilled dough into a rectangle 20 by 5 inches, cut in half crosswise, and chill one half. Roll remaining half into a rectangle 15 by 5 inches if you are forming by hand, and cut into 3 crosswise. Chill 2 of the 3 pieces.

Roll remaining piece into a 5½-inch square, and cut on the diagonal into 2 triangles. Lengthen one triangle to 7 inches, rolling it out with your pin; stretch the base an inch, pulling the two ends with your fingers.

Finally, holding point of triangle with one hand, roll up from base to point with other hand.

Bend the two ends down to form a crescent shape, and place on a buttered baking sheet, point of former triangle resting inside the curve of the crescent. Form rest of dough in the same manner.

If you are using a croissant cutter, roll dough rectangles 5½ inches wide and cut; form as described.

☼ Formed croissants may be covered airtight and frozen for a week or so.

Final rise before baking. Cover loosely with floured plastic or a towel; set at around 75 degrees. Dough should almost triple in size, and look and feel light and puffy. It is this final rise that makes the croissants light and airy. Time: 1½ hours or more. (Preheat oven to 475 degrees in time for next step.)

Baking: *oven at 475 degrees.* Just before baking, paint the croissants with egg glaze. Set in middle level of preheated oven for 12 to 15 minutes, until nicely puffed and brown. Cool 10 to 15 minutes on a rack before serving.

☼ To keep baked croissants, freeze them as soon as they are cool; unwrap and set on a buttered baking sheet in a 400-degree oven for 5 minutes to thaw and warm through before serving.

Pizza variations

I certainly never thought I'd get into the pizza business, but I fell into it after we had invented our baker's oven with steam contraption and tile-lined oven rack. Soon after this great discovery, we went to a waterside restaurant in Nice, where our host, who had grown up with the proprietor, enthusiastically suggested a first course of pizza.

"Come and see how he makes it," urged Marcel, propelling us to a corner of the dining room where flames were flickering in the open hearth of a beehive-shaped brick oven. As we peered over the work counter in front of it, Marcel introduced us to Umberto, who proffered a floury hand, then slid an uncooked pizza from a long-handled wooden paddle into the oven, slithered a cooked one from it onto his paddle, and swished it off onto a serving dish, where a passing waiter bore it away.

"We'll have the classic herb, cheese, and tomato," said Marcel, and Umberto's big hand reached under a towel covering dozens of balls of dough. He selected a medium-sized piece, floured his wooden work surface, rolled, turned, and pulled the dough into an ample circle. He sprinkled his wooden paddle with cornmeal, and spread the dough upon it. Rapidly he spooned on a thick sauce of fresh tomatoes, strewed over it chunks of cheese the size of gambling dice, and sprinkled everything liberally with olive oil.

"*Ça va?*" He held the paddle out to us, and we breathed in the lusty aromas of Provence as he circled it down into the oven, poised the end of the paddle on the oven floor, and with a little jerk of his wrist, slid the pizza off onto the hot surface. He poked up the fire inside the oven, pulled out a finished pizza, added an order of barbecued rabbit and a platter of sausages—the oven was used for everything, including steaks —and in a few minutes out came our pizza. The cheese had melted into big bubbling blobs and the edges of the dough looked browned and crisp. We took it hungrily to our table—the bottom was softly crunchy, the top was tender and almost crisply breadlike. The flavor was heavenly, and we ate every crumb.

When Paul and I got home to our little house in the hills of the *arrière pays*, we had but a single thought: "Let's make a pizza!" We had the perfect setup: There was leftover raw French bread dough in the freezer; the paddle could be the sliding board we used for our French bread; and we had the tiles for the oven, to make the hot baking surface. Next day we had pizza for lunch, and that gave birth to our television program.

If you are ever in Nice, at the big open market that borders the old town and stretches for a mile or more under the plane trees beyond the Place Gambetta, look for the outside stand that sells pizza, and that fragrant onion tart, *pissaladière,* and *socca,* an enormous crêpe made out of chick-pea flour. Then wander up into *la vieille ville,* if you are there in the very early morning, and see how pizzas are made in the ancient vaulted bakery that contains only a built-in brick oven and just enough room for the handsome bearded baker to move his paddles about and to mix his doughs and batters on two crude work tops. We filmed all of this for our program "Pizza Variations," and perhaps you saw the delivery boy on his bicycle rattling down the old streets with his load of pizzas, *pissaladières,* and *soccas* bouncing behind, as he shuttled to the stand in the market, and back up again for another load.

Here, then, is how to turn your kitchen into a pizzeria, and for details on making your own baker's oven, see the directions on page 466. Although you can form and bake a pizza in a pizza pan, you will not get the same splendid results as when you do it the professional way described here.

Your own homemade pizza

For two 16- to 18-inch pizzas

For your oven
The hot tiles, shingle (sliding board), and cornmeal described on page 466

Pizza dough
1 package fresh or dry-active yeast completely dissolved in ⅓ cup tepid water (100 degrees)
3 cups all-purpose flour (preferably unbleached) and ¾ cup plain bleached cake flour
2¼ tsp salt
1¼ to 1⅓ cups tepid water
3 Tb olive oil

The pizza topping (for 2 pizzas)
About 4 cups fresh tomato pulp (tomatoes peeled, seeded, juiced, and diced), or 3 cups drained, peeled, canned Italian plum tomatoes, diced

3 cups sliced fresh mushrooms tossed in 3 Tb olive oil
4 Tb capers
4 cups mixed diced cheese as follows: equal
   parts of Mozzarella, sharp cheddar, and Swiss,
   all cut into ½-inch dice
2 tsp oregano, thyme, basil, or a mixture
   like Italian seasoning
Olive oil

Making the dough. While the yeast dissolves, measure the flour, salt, and tepid water into a bowl, then add the yeast. *Either:* Mix and knead by hand, following the French Bread recipe, page 461, and then knead in the oil after the dough has massed and rested 2 minutes; *Or:* Use a heavy-duty electric mixer with dough hook as follows: Mix all ingredients in machine for a minute or so at low speed, until dough masses on hook. Let rest 2 minutes, then pour in the oil and continue mixing at low speed for another minute or more until the dough has absorbed the oil. Turn out onto work surface and let rest 2 minutes, then knead vigorously by hand for a minute or so to be sure dough is smooth and elastic; it will be soft and slightly sticky, like the dough for French bread.

Rising the dough. Following the method for French bread dough, page 463, let rise to triple its original volume at a temperature of around 75 degrees—3 hours or more. Deflate, fold in 3, replace in bowl, and let rise again to almost triple—about 1½ hours—but this second rise may be completed overnight in the refrigerator. When completed, deflate the dough and cover with a plate and a 5-pound weight to prevent it from rising until you are ready to make your pizza.

✲ Risen dough may be frozen for a week in a covered bowl; thaw overnight in the refrigerator, or for several hours at room temperature.

Forming the pizza. At least 45 minutes before baking, line oven racks with tiles, set on lower level and upper-third level, and preheat oven to 450 degrees. About half an hour before you wish to serve, turn dough out onto a floured surface and cut in half. (Refrigerate or freeze second half if you are not cooking 2 pizzas.) Flatten with palms of hands and form into a ball as follows: Fold left side two thirds of the way over to right side, flatten dough slightly by pushing it with the palm of your hand from right side toward left side; fold far side almost down over near side, rotate dough a quarter turn clockwise, push again, and continue thus rapidly a number of times to form a round cushion of dough smooth on the bottom. Turn the dough over, smooth bottom side up, and rotate for several turns between the palms of your hands, tucking edges underneath, to make a neat ball shape. Flatten into a disk with a floured rolling pin, but as soon as dough resists you and becomes rubbery stop rolling; flour top and bottom, and cover with a sheet of floured plastic. Let rest 3 to 4 minutes, roll again. Let rest again when dough resists you, and continue. In 10 to 15 minutes, you will have been able to enlarge the circle to a diameter of 14 to 16 inches; it should be about $\frac{3}{16}$ inch thick.

Sprinkle the shingle liberally with cornmeal. If dough seems at all sticky, flour both sides heavily, roll up on pin; starting at far end of shingle, unroll the dough upon it. Pat quickly out into shape if necessary, then rapidly garnish the surface with the tomatoes, mushrooms, capers, and cheese; sprinkle on the oregano or other herbs, and drizzle over it a few drops of olive oil.

Immediately open oven door, lay far edge of shingle at far edge of heated tiles, give a preliminary jerk or two to start the pizza moving, then smoothly give the shingle a quick sweep toward you, leaving the pizza on the hot tiles. Bake for 12 to 14 minutes, until edges of dough have puffed slightly and begun to color lightly, and cheese has melted. Slide shingle under the pizza, and unmold onto a serving board or tray.

Pissaladière niçoise (*Onion tart with anchovies, olives, and cheese*). This is exactly like a pizza, but the topping is 4 cups sliced onions cooked to very soft and translucent in 4 tablespoons olive oil, cooled slightly, then spread on the dough. Decorate with anchovy fillets arranged like the spokes of a wheel and either whole tiny black olives or sliced pitted olives. Spread on ½ cup of grated Swiss cheese, or a combination of Swiss and Parmesan, a sprinkling of oregano, and a drizzle of olive oil. Bake like the pizza.

Socca

―――◆―――

NIÇOISE CHICK-PEA
CRÊPE

When you are shopping in the early morning at that great open market of Nice, the outdoor pizzeria offers portions of hot *socca*, scooped out of an enormous round copper platter into brown paper cones. The Niçois eat their portions of chick-pea crêpe just as it is, with perhaps a sprinkling of salt. You could serve yours at a cocktail party, letting each guest tear off and scoop his bit onto a paper napkin. Or let it be an unusual first course, accompanied by a fresh tomato sauce.

For a 12-inch socca,
serving at least 6 people
as an appetizer

⅔ cup chick-pea flour (often available in
    health-food stores or Italian markets)
¼ tsp salt
1 cup cold water
3 to 4 Tb olive oil

Equipment: A 12-inch round pizza tray, no-stick
recommended; a sieve

Preheat tile-lined oven rack in a 450-degree oven for 45 minutes before baking. Beat the chick-pea flour, salt, and water together, or mix in blender. Let stand 30 minutes. Smear baking tray with a tablespoon of the oil; pour the chick-pea batter through a sieve into the pan, adding enough to cover surface by about ⅛ inch. Drizzle on 2 to 3 tablespoons more oil, and spread with a spatula. Ten minutes before you wish to serve, set pan on the hot tiles in upper third of hot oven for 4 to 5 minutes, until crêpe begins to seethe, showing it has set. Then set close under a moderately hot broiler, rotating pan several times, for 3 to 4 minutes until lightly browned. Serve hot, tearing or cutting strips crosswise, beginning at one edge of circle.

Grand finales, part 1: desserts

*I*t is definitely not a party without a dessert, whether it's a store-bought ice cream or shortcake with frozen strawberries. But what fun for all concerned when it is a *spécialité de la maison,* tasting of the best and freshest ingredients. I know this does not appeal to every cook: witness a letter I shall paraphrase from a disgruntled lady viewer in *Le Far West* after our television program "Ice Cream." "Last evening's presentation confirmed my growing feeling that Julia Child's time has come," she wrote her local PBS station. "The effort and materials wasted in composing *bombe glacée* and some grapefruit sherbet seemed short of ridiculous—especially when one can go out and purchase any number of marvelous flavors all around the country. I do believe Julia is becoming part of the past, like Escoffier—removed from reality. Besides," she concluded, "I don't like her new hairdo." So I have put ice cream way in the lower-middle level of this chapter, and shall start out on apple desserts—handmade in the old-fashioned way.

Apple desserts and tarts

It seems to me I have had more than most people's share of collapsing apple desserts, and every one of them has been my own fault because I chose the wrong kind of apple. And every collapse has been in public, too, right over the television air. The first was in black-and-white TV, an apple charlotte, that lovely dessert of carefully flavored thick applesauce baked in a colonnade of butter-soaked bread strips that brown in the oven; you unmold the charlotte after baking, and it stands upright and handsome with its fragrant aroma of butter, apples, and spices. I unmolded it all right, and it looked just fine on the screen for about 30 seconds, until the walls slowly began to sag and the whole dessert deflated like an old barn in a windstorm. I could only say, hiding the tears in my voice, that I didn't like too thick an applesauce anyway. But the bitter truth was that I had stupidly chosen the wrong apples; I had made my applesauce out of Gravensteins or McIntoshes, and those two apples just do not have the necessary body to produce a thick mass that will hold up in a molded condition. I did notice as I boiled and boiled them, and they sputtered their juices up to the ceiling, that they never reduced the way they were meant to. Had I been more experienced and applewise, as I look back on it now, I would have seen it was not right. I would have started all over again with the right apples. Or at least I could have saved the day by stirring in some fresh white bread crumbs sautéed in butter—or some cake crumbs; that would have given the necessary body and the charlotte would have held its ground.

Another sad episode was in full color, with a *Tarte Tatin,* the upside-down apple pie creation on page 497. I had worked out a great new system of cooking the whole tart in a frying pan, and was delighted with myself. When we started the show the tart was in the oven, was to come out at the appointed time, was to sit in its pan over high heat to do a final caramelization and drying out of the bottom, then was to unmold beautifully, brownly, and with its apple slices in perfect symmetry on its serving dish.

"Don't you think," urged Ruthie, my producer, before the show, "don't you really think it would be a good idea to unmold it first and put it back, just to be sure everything is all right?" "No, no, no, no!" said I, imperiously. "Everything must be exactly as it is, no tricks, I want people to see the whole tart just as it would be at home. But there won't be any problems!" Hah!

When the time came to remove the tart from the oven, I could see it was still too juicy. I put it on the stove at full heat, as long as my time allowed, but could see it was not going to work. Of course, I had to un-mold it anyway, and it plumped messily onto the dish. "Never you mind," I said courageously to my viewers, "that does happen." So I scooped the apples in place as best I could, sprinkled all with powdered sugar, and browned it rapidly under the broiler. I was using Cortlands, so I thought, but either had gotten McIntosh by mistake, or the Cortlands were old and punky, and would not keep their shape in slices as they should have.

Now that I have been too often deceived in public, I am very careful indeed about the apples I choose for special desserts like charlottes and upside-down tarts. After quite a bit of correspondence with the Department of Agriculture, the Fresh Fruit and Vegetable Association, and the International Apple Association, I offer you the following guide:

HOW TO AVOID THE WRONG APPLE. It is not always easy to find the right apple for cooking, since many markets are very limited in their choice—because we, the public, do not express ourselves. Apple choices depend, of course, on the time of year and also on the area where you live. If you are fortunate enough to be in a region growing apples for pie makers and apple-slice canners, you will have much the best choice. What we are concerned with now is apples that will hold their shape for baking and for tart making, and here they are:

> Golden Delicious, Rome Beauty, York Imperial, Greenings, Newtons, Monroes, Northern Spy. (Others reputed to be good but that I have not personally tried are: Staymen, Winesap, Baldwin, Grimes Golden.) Cortlands have worked for me when new, fresh, and firm. I have had disasters with the Gravensteins and the McIntosh. When you must absolutely have baked apples or apple slices that will hold during cooking, however, the Golden Delicious is the old reliable.

HOW MANY APPLES DO I NEED?

> 3 medium apples = 1 pound, and make 2⅔
> cups sliced apples
> 12 medium apples = 4 pounds, and make about
> 3 quarts of sliced apples

Pommes Rosemarie

APPLES ROSIE;
SLICED APPLES
BAKED WITH
BUTTERED CRUMBS
AND SPICES

This is a kind of apple Betty, which was devised by my California friend Rosie. We used it on our program "Kids Want to Cook," because it is easy to do, delicious to eat, takes nicely to an accompaniment of whipped cream or vanilla ice cream, and gives a good workout with the knife. It is best to have rather firm cooking apples for this, so the slices will stay whole; but if you have only Macs or Gravensteins, you can still make the dessert; it will just take longer to cook because they are so juicy. (*Note:* This very detailed recipe is designed for young beginning cooks.)

For 6 people

Baking time: 1 to
1½ hours

About 4 pounds (12 medium-sized) cooking apples,
such as new Cortlands, Rome Beauty, or others
from the suggestions preceding this recipe
1 lemon
½ to ¾ cup sugar (depending on sourness
of apples)
1 tsp cinnamon
½ tsp mace or cardamom
2 cups lightly pressed down fresh white
bread crumbs
4 ounces (1 stick) butter

Equipment: A 2½- to 3-quart baking dish about
3 inches deep, with cover; buttered
aluminum foil cut to fit top of dish
Optional accompaniment: A bowl of whipped
cream, or vanilla ice cream

Preparing the apples. One at a time, with a small sharp knife, cut apples in half lengthwise, through stem end, then cut the half in half. Dig out the bit of core in the center of each quarter with your knife, then shave off the peel. Cut the apple quarters into 3 or 4 lengthwise slices—I find the fastest way to do this is to hold the apple piece with its curved side down on the cutting board, and then slice. This is dog work, but go as fast as you carefully can, dropping the slices of each apple as finished into a large mixing bowl. When all apples are sliced (you will have 2½ to 3 quarts if you measure them), grate the zest (colored part of peel only) of the lemon over the apples, and squeeze in the juice. Sprinkle on the sugar, the cinnamon, and the mace or cardamom. Toss the apples about to coat them with all the flavorings. Taste, and sprinkle on more sugar if too sour.

So that the oven will be hot when you are ready to bake, slide rack onto lower-middle level, set thermostat to 425 degrees, and turn the oven on.

The buttered crumbs. Prepare the bread crumbs, first by slicing the crust off the bread—you will need about a third of a 1-pound loaf to make 2 cups of crumbs. Either rub the bread against the large holes of a grater, or tear into smallish pieces and whirl it a handful at a time in an electric blender. Then cut the butter into eighths for quick melting, and set it in a saucepan over moderate heat until bubbling; stir in the crumbs.

Assembling and baking. Spread one fourth of the buttered crumbs in the bottom of the baking dish, cover with half the apple slices, and spread over them half the remaining crumbs. Spread on the rest of the apples, pour on any juices, and cover with the last of the crumbs. Lay the foil, buttered side down, over the dish, and set on a cover. Bake for 30 to 40 minutes, until juices have bubbled over crumbs on top. Then uncover and let apples cook until the juices are thick and syrupy when you tip the dish, about 30 minutes more.

✪ If you want to keep the apples warm, set baking dish over simmering water or on an electric warming plate until you are ready.

Serve Apples Rosie just as is, or bring a bowl of whipped cream or vanilla ice cream to the table, and a bowl of sugar, too.

Alaska aux pommes; pommes mascotte

———◆———

MERINGUE-TOPPED
BAKED APPLES
FLAMED IN WHISKEY

How to dress up the humble baked apple—cook it in wine, wrap each in a cloak of meringue and brown in the oven; then, if you are in the mood for drama, flame them at the table in Bourbon whiskey. How well I remember this show, the finish to our program "Spaghetti Dinner Flambé." We decided to heat the whiskey in a fireproof glass bowl because the whole bowl becomes engulfed in flames, and it is beautiful. I don't know why, but bowl after flameproof bowl broke as we filmed it, and when we finally got the sequence done, the flames didn't show up at all on the TV screen. There I was, apparently dipping hot air out of an empty bowl, talking away about the wonder of it all. Blue alcohol flames, it appears, are very hard to catch with the TV camera, and we hadn't yet developed the right technique. Well, it works nicely at home, anyway, and makes a delicious dessert—but you may be safer using a pan rather than a flameproof bowl for the finale.

For 4 people

4 baking apples (Golden Delicious recommended)
½ lemon
A filling for the apples, such as bottled
    Nesselrode, or chopped candied fruits
    and nuts, or raisins
The zest (yellow part of peel only) of ½ lemon
½ cup dry white Vermouth, cider, apple
    juice, or apple nectar
⅓ cup sugar
2 Tb melted butter
4 rounds of pound cake or yellow cake,
    ⅜ inch thick, toasted
½ cup apricot jam, sieved into a small saucepan
2 egg whites
⅛ tsp cream of tartar
⅓ cup sugar
¼ tsp vanilla
Optional: About ½ cup Bourbon whiskey

Baking the apples. Preheat oven to 350 degrees. One at a time, core the apples, shave a slice off large end so apple will stand firmly upright, peel, and rub with cut lemon, dribbling also a few drops into the core, to keep apples from darkening. Arrange in a heavily buttered baking dish just large enough to hold the apples comfortably, fill cores with whatever you have chosen. Add the zest of lemon, and pour around the apples enough Vermouth or other liquid to make about ½ inch in the dish. Sprinkle the sugar over the apples; cover each with ½ teaspoon of melted butter. Bake in middle level of preheated oven, basting with juices every 10 minutes or so, for about 40 minutes; apples should be tender when pierced with a knife, but must not be overcooked and lose their shape.

☼ May be baked in advance and reheated.

The meringue and final baking. Shortly before you are ready to prepare the meringue and finish the apples, preheat oven to 500 degrees. Paint the toasted cake rounds with the remaining melted butter, and spread with a light coating of sieved apricot jam. Place a warm apple upon each. Beat the egg whites until foaming, beat in the cream of tartar, and gradually increase to fast, until egg whites form soft peaks; gradually beat in the sugar and continue until egg whites form stiff peaks; then beat in the vanilla. One at a time, spread a cloak of meringue around the apples, leaving the top of the filled core free; transfer each apple, as it is done, to a fireproof serving platter. Set in upper-middle level of 500-degree oven for about 2 minutes, just until meringue is lightly browned.

✿ If you are not serving immediately, apples will keep perfectly in a warming oven at 140 degrees for an hour or more.

Serving. For serving, pour apple-cooking juices into pan with remaining apricot jam and blend over heat; add more sugar if necessary, and pour into a warm sauceboat. If you wish to flame the apples at the table, heat Bourbon in a pan or (if you are sure of it) in a fireproof bowl, ignite with a lighted match, and, spooning high for drama, dribble flaming liquid over each apple as you serve it.

La tarte des demoiselles Tatin

———◆———

UPSIDE-DOWN
APPLE TART

While there is nothing more American than apple pie, there is also nothing more French than *tarte aux pommes*. Their typical apple tart has a bottom crust only. To achieve the norm, the sisters Tatin, who kept an inn at Lamotte-Beuvron just south of Orléans on the Loire, developed an upside-down wonder that has become a restaurant favorite in Paris ever since. The apples caramelize in the bottom of the pan, the crust cooks on top, and when the tart is done it is turned upside down on the serving dish, where the crust takes its accustomed place.

For an 8-inch tart,
serving 6 people

For the crust

*1 cup all-purpose flour (scoop dry-measure cup
into flour and sweep off excess)*
¾ stick (3 ounces) chilled butter
2 Tb chilled vegetable shortening
1 Tb sugar
Pinch salt
⅓ cup iced water

**For about 3½ quarts sliced apples (better
too many than too few!)**

*5 to 6 lbs. firm cooking apples that will hold
their shape, such as Golden Delicious (other
suggestions are on page 493)*
The grated rind of 1 lemon
The juice from ½ lemon
½ cup sugar

Plus the following

3 Tb soft butter
About 1 cup sugar
4 to 5 Tb melted butter
*If needed: Confectioners' sugar in a fine-meshed
sieve*

*Equipment: A heavy frying pan about 9 inches
top diameter and 2 inches deep (to go into
oven) ; a pizza pan, to catch drippings
in oven; a serving dish*

The crust: pâte brisée fine, sucrée. Measure the flour into the bowl of
an electric mixer (or a 2-quart bowl if your mixer is hand-held). Cut
butter into ½-inch bits, and add to flour along with the shortening, sugar,
and salt. Blend fat and flour together until mixture looks like coarse
meal—several minutes, if you are using a portable; then add the iced
water and blend rapidly for a few seconds until pastry masses together.
Turn out onto a board. Knead briefly into a ball, wrap in wax paper or
plastic, and chill for 2 hours or overnight. (Flour must have time to
absorb the liquid; for easy rolling, gluten in flour must relax and fat
must chill.)

The apples. Peel, quarter, and core the apples; cut into lengthwise
wedges about ¾ inch at the thickest portion. Toss in a large bowl with

the lemon rind and juice and the sugar, and let apples sit for at least 30 minutes so that they will render excess juice. (Juice may be reserved and boiled down until syrupy, then poured over the finished and unmolded tart, later.)

Assembling. Preheat oven to 425 degrees. Smear the soft butter inside the pan, making the heaviest layer on the bottom; spread in a layer of sugar ⅓ inch deep. Arrange a neat design of apple slices in bottom of pan—this will eventually be the top of the dessert; sprinkle on a tablespoon of melted butter and another of sugar. Continue filling pan in layers; the apples can now be arranged less carefully, since they will sink down as they cook. Roll the dough ³⁄₁₆ inch thick, cut into a circle very slightly larger than top of pan; roll up on pin and unroll over apples. Tuck edges down against edges of pan, and pierce 6 steam holes ¼ inch in diameter through top of dough.

Baking. Set pan over moderately high heat on the stove, and cook 4 to 5 minutes, allowing apple juice to bubble up and to thicken into a heavy syrup. Then set in middle level of preheated oven; slide drip tray onto a rack just below the tart. Bake for about 30 minutes, until crust is crisp and brown, and juices are very thick—a very important point! With a heavy pot holder, remove pan and set over moderately high heat on the stove for several minutes, shaking pan by handle so that apples will not stick on bottom; this will usually caramelize the bottom of the apples. When juices have all but evaporated, the tart is ready for unmolding.

Unmolding. Hold pan and platter side by side; tilt the two together at an angle, then quickly reverse pan over onto platter to unmold tart. If you had the right kind of apple, and if you allowed the juices to thicken and then to evaporate as they should, tart should unmold with the apple design neatly in place on top while the crust is underneath. Rearrange any slices that may be out of order or, if tart has not unmolded properly, scoop the apples in place with a spatula and make them look as neat as possible.

Trouble-shooting. Although apples should be a nice caramel brown, they sometimes are not. To caramelize them, sprinkle top surface with a ⅛-inch layer of confectioners' sugar, cover exposed surface of platter with foil, and set under a medium-hot broiler; watch carefully, rotating platter if necessary, until sugar has caramelized evenly—3 or 4 minutes.

Serving. Serve the tart hot, warm, or cold, with whipped cream or with the heavy French cream described in the following recipe.

Crème
fraîche

A HOMEMADE
VERSION OF HEAVY
FRENCH CREAM

Most French cooking with cream, in Paris at least, has always been done with the rich, heavy kind that has a slightly nutlike and slightly acid flavor; it is something akin to our sour cream but much less acid, and it has a much higher butter-fat content. While our sour cream has 18 percent butter-fat, the French cream, called *crème fraîche* or *crème double,* has at least 35 percent—which is comparable to our heavy cream. Any fresh cream, if left alone, will thicken like French cream, since its natural lactic acids and ferments work in it, thickening it and also preserving it. Pasteurization kills these ferments. In our sweet cream, ferments are not returned after pasteurization; in French cream, they are, so the French pasteurized heavy cream thickens and takes on its characteristic slight acidity and nutlike flavor. (The term "sweet cream" means unfermented cream, by the way, and French sweet cream is called *fleurette.*)

You can make a reasonable facsimile of French *crème fraîche* yourself, using American heavy cream and blending it with sour cream; you let it sit until the ferments have acted and the cream has thickened, then you refrigerate it. Fortunately this works either with the new super-pasteurized heavy cream or with regular heavy cream.

Why bother with it? First, it preserves regular cream for 10 days at least, meaning you can always have thick cream on hand even if you want but a dab of it. Then, it's easy to use, since you dip out as much as you want in a spoon, as though it were sour cream. It will boil without curdling, which is not the case with sour cream. It tastes good on berries and with apple pies. Whether it is an essential ingredient to French cooking, as some people claim, I am not so sure. But I always have a large glass jar of *crème fraîche* in my refrigerator because I like the comfortable looks of it, and I am used to cooking with it.

Note: In Volume I of *Mastering,* way back in 1961, we suggested using a teaspoon of buttermilk per cup of cream, as a fermenting agent; it is a nuisance, however, to have a whole quart of that around unless one is a buttermilk fiend. Yoghurt does the same work. I now prefer sour cream to either, since it produces a slightly less acid *crème fraîche.*

For 1½ pints of crème fraîche

½ pint commercially soured cream
1 pint heavy cream

Turn the soured cream into a saucepan, and gradually stir in the heavy cream to make a smooth blend. Heat gently just to take off the chill and to start up the action, but do not go over 85 to 90 degrees or you will kill the ferments; then pour into a container. Set partially covered at around 75 degrees for 6 to 8 hours, or overnight, until the cream has thickened; stir up, cover, and refrigerate. (If temperature is colder, cream will simply take longer to thicken; if hotter, watch that it does not over-ferment.) When your supply is almost exhausted, blend in more heavy cream and repeat the process.

Tarte aux pommes; tarte aux poires

———◆———

APPLE TART;
PEAR TART

Most of us are used to pies and tarts that are formed and baked in pans or rings, and have even, predictable sizes. But there is also the free-form tart, where you roll your dough any size and shape you wish, form edges around it to hold in your filling, and you are then much more flexible in the number of people you can serve. Here is a pure, very simple way of making a fruit tart, using the free-form system: the raw shell is formed and painted with fruit glaze; then overlapping slices of apple or pear are arranged in a neat design over it and sprinkled with sugar; the tart is baked, and given a glittering coating of glaze when it emerges from the oven. It makes a lovely dessert, served with a bowl of *crème fraîche,* whipped cream, ice cream, or nothing else at all, and it is a glorious object to present at a tea party or an evening get-together.

Notes on dough and form. You can, of course, form and bake your tart in a pie shell or quiche ring, but in that case I think it is best to prebake the shell first (described and illustrated, page 608) to prevent a soggy bottom crust. The free form, in my experience with this type of fruit tart, does not run into soggy problems. Which dough to use, French pie dough or French puff pastry? The puff pastry, rolled thin, gives an attractive flaky bottom crust, while the sides, rolled thicker, puff up to hold in any juices. Puff pastry is preferable, then, if you have it, but a good pie dough, such as the one suggested, is an excellent alternative. Does this recipe differ from the one in Volume II of *Mastering?* Yes! A slightly different system for forming the shell, but essentially the same procedure. No harm in having a good tart two ways! Why the rectangular form? I think it makes easy serving; you cut it in half or in thirds lengthwise, then into crosswise pieces as large or as small as you wish.

Illustrations for making the tart shell are on page 609.

For a rectangular tart about 12 by 14 inches, serving 8 to 12

Either: The free-form shell of French pie dough described on page 609
Or: Enough chilled dough to make the puff pastry shell described here, for which you will need half the recipe for French puff pastry on page 611
Or: All of the mock puff pastry on page 48
Either: 3 or 4 firm, crisp cooking apples or Golden Delicious apples
Or: 5 or 6 firm, ripe unblemished pears
1 cup apricot glaze (described in the next recipe)
¼ cup sugar

Equipment: Large baking sheet; a ruler (to measure thickness of dough); a pastry brush; a board or tray covered with foil, large enough to hold the tart for serving

Free-form rectangular shell of French puff pastry. Choose your largest baking sheet, and butter it. Roll the dough into a rectangle 14 inches long and no less than ¼ inch thick; cut 4 lengthwise strips ¾ inch wide from it, and refrigerate. Roll remaining dough rapidly into a 12- by 14-inch rectangle about ⅛ inch thick; roll rectangle up on your pin, and unroll it onto your baking sheet. (Refrigerate for 10 minutes or so if pastry has softened too much for easy handling.) Pat it out to the proper size with your fingers, and trim edges evenly. Paint a ¾-inch border of cold water all around top edge of dough, then press the reserved strips in place, overlapping and moistening one end of each at each of the corners to make a continuous border of pastry. Trim off protruding ends. Pressing top of pastry strips with your fingers as you go, seal them to the bottom dough by pressing a decorative edging around outside sides, using the tines of a fork, held upright, or the back of a knife. Press a decorative design also on top of strips. Cover and chill for half an hour, to relax the dough.

✲Shell may be formed a day in advance; cover and refrigerate it. Or you may freeze it for weeks, but let thaw at room temperature for half an hour before continuing.

Baking the tart. Preheat oven to 450 degrees. Peel and core the fruit, and cut into thin, even, lengthwise slices. Paint the inside of the shell with a thin coating of the glaze. Arrange the slices of fruit in an overlapping series of rows over the bottom of the shell, and sprinkle on the sugar. Bake in middle level of oven 20 minutes, until tart sides have risen and begun to brown; reduce oven heat to 400 degrees and bake another 20 minutes, or until sides feel crisp. (For a pie-dough shell, bake at 425 degrees.) When done, paint both fruit and tart edges with the glaze. Slide tart onto serving board or tray, if you are serving it hot or warm, or onto a rack if you are serving it cold, later.

✵ With puff pastry, the sooner you serve and eat the tart the better. If it must be done ahead, it keeps best when frozen after baking. I have often frozen leftovers of this tart; thawed in a 400-degree oven until it has re-crisped, and painted with a little more glaze, it is delicious.

Trouble-shooting. You shouldn't have any trouble with collapsing puff pastry sides if they are a full ¾ inch wide, if you sealed them well to the bottom dough in the first place, and if the shell rested before baking; but it can happen. Therefore watch the tart the first 20 minutes, and if you see signs of them swaying inward, quickly brace them up with toothpicks. An outward collapse can be prevented by bracing the sides with several thicknesses of foil, or a bread pan.

Glaçage à l'abricot et à la gelée de groseille

———

APRICOT AND
CURRANT GLAZES

That which glitters on a French fruit tart is apricot jam or red currant jelly, boiled briefly with sugar until it is sticky enough to adhere to the fruit. The glaze is also painted on the inside of the pastry shell to act as an edible waterproof coating.

To make apricot glaze, rub about a cupful of apricot preserves through a sieve into a saucepan, stir in 2 tablespoons of sugar, and boil for several minutes until last drops falling from spoon are thick and sticky and make a thread when taken between your thumb and forefinger (228 degrees). (It won't burn you—have a cup of cold water beside you, and dip your fingers into it first; professionals simply lick their fingers before taking up the syrup.) Set the glaze over hot water until you are ready to use it; any that is left over will keep in a screw-top jar. (If glaze seems too thick and sticky when you are about to use it, thin out with droplets of hot water.)

Make red currant glaze the same way, but no prior straining is needed.

———————◆———————

Fresh fruit tarts

Summer is the season for fresh strawberry tarts, or sliced fresh peaches laid over a wine-flavored pastry cream. During the fall and winter you can make designs of fresh grapes and bananas plus a variety of canned fruits cunningly disguised in wine and hidden under handsome glazes.

THE TART SHELL. For such tarts you need a fully baked pastry shell. Of course, you may use a store-bought one, or a commercial frozen shell that you prebake before filling, so let nothing daunt you. But your own home-made pastry is always a treat to family and friends. I like the free-form rectangle of French puff pastry described for the preceding apple and pear tart. To prebake it, line the inside of the raw pricked shell with aluminum foil and, to weight down the bottom of the dough, fill with beans or chick peas (kept in a big jar just for this purpose; I've still my original batch that began service in the early 1950's). And there are little pieces of aluminum the size of baking-chocolate bits or drops, made especially for holding pastry bottoms in place; you'll find them in import shops.

Bake shell 20 minutes at 450 degrees until sides have risen, begun to brown, and bottom has set. Remove foil and beans, prick bottom of shell lightly again to keep it from rising, and lower thermostat to 400 degrees. Bake 5 minutes or so more, until lightly browned. Let cool and set 10 minutes, then slide onto a rack. The shell is now ready to use. (For pie-dough shells, bake at 400 degrees, following the same general system.)

✺ Baked shells may be wrapped airtight when cool, then frozen.

Crème pâtissière

———◆———

PASTRY CREAM;
CUSTARD FILLING

Crème Pâtissière, one of the fundaments of French *pâtisserie,* is a custard filling that goes into tart bottoms and is piped into chocolate eclairs; it can also be combined with whipped cream, beaten egg white, ground almonds, caramelized nuts, or other delicacies, to form numerous desserts. You are always wise to make the initial mixture very thick, because while it is difficult to thicken when already made, you can very easily thin it out, after cooking, with more milk or with cream. Any pastry cream you do not use up you can freeze. (*P.S.:* We have *Crème Pâtissière* in *Mastering I* and *The French Chef,* but each recipe gives a slightly different view, just to show that there is more than one way of looking at a custard.)

For about 2½ cups

2 cups milk in a small saucepan
6 egg yolks in a 2½-quart heavy-bottomed stainless or enameled pan
½ cup sugar
½ cup all-purpose flour (measure by scooping, then leveling with a knife)
3 Tb butter
1 Tb vanilla extract; or ½ Tb vanilla and 1 or 2 Tb rum, kirsch, orange liqueur, Cognac, strong coffee, or etc.
A pinch of salt
If needed: 2 or more Tb heavy cream

Equipment: A portable electric beater, or a large wire whip; a wooden spoon

Heat the milk. Meanwhile, start beating the egg yolks, gradually pouring on the sugar, and continue beating for several minutes until thick and pale yellow. Beat in the flour to mix thoroughly. By dribbles, beat in two thirds to three fourths of the hot milk; set rest of milk aside. Stir custard mixture over moderately high heat with mixer or whip, reaching all over bottom and sides of pan—and do not worry about curdling the egg yolks; they are in a flour-based sauce and will come to no harm. The custard will begin to show signs of lumping as boil is reached; beat vigorously to smooth it. The cream should be very thick, like a heavy mayonnaise, but if it is too thick and stiff, thin out with droplets of milk throughout the cooking.

Lower heat to moderate and stir with a wooden spoon, again reaching all over pan 2 to 3 minutes more, to cook the flour. Remove from heat and beat in the butter, a tablespoon at a time, then the flavoring and salt. Spread plastic wrap upon surface to prevent a skin from forming, and chill. Taste carefully before using, and if it's too stiff beat in a little fresh cream by dribbles; the custard, however, should remain thick so that it will hold in a pastry shell.

Tarte aux fraises

━━━◆━━━

FRESH STRAWBERRY
TART

Make this with or without pastry cream. Paint the inside of a fully baked tart shell with warm red currant or apricot glaze, and let the glaze set 5 minutes. If you are using *Crème Pâtissière*, spread a ½-inch layer in the shell—no more, or the cream will spread out when the tart is cut and served. Arrange fresh hulled strawberries, close together and pointed ends up, in the cream or on the shell. Spoon warm glaze over the strawberries. Refrigerate until serving time.

VARIATIONS

Make other fruit tarts exactly the same way, using mixed wild berries, peaches, grapes, sliced bananas, or canned fruits, alone or mixed in attractive designs. Here is an example:

Tarte des quatre saisons

PEACH AND APRICOT
TART WITH BANANAS
AND ALMONDS

For 4 to 6 people

A No. 2 can (20 ounces) each of sliced peaches and
    of apricot halves
½ cup apricot jam, sieved
The grated rind and strained juice of 1 lemon
¼ cup sugar
A 9-inch fully baked pastry shell, or a free-form shell
    (page 609), on a serving dish
2 ripe but firm bananas, sliced
About ⅓ cup sliced almonds

Drain the juices of the canned fruits into a saucepan, blend in the sieved apricot jam, lemon, and sugar, and stir over moderately high heat until sugar has dissolved completely; boil rapidly for several minutes until last drops to fall from spoon, when lifted and drained, are thick and sticky. Paint inside of shell with a coating of this syrup. Then add the drained fruit to the remaining syrup and boil slowly for 5 minutes. Lift pieces of fruit with a fork and spoon to drain, arrange them attractively in the shell, decorate with slices of banana and the sliced almonds. Boil the remaining syrup again, until thick and sticky, then spoon it over the fruit to make a glittering over-all transparent covering.

☼ May be assembled several hours in advance of serving.

Accompany, if you wish, with lightly whipped and sweetened cream, *crème fraîche,* or vanilla ice cream.

Tarte au citron, La Pitchoune

———◆———

LEMON TART
DECORATED WITH
GLAZED LEMON
SLICES AND LEMON
PEEL

While I was finishing up this book in the south of France, Mary Frances (M. F. K.) Fisher wrote one of her elliptically charming letters, recalling Marseille, and Aix, and our own region around Grasse. And she spoke of lemon tarts; that the one she remembered at Saint-Rémy hadn't the appealing homey quality of a certain Mme. Gatti's lemon tart from our region. I know Mme. Gatti, and Mme. Gatti was delighted to be so praised by Mme. Fisher. Mme. Gatti said she'd bring me her tart and her recipe for it, but so far I've had neither the one nor the other. In the meantime, since *Tarte au Citron* is a specialty of a number of restaurants in the area, I began looking them up, and tasting them at various establishments. We have, of course, two dandy lemon tarts in Volume I of *Mastering*, one a lemon soufflé tart, and the other a lemon tart with ground almonds. But I had another idea: I wanted lemon slices on top, edible lemon slices, so you'd know right away it was lemon tart, and I didn't want it to taste like our American lemon pie—there would be no point in that. So here is my *Tarte au Citron.*

Notes. This is not a quick tart, but it is a beautiful one, and Rome was not built in a day, so they say. It is a shell filled with lemon custard mixture and baked; then it is decorated with glazed lemon slices and lemon peel, and the whole structure is glazed. The lemon slices are the tricky part, but you can do them several days in advance of baking. The custard mixture of lemon, sugar, and eggs is beaten into a thick foam in the electric mixer, giving it a light, creamy quality when baked. There is a secret touch in here too, a little finely grated raw apple—and why not? This was a suggestion from the good Mme. Saint-Ange, in her endearing now out-of-print masterpiece, *La Cuisine* (Paris: Larousse, 1927 and reprints).

For 8 to 10 people

A 5- to 6-cup partially baked tart shell (such as one in a 9- by 1½-inch flan ring, or in an 11- by ¾-inch fluted false-bottomed tart tin, page 606)

For the glazed lemon slices and glazed lemon peel
4 bright, firm, clean, fine lemons
1⅓ cups sugar
A scant ½ cup water
½ cup apricot jam forced through a sieve

The lemon tart filling
1 medium-sized apple
3 "large" eggs
⅔ cup sugar
The grated rind of 2 lemons
⅓ cup strained fresh lemon juice

Equipment: For beating the eggs, a portable or table-model electric mixer with a round-bottomed cul-de-poule type bowl (page 636) ; a grater for the apple

The glazed lemon peel and lemon slices. For the peel, remove the zests (yellow part only) of the lemons in long strips with a vegetable peeler, pile strips by twos or threes and cut into julienne matchsticks about 2 inches long by $\frac{1}{16}$-inch wide; blanch (simmer in 1 quart of water) 10 to 15 minutes, or until just tender. Drain, rinse in cold water, dry in paper towels, and place in a small bowl. Meanwhile, cut all white part of peel off the lemons, and cut lemons into crosswise slices $\frac{3}{16}$-inch thick, making sure you remove the seeds without injuring the slices.

Choose a heavy-bottomed 6- to 8-cup saucepan, and in it boil the sugar and water to the soft-ball stage (bring sugar and water to boil, swirling pan by handle until liquid is perfectly clear and limpid—indicating sugar has melted; cover and boil rapidly, peeking now and then, until bubbles thicken, and sugar has reached the soft-ball stage—238 degrees; a dribble will form a soft ball when dropped into cold water). Immediately stir 3 tablespoons into the blanched peel, and carefully add the lemon slices to the syrup. Bring just to the boil, letting syrup bubble over top of lemon slices, then set aside, spooning syrup from bottom of pan carefully up over slices several times during the next half hour to prevent syrup from coagulating in bottom of pan. Lemon slices should sit in the syrup at least an hour, to absorb the sugar.

✼ May be done several days in advance; cover and refrigerate.

Baking the tart. Preheat oven to 350 degrees. Peel and core the apple, and force through the small holes of the grater into the bottom of the partially baked shell; spread the apple evenly over the surface. Beat the eggs, sugar, and grated lemon rind for 4 to 5 minutes until very thick and creamy, like a heavy mayonnaise. Then, by driblets, beat in the lemon juice—this will thin out the mixture somewhat, but it remains creamy and foamy. Pour into the shell, filling it within $\frac{1}{16}$ inch of the rim all around—if there are any low places in the rim of the shell, slip a double thickness of aluminum foil under that portion of shell and against outside rim to prevent spill-over. (You will probably have a little more filling than you can use; it makes a pleasant drink.) Immediately set in middle or lower-middle level of preheated oven and bake 20 to 30 minutes, until filling has puffed slightly, browned on top, and is set (it doesn't sway and ripple if shaken gently). Do not touch the top; it is very tender. Remove from oven and let cool 15 minutes, then very carefully unmold onto a serving dish.

Decoration and glazing. The top of the tart is now to be decorated with a ring of lemon slices, and a strewing of candied peel; then the sugar syrup is to be boiled down with apricot jam to make a glaze—a gorgeous covering glitter. Very carefully, with 2 forks, lift the lemon slices one by one out of their syrup and arrange around the circumference of the tart, overlapping them if you have enough. Again with forks, lift the peel out of its syrup and strew in the center. Combine the 2 syrups in the pan, blend the sieved jam into it, and boil down rapidly to the thread stage—last drops of syrup to fall from spoon are thick and sticky. Spoon as much of the glaze over the lemon slices and peel as you wish and you may also want to paint the outside of the shell with glaze. The tart is now ready to serve.

✼ Tart is at its best when eaten the day it is baked, but leftovers kept in the refrigerator always taste good too.

Fruits poached in wine, and a pear and meringue fantasy

What to make for dessert when you are having a grand dinner party and the rest of the menu has been rather rich and elaborate? Often a fruit dessert of some kind is your best answer, and when you poach your fruits in wine you can serve them just as they are, or you can combine them with something else and serve forth a delightful and original creation. One suggestion described in this section is pears poached in red wine, bananas poached in white wine, all beautifully glazed, and arranged together over a mound of ice cream perched on a meringue shell. But first I shall start with a rundown on poaching fruit, since it is a most useful technique when you have an oversupply of ripening fruit that will not last another day. Use it also when you have pears that won't quite ripen, or apples that are not quite crisp enough to eat raw, since a slow simmer in wine or sugar syrup will almost always turn these otherwise disappointing objects into something most agreeably edible.

Compote de fruits

FRUITS POACHED IN WINE OR A SUGAR SYRUP

To poach fruits in syrup means to submerge them in a sweetened liquid and to cook them at just below the simmer—to prevent them from disintegrating—until they are tender; then they must sit in their cooking liquid 20 minutes or so to imbibe its sweetness and flavor. You can now eat the fruits just as they are, with a little of their lovely syrup, accompanying each mouthful with a bite of homemade cake or cookies. Or you can dress the dish up, serving poached peaches, for instance, on little rounds of cake and spooning a purée of raspberries or strawberries over them. Or serve poached pears on vanilla ice cream, and coat them with hot chocolate sauce and a dollop of *Crème Chantilly*. And once poached, the fruits can sit in their syrup in the refrigerator for a number of days; thus poaching is also a preservative.

Sugar proportions for sugar syrups. The proportions of sugar to liquid, for poaching raw fresh fruits, are invariable—1½ cups of sugar per quart of liquid, or 6 tablespoons per cup. If you want to go into the mathematics of it, they are based on the metric system, where a liter is slightly more than a quart (4⅓ cups), and 25 grams is slightly less than an ounce (which is approximately 30 grams). Sugar syrups are measured in degrees, based on the amount of sugar per liter of liquid—25 grams per liter makes 1 degree. In cups and spoons this would make 2 tablespoons of sugar per quart of liquid. A fruit-poaching syrup is always at 12 degrees, or 300 grams of sugar per liter, making, for us, 24 tablespoons or 1½ cups of sugar per quart. (In France you use a sugar hydrometer, a *pèse sirop*, a glass tube device with a weight in it, that fits in a small container; you fill the container with your syrup, plop in the hydrometer, and it registers the degree of sugar density, thus avoiding all mathematics and human errors.)

Pears poached in red wine

3 or more pears, firm, ripe, and unblemished
(Bartlett, Anjou, Bosc, Comice, Hardy, Clapp, or Nelis)
1 quart of water and 2 Tb lemon juice in a bowl
2 cups red wine (Mâcon, Gamay, or the like)
in a 3-quart pan
The zest (colored part of peel only) and 2 Tb
of juice from 1 lemon
¾ cup sugar
1 stick or ½ tsp cinnamon

Peel, halve, and core the pears, dropping them into the lemoned water as you go, to prevent discoloration. Meanwhile, simmer wine with zest, additional lemon juice, sugar, and cinnamon, to bring out flavor of ingredients (5 minutes or so). Drop in the pears, bring just to the simmer (add a little more wine, or water, if fruit is not covered by liquid, plus a little sugar, measuring it in: proportions are 6 tablespoons sugar per cup of liquid). Lower heat and maintain liquid at the not-quite-simmer for 8 to 10 minutes, just until pears are tender when pierced with a knife. Let cool in syrup for at least 20 minutes.

Serve warm, cool, or chilled. Store in a covered bowl in the refrigerator.

Bananas poached in white wine

3 or more firm, unblemished, barely ripened bananas
2 cups dry white wine (Mâcon, Pinot Blanc, or any
white wine that is fairly strong but not sour)
¾ cup sugar
1 Tb pure vanilla extract
A 3-inch stick of cinnamon

If you want to serve the bananas whole, plan to poach and serve them in the same dish, but if you are using them with other fruits or in a decoration, they are easier to handle when cut in half crosswise, and each half then cut in half lengthwise. Simmer the wine with the sugar, vanilla, and cinnamon for 5 minutes, stirring occasionally, then add the bananas and cook at below the simmer about 5 minutes or until bananas are just tender. Let them sit at least 20 minutes in their cooking liquid, and they are done.

Apples poached in sugar syrup. Use the preceding proportions substituting water for white wine, and you may also wish the zests (yellow part of peel only) of a lemon. Peel and core the apples, leaving them whole or quartering them, and poach in exactly the same way, but for about 15 minutes.

Peaches and apricots. Poach peaches and apricots whole, either in sugar syrup or in white wine, but do not peel them until they have steeped their 20 minutes after their 8 minutes of cooking.

Fantaisie glacée aux poires et aux bananes

———◆———

PEAR AND MERINGUE
FANTASY, AN ICE
CREAM PIE TOPPED
WITH FRUITS
POACHED IN WINE

Here is a dessert you can adapt to the seasons, since it consists of a large crisp circle of baked meringue on which you mound a dome of ice cream or sherbet; this in turn you surround with whatever wine-poached fruits that appeal to you, and you finish them off with curlicues of whipped cream. It is a dessert that looks wonderfully complicated and professional, but, like many such concoctions, is merely a matter of assembling the parts. And the parts you can have well in hand ahead of time: the baked meringue will keep for weeks in the freezer, the poached fruits will keep several days in the refrigerator; even the heavy cream can be whipped and will stay up for several hours. But be sure to test the ice cream—if it is the very firm type, let it soften in the refrigerator 20 minutes before you plan to serve. Final assembly, then, will not take you more than 2 or 3 minutes.

MERINGUE NOTE. The meringue mixture here is beaten egg whites, sugar, and pulverized almonds, hazelnuts, or pecans. It is the nuts that give an otherwise plain meringue much more taste, and a tenderer as well as crisper texture. It is known variously as a *fond parisien,* or *fond de Succès,* or *fond de Progrès* (both names of French cakes), or *broyage suisse,* and whatever you choose to call it, this is a most useful mixture for your repertoire. It takes but a few minutes to whip up in an electric mixer, and, since you pipe it or spread it on baking sheets in any size and form you want, you are not forced into the limits of a cake pan. Thus you can use the meringue for big desserts, as here; you can make individual sizes or *petits fours;* or you can pile large-size baked meringues one on the other with a rich butter cream between each, to produce a wonderfully fancy cake, as suggested on page 582.

For a meringue-nut shell about 10 inches in diameter

For 6 to 8 people

Soft butter, and flour

3 egg whites in a very clean, dry beating bowl

⅛ tsp cream of tartar

Pinch of salt

2 Tb sugar (to beat into the egg whites at first)

1 tsp pure vanilla extract

4 drops almond extract

½ cup sugar (to fold into the beaten egg whites later)

3 ounces (about ¾ cup lightly packed) pulverized almonds, or a combination of pulverized almonds and either hazelnuts or pecans

1 Tb cornstarch, to be sieved into the nuts

The other ingredients

3 pears peeled, halved, cored, and poached in red wine, and 3 bananas peeled, quartered, poached in white wine (or other fruits of your choice), page 512

½ cup red currant jelly

¾ cup apricot jam, forced through a sieve

About 1 quart excellent vanilla ice cream, or the grapefruit sherbet on page 539, or another sherbet or ice cream of your choice

1 cup heavy cream, whipped, and flavored with vanilla and confectioners' sugar (may be prepared in advance; see page 556)

Equipment: An electric mixer, either hand-held or
table model, and a no-stick pizza pan or baking
sheet; a rack set over a tray to hold the poached
fruit for glazing; a pastry bag with cannulated
tube for whipped cream decorations

Forming and baking the meringue-nut shell *(Fond parisien)* : *about 2 hours.* Preheat oven to 250 degrees. Smear butter on pizza pan or baking sheet, roll and shake flour around in it to cover surface completely, and knock out excess. Trace a 10-inch circle in center of pan. If egg whites are chilled, stir over hot water briefly to bring to room temperature. Then start beating them rather slowly at first, using an electric beater (or a large balloon-shaped whip). When foaming, beat in the cream of tartar and salt, and gradually increase beating speed to fast. When egg whites form soft peaks, sprinkle in the 2 tablespoons of sugar, the vanilla, and almond extract; continue beating until eggs form stiff shining peaks. Now, by 2-tablespoon sprinkles, rapidly fold in the sugar, alternating with the pulverized nuts mixed with the cornstarch, using a rubber spatula and plunging it down into the bottom of the bowl, scooping it up, rotating bowl as you go, and deflating the egg whites as little as possible.

With a rubber spatula, spread the meringue mixture into the marked circle in the pan, pushing it up around the circumference to make a raised edge all around about ½ inch wide. This will give you a free-form dish or pie-shell shape that will come out of the oven in exactly the same shape and size it went in.

Bake in lower-middle or middle level of 250-degree oven for 1½ to 2 hours, lowering heat to 225 or 200 degrees near end of cooking if shell colors more than a café-au-lait shade. Shell is done when you can very gently pry it loose from baking surface with a spatula—do not force it or you will damage the shell. It will come loose only when it is ready to do so.

✵ Keep the meringue in a dry place if you are using it shortly, or in a warming oven at 100 degrees; or wrap airtight and freeze it.

Glazing the meringue and the poached fruit. When you are ready to glaze the fruit, to make it glitter as a decoration around the mound of ice cream, you can do so several hours in advance and, if need be, spoon a final coating of syrup over it just before serving. Proceed as follows:

Arrange the poached fruit, rounded side up, on cake rack set over tray, and chill. You will need a red-wine glaze and a white-wine glaze: remove 1 cup of each wine from the poached fruit containers, and place in separate saucepans. Into the red-wine glaze liquid, beat the currant jelly and 3 tablespoons of the strained apricot; boil down rapidly to the thread stage—last drops to fall from spoon are thick and sticky. Meanwhile, mix 1 cup of the white-wine poaching liquid with the remaining apricot and boil it down rapidly, also to the thread stage. (Keep over hot water or reheat to liquefy before using.)

At some convenient time, paint top and sides of meringue shell with warm white-wine-apricot glaze, let set a few minutes, then place on a serving dish, and mound the ice cream on the shell, leaving raised border free (on which to rest the fruit, later) ; cover with an upside-down bowl, and set in the freezer.

Remove fruit from refrigerator, and spoon red-wine glaze over the pears and white-wine glaze over the bananas; return fruit to refrigerator.

Assembling the dessert just before serving. (You will have whipped the cream and turned it into a cheesecloth-lined sieve set over a bowl in the refrigerator. And if ice cream is of the hard variety, you will have set it in the refrigerator for 20 minutes before serving. Also, as a precaution, set the 2 pans of glaze in hot water or on a warming device just in case fruits need more glitter.)

Now, remove the ice cream–meringue assembly from the refrigerator, and the fruits. Reglaze the fruits if need be, and rapidly arrange them upright, alternating pears and bananas, on the edge of the meringue, leaning against the ice cream. Scoop whipped cream into the waiting pastry bag, pipe curlicues on top of the dessert and in strategic places around the edge, and bring the dessert into the dining room. Be sure to display it, so everyone can see, since a proper *présentation* is not only always correct, but also desirable for any beautifully arranged dish such as this one—good cooking appeals to all the senses, in other words.

A fancy custard

There are chopped almonds all around the sides, and under its glittering top is a chic design of colorful fruits. It looks worldly, complicated, and too professional to be homemade. Yet this handsome molded dessert is just an everyday Cinderella custard dressed up with cake, fruits, a whisper of rum, and apricot jam. Like all custards, it is quick to do, and like so many French recipes, it uses familiar ingredients, but does so with a flair. The custard mixture is the French formula for *crème renversée*—eggs and egg yolks beaten briefly with sugar before hot milk is poured on. Rather than being baked as is, it is poured into a dish that has been decorated with glacéed fruits and lined with leftover or store-bought cake or brioche, and flavored with rum. After baking, the custard is unmolded. Serve it as a single large custard, or cut the baked dessert into individual portions, glazing each with apricot jam and brushing the sides with almonds.

A NOTE ON GLACÉED FRUITS. Glacéed fruits should be, can be, absolutely delicious, but you must really buy them in a specialty shop to get anything worthwhile. I was never a candied fruit enthusiast, in fact, quite the opposite, until I tasted my first glacéed tangerine at Maiffret's in Cannes, on the rue d'Antibes, about halfway up from the Old Port end, on the left. You can't miss it because a giant cornucopia filled with all manner of glacéed fruits spills out at you in their window—whole pineapples, whole lemons, strawberries, the small sweet tangerines of the Midi, bright red cherries, figs. Go in and buy a small bag, and after the first bite you will be hooked, I wager. The lemons taste sweetly, sourly lemony, the figs figgy, and even the strawberries are themselves. If you are polite and earnest, you might be invited backstage where the fruits are made. There may be great tubs of lemons soaking to soften them for the fray. The steam kettles will be boiling up syrup and pineapple slices in small lots, and batches of cherries are steeping in earthenware bowls, tier upon tier. Bins of readied melon slices wait for their final glaze, and trays of candied oranges sit drying. It takes several weeks for the fruits to steep in ever renewed and ever stronger syrup until the final candying and preserving are complete, and it is all hand work. It was in Cannes, at that very store, that we filmed a colorful sequence on glacéed fruits, to honor this fast-dying craft and to show its beauty. That film, in turn, gave birth to our program and this dessert, *Glamour Pouding*. (The store does a large mail-order business all over the world: Maiffret, Fabrique de Fruits Confits et Chocolats, 53, rue d'Antibes, 06400 Cannes, France.)

Glamour pouding

MOLDED CUSTARD
WITH RUM-
FLAVORED GLACÉED
FRUITS AND CAKE

For an 8-cup baking
dish or pan, serving
8 to 9 people

Use whatever combination of glacéed fruits that appeals to you; described here is the simplest, which should be available anywhere. Choose a high baking dish like a soufflé mold, or a round or square cake pan; for individual servings, the square pan makes a custard easy to cut into 9 portions.

The fruits
About 25 whole glacéed cherries
¾ cup mixed diced glacéed fruits (such as
*   fruit-cake mix)*
⅓ cup dark rum

The custard mixture
5 whole "large" eggs
5 egg yolks
¾ cup sugar
1 quart milk heated in a saucepan
1 Tb pure vanilla extract

For assembling the custard
About 1 pound yellow cake, sponge cake, pound
*   cake, or brioche (such as a 9- by 1½-inch round*
*   or 9- by 3- to 4-inch loaf)*

Decorations
1 cup apricot jam
2 Tb sugar
Chopped almonds (or walnuts)

Preheat oven to 350 degrees.

Preparing the fruits. Cut the cherries in half through the stem side, rinse in boiling water, drain, and put in a small bowl. Rinse the diced fruit in boiling water, drain, and put in another bowl. Stir 2 tablespoons of rum into the cherries, and the rest into the diced fruit.

The custard. Blend the eggs and egg yolks in a mixing bowl with a wire whip, and beat in the sugar, beating for a minute or two to be sure all is well blended. By driblets, beat in the hot milk, then the vanilla extract.

Assembling. Provide yourself with an 8-cup baking dish, cake pan, or square pan 8 by 8 by 2 inches, and line the bottom with buttered wax paper. Drain the cherry maceration into the diced fruit, and arrange the cherries in an attractive design, cut side down (this is the side that will show), in the baking dish or pan—if you are using a square pan, mark squares in the wax paper to guide you for decorating and cutting, and compose a decoration for each square. Cut cake into wedges, strips, or squares, about ½ inch thick, and fit closely over the decorations. Slowly ladle in the hot custard mixture, letting cake absorb the liquid. When top of cake is covered, spread on the diced fruit and their rum maceration. Put more pieces of cake on top, slowly ladle on more custard, and when absorbed, ladle on driblets more, until all custard is used, and pan is filled almost to rim. (Proportions of cake to custard are not too important here, although if you have too much cake your dessert will be pudding-like rather than custardy.)

Baking. Set custard in a larger pan of boiling water in lower-middle level of preheated oven—water should come a half to two thirds up outside the custard dish. Regulate heat throughout baking so that water in pan never actually simmers: it should barely bubble. Custard should be done in about 1 hour, depending on shape of dish or pan; a skewer, toothpick, or knife plunged down through center should come out clean, and you can gently pull custard free from sides of dish. Let settle 20 minutes on a rack before unmolding.

Apricot glaze. While custard is sitting, push the apricot jam through a sieve into saucepan, stir in the sugar, and bring to boil. In a minute or so, when last drops to fall from spoon are sticky and thick, and form a thread when taken between thumb and forefinger, the glaze is ready to use. Keep warm over hot water until you have finished decorating with it. Scrape any leftovers into a screw-top jar and reserve for another time.

Unmolding, decorating, and serving. If you are serving the custard whole, unmold directly onto serving dish, peel off wax paper, and slip fresh sheets of wax paper under edges of dessert all around. Paint entire surface with the warm apricot glaze, brush almonds against sides, and pull out the protecting wax paper sheets. If you are making individual servings from a square, cut portions one by one; hold on a spatula or pancake turner while you paint with apricot glaze; brush sides with chopped nuts, and arranged on a serving dish. Cover it with an upside-down bowl and refrigerate until serving time. You may wish to accompany the dessert with a custard sauce, or a fruit sauce, such as frozen strawberries or raspberries thawed and pushed through a sieve.

Note: Decorating with chopped nuts. To brush chopped nuts against the sides of a cake or dessert, simply pick up a handful and, holding your hand like a spatula, brush the nuts off against the sticky sides; a coating of nuts will adhere, and the rest will fall off onto wax paper, a tray, or whatever you have put under the dessert to catch them.

A Bavarian combo

Cold soufflés, molded desserts, chiffon pies, and custard tarts

Of all luscious, creamy, light, and heavenly French desserts, a perfectly executed *Bavarois* may well be the most and the best. A combination of custard sauce, beaten egg whites, and whipped cream with just enough gelatin to hold everything together, it can stand majestically on a silver salver either by itself as a Bavarian cream, or corseted with ladyfingers in the guise of a Charlotte Russe. Piled into a cylindrical mold and walled with wax paper until the gelatin has set, it becomes a cold soufflé. And poured into a sugar crust, it is a chiffon pie. Here is the mother formula, with special flavoring suggestions at the end of the recipe.

Bavarois à la vanille, ou au café

BASIC VANILLA OR
COFFEE BAVARIAN
CREAM

2 Tb (2 packages) *plain unflavored gelatin*
½ cup milk or strong coffee in a small pan (or other liquid; see notes at end of recipe)
1⅔ cups additional milk in a second pan
1 cup sugar
8 egg yolks in a third pan—a heavy-bottomed 2-quart stainless or enameled one
1 tsp pure vanilla extract (or more, but see flavor notes at end)

For about 2 quarts,   *5 egg whites in a clean dry beating bowl (stir a mo-*
serving 8 to 10   *ment over hot water if chilled)*
                          ⅛ tsp salt
                          ¼ tsp cream of tartar
                          ½ cup chilled heavy cream in a 3-quart
                             metal mixing bowl

                          Other equipment: A wire whip; a wooden spoon;
                             a fine-meshed sieve set over another 3-quart
                             metal bowl; a rubber spatula; a clean dry
                             beater for egg whites; a large bowl with
                             2 trays of ice cubes and water to cover them

Custard sauce with gelatin (*Crème anglaise collée*). Sprinkle the gelatin into the ½ cup of milk, and set aside to soften; heat the 1⅔ cups milk. Meanwhile, gradually whip the sugar into the egg yolks, beating several minutes until yolks are pale and thick. Then, by dribbles, beat the hot milk into the yolks and sugar, thus heating the yolks slowly to prevent curdling. Set directly over moderate heat and stir slowly with a wooden spoon, reaching all over bottom and sides of pan as the yolks slowly warm; remove pan from heat instantly if there is any suggestion of lumping, stir for a moment, then continue over heat. Indications that mixture is heating enough to thicken are the appearance of very fine bubbles of foam on the surface, and then wisps of steam. Continue until mixture has thickened into a custard—meaning it will coat the spoon with a quite thick, creamy layer. It cannot come to the simmer or the yolks will scramble, but you must heat it to the creamy custard stage. Immediately remove from heat; stir for a good minute to cool the custard and stop the cooking. Finally stir the softened gelatin mixture over heat to dissolve it; beat into the hot custard. To be sure all gelatin has gone in, rinse gelatin pan with hot custard, and scrape residue back into custard with a rubber spatula— gelatin granules must be completely dissolved. Strain, stir in the vanilla, and set aside.

The egg whites. At once, start beating the egg whites, slowly at first until they begin to foam. Add the salt and cream of tartar, increasing speed to fast until the egg whites form stiff shining peaks. Fold the egg whites into the hot custard. (Heat of custard cooks the whites slightly, and gives them a light puff.)

Lightly whipped cream (*Crème Chantilly*). Set bowl of cream in the ice. Circulating beater or a large whip to incorporate as much air as possible, beat for several minutes until cream doubles in volume and holds its shape softly when lifted in a spoon. Set aside.

Finishing the Bavarian cream mixture. Set the custard–gelatin bowl in the bowl of ice, and fold gently with rubber spatula every few minutes, to cool the custard evenly and to prevent sides and bottom from setting. When cool, thick, and almost set—8 to 10 minutes—whip the cream a moment if it has lost its shape, then fold it into the custard. Immediately prepare to mold and chill the *Bavarois* to make one of the following desserts:

Soufflé froid (*A cold soufflé*). Choose a decorative cylindrical serving dish about 7 inches in diameter and 3 inches deep.

Fold in half lengthwise a sheet of wax paper long enough to encircle the mold; pin it in place as illustrated, letting collar stick 3 inches above rim of mold. Pour in the Bavarian cream mixture—don't worry, collar will hold it in place—the cream should rise 1½ to 2 inches above rim of mold.

Cover top of collar with plastic, and chill 4 to 5 hours or overnight. To serve, remove collar, peeling it gently from sides of dessert. Brush ground nuts, ground macaroons, or *pralin* (caramelized ground nuts, page 643) against sides, and sprinkle a dusting on top to simulate a browned soufflé. (Notes on how to brush nuts around a dessert are on page 519.) Keep the soufflé refrigerated until ready to serve.

Bavarois* or *Charlotte Russe (*A molded dessert*). Either rinse a 2-quart plain or fancy mold in cold water, or line a cylindrical mold with upright ladyfingers or strips of sponge cake. Scoop in the custard, cover, and chill 4 hours at least. To unmold, dip in very hot water for several seconds, then reverse onto a chilled serving plate.

Chiffon pie or tartlets. Paint baked pie shells or tartlet shells with apricot glaze, page 503, fill with the Bavarian cream, and chill several hours. Decorate with fruits, nuts, chocolate, or whatever suits your fancy.

SPECIAL FLAVORINGS FOR
BAVARIAN CREAM

Toasted hazelnuts or almonds. Spread 1½ cups nuts on a baking pan, and toast them in a 350-degree oven 15 to 20 minutes, stirring up several times until a light brown. Purée in an electric blender with a cup of almost boiling milk; let steep an hour. Strain, pressing juices out of nut residue; let this be part of the 1⅔ cups milk called for in the recipe. Additional flavoring, besides vanilla, could be several spoonfuls of Bourbon whiskey or Cognac.

Orange, strawberry, or raspberry Bavarian cream. Dissolve the gelatin in 1 cup strained orange or berry juice, and use only 1¼ cups rather than the 1⅔ cups milk called for, plus the grated peel from 2 oranges. Decorate with fresh orange segments or berries.

Chocolate Bavarian cream. Beat ⅔ instead of 1 cup sugar into egg yolks, and use 1⅓ cups rather than 1⅔ cups milk; melt 8 ounces semisweet baking chocolate in this milk before beating it into the yolks and sugar.

Tipsy Bavarians. Cut stale sponge cake or ladyfingers into 24 strips 1 by 3 by ½ inches and lay in a plate. Make a syrup of ¼ cup sugar dissolved in ⅓ cup hot water and ⅓ cup Bourbon, dark rum, or Cognac. Just before molding the custard, pour the syrup over the cake, and make layers of cake and Bavarian cream. Chill, as for the *Bavarois,* page 521.

Sauces to serve with Bavarians. Depending on the custard flavorings, serve a caramel sauce, whipped cream, chocolate sauce, chestnut or Nesselrode sauce, or a strained fresh-fruit sauce (raspberries, peaches, strawberries put through a sieve and sugared) .

ALCOHOLIC NOTE. Very soon after this program was aired, David Ives, the head of WGBH, our Boston PBS station, received a long letter from a doughty old Rhode Island temperance girl of eighty-eight. "I saw that Julia of yours the other night," she wrote, "putting teaspoon after teaspoon [sic] of booze in her dessert, and all the while saying it was good for the children. I know that Julia. She's a tool of the liquor interests—she's always pushing booze." Well, you don't have to booze it up; just use more vanilla. And, as I have been told by some AA people, never put even a drop of wine or liqueur—or booze—in anything if you are having an alcoholic at your table, since just a whiff of it can send them off.

Chocolate mousse

It's a sin, wickedly rich and fattening, but every spoonful is glory, and that's what chocolate mousse is supposed to be. We did it on the second program of "The French Chef's" second season in living color. This group of twenty-six shows was designed to give the accomplished cook a refresher course, while at the same time taking the beginner on a tour of the French classics. The only way to begin cooking is to start right in, and *Mousse au Chocolat* is a small treasure of culinary basics.

This recipe, then, I am directing to those of you who are new to cooking. You'll always be melting chocolate, that's for sure. You'll be boiling up sugar syrups for fruit sherbets, cake frostings, caramels, and glazes for fruit tarts. Every time you want a custard sauce, a Bavarian cream, or a hollandaise you'll be warming and thickening egg yolks, and the sooner you take the bugaboo out of that the better. And then you have egg whites—how to beat them and how to fold them into whatever they are destined for. Mastery of this operation opens up endless vistas of soufflés, cakes, *mousselines, roulades,* and even *bûches de Noël.* What better way is there to learn five fundamentals of *la cuisine universelle,* and to eat them too?

RÉSUMÉ OF RECIPE: Egg yolks are combined with a sugar syrup, and beaten over hot water until they have poached and thickened, like a custard sauce; they are then beaten until cool and even thicker. At this point melted chocolate and butter are folded into them, and finally stiffly beaten egg whites. It is clever to use butter rather than whipped cream, because the butter along with the chocolate firms up when chilled, giving the mousse enough body to be unmolded, if you so wish. Yet the beaten egg whites keep it light in texture.

☼A chocolate mousse may be made a day or two before serving, and it may be frozen.

Mousse au chocolat

◆

For about 5 cups,
serving 8 to 10

4 "*large*" *eggs*

*1½ Tb instant coffee dissolved in ¼ cup
 hot water in a small saucepan*

¾ cup sugar

*¼ cup dark Jamaican rum, orange liqueur,
 Cognac, frozen orange juice, or strong coffee*

*Either: 4½ ounces "German's" or "Dutch"
 semisweet baking chocolate and 1½ ounces
 unsweetened baking chocolate*

Or: 6 ounces semisweet baking chocolate

6 ounces (1½ sticks) unsalted butter

*A pinch of salt and a scant ¼ tsp cream of
 tartar (for egg whites)*

*Equipment: A small glass jar (for separating
 egg whites)*

 *A 2½- to 3-quart stainless steel bowl or
  saucepan (for egg yolks), and a wet potholder or heavy pan to hold it steady
  for beating*

 *A clean, dry 2½-quart mixing bowl, preferably
  of stainless steel (for beating egg whites)*

 *A portable electric beater with, if possible, extra
  blades; or a large wire whip (for egg yolks,
  chocolate, and egg whites)*

 *A cover for the small saucepan now holding
  the coffee*

 *A larger pan with 1 inch or 2 of simmering
  water, to hold the small pan (for melting
  chocolate)*

 *Another and even larger pan with simmering
  water, to set the egg-yolk pan into*

 1 or 2 rubber spatulas

 *Useful: an electric mixer on a stand, for
  final beating of egg yolks*

Egg yolks and sugar—preliminary blending. Start separating the eggs, dropping the white from Number One egg into the jar, and the yolk into the stainless bowl or pan. Be sure there is no speck of yolk in the white—scoop it out with a bit of shell if there is, then transfer white into the egg-white beating bowl. Continue with the rest of the eggs. Set whites aside, out of the way. Using portable beater or wire whip, beat the yolks for 2 to 3 minutes until pale, lemon colored, and thick; this is a kind of anti-curdle insurance, and prepares them for being heated. You are now ready for the sugar syrup.

Set pan with coffee over high heat, blend in the sugar, and bring to the boil, swirling pan by its handle. Let boil a moment or two, swirling, until sugar has completely dissolved—liquid will be clear rather than cloudy. At once, bring hot liquid over to egg yolks; begin beating the yolks at moderate speed while you slowly dribble the hot syrup into them. Then set aside for a moment while you prepare the chocolate for melting.

Melting the chocolate. Stir the ¼ cup rum or other liquid into the now empty sugar-boiling pan, and break the chocolate into it. Remove larger pan of simmering water from heat, place chocolate pan in it, stir up once, cover pan, and let chocolate melt slowly while you continue with the egg yolks.

Egg yolks and sugar—thickening over hot water. Set the egg-yolk pan in the second pan of water, and keep water at just below the simmer. Beat the yolk mixture rather slowly but continuously with portable mixer or whip for 5 minutes or longer, until it doubles in volume and becomes a thick cream that is hot to your finger. When warm and thick, scrape into the bowl of your electric mixer (or place egg-yolk pan in a large bowl of cold water). Beat at moderate speed 5 minutes or so, until cool, and when you lift a bit on a spatula it dribbles off in a thick ribbon that takes several seconds to dissolve and absorb back into the surface of the main body.

Combining egg yolks with melted chocolate and butter. Remove chocolate pan from the hot water and stir up; if not quite melted, renew hot water, and beat a few seconds, until chocolate is perfectly smooth and shining. Remove from hot water. Cut butter into 1-inch pieces, and beat it rapidly piece by piece into the chocolate, using electric mixer or whip. Scrape chocolate over egg yolks, then combine the two with a rubber spatula by cutting straight down through the center with edge of spatula, drawing spatula to edge of pan, then bringing it up to the surface in a scooping motion. Continue thus, rotating pan, and scooping rapidly until yolks and chocolate are fairly well combined. They will get more mixing later, and you need not be thorough as long as you are fast—about 30 seconds in all.

Beating the egg whites. At once, before chocolate and butter have time to cool and thicken, get to the egg whites. If they are chilled they won't mount properly: set bowl in hot water and stir about for a few seconds until the chill is off, testing with your finger to see if they are room temperature. Being sure your beater is perfectly clean, start whipping the egg whites at moderate speed for a minute, until they are broken up and foaming. Add the salt and cream of tartar, and gradually increase speed to fast—circulating beater all about the bowl to incorporate as much air as possible, and taking about a minute to arrive at top speed. Continue until beater leaves definite traces in the egg whites, then begin testing. Egg whites should form stiff shining peaks when lifted in wires of beater, just the tops of the peaks bending down slightly. Proceed at once to next step. ("Stiff but not dry" is a phrase often used, but it is the shine and the sheen of them that you look for, since if you overbeat egg whites they lose that look, begin to break down, and to turn grainy. But if this does happen, add another egg white, and beat again.)

Completing the mousse. Immediately turn one fourth of the beaten egg whites out on top of the chocolate with your rubber spatula; scoop and fold in rapidly to loosen the chocolate mixture. Turn the rest of the egg whites on top, and rapidly fold them in, just as you combined the chocolate and egg yolks, by rapid scoops with your spatula, rotating the pan or bowl as you do so. The whole process should not take more than a minute, and remember you are trying to deflate the egg whites as little as possible. The mousse is now finished, and needs only to be chilled, or frozen. Following are some suggestions:

SERVING SUGGESTIONS

For chilled mousse. Heap the mousse into an attractive serving bowl, or into individual *coupes,* glasses, bowls, or little pots. Cover, and chill 2 hours for individual servings, 4 hours or overnight for a large bowl. The mousse will keep perfectly under constant refrigeration for 3 to 4 days.

For frozen mousse. Rather than chilling the bowl (or individual servings), you may wrap the mousse airtight and freeze it; serve either frozen or thawed. Another idea is to mold the mousse in sugar cookies as follows: Choose a fairly straight-sided 5- to 6-cup rounded metal dish or charlotte mold, and line the bottom with a round of wax paper. Spoon a little of the mousse into the bottom, half an inch or so, but do not let it touch the sides of the mold. This is to brace the cookies. Place upright sugar cookies (or ladyfingers, or thin strips of sponge cake) slightly overlapping each other around the sides of the mold, their most attractive sides against the mold. Fill with the mousse, cover airtight, and freeze. (Trim off protruding cookie ends just before unmolding.) To unmold, dip mold about 10 seconds in a bowl of very hot water; remove from water, and turn serving dish upside down over mold. Reverse the two, and the mousse should come out very easily because of the paper on the bottom and the cookies around the sides. Peel paper off top of mousse. If you are not serving immediately, cover with a big bowl and refrigerate.

Strawberry soufflé for dessert

Soufflé for dessert! There is always an excitement about it, and not only in the breast of the cook—a soufflé makes any dinner a party. While most dessert soufflés are mixtures of pastry cream or a milk sauce plus egg yolks and beaten egg whites, fruit soufflés like this one are nothing but the pure fruit itself—raspberries, apricots, or strawberries, plus sugar and egg whites, and a touch of starch for tenderness. They are light and lovely, and you rise from the table satisfied yet not surfeited. (This is another very detailed recipe, designed for those who are new to soufflés; more are in *Mastering*, Volume I, and in *The French Chef Cookbook*.)

BEET SUGAR AND CANE SUGAR. The chemical formula for pure sugar is:

$$C_{12}H_{22}O_{11}$$

Whether it comes from beets, cane, palm trees, maple trees, sorghum, or watermelons, pure sugar is pure sugar. There may be some differences in how finely it is ground or how it is packaged and presented, but, according to exhaustive research by the U.S. Department of Agriculture, as stated in "Bulletin 535," there is no chemical test that can distinguish pure crystallized sugar as coming from any particular source. According to our taste tests, too, since the U.S. Sugar Beet Association was kind enough to send us a half dozen samples of their sugar from various manufacturers, we were unable to tell the slightest difference when comparing beet and cane sugars. However, the myth persists (and who in the world could be nourishing such a concept?) that cane sugar is the only pure sugar. I was in this trap myself, having picked up some remarks from the French during my formative years that I foolishly never verified. I stated my erroneous opinion loudly over the air during the following soufflé program, and it was not until then that the truth was revealed to me in a spate of letters from viewers, amazed at my ignorance. Even the other day, at the time of this writing, a distinguished food authority in the international *Herald Tribune* claimed that "most gourmets still prefer cane to beet sugar." It is interesting to note, however, that in recent years many packages of American sugar do not say anything more about their product than that it is pure sugar, and I have yet to hear a gourmet squawk.

TECHNIQUES FOR FRESH FRUIT SOUFFLES

A soufflé of fresh strawberries, my first, in a New York restaurant, so overwhelmed me that I went right home and made one. It was a purée of fresh strawberries folded into an Italian meringue, given a bit of body and help with a spoonful of cornstarch. It turned out beautifully. I then made it for a television show, and put it into the first edition of this book. But, alas, I have had trouble with that particular formula ever since. It is just too fragile, too collapsible, and so I determined to find another way to go about it.

The difficulty with fresh strawberries is that they are juicy, so much so that they water down anything they cook with. The classical approach is to purée them and to boil them down into a thick strawberry-sugar syrup, thereby evaporating that excess juice. However, when you boil strawberries and sugar long enough to thicken, you end up with strawberry jam. But that's not what fresh strawberry soufflé is about—it's about the taste of fresh strawberries. While pondering these problems aloud to Anne Willan, director of the La Varenne cooking school in Paris, she suggested slicing rather than puréeing the strawberries since she had sliced fresh pears for a sherbet and found her recipe much improved.

I then tried sliced berries, and I macerated them in sugar to force out some of their juices before folding them into my egg whites. This produced a beautiful-looking soufflé, but it had the texture of cotton batting. To improve the situation I tried to give more body first with cornstarch, then with egg yolks, and finally with pastry cream. But using these thickeners caused the soufflé to need more time in the oven, which meant the strawberries exuded the rest of their juices, which sank unhappily to the bottom of the soufflé dish.

Obviously, however, slicing and macerating seemed to be part of the solution, and finally, in Version 29, I found the whole of it. I folded the sliced and drained strawberries into my sugar syrup, boiled them up for a moment, and drained them again. Then I boiled down their newly exuded juices to a thick syrupy state, and folded the strawberries again into the syrup, letting them cool and thicken for a few minutes before combining them with the egg whites. Done this way, they lose none of their primal taste, and they bake into what I consider to be a proper fresh strawberry soufflé. And what an amazingly simple solution it is!

This system can certainly be adapted to other fresh fruits, but I am too oversouffléed at this writing even to consider it. However I do have one final remark: you must surely use a wide soufflé or baking dish for this type of mixture—mine holds 2½ quarts and is 8½ inches across. I did some of my early soufflés in a charlotte mold 6 inches in diameter and, because the soufflé is so light, it rose right up and up and up, and hit the top of my oven! A wide mass, on the other hand, cannot muster the body strength to play such dirty tricks on you.

Soufflé aux fraises

STRAWBERRY SOUFFLÉ

For a 2½-quart soufflé dish 8 to 9 inches in diameter, serving 6 people

3 pints of fresh strawberries (an extra pint if you wish to serve a strawberry sauce, see end of recipe)
⅓ cup sugar (more or less, depending on berries)
1 tablespoon red wine vinegar (a Venetian touch)
½ Tb soft butter and 1 or 2 Tb of sugar for baking dish
⅔ cup sugar in a heavy-bottomed 2-quart saucepan
⅔ cup (about 4) egg whites in a clean, dry beating bowl

For the egg whites
Pinch of salt
¼ tsp cream of tartar
2 tablespoons additional sugar
The grated rind of 1 lemon

Optional sauce
Whipped cream, custard sauce, and/or fresh strawberry purée

Macerating the strawberries. Hull and wash the strawberries, slice them rather roughly, and toss in a large bowl with the sugar and vinegar; let macerate (stand) half an hour, so that the juices will exude. Then drain in a colander set over a bowl.

Miscellaneous activities. Preheat oven to 425 degrees and place rack on lower third level. Smear baking dish (which should be fairly straight sided) with butter, roll sugar around in it to coat bottom and sides, and shake out excess sugar; no collar is needed. Prepare the rest of the ingredients.

Boiling the berries. Pour ¼ cup of juices drained from the berries into the saucepan of sugar. Set over high heat and, swirling pan by handle, bring just to the boil; remove from heat, swirling, until sugar is completely dissolved, then return over high heat. Cover pan and boil a minute or so, until bubbles thicken and sugar is at the soft-ball stage (238 degrees). Fold 2½ cups of the drained, sliced strawberries into the hot syrup and bring to the boil, folding, for 1 minute. Then drain the strawberries through a sieve set over a bowl. Return juices in bowl to saucepan and boil down rapidly until thickened (but be careful not to scorch or burn them); add any more juices that have accumulated in bowl as you boil. Finally fold the strawberries again into the syrup, add the grated lemon rind, and set aside for a few minutes to thicken as the syrup cools.

Finishing the soufflé mixture. Being sure that your oven is at 425 degrees, start in on the egg whites by first stirring them for a minute or so over hot water to take off their chill. Then beat slowly for a moment until they have foamed up, beat in a small pinch of salt and ¼ teaspoon cream of tartar, and gradually increase speed to fast, until egg whites form stiff, shining peaks. Sprinkle in the 2 tablespoons sugar, and beat a few seconds more to stiffen them further. Immediately scrape the strawberry mixture into one side of the egg whites, and rapidly but delicately fold them together.

Baking and serving. At once turn the soufflé mixture into the prepared baking dish, either smoothing the top with a spatula or leaving it in its rather rough state—which I prefer—and set it in the oven. The soufflé will take 10 to 12 minutes to bake, rising some 2 inches above the rim of the dish, and the top will brown nicely. A skewer inserted into the side of the puff will come out almost clean. Bring it to the table at once (although it will wait, if necessary, for several minutes in turned-off oven, door ajar). To serve, plunge spoon and fork back-to-back vertically into top of soufflé, and tear it apart for each portion; surround each with optional whipped cream, custard sauce, and/or strawberry purée.

For fresh strawberry purée or sauce. Hull and wash a pint of strawberries, and purée in a blender, food processor, or vegetable mill, then beat in sugar and lemon juice to taste.

Crêpes

Crêpes are a must in any cook's bag of fundamentals, not only because they are so easy to make—they are always among the first dishes one is taught in any beginners cooking class—but also because, with a stack of those paper-thin French pancakes on hand in the freezer, you can look forward to any emergency situation that will draw them out. Flashy desserts like the ones described here are quick to produce, as are rapid main courses such as crêpes rolled up with a creamed filling of some sort, even be it chopped hard-boiled eggs, herbs, and cheese rather than a *velouté* of fresh lobster, or a filling of ham and mushroom *duxelles*. Thus, although I have dealt with them in other books, I still have more to say about crêpes, including cooking them upside down. First, however, following a note on flour, is an all-purpose formula for making the batter.

WONDRA AND INSTANT-BLENDING FLOUR VERSUS REGULAR ALL-PURPOSE FLOUR. I have suggested Wondra or instant-blending flour for crêpe batters since it mixes up so easily in a quart measure and you can use it right from the measure after a 20- to 30-minute rest. (Crêpe batters must rest so that the flour particles will absorb the liquid, swell, and soften, and cook up into a light and tender pancake.) Batter made with regular flour needs a longer rest—2 hours; make them either in an electric blender, where all the ingredients are whirled about for 30 seconds or so until perfectly smooth, or gradually blend liquids into flour by hand or with a mixer, beat out the lumps, and strain the batter. Thus my preference is purely for convenience, since I do not find any difference in the final crêpe whichever of these flours I have used.

Pâte à crêpes ordinaire

———

ALL-PURPOSE
CRÊPE FORMULA

This is the formula to choose when you are making lots of crêpes and want extra ones to store in your freezer. Since you do not need sweet crêpes to create a dessert, this formula can be used for any purpose, and for crêpes cooked upside down as well as crêpes cooked right side up.

For 2⅓ to 2¾ cups of batter, making about 20 crêpes 5½ inches across

3 "large" eggs broken in a 4-cup measure (or a bowl)
⅔ cup milk
⅔ cup water, plus droplets more if needed
¼ tsp salt
For crêpes cooked in the usual manner: 3 Tb
*   dark sesame oil or fresh peanut oil (for upside-*
*   down crêpes, see notes in recipe, page 534)*
1 cup Wondra flour or instant-blending flour,
*   (for regular flour, see notes preceding recipe)*
A little peanut oil for greasing crêpe pans

Equipment: A wire whip; 1 or 2 frying pans or
*   crêpe pans (see below) measuring spoons;*
*   a large kitchen spoon or ladle to hold measured*
*   batter; a flexible-blade spatula; 24 wax paper*
*   squares 6 inches to a side, and a dish*
*   on which to stack the cooked crêpes*

The crêpe batter. Beat the eggs to blend whites and yolks, then beat in the liquids, salt, and oil; gradually beat in the flour. Let stand 20 to 30 minutes (or longer, if need be, in the refrigerator).

Cooking crêpes in a pan, in the usual manner

Stir up your batter to be sure it is smooth, then pour 2 tablespoons of it into your big spoon or your ladle, and take mental note of how full it should be for each crêpe. Set the crêpe-stacking dish and wax paper squares by your side. Place pan (or pans) over moderately high heat and brush lightly with oil (usually only necessary for the first crêpe). Flick a few droplets of water into the pan: they should sizzle. Pour in a small spoonful of batter as a test: it should sizzle, form little bubbles in the surface, and brown. Now put sufficient batter into your big spoon or ladle, and you are ready to go.

Choose a pan with 5½-inch bottom diameter, such as the American iron
skillet at left, or the low-sided French crêpe pan in the middle. However,
my choice is the heavy duty aluminum pan at right because its heat-resistant
handle needs no potholder, and its no-stick interior makes for easy flipping.

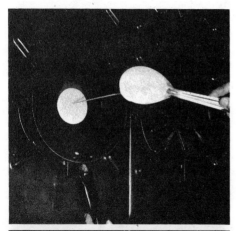

Grasping handle in one hand, pour the batter into the center of the hot pan.

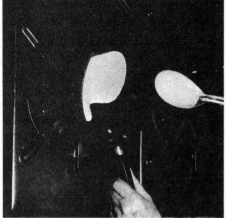

Immediately tip pan rapidly around to spread batter all over bottom surface. Set directly on burner, and bubbles will almost immediately appear throughout batter.

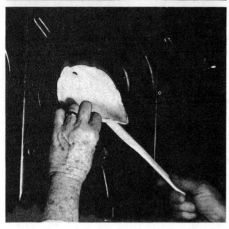

Let cook about half a minute, or until an edge when lifted is brown underneath; when you shake the pan hard, the crêpe will usually come loose. Flip crêpe over onto its other side, either by tossing it in the air, or by turning it with a spatula.

In either case, cook 15 to 20 seconds more; this side will brown only in spots, and is considered the underside that is never exposed to the public. Place a wax paper square on the stacking plate, slide the crêpe onto it, and cover with another square of paper—to prevent the crêpes from sticking to each other later. (Your first crêpe is often not a beauty because your pan may not be hot enough, or too hot—adjust the heat and keep going. I often find, when I've not done them in a while, that I've lost my touch and it takes several crêpes before I get the batter quickly, evenly, and thinly spread in the pan, and the heat just right. The crêpes should not be more than $\frac{1}{16}$ inch thick, and they should be light and delicate in texture; they must have enough body to hold together, however, or you cannot roll or fold or fill them. If, after making several, you think the batter is too heavy, thin it by beating in more water by droplets.)

Storing or freezing crêpes. If you are making the crêpes ahead, you may cover and refrigerate them; they will keep for 2 days or so. Or you may freeze them, and in this case I find it a good idea to separate them into piles of 4 or 6 with a big square of aluminum foil, just in case that is all I may want to use; then wrap airtight. To thaw, place in a covered dish in a 300-degree oven for 10 minutes or so, until warmed through enough so that you can separate them easily.

Cooking crêpes upside down, on the bottom of a pan

It is amusing and very easy indeed to cook crêpes on the bottom of an upside-down pan. You heat the pan to sizzling, dip its bottom in the batter so a thin layer will stick to it, then set the pan upside down over heat to cook the crêpe. Although you can get an upside-down crêpe-making outfit, I see no reason to spend all that money when you can rig a setup yourself with what you have on hand.

Use the all-purpose batter formula on page 531, but omit the oil (this batter will make about 30 crêpes 5½ inches across). Soak 4 thicknesses of paper toweling in peanut oil, and place on a plate beside you (I keep a stack of aluminum pie plates for this sort of thing). Have a wad of paper towels handy, and a potholder, a plate for scraps, a stacking plate, 3 dozen 6-inch wax paper squares, and a flexible-blade spatula. Stir up the batter and pour into a pie plate just large enough to hold the bottom of whatever frying pan you have decided upon.

Choose an iron frying pan with bottom diameter 4½ to 5½ inches across, and turn it upside down over a burner on top of the stove—moderately high flame for gas; highest heat for electricity. Flick droplets of water on bottom of pan until they sizzle, indicating it is hot enough. Then rub bottom of pan over the oiled towels and wipe off excess; you need just a film on the surface.

Immediately set just the bottom of the pan in the batter—it should sizzle; leave it barely a second and lift it out.

Bottom of pan will be coated with a thin layer of batter.

Hold pan upside down over heat and cook until edges of crêpe begin to brown—40 seconds or so. Gently dislodge it from the pan with your spatula.

Turn the crêpe and cook for 10 seconds or so on its other side. This other side, as usual, will be only a spotty brown, but it will be cooked and not soggy raw.

Here, on the left, are crêpes turned on their best sides, and on the right they are underside up. Stack the crêpes, as they are made, between squares of wax paper—unless you are using them immediately, in which case the paper is not necessary.

Remarks. Your crêpes will be thinner, usually, made this way than in the conventional way, and you can keep several pans going at the same time. Once in a while you may find that the crêpe will not adhere to the bottom of the pan when you dip it into the batter: it falls back in, making a lumpy mass. This can be caused by a pan so hot that the batter cooks immediately and falls off; or the pan may be too profusely oiled. Strain the batter, wipe the pan clean, cool it off, and start again.

A formula for sweet crêpes

Here is a light and delicate sweet crêpe batter for dessert dishes, so delicate a batter that I think it's safer to cook it in a pan, in the conventional manner described on page 532. (Beat up the eggs, then the liquids, sugar and salt, and gradually beat in the flour; let batter rest 20 minutes before using.)

For 16 to 18 crêpes 5½ inches across

2 eggs and 2 egg yolks in a quart measure
½ cup water
½ cup milk
3 Tb dark sesame oil, or melted butter, or salad oil
¼ cup kirsch or orange juice, or a
*   mixture of the two*
¼ cup sugar
⅛ tsp salt
1 cup flour (Wondra or instant-blending
*   recommended)*

Instant desserts made with crêpes. The simplest dessert of all is to butter the underside of the warm crêpes, sprinkle with granulated sugar, roll or fold them so the good side is in view, and serve them as is. Or spread them with jam instead of sugar. To carry this another step, then arrange them (jam-filled or only sugared and buttered) in a buttered baking dish, sprinkle with sugar and melted butter, and run them under the broiler for a few seconds to caramelize the top lightly. Finally, to be even more elaborate, you heat orange liqueur, or Cognac, or bourbon whiskey in a small pan, bring the hot caramelized crêpes and the warm liqueur to the table, pour the liqueur over the crêpes, and flame them. Here are two more ideas, of a more formal kind.

Crêpes flambées, Sainte Claire

FRENCH PANCAKES
WITH APRICOT
FLAVOR, FLAMBÉED

For 4 to 6 people

When you want a flaming crêpe dessert, this one has a delightful flavor, and you can do everything at the table in a chafing dish, or assemble in the kitchen and flame at the table.

12 5½-inch crêpes, from either of the
    preceding batters
1 cup canned apricot nectar (or syrup
    from canned apricots)
The grated peel of 1 orange
2 to 3 Tb butter
A chafing dish or serving skillet
2 Tb sugar
⅓ to ½ cup Cognac (or bourbon whiskey)

Either in advance, or at the table in the chafing dish, heat the apricot nectar, orange peel, and butter until the butter has melted. Dip each crêpe into the syrup and fold in half or into quarters, best side exposed to view. Arrange slightly overlapping each other in the dish. Just before serving, heat to bubbling hot, sprinkle on the sugar, and pour in the liqueur. Heat again to bubbling, and ignite either by tilting pan into heat or by touching a lighted match to the surface. Swish pan by handle until the flames subside, then serve onto very hot plates.

Crêpes à la pagode, en flammes

FRENCH PANCAKES
WITH WALNUT AND
KUMQUAT FILLING

Nineteenth-century France was romantically invaded by Chinese influences, and could the title here refer to the kumquats? Might they have been grown exotically under a Chinese pagoda? We shall probably never know, but this unusual combination of walnuts and kumquats, along with plenty of good fresh butter and Cognac, makes a most welcome change from the ubiquitous *Crêpes Suzette*. A dessert you can assemble in advance and refrigerate until you want to heat and serve it.

For 6 people

18 crêpes 5½ inches in diameter, from either of the preceding crêpe-batter formulae

The walnut and kumquat filling
1½ sticks (6 ounces) soft unsalted butter
1 cup sugar
3 "large" eggs
1½ cups (about 6 ounces) pulverized walnut meats
3 Tb kirsch or Cognac
6 kumquats in syrup, seeded and finely diced

For baking and flaming
¼ cup sugar
4 Tb melted butter
½ cup chopped walnuts
4 to 6 kumquats cut into julienne (very thin strips)
⅓ cup of the kumquat syrup
½ cup Cognac

Making the crêpes and the filling: *may be done several days in advance.* Make very thin crêpes in the usual way. Beat all the ingredients for the filling together; cover and freeze for half an hour, or until congealed (this is to keep filling from immediately spreading when crêpes are baked) .

Assembling: *may be done in advance.* Reserve ⅓ cup of the filling in a small saucepan for later. Lay a crêpe, underside up, on a sheet of wax paper. Place a 2-tablespoon lump of filling on bottom half, and fold top half over to form a half-moon shape. Place it in a heavily buttered baking dish about 12 inches in diameter and arrange the rest slightly overlapping.

✡ Cover and refrigerate; will keep a day or two, or may be frozen.

Baking and serving: *about 15 minutes at 425 degrees.* Sprinkle the crêpes with the sugar, dribble on the melted butter, and strew over them the walnuts and kumquat strips. Bake about 15 minutes in upper level of preheated oven until lightly browned and bubbling hot; keep warm if not to be served shortly, and reheat on top of stove just before serving. Bring reserved ⅓ cup of filling to the simmer with the kumquat syrup and 2 Tb Cognac; keep warm. Just before serving, pour hot sauce over hot crêpes, heat remaining Cognac in pan, and pour over. Bring immediately to table, and ignite. Spoon flaming liquid over crêpes, and serve on very hot plates.

Sherbets, ice cream, and a homemade bombe

A splendid dessert ready to serve at a moment's notice—that is the wonder of having ice creams and sherbets in storage, especially when they are your own homemade special brand. These are all non-cranking formulae, which you mix up and set in your freezer. The sherbets need a beating or two midway through to break up their ice crystals; mixtures with whipped cream in them freeze just as they are. I shall start with sherbets.

Mousse glacée aux pample-mousses

GRAPEFRUIT SHERBET

Grapefruit sherbet? I first had it in England, at a fine small restaurant run by a retired banker in Chichester, where we dined before seeing a revival of *Private Lives*, done beautifully with a London cast at a summer theater set in a vast expanse of English lawn. I kept thinking of that deliciously refreshing and unusual sherbet all through the play, and as soon as I got home to America, and pink grapefruit came into season again, I began play-

ing around with the idea. Whether or not the following version ap-
proaches the original I now have no idea, but it pleases me to think of it
as *Le Sorbet de Chichester,* pronouncing the sound of the town *à la française*—Shee-shest-aire.

For about 2 quarts,
serving 6 to 8

3 or 4 grapefruit, the pink-fleshed kind,
     if possible
3 egg whites at room temperature, in the clean,
     dry 2½- to 3-quart bowl of an electric beater
A scant ¼ tsp cream of tartar
A pinch of salt
1¼ cups sugar
⅓ cup water
Optional: 2 to 3 Tb kirsch

Preparing the grapefruit. With a vegetable peeler, skin off the zest
(colored part of peel only) of the grapefruits. Simmer zests 15 minutes
in 2 quarts of water; rinse in cold water, drain, and pat dry. Cut half the
zests into strips 1½ inches long, then, piling 2 or 3 together, slice them
into julienne matchsticks less than $\frac{1}{16}$ inch wide; place in a small bowl
and reserve for final decorations. Cut the remaining white peel from the
grapefruit to expose the flesh; cut out the segments of flesh from between
the membranes of the fruit and purée it through the coarse blade of a
vegetable mill, in a blender, or chop fine. Place in a 4-cup measure, and
squeeze in enough juice from the remains (a potato ricer is fine for this)
to make about 3 cups of combined pulp and juice. Purée the rest of the
blanched peel in an electric blender with a cup of the grapefruit juice
(or mince very fine) , and pour into measure with pulp and juice.

Meringue italienne (*Italian meringue mixture*). Start beating the egg
whites slowly; when foaming, beat in the cream of tartar and salt, and
gradually increase speed to fast until egg whites form stiff shining peaks.
Turn speed to very slow, and continue beating while preparing a sugar
syrup as follows: Bring sugar and water to the boil in a small saucepan
over high heat, swirling pan gently by handle until sugar has dissolved
and liquid is completely clear. Cover pan, and boil without stirring for
a minute or so until bubbles begin to thicken; uncover and boil rapidly
to the soft-ball stage (238 degrees) . Immediately pour about 3 tablespoons into bowl of peel strips, then, beating the egg whites at moderate
speed, dribble the remaining syrup into them. Continue beating at high
speed for 5 minutes or so, until egg whites are cool, and form stiff
satiny peaks when a bit is lifted. Beat the grapefruit flesh and juice into
the meringue.

Freezing the sherbet. Turn the sherbet mixture into a shallow pan or into ice trays, and freeze at zero degrees or less for an hour or more, until mushy and almost set (if frozen solid, let soften). Scrape into a mixing bowl or bowl of electric mixer and beat vigorously to break up ice crystals and unify consistency. Turn into a serving bowl, a metal mold, or individual cups. Cover, and freeze at least 2 hours for individual portions; 4 hours for bowls or molds.

Serving. Sherbet should soften slightly before serving. For individual portions, set in refrigerator 10 minutes. For a bowl, or for scooping, allow half an hour. If it is to be unmolded, dip mold into warm water, and reverse onto a chilled platter, cover and freeze half an hour to set dribbles, then place still covered in refrigerator for 30 minutes.

Just before serving, decorate with the julienned peel and syrup, into which you may wish to stir a spoonful or so of kirsch.

A MORE CONCENTRATED SHERBET

Just while I was working on this chapter, I picked up Gault and Millau's lively magazine on travel and gastronomy, *Le Nouveau Guide,* and there was the sherbet formula used by many of the well-known restaurants in France. I tried it with some fresh strawberries, and the result was most definitely 3-star. It is, however, high in sugar calories, if that is of concern to you—1,728 of them per quart, as opposed to 576 calories for 2 quarts of sherbet made according to the preceding system. A large amount of sugar cuts down on the formation of ice crystals, and serves the same purpose as the egg whites in the Italian meringue. Too much sugar, however, and your sherbet won't freeze; the limits for ripe raw fruit are 2¾ cups of sugar per quart of fruit and/or juice. Which formula to choose? The one with the meringue makes double the amount, while the following recipe produces half as much and triples the calories, but the result is wonderfully rich on the tongue.

Sorbet aux fraises ou aux framboises

FRESH STRAWBERRY OR RASPBERRY SHERBET

The formula here is ⅔ cup of sugar and 1 tablespoon of lemon juice for each cup of fruit purée.

About 1½ quarts of fresh berries
(to produce 3 cups of purée)
2 cups sugar
3 Tb fresh lemon juice

For 1 quart of concentrated sherbet, serving 6 to 8

Put the berries through the finest blade of a vegetable mill, or force through a fine sieve, to eliminate all seeds; measure 3 cups into a metal bowl. Add the sugar and lemon. Set over a larger bowl filled with a tray of ice cubes, water to cover them, and 2 tablespoons of salt. Beat the purée over the ice with a portable electric mixer or a wire whip for several minutes, and while it chills, the sugar should dissolve completely—beat until you cannot feel the faintest granule of it on your tongue. Mixture will now be thoroughly chilled and will freeze quite rapidly; cover, set at zero degrees or lower, and beat up once or twice during its freezing to break up ice crystals.

OTHER FRUITS FOR SHERBETS

Use either of these two formulae for grapefruit, oranges, or tangerines (with the pulp and peel system described on page 540), ripe peaches, apricots, strawberries, raspberries, blackberries, and, of course, experiment on your own. When it comes to home-stewed fruits, which can make delicious sherbets, use the formulae on pages 511–12, but you will need more sugar—rather than the 1½ cups per quart called for in simple poaching, use 2 to 2¾ cups of sugar per quart of liquid, depending on the sweetness of the fruit. (Technically, this makes a syrup of 18 to 22 degrees rather than one of 12 degrees, as explained in the sugar-proportion notes on page 510.) How much sugar is in canned and frozen fruits? Who knows, since it is rarely noted on the label. Here you will have to experiment, guess, and depend on your sweetness memory as to how much additional sugar is needed.

Glace au chocolat

———◆———

CHOCOLATE
MERINGUE ICE
CREAM

For about 3 quarts

This is a delicious ice cream that remains rather soft even after freezing, and is an ideal mixture to use inside a *bombe glacée,* as well as being an ice cream to serve in individual cups or a large bowl.

The Italian meringue

3 egg whites, a scant ¼ tsp cream of tartar,
and a pinch of salt
1 cup sugar and ⅓ cup water in a small saucepan

The chocolate and the cream
1 cup milk in a saucepan
¼ cup strong coffee
6 ounces semisweet baking chocolate
1 ounce unsweetened chocolate
½ pint heavy cream in a metal mixing bowl set
over a larger bowl with ice cubes and water

Make the Italian meringue as described in the recipe on page 540. Meanwhile, heat the milk, coffee, and chocolate to the simmer, stirring, until chocolate is melted and perfectly smooth; simmer, stirring, for a few minutes while chocolate thickens into a quite heavy cream. Stir over ice until cool but not set; then put aside. Set the bowl of heavy cream in ice, and whip into *Chantilly* (until it holds its shape softly when lifted in a spoon). Fold the cool chocolate into the meringue mixture, then fold in the whipped cream. This ice cream needs no mid-freeze beating; turn immediately into a bowl, mold, or cups, cover, and freeze at least 4 hours.

Bombe glacée au chocolat

MOLDED VANILLA
AND CHOCOLATE
ICE CREAM

Line a chilled fancy metal mold or metal bowl with slightly softened vanilla ice cream (best-quality store-bought, or use the preceding formula minus chocolate mixture, plus another half pint of heavy cream for whipping, and a tablespoon of pure vanilla extract); lining should be ⅜ to ½ inch thick all around. Freeze uncovered half an hour or until set. Push up lining all around with the back of a spoon, to be sure inside rim of mold is well covered. Turn in enough of the unfrozen chocolate meringue ice cream to fill the mold; cover airtight and freeze at least 4 hours. Unmold in warm water onto a chilled serving dish; cover with an upside-down bowl and freeze another half hour at least before scraping dribbles from serving dish. Set in refrigerator 20 to 30 minutes to soften, before bringing to the table.

Grand finales, part 2: cakes and petits fours secs

Cake with a halo—gâteau Saint-Honoré

Gâteau in a cage—gâteau des Trois Mages, under a caramel dome

Homemade cakes
Electric mixers and the right bowl
Cake formulae and techniques
Pain de Gênes—an almond cake
Le Brantôme—a VIP walnut cake
Brandy-butter filling and glace royale
  frosting
L'Éminence Brune—a chocolate cake

Working with chocolate
Types of chocolate and substitutions
To melt chocolate for decorations
Chocolate cutouts, lettering, cigarettes
Crème au beurre—French butter-cream
  frosting and filling

The Génoise jelly roll
Génoise cake batter
Génoise cake
Gâteau roulé—sponge sheet for jelly roll
Bûche au chocolat, bûche de Noël—
  chocolate log cake

Layer cakes
La grande bouffe aux écailles et au
  chocolat

Mrs. Child's famous sticky fruit-cake

Petits fours secs
Madeleines à la génoise
Madeleines de Commercy, with the
  hump on top
Langues-de-chat—cats' tongue cookies
Tuiles aux noix—walnut wafers

Spiced dough for gingerbread houses,
  gingerbread men, cutouts, cookie
  molds, speculos

An almond feuilleté—Le Pithiviers

W hen is a cake not a cake but a dessert? It is indeed hard to say, and these do seem to fall into both categories. Certainly the first two could be described as dessert cakes, the *Saint-Honoré* and the cream-filled *Gâteau* in a cage. The walnut and chocolate cakes could be either, as can the jelly roll, Yule log, and fancy layer cakes. Any one of them makes a grand finale to even the most modest meal, and all are equally appropriate at tea parties, buffets, solemn family gatherings, and champagne receptions.

———————◆———————

Cake with a halo

A halo of *pâte à choux* crowned with tiny puffs, filled with luscious liqueur-flavored pastry cream, and decorated with fruits—this is the famous *Gâteau Saint-Honoré*, named after the patron saint of bakers and pastry chefs. Here, for this handsome dessert, all the parts may be prepared ahead, even frozen for several weeks, and the final assembling is done at leisure shortly before serving. The shell consists of a bottom disk of pie-crust dough, and a halo and puffs of *pâte à choux* that are fixed upon it with caramel syrup; the filling may be whipped cream, or ice cream, or the traditional *Crème Saint-Honoré*—a pastry cream with gelatin, beaten egg whites, and whipped cream. The fruit decorations are whatever is in season.

Gâteau Saint-Honoré

———————

RING OF CREAM
PUFFS FILLED WITH
WHIPPED CREAM OR
PASTRY CREAM AND
FRUITS IN SEASON

For a 10-inch dessert,
serving 8 people

The important consideration in this recipe is the shell, since you have your wide choice of filling. If you are planning on a *Crème Saint-Honoré*, however, because its base is the custard filling, *Crème Pâtissière*, I suggest that you make more *choux* pastry than you need, and you can turn the extra amount into pastry cream. (They are almost the same formula, actually, so it would be a silly waste of time to go through the same motions twice.)

The bottom disk of pie-crust dough
Sufficient pie-crust dough to make a disk 10 inches in diameter (page 604, or your own formula)

Pâte à choux—cream-puff pastry for halo, 22 puffs, and pastry-cream filling
(for about 4 cups, enough for pastry cream as well as puffs; if you don't want the pastry cream, use ⅔ of the ingredients listed)
2 cups water in a heavy-bottomed 3-quart saucepan
1¼ sticks (5 ounces) butter cut into ½-inch pieces
¼ tsp salt
1 Tb sugar
1½ cups all-purpose flour (measure by scooping dry-measure cups into flour and sweeping off excess)
6 "large" eggs
½ to 2 additional eggs, as needed
Egg glaze (leftover egg from above plus a tsp of water, or 1 egg beaten with 1 tsp water)

Other ingredients
½ cup sugar and 3 Tb water (to make a caramel)
A filling for the Saint-Honoré: see suggestions at end of recipe

Equipment: Useful for making choux pastry, a
portable electric beater (or a wooden spoon) ;
for forming and baking halo and puffs, a large
pastry sheet (12 x 20 inches at least, and no-stick
if possible) , a large pastry bag with ½-inch
round tube opening, a pastry brush, and a
cake rack set over a tray; a small heavy
saucepan with cover for the caramel

The bottom disk of pie dough. Roll dough ³⁄₁₆-inch thick. Using a cake pan or bowl, cut out a circle approximately 10 inches in diameter, roll circle of dough up on your pin, and unroll onto baking sheet. Prick all over at ¼-inch intervals with pastry pricker or fork, and refrigerate the disk until you are ready to bake it.

The choux pastry (for halo and puffs). Measure out all ingredients. Preheat oven to 425 degrees. Bring the water slowly to the boil with the butter, salt, and sugar. When butter is melted, remove pan from heat and immediately pour in all the flour; at once beat it in, either by electricity or by hand. When smoothly blended, beat with a wooden spoon over moderate heat for 2 to 3 minutes to evaporate excess liquid: pastry should clean itself off sides and bottom of pan, and begin to film the bottom of the pan. Remove from heat, make a well in center of hot pastry, and beat in 1 of the 6 eggs, beating until egg is absorbed and pastry is smooth (an electric beater works well and quickly here) . Continue with 5 more eggs, one at a time. Pastry should hold its shape when lifted with a spoon: if too soft, you cannot form and bake it properly; on the other hand, it is the eggs that give the puff and you want to add more if possible. Break 1 of the additional eggs into a small bowl and blend with a fork; add dribbles to the pastry, beating vigorously until absorbed. Beat in as much of the additional eggs as you think the pastry will safely take—a bit too little, however, is better than a bit too much.

Forming halo and puffs. Now you are to form a circle of *choux* pastry—I call it a halo—that will sit on top of the disk of pie dough; on that halo, after it has baked, will be a circle of tiny brown puffs, side by side. To guide you in forming the halo, use the same round cutting device you used for the bottom disk of pie dough; dip its edge in flour and set on another pastry sheet to give you a faint guideline, then lift it off. Fill pastry bag with the warm *pâte à choux,* and squeeze a line of pastry the thickness of your thumb around inside edge of circular mark. This is the halo. Squeeze out 20 to 22 tiny puffs 1¼ inches in diameter, spacing them ¾ inch apart inside and outside the halo; add some to baking sheet containing pastry-dough disk if you need more room. (Squeeze remaining pastry back into saucepan; you will have about 1¼ cups, to be turned into a pastry cream while puffs are baking.) Smooth out halo with a rubber spatula dipped in cold water. Paint top of halo with egg glaze; paint tops of puffs, pushing them into a dome with pastry brush as you glaze them.

Baking bottom disk, halo, and puffs. To prevent pie-crust disk from rising, butter the underside of a cake pan, and lay right on top of disk. Bake in upper and lower-middle levels of preheated 425-degree oven. When just beginning to brown lightly, in about 20 minutes, the pie-crust disk is done; remove to a rack. When puffs and halo have risen and browned, in 30 minutes or so, turn oven down to 350 degrees until they feel crisp; turn oven off, leave door closed, and let dry out for 10 minutes, then leave door ajar, and let them dry out 15 minutes more. Cool on a rack.

✿ May be baked ahead; when cool, wrap airtight, then freeze. Defrost at room temperature; puffs may be crisped in a 350-degree oven for 10 to 15 minutes.

Assembling the Saint-Honoré shell. The various pieces are now to be assembled into their whole, and glued together with caramel. Place the pastry disk on a serving plate, and have the halo and puffs at hand, plus 2 forks for dipping and arranging. Make the caramel as follows: Bring the ½ cup of sugar and 3 tablespoons of water to the boil in a small saucepan, swirling pan by handle as boil is reached to be sure sugar dissolves and liquid is perfectly clear and limpid; cover pan and boil rapidly without stirring, until bubbles are thick and large, then uncover pan. Boil over high heat, swirling pan lightly by handle as sugar begins to brown, then remove from heat, swirling pan until bubbling ceases. Immediately spoon a few drops of caramel around edge of pastry disk and affix halo on. top. Then rapidly, one by one, dip bottom of puffs into caramel and arrange side by side in a circle on top of the halo—reheat caramel if necessary. Spoon up syrup and let it dribble from end of spoon, waving it over the puffs to decorate them, until all the syrup is used. The shell is now ready for filling.

☼ May be assembled several hours ahead; if longer, cover airtight and freeze. (Keeps freshest when frozen.)

Note: For the ultimate in *Saint-Honoré* elegance, you may pipe whipped cream or pastry cream into both halo and puffs, using a pastry bag. Then, however, you would have to assemble and serve the dessert at once because the cream would gradually soften the pastry.

Filling the Saint-Honoré. Fill the *Saint-Honoré* shell just before serving, with sweetened whipped cream and fresh fruits such as sliced peaches or strawberries, or with scoops of ice cream or sherbet and fruits. Or follow tradition with a *Crème Saint-Honoré,* described in the next recipe.

Crème Saint-Honoré

CUSTARD FILLING
WITH BEATEN EGG
WHITES, GELATIN,
AND WHIPPED
CREAM

For about 4 cups

Use *Crème Saint-Honoré* as a filling not only for the *Gâteau Saint-Honoré,* but also for baked pie shells, or serve it in a bowl to accompany fresh berries or sliced fresh fruits, or layer it in a serving dish with chunks of sponge cake soaked in rum-flavored sugar syrup and decorated with fresh fruits, glacéed fruits, or chopped nuts and grated chocolate. It is a cream of many uses, in other words.

1½ envelopes (1½ Tb) plain unflavored gelatin
⅓ cup kirsch, orange liqueur, rum, Bourbon,
    or orange juice
1¼ to 1½ cups leftover choux pastry from preceding
    recipe (or 2 cups warm Crème Pâtissière—
    pastry cream—page 504, and omit the sugar,
    milk, and vanilla called for here below)
⅔ cup sugar
¾ cup milk, more or less
2 tsp pure vanilla extract
4 egg whites, a pinch of salt, and ⅛ tsp cream
    of tartar

1½ cups (¾ pint) heavy cream—½ cup is for
whipped-cream decorations
3 Tb confectioners' sugar and 1 tsp pure vanilla
extract for the above decorations

Sprinkle the gelatin over the liqueur, and let dissolve while preparing rest of ingredients. Meanwhile, place the leftover *choux* pastry in a heavy-bottomed enameled or stainless saucepan; beat in the sugar with a wire whip, then dribble in ½ cup of the milk, beating. Heat slowly to the simmer, beating until perfectly smooth. It will be very thick: beat in more milk by droplets until it has thinned out to a very heavy cream; remove from heat. (This is now equivalent to 2 cups of warm pastry cream, and shall be referred to as such.) Beat the dissolved gelatin-liqueur into the warm pastry cream, then the vanilla extract. In a clean separate bowl, beat the egg whites until foaming, beat in the salt and cream of tartar, then beat until egg whites form stiff shining peaks as described on page 636; fold them delicately into the warm pastry cream.

Set the pan of pastry cream over ice—a tray of ice cubes, and water to cover them, in a large bowl. Fold the cream gently for several minutes until it is chilled but not set; remove pan from ice. Pour the heavy cream into a separate bowl, set over the ice, and beat into *Chantilly*—until it makes soft peaks, page 556. Fold two thirds of the *Chantilly* delicately into the chilled pastry cream, and your *Crème Saint-Honoré* is completed.

✵ If you are not to serve immediately, set the *Crème Saint-Honoré* in the refrigerator; turn the remaining *Chantilly* into a sieve lined with washed cheesecloth, set over a bowl, and refrigerate it also. If you are to have sliced peaches or strawberries, prepare them and let macerate with lemon juice and sugar to taste, in the refrigerator.

Filling a Gâteau Saint-Honoré. At serving time, spoon a 1-inch layer of chilled *Crème Saint-Honoré* into the shell, cover with a thin layer of fruits, then with another inch of the cream, and continue until shell is filled, ending with a topping of fruit. (Do not make fruit layers too thick or they may sink through the cream; pass any extra fruit separately.) Turn the reserved whipped cream into a bowl and beat a minute or two more, until quite stiff; sift and fold in the confectioners' sugar, and fold in the vanilla extract. Either place decorative spoonfuls of whipped cream over the dessert or, for a professional effect, pipe it in curlicues from a pastry bag with cannulated tube. Serve at once.

Gâteau in a cage

Here is a glittering dessert that will dazzle your guests—a layer cake filled with *crème Chantilly*, liqueur syrup and fruits, and enclosed in a caramel cage. It is the invention of Chef Jean Deblieux, *maître sucrier* and *pâtissier*, who graciously let us film him at work in his basement atelier on the rue de l'Étoile in Paris.

Le gâteau des Trois Mages; le gâteau Deblieux

DESSERT CAKE
WITH WHIPPED
CREAM AND FRUITS
IN A CARAMEL CAGE

For a 9-inch cake,
serving 8 to 10 people

For the cage (top and bottom)
1 cup sugar
¼ cup corn syrup in a 1-cup measure
⅓ cup hot water

*Equipment for cage making: A heavy saucepan
    with cover, for sugar boiling (about 1½ quart
    size) ; a mold for the cage— a stainless-steel
    bowl about 10 inches top diameter, 6 inches
    deep, and heavily buttered on the outside; a 9-
    by 1½-inch metal cake pan for the bottom cage,
    also heavily buttered on outside (you may wish
    to omit this bottom cage) ; to prevent hot
    caramel from dripping on bare hand—a very
    heavy rubber or leather glove; a large metal
    kitchen spoon for caramel dripping*

The cake
*A round 9- by 1½-inch cake such as the almond cake
    on page 559, the Génoise on page 577, or a
    store-bought sponge cake or yellow cake*
*Liqueur-sugar syrup (¼ cup sugar dissolved in
    ½ cup hot water, and flavored with 1 tsp
    vanilla extract and 3 Tb kirsch or rum)*
*½ cup raspberry or strawberry jelly melted with
    3 Tb water in a small pan*

*2 cups crème Chantilly (½ pint heavy cream lightly
　beaten, sweetened, and flavored; see
　end of recipe)*
*2 to 3 cups fresh strawberries or raspberries, or
　frozen berries thawed and drained, or glacéed
　chestnuts, or Nesselrode (glacéed fruits and
　chestnuts in rum and syrup, in jars
　at fancy food shops)*

Caramel syrup. Pour sugar into pan, and corn syrup into measure. Add hot water to corn syrup, mix to blend, and scrape into sugar pan. Set over highest heat and, swirling pan occasionally by handle but never stirring with a spoon, bring to the boil. Remove from heat for a moment, swirling; look carefully to be sure sugar has completely dissolved, and syrup is perfectly clear and limpid. (If sugar does not dissolve at this point, it will usually crystallize as it comes near the caramel stage later; when it is thoroughly dissolved, you will have no trouble.) Cover the pan and boil 3 to 4 minutes. (Steam, condensing on underside of cover, runs down inner sides of pan and washes off any sugar crystals that might be forming.) When bubbles are large and thick, the caramel stage is almost at hand: stand over syrup every moment from now on, swirling pan gently by handle from time to time, and in a minute or so syrup will begin to turn a golden color. Remove from heat as soon as it is a deep golden yellow, since it will continue cooking and darkening slightly for several seconds.

Immediately begin to lift spoonfuls of syrup and dribble back into the pan off the tip of the spoon; continue until syrup cools enough to form a thick, heavy thread. Then set over very low heat, regulating it so that syrup remains at this heavy-thread consistency. (You may stir it up, from time to time, but do not let it boil again if you can help it, or it will darken; do not use the caramel when it is too hot, or it will burn the butter off your bowl and you will not be able to unmold the cage.)

Caramel cage. Protecting your hand with a glove or a heavy towel, hold the buttered bowl upside down over the caramel pan, and slowly swirl thick threads of caramel off end of spoon over its surface, making an interlocking web of spirals all over outside of bowl using about ½ the caramel. Set bowl upside down on work surface, and let cool 30 seconds, or until caramel has begun to harden but is still faintly warm to the touch. Very gently push the web of caramel toward bottom of bowl from the edges all around, until you feel and see it loosen; carefully turn bowl right side up, and very carefully push it free of its caramel dome.

Cover outside of cake pan in the same manner, making a bottom case for the cake—you may wish to omit this however. The final assemblage of top and bottom will look like this.

Caramel note: This may not work for you the first time, or even the second time. Points to remember are: 1) The caramel must not be too hot—if it bubbles as it hits the metal surface, it burns off the butter. You may be wise in letting the caramel cool, then reheating it, just until it liquefies and falls from the spoon in a very heavy thread—the heavy thread is the indication that the caramel is just right. 2) Be sure your bowl does not curve in at the top—it must slant out enough so that the cage can be unmolded. 3) Any caramel left over from an unsuccessful attempt is not wasted: it is already mixed with butter, so melt it again until malleable, and turn it into taffy, in the age-old pulled-out way.

☼ Store dome and bottom case either in a warming oven at around 80 degrees, or in the turned-off oven, or in the refrigerator or freezer. They will keep for a day or two in oven or refrigerator; although they may become slightly sticky unless covered airtight, they will keep for weeks when frozen.

Assembling the cake in the cage. Trim cake to be sure it will fit into bottom case of caramel. With a long, thin, very sharp knife split the cake horizontally into three layers. Place caramel case on serving platter, and turn top layer of cake upside down into case. Sprinkle with a tablespoon of the liqueur-sugar syrup, and paint with 2 tablespoons of melted jelly. Spread with ⅓ of the *crème Chantilly* and ⅓ of the fruits. Repeat with second layer of cake. Turn final layer of cake upside down (crumb side up) over the filling, sprinkle with syrup, spread with jelly, and *crème Chantilly*. Arrange remaining fruits decoratively over the top, and place the caramel dome over all. Refrigerate for 30 minutes or until serving time.

☼ Cake may be assembled an hour or so in advance.

Serving. Tap dome to break it, then cut cake into pie-shaped pieces giving a little of the caramel to each guest along with the cake. Champagne demi-sec, sparkling Vouvray, a Sauternes, or a Barsac would go very well with this dessert.

Crème Chantilly

½ pint chilled heavy cream
½ cup confectioners' sugar in a sieve
½ tsp pure vanilla extract

LIGHTLY BEATEN
CREAM, À LA
FRANÇAISE

For about 2 cups

Equipment: A 2½- to 3-quart round-bottomed metal bowl; a larger bowl containing 1 tray of ice cubes and water to cover them; a large balloon-shaped wire whip, or a portable electric beater

Pour cream into metal bowl and set over ice cubes. (You will never have trouble whipping cream if you always beat it over ice.) Incorporating as much air as possible, beat the cream using an up-and-down circular motion with a whip, or rotate beater around bowl if it is electric. In 3 to 4 minutes cream will begin to thicken, and if it is to be used as a sauce, it is thick enough when beater leaves light traces on surface; for the foregoing cake, beat a few seconds longer, until cream holds softly in wires of whip, and holds its shape when lifted.

✿When you are whipping the cream in advance, keep over ice if the wait is up to half an hour, and whip a few seconds again before using. For a longer wait, line a sieve with a double thickness of well-washed cheesecloth, set the sieve over a bowl, turn the cream into the sieve, and refrigerate; decant the milky liquid oozed out of the cream, and turn the whipped cream into the empty chilled bowl.

Just before using the whipped cream, sift on the sugar, add the vanilla, and fold them in with a rubber spatula.

Homemade cakes

The two preceding recipes are not cakes in the batter sense of the word, where you start out with flour, eggs, sugar, a cake pan, and a preheated oven. The following recipes are the real cakes, but modern ones. Since the invention of the electric mixer, the whole world of cakery is infinitely simplified, and I would even go so far as to say that if you don't have at least a portable mixer, don't bother with cakes at all. Reading over some old pre-mixer French recipes one wonders how they ever managed in those days: "After you have beaten the butter and sugar with a wooden spoon, beat in the eggs one by one, beating 10 to 15 minutes between each to make a frothy mass." Of course, in that era, even quite modest homes had cooks, and cooks had kitchen maids to help. One can picture that raddled little helper sitting on a stool in a dark corner, her bowl between her knees, her poor little arm beating, beating, beating, a wisp of hair escaping from her mussy white cap; every once in a while cook gives her a contemptuous look and orders her to beat ever faster and more vigorously. Those cakes took grueling hours to make, while a mixer does the same work in a few minutes. There will always be some around who declare it is just not the same with a mixer, but that is the bramblebush syndrome—it must hurt or it can be no good. Let these romantics make their cakes by hand, then, while we go to heights unheard of, by machine. But first, let us speak of those machines.

ELECTRIC MIXERS

The most important consideration when you are using an electric mixer for beating up egg whites or whole eggs and sugar is that the entire mass of material must be kept in continual motion. This means that you must have a round-bottomed bowl, *cul-de-poule* shaped—like the curved bottom of a live chicken. Otherwise, when directed to beat eggs and sugar until they make a thick mayonnaiselike cream, you will never make it in a wide-bottomed bowl no matter how long you beat. Some mixers are designed with the correctly shaped bowl, and a beater that not only rotates but also circulates rapidly about the bowl. Other mixers have a flat-bottomed bowl that beats only a portion of the eggs at a time; if you have one of these (and what non-cooking oaf designed them, one wonders), find a round-bottomed bowl that will fit on the stand, and use that. If you have a portable hand mixer, choose the proper bowl and you will be in business; it will simply take a little longer to beat, and you will have to stand over your work, of course, for the 4 to 5 minutes necessary. Please see the illustrated discussion of mixers on page 636.

CAKE FORMULAE AND TECHNIQUES

Cakes fall into two categories, the separated egg type known as the *biscuit* or sponge cake, and the whole egg type known as the *Génoise*. The separated egg type of cake is somewhat the same technique you use for a soufflé: you make a batter of egg yolks and sugar, and you fold stiffly beaten egg whites and flour into it. It puffs like a soufflé in the oven, but the puff remains because you have just enough flour in the mixture for it to cook firm and stay up.

The whole egg *Génoise* type of cake, on the other hand, formerly was the province only of accomplished cooks or professionals because of the enormous amount of beating required to make the whole eggs hold in a creamy thick mass; with the electric beater, however, that problem is solved. The only exception to the long-beaten *Génoise* type of whole egg cake has been the domestic pound cake, the *Quatre Quarts Ménagère,* suggested in many French cookbooks for the average French housewife, *la ménagère.* She is directed to beat the sugar and butter into a *pommade* (a creamy fluffy consistency), then she is simply to stir in her eggs and flour plus a bit of baking powder to puff things up, and with no more ado she turns it into her pan and bakes it. A very simple recipe it is, and the resulting cake is about what one might expect—and deserve—for so little effort.

However, set out these very same *Quatre Quarts Ménagère* ingredients and proportions minus the baking powder (which will not be needed), put the machine to them, and you'll be surprised at the difference. Beat the butter and sugar into a *pommade* with your electric mixer, then add the eggs one by one, whipping each fast for 2 to 3 minutes before breaking in the next, and you fold in the flour. Just because of that vigorous beating of the eggs you improve the texture and quality of your batter, and you get a very good cake, a bit heavy to be sure, but that is pound cake.

Now take a further step, again with these identical ingredients and proportions, and turn them around. Beat the eggs and sugar (rather than butter and sugar) into a thick mayonnaiselike cream, beat the butter separately, to the same mayonnaiselike consistency, and combine the two; fold in the flour, and you find that with those exact same materials combined in another way you have to use a 9-inch pan rather than an 8-inch pan. You end up, in other words, with a much lighter and bigger cake. Thus, once you have made a cake or two and the fear has gone out of you, do feel free to experiment. You know what the idea is all about, and if a particular type of recipe doesn't turn out the way you want but the conception is worthy, try out improvements on your own. Some will succeed while others fail, but they will be edible, usually, and it is just as important to know what won't work as what will.

Pain de Gênes

Here is an easy example of the whole egg cake made in an electric mixer—or with a portable hand-held electric beater. (Another and more classic example is the modern, not *ménagère, Quatre Quarts* pound cake in Volume II of *Mastering.*) Most traditional recipes for the following almond cake start out with the butter-sugar *pommade* described in the previous section; then beat in the eggs, and fold in the flour and almonds; this gives enough batter for a 4-cup 8-inch round cake pan. Here, however, beating the sugar and eggs first and then combining them with a butter *pommade,* you get 2 cups more batter, enough for a 9-inch cake pan. Why one would want a smaller and heavier cake when one can have a lighter and bigger cake with the same ingredients I have no idea. Habit and tradition, perhaps, plus lack of thinking in terms of what electrical machinery can do for a cake.

For a 9- by 1½-inch, 6-cup cake pan

3 *"large" eggs*
¾ *cup sugar*
2 *tsp pure vanilla extract*
¼ *tsp almond extract*
1 *stick (4 ounces) unsalted butter*
⅓ *cup all-purpose flour (measure by scooping dry-measure cup into flour and sweeping off excess)*
4 *ounces (¾ cup lightly pressed down) ground blanched almonds (you can do them ¼ cup at a time in the electric blender)*

Equipment: Either a table model or a portable electric mixer and a round-bottomed mixing bowl (page 636) ; a flour sifter set over wax paper; a rubber spatula; a cake rack

Preheat oven to 350 degrees and set rack in middle or lower-middle level. Butter inside of cake pan, line bottom with a round of wax paper, butter that, and roll flour around in pan to cover inside completely; knock out excess. Turn the ⅓ cup of flour into the sifter, and have the almonds ready.

The eggs and sugar. Break eggs into the mixing bowl and, if chilled, set in hot water and stir about for a minute or so to take off the chill—very important, since if eggs are cold they will congeal the butter, which is to go in later. Gradually beat in the sugar, then the vanilla and the almond extract; now beat at high speed for 5 minutes or more, until mixture is thick, like a heavy mayonnaise.

The butter. Meanwhile, cut the butter into a metal mixing bowl and beat briefly over hot water to soften it, then beat over cold water until creamy and the consistency of heavy mayonnaise—exactly the same consistency as the egg-sugar mixture.

Finishing the batter. Remove egg mixture from beater stand. Stir 2 to 3 spoonfuls of it into the creamed butter and set aside. With a rubber spatula, rapidly and delicately fold into the egg-sugar mixture alternate quarter cupfuls of almonds and sprinklings of flour. When almost absorbed, fold in the butter by scoopfuls. (See page 639 for directions on folding.)

Into the cake pan. Immediately, rapidly, and delicately, with your rubber spatula, turn the batter into the prepared pan. Bang pan once lightly on table to settle the batter.

Baking. Immediately set the cake in the middle level of the preheated 350-degree oven, and bake about 30 minutes. Cake is done when the top feels spongy to your finger, and when the faintest hairline of shrinkage shows between cake and pan. Remove pan to a rack and let cool 10 minutes. Then run a knife around inside edge of pan, and unmold cake onto rack. Let cool.

Serving. Serve as is, top sprinkled with confectioners' sugar if you wish. It goes well with tea or with fruits. Or you may split the cake and use the brandy-butter filling suggested for the walnut cake (next recipe), for instance, plus a *glace royale* topping and sidewalls of toasted almonds.

Le Brantôme

WALNUT LAYER
CAKE WITH BRANDY-
BUTTER FILLING
AND GLACE ROYALE
FROSTING

Rather than a pound cake, a sponge cake, an angel or a lady cake, a Genoa or an almond cake, a chocolate or a spice or a caramel cake—when you know they're coming, bake them a walnut cake, with a whipped cream batter, a brandy filling, chopped nut sidewalls, and a white-frosted top covered with sweet words of love. (I couldn't resist that little teaser we used when I did the *Brantôme* on one of our TV programs; it is a delicious light cake that does really taste of walnuts. And it's a different technique for using the whole eggs and sugar beaten thick: after incorporating the flour, you fold in whipped cream rather than a butter *pommade*.)

For two 9-inch cakes layered together, serving 10 to 14

3 "large" eggs
1½ cups sugar
⅛ tsp salt
2 tsp pure vanilla extract
1 cup (4 ounces) walnut meats, pulverized in the electric blender
1½ cups all-purpose flour (measure by scooping dry-measure cups into flour and sweeping off excess)
2 tsp double-action baking powder
1½ cups chilled heavy cream

Equipment: An electric mixer and a round-bottomed mixing bowl (page 636) for beating the eggs; 2 6-cup cake pans (such as round, 9 by 1½ inches), buttered, bottoms lined with buttered paper, and floured lightly; a flour sifter or sieve set on a 12-inch square of wax paper; a 2½-quart metal bowl for cream beating, and a larger bowl with a tray of ice cubes and water to cover them; a portable electric mixer or large balloon-shaped wire whip for cream, also

Preheat oven to 350 degrees.

(*Organization note.* I am assuming you have a mixer on a stand, so that you can start the eggs and sugar, and prepare the ingredients called for in paragraph 3 while the eggs are beating. If you've a portable mixer, however, begin first with the items called for in paragraph 3: then beat up the eggs, and follow on with the rest of the recipe.)

Break the eggs into the mixing bowl; gradually beat in the sugar using moderate speed, then continue beating at high speed for 5 minutes or more, until mixture is thick and the consistency of whipped cream. Beat in the salt and vanilla.

While eggs are beating prepare the cake pans; grind the walnuts; measure out the flour and baking powder and place it in the flour sifter. Then whip the cream into *Chantilly,* meaning it should double in volume and hold its shape softly when a bit is lifted and dropped back onto the surface.

When eggs are thick and creamy, sift a quarter of the flour on top, and fold it in with a rubber spatula—plunge spatula like a knife down into center of mixture, draw it to the side of the bowl and up to the surface in a rapid scoop, bringing some of the eggs up over the flour; rotate bowl slightly, and continue rapidly and gently for several scoops until flour is almost incorporated. Sift on and fold in another quarter of the remaining flour. Then scoop the whipped cream on top of the mixture, sift on more flour and a sprinkling of nuts, and continue folding, alternating with sprinkles of flour and nuts until all are incorporated.

Turn the mixture into the two pans, dividing it as evenly as possible. They will be about three quarters full. With spatula, spread batter evenly in the pans. Place at once in middle level of preheated 350-degree oven, spacing pans diagonally from each other at far and near corners of rack. (Or use 2 racks, and switch pans from one to the other halfway through baking.) Bake about 25 minutes—cakes will rise to top of pans, then sink lightly and brown; they are done when they show the faintest hairline of shrinkage from sides of pan. Let cool 10 minutes, then unmold on racks.

When cold, you may ice them, or you may wrap airtight and refrigerate or freeze them.

FILLING AND FROSTING SUGGESTIONS

Brandy-butter filling
1 egg in a small saucepan
3 Tb Cognac or Armagnac
2 Tb butter
½ Tb cornstarch
1 cup sugar
2 to 4 more Tb butter, unsalted

About 1½ cups warm apricot glaze (1½ cups
apricot jam, sieved, and boiled with 3 Tb sugar
to the thread stage, 228 degrees)
About 1½ cups chopped walnuts

Glace royale frosting
1 egg white in a small mixing bowl
¼ tsp lemon juice
2 cups or more, confectioners' sugar sifted
1 tsp or so Cognac or vanilla extract
Optional: Melted bitter chocolate or food coloring

For the brandy-butter filling. Beat the egg, brandy, 2 tablespoons butter, cornstarch, and sugar together over moderate heat and let boil, stirring, for 2 to 3 minutes, to cook the starch. Remove from heat, and beat in 2 to 4 additional spoonfuls of butter. The filling will thicken more as it cools.

Spread as much of the filling as you wish on top of one of the walnut cakes, and set it upon a circular cake rack over a tray. Turn the other cake upside down upon it. Using a pastry brush, paint top and sides of cake with the warm apricot glaze (for flavor, and also to keep crumbs down on top and provide sticky sides for the nuts). Immediately, before the glaze has set, brush chopped walnuts around the walls of the cake. Transfer cake to a serving dish.

For the glace royale. (This is easiest to make in a small bowl with a portable electric mixer.) Start beating the egg white, lemon juice, and a cup of confectioners' sugar, beating in more until you have a thick white paste. Beat in a teaspoon of flavoring, then continue beating several minutes until frosting is thick, smooth, and stands in peaks—you may need to beat in a little more sugar if frosting does not thicken enough, but do not do so until you have worked the mixture several minutes, and given the egg white and lemon time to do their job of stiffening.

☼ If you are not using it immediately, or will have leftovers, scoop into a jar, lay 4 thicknesses of damp paper towels on top, and cover airtight.

Frosting the cake. Spread a thin layer of frosting over the glaze on top of the cake. If you wish to make decorations or write messages, mix a little melted chocolate into about an equal amount of frosting, or use drops of food coloring, and squeeze the colored frosting through a paper decorating cone, page 572—and see also the chocolate decorations suggested in that same section.

✪ Decorated cake will keep nicely for several days under refrigeration, covered with an upside-down bowl.

Gâteau au chocolat; l'Éminence Brune

BITTERSWEET
CHOCOLATE CAKE

This is a very special chocolate cake—very chocolaty, brown, bittersweet, and buttery, yet very light and delicate in texture. It really needs no icing at all, but is nevertheless filled and covered with a glittering chocolate-butter glaze. Like most French chocolate cakes it is moist, and, even by other standards, slightly underdone. As for technique, rather than being a whole-egg batter, this is the separated egg method where you beat the yolks and sugar, add the melted chocolate, and fold in stiffly beaten egg whites. To keep the cake light, sifted cornstarch rather than flour goes in. You can make a chocolate cake with no starch at all, by the way, but to my mind you produce more of a pudding than a cake.

The chocolate

For an 8-inch cake
serving 8 or more

2 tsp instant espresso coffee
¼ cup boiling water
7 ounces semisweet baking chocolate
2 ounces unsweetened (bitter) chocolate

The cake pans

Two 8- by 1½-inch round one-piece cake pans
  (4-cup capacity)
2 tsp soft butter
2 rounds of wax paper cut to fit bottom of pans
¼ cup flour

The batter

4 "large" eggs (if chilled, set in tepid water
  for 5 minutes)
⅔ cup sugar (extra-fine granulated if possible)
4 ounces (1 stick) soft unsalted butter
¼ tsp cream of tartar and a pinch of salt
2 Tb additional sugar

*¾ cup cornstarch (to measure, sift directly into
dry-measure cups and sweep off excess)*

For the chocolate and butter glaze
1 tsp instant expresso coffee
2 Tb boiling water
4 ounces semisweet chocolate
1 ounce unsweetened chocolate
2 ounces (½ stick) unsalted butter

*Equipment: For melting chocolate, a covered 6-cup
saucepan and a second pan of simmering water
that will hold the first; a clean dry beating bowl
for the egg whites, and 3- to 4-quart mixing
bowl for the yolks; a portable electric beater
with, if possible, 2 sets of blades; a sifter set over
wax paper; a cake tester or wooden toothpick*

Preheat oven to 350 degrees, and set rack in lower-middle level.

The chocolate. Blend the coffee and water in the pan, set in larger pan of simmering water, and remove from heat. Break up the chocolate, stir it into the coffee, cover, and set aside to melt slowly until you are ready to use it.

The cake pans. Smear butter inside both cake pans, covering them completely. Place wax paper in bottom of each, butter it, then roll flour around in first pan to coat inside completely. Knock flour out into second pan, coat it, and knock out excess flour.

The batter. Separate the eggs, dropping the whites into the beating bowl, and the yolks into the mixing bowl. Start beating the egg yolks, gradually adding the sugar, and continue beating until yolks are thick, pale yellow, and, when a bit is lifted in blades of beater, it drops off in a thick ribbon that slowly dissolves on the surface of the mixture—about 3 minutes of beating.

Finishing the chocolate. Chocolate should now be soft. If not, remove pan and reheat water; remove from heat, set chocolate pan in again, and beat the chocolate with the portable mixer until perfectly smooth. Beat in the butter, 2 tablespoons at a time, then gradually beat the chocolate and butter into the egg-yolk mixture.

The egg whites. Immediately change beater blades (or rapidly and thoroughly wash and dry dirty blades), and proceed to the egg whites. Start beating at moderately low speed for a minute or so, until foaming, and beat in cream of tartar and salt. Gradually increase speed to fast, and continue beating until egg whites hold their shape in soft peaks; gradually beat in the 2 tablespoons extra sugar, and continue beating until egg whites form stiff shining peaks; they are now ready to be folded into cake batter. (Time: 3 to 4 minutes—circulate beater constantly around bowl for fastest action.)

Folding. Being sure chocolate and egg-yolk mixture is smooth and soft—stir over hot water if it has stiffened— sift on one quarter of the cornstarch, and scoop in one quarter of the egg whites; stir in with rubber spatula. Then scoop rest of egg whites on top, sift on one third of the remaining cornstarch, and begin to fold as follows:

Plunge rubber spatula down from top center of egg whites to bottom of bowl, bring to edge of bowl, then turn it as you lift it back up to the surface, thus bringing a bit of the chocolate up over the egg whites. Rapidly repeat the movement several times, rotating the bowl as you do so. Sift on half the rest of the cornstarch, continue with several rapid scoops of the spatula, then sift on the last of the cornstarch, and continue folding until blended. The whole process should not take much more than a minute, and your object is to deflate the egg whites as little as possible.

Into the cake pans. At once turn the batter into the two prepared cake pans, running it up the edge all around with your spatula to prevent cakes from humping in the middle as they bake. Pans will be about half full. Bang once on work surface to settle the batter, and place in preheated oven, one near rear corner of rack, and the other diagonally across near front corner.

Baking. Set timer for 15 minutes. Cakes will rise to about top of pans, and are done when only the center shakes a little when moved gently. A cake tester should come out almost clean when inserted around the edges, but have a number of wet brown specks attached to it when plunged into the center 2 inches.

Cooling and unmolding. Set pans on racks, for air circulation, and let cool. Cakes will sink slightly, and will shrink from sides of pan. Because cake texture is very soft and delicate, you will find them easiest to unmold when chilled and firm; thus, when cool, wrap and refrigerate for an hour or so.

Filling, icing, and serving. Melt the chocolate with the coffee as described on page 565, then beat in the butter. If too liquid for easy spreading, beat over cold water until lightly thickened. Unmold one of the cakes directly onto serving plate, and stick pieces of wax paper underneath all around to catch icing dribbles. Spread top with a ⅛-inch layer of icing. With the help of a flexible-blade spatula, unmold second cake on top of first. Cover top and sides with icing. Peel out the wax paper strips from under cake. If you are serving soon, leave at room temperature. Otherwise cover with an upside-down bowl and refrigerate (or freeze), and let come to room temperature for an hour or so before serving, to let the chocolate icing regain its bloom and the cake its texture.

------◆------

Working with chocolate

Chocolate leaves, flowers, silhouettes, sheets of chocolate, and chocolate cigarettes are much simpler to do than most of us would think. All you need is properly melted chocolate and a smooth surface to work on. You are then ready to produce *petits fours* with chic brown walls, desserts covered with curls, and cakes bearing fancy decorations and sweet messages, all in chocolate. Here, following a few words on the nature of chocolate, are directions for melting it, three of the basic decorating techniques, and the perfect background for your fantasies in chocolate—French butter-cream frosting and filling.

TYPES OF CHOCOLATE

Every manufacturer has his own secret formula for chocolate: how much pure chocolate, cocoa butter, sugar, flavorings, and other ingredients are combined together, how long it is processed, at what temperature, and so forth. Here is a roster of the types of chocolate one can buy, from information provided me by various kindly manufacturers, particularly the Nestlé Company, and the Hershey Chocolate Company.

Unsweetened baking chocolate, sometimes called bitter chocolate, is pure chocolate, as we buy it packaged in our markets. To make it, the cacao bean is pressed and rolled until its natural cocoa butter liquefies, and the nibs, as the roasted and shelled beans are called, can be molded into a cake. Technically, this is then called chocolate liquor; it has a cocoa butter content of 54 to 55 percent. All the other chocolate types, as well as cocoa, are made from it; the cake is pressed to remove as much of the cocoa butter as the manufacturer desires. For cocoa powder, the pressed cake is then simply pulverized. For semisweet baking chocolate and candy bar chocolate, it is combined with sugar, vanilla or other flavorings, or special ingredients, ground to a smooth paste between rollers, and finally "conched," meaning heated in tubs with great rollers plowing back and forth to smooth and refine the chocolate before it is tempered, molded, cooled, and packaged.

Semisweet baking chocolate is unsweetened chocolate liquor blended with sugar and cocoa butter; most manufacturers stay with a pure chocolate ratio of 35 to 38 percent, and a cocoa butter content of 28 to 32 percent.

Brand-name semisweet or sweet chocolate, such as *Baker's German's Sweet Chocolate* (General Foods), *Eagle Sweet Chocolate* (Ghirardelli and Maillard), *Pennsylvania Dutch Sweet Chocolate* (Hershey), *Godiva* (Pepperidge Farm). These are all special and secret formulae, probably more refined and smoother than plain semisweet chocolate. They average 32 percent cocoa butter and 35 percent pure chocolate. I find them all interchangeable, but if a recipe calls for one of them and I have only plain semisweet, I use 1 ounce of unsweetened chocolate for every 4 of semisweet.

Chocolate bits or morsels have more viscosity than regular chocolate, meaning they are supposed to keep their shape when baked in cookies, etc. They average 29 percent cocoa butter and 29 percent pure chocolate, and can be used like semisweet chocolate in general cooking and baking.

Couverture chocolate is of extra-fine quality for professional candy and pastry work, and there are many formulae, depending on the use for which it is destined, such as for dipping candies, glazing cakes, and so forth. The average cocoa butter content is 34 percent, but may vary between 31 and 40 percent. The pure chocolate content varies between 38 and 80 percent, but 40 is the average.

French chocolate. The best type for baking and general cooking is *chocolat à croquer,* or eating chocolate. It averages 30 percent cocoa butter and 50 percent pure chocolate. To make an equivalent, use 1 ounce of unsweetened chocolate for every 3 to 4 ounces of regular semi-sweet or brand-name sweet chocolate.

Swiss or European bitter chocolate is a term I've occasionally run into in recipes, and I don't really know what is meant by it. I simply use my formula of 1 ounce of unsweetened chocolate for every 3 of semisweet baking chocolate. (I don't think these special chocolate requirements are as important as "they" would have us believe!)

SUBSTITUTIONS: WHEN YOUR RECIPE CALLS FOR ONE KIND OF CHOCOLATE AND YOU HAVE ANOTHER

When you want unsweetened baking chocolate and you have cocoa:
> For each ounce of chocolate required, blend 3 level tablespoons unsweetened cocoa powder with 1 tablespoon unsalted butter, shortening, or cocoa butter (buy it at a pharmacy).

When you want semisweet baking chocolate and you have cocoa:
> Proceed as above, but add 3 tablespoons sugar.

When you want semisweet chocolate and have only unsweetened chocolate:
> To make 6 ounces of semisweet chocolate, use 2 ounces unsweetened chocolate, 7 tablespoons sugar, and 2 tablespoons unsalted butter, shortening, or cocoa butter.

When your recipe calls for a name-brand "sweet chocolate," like German's, Dutch, Eagle, or a French brand:
> Use regular semisweet baking chocolate, either just as it is, or enrich it with a little unsweetened chocolate—1 ounce of unsweetened chocolate for every 3 to 4 ounces of semisweet.

How to melt chocolate for decorations

Chocolate for use in general cooking and baking is usually, in this book anyway, melted with several tablespoons of coffee, rum, or liqueur, to give it added flavor. Chocolate for decorations, however, is melted as is, and it should reach a temperature of only 110 degrees, since it burns easily, and when it burns it darkens and stiffens. Also, at 110 degrees, all the elements that it contains—its sugar, cocoa butter, and so forth—are liquefied to blend into a perfectly smooth, thick, glistening cream; then you let it slowly cool until the pan is almost cold, but the chocolate is still liquid, and it is ready to use. Here are directions for the chocolate to use, and 3 ways of melting it.

The chocolate. Use either semisweet baking chocolate, or unsweetened chocolate, or the combination I particularly like: 1 ounce of unsweetened chocolate for every 4 ounces of semisweet chocolate. Then proceed in one of the following ways.

The hot water method is always sure and is easy to control. Break the chocolate up into a saucepan. Place another and larger pan filled with an inch or two of water over heat and bring to the boil; remove from heat, and set the chocolate pan in it. Cover the pan and let the chocolate melt and soften for 5 minutes or so, then stir it up until it is smooth and glistening—you may have to heat the water in the warming pan briefly if the chocolate has not melted sufficiently.

The warming oven takes longer but is highly efficient. Break the chocolate up into a saucepan and set in an oven that you can regulate so it does not go over 110 degrees, and leave the pan for an hour or so, until the chocolate has melted. This is the *étuve* method used by professionals, and they always have several pans of melted chocolate ever at hand. When they have finished using the chocolate, back it goes into the oven, with more chocolate added to the pan as needed.

The microwave oven needs watching. It is surprisingly successful, but I don't find the chocolate always melting as smoothly as in the preceding two methods, probably because you don't have quite as much control; in addition, you must watch that you don't overcook. For a 4- to 6-ounce bar, fold back the paper leaving a layer on bottom and sides, but the top of the chocolate may be uncovered; microwave 3 minutes, leave 1 minute, then work the chocolate about with a spatula to smooth it. If not quite melted, microwave half a minute more. For 4 to 6 separately wrapped ounces, place closely together paper-opening-side up, microwave 3 minutes, leave 1 minute. The microwave is also useful for remelting scraps left over from the following decorations: place them in a Pyrex dish and microwave a minute or so uncovered, watching you do not overcook. Leave 1 minute, then stir up until perfectly smooth.

Sheets of chocolate for decorations

For these, melted chocolate is spread thinly over sheets of wax paper, then either cut into shapes or left as is to be broken later into rough squares or triangles. Use the decorations on the tops or around the sides of frosted cakes or *petits fours.*

For 3 or 4 sheets of chocolate, each about 12 inches square

5 ounces of perfectly melted chocolate, as described in the preceding recipe

Equipment: 4 sheets of wax paper 14 inches long, or heavy flexible plastic or acetate (available in art supply stores, and reusable) ; baking sheets, trays, or racks large enough to hold the sheets of paper; a flexible-blade spatula for spreading, and a table knife and ruler or cookie cutouts if you want special designs

Let the melted chocolate cool slowly, stirring frequently, until pan feels almost cold to your hand but the chocolate is still liquid and glistening. With a spatula spread the chocolate as evenly as you can over the paper, making a layer less than ⅛ inch thick.

Free-form shapes. If you are to make rough broken squares or triangles, let the chocolate cool until set, either at room temperature or in the refrigerator. When it is time to decorate your cake or *petits fours,* bend the paper backward to release it from the chocolate, and break off pieces of chocolate (usually 2-inch squares) ; insert them edgewise into the soft frosting of your cake, starting at the center and spiraling successive pieces outward to give a raised flower-petal effect. This free-form type of decoration can be very effective, and there are no rules except your own ingenuity. You may wish to finish the decoration by sprinkling a little confectioners' sugar through a fine-meshed sieve over the chocolate leaves.

Cutouts. When you want cutouts, such as squares or diamonds, or rectangles to form chocolate sidings for *petits fours,* or shapes made with a cookie cutter, spread the chocolate on the paper as described in the preceding paragraph, but let it cool only until it has barely begun to set— until the surface clouds over. For squares, diamonds, or rectangles, cut down through the chocolate with the dull edge of a table knife, using a ruler to guide you; or press into the chocolate with a cookie cutter. When the chocolate has set and hardened, remove the squares, diamonds, or rectangles by bending the paper back to release them; for cookie-cutter shapes, carefully break off chocolate from around the design, and lift the designs off the paper.

Storing chocolate designs. Place in a covered can or pan between sheets of wax paper and keep in a cool place, or under refrigeration. Store all scraps and melt again when you need more chocolate.

Chocolate silhouettes and lettering. When you want to place figures or lettering on a cake frosting or around its sides, or want figures that you can stand up on the cake, you can squeeze melted chocolate out onto paper or plastic sheets through a paper decorating cone (see next paragraph), but make paper cutouts or line drawings first, to lay under your paper or plastic and guide your movements. Then melt and cool the chocolate as directed in the preceding recipe, pour it into the cone, and squeeze out your designs, making them almost ¼ inch thick if you are to stand them upright. Let them cool and set, then peel the paper off the back of the chocolate.

To make a paper decorating cone. Cut heavy freezer or bond paper into a right-angle triangle with short sides about 15 and 12 inches. Grab the triangle by its hypotenuse with your left hand, thumb on top and opposite the right angle; this part of the hypotenuse is to become the point of the cone. Curl the 2 ends of the hypotenuse around your thumb to meet at the right angle opposite, and you have formed the cone shape; secure ends with a straight pin, and cut the point of the cone to make any size opening you need.

Chocolate cigarettes, chocolate curls, chocolate tubes. When you spread a layer of melted chocolate out on a smooth surface, let it set, and do some fancy knife work on it, it will curl itself up into cigarette shapes, and you can press these into the soft frosting on the top or around the sides of cakes and *petits fours.* They take a certain dexterity to achieve and, if you are like me, will muss up a bit of chocolate before you master the movement; then all goes beautifully until the next time, several months later, and you have forgotten those clever feelings you had developed. Here you will need a smooth working surface such as marble, glass, or plastic, a flexible-blade spatula with metal surface about 7 inches long, and a flexible-blade straight-edged knife with a cutting edge 7 to 8 inches long.

Melt and cool the chocolate as described on page 569, and when pan is almost cold to your hand, but chocolate is still liquid and glistening, spread a band of it 16 to 18 inches long out in front of you; make it 3 inches wide—or slightly wider or narrower, according to your decorative intentions. It should be less than ⅛ inch thick. Rapidly spread it several times back and forth with your spatula, scraping it off the surface, and smoothing it back on, until it begins to set. Then leave it for a minute or so, until the surface clouds over and it has almost but not solidly congealed.

Now you are ready to curl the chocolate. Start an inch from the near end of the band of chocolate, and holding the knife in both hands, its blade almost parallel to your work surface, turn it at an angle—at a diagonal to the length of the band. Push the knife blade several inches straight out in front of you, and the chocolate should curl up as it leaves the surface.

Continue down the band, making curls as you go, and when you have finished, lay down another band of chocolate and repeat the process. (Don't be discouraged if at first you don't succeed; keep curling, and remember that diagonal angle of the knife, which is the secret.)

Store the cigarettes in layers separated by wax paper, in a container placed in a cool place or under refrigeration. Broken curls and slivers can also make attractive decorations, strewn over the surface of a soft frosting; or remelt them.

Crème au beurre classique, au sucre cuit

CLASSIC FRENCH
BUTTER-CREAM
FROSTING AND
FILLING

This is the traditional French butter cream, made with egg yolks and 1 whole egg, onto which hot sugar syrup is poured; it is then beaten over hot water until thick and foamy, and beaten again until cool and even thicker before butter and flavoring go in. It is utterly delicious. Flavor it with liqueurs or rum or chocolate, and you can freeze any leftovers. Use it as a frosting or a filling for cakes and *petits fours,* or sandwich it between cookies. I have suggested here that you use the electric blender, as well as an electric mixer, although you can do all by hand, as indicated. (Note also the alternate butter cream with Italian meringue, used for the *Bûche de Noël* on page 580.)

For about 2 cups,
enough to fill and frost
a 9-inch cake

⅔ cup sugar and 3 Tb water in a small
saucepan, with cover
1 egg and 3 yolks in the jar of an electric blender
(or in a stainless saucepan)
2 sticks soft unsalted butter
1 tsp pure vanilla extract
2 to 4 ounces melted chocolate (see
directions on page 569)

Equipment: A wire whip, an electric mixer,
and, if you have it, an electric blender

Shaking pan gently by handle, bring sugar and water to boil over high heat; when liquid is perfectly clear, cover for a minute, until bubbles have begun to thicken. Uncover, and boil to the soft-ball stage, 238 degrees. Immediately turn on blender, and slowly dribble the hot syrup onto the whizzing egg yolks, then pour mixture back into sugar-boiling pan (or beat the egg yolks in a separate saucepan, dribbling the hot syrup onto them).

Set over barely simmering water, and beat slowly with wire whip until mixture is too hot for your finger, and has thickened enough to form a fat ribbon when lifted and dribbled off wires of whip. Remove from heat, and beat in an electric mixer (or by hand over cold water) until cool. Beat in the butter by 2-tablespoon bits, and finally the vanilla, and as much of the chocolate as you wish. Beat over ice, until of easy spreading consistency. Use for both fillings and frostings.

✦ Will keep several days under refrigeration, or may be frozen. To reconstitute frozen butter cream, thaw it, then beat in several tablespoons of soft butter to bring back its original consistency.

Other flavors for butter cream. For vanilla flavoring, add 1 tablespoon rather than 1 teaspoon of pure vanilla. For rum flavoring, or kirsch or orange liqueur, beat in 2 to 3 tablespoons after the butter has gone in, and if the butter cream begins to separate, beat in several more tablespoons of butter to smooth it out. For coffee flavoring, dissolve a tablespoon or so of instant espresso in a tablespoon or two of hot water, let cool, and beat in as for the liqueur.

The Génoise jelly roll, a bûche, and a bouffe

Five good reasons for making the *Génoise* type of cake batter are: one, the cake itself, since it is the perfect all-purpose type for icing and filling, for layering with fruits and whipped cream, or to use as a wedding cake. And two, three, four, and five, that the same formula will produce *petits fours,* cupcakes, *Madeleines,* and the sponge sheet that makes jelly rolls and Yule logs. As you will see, the *Génoise* is almost like a *Quatre Quarts* pound cake and the preceding almond cake on page 559; the *Génoise* simply has more eggs, and produces a lighter and drier cake. This particular recipe is also a *Génoise* with a difference because it is made with browned butter rather than plain melted or creamed butter, which gives it a special taste and texture.

Pâte à génoise

GÉNOISE CAKE
BATTER, FOR
MAKING CAKES,
PETITS FOURS, CUP-
CAKES, MADELEINES,
AND SPONGE SHEETS

For about 6 cups of
batter, which will
produce any of the
following: 1 cake in
an 8-cup pan, such
as a square one 9 by
1½ inches; 2 round
cakes 8 by 1½ inches;
16 cupcakes baked

4 *"large" eggs*
⅔ *cup sugar*
2 *tsp pure vanilla extract*
The grated rind of 1 lemon
1¼ *sticks (5 ounces) unsalted butter*
1 *Tb flour (for preparing pans)*
⅔ *cup all-purpose flour (measure by scooping
 dry-measure cups into flour and sweeping
 off excess)*
⅓ *cup plain bleached cake flour*

*Equipment: An electric beater (preferably one
 on a stand, but a portable will do) , and a
 round-bottomed beating bowl (page 636) ;
 cake pans, or whatever the batter is to be
 baked in; a small bowl and pastry brush for
 preparing pans; a flour sifter set on wax
 paper; rubber spatulas*

(continued)
in ½-cup containers
or muffin tins; 4
dozen Madeleines 3
inches long; a sponge
sheet in a 12- by 16-
inch pan; a sponge
sheet thinner than the
preceding one, and a
dozen Madeleines

Preliminaries. Preheat oven to whatever degree called for in your directions (see following recipes), place rack in lower-middle level, and collect all ingredients. If you do not have a mixer on a stand, brown the butter and prepare the pans now; otherwise do it while the eggs are beating.

Beating the eggs and sugar. Break the eggs into the mixing bowl and, if chilled, stir them over hot water to take off the chill. Beating at slow speed, gradually sprinkle in the sugar, then add the vanilla and lemon rind and beat at high speed 5 minutes or longer, until eggs have doubled in volume, and are the consistency of a heavy mayonnaise.

Browning the butter and preparing the baking pans. Meanwhile, cut the butter into ½-inch bits and melt slowly in a small saucepan over moderate heat. When butter foams up, swirl pan and continue cooking it until very lightly browned. Remove from heat and dip out 2 tablespoons into a small bowl, and mix with the tablespoon of flour; use this to grease the cake pans, jelly roll pan, or cookie cups as described in each recipe. Stir rest of browned butter over cold water, until tepid but still liquid. Scoop the ⅔ cup flour and the ⅓ cup cake flour together into the flour sifter.

Completing the batter. When egg-sugar mixture is ready, remove bowl from stand. If eggs still feel cold, beat with a wire whip over hot water for a minute or two until tepid: cold eggs will congeal melted butter. The butter, in turn, must also be tepid, but liquid, since hot butter will sink down in the batter rather than remaining in suspension throughout it; beat over cold water if necessary. Now sift one third of the flour over the egg-sugar mixture and rapidly fold it in with a rubber spatula; when almost absorbed, begin alternating with driblets of butter and siftings of flour, folding rapidly and continuously until all of both are used. (Directions for folding are on page 639.)

At once proceed to one of the following recipes.

Génoise fine

GÉNOISE CAKE,
FOR LAYER CAKES
AND PETITS FOURS

Have oven preheated to 350 degrees. If you want a square cake or one to cut into *petits fours*, use an 8-cup pan, such as a 9 by 9 by 1½-inch square; or you may wish to use two 4-cup pans, round ones, 8 by 1½ inches. Paint interior of pan with the browned butter and flour mixture, line bottom with wax paper, and paint that also. When batter is ready, immediately turn it into the pan or pans, and, if more than three quarters full, surround with a collar of buttered foil that rises an inch over the rim. Bake immediately in middle or lower-middle level of oven for 25 to 30 minutes, until puffed and browned, and cake shows a faint hairline of shrinkage from pan. Remove pan to a rack to cool 10 minutes, then run a knife around cake at edge of pan, and unmold onto a rack. Let cool. If not to be filled shortly, wrap airtight and refrigerate, or freeze.

Gâteau roulé

SPONGE SHEET
FOR JELLY ROLLS,
BÛCHES, LAYER
CAKES, AND PETITS
FOURS

Preheat oven to 375 degrees, set rack in lower-middle level, and choose either a jelly roll pan about 12 by 16 inches, or a large baking sheet. Spread a sheet of wax paper in pan or on baking sheet, letting it hang 2 inches over each of the two ends (for easy unmolding, later). Paint the wax paper with the browned butter and flour mixture, and also the long sides of the jelly roll pan, if you are using one. Provide yourself with ½ cup or so of confectioners' sugar in a small fine-meshed sieve.

When batter is ready, spread it evenly in the pan (or on the sheet), and set immediately in preheated oven. Bake 12 to 15 minutes, until top of cake is barely starting to color, and is lightly springy—if you bake it too much it will crack when you start to roll it later. Remove from oven and immediately sprinkle top with a $\frac{1}{16}$-inch layer of confectioners' sugar; cover with a sheet of wax paper, and a damp towel. Set a tray or a baking sheet on top and reverse the two; let cool 10 minutes thus, upside down, then, holding one end of the wax paper overhang, gently remove baking pan, and carefully peel wax paper off cake.

✿ If you are not to fill and roll the cake now, sprinkle with confectioners' sugar, cover with a clean sheet of wax paper, roll up loosely, and wrap airtight. Refrigerate or freeze, but if you freeze it, be sure to thaw it before unrolling, or it will break apart.

SERVING SUGGESTIONS

Jelly roll cake. Unroll the cake, if it has been stored, and sprinkle with droplets of kirsch, rum, or orange juice. Spread with a cup or so of jam or jelly, roll up either from one of the short or the long ends, and transfer to a serving platter. Just before serving, sprinkle with confectioners' sugar and decorate, if you wish, with preserved fruits such as kumquat halves or cherries. (You can, of course, use fresh fruit mixtures, whipped cream, or anything you find attractive, delicious, and/or amusing.)

Bûche au chocolat; bûche de Noël

———◆———

CHOCOLATE
LOG CAKE

This elaborately silly log-shaped cake need not be confined to Christmas alone. It is equally appropriate decorated with American flags and an ax for George Washington's birthday, or with flags and sparklers for the Fourth of July. Any celebration, in fact, that would benefit from a handsome chocolate dessert could call for a chocolate log. It is nothing but a jelly roll with chocolate frosting that is roughened to look like tree bark, and it is trimmed with mushrooms and other woodsy shapes made out of meringue while a wispy veil of spun sugar hovers over all.

Although a *bûche* is that simple, really, we had a terrible time in our television studio when we did our last one, and I remember that day so vividly as I write about *bûche* here. For some reason we got a late start, and, to make matters worse, the sponge sheets, carefully prepared in advance and rolled up in the freezer for safe keeping, had not been thawed. Naturally they broke into pieces as they were unrolled, and our team of volunteer cooks had to work like fury baking fresh ones.

By the time the cameras got rolling we were all a little slaphappy, particularly me. Midway through the show the log was ready for frosting, and something went wrong with the butter cream—it wouldn't stick onto the cake. I kept assuring my viewers, "Never mind how messy it looks now, you'll see how beautiful it will be in a moment." (Thinking back on it now, I am quite sure my troubles occurred because the cake was warm and soft, having just been made.) Ruthie kept sending up signals that were held in front of the camera for me to see: "Fix front of *bûche!*" It appeared that the front of the cake, which the camera could see but I couldn't, kept dropping off patches of frosting, leaving unsightly holes, like gaping wounds. I would turn the log around; again the side facing the camera would start slipping. Finally the *bûche* did get done, in our 28 minutes of taping time, and what with artful poking and patting and patching it was quite handsome, loglike, and festive with its final decorations in place. All I can say about this performance is that anyone seeing it must have felt much assured, and must certainly have said, "If she, that bumbling creature, can do it, I can do it!" So be it.

This recipe consists first of a sponge sheet—the *Génoise* formula in the preceding recipe, or another one if you wish. The second part of it is Italian meringue—beaten egg whites with hot sugar syrup whipped into them—very easy to do with an electric mixer. A little of the meringue is formed into mushroom shapes and baked, and the rest becomes a chocolate base for filling and frosting. For the filling, the base is made soft and rich with butter, but for the frosting it is stiffened with cocoa and confectioners' sugar so that it will withstand party lights and excitement without collapsing. (If you have done the *bûche* in *The French Chef Cookbook,* you will note that it differs from this only in the cake and in the frosting.)

The Italian meringue, for mushrooms, filling, and frosting

For a bûche serving
10 to 12

3 egg whites
A pinch of salt
A scant ¼ tsp cream of tartar
1⅓ cups sugar
½ cup water

The chocolate meringue base, for filling and frosting

12 ounces semisweet baking chocolate melted
with ⅓ cup strong coffee (page 525)
1 Tb pure vanilla extract
Optional: 2 to 3 Tb dark Jamaican rum
½ stick (2 ounces) soft unsalted butter

For the filling
½ stick additional butter

The cake
A baked and chilled sponge sheet, about 11 by 17 inches, such as the Génoise on page 577

For the frosting
2 to 3 tablespoons unsweetened cocoa
½ cup or more confectioners' sugar in a fine-meshed sieve

For the spun-sugar moss—a caramel
1 cup sugar
⅓ cup water
3 Tb white corn syrup

Equipment: An electric mixer for the meringue, preferably a mixer on a stand; a pastry bag with a ⅜-inch tube, a separate tube with a ⅛-inch opening, or a paper decorating cone, and a buttered and floured baking sheet (no-stick preferred), for the mushrooms; a serving tray or foil-covered board for the bûche to sit on; an oiled broomstick suspended between 2 chair backs, and newspapers on the floor, for the spun sugar

The Italian meringue. (If egg whites are cold, set bowl in hot water and stir with wire whip to take off chill.) Beat the egg whites at moderate speed for a moment until they begin to foam; add the salt and cream of tartar and beat at moderately fast speed until egg whites form stiff shining peaks when lifted in a spoon or spatula. Set aside or turn to low speed.

Meanwhile, place sugar and water in a small, heavy saucepan and set over high heat. Swirl pan gently by its handle (do not stir) until sugar has dissolved completely and liquid is perfectly clear. Cover pan and boil rapidly without stirring for a moment or two; uncover pan when bubbles begin to thicken, and boil rapidly to the soft-ball stage, 238 degrees.

Beating egg whites at moderately slow speed, pour in the sugar syrup in a thin stream. Continue beating at high speed for at least 5 minutes, until mixture is cool. It will be satin smooth, and form stiff peaks when lifted with a spoon or spatula.

Meringue mushrooms. Preheat oven to 200 degrees. Scoop about one quarter of the Italian meringue into pastry bag. The mushrooms are made in two parts: ½-inch domes for the tops and small pointed cones for the bottoms; 6 to 8 of each are sufficient. Make the domes with the pastry bag on the baking sheet. Then, for the smaller cones, insert tube end of pastry bag into a ⅛-inch tube or into a paper decorating cone, and squeeze the meringue through this smaller opening. Return any unused meringue to main mixture. Bake about an hour, until mushroom parts push easily loose from baking sheet.

✴ If made in advance, keep in a warming oven or wrap airtight and freeze.

Filling and frosting the cake. Being sure the melted chocolate is perfectly smooth, beat it into the Italian meringue, along with the vanilla, optional rum, and ½ stick of butter. Remove about two thirds of the mixture to a bowl, and reserve. Beat the additional ½ stick of butter into the remaining meringue, spread over the sponge sheet, and roll up, starting at one of the long sides. Place cake on serving tray or board, seam side down, and slip a length of wax paper along each side. Cut off a bit from each end, on the bias; insert a piece of the cut-off cake into the rolled-up cake to serve as a branch or bump on the log-to-be.

Beat 2 or more tablespoons of cocoa into the reserved meringue mixture to give it some body; if too soft to spread, refrigerate or beat over cracked ice. When of correct spreading texture, frost the cake, but leave ends unfrosted; roughen frosting with a fork to give a barklike effect.

With a small knife, pierce a hole in bottom of each mushroom cap, fill with frosting, and insert conical stem. Arrange the mushrooms upon the log wherever you think they should be. Sprinkle cake with confectioners' sugar to give a light snowy effect; sprinkle tops of mushrooms with a little cocoa in a fine sieve. Arrange leaves or flowers around the log if you wish, or other decorations. Refrigerate until serving time.

Optional spun-sugar moss. If you wish spun-sugar moss, make it shortly before serving or the moss may get gummy. Dissolve sugar and water with corn syrup, then boil, following directions for the Italian meringue sugar syrup, but continue boiling until syrup has turned a light caramel.

Let syrup cool a few seconds, stirring with a table fork, until it forms thick threads. Then dip fork into syrup and wave it over the broomstick, letting threads hang down from it as shown. Reheat syrup as necessary, until you have as much spun sugar as you wish. Sweep the moss off the broomstick, drape it over or around the log, and serve.

Layer cakes made
from sponge sheets or
meringue disks

You can make an easy-to-serve and elegant rectangular layer cake from either the meringue-nut mixture on page 512, which you can form in any size and shape you wish, or a sponge sheet that you cut into strips. Here, in outline form, is one idea.

La grande bouffe aux écailles et au chocolat

———◆———

RECTANGULAR
LAYER CAKE OF
GÉNOISE,
CHOCOLATE
BUTTER CREAM,
AND ALMONDS

For 12 or more
servings, a cake 12
inches long, and 4
inches high and wide

A baked sponge sheet about 11 by 17 inches, such as the Génoise on page 577
A liqueur-sugar syrup (¼ cup sugar dissolved in ½ cup water and flavored with 2 to 3 tablespoons dark Jamaican rum, Bourbon, kirsch, or orange liqueur)
A butter-cream filling and frosting, such as the one with Italian meringue on page 581, or the classic on page 573. (Divide in half, to be sure you will have enough for frosting as well as filling.)
1 cup or more toasted shaved almonds

When baked, cut the sponge sheet into 4 crosswise strips 4 inches wide, going right through cake to paper, and being sure each strip will separate with its paper: keep paper on the strips for easy lifting.

Lift one strip by its paper and turn upside down on serving platter or foil-covered board; peel off paper. (Insert pieces of wax paper under edge of cake strip all around, to catch frosting dribbles.) Sprinkle the cake strip with 2½ tablespoons of liqueur syrup, and spread with a layer of filling (sprinkling over it any cake crumbs you may have accumulated) . Continue with the second and third strips in the same manner, piling them one upon another with filling in between. Then lay the fourth strip on top, and spread the reserved butter cream over top and sides of cake, smoothing it nicely, especially on top, with a wet metal spatula. Brush the toasted shaved almonds against the sides of the cake (these are the *écailles*—fish scales) , and remove the strips of waxed paper. Refrigerate until ready to serve.

Mrs. Child's famous sticky fruitcake

—◆—

A CHRISTMAS CAKE

This cake isn't sticky at all, but it started out that way during my first experiments, and the name has remained, as a family joke. I decided to work up a very fruity and nutty mixture that was easy to do all alone, with no friendly helping hands, and this is it. It's not a budget cake, unfortunately, since a large amount of fruits and nuts can never be an economy affair. But it is so rich and filled with good things that only a small slice should suffice, meaning that one luxury cake can go a long way. It is my habit to make a large amount of anything like this, particularly since it keeps for months and small fruitcakes make wonderful gifts, but you may cut the recipe in half or in thirds if you wish.

The fruit and nut mixture:
to be macerated 12 hours

For 16 cups or more of fruitcake batter, to fill a 16-inch angel loaf pan 4¼ inches deep, or two 9-inch 8-cup pans, or whatever combination and size of pans you wish, including miniature 1-cup loaf pans

4 pounds (2 quarts) diced mixed glacéed fruits: part of this may be diced dried dates, pitted tenderized dried prunes or apricots, or raisins, or currants

1 pound (2 cups) prepared store-bought mincemeat

1 pound (1 quart) mixed unsalted whole or chopped nut meats (such as walnuts, pecans, almonds, cashews, filberts)

⅔ cup dark Jamaican rum
⅓ cup Cognac or Bourbon
1 Tb instant coffee (espresso coffee suggested)
¼ cup dark molasses
1 tsp cardamom
½ tsp each: cinnamon, cloves, allspice, mace
1½ tsp salt

The dry ingredients
3½ cups all-purpose flour (measure by dipping
*   dry-measure cups into flour and sweeping*
*   off excess)*
1 Tb double-action baking powder

The remaining ingredients
½ pound (2 sticks) butter
2 cups white sugar
⅓ cup light-brown sugar
2 Tb vanilla
6 "large" eggs

Optional decoration after baking
1 to 1½ cups apricot glaze (apricot jam pushed
*   through a sieve, boiled to the thread stage*
*   [228 degrees] with 2 Tb sugar per cup of*
*   strained jam, page 503)*
A dozen or so glacéed cherries
A dozen or so whole pecan or walnut halves

Macerating the fruits and nuts. Turn the candied fruits into a very large mixing bowl, pour on boiling water to cover, stir about for 20 to 30 seconds, then drain thoroughly; this is to wash off any preservatives. Return fruit to bowl, add the mincemeat, nuts, liquors, instant coffee, molasses, spices, and salt; stir about. Cover airtight, and let macerate for 12 hours (or longer) .

Completing the cake mixture. Stir half the flour into the fruits and nuts, sprinkle over the baking powder and the rest of the flour, and stir to blend. Using an electric mixer, beat the butter and sugars together in a separate bowl until light and fluffy, then beat in the vanilla, and the eggs, one at a time, beating 30 seconds after the addition of each egg. Blend the egg-sugar mixture into the fruits.

Baking. Preheat the oven to 275 degrees. Butter your cake pan (or pans), line bottom with wax paper, butter that, roll flour around in the pan to coat interior, and knock out excess flour. Turn the batter into the pan, filling it to within ¼ inch of rim (and mold any extra cake mixture in a muffin tin). Bake in middle level of oven for 2 to 2¾ hours or longer, depending on size and shape of pan. Cake will rise about ¼ inch, top will crack in several places, and it is done when it shows the faintest line of shrinkage around edge of pan in several places; a skewer, plunged down into cake through a crack, should come out clean (or, at most, showing a residue of sticky fruit). Remove cake from oven and place pan on a rack to cool for 20 to 25 minutes; cake should shrink a little more from sides, showing it is ready to unmold. Turn cake upside down on rack and give a little shake to unmold it. Peel paper off bottom, and turn cake carefully right side up—you will need some fancy maneuvering if this is a big cake, like boards for bracing and turning.

Additional flavoring. If you wish more Cognac or rum or Bourbon flavoring, pour a spoonful or two over the cake 2 or 3 times as it cools.

✣ *Storing the cake.* When cold, wrap in plastic, then in foil, and store in a cool place. Will keep for months, and flavor matures with age, although the cake makes delicious eating when still warm from the oven.

Optional decoration. If you wish to make a luxurious spectacle of this cake, first paint the top and sides with warm apricot glaze, page 503 (be sure glaze has really boiled to the thread stage, so it will not remain sticky when cool).

Press halved glacéed cherries and nut meats into the glaze and, for a loaf cake like the one illustrated, make a line of cherries down the center flanked on either side by nut meats.

Paint a second coating of glaze over the fruits and the top of the cake. Let set for half an hour at least, allowing the glaze to dry and lose its stickiness. (Although you can still store the cake after glazing, I usually glaze it the day I serve it.)

Petits fours secs

Madeleines two ways, Cats' Tongues, and Tiles

Madeleines, those buttery, shell-shaped mouthfuls, were made unforgettable by Marcel Proust in *Swann's Way.* Near the end of the first chapter, in case you haven't read the book, Proust describes how his mother sent out for some of those little cakes, short and plump, called *petites Madeleines,* which seem to have been molded in the ribbed cavity of a scallop shell; at the instant a mouthful of tea, mixed with the crumbs of the *Madeleine,* touched his tongue he shivered, and a delicious pleasure invaded him—so begins one of the great classics of French literature, as well as life everlasting to that little cake. *Madeleines* are not particularly exciting in flavor but they are not meant to be; they are an accompaniment to tea, or to fruits or sherbets. Served in a pretty dish, they are charming indeed and, since they freeze perfectly, you might as well make 4 dozen while you're at it. Then you will have *Madeleines* on hand when you need something especially nice to bring forth.

After our television show "Madeleines and the Génoise Jelly Roll," a young French woman wrote me saying she wished I had shown the recipe for the *Madeleines de Commercy,* that hump up in the middle. So here they are both ways, the one crisp and light made from *Génoise* batter, and the other more solid, with its hump.

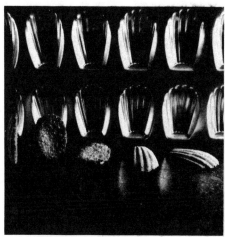

Madeleine pans are cookie sheets with, usually, 12 shell-shaped depressions in them about 3 inches long and ½ inch deep, made either out of tinned metal (*tôle étamée*) or of aluminum. My husband decided that some early cook must have baked his cakes in cockle shells, and we tried it with ribbed scallop shells—it works very nicely. If you have neither the right pan nor the right shell, you can use muffin tins, but then you cannot call your cakes *Madeleines* since *Madeleines* must be shell-shaped.

Madeleines à la génoise

LIGHT MADELEINES
MADE FROM
GÉNOISE CAKE
BATTER

For 4 dozen 3-inch
Madeleines, baked in
Madeleine pans

These are particularly good with fruits and sherbets, since they are light and delicate. The use of browned butter in the batter makes a much crisper and tastier little cake than the usual batter with plain butter. The browned butter mixed with flour, in addition, assures you of safe unmolding.

The Génoise cake batter on page 575
The small bowl containing 2 Tb browned
*   butter and 1 Tb flour*
4 Madeleine pans, each with 12 shell-shaped
*   depressions 3 inches long*

Preheat oven to 375 degrees, and place racks in upper and lower-middle levels. While the eggs and sugar are beating, paint the *Madeleine* cups lightly with the reserved browned butter and flour mixture; go over them again with a dry brush to remove any pools of butter. When batter is done, immediately start filling the pans about ½ full (1 tablespoon). Do *not* bang pan on table when filled; immediately place in oven, set kitchen timer for 12 minutes, and fill the remaining pans as rapidly as possible, setting each in the oven—2 pans to each rack. *Madeleines* are done when lightly browned, and when you can dislodge them from the cups. Unmold immediately with the point of a table knife, and cool, shell side up, on a rack.

✣ When cool, store in a warming oven or, if you are not serving them within a few hours, cover airtight and freeze them.

Serve as is, or turn ribbed side up and sprinkle with confectioners' sugar.

Les Made-
leines de
Commercy

THE MADELEINES
WITH THE HUMP
ON TOP

This is quite a different *Madeleine*, heavier, more like a pound cake. It is the Proustian model, which he dipped in his tea, to the profit of the bakers of Commercy, who now send them all over France. The following recipe is one I have adapted from *Le Nouveau Mémorial de la Pâtisserie et des Glaces*, by Pierre Lacam (91560 Crosnes, France: Editions Seurre-Lacam, 1946 and reprints). Lacam's method does make a hump because the batter rests an hour, allowing the butter to congeal in it, then it goes in a lump into the *Madeleine* cups. Some spreads out to fill the cups as it bakes, but a portion remains and swells into the characteristic hump. The *Madeleines* then, of course, must be served hump side up, and why they are baked in shell-shaped molds when the ridges don't show only the ancient bakers of Commercy can say, if they could but mumble to us from their tombs.

For 2 dozen Madeleines
3 inches long

2 "large" eggs beaten in a 1-cup measure
⅔ cup sugar
1 cup all-purpose flour (measure by scooping
dry-measure cup into flour and sweeping
off excess)
1 stick (4 ounces) butter for batter, and 1½ Tb
for buttering the molds (5¼ ounces in all)
1 Tb flour in a small bowl
Pinch of salt
½ tsp pure vanilla extract
The grated rind of ½ lemon
3 drops of lemon juice (or 2 of lemon and 2 of
bergamot, a citrus-flavored essence you may
find in a specialty-food shop)

Equipment: 2 Madeleine pans each with 12
shell-shaped depressions 3 inches long; a
small bowl for the flour-butter mixture to
grease molds, and a pastry brush

Preliminaries. All ingredients must be tepid here to prevent the melted butter from congealing in the batter before it has blended as it should. Stir the eggs in their container over warm water until tepid; set sugar and flour in the oven for a few minutes, also until tepid. Then bring out all your ingredients and equipment, and measure 1 tablespoon of the flour into the small bowl reserved for greasing the molds.

The batter. Measure three quarters of the eggs into a mixing bowl with the sugar and the flour, and beat vigorously with a wooden spoon to blend into a heavy cream—if very stiff, beat in a droplet or so of the remaining egg. Set aside for 10 minutes. Meanwhile, melt all of the butter in a saucepan, and let it boil until it begins to brown very lightly. Blend 1½ tablespoons into the bowl with the tablespoon of flour, and reserve. Stir the rest of the browned butter over cold water until cool but still liquid. Finally, beat the remaining bit of egg into the batter, and stir in the cool butter. Stir in the salt, vanilla, grated lemon, lemon juice (and bergamot, if you have any). Cover the batter, and set aside for 1 hour (or longer, if need be). Meanwhile, paint the *Madeleine* cups with a light coating of the browned butter and flour mixture, wiping up any pools that form in bottom of cups; set aside (refrigerate in hot weather).

Baking. Preheat oven to 375 degrees in time for baking. After its hour-long rest, batter will be fairly stiff. Using a spoon and rubber spatula, dislodge a rather generous tablespoon lump of batter into each *Madeleine* cup, but do not spread it out; it must stay in a lump in the middle of the cup. Bake in middle level of preheated oven about 15 minutes. Batter will spread out to fill the cups, and will gradually swell up into a hump in the middle. The *Madeleines* are done when lightly browned around the edges, and when they begin to shrink very slightly from the cups. Unmold onto a rack, humped side up.

✲When cool, wrap airtight and freeze if not to be served promptly.

Serve as is, or sprinkle tops with a dusting of confectioners' sugar.

Langues-de-chat

CAT'S TONGUE COOKIES; FINGER-SHAPED COOKIES

For about 30 cookies, 4 inches long and 1¼ to 1½ inches wide

These crisp little wafers go with ice creams and fruit desserts, and are wonderful to have on hand when you want a molded magnificence, since you can use them rather than ladyfingers. They freeze perfectly, too, so you might make a lot while you're at it.

½ stick (2 ounces) soft unsalted butter
⅓ cup sugar
The grated rind of 1 lemon
¼ cup egg whites (about 2 "large" egg whites)

⅓ cup all-purpose flour (measure by scooping dry-measure cup into flour and sweeping off excess)

Equipment: 2 or more buttered and floured cookie sheets, the largest you have, and no-stick recommended; a 12- to 14-inch pastry bag with ⅜-inch round tube opening; a flour sifter set over wax paper; an electric beater or wooden spoon; a rubber spatula and a flexible-blade spatula; a cake rack

Preliminaries. Preheat oven to 425 degrees and set racks in upper- and lower-middle levels. Prepare pastry sheets, assemble pastry bag, and set out all your ingredients and equipment.

The batter. The mixture here is only butter and sugar beaten to a *pommade* (a light and fluffy consistency), then mixed with plain egg white, and finally with flour; the trick is to keep it light and fluffy so it has enough body to hold in a pastry bag and be squeezed out. Proceed as follows: Using an electric beater or a wooden spoon, whip the butter, sugar, and grated lemon rind in a small bowl until they form a fluffy *pommade*—if you have softened it too much and it has turned limp and almost liquid, beat over ice water to bring it back to a fluffy, almost foamy, state. Beat the egg whites briefly with a fork, just to break them up. Pour ½ tablespoon of them into the butter-sugar mixture and rapidly cut it in with a rubber spatula, giving 3 or 4 brief scoops. Do not try to mix thoroughly because you do not want to soften the batter; rapidly cut in the rest of the egg whites by ½ tablespoons. Then sift on one quarter of the flour, rapidly cut it into the mixture, and continue with the rest in small portions. Stand the pastry bag in a cup, spread the top open, and scoop in the batter.

Forming the cookies. Using quick straight strokes, form lines of the batter on the prepared cookie sheets, making lines 3 to 4 inches long and the width of your finger, spaced 3 inches apart—they will spread in the oven.

Baking. Bake 2 sheets at a time in upper- and lower-middle levels of preheated 425-degree oven. In 6 to 8 minutes, when ⅛ inch around their circumference has browned, the cookies are done. Remove from oven and immediately, with a flexible-blade spatula, dislodge cookies onto a rack. They will crisp as they cool.

☼ Store in a warming oven, or wrap airtight and freeze.

Tuiles aux noix

WALNUT WAFERS

Tuile means tile, in this case the old-fashioned long curved tile you still find on old farmhouses in France. To give cookies a tile shape, you scoop them from their hot baking sheet and rest them for a moment on a rolling pin or a bottle, where they crisp into a curve. *Tuiles* are usually made of a batter with almonds, but here it's chopped walnuts, and a very thin, light, and delicious wafer it makes. You may prefer them flat, however, particularly if you want to store them, since the curved shape is fragile and takes up room. Serve them with tea, with fruits, with sherbets.

For 24 wafers 3½ inches across

1 cup (4 ounces) chopped walnut meats
½ cup sugar
½ stick (2 ounces) soft unsalted butter
Pinch salt
2 Tb heavy cream
¼ cup egg whites (about 2 egg whites)
¼ cup all-purpose flour (measure by scooping
    dry-measure cup into flour and sweeping
    off excess) ; place in a sifter or sieve set over
    wax paper
1 Tb rum or kirsch

Equipment: 2 large baking sheets, about 14 by
    16 inches, and no-stick if possible, buttered
    and floured; an electric blender (to pulverize
    walnuts) ; a flexible-blade spatula; a rolling
    pin or 2 bottles on which to shape cookies
    if you want the tile shape; a cake rack

Preliminaries. Preheat oven to 425 degrees. Prepare baking sheets. Set ½ cup of nuts aside, and pulverize the rest, ¼ cup at a time, with some of the ½ cup sugar, in the electric blender (blend just enough to powder them but be careful not to overdo it and turn them into a damp mass). Set out the rest of the ingredients and equipment. If you are using a rolling pin or bottle to form the cookies, brace underneath each side of it with a pot holder, for instance, to keep it from rolling about.

The batter. If butter is hard, beat in a metal bowl over warm water for a moment to soften, then over cold water to cream and fluff it. Fold in the pulverized walnuts plus sugar, the pinch of salt, and the cream. Break up the egg whites with a fork, and fold them into the walnut mixture rapidly, by ½ tablespoons, keeping the batter fluffy and light. By sprinkles, fold in the flour and finally the rum or kirsch.

Forming the cookies and baking. The wafers are to be formed in 4 batches of 6, and while one sheet is baking, you form the next. Divide batter into 4 equal parts. Taking one of them, drop ½ tablespoon blobs of batter, spaced 6 inches apart, on one of the baking sheets; spread out with the back of a spoon into 3½-inch disks. Top each with a big pinch of the reserved chopped walnut meats. Set the filled sheet in the middle level of the preheated oven and bake about 6 minutes, just until the edges of the cookies brown. Then set baking sheet on open door of oven to keep warm, and one at a time rapidly sweep a cookie off the baking sheet with the side of your flexible-blade spatula, either onto the rolling pin or bottle for a curved shape, or onto cake rack for a flat shape. Cookies crisp into shape in a matter of seconds. Continue with the rest. Then close oven door and let oven regain its temperature while you continue forming a new batch. (When you reuse a baking sheet, be sure to rinse it off in cold water; it must be cool before you form the cookies.)

✥ Keep wafers crisp in a warming oven, or arrange in an airtight container and freeze them.

Spiced dough for gingerbread houses, gingerbread men, cutouts, cookie molds, speculos

Once on a visit to Brussels we found an old wooden cookie mold, a *speculos,* that had carved into it a large-nosed woman with a bustle, making a figure some 18 inches high. I had always intended to work up the proper dough for that mold and never got around to it until *Life* magazine, during one of its last regular issues, did an article on Christmas baking and asked me to contribute. Delighted to be forced into action, I finally settled on the following dough, which I have since given out to a number of fancy cookie makers—or makers of fancy cookies—who have had great success with it, as have I. It is a spicy dough that hardens nicely as it bakes, and the cookies will keep for months; I've had my Belgian-woman-cookie around for several years, now, as well as a number of smaller molded forms that I place about our Christmas tree. It's a fine dough, too, for gingerbread houses, gingerbread men, and so on and so forth. It also makes very good eating—when reasonably fresh.

For about 3 cups of dough, enough for 2 dozen or so small cookies or 1 18- to 20-inch gingerbread man	1 stick (4 ounces) butter ½ cup dark-brown sugar ½ cup white sugar 2 "large" eggs ⅛ tsp salt 1 tsp cinnamon ½ tsp ground cloves ½ tsp nutmeg 1 tsp ginger 1 tsp cardamom 2 to 2½ cups all-purpose flour

In an electric mixer, cream the butter and 2 sugars until light and fluffy. Beat in the eggs and seasonings, and continue beating until light and thoroughly mixed—2 minutes or so. Gradually beat in as much flour as you can, until machine clogs. Turn out onto work surface, and vigorously knead in more flour to make a very stiff dough. Wrap airtight and refrigerate at least 24 hours.

Forming the dough

For cookie cutters. Roll chilled dough ¼ inch thick, cut into shapes, and arrange on buttered and floured baking sheets.

Free-form shapes and gingerbread houses. (Here, be sure all dough you are not working on is kept refrigerated; if it warms and softens, you are lost. It is also helpful to have a pattern cut from heavy brown paper, and to use rather big, uncomplicated shapes—thin legs, narrow lines, and tiny decorations tend to bake out of shape and cook unevenly.) Roll dough into squares, oblongs, or whatever general shape you intend to make, roll it up onto your pin, then onto a floured and buttered baking sheet; cut into the shape you have chosen.

Speculos molds: wooden or plastic molds with forms and figures carved into them. Flour the molds heavily and thoroughly; shake off excess flour. Roll the chilled dough ¼ inch thick, and in the general shape of the mold. Roll dough up on your pin, then out into the mold. Press dough into mold with thumbs and fingers to catch all parts of the design, and work off excess dough around edge of design with your thumb. Unmold on buttered and floured baking sheet. Go over design with a knife, if necessary, to point up any blurred details.

Baking and decorating

Bake in a preheated 350-degree oven 12 to 15 to 18 minutes, or longer if dough is thicker than ¼ inch, until cookie feels dry and firm to touch, and edges are barely beginning to color. Cool on a rack. Decorate with royal frosting, page 563, or coloring from decorating squeeze tubes.

An almond feuilleté

Certainly one of the most glorious reasons to master French puff pastry is the *Pithiviers,* a rum-flavored almond cream baked between two layers of that buttery wonder dough, *pâte feuilletée,* known variously as flaky pastry and thousand-leaf dough as well as French puff pastry. Its hundreds of very very thin layers of dough, sandwiched between hundreds of layers of butter, puff into such an airy and tender delight when it is baked that it literally does melt in your mouth, and to have that happen with a rum and almond filling, too, is one of life's unforgettable experiences.

Although the *Pithiviers* appears in Volume II of *Mastering*, I particularly wanted to repeat it here to give you an example of the round puff pastry tart, since you can use the same system for the Ham Tart on page 70, making it round rather than rectangular. Although a round tart is easy to assemble once you have your chilled pastry dough, it does demand more pastry, and there are certain tricks to making the top and bottom layers stick together until they have baked closed to hold in the filling.

DOUGH NOTES. Do remember, as with all puff pastry affairs, to refrigerate any dough you are not working on, to work fast on the dough at hand, and not to delay in putting it all in the refrigerator if it softens and becomes hard to handle. I have indicated two rest periods to firm the dough and to relax it, but you may find that one is enough. Count on 1 hour for assembling, which includes chill periods, and another hour for baking. The sooner puff pastry is served after baking, the more wonderful it tastes; however, storing and ahead-of-time notes are at the end of the recipe.

Le Pithiviers

ALMOND CREAM TART IN FRENCH PUFF PASTRY, TO SERVE AS A DESSERT, OR WITH TEA

For a round tart 8 inches in diameter, serving 6 to 10

The almond cream
⅓ cup sugar in a mixing bowl
½ stick (2 ounces) soft butter
1 egg
½ cup, lightly packed, ground blanched almonds (about 2½ ounces)
¼ tsp each: almond and vanilla extracts
1½ Tb dark rum

The pastry
French puff pastry made with 3½ cups flour, chilled and ready to roll, page 611

Egg glaze
1 egg beaten with 1 tsp water

*Equipment: A rolling pin with rolling surface 16 to
18 inches long; a baking sheet; a circular cutter
8 inches in diameter, such as a bowl or a quiche
ring; a pastry brush; a steam vent (a buttered
pastry tube, a funnel, or foil; a small sharp knife)*

The almond cream. Beat the sugar and butter until soft and fluffy, using a wooden spoon; then add the egg, almonds, almond and vanilla extracts, and rum, beating to blend. Turn into a small bowl, cover, and freeze 30 minutes or until ready to use.

Rolling out the pastry. The *Pithiviers* consists of a lump of almond cream baked between 2 circular layers, or disks, of puff pastry. Roll the chilled pastry into a rectangle 14 inches long and 7 to 8 inches wide; halve crosswise and refrigerate one half. Roll remaining half rapidly into a 9½-inch square ⅜ inch thick—be sure dough is not thinner, or it will not puff properly in the oven. Lift dough to let it shrink back if it will, roll again if necessary, then center cutter on the dough. Being sure there is a ½-inch border all around, cut out an 8-inch disk. Run cold water on baking sheet; roll disk up on pin and unroll onto baking sheet (sheet is dampened so bottom layer will have a grip, and can puff later). Refrigerate. Roll out second half of dough, cut into an 8-inch disk; place on wax paper on top of first disk and chill until hard and firm—20 to 30 minutes.

Assembling. Remove bottom disk (on its baking sheet) from the refrigerator. With your fingers, push it out all around from center outward, to about 9 inches. Form the chilled and hard almond cream into a round cake 4 inches in diameter, and center it on the dough.

Rapidly roll out the second disk of dough, enlarging it to 9 inches. Paint circumference of bottom disk with cold water, roll top disk up on pin, and unroll over bottom disk. Seal the two layers of dough together first by pressing all around circumference of almond cream with the side of your hand, pressing hard to seal. Make a little hole in top of dough down into the cream, to let air escape.

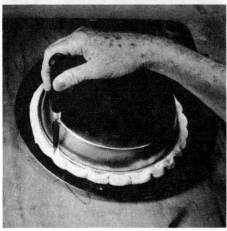

Then press the dough firmly with the flat of your fingers from edge of cream outward to edge of dough, to seal. Your object is to hold the almond cream in its lump, since it will slowly expand outward as the pastry bakes, and you want to prevent it from leaking out the edges. Chill again for 20 to 30 minutes until hard and firm. (Preheat oven to 450 degrees if you are baking after the next step.)

Scalloped edging. Remove pastry from refrigerator, and center your 8-inch cutter on top of it; you should have about ½ inch of dough protruding all around. With a sharp small knife, cut a decorative scalloped edging all around the circumference. Press cutter into dough to make a definite indentation and final seal. If you wish, press the tines of a fork outside the edging, all around.

☼ You may cover and freeze the *Pithiviers* at this point.

Glazing and top decorations. Just before baking, paint top of pastry with egg glaze, being careful not to drip glaze down sides of edging (glaze over edging may hold down the puff). Insert a buttered pastry-tube nozzle, small funnel, or foil funnel into air hole, to let out steam during baking; push it right down into the almond cream so it will not topple over as pastry rises. Paint with a second coating of glaze. Then, using the point of your knife, cut down through glaze and almost ⅛ inch into the dough to make decorative designs all over top of pastry out to edging: during baking the lines remain pale and the glaze browns. The usual pattern for a *Pithiviers* is a wheel of swirling spokes, starting at the steam hole and curving gracefully out to the edge, where they spread out ½ inch apart.

Baking. At once, set pastry in lower-middle level of preheated 450-degree oven and bake 20 to 25 minutes, until pastry has tripled in height and started to brown nicely. Turn thermostat down to 400 degrees, and peek every 5 minutes or so to be sure it is not browning too much. If necessary, cover loosely with a sheet of foil. It will need another 25 minutes of baking, and is done when the sides are firm to the touch. It is better to bake a little longer than to bake too short a time and risk underdone pastry. (When done, you may, if you wish, sieve a ⅛-inch layer of confectioners' sugar over the *Pithiviers,* and return for 5 minutes to a 500-degree oven, for a caramel glaze; with 2 coats of egg glaze, however, I don't find the sugar glaze necessary.)

Serving. Serve the *Pithiviers* hot, warm, or cold, but it is at its best fresh from the oven. Cut into wedges like a pie.

✿ If you cannot serve within 2 to 3 hours, keep the *Pithiviers* in a warming oven at around 100 degrees for a day or two. Otherwise let it cool, wrap airtight, and freeze; thaw for 30 to 40 minutes in a 350-degree oven.

Fundaments

I have put some of the fundamentals of cooking—the sauces, the pastry doughs, the wines—at the end rather than at the beginning of this book. I hate lists of things to start off with. It's like having your very first French class nothing but conjugations of verbs when what you want to know is how to pass the time of day or order a dinner. Or your first session at the piano is but a run up and down of scales and arpeggios and you want the Brahms Lullaby. Or, and perhaps even worse, your first cooking lesson is on how to pluck and eviscerate a fowl and you don't even know how to poach an egg, and the egg, of course, should come first! In addition to such considerations, much of the dough, sauce, and wine information is scattered through many chapters of the text, and it is good to have them gathered together here, in one group.

———◆———

French pastry doughs for pies, tarts, pâtés en croûte

Nothing makes one feel more like a real cook than turning out a decent pie dough for a quiche or a tart or a turnover, or for some little *amuse-gueule* cocktail appetizers. It is silly to buy a mix when your own tastes so much better and is so easy with an electric mixer. So if you've been afraid to make your own, try the following recipe with your machine; I can practically guarantee you'll bake it right the first try. The reason I so much favor the machine over the bare hand is that your primary step in making dough is to blend fat and flour together so that the fat is broken into tiny particles, each of which is coated with flour; the fat must remain cold and that means quick work. If you do it by hand, and are new to cooking, it can be a long, messy business and those hot, nervous hands can melt the fat; then the pie dough bakes into cardboard. By machine that horrid problem doesn't arise. Of course it is useful to have the knowledge in your bare hands, too, in case the electricity goes off, but that can come later. The important thing is for you to make that dough, and to bake that crust, and to realize that the only thing you have to fear is fear itself—that great F.D.R. phrase that applies so poignantly to cooking too.

Pâte brisée fine, électrique

ALL-PURPOSE BEST-QUALITY FRENCH PASTRY DOUGH FOR PIE CRUSTS, TART SHELLS, QUICHES, TURNOVERS, TARTLETS, AND APPETIZERS—MADE IN THE ELECTRIC MIXER

For about ½ pound of flour, enough for two 8- to 9-inch shells

1¾ cups (8 ounces) all-purpose flour, preferably unbleached (or "instantized," or "Wondra," or "instant-blending") : measure by scooping dry-measure cups into flour and sweeping off excess
1 tsp salt
1¼ sticks (5 ounces) chilled butter
2 Tb (1 ounce) chilled lard or shortening (to tenderize American flour)
⅓ to ½ cup ice water

Place flour and salt in bowl of mixer (or a mixing bowl). Rapidly cut chilled butter into lengthwise quarters, then into ¼-inch pieces, and drop into flour. Cut chilled lard or shortening into small pieces and add them too. Now you are going to mix the flour and butter until the butter is reduced to tiny bits less than $\frac{1}{16}$ inch in size, each bit being coated with the flour. To do so, turn on beater to moderate and start mixing—circulating beater all about the bowl if you are using a portable, or standing right over it every second if using a table model.

In a minute or so the mixture should look like a very coarse cornmeal, and the first part of the job is done. Be careful, however, not to overmix and soften the butter, turning things into a paste—it should be light and dry.

Pour in ⅓ cup of the ice water and continue mixing for just a few seconds, until dough masses in blades of beater. Add more water by droplets to unblended bits.

Scrape out of mixer onto a working surface, and gather the dough into a ball, pressing it firmly into a thick cake 4 to 5 inches in diameter. Consistency should be pliable rather than stiff, but not damp and sticky. Flour lightly, wrap in a sheet of plastic and a plastic bag, and refrigerate for at least 2 hours, to give flour time to absorb liquid, to relax gluten in flour so the dough will roll easily, and to chill the butter—again for easy rolling.

✦ Dough will keep for 2 to 3 days under refrigeration, but if you have used unbleached flour, it will gradually turn grayish—you can still use it if color is not pronounced, however. For longer storage, freeze the dough, where it will keep perfectly for months.

Electric super-blender-food-processor pie crust dough

Pie crust dough is sinfully easy in the marvelous machine illustrated on page 154; when my editor, Judith Jones, as well as my colleague, Simca, saw it in action they each immediately bought one. "If only for pie dough," said Judith, "it's worth the price to me." I have found that 2 cups of flour is the limit for easy mixing, but since it takes literally less than 10 seconds to make a dough, you can do large lots as well as small, dumping out one batch and adding another until your quota is filled. The following system works well for me, using the preceding proportions for a *Pâte Brisée Fine,* or any of the succeeding formulae.

Use either the plastic or the regular blade in the machine. Put in the flour and salt. Rapidly cut butter and lard or shortening into ½-inch bits and drop into machine. Turn on for 3 seconds. Stop. Add all but 2 tablespoons of the ½ cup of ice water and turn on machine—in 2 to 3 seconds, the dough has just begun to mass on the blade, and the pastry is done.

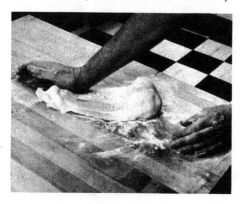

Turn it out onto your work surface and with the heel of your hand (not the palm), rapidly and roughly smear it 6 to 8 inches out in front of you, by 3-spoonful bits —a lump the size of a small egg— to make a final blending of butter into the dough.

If pastry seems dry, you can at this time sprinkle on droplets of water as you smear—it should be malleable, but not damp and sticky. Form into a cake 5 inches in diameter, flour lightly, wrap in plastic and a plastic bag, and chill for at least 2 hours before using.

OTHER DOUGH FORMULAE

Make the following doughs in exactly the same way as in either of the two systems described, first blending the flour and butter, then adding the liquid, massing the dough into a cake, and chilling 2 hours before using. I shall give all these proportions for 1¾ cups of flour, or about ½ pound, but why not double the recipe, and keep the overflow in the freezer?

Pâte brisée à l'oeuf

A LIGHT CRISP
DOUGH DESIGNED
FOR TART SHELLS

This dough is particularly recommended when you are making upside-down molds or pastry turnovers.

1¾ cups all-purpose flour
1 tsp salt
1⅛ sticks (4½ ounces) chilled butter
2½ Tb (1¼ ounces) chilled lard or
*   vegetable shortening*
A scant ½ cup liquid, consisting of ½ egg plus
*   the necessary ice water*

Pâte brisée sucrée

SWEET DOUGH, FOR
DESSERT TARTS

I like this for the Upside-down Apple Tatin, page 497, the Lemon Tart, page 507, and the Pear or Apple Tarts on page 501.

1¾ cups all-purpose flour
Pinch of salt

2 to 2½ Tb sugar
1¼ sticks (5 ounces) chilled butter
2 Tb (1 ounce) chilled shortening
⅓ to ½ cup ice water

Pâte sucrée aux jaunes d'oeufs

A LIGHT DOUGH
FOR PREBAKED
TART SHELLS

I recommend this one for strawberry and other fresh fruit tarts.

1¾ cups all-purpose flour
Pinch of salt
2 to 2½ Tb sugar
1⅛ sticks (4½ ounces) chilled butter
2½ Tb (1¼ ounces) vegetable shortening
A scant ½ cup liquid (1 egg yolk plus necessary ice water)

Pâte à pâté

PASTRY DOUGH FOR
PÂTÉS EN CROÛTE,
MEAT PIES, MEAT
TURNOVERS

Here, the proportions are for 1 pound of flour, since you usually need more dough for a pâté than for a tart. Double the following proportions if you are doing the free-form Pâté Pantin on page 372, to be sure there is enough dough.

3½ cups (1 pound) all-purpose flour
2½ tsp salt
1 stick (4 ounces) chilled butter
6 Tb (3 ounces) chilled lard
¾ to 1 cup liquid (2 egg yolks plus necessary ice water)

PIE DOUGHS AND THE METRIC SYSTEM

When we finally convert to the metric system, pie doughs will be much easier to calculate. The all-purpose *Pâte Brisée Fine*, for instance, is based on 4 parts butter to 5 parts flour, or the butter is at 80 percent. The translation from cups and spoons would be as follows, which may be useful to you when cooking abroad:

1¾ cups all-purpose flour — 250 grams flour
1 tsp salt — 5 grams salt
6 ounces butter and shortening — 200 grams butter
⅓ to ½ cup ice water — 1 deciliter ice water, plus droplets more, as needed

Forming and baking tart shells

Forming tart shells. A French flan ring (front row and two right rear rings in illustration) set on a buttered baking sheet is the perfect mold for a tart shell, as is the fluted false-bottomed tart mold now available in either white metal or black (two molds illustrated at left rear) in most import shops. If you have neither one, take a cake tin 1½ inches deep or two matching pie plates. Whatever mold you choose, butter the inside surface before rolling out your dough. (Although black metal molds, by the way, have been much touted as producing browner, crisper, and finer pie shells than white metal, I was unable to find any appreciable difference in a recent baking contest comparing the two.)

Use one of the preceding chilled doughs; beat with your pin to soften. (And do get yourself a rolling pin with rolling surface of 16 to 18 inches, as illustrated; a broom handle is better than a too-short rolling pin.) Then roll it into a circle ³⁄₁₆ inch thick and 2 inches larger than your mold.

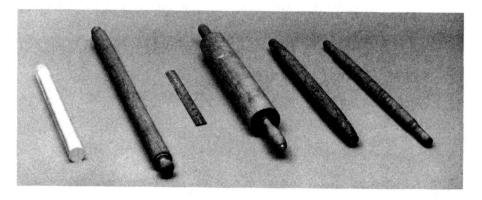

Roll dough up on your pin and unroll over mold. Lift edges to settle it in the bottom of the mold.

Then, with your thumbs, work about ⅜ inch of dough gently down sides of mold to make sides thicker and sturdier than bottom.

Roll pin over top of mold. Trim off excess dough all around.

Then push up a ⅛-inch ridge of dough all around rim.

Either with a pastry pinch (metal tweezers with flat serrated pinching ends ½-inch wide) or with dull edge of a table knife, make a decorative pattern around rim. Prick bottom of pastry with a fork at ¼-inch intervals. Refrigerate at least ½ hour.

Prebaking tart shells. Whether your formed tart shell is homemade or raw store-bought, prebaking before filling will assure you of a crisp bottom crust. The empty raw shell must be braced while baking, to keep it in shape.

For homemade shells, butter a large sheet of lightweight aluminum foil, and set buttered side down in chilled pastry shell, pushing foil gently up all around edges of dough. Fill completely with aluminum bits made especially for the purpose, or with dried beans, peas, or rice—which may also be kept for this purpose and used for years.

If you are not ready to bake, refrigerate the shell. Bake in lower-middle level of preheated 450-degree oven for 7 to 8 minutes, until pastry is set but still slightly soft. Remove liner, prick bottom of dough again with a fork. (If edges have sunk down, push up gently with a spatula, or patch, if necessary, with raw dough.) Return foil and beans, and bake another few minutes, and when pastry is set, remove liner and bake another 2 to 3 minutes until shell has just begun to color and to shrink slightly from edges of mold. Remove from oven, let cool and set 10 minutes, then gently unmold onto a rack to crisp. Before filling and baking, set on buttered baking sheet, and if you are using a flan ring, set it around the shell for safety.

For store-bought shells, follow package directions, but bake until shell is only beginning to color. After cooling, return shell to its aluminum pan for baking with a filling, and unmold from pan for serving.

☼ Both raw and prebaked shells may be wrapped airtight and frozen.

Free-form shell for tarts and quiches

I have lately become wedded to the free-form square or rectangular shell that I can make any size I want, but is usually a rectangle about 12 by 14 inches that sits on a serving board. It serves 12 people nicely, or double the number if it's a cheese quiche–type of affair for cocktails. A shell made of puff pastry is described at the end of this recipe; here is how to make one out of pie dough.

Make double the amount of the *Pâte Brisée Fine* recipe on page 602 (3½ cups or 1 pound of flour). What you want is a bottom dough, and strips of dough about ¾ inch wide to make the sides all around; if it is to be a fresh fruit tart, the sides need be only ⅛ inch thick, but for baked fruit tarts and quiches you should have double strips, one laid upon the other, to give more depth. Thus, roll the dough out into a large square or rectangle ³⁄₁₆ inch thick, and cut strips for the edging as well as cutting the bottom piece, which you roll up on your pin and unroll on a lightly buttered pastry sheet.

Paint a ¾-inch border all around with cold water, and press strips of dough in place on the two long sides. Wet ends of strips, and press strips of dough on the two short sides, overlapping both ends. If you are doing double strips for a quiche or filled tart, then press extra strips on top of the first, being sure corners are well sealed. Refrigerate for half an hour or longer before baking.

When well chilled, prick bottom of pastry with the tines of a table fork at ¼-inch intervals, and line bottom and sides with aluminum foil, then fill with aluminum bits or beans. Bake 10 minutes or so in the lower-middle level of a preheated 400-degree oven; lift foil and beans to see if pastry has set; if not, bake a few minutes more. Remove foil and beans, and, if you want a fully baked shell for fresh fruit tarts, bake 5 minutes or so more, until lightly browned.

Use with any of the quiche recipes on page 59, or the tart suggestions starting on page 497.

Other suggestions for free-form tart shells. You can combine doughs for free-form tart shells, making the bottom out of *Pâte Brisée* and the strips out of real or mock puff pastry—thus the strips will rise and make more dramatic sides to hold in the filling. (Mock puff pastry is *Pâte Brisée* rolled with extra butter, page 48; real puff pastry is the following recipe.) For the puff pastry shell, described on page 502, you roll the bottom quite thin, and prick it thoroughly to keep it from rising; leftover bits of puff pastry, reconstituted, can be used here.

French puff pastry

Foods have highs and lows of style, just as do clothes, furniture, shoes, and people. Most of the in-group food and drink modes are initiated by the famous so-called three-star restaurants in France, as rated from one for *good* to three for *prodigious* by the French dining and lodging manual, *Le Guide Michelin.* The great three-star eateries receive wads of publicity, loving articles by our own traveling gourmet correspondents, and soon the whole world knows that the chic dish of the moment is, let us say, thin slices of breast of duck and a sauce of green peppercorns, or that the *apéritif* of the year is champagne with a few drops of raspberry syrup. Some time ago the *Tarte Tatin,* our upside-down apple tart on page 497, was the dessert supreme. In the last few years puff pastry has made a comeback, with a *feuilleté* of asparagus or of truffles suggested as a first course, or one of raspberries or wild strawberries for dessert. And what a delight to have it back in vogue again, since, when made as it should be, puff pastry is a marvel of buttery delicacy that literally melts in your mouth.

It is the pastry for Napoleons, *vol-au-vent,* patty shells, Wellingtons, fancy tarts, turnovers, cookies, cakes, and is, in fact, the dough that can make you famous. Rather than being a solid piece, it is many layers of dough each separated by a paper-thin layer of butter. When baked, every layer swells individually, and the pastry puffs at least 5 or 6 times its original height. This is all done by a series of simple rollings out and foldings up, so that one initial layer of dough spread with a single layer of butter multiplies itself by geometric progression.

Because of its high butter content and its multiple rollings, the dough needs ample chilling and resting. Count on a minimum of 4 hours from the time you start to the time you form and bake puff pastry. Once made, however, the pastry will keep for months in the freezer—as soon as you have thawed it, you can produce any number of quickly assembled splendors in a matter of minutes, such as the beautiful almond tart, *Le Pithiviers*, on page 595, the *Feuilleté au Jambon* on page 70, or the *Talmouse* appetizers on page 55. Besides, puff pastry is very satisfying to create, and when you toss it off effortlessly, you feel serenely calm and important—at least I do. Although it strikes fear into the hearts of many, I was fascinated to know, after our TV program on it, "Flaky Pastry," that our fearless young floor manager, who was not a cook at all, went home and made it the next day. "No trouble whatsoever, and why should there be?" said he, with simple authority.

A NOTE ON FLOUR. In my experience, and I've done batches and batches of it for our television shows, the lightest and highest-rising puff pastry is made with unbleached all-purpose flour. If you cannot find it in your regular market, look for it in health-food stores. However, since our all-purpose flour, whether bleached or not, is designed more for yeast doughs than for pastry doughs, it has more gluten content than, say, regular French flour, which is designed more for pastries than for breads. To make a dough that will roll out easily, then, you need to reduce the gluten content, since it is the gluten that turns rubbery in a dough and makes it spring back or refuse to stretch out when you roll it. That is the reason for the cake flour in the following proportions.

If you cannot find unbleached flour, substitute ¼ cup fresh peanut oil for the 2 ounces of butter in the initial dough proportions; this will help matters to some degree, since oil seems to have a tenderizing effect on bleached flour.

Pâte feuilletée

FRENCH PUFF PASTRY

Puff pastry consists of an initial dough, really a kind of *Pâte Brisée* or pie dough, and a mass of softened butter. The butter is spread on the dough, the dough is folded to enclose it, then the two are rolled out together, folded, rerolled, folded, and it is this manipulation that extends the butter between the layers of dough. You have to stop between each pair of rolls and folds—called turns—and let the dough rest, allowing the butter to chill or it would ooze out; in addition you are resting the gluten, which otherwise tightens up and refuses to be rolled out.

Note: The proportions of flour to butter here are one to one—1 pound of each.

The initial dough: La Détrempe

For 2½ pounds of puff pastry, enough for a round tart 8 to 9 inches in diameter, like Le Pithiviers, page 595, plus enough leftovers for a rectangular tart, like Ham Feuilleté on page 70, or for cocktail appetizers, or the preceding free-form tart shell

2¾ cups unbleached all-purpose flour (measure by dipping dry-measure cups into flour and sweeping off excess)
¾ cup plain bleached cake flour
2 tsp salt
½ stick (2 ounces) chilled butter (unsalted if possible, since it is usually firmer; and this must be stick butter, not creamed or whipped butter)
About 1 cup ice water

The main part of the butter

3½ sticks (14 ounces) chilled butter (see notes above)

Equipment: An electric mixer (or mixing bowl, and pastry blender or your own hands) ; a ½-cup dry measure (to reserve flour for main part of butter) ; a rolling pin with rolling surface 16 inches long (see discussion, page 606) ; a pastry scraper or stiff spatula; useful— a pastry marble (chilled in refrigerator in hot weather)

The initial dough. Toss and blend the 2 flours in the mixing bowl; scoop out ½ level cup and reserve for next step. Blend the salt into the remaining flour, cut the chilled butter rapidly into lengthwise quarters, then into ¼-inch bits, and add to the flour. Rapidly break butter into flour, using an electric mixer as described for *Pâte Brisée* on page 602 or with the balls of your fingers, until mixture resembles small oatmeal flakes. Blend in the water with a rubber spatula, pressing dough together as it masses; turn out onto work surface and press into a rough ball, kneading briefly once or twice to mass the dough together. Set at the side of your work surface.

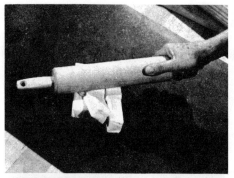

The butter. Soften butter by beating it with rolling pin, then smearing it out by bits with the heel (not the warm palm) of your hand.

When somewhat softened, smear in the ½ cup reserved flour. Work with heel of hand and spatula, smearing out and gathering up, until perfectly smooth and spreadable, but still cold. Scrape into a lump at the side of your work surface.

First dough and butter layer. Scrape work surface clean, and flour it lightly. Push, pat, and roll the dough into a rectangle about 16 by 8 inches, its length stretching in front of you.

Using your fingers and the scraper or spatula, spread the butter on the forward two thirds of the dough rectangle, leaving ½ inch unbuttered dough around top and sides. Both butter and dough will look rough and uneven, which is normal.

Turn No. 1. Dough is now to be folded and rolled out 4 to 6 times in all, and each roll and fold is called a "turn." Fold the unbuttered third of the rectangle toward the middle.

Fold the buttered top down to cover it, as though folding a business letter. Rotate dough so top flap is to your right. You now have 3 layers of dough and 2 of butter.

Turn No. 2. (Dough will be soft and sticky; if you find it too difficult to handle, wrap in plastic and refrigerate for 30 minutes, then continue.) Lifting and flouring it lightly as necessary, and using firm even strokes, roll dough out into a rectangle 18 to 20 inches long and 8 to 10 inches wide. Fold the two ends so their edges meet on top in the middle. Then fold in two, like a book, and rotate so the opening is to your right. With balls of fingers, make 2 depressions in top of dough to indicate the 2 turns. Wrap in plastic, place in a plastic bag, and refrigerate for at least 40 minutes, or overnight if you wish. You now have 9 layers of dough and 8 of butter.

Turns No. 3 and 4. If dough is cold and hard, beat evenly back and forth and across for a minute or more, to soften the butter and to start the dough moving—it is very important to soften hard butter at this point, or it will flake and break up rather than spreading itself evenly the length of the dough. Roll dough into a rectangle 10 by 20 inches; fold in thirds, as in Turn No. 1. Rotate so top flap is to your right; roll and fold again. Mark 4 depressions in the dough with the balls of your fingers, to indicate the 4 turns. Wrap and refrigerate—for 2 hours if you are then to use it, for 1 hour if you are making more turns.

✳ You can use the dough at this point, for turnovers, or such things as the Ham Tart on page 70. Or if you wish to refrigerate the dough for several days, or to freeze it for several months, this is the best point at which to do so.

Turns No. 5 and 6. For *vol-au-vent,* patty shells, fancy tarts like *Le Pithiviers,* or in any case where you want the maximum of puff and lightness, give the dough 2 more turns, exactly like Turns No. 3 and 4. Wrap and refrigerate for at least 2 hours before rolling out the dough.

Mock puff pastry. This is turning plain pie dough into a puffing dough; see directions on page 48.

Reconstituting puff-pastry leftovers. Arrange the dough on your work surface so it is all in one layer; cut and arrange the pieces so they form a rough rectangle. Paint edges with cold water and seal together with your fingers. Roll out into a larger rectangle as best you can, spread the top two thirds with a teaspoon or so of soft butter, fold into thirds, as though folding a business letter, wrap, and chill an hour or so. Give 2 more turns, wrap, and chill at least 2 hours—overnight is better, to relax the dough. Use the dough for tarts, turnovers, or appetizers; or store in the freezer.

The sauce roster

Sauces that are integral parts of a dish are, in almost every instance, parts of the recipes in this book. The section here, then, is in the form of a meander and an *aide mémoire,* except for a complete treatise on the hollandaise family, which took up a whole program. Most of these sauces, of course, have appeared in the two *Masterings* as well as in *The French Chef Cookbook,* but there is no harm in the retelling, since, knowing you have probably seen and read much of it before, I have in each instance looked at the subject from a different angle. One never ceases to learn and still, after more than twenty-five ·years in the business, I, at least, am continually running into a new discovery or another point of view.

THE WHITE SAUCE FAMILY

Béchamels, veloutés, cream sauces, fish sauces,
cheese sauces, soufflé and soup bases

The traditional white sauce family began taking a beating in the early 1970's from those who presume to speak for the *nouvelle vague,* the new wave of French cuisine, the so-called young Turks who run the Michelin-given three-star restaurants in France. Down with flour, is the word, *à bas* Escoffier, down with the old and up with the new. But since none of the new chefs has so far put anything down in writing, we must rely on information that comes to us second hand, from food writers and publicists. We do have Raymond Oliver's several books, including his monumental *La Cuisine,* translated from the French by Nika Hazelton and Jack Van Bibber (New York: L. Amiel, 1969). Oliver, owner of the beautiful Grand Véfour restaurant in Paris, is the elder statesman of the group, but his books were written before the cult of the new came into being. He uses a *roux* of flour and butter cooked together for his traditional *béchamels* and *veloutés,* as does the distinguished former chef of the Kennedy White House, René Verdon, in his *French Cooking for the American Table* (New York: Doubleday, 1974). Other noteworthy examples are Jacques Pépin's fish sauces with *roux* in his interesting *Chez Moi, A French Chef Cooks at Home* (New York: Simon & Schuster, 1975). Even the great Fernand Point, the presumed father of the new school of chefs, and at whose restaurant, La Pyramide, at Vienne, many of them trained, suggests a little *roux* moistened with milk and cream to pour over his delicate mousse of pike, his *Quenelles à la Crème,* before they brown lightly in the oven.

According to the writers for the new cult, however, we are to shun the *roux* absolutely: we must use reductions and essences, and we must mount them with lashings of butter and cream, and with egg yolks. Well, this is all fine for luxury restaurants, but if we home cooks follow that lead we'll be giving everyone in the family not only severe avoirdupois, but constant bilious attacks that will lead to eventual fatty degeneration of the liver—to say nothing of flooding the freezer with an oversupply of egg whites. The vogue will pass, since the point of the *roux*-thickened sauces, the *béchamels* and *veloutés,* is simple and logical: this type of sauce is far less rich, less fattening, and more economical than a sauce thickened with the large quantities of cream or butter and/or egg yolks required for a non-*roux* sauce. Yet when the *béchamel,* and especially the *velouté,* is knowingly concocted and carefully flavored, it is absolutely delicious. In fact, to me, this family of sauces is fundamental to French home cooking. Without them, how would we have our comfortable hard-boiled egg dishes, like *Oeufs à la Tripe* and *Oeufs Chimay?* What would be the alternative to the creamy inner sauce for the lasagne, or the filling for the spinach turnover, and how would we make our cheese or chicken croquettes?

Fortunately, these sauces are very quickly made, and there is nothing mysterious about them. They consist of a cooked *roux,* a hot liquid that is smoothly blended in, such as milk, vegetable juices, chicken stock, fish poaching liquid, and a brief simmer; perhaps you enrich them at the end, with a dollop of butter, or cream, or a combination of cream and egg yolks. But the enrichment can be very reasonable indeed, measured to your waistline.

Certainly the *roux* is the key to the *béchamel* and the *velouté,* however, since if it is not cooked slowly and thoroughly the sauce will be pasty and floury. It is actually the uncooked or poorly cooked *roux,* in my opinion, that has given flour a bad name in sauces. But since it takes only 2 or 3 minutes to cook flour and butter together, and since there is nothing difficult about it whatsoever, there is no excuse at all for a badly made sauce. Why, then, do so many American recipes read: "Melt the butter, blend in the flour, then beat in the liquid." Why? Are we too dumb or too lazy to stir flour and butter over moderate heat for 2 to 3 minutes? Are 2 to 3 minutes too much time to take? Or are we always cooking in flimsy pans that burn the *roux?* I don't understand it at all, and if you run into any of those recipes—and you will—just change them to read, "Melt the butter, blend in the flour, *stir over moderate heat until butter and flour foam together for 2 minutes without coloring more than a buttery yellow, remove from heat, and when roux has stopped bubbling, pour in all the hot liquid at once, vigorously beating with a wire whip to blend roux and liquid smoothly."* That makes 56 words instead of 12; perhaps it is just to save space that they don't cook the *roux.* But save space and ruin a sauce?

Sauce béchamel; sauce velouté

BASIC WHITE SAUCE

For 2 cups of general-purpose sauce (1½ tablespoons flour per cup of sauce)

2 cups of liquid (milk, stock, and/or vegetable juices)
2 Tb butter
3 Tb flour
Salt and pepper to taste

Equipment: A heavy-bottomed saucepan in which to cook the sauce, and another saucepan in which to heat the liquid; a wooden spatula or spoon to cook the roux, a wire whip with which to blend liquid into roux, a rubber spatula for cleaning sauce off sides of pan

Heat the liquid to below the simmer. Meanwhile melt the butter in the heavy-bottomed pan, then blend in the flour with your wooden spatula or spoon—you should have just enough butter so that mixture makes a loose paste—stir in a little more if need be. Stirring slowly, cook over moderate heat until butter and flour foam and bubble slowly for 2 minutes without coloring more than a buttery yellow. Remove pan from heat and wait 30 seconds or so until *roux* has stopped bubbling. Then, all at once, pour in the hot liquid, vigorously beating with your wire whip to make a perfectly smooth blending. With spoon or rubber spatula, scrape all around inside corners of pan to be sure all *roux* has been absorbed into the liquid, and beat again for a few seconds.

Now set saucepan over moderately high heat and bring to the slow boil, stirring rather slowly, taking a second to circulate your wire whip about the pan. Boil slowly, stirring, for 2 minutes. If you have used milk only, stir in ¼ to ½ teaspoon of salt and several grinds of white pepper; if you have stock or other liquid, taste, and correct seasoning. If it is a milk sauce, the initial cooking is done; if it is a sauce with stock, you may want to simmer it longer, but this depends entirely on how strong and well-flavored the stock was to begin with, and other considerations that your particular recipe will discuss with you.

✻ If you are not to use the sauce immediately, clean off sides of pan with a rubber spatula, and you will have to do something about the top of the sauce to prevent it from crusting over. You can lay a piece of plastic wrap right on top, which will prevent a crust, but you lose a little sauce when you remove the plastic. Or take a small piece of soft butter, drop it on top of the sauce, and spread it all over with the back of a spoon. Or take a tablespoon of milk, cream, or stock, dip it gently on top of the sauce by tipping the spoon over the surface, and smear the liquid around with the back of the spoon.

Additions and enrichments to white sauces. The plain *béchamel* white sauce is a base only, to be mixed into something else, to be flavored with cheese, to be simmered with cream and herbs. The *veloutés* with their base of stock or other liquid are usually enriched with butter, or cream, or cream and egg yolks. An excellent example of what you can do with *veloutés* is the *Sauce Parisienne* with the shrimp mousse on page 153. Others are the white-wine *velouté* for the sole fillets, on page 135, and the glazing sauce for the braised ham *Duxelles,* page 309. Examples of putting a *béchamel* to work are the onion-flavored inner sauce for the lasagne on page 351, and its double duty for the soufflé *roulade* with broccoli on page 109.

BROWN SAUCES

A serious brown sauce in the classic manner is much more of a problem than any of the white sauces, because it takes several hours of simmering. Our one example is the *Semi-Demi-Glace* with the roast tenderloin of beef on page 282; it's a lovely sauce when you have the time and the homemade brown meat stock to simmer with it. Other brown sauces, less formal but nonetheless good, are made from the deglazing of roasting pans and sautéing skillets: you have finished cooking the meat or poultry, you skim out all but a spoonful of fat, throw in a chopped shallot or scallion and cook a moment, then stir in a bit of wine and scrape up all coagulated cooking juices into it, add some meat stock, and boil it rapidly until reduced to the syrupy state; you swirl in a little butter for a light liaison and enrichment, and pour it over your meat. It is a delicious type of sauce, a pan gravy, a *petit jus*, just a spoonful per serving; use it for anything you roast or sauté, like liver, kidneys, hamburgers. It tastes of the food that it sauces, it doesn't mask it or drown it, it simply extends and complements the original. These appear throughout French cooking and throughout this book, as integral parts of such recipes as the roast lamb on page 290, the roast turkey on page 236, and many others.

Then you have the brown sauces that are parts of a stew or a braise, that make themselves as the food is cooking. You may have thickened it with a *roux* before the braising begins, as for the braised beef *en Daube* on page 266, and the *Coq au Vin* and Chicken Fricassee on page 199, where all you do at the end is to degrease and flavor the final savory product. Or you may choose the *beurre manié* way, where you thicken the cooking liquid at the end with a flour-butter paste, like the sauce for the *Boeuf Bourguignon* on page 263. Or you may be entirely fat free, and use the methods discussed on page 270.

In addition to these, you have what Escoffier calls the small composed sauces, like the one for sautéed chicken with tomato, mushrooms, and herbs, page 189, or the deglazing sauce with wine and cream for hamburgers on page 314.

Except for the mock *Demi-Glace,* there is nothing either time-consuming or difficult about any of these sauces, and they do much to make the delight of any dish.

TOMATO SAUCES

A good tomato sauce is essential to any cooking of the Western world, and the one in the lasagne recipe, on page 351, with its use of both canned and fresh tomatoes, is a fine example. Make a lot while you're at it, and keep the extra in the freezer. Fresh tomato *fondue* is another useful flavoring—tomatoes peeled, seeded, juiced, chopped, and simmered in butter or olive oil with a bit of chopped shallot, perhaps a clove of crushed garlic, salt, pepper, and thyme or basil. This too can be frozen, and when you stir a spoonful into the deglazing sauce of a steak or a roast, you have added, perhaps, just the famous *je ne sais quoi de saveur* to give a sophisticated final touch to that particular meal.

OIL AND VINEGAR SAUCES: THE VINAIGRETTES

Vinaigrettes, or "vinegarettes" as a friend of mine calls them, often contain lemon juice and no vinegar at all, but are usually salad dressings. Their delectability lies in the perfection of their ingredients: the best and freshest oil, the freshest lemons, the finest wine vinegar; when you have these, you need few other elaborations besides a little chopped shallot or scallion, or hard-toasted French bread rubbed with a clove of garlic and crumbled into your salad, or a little dry or Dijon-type mustard whipped with the lemon or vinegar. Herbs, of course, are heavenly additions—fresh chives, chervil, tarragon, basil, even fresh parsley.

However, I am particularly fond of the garlic dressing for the *Salade Niçoise* on page 436, with its combination of both lemon juice and vinegar, and here is a variation on that.

Variation on garlic dressing. Pound a clove of garlic in a small mortar with half a teaspoon of salt and the minced zest (yellow part only of peel) of half a lemon; beat in a tablespoon of lemon juice, then 4 of good olive oil, and finally a tablespoon or so of sesame paste, a few grinds of pepper, and a sprinkling of fresh minced basil. Serve this sauce with hard-boiled eggs, with cold artichokes, or over the cold baked eggplant halves on page 399; it is good also with sardines or tuna, and with broiled fish, as well as with a salad of cold green beans or cooked dried beans or lentils.

MAYONNAISE

Never-fail methods for making your own perfect mayonnaise, that thick ambrosial sauce that tastes so deliciously of fresh eggs, fresh fine oil, and fresh lemons, are on page 439, showing you how to make it entirely by hand, or with the electric mixer, or in the electric super-blender-food-processor. Another mayonnaise mixed with herbs, capers, and hard-boiled eggs is served with the cold lobster on page 177, and would be equally good with cold roast veal or pork, cold fish or chicken, or cold vegetables.

Then there is *green mayonnaise,* lovely with cold fish, eggs, chicken, shrimp, and vegetables; to make that you use the regular mayonnaise formula, and for each 2 to 2½ cups of it you have about ¾ packed cup of fresh greenery like a combination of parsley, chives, basil, tarragon, plus some spinach and watercress leaves: drop them for 2 minutes in boiling water, drain, and squeeze dry in the corner of a towel, purée them in an electric blender with a few tablespoons of oil, gradually beat the purée into the mayonnaise, and you have a beautiful, herbal, pale-green sauce.

Other purées that can go into mayonnaise to lighten it or change its character could be a purée of green asparagus tips or of artichokes—scraped leaf bottoms or the cooked bottom itself—squeezed in the corner of a towel to extract excess juice. A purée of canned red pimiento stirred into mayonnaise along with chopped green herbs is an idea from my colleague, Simca, who uses it most effectively with cold poached fish or cold poached eggs. Then you can lighten mayonnaise by stirring in a spoonful or so of *crème fraîche* or sour cream, as discussed in the sour-cream sauce paragraphs on page 442. Again, you could lighten it by folding in a beaten egg white or two; or you can give it more body when you want it to cover cold poached fish or poultry—sieve in a couple of hard-boiled eggs. In other words, while it is divine and soul-satisfying just as it is, consider mayonnaise a springboard for color and creativity.

THE HOLLANDAISE FAMILY

Among the famous sauces of France, hollandaise certainly ranks in the top echelon. The doyen of the hot egg-yolk-and-butter family, hollandaise is flavored with lemon, while its sister, *béarnaise,* has the stronger personality of pepper, vinegar, tarragon, and shallots. Otherwise they are the same sauce, with the same proportions and same techniques of making.

You can do either one in the electric blender, but handmade sauce is almost as fast. Although for handmade sauce you do have to thicken the egg yolks over heat before you beat in the butter, you don't have the messy job of digging it out of the machine afterward. And if you want more than the ¾ cup or so that the machine produces, hand work is infinitely speedier for large amounts. In addition, learning to have complete confidence in the handling of egg yolks under all circumstances gives one a satisfying sense of cleverness and power.

RULES TO REMEMBER. To make hollandaise or *béarnaise* by hand, you thicken egg yolks with lemon juice or vinegar flavoring over heat, then beat in butter, to make a warm, thick, creamy sauce. The two things to watch for are heating the yolks without scrambling them, and then adding the butter in such a way that the sauce thickens. Keep the following points in mind and you will never fail.

1. Before doing anything else, beat the plain yolks for a minute or more to cream them. This readies them for coming events.

2. Always add some liquid and some butter to the yolks before cooking them. This prevents heat shock.

3. Let the yolks heat gradually to prevent scrambling.

4. Start beating butter into the warm cooked yolks by teaspoon bits or dribbles until the emulsion (thickening) process begins.

5. Do not exceed maximum butter proportions of 3 ounces per yolk or emulsion will break down and sauce will thin out.

6. Keep finished sauce over barely warm heat to prevent curdling, and serve in a warm bowl, not a hot one.

7. It is quick and easy to reconstitute a thinned-out or curdled sauce.

Sauce hollandaise

WARM EGG-YOLK-AND-BUTTER SAUCE WITH LEMON FLAVORING, TO ACCOMPANY POACHED EGGS, POACHED AND BOILED FISH, ARTICHOKES, ASPARAGUS, BROCCOLI

For 1 to 1½ cups, serving 4 to 8

1 Tb lemon juice in a small saucepan
2 Tb water
¼ tsp salt
6 grinds of white pepper (a big pinch)
3 egg yolks in a heavy-bottomed 6-cup stainless or enameled saucepan
2 Tb cold butter
1½ to 2 sticks (6 to 8 ounces) soft butter or melted butter, beside you
Additional salt, pepper, and lemon juice

Other equipment: A wire whip; a pan of cold water set beside you at the stove; a rubber spatula

Preliminaries. Simmer the lemon juice, water, salt, and pepper until reduced to 2 tablespoons—to concentrate the pepper flavoring. Meanwhile, beat the egg yolks for a minute or more, until thickened into a rather sticky cream. Cool the lemon juice reduction by setting pan in the cold water, then beat by driblets into egg yolks. Place 1 tablespoon of the cold butter in the pan (by gradually melting as the yolks are warmed, this softens the shock of heat).

Cooking the egg yolks. Set pan over moderate heat, stirring constantly and rather slowly with wire whip, reaching all over bottom and corners of pan. (Be ready to move it rapidly off and on heat, or to cool pan in cold water if there is a suggestion of curds or scrambling.) In a minute or so, foam will appear on top of yolks, then a wisping of steam, indicating that they are heating. Continue until the yolks are thick and smooth. At once remove pan from heat; immediately beat in second tablespoon of cold butter to cool the yolks. Continue beating for a moment to stop the yolks from cooking.

Beating in the butter. Begin beating in the butter by teaspoon gobs, or by driblets; as each addition is absorbed by the yolks, add another, and continue without stopping until sauce thickens into a heavy cream. As soon as sauce has thickened, you know the emulsion process has been established and you may pause. If you are serving immediately, beat in as much of the butter as you wish. If you are making the sauce in advance, stop at this point and set it aside; beat in hot melted butter by dribbles to heat the sauce just before bringing it to the table. In either case, correct seasoning before serving, beating in more salt, pepper, and lemon if you feel them necessary. For a lighter sauce, beat in droplets of hot water, vegetable cooking juices, or stock—a tablespoon or two, just before serving.

Trouble-shooting

If sauce refuses to thicken (because you beat in the butter too fast), stop where you are; beat a teaspoon of lemon juice and a tablespoon of the sauce in a small bowl until sauce begins to thicken, then beat in the rest of the sauce by small dribbles. Continue where you left off.

If finished sauce begins to separate, curdle, or thin out (you kept it too warm, or you exceeded the butter proportions), beat in a tablespoon of cold water; if this does not work, use the system discussed in the paragraph above.

If sauce is lumpy (you've kept it too warm and the yolks have scrambled), push through a strainer to even the lumps, then disguise it with chopped hard-boiled egg, capers, and minced parsley.

Sauce mousseline. Whip ¼ cup of heavy cream, and fold it into the hollandaise just before serving. This is lovely with boiled salmon, trout, or striped bass, fish soufflés, and asparagus.

Sauce béarnaise

———◆———

WARM EGG-YOLK-
AND-BUTTER SAUCE
WITH VINEGAR AND
HERB FLAVORING,
TO ACCOMPANY
POACHED EGGS,
BROILED OR FRIED
FISH, BROILED
CHICKEN, STEAKS

For 1 to 1½ cups,
serving 4 to 8

¼ cup white- or red-wine vinegar
¼ cup dry white wine or dry white Vermouth
1 Tb minced shallots or scallions
½ Tb dried tarragon (or 1 Tb fresh)
¼ tsp cracked peppercorns
¼ tsp salt

Simmer the vinegar and wine or Vermouth with the shallots or scallions, tarragon, pepper and salt for 8 to 10 minutes, until liquid has reduced to about 2 tablespoons. Cool, then strain: substitute this for the lemon juice reduction in the preceding hollandaise recipe. If you want a particularly strong, tart flavor, you may wish to use only 1 stick of butter.

Electric blender béarnaise is on page 387.

———◆———

Wine for drinking, cooking, and tasting

There are so many good books out nowadays on the choosing of wines for drinking that it would be foolish of me to go into this vast subject at all except to observe that the first consideration, always, is that the food should enhance the wine and the wine should complement the food. When one overpowers the other, you have a mismanagement. Fortunately, the only way to learn about wines is to drink them. (Although I have given wine suggestions for all main-course dishes in this book, I realize full well that my domestic choices are sketchy: great improvements are now taking place in West Coast wine production, and I make no pretense at all of being an up-to-date authority.)

Wines for cooking should be young, healthy, and usually dry. White wine is the one most often called for and the hardest to find at a reasonable price. It should be dry, have a good body, and not the slightest sourness. You will have to taste them, ask friends and chefs in your area, and experiment. As always, I use a light white French Vermouth more than anything else . . . Noilly Prat, Boissières, Martini Blanc are those I've had the most success with. (I've not yet found a domestic Vermouth I like in cooking.) Red wines are much less of a problem, and are much less used in cooking; an honest Chianti, Zinfandel, or Gamay is usually sensibly priced and works out beautifully. But whatever wine you use, be sure you taste it carefully first—if it is not good to drink, it will not be good to cook with.

A CHEESE AND WINE-TASTING PARTY

When you want a change from the usual cocktail routine, or would like to give an informal after-dinner get-together, a cheese and wine tasting party is both easy to organize and fun for hosts and guests alike. No outlandish equipment is needed; you arrange the wine and glasses, along with cheese and other edibles, all together on one large table, or use a series of card tables with one or two wines at each. You need only one glass per guest plus a few extras to replace strays; after each sampling, which consists of an ounce or so, the guest rinses his glass from a pitcher of fresh water, pours that into a tub on the floor, and proceeds to the next bottle. Wines and cheeses may range from the simple jug and domestic cheddar to vintage rarities. We suggest here a middle way, which you can plan according to your cash reserves.

THE WINES. One bottle of wine contains 24 ounces; you will need at least ½ bottle per person plus several in reserve, particularly if your group numbers less than 16 people. The following list is for 16 to 20 guests, and compares French wines with their California cousins, known as varietals because they go by the name of the grape that produced them. Start with the lightest wines, and move along to the heavier ones.

An Alsatian Riesling and its American counterpart, Johannisberger Riesling. Chill an hour or two; open just before serving.

A French *rosé* from Tavel or Anjou, and a California Grenache *rosé*. Same as above.

A French Beaujolais and a domestic Zinfandel or Gamay. Let sit for several hours at cool room temperature—60 to 62 degrees would be ideal —or chill 20 minutes in the refrigerator; open just before serving.

A French red Bordeaux, such as a Médoc, and a California Cabernet Sauvignon. Let *chambrée*, or sit, at room temperature of around 65 (or 70) degrees for several hours; open the French wine 2 to 3 hours before serving and the domestic one an hour before.

A French white Burgundy and a domestic Pinot Chardonnay. Chill about an hour—wines should be very cold but not so iced as to lose character; open just before serving.

A French red Burgundy and its American cousin, Pinot Noir. These are usually served 2 to 3 degrees cooler than the red Bordeaux—around 62 to 65 degrees if possible; open about 1 hour before serving.

THE CHEESES. Although professional wine tasters require absolute quiet and no distractions other than little cubes of bread between sips to pursue their trade, informal parties like this may take liberties with tradition. A collection of cheeses could include the blue family, from Roquefort to Danish and domestic; these would go with the Burgundies and Pinots. Soft cheeses like Brie, Camembert, and Liederkranz are happy with red Bordeaux and Cabernet Sauvignon. Cheddars and Swiss cheese go with Beaujolais, Zinfandel, and Gamay wines, while Rieslings and rosés need the milder cheeses like Monterey Jack. Place the cheeses on boards or trays near the appropriate wines, with a separate knife for each cheese, and either chunks or thin slices of French bread within easy reach.

STORING CHEESE. I think the best place to store ripe and ready-to-eat cheese is in the refrigerator, where the temperature is around 37 degrees. I wrap each piece airtight in plastic, and place the lot in a large plastic bag, itself closed airtight with a twisted wire or plastic fastener. (I do have a glass-jar cheese container, with sunken well to hold the solution of vinegar, salt, and water that is supposed to preserve the cheese; it seems to work satisfactorily, but doesn't hold enough cheese to be practical for our household.) For serving, do let cheese sit half an hour or so at room temperature, to take off the chill and to bring out the flavor.

CHEESE ETIQUETTE: HOW TO HELP YOURSELF. There is a politeness in the way you cut a piece of cheese for yourself, and the rule is to do so in such a way that the cheese remains in the same general shape it had when it was presented to you. For instance, a Brie cheese is usually served in a pie-shaped wedge. That means you should cut yourself a slice from one of the long sides, and the cheese will continue looking like a Brie for the next guest. If you rudely cut off its nose—its point—you have not only ruined its looks, but you have unwittingly and ungraciously lopped off its identity. You've turned it into an anonymous leftover.

On the other hand, if the Brie is served as a whole large wheel, you cut yourself a wedge, neatly and nicely, as though it were a pie. The whole Camembert, shaped like a small round cake, is also cut into wedges. However it does become more difficult when you are faced with a short fat wedge of Roquefort, or a block of Gruyère or cheddar, but you are playing the right game when you do your best to leave the cheese in its original shape.

Incidentally, we were shown by some English friends a fine way of cutting large cylindrical shapes, like Stiltons and whole cheddars. You slice off the top covering and save it. Then, holding your knife parallel to the top of the cheese, you cut slivers round and round the top, keeping the cylindrical shape. Before storing the cheese, replace the top, and cover with plastic wrap.

COOKED TIDBITS. Although you need nothing hot from your kitchen, you may wish to add your own personal touch to the party. You might serve a cheese quiche in the free-form shell described on page 609, which you can cut into bite-sized pieces. The *Croque Monsieur* and *Croque Madame* on page 42 are other possibilities. On our television program we did the Cheddar Cheese Tartlets on page 47, and the little Cheese Croquettes on page 45. I do think that something homemade, however simple, shows that you care and want to honor your guests.

A culinary gazetteer

*Here is the collecting spot for everything I felt needed
mentioning that is not dealt with elsewhere, or
that wanted more expansive treatment
than a mere listing in
the index*

AROMATIC. Aromatic vegetables, aromatic broth, aromatic liquid, and so forth—anything that foods cook with that gives them flavor. The aromatics are usually carrots, onions, celery, garlic, and herbs, as well as wines and liqueurs. Cooking with aromatic ingredients, particularly in the poaching and braising of meats and vegetables, and the making of stocks and sauces, is one of the keys to good French cooking.

BAKING POWDER. Although baking powder appears in only one recipe in this book, I am mentioning it here because we get frequent queries in our French Chef office. Baking powder is a quick chemical substitute for yeast; it puffs up a dough, making it light and increasing its volume. Our most familiar example is baking powder biscuits, but you can make baking powder doughnuts as well as baking powder cakes and bread. There are two kinds of baking powder usually available: single action, which works on the dough only when it is in the oven, and double action, which works both in the cold dough and in the oven. According to Belle Lowe's *Experimental Cookery* (New York: John Wiley & Sons, 1961) a teaspoon of either type is generally sufficient for 1 cup of flour. The French name for baking powder is *levure alsacienne, levure chimique,* or *levure en poudre;* the directions on my 15-gram package declare that its contents, 2½ teaspoons, are sufficient for 500 grams, or 3¾ cups, of flour. Baking powder in high-altitude cookery is a story in itself; see the high-altitude entry in this list for how to obtain that information.

BAY LEAVES. You will notice I always stress "imported bay leaves"—because the domestic California bay has a stronger, oilier, and substantially different taste from that of the Mediterranean bay.

BLANCH. To blanch, usually in boiling water: this is to drop green vegetables into a large amount of boiling water either to cook them rapidly until limp, as for spinach or cabbage leaves that are to have further cooking; or to blanch them until almost tender, as for green beans that are to be tossed in butter. It also means boiling pieces of bacon to remove excess salt and the smoky flavor, or boiling tripe to freshen it before proceeding to the final cooking.

BOIL, SIMMER, POACH, TEPID, WARM, HOT, etc. Except for BOIL, *Webster* gives no temperature pronouncements for other states of liquid over heat, and I am therefore free to give my own, which I arrived at by holding my Weston Instant Pocket thermometer in a saucepan of water. Looking carefully at water as it comes to the boil is a good idea, actually, since you are observing the liquid yourself, and feeling it, and knowing, therefore, what the terms should mean. (Temperatures are for tap water at sea level.)

Tepid, 85 to 105 degrees, around body temperature: the chill is off and warmth is perceptible.

Warm, 115 to 120 degrees: the liquid is definitely warm, comfortable to the hand, but not hot.

Hot, 130 to 135 degrees: it is much too hot for your hand.

Poach, 180 to 190 degrees: it is beginning to move, to shiver, to *frémir*— just right for poaching fish and eggs.

Simmer, 190 to 200 degrees: there is more movement, and little bubbles appear in the liquid.

Slow boil, 205 degrees: even more movement and bigger bubbles.

The real boil, 212 degrees: the liquid is seething and bubbling and steaming.

BRAISE. To cook food, usually meat—but it can be onions, carrots, sauerkraut, or cabbage—in a covered pan with more or less liquid, depending on how long the food is to cook. Braising is distinct from stewing, where the food is submerged in liquid, and distinct from covered roasting or *poêléing,* where no liquid is added. Braising is a combination of cover roasting and steaming, used wherever foods will benefit from moist cooking.

BREAD CRUMBS. You'll want bread crumbs to sprinkle over the top of a dish that is to be baked or browned; to mix into a filling to bulk it up or to absorb moisture; to coat chicken Kiev or a fillet of fish that is to be deep fried or broiled—in fact, it is useful to have bread crumbs always at hand. I prefer them fresh, made out of a French or Italian type of white bread, or any nonsweetened homemade type of white bread with body and texture. Slice off the crusts, cut the bread into half-inch cubes, and crumb these in an electric blender, about ¾ cup at a time. Store the crumbs in an airtight plastic bag in the freezer, ready for instant use; they will keep a month or more.

BUTTER. Unless your recipe is specific, salted and unsalted butters are interchangeable. I am talking about butter that comes in packages containing either wrapped sticks or a solid one-pound block—that is, not whipped butter. One uses unsalted butter for cakes, cookies, and desserts, and I personally prefer unsalted butter for pie doughs and puff pastry, since most brands I have tried seem to have less water content than salted butter; they seem more solid, in other words, and that is desirable for pastries. When I was starting my cooking career in Paris, speaking of solidity, our chef insisted on *beurre des Charentes* for his puff pastries, since he considered butter from that region of France to have the most body. I still use it when I'm there, but I buy a lighter butter for the table, *beurre d'Isigny*. French butters are made from *crème fraîche*, the slightly fermented heavy cream described further on, and each region of France has its own native lactic ferments that give (or used to give) the butter from each area its own special regional character. Fine French butters are never salted, but you will find salt added to some farm butters, where it acts as a preservative. American butter, on the other hand, is made from sweet unfermented cream and has a neutral taste because the natural ferments have been pasteurized out; actually, then, we should call all our butter, salted or not, "sweet butter," since it comes from sweet cream. Thus, to avoid any confusion, I always use the term "unsalted butter."

Washing butter. You will run into recipes, mostly old ones, that direct you to wash the butter and to knead it until it is waxy: knead it in a damp towel until it is malleable, then knead in a basin of cold water, then knead, still in the towel, on your work surface, mopping up moisture with paper towels. This method was used in the old days to remove salt and residual moisture, and also to freshen the taste of the butter if it had been kept too long. It is rather fun to do, and a good trick to know about if you run into an inferior grade of butter that oozes moisture droplets, or if you have a butter with questionable taste.

Clarified butter. This means butter that has been rid of its milky residue: cut it into small pieces and melt it over moderate heat, skim off the foam, then pour the clear yellow liquid off the milky residue in the bottom of the pan. The clear liquid is clarified butter, and you use it for sautéing chicken breasts, white-bread croutons, calf's brains, or anything fine and delicate that you want to sauté in butter. It is the milky residue, if left in, that turns brown, then black and bitter. Clarified butter, by the way, will keep for weeks in a covered jar in the refrigerator; it is the same as *ghee* used so extensively in the cooking of India.

Butter substitutes. There is no substitute for the taste of butter; however, you may use the other spread instead of butter in any recipe, since the cooking reactions will be substantially the same.

BUTTERED AND FLOURED. For cake pans, pastry sheets, cookie molds. Rub a film of soft butter over baking surface, sprinkle on flour and tilt in all directions to coat entire surface with the flour; knock off excess by banging edge of upside down mold on edge of sink. (This coating prevents batters from sticking to baking surface during cooking.)

CHEESECLOTH. They don't sell cheesecloth in France the way they do here, and if you want some there, go to a pharmacy and ask for *"gaze à pansement"* (bandage gauze). It took me years to figure out that one. Whether French or American, cheesecloth needs a washing in soap and warm water to remove the medical chemical taste it would otherwise impart to cooking.

TO COAT A SPOON. This term is used to give some indication of how thick a sauce should be. If it is watery, it will merely wet the spoon, but if it is a thick mayonnaise it will cling all over the surface, in a thick layer. On the other hand *crème anglaise* will simply coat the spoon rather lightly, but you can see the layer there, meaning the sauce has thickened.

CORRECT SEASONING. This means taste the food and decide what else it needs in the way of salt, pepper, Cognac, garlic, tarragon, cinnamon, red wine, or whatever—the fateful decision is entirely your own.

COURT BOUILLON. A flavored liquid in which to simmer or poach vegetables, fish, or other ingredients; the liquid is usually wine diluted with water, plus aromatic vegetables—carrots, celery, onions—and herbs, all simmered together to make an aromatic broth.

CROSS-HATCHING. Criss-cross marks made with the point of a knife through the wet egg glaze on a pastry dough before it goes into the oven, to break up the glaze and produce a decorative pattern as the pastry browns. For pie-dough toppings the knife point merely grazes the pastry, but for puff pastry, which is thicker, the cut goes down $\frac{1}{16}$ inch into the dough, which then opens up into a handsome design as it bakes.

DEGLAZE. This means to gather up the coagulated cooking juices from a pan after the food is done, and to incorporate them into your sauce. Deglazing is another one of the keys to fine food, since those coagulated juices are the essence of flavor that has exuded from the roast chicken or sautéed hamburger, to take examples, and has been concentrated in the coagulation adhering to the pan. To gather up that flavor, you pour a little wine, or stock, or even water into the pan set over heat; scrub hard with a wooden spoon to loosen and dissolve the coagulation into the hot liquid. Then you add the liquid as is into a ready-made sauce, or you boil down the liquid until it is thick and syrupy, swish in a bit of soft butter to enrich it, and pour that over your meat, thus making one of the simplest and most delicious of sauces.

DEGREASE. To skim the fat off the surface of a stock, a soup, a stew, a sauce, do it with a spoon, which takes time and patience. But if you have plenty of time, use the simplest and most foolproof method: chill the liquid, and lift off the fat when it has congealed. Or provide yourself with one of the degreasers illustrated here.

DEGREASING DEVICES (*from left to right*)

A handsome glass object with plastic-tipped plunger: when you remove the plunger the clear liquid pours out the bottom spout, and the plunger stops the flow when the fat appears at the exit.

A Pyrex pitcher with spout starting at the bottom: pour out the clear stock until the fat appears in the spout.

A glass jar and a bulb baster: either suck the fat off the top of the liquid, or draw the liquid off from under the fat.

The separatory funnel: the fat rises to the top of the bulbous container, the liquid is drained from the bottom tube, and a faucet shuts off the flow when the fat appears. (This model had a broken bottom tube, and I bought it for half price at a chemist's supply house.)

DIET COOKERY. I have purposely avoided any dietary comments in this book because the situation seems to be one of ever-sifting sands, where one theory is all the rage and is then superseded by another. The point of the book, anyway, is to concentrate on the techniques of cookery, since they can be applied to whatever ingredients you use.

EGGS. All eggs called for in the recipes here are U.S. Graded Large Eggs; it is useful always to have the same size, then at least you have one constant factor in your ingredients. A "large" egg weighs 2 ounces; the white measures 2 tablespoons and the yolk 1 tablespoon. Egg whites freeze perfectly in a screw-topped jar, and can be defrosted and refrozen with no harm. Egg yolks will also freeze, but they do not soften completely when thawed; to use them in hollandaise or mayonnaise, let them thaw, then beat them in an electric blender with a fresh yolk and a little vinegar or lemon juice, and when they are a smooth cream, proceed with your sauce.

EGG WHITES, THE BEATING OF. With electric beaters, either portable or the table-model types shown on these pages, there is no difficulty whatsoever in beating egg whites. I am certainly not against the handsome hand-held balloon whip and the beautiful unlined hammered copper bowl, but I now think these requirements put egg whites into that all too familiar Cloud Coo-Coo Land inhabited by the We Happy Few, and we want to de-emphasize that around here. However, whether you stick to the old-fashioned hand or take up modern means, these are the few simple rules to remember when you are beating egg whites:

1. *Choose the right bowl.* It should be of stainless steel or of tinned metal (or, of course, of hammered copper) ; porcelain and glass bowls allow the beaten whites to fall down their slippery sides, and lose volume. Unfortunately, many table model beaters have slippery-sided porcelain or glass bowls; don't buy that kind of beater, or change to another bowl. It is important, also, that the bowl be of such shape that the whole mass of egg whites will be in motion at once; i.e., the bowl should not be too wide, and it should have a rounded bottom—*cul de poule,* as the French say, shaped like the bottom of a setting hen.

Here is the typical wrong bowl; it is so wide that only part of the egg whites are in motion. Although it had beaten the egg whites for almost a minute at high speed when this picture was taken, the food coloring has still not blended into the whole.

Substitute a stainless-steel round-bottomed bowl for the wrong bowl, using the same beater, and the food coloring blends in 15 seconds or so.

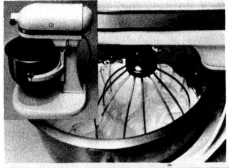

Here is a well-designed beater, where the whip rotates about itself as well as circulating around the bowl. Look for this system when you are buying a beater.

Here are the attachments: dough hook—*for kneading doughs or heavy meat mixtures;* whip—*for egg whites, eggs and sugar, and light fluffy mixtures;* flat beater —*for pastry doughs (blending butter and flour) and meat mixtures;* splatter shield— *to prevent flour from flying out of the mixer and messing up your work area.*

2. *Bowl and beaters must be clean.* Bits of egg yolk or oil or grease prevent the egg whites from mounting; presumably they form a film over the air bubbles, which then cannot expand—at least that theory sounds like a reasonable explanation of the fact. (That's why plastic bowls are out; they may retain oil or grease in their pores, which could then exude in the egg whites.)

3. *Egg whites must be warmed if chilled.* Set them, in their beating bowl, in a basin of hot water, and stir about with your impeccably clean finger to take off the chill. (If they are chilled, as I found out from our TV experiences, they form white flecks, and do not mount properly.)

4. *Start slow.* If you start beating too fast, you won't break up the mass of clinging white, and you won't get the volume you're after. Beat slowly for almost a minute, until the white is loose and has begun to foam.

5. *Then beat in cream of tartar and salt.* Add ¼ teaspoon of cream of tartar and a pinch of salt for 4 egg whites. These are stabilizers; they will help prevent the egg whites from breaking down once you've finished beating them.

6. *Gradually increase speed to fast.* Take about a minute to reach full speed—and the whole mass of egg whites should be in motion, which is the reason for having the correctly shaped bowl.

7. *Do not overbeat your egg whites: stand right over them all the time.* Beat until the egg whites form stiff shining peaks and hold in the wires of the beater—two or three minutes of beating, depending on your equipment; when a bit is lifted with a rubber spatula, it clings to the spatula and forms a shining peak. The sheen and the shine are the clues; "stiff but not dry" is another expression for the same condition. Overbeaten egg whites are dull, begin to break up, to fleck; they have lost most of their puffing abilities. But if you have overbeaten, add another egg white and beat again; the sheen and the shining peaks will return. An extra egg white will not change your proportions; it will, on the contrary, restore them to what they should be.

8. *Use your egg whites at once.* (But if for some reason you cannot, beat them again before using, adding another egg white.)

Troubles, and two general remarks. If your egg whites refuse to mount, you are beating them in a greasy bowl or with greasy beaters; you'll have to start all over again with fresh egg whites and clean dry equipment. A slight help in keeping egg whites up, when you are doing a dessert or cake, is to beat into them (for 3 to 4 whites) 2 to 3 tablespoons of the sugar called for in the recipe, beating it in by sprinkles just before the egg whites have reached their full volume, then beat to the stiff shiny stage. You should never have any trouble at all when you follow the 8 steps listed, but however well you beat them, you must fold them into the rest of your ingredients without losing a bit of their volume, and for this important process, see the entry under FOLD, a little farther on.

FLOUR. Whenever flour is called for in this book, it is all-purpose white flour unless otherwise specified; I prefer the unbleached to the bleached for pastry doughs because bleached flour produces a certain brittle texture in the baked dough. A discussion of French versus American flours for pastry making is on page 610. In all cases where cups of flour are called for be sure to measure as follows, for accurate weight: dip dry-measure cup in flour container, and sweep it off level with lip of cup, using the flat edge of a knife or spatula; if the flour is to be sifted, do so after measuring it, not before, since sifting changes the weight. A table of flour measurements is on page 674, giving cups, pounds, and metric equivalents.

Cake flour, by the way, is made from a special part of the wheat grain near the germ; it is mostly starch with very little gluten. You can substitute cornstarch (corn flour in England; *crème de maïs* in France) for cake flour in any recipe that calls for cake flour (or, for that matter, you may substitute all-purpose flour for cake flour, using 2 tablespoons less for each cup specified). When you have only French flour, use half French flour and half *crème de maïs* (cornstarch) to substitute for cake flour.

Pastry, flour, bread flour, high gluten flour. Flour is composed, among other things, of starch and gluten. The more gluten, or protein as it is sometimes called, the stronger the flour—meaning that a yeast dough made with that strong, hard-wheat, flour will rise high and stay risen. Strong flour, then, is desirable for many kinds of bread, such as white sandwich loaves and brioches. Although all-purpose flours are designed for yeast doughs, you will also at times see packages labeled "bread flour," or "high gluten flour," made especially for yeast doughs. But a strong flour is not desirable for tart, turnover, and puff pastry doughs because continual rollings out, foldings, and shapings so activate the gluten that the dough becomes rubbery and hard to handle. It used to be easy to find flour with a low gluten content, called pastry flour; sometimes it is available in health-food shops, but you can create your own by including a certain proportion of plain cake flour with your all-purpose flour, as discussed in the French puff pastry section on page 610.

Bleached and unbleached flours. When flour is just milled, it is yellowish in color; when stored a certain amount of time, it will bleach itself naturally. But the process may be hurried up by chemical means, known as bleaching. This not only whitens the flour, but also preserves it so that it will not turn sour or go off in flavor; bleaching also prevents a pie dough kept in the refrigerator for several days from turning gray. I prefer unbleached flour for pastry doughs, however, because they seem easier to handle, and doughs made with unbleached flour are tenderer when baked. If your regular market does not carry unbleached flour, try a health-food store. At the present time, by the way, French household flour is still unbleached.

Instant-blending flour, granular flour, Wondra flour. These are flours that have gone through a patent process that renders them free-flowing, with a texture like finely granulated sugar. They need no sifting, and do not lump when mixed with cold liquids. I like them for crêpes, and also for pie dough made in the machine. However, I do not find them as smooth as regular flour when used in sauces. You will see the same kind of flour in French markets, often called *farine sans grumeaux*—flour without lumps.

FLUFF. To fluff with a fork, as for cooked rice: lift the rice lightly with the fork, and toss it to separate the grains as you toss in butter, salt, pepper, cheese, or whatever.

FOLD. To combine a lighter mixture, such as beaten egg whites, into a heavier mixture, such as a sauce base or cake batter. Folding is the key to soufflés and cakes, since your object is to deflate the eggs as little as possible while you rapidly combine them with the rest of the batter. If your basic batter or base is cold and stiff, you must lighten it in some way, such as by stirring over moderate heat to decongeal it, or by stirring in some of the egg whites to loosen it; it must be the consistency of whipped cream before you begin folding. Then scoop the beaten egg whites on top of the sauce or batter and, holding your rubber spatula like a knife, cut with a plunge down through the center of the mixture to the bottom of your pan or bowl, rapidly draw it toward you to the edge of the pan and, turning it sideways, lift up to the surface, bringing a bit of the batter up over the egg whites. Rotate the pan a quarter turn clockwise, repeat the motion, and continue plunging down the spatula, turning it, and lifting it up—it's a scooping motion, really, taking only a second from start to finish. Ten to a dozen scoops, taking as many seconds, and the operation is complete, except for a rapid scoop or two around the edge and bottom of the pan to be sure all is incorporated. If you have beaten your egg whites perfectly, as described a few items back, but yet have trouble with cakes that do not rise enough, or with soufflés that are unspectacular, it is very probable that you have not attacked folding with enough exuberant abandon—it needs big rapid movements, and just remember your object: to deflate those eggs, your puffing medium, as little as possible.

GARLIC. There is no substitute for fresh garlic, and since it is always available, why risk ruining the taste of a dish with anything else? And fresh garlic is so easy to use, either in a garlic press, or in any of the following ways:

Mince no. 1. Place whole unpeeled garlic on work surface, lay the large flat side of a big knife blade upon it and smash down hard with your fist; the garlic splits, the peel comes off easily, and you can mince with ease.

Mince no. 2. Put the garlic, peeled or not, between 2 sheets of wax paper and proceed as in No. 1—this keeps the garlic off your work surface.

Mince no. 3. Place a peeled clove of garlic on your work surface, hold it down with your left thumb and scrape down its side with the blade of your knife to turn it into a purée.

Mince no. 4. For this you use a small mortar—purée the garlic into it with a press, or smash it and place it in the mortar, then pound it with a bit of salt to make a very smooth paste.

To get garlic off your fingers. Rinse your hands in cold water, rub with table salt, wash with soap and tepid water, then hot water. Repeat if necessary. (Hot water at first sets the odor, while cold water rinses it off.)

HERBS AND SPICES. Unless otherwise indicated, all herbs called for like thyme, tarragon, rosemary, etc., are dried. How to decide the relationship between fresh and dried herbs? I frankly have no idea, and will venture only a guess estimate of 3 or 4 to 1. Dried herbs must smell fresh and fragrant: rub a pinch between your thumb and forefinger and the essential perfume should be released . . . if it smells and tastes like dried grass, throw it out. Then, how to decide on measurements for fresh herbs? How big are the leaves, for instance, and do you press them into your measuring spoon? Again, I think one can only indicate, and expect the cook to use common sense. I do give tablespoon measures for chopped parsley, but merely as an idea of how much.

HIGH-ALTITUDE COOKERY. At any altitude over 3,000 feet, many recipes, especially those for cakes, soufflés, and yeast doughs, need some readjustment, such as a decrease in leavening and/or in sugar, and an increase in liquid. Much useful work on the subject, along with a number of pamphlets and recipes, has been done in Colorado. For information, write:

> Colorado State University
> Experiment Station, Cooperative Extension Service
> Fort Collins, Colorado 80521

TO HOLD ITS SHAPE. Speaking of a warm *choux* pastry, or a fish mousse mixture, you will be directed to beat it "until the mixture holds its shape in a spoon." This means when you lift up a gob of it with a spoon or a spatula, it mounds in a lump, holding itself in the shape of a mounded lump rather than dissolving back into a thick mass.

MEASURES. A discussion of measurements and comparison tables between the American system and the metric system begins on page 667.

MERINGUES, THE WEEPING OF. This sad condition is one that brings a frequent question into our French Chef office: "Why does the merinque topping on my pie weep?" According to information I have gathered from the former Poultry and Egg National Board, and from Belle Lowe's *Experimental Cookery,* there could be three reasons:

1. The meringue was not properly made: beat the egg whites until they foam and begin to take on shape, then beat in the sugar gradually and be sure it dissolves completely—so that you can feel no granule on your tongue at the end of your beating. Use 2 tablespoons of regular table sugar or superfine sugar per each "large" egg white (or for each 2 tablespoons of egg white).

2. The meringue must be spread on a warm filling.

3. The meringue was overbaked: it should be ¾ to 1 inch thick, and baked 6 minutes at 425 degrees F., or 8 at 400 F., or 18 at 350 F.

On the other hand, you could try the other type of meringue, made with boiling sugar syrup, the *Meringue Italienne* described on page 580, and you would be trouble free.

MICROWAVE OVENS—RADAR OVENS. I love a large piece of fish braised by microwave, and a roast chicken browned first and then finished by microwave. The oven does produce wonderfully juicy flesh when the flesh is tender to start with, but you have to watch the cooking like a hawk, since a minute or so too long can dry out the meat in a flash. I used my microwave a lot for cooking when I first got it; I was having fun with it, and trying it out. Now I use it constantly and find it a tremendous convenience, but I rarely cook in it. I defrost frozen bones, stocks, egg whites, and bread; I warm a chilled glass of milk or an ice-cold apple in it. I use it for melting chocolate and softening butter, for drying out wet newspapers, and for thawing frozen pie dough. If price had been of no consequence when I bought my new big oven, however, and if they had been in existence then, I'd have got myself a full-size self-cleaning regular oven with microwave—all in one single oven. Then I would be using it a great deal for cooking, I think, because I could switch from one system to the other at will. *Warning:* I have learned from experience never to leave the oven in operation when I am not right in the kitchen to oversee it, since if you are cooking a small object, over-microwaving can burn it up, and an overcooked fully dried-out newspaper will catch fire. That latter lesson cost me thirty-five dollars in oven repairs.

OIL. Oils for frying, sautéing, and salad dressings must be of excellent quality because, obviously, they impart their flavor to the food. I've gone into frying oils on page 410, but will recapitulate here—I think that deep frying is acceptable only when done in fresh pure new peanut oil; it is, then, for me at least, a luxuriously expensive but delicious way to cook. Just as important as your frying oil is the oil you use for the browning of meats, or the oil you blend with butter for the sautéing of chicken, or steak, or vegetables. I prefer a good grade of pure Italian olive oil for this, but will accept pure peanut oil. Finally, and crucial, is the selection of oil for salad dressings and mayonnaise; for this I always choose a fine light French oil with a label stating where it was made, and that it is a pure, natural, virgin oil. Virgin means the oil is the first pressing, done without heat—*première pression à froid.* Such an oil is not easy to find, and you may well have to send to a mail-order house for it. Where we live, we've induced our wine merchant to stock a fine French virgin oil that he imports along with his wine shipments.

OLIVES. Olives are frequently called for in the dishes of Mediterranean France, and for the most part these are the tiny black olives of Nice, put up simply in brine with a light herbal flavoring. Invariably imports—that is, if you can get them at all—but I've seen, in some delicatessens, the small black olives of Italy, which are worthy substitutes. Our bland black olives are usable, but are more decorative than tasty, and I prefer instead the dry imported oil-packed olives; these should be simmered 10 minutes or so in water to remove some of their overly strong taste before you add them to any recipe.

OVEN, PLACEMENT OF FOODS IN. In any well-constructed oven, the heat rises from the lower part, circulates up the sides to the top, and descends, in a movement known as heat convection. Thus where you place a pan in the oven is important. When you are looking for general all-around heat, for roasting meat or baking a cake, as examples, you place your pan so that it is centered in the oven. That would be in the middle or lower-middle level for the cake, and the lower middle or lower third of the oven for a big roast. When you want something to brown on top as it cooks, like a *quiche,* or a *gratin* covered with cheese or bread crumbs, you place it in the upper-third level, where the heat convection flow is strongest—it has traveled up the sides of the oven where the two streams of heat meet and then converge in their descent, browning the surface of the *quiche* or *gratin.* Try this yourself the next time you have a dish to brown, and you will see how much faster it browns in the upper third of the oven than in the middle. On the other hand, a soufflé needs a push from the bottom to speed its rise, and you set that in the lower level of the oven. A separate problem is that of cooking several dishes at once in the same oven. If you have 2 baking sheets on 2 racks in the oven, for instance, rapidly exchange their positions once or twice during baking so they will cook evenly. For 2 cake pans, set them on the same rack if possible, but diagonally opposite each other, leaving airspace between; shift them if they seem to be baking at different speeds. In other words, watch what is happening and take action if you think it necessary. You will probably find, too, that the timing for several pans will be longer than for one, and it may be wise to raise your thermostat 25 degrees or so, particularly for meat dishes; thus, for several pans, allow extra minutes in your timing schedule, just in case.

PEPPER. Pepper must taste fresh and aromatic, and the freshest usually comes from grinding peppercorns in a pepper mill. Be sure you get a pepper mill that will really grind, however, since some appear to be purely decorative. The French Peugeot is one brand that has always been reliable, in my experience. White pepper, needed for white sauces, fish mousses, hollandaise, and the like, is the mature peppercorn with its outer coating rubbed off; black pepper is the immature berry, harvested when red, and sun or kiln dried until the outside becomes shriveled, hard, and dark. The heavier the peppercorns, the better the grade; Alleppey, Tellicherry, and Lampong are three of the top names in the hierarchy. In the late 1960's green peppercorns came into vogue, packed in water and sold in cans or jars; they give a pleasant, fresh and mildly peppery taste to stews and sauces, and should be pounded into a paste to give out their full flavor—unless you want to show off to your guests that you are using them, in which case you leave some whole. An open jar of them will keep a week or more in the refrigerator but they can go sour, and you are better off freezing what you don't use.

POACH. See BOIL, SIMMER, etc.

PRALIN—NUT BRITTLE. This delicious mixture of caramel and the nuts of your choice is easy indeed to make, freezes for months and months, and is then ready at once to sprinkle over ice cream or custards, to be mixed into dessert creams and sauces, or to brush around the sides or over the tops of cakes and *petits fours*. For about 1½ cups: spread almonds, walnuts, pecans, filberts, or peanuts (with or without their skins) on a baking sheet and toast to brown very lightly in a 350-degree oven, turning several times for 10 to 20 minutes. Then make a caramel: heat 1 cup of sugar with ⅓ cup of water in a small saucepan, swirling pan by its handle as syrup comes to the boil, allowing sugar to melt completely and liquid to become crystal clear; cover pan and boil over high heat until bubbles thicken, then uncover and boil, swirling pan by handle as syrup turns a light caramel brown. Stir in the toasted nuts until they are enrobed completely, then turn out onto a lightly oiled or buttered pastry sheet or marble. When cold and set, crack into pieces, break up, then pulverize in an electric blender, and the *pralin* is ready to use. Store in an airtight jar, in the freezer.

REDUCE—REDUCTION. Cooking terms meaning the boiling down of stocks and cooking liquids to concentrate their flavor—a most important process in any good cooking, particularly French.

ROUX. Flour and butter cooked together, the thickening agent used for brown sauces, and white ones. For brown *roux,* see the mock *Demi-Glace,* page 282; for a discussion of white *roux,* see the introduction to the white sauce family on page 616.

SALT. In France, you can buy *sel gris,* rock salt, for cooking, and it is convenient because you put it in an open jar, and reach in for a handful when you want to salt your vegetable cooking water. I use Kosher salt as a substitute. One often reads paeans of praise for sea salt, which is claimed to be saltier, healthier, and better in every way than other salts; I cannot tell any difference at all between sea salt and regular store-bought salt, but I would never have won the contest of princess and the pea, either. By the way, if you have oversalted a soup or a sauce, you can help the situation by simmering in it for 5 minutes a grated potato, which absorbs some of the excess, and then you strain the soup or sauce and hope for the best.

SCALD. To scald milk means to heat it to just under the boil, until a skin forms over its surface. In the old days before pasteurization milk was scalded to kill the bacteria in it, since wild bacteria could interfere with the action of live yeast cells in one's bread dough. I don't think scalding modern pasteurized milk serves any useful purpose nowadays, and I therefore prefer to use the terms hot milk or boiling milk, or whatever describes its temperature.

SCALLIONS. Green onions, with a white undeveloped bulb, and long thin green leaves. Use the bulb as a substitute for shallots, and mince the tender part of the green when you have no fresh chives.

SCORE. This means to draw the blade of a sharp knife over the surface of something to make very shallow cuts about $\frac{1}{16}$ inch deep. You score the milky side of a fish fillet to cut the membrane covering, so it will not draw up when the fish is cooked; you score the membrane of a flank steak for the same reason.

SEASONING. See CORRECT SEASONING.

SHALLOTS. Small onion-shaped bulbs with a mild onion flavor; they are tender and cook quickly, so are ideal for sauces and as a fast flavor enhancer. The true shallot, *échalotte grise,* is shaped rather like a clove of garlic, with a hard grayish brown skin; it has a faint suggestion of garlic along with its onion. The red shallot, or *échalotte-oignon,* reddish brown and bulbous, is the shallot we usually find in our markets, however.

SIMMER. See BOIL, SIMMER, etc.

SKIM. To remove the scum from a liquid, with a big spoon, or with a spoon-shaped sieve; also to *degrease,* q.v.

SPICES. One usually thinks of spices as being in the clove, cinnamon, mace, and nutmeg family, but it is hard to make an absolute difference between herbs and spices, since there are overlappings. I like to have an herb and spice combination, *épices fines,* on hand for mixing into pork roasts and chops, meat *pâtés,* and the like, and I keep it in a screw-toped jar (2 tablespoons each of ground bay, clove, mace, nutmeg, paprika, and thyme; 1 tablespoon each of ground basil, cinnamon, and savory; 5 tablespoons of ground white peppercorns). In French recipes you will run into *quatre épices,* which is usually a mixture of pepper, clove, ginger or cinnamon, and nutmeg, but every manufacturer has his own formula. If I don't have any *quatre épices,* I use allspice.

STOCKS AND BOUILLONS. Along with aromatic ingredients and the reduction of cooking liquids, stocks and bouillons are certainly fundamental to all good cooking, because they give that certain depth and sophistication of flavor that you will never get with water alone. If you have no homemade stock on hand you must, of course, resort to canned beef bouillon, canned chicken broth, and canned clam juice. But these substitutes can always be enriched and dissembled so that their standard flavors are not recognizable. For details, please consult the index.

SUGAR. Unless otherwise specified, all sugar called for in this book is regular granulated table sugar, either cane or beet, since they are interchangeable. Here are notes on various types of sugar.

Barbados and Demarara⁻ sugars are unrefined cane sugars of a brownish tinge, used mostly in Britain.

Brown sugar can be either light or dark, with the latter having the stronger flavor. (To soften brown sugar that has hardened, place in a jar, sprinkle with a few droplets of water, cover airtight, and set in a warming oven, over a gas pilot light, or on a radiator until softened. If you keep brown sugar in an airtight container, it should not harden.)

Caster sugar is a British term for finely granulated table sugar, in contrast to the more coarsely ground "granulated sugar" used in cooking.

Confectioners' sugar or powdered sugar can be a more or less fine powder, the 4XXX variety being the finest.

Flavored sugars (lemon, orange, vanilla) are sugar pounded, ground, or steeped with fruit peels or vanilla bean.

French sugar terms: Sucre semoule, a coarse grind for preserving; *sucre en poudre,* regular table sugar; *sucre glace,* confectioners' sugar.

Instant or superfine granulated sugar or bar sugar, a very finely ground sugar that will melt quickly; it is available everywhere, so just look at the labels.

Moist sugar, an old-fashioned light-brown sugar chopped off a big block— the way it used to be sold.

TEFLON. I have been an enthusiastic supporter of Teflon-lined pans ever since they came on the market. I think they are wonderful for breads and muffins, for baking sheets, for electric skillets, and especially for frying pans. Although one cannot expect the Teflon lining to be permanent, my medium-sized all-purpose heavy-duty everyday Teflon-lined frying pan has lasted so far for five years and now gives only slight signs of age; but I use only wooden instruments in it, and am very careful never to scour it.

TEPID. See BOIL, SIMMER, etc.

TOSS. Tossing food in the pan is better than stirring it, since the toss is less likely to break it apart or mash it. And because you should make a habit of tossing wherever possible, always cook in a large enough pan, filled by no more than half; its sides should be high enough so that the ingredients don't hop out onto the stove. The French *sauteuse* saucepan with outward slanting sides 3 inches high is ideal for vegetables, and any frying pan you own should have outward sloping sides 2 inches high. Hold the pan handle firmly, palm underneath it and thumb on top, then jerk the pan sharply toward you, making the food bang against the far side of the pan and turn over onto itself; repeat the movement rapidly, also swirling the pan to vary the action. *Faire sauter* would be the equivalent expression in French, from which comes the term *sauté*, which is exactly the way you do sautéed mushrooms in a hot frying pan.

VANILLA. Always use pure vanilla extract; vanillin or imitation vanilla flavoring never succeeds in giving anything but a cheap imitation of the original. The real vanilla bean is favored by many fine cooks, but lately I've not had much luck with it; after steeping the bean in warm syrups or hot milk, I've always had to add vanilla extract to get the right effect.

VINEGAR. Wine vinegar is used exclusively for cooking in this book—except when vinegar goes into egg-poaching water. Buy an excellent brand, and taste it to be sure it is mild enough and pleasant in flavor. There are some good domestics, and often you can find French wine vinegars from Orléans. White or red wine vinegars are interchangeable, although you may at times want white vinegar for pale purposes, such as flavored butters or béarnaise sauces.

WEIGHTS AND MEASURES. See page 667 for complete discussion, including notes on the metric system.

WINE. Wines for cooking, drinking, and tasting—see page 624. Wines to accompany all main-course dishes are always suggested in the introductory paragraphs of those recipes. By the way, don't throw away leftover wine or even wine that has begun to go off for drinking—boil it down by half, bottle it, refrigerate it, and use it for cooking; the boiling pasteurizes it, and it will keep nicely for weeks.

Learning about meat

Official names and aliases, descriptions,
French equivalents, and the
cooking method for
each cut

The only way to learn about meat is to start in and train yourself. Rib chops, loin chops, porterhouse steaks, and legs of lamb are easy, but when you want to save money you have to learn the complications of the money-saving cuts in the hind leg and the shoulder, the flank and the brisket. The following drawings and tables will, I hope, help you on your way. In each case I have described the cut as it would relate to the human body, and I've tried to name French equivalents for all when possible (the French meat-cutting system is very different from ours), in case you might find yourself living and cooking in France, or wanting to translate recipes from French cookbooks. In the column labeled COOKING METHOD, the terms roast, broil, or sauté mean that you cook by dry heat and have a first-class top-quality cut; braise or stew are for the less tender cuts that need moist heat and longer cooking.

Primal (wholesale) cuts and bone structure of beef

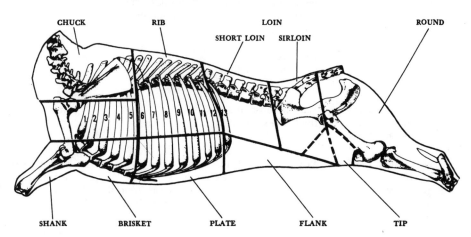

BEEF (*Boeuf*)

OFFICIAL NAME OF CUT (*other names*)	DESCRIPTION	FRENCH EQUIVALENT	COOKING METHOD
BEEF CHUCK, WHOLE	The shoulder section containing ribs 1–5, the shoulder blade, upper arm, and neck	ÉPAULE (shoulder blade, upper arm, lower arm, but not neck and not ribs	· · ·
BEEF CHUCK, ARM HALF	The upper arm from above the elbow, and middle section of ribs 1–5	· · ·	· · ·
ARM POT ROAST (chuck arm; chuck round bone; lower half clod)	The main part of the upper arm, not including knuckle at shoulder end	JUMEAU À POT-AU-FEU (outside upper arm) MACREUSE À BIFTECK (inside upper arm)	Braise
CROSS-RIB POT ROAST (Boston or English cut; thick rib roast; bread & butter cut)	Meaty portion on top of ribs 3–5	(Part of CÔTES DÉCOUVERTES)	Braise
SHORT RIBS (barbecue, English short, braising, kosher, or flunken short ribs; brust flanken)	Middle portion of ribs 1–5 with more or less meat on top of them (most meat when labeled "flunken" or "flanken")	PLAT DE CÔTES DÉCOUVERTES (ribs 2–5) CÔTE CHARBONEUSE (1st rib)	Braise
BEEF CHUCK, BLADE PORTION	The shoulder blade section; includes neck vertebrae 6–7, and upper part of backbone and ribs 1–5 (cross cuts of bone look like the number 7)	PALERON (shoulder blade section only)	· · ·
BLADE ROASTS, TOP OR UNDER BLADE ROASTS, 7-BONE POT ROAST	Various cross cuts of the blade section	· · ·	Braise
BEEF CHUCK EYE ROAST (boneless chuck roll or fillet; inside chuck roll)	Prolongation of rib eye in shoulder area	BASSES CÔTES (ribs 3–6) SURLONGE (dorsal vertebrae 2–3)	Braise (roast at your own risk)

OFFICIAL NAME OF CUT *(other names)*	DESCRIPTION	FRENCH EQUIVALENT	COOKING METHOD
MOCK TENDER (chuck eye, fillet, or tender; Scotch or Jewish tender; medallion pot roast; fish muscle)	Conicle-shaped muscle from top of blade, small side	MACREUSE À POT-AU-FEU	Braise; stew
TOP BLADE ROAST (flat iron; triangle; upper half clod)	Other top section from other side of blade; larger	JUMEAU À BIFTECK	Braise
BEEF CHUCK, NECK POT ROAST	The neck end, with 7 neck vertebrae; usually boned	COLLIER (includes LA GRIFFE, VEINE MAIGRE, VEINE GRASSE)	Braise; stew; grind
BEEF BRISKET, WHOLE	The chest, including ⅔ of breastbone, and lower ribs 1–5	POITRINE	· · ·
BEEF BRISKET, POINT HALF (front, point, or thick cut)	Boneless front half of brisket	GROS BOUT DE POITRINE	Braise; stew
EDGE CUT; HALF POINT	The above, halved lengthwise	· · ·	Braise; stew
BEEF BRISKET, FLAT HALF	Boneless back half, brisket	· · ·	Braise; stew
BEEF BRISKET, MIDDLE CUT	Cross cut of brisket, middle section (choicest cut)	MILIEU DE POITRINE	Braise; stew
BEEF PLATE, WHOLE	The lower part of the beef, opposite the rib section; includes lower part of ribs 6–13 and final ⅓ of breastbone	TENDRON	· · ·
BEEF PLATE, SHORT RIBS	The flat ends of ribs 6–9, usually 2 inches long	PLAT DE CÔTES DÉCOUVERTES	Braise; stew
RIBS & SPARERIBS	Same as above, but top layer of meat stripped off	· · ·	Braise; stew

OFFICIAL NAME OF CUT (*other names*)	DESCRIPTION	FRENCH EQUIVALENT	COOKING METHOD
BEEF PLATE, WHOLE BEEF PLATE, ROLLED (Yankee pot roast)	(*continued*) Boneless meaty part of plate, rolled and tied	BAVETTE À POT-AU-FEU	Braise; stew
FORE SHANK & HIND SHANK	Usually only the fore shank is seen; cross cuts, bone in	GÎTE GÎTE DE— DEVANT (fore) ; DERRIÈRE (hind)	Braise; stew
BEEF RIB ROASTS BEEF RIB, WHOLE	The rib roast section, including backbone and ribs 6–12	MILIEU DE TRAIN DE CÔTES: ENTRECÔTES (rarely cut as a rib roast in France; usually steaks, or boned roasts and stew meat)	• • •
BEEF RIB ROAST, LARGE END; SMALL END (Standing rib roast)	Ribs 6–9 are large end; ribs 9–12 are small end	• • •	Roast
BEEF RIB, RIB EYE ROAST (Delmonico or rib-eye pot roast; regular roll roast)	Ribs 6–12 boned out, and just eye of meat remains	• • •	Roast
BEEF RIB, ROLLED CAP POT ROAST	The boned-out covering flap of meat, left from rib-eye roast	• • •	Braise
(Spencer roll)	Rib roast with tail and bones removed	• • •	Roast
BEEF RIB, BACK RIBS (riblets; finger ribs)	The ribs left over from the boning of a rib roast	PLAT DE CÔTES: Ribs 9–11, CÔTES COUVERTES; Ribs 3–8, CÔTES DÉCOUVERTES	Braise; stew
BEEF RIB, SHORT RIBS	Lower part of ribs, trimmed from a rib roast	HAUT DE CÔTES, or part of PLAT DE CÔTES	Braise; stew
BEEF LOIN BEEF LOIN, WHOLE	The short loin (small of back) , and sirloin (hip section) , including backbone, front part of hip bone, and sacrum bone	ALOYAU	Roast (but seldom done whole)

OFFICIAL NAME OF CUT (*other names*)	DESCRIPTION	FRENCH EQUIVALENT	COOKING METHOD
THE SHORT LOIN	The small of the back from front end of hip-bone to 13th rib; contains the top loin (large muscle) the tenderloin (inside muscle), and backbone	FAUX-FILET or CONTRE-FILET (top loin) & FILET (tenderloin)	Roast (but seldom done whole)
BEEF LOIN, TOP LOIN ROAST (shell, loin strip, New York strip, club sirloin, Delmonico)	The top of the loin, the large outside muscle (can be boned out or not)	FAUX-FILET or CONTRE-FILET	Roast
BEEF LOIN, TENDER-LOIN ROAST (short-loin tenderloin; filet mignon roast)	The underside of the loin, the small muscle, always boned, but minus the butt end of the tenderloin, which lies in the sirloin section	FILET (*Filet entier* includes butt end)	Roast
(Heart of tenderloin)	From vertebrae 2–5	COEUR DE FILET; CHÂTEAUBRIAND	Steaks & roasts
TENDERLOIN TIPS	Small end	FILET MIGNON; QUEUE	Steaks & roasts
(tenderloin butt; New York butt)	Butt end, in sirloin	TÊTE DE FILET; BIFTECK	Steaks & roasts
BEEF LOIN, SIRLOIN STEAKS (various)	The hip-bone area, front part, including sacrum	RUMSTEAK & CULOTTE	Steaks & roasts
. . .	A prolongation of rump end of sirloin down the tip section (front) of the leg	AIGUILLETTE BARONNE	Braise
BEEF ROUND	The hind leg, from back end of hip bone to ankle	CUISSE	. . .
BEEF ROUND, RUMP ROAST (standing rump roast)	Above back end of hip bone	RUMSTEAK	Braise; roast if top quality

OFFICIAL NAME OF CUT (*other names*)	DESCRIPTION	FRENCH EQUIVALENT	COOKING METHOD
BEEF ROUND (*continued*)			
BEEF ROUND, TOP ROUND ROAST (inside round; top-side)	Inside muscle of upper leg, the largest muscle	TENDE DE TRANCHE; NOIX	Braise (roast top-quality 1st cuts near rump)
BEEF ROUND, BOTTOM ROUND ROAST (gooseneck or outside round; silverside)	Outside muscle of upper leg with round eye muscle	GÎTE À LA NOIX SEMELLE	Braise (roast top-quality 1st cuts near rump)
BEEF ROUND, EYE ROUND ROAST	Round eye muscle of bottom round	ROND DE GÎTE À LA NOIX	Braise
BEEF ROUND, HEEL OF ROUND (Pike's Peak; Diamond; Denver or Horseshoe roast)	Gristly portion at back of leg above ankle	NERVEUX DE GÎTE À LA NOIX	Braise; stew
BEEF ROUND, TIP ROAST (sirloin tip; veiny; face; knuckle)	The front of the leg, from hip to knee	TRANCHE GRASSE	Braise (roast if top quality)
. . .	Gristly end of tip	NOURRICE	Braise; stew
BEEF STEAKS			
BEEF CHUCK, SHOULDER STEAK (London broil; clod steak; arm steak)	Steak from upper arm; top quality	MACREUSE À BIFTECK	Broil; sauté
BEEF CHUCK, UNDER BLADE STEAK (bottom chuck; under cut; chuck fillet)	Steak from underneath the shoulder blade; top quality	PIÈCE PARÉE	Broil; sauté
BEEF CHUCK, TOP BLADE STEAK (book, butler, lifter, petite or top chuck steak)	Steak cut from triangular shaped piece, from top of shoulder blade	JUMEAU À BIFTECK	Broil; sauté
BEEF PLATE, SKIRT STEAK (diaphragm; London broils; London grill steak)	Meaty part of diaphragm, opposite rib section (often rolled and skewered into shape)	HAMPE	Broil; sauté

OFFICIAL NAME OF CUT (*other names*)	DESCRIPTION	FRENCH EQUIVALENT	COOKING METHOD
BEEF FLANK STEAK	Meaty part of flank, opposite loin section	FLANCHET; BAVETTE À BIFTECK	Broil or roast whole
BEEF RIB STEAK; RIB EYE STEAK	Any steak cut from the rib-roast section, bone in, or boneless, and/or tail-less	ENTRECÔTE	Broil; sauté
BEEF LOIN, T-BONE STEAKS; PORTER-HOUSE STEAKS	Any cross-cut steak from the loin, bone in, including loin strip and less or more tenderloin	(A cross cut of the loin is not the French way of doing things)	Broil; sauté
BEEF LOIN, TOP LOIN STEAKS (shell, strip, club, sirloin strip, Delmonico, NY strip, Kansas City)	The loin strip, with or without bone	FAUX-FILET; CONTRE-FILET (Boneless)	Broil; sauté
BEEF LOIN, SIRLOIN STEAKS (WEDGE BONE; ROUND BONE; PIN BONE; SHELL; TOP SIRLOIN) (rump; New York sirloin; flat bone; wedge bone; hip steak)	Cross cuts from the front section of the hip named according to shape of visible bone, and boned or portioned at will	(No French equivalents, since no cross cuts; however, this cut does furnish RUM-STEAKS and BIFTECKS)	Broil; sauté
BEEF ROUND STEAKS	Steaks cut from the hind leg; presumably the first cuts, nearest the rump, will produce steaks when they come from a top-quality well-hung animal—an uncertain factor in my experience, except for the tip steak	(French cutting methods very different for the leg. Steaks come from TRANCHE GRASSE (tip) ; and LA POIRE or BOULE DE TENDE (top round) . They are quite firm!	Braise; broil or sauté at your own risk

MISCELLANEOUS

BEEF ROUND, CUBES FOR KABABS	Usually from the sirloin tip (I have always found these too tough for broiling)	• • •	First-class stew meat, in my opinion
(HANGING TENDER; HANGER)	Strip of meat along inside of backbone	ONGLET	Roast; broil; sauté

FRESH PORK (*Porc*)

Primal (wholesale) cuts and bone structure of pork

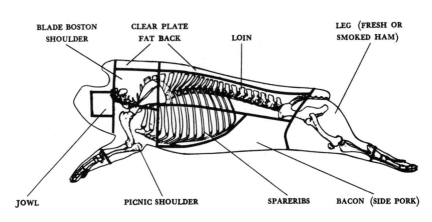

BLADE BOSTON SHOULDER • CLEAR PLATE FAT BACK • LOIN • LEG (FRESH OR SMOKED HAM)

JOWL • PICNIC SHOULDER • SPARERIBS • BACON (SIDE PORK)

OFFICIAL NAME OF CUT (*other names*)	DESCRIPTION	FRENCH EQUIVALENT	COOKING METHOD
FRESH PORK SHOULDER			
FRESH PORK SHOULDER WHOLE (New York style shoulder)	Shoulder blade, and upper and lower arm	BOUT DE DEVANT (*palette, échine & dessous de col*), but only part of upper arm	Roast or braise
BLADE BOSTON ROAST (pork butt, Boston butt, Boston shoulder)	Shoulder blade section, except for small end at arm	PALETTE (includes part of upper arm)	Roast or braise
ARM PICNIC (Picnic shoulder)	Upper arm and small end of shoulder blade	No exact equivalent; part is in *palette*, part in *jambonneau*	Roast or braise
PORK HOCK (pork shank)	Lower arm from elbow to wrist (ankle)	JAMBONNEAU (*jarret de devant*), also includes part of upper arm	Roast or braise
FRESH PORK LOIN	The whole loin (backbone section) from tail to neck including upper half of ribs	LONGE DE PORC	. . .

OFFICIAL NAME OF CUT (*other names*)	DESCRIPTION	FRENCH EQUIVALENT	COOKING METHOD
SIRLOIN (loin end, hip bone)	Hip bone end of loin	POINTE DE FILET	Roast; broil; chops
CENTER LOIN	The small of the back	MILIEU DE FILET	Roast; broil; chops
CENTER RIB	Ribs 6–13	CARRÉ	Roast; broil; chops
BLADE LOIN (7-rib roast)	Shoulder end of loin	ÉCHINE	Roast; braise
TENDERLOIN (pork tender)	Tenderloin, from small of back, underneath	FILET MIGNON	Roast; broil; sauté
TOP LOIN (strip loin)	Loin strip from small of back, opposite tenderloin	NOIX DE FILET	Roast; broil; sauté

PORK LEG (fresh ham)

PORK LEG, FRESH HAM	The whole leg section including lower half of hip bone, upper leg, and lower leg	JAMBON FRAIS, ENTIER	Roast, poach, braise
PORK LEG, RUMP PORTION (leg butt, leg roast sirloin portion)	Cross-cut roast from the hip end (large end)	No traditional equivalent for these 2 cuts, but the term *rouelle* would be	Roast; braise
PORK LEG, CENTER ROAST	Cross-cut roast from center of leg	descriptive (as for *rouelle de veau*)	
PORK LEG, SHANK PORTION	Small end or shank end	JAMBONNEAU (*jarret de derrière*)	Roast; braise

PIG'S FEET (pig's trotters)

	Front and hind feet, removed at wrist or ankle (front feet considered best)	PIEDS DE PORC (front are *pieds de devant*)	Braise; stew

RIBS

PORK LOIN BACK RIBS (country back bones; ribs for barbecue)	The ribs, leftover from a boned loin of pork	· · ·	Roast; braise; stew
PORK SPARERIBS	The chest ribs, minus the breastbone	PLAT DE CÔTES	Roast; braise; stew

OFFICIAL NAME OF CUT (*other names*)	DESCRIPTION	FRENCH EQUIVALENT	COOKING METHOD
FRESH SIDE PORK (fresh belly; streak of lean; pork belly)	The belly or underside of the pork, from which bacon is made, corresponds to the brisket of beef	LARD DE POITRINE FRAIS	Boil; broil; sauté
JOWL (cheek; chap; chaw)	From the head; the cheek	Part of LA HURE, head	Boil; broil; sauté
FATBACK; CLEAR PLATE	The hard fat just under the skin of the loin (or back)	LARD GRAS	For larding meat; for barding (tying around roasts); for lining *pâté* molds
LEAF LARD	Fat from around the kidneys; the choicest fat for cooking	PANNE DE PORC	For general cooking and sausage making

LAMB AND MUTTON (*Agneau et Mouton*)

Primal (wholesale) cuts and bone structure of lamb

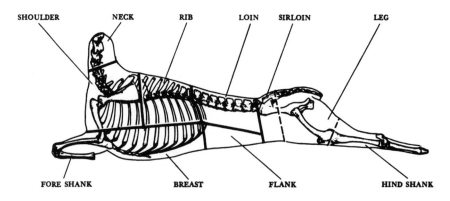

OFFICIAL NAME OF CUT (*other names*)	DESCRIPTION	FRENCH EQUIVALENT	COOKING METHOD
LAMB SHOULDER			
LAMB SHOULDER SQUARE CUT WHOLE (shoulder block; shoulder roast)	The neck, shoulder ribs 1 to 5, shoulder blade, upper arm section	ÉPAULE (shoulder blade, upper arm, lower arm but not the shoulder ribs). Usually boned and rolled	Roast; braise
CUSHION ROAST	The same, boneless but not rolled; can be stuffed	• • •	Roast; braise
BLADE ROASTS (or CHOPS) (shoulder blocks)	Shoulder blade section	PALETTE	Roast; braise
ARM ROAST (or CHOPS)	Upper arm section	COUDE	Roast; braise
NECK SLICES or STEW	Neck section	COLLET	Braise; stew
LAMB BREAST	The breast from neck end to 13th rib	POITRINE	Braise; stew; bone and stuff
LAMB BREAST RIBLETS AND SPARERIBS	Chest ribs in single pieces or in a block	(The term *tendron* would be equivalent as in *tendrons* of veal)	Braise; roast
LAMB SHANK (fore shank; trotter)	The lower arm	Included as part of ÉPAULE (shoulder)	Braise
LAMB RIB ROAST (rib rack; hotel rack)	The rib-roast section includes ribs 6–12	CARRÉ, CARRÉ COUVERT	Roast
(Short ribs—would be included as part of riblets and spareribs from lamb breast cuts)	Rib ends	HAUT DE CÔTELETTES	Braise; stew
LAMB LOIN (trimmed)			
LAMB LOIN ROAST (saddle roast)	½ of the small of the back from hip to 13th rib, minus flank	FILET	Roast
DOUBLE LOIN ROAST (saddle of lamb)	The whole of the small of the back, in one piece, minus flanks	SELLE ANGLAISE; SELLE D'AGNEAU; LES DEUX FILETS RÉUNIS	Roast

OFFICIAL NAME OF CUT (*other names*)	DESCRIPTION	FRENCH EQUIVALENT	COOKING METHOD
LAMB LEG			
LAMB LEG WHOLE (leg, sirloin on; leg-o-lamb; full-trimmed leg roast)	The hind leg, from the ankle, including all of the hip section	GIGOT ENTIER	Roast; poach
LAMB LEG, SHORT CUT SIRLOIN OFF	The hind leg, upper half of hip removed	GIGOT RACCOURCI	Roast
LAMB LEG, SIRLOIN HALF (butt half)	The hip section only	LA SELLE	Roast
(Hind saddle of lamb; saddle of lamb)	The 2 legs and the whole double loin in 1 piece	LE BARON D'AGNEAU	Roast
CHOPS & STEAKS			
LAMB SHOULDER, BLADE CHOPS	Chops cut from shoulder blade section	(from the PALETTE)	Braise
LAMB SHOULDER, ARM CHOPS	Chops cut from the upper arm section	(from LA COUDE)	Braise
. . .	French shoulder chops, ribs 1–5, but not including shoulder blade	CÔTELETTES DÉCOUVERTES	Braise; broil
LAMB RIB CHOPS (rack lamb chops)	Chops cut from the rib section, ribs 6–12	CÔTELETTES SECONDES (from ribs 6–8) CÔTELETTES PREMIÈRES (from ribs 9–13)	Broil; sauté
LAMB LOIN CHOPS	Chops cut from the loin (small of back)	CÔTELETTES DE FILET	Broil; sauté
LAMB LOIN DOUBLE CHOPS (English chop)	Chops cut from the 2 sides of the loin, not separated	TRANCHES DE SELLE ANGLAISE	Broil; sauté
LAMB LOIN, DOUBLE CHOP BONELESS	Boned-out double lamb chops	NOISETTES D'AGNEAU (May also be boneless rib chops)	Broil; sauté
LAMB LEG, SIRLOIN CHOPS	Chops cut from hip section of leg	TRANCHE DE SELLE D'AGNEAU	Broil; sauté
LAMB LEG, CENTER SLICE (steak; leg chop)	Cross-cut through bone of upper leg	(Rare in France, would correspond to a ROUELLE of veal)	Broil; sauté

VEAL (*Veau*)

Primal (wholesale) cuts and bone structure of veal

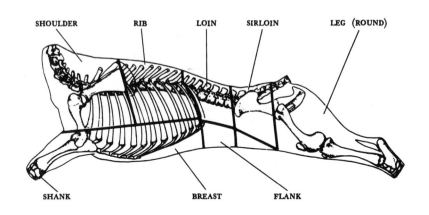

SHOULDER   RIB   LOIN   SIRLOIN   LEG (ROUND)

SHANK   BREAST   FLANK

OFFICIAL NAME OF CUT (*other names*)	DESCRIPTION	FRENCH EQUIVALENT	COOKING METHOD
VEAL SHOULDER, WHOLE	The neck, the shoulder blade section, the upper arm, shoulder ribs 1–5	ÉPAULE (shoulder blade, upper arm, lower arm, but not shoulder ribs)	(Never sold whole for cooking in one piece)
VEAL SHOULDER, ARM ROAST (round bone roast)	The upper arm section including some rib ends	COUDE (most of upper arm, and elbow)	Braise; roast
VEAL SHOULDER, BLADE ROAST	The shoulder blade section	PALETTE	Braise; roast
· · ·	Containing small end of shoulder blade and end of upper arm	ROUELLE	Braise
VEAL NECK	Contains the 7 neck vertebrae; usually boned	COLLET (not part of ÉPAULE)	Stew; braise
VEAL BREAST	The whole chest and plate section, including breastbone and 13 rib ends	POITRINE (brisket) and TENDRON (plate)	Braise; stuff and braise

OFFICIAL NAME OF CUT (*other names*)	DESCRIPTION	FRENCH EQUIVALENT	COOKING METHOD
VEAL SHANK	Lower arm, elbow and wrist (ankle) usually cross cut in slices with bone	JARRET DE DEVANT (knee is CROSSE)	Braise
VEAL RIB ROAST (rack)	The rib roast section includes ribs 6–12	CARRÉ COUVERT	Roast
VEAL LOIN ROAST	The small of the back, from tip of hip bone to 13th rib	LONGE; ROGNONNADE	Roast
VEAL LEG, WHOLE (veal round; leg of veal)	Whole hind leg of veal from the ankle, and including all of the hip section	CUISSEAU ENTIER	(Rarely sold in 1 piece for cooking)
VEAL LEG, SIRLOIN ROAST	The front part of the hip bone section	QUASI	Roast
VEAL LEG, RUMP ROAST	The back, rump, or aitch bone section of the hip bone	LA CULOTTE	Roast
VEAL LEG, TIP ROAST	The front of the upper leg to the knee or knuckle	NOIX PÂTISSIÈRE	Roast
VEAL LEG, CENTER ROAST	The back of the upper leg, corresponding to top and bottom round of beef	NOIX and SOUS NOIX	Roast
VEAL LEG, ROUND ROAST	The whole upper leg	(Rare in France)	Roast
VEAL LEG, HEEL ROAST	The gristly end of the bottom round	(Part in SOUS NOIX, and part in JARRET)	Braise
VEAL LEG, SHANK	The hind shank	JARRET (includes some of HEEL)	Braise—osso bucco
CHOPS, STEAKS, SCALLOPS			
VEAL SHOULDER, BLADE STEAK; ARM STEAK	Steaks from shoulder blade and arm	CÔTES DÉCOUVERTES (without shoulder blade portion)	Braise

OFFICIAL NAME OF CUT (*other names*)	DESCRIPTION	FRENCH EQUIVALENT	COOKING METHOD
VEAL RIB CHOPS	Chops from ribs 6–12	CÔTES COUVERTES SECONDES \ (ribs 6–8) CÔTES COUVERTES PREMIÈRES (ribs 9–12)	Broil; sauté
VEAL LOIN CHOPS & KIDNEY CHOPS	Chops from the small of the back, the loin, with loin strip and tenderloin and sometimes kidney	LONGE; ROGNONNADE (usually not cut into chops)	Broil; sauté; braise
VEAL LEG SIRLOIN STEAK or ROUND STEAK	Cross cuts from the sirloin or the center portion of the leg, bone in	OS BARRÉ (rump steak) MILIEU DE ROUELLE (center cut of leg) TALON DE ROUELLE (shank end of leg) FRICANDEAU (2 inches thick from sirloin or center cut leg)	Braise; sauté and cover-cook
VEAL CUTLETS (scallop; scallopini)	Thin boneless pieces 3 to 5 inches long and 2 to 3 inches wide— best are cut from top round or bottom round of leg	ÉSCALOPES DE VEAU	Sauté
VEAL LOIN, TOP LOIN CHOPS	Boneless loin strip or rib-eye slices	GRENADINS DE VEAU (Also cut from the leg, always tied into a round shape and barded)	Sauté

Weights, measures, and the metric system

———————

America is the only major country that has not yet converted to the metric system, and certainly in another generation we shall happily and comfortably have done so. Then we shall never again have to mutter for remembrance, "A pint's a pound, 2 pints to a quart, 4 quarts to a gallon, and if I want to find out how many ounces there are in that gallon—?" We won't be wondering whether there are 8 or 16 tablespoons to a cup, nor whether a cup's a pint or a half pint, nor shall we have sinking spells when we must figure out the ounce equivalent of ⅘ of 3¾ cups of flour. All will be blissfully easy because it will all be calculated in decimals, and it will be logical and regular, and we shall be using the same system as almost everyone else in this one world of ours.

The great convenience in the metric system is that everything is in units of 10. Going back to that ⅘ of 3¾ cups of flour again as an example, in metrics this would be ⅘ of 500 grams of flour. The answer of 400 registers almost immediately in your brain, as though you'd punched it out on a lightning-fast electronic calculator. But in metrics all is so easy you don't need a calculator. I happen to be used to metrics because I started my cooking career in France, and have been converting ounces to grams ever since; I cook in metrics for convenience, then translate back into ounces when I am writing recipes. Except for Centigrade temperatures, for which I have yet to develop a head and a feel, I find weights and measures very easy to transfer from one system to the other because of their very close relationship. Unless you need absolute accuracy, just remember that a liter's a quart, and a kilogram's 2 pounds; there are 3 centimeters to the inch, and 30 to the foot, while the meter is 39½ inches long.

The liquid and the dry measures, however, are what concern us most in cooking, and since the changeover to metrics is almost upon us, I think we must take action now to urge anyone who is writing about food to use the large simple metric units for liquid measures adopted long ago by the French—a liter, ½ liter, ¼ liter, and the deciliter (¹⁄₁₀ liter) and half deciliter. These convert so easily into our present cup and spoon measurements that we can keep right on using what we have. The ¼ liter is our 1 cup—plus 1¼ table-spoons if one must be that accurate, and one rarely needs to be. Thus we can use our handy cup measures for both liquid and dry ingredients, just as we have always done.

Professionals and scientists must, of course, be precise down to the fraction of a fraction, and anyone tripling and quadrupling recipes had better watch their milliliters, but we in everyday home cooking can take a far more relaxed attitude. On the other hand, it is useful to be able to translate from one system to the other, and here are some tables of equivalents to start you thinking in terms of the more simplified metric future. And, by the way, if you are doing professional work, the U.S. Government has put out a dandy 251-page manual with tables converting grams to ounces, pounds to kilograms, ounces to milli-liters, quarts to liters, and so on and vice versa:

> *Units of Weights and Measure,* Definitions and Tables of Equivalents. National Bureau of Standards, Miscellaneous Publication Number 286, U.S. Department of Commerce (available from the U.S. Government Printing Office, Washington, D.C. 20402. Under $3.00).

LIQUID MEASURE

*Cups, quarts, ounces, pounds, and
their metric equivalents*

Nearest convenient equivalents (with nearest actual equivalents in parentheses)

CUPS AND SPOONS	QUARTS AND OUNCES	METRIC EQUIVALENTS	FRENCH TERMS
4⅓ cups	1 quart 2 ounces (1.056 quarts)	1 liter 1,000 milliliters	1 litre
4 cups	1 quart	1 liter less 1 deciliter (0.946 liter)	· · ·
2 cups (plus 2½ Tb)	17 ounces (16.907 ounces)	½ liter	demi-litre
2 cups	1 pint; 16 ounces	½ liter less 1½ Tb (0.473 liter)	· · ·
1 cup (plus 1¼ Tb)	8 ounces (8.454 ounces)	¼ liter	quart de litre
1 cup	8 ounces	¼ liter (0.236 liter)	· · ·
⅓ cup (plus 1 Tb)	3½ ounces (3.381 ounces)	1 deciliter ¹⁄₁₀ liter 100 milliliters	1 décilitre 1 demi-verre
⅓ cup	2⅔ ounces	1 deciliter less 1⅓ Tb (0.079 liter)	· · ·
3⅓ Tb	1¾ ounces (1.690 ounces)	½ deciliter 50 milliliters	demi-décilitre
1 Tb	½ ounce	15 milliliters 15 grams	cuillère à soupe or à bouche; verre à liqueur
2 tsp	⅓ ounce	10 milliliters 10 grams	cuillère à entremets
1 tsp	¹⁄₁₆ ounce	5 milliliters 5 grams	cuillère à café

CONVERSION FORMULAE: To convert: Quarts to liters, multiply the quarts by 0.94635; Liters into quarts, multiply the liters by 1.056688; Ounces into milliliters, multiply the ounces by 29.573; Milliliters into ounces, multiply the milliliters by 0.0338.

WEIGHTS

Pounds and ounces vs. metrics

POUNDS & OUNCES (*most convenient approximation*)	METRIC (*and usual French units underlined*)
2.2 pounds	1 kilogram—1,000 grams
1.1 pounds	500 grams (une livre)
1 pound (16 ounces)	454 grams
9 ounces	250 grams (une demi-livre)
½ pound (8 ounces)	227 grams
4⅜ ounces	125 grams
¼ pound (4 ounces)	114 grams
3½ ounces	100 grams (un hecto—hectogramme)
2⅔ ounces	75 grams
1¾ ounces	50 grams
1 ounce	30 grams (28.3 gr.)
1 scant ounce	25 grams
½ ounce	15 grams
⅓ ounce	10 grams
⅙ ounce	5 grams

CONVERSION FORMULAE: To convert: Ounces into grams, multiply the ounces by 28.3495; Grams into ounces, multiply the grams by 0.035274.

TEMPERATURES

Fahrenheit vs. Centigrade

FAHRENHEIT	CENTIGRADE	FAHRENHEIT	CENTIGRADE
50	10	302	150
51.2	12	325	163
60	16	350	177
68	20	375	190
75	24	390	200
80	26.7	400	204.4
86	30	410	210
95	35	425	218
100	38	428	220
104	40	437	225
110	44	450	232
122	50	475	246
212	100	500	260
225	107.2	525	274
250	121	550	288
275	135	575	302
300	149		

CONVERSION FORMULAE: To convert Centigrade to Fahrenheit: Multiply by 9, divide by 5, add 32; Fahrenheit to Centigrade: Subtract 32, multiply by 5, divide by 9.

AMERICAN OVEN TEMPERATURES AND TERMS
VS. CENTIGRADE AND FRENCH TERMS

FAHRENHEIT DEGREES (*American terms*)	CENTIGRADE DEGREES (*French terms*)	FRENCH THERMOSTAT SETTINGS (*approximate*)
160	71	No. 1
212	100 (très doux; étuve)	
221	105	No. 2
225 (very slow)	107 (doux)	
230	121	No. 3
300 (slow)	149 (moyen; modéré)	
302	150	No. 4
350 (moderate)	177 (assez chaud; bon four)	
375	190	No. 5
400 (hot)	205 (chaud)	
425	218	No. 6
475 (very hot)	246 (très chaud; vif)	
500	260	No. 7
525	274	No. 8
550	288	No. 9

MISCELLANEOUS MEASUREMENTS

Although a pint of water is a pound and can be contained in a 2-cup measure, a pound of flour is 3½ cups and a pound of sugar is not quite 2½ cups. Half a pound of melted cheese makes 1 cup, but how do you measure grated cheese in a cup? Lightly pressed in place it weighs 3½ to 4 ounces, but if you push it down tight it could weigh 6 to 7 ounces. The same with fresh bread crumbs and, more seriously, with flour, because if you bang the measuring cup on the table you can pack in an ounce or so more.

Thus cups are not the ideal measuring instruments for fluffy foodstuffs, but cups, I suspect, are what we shall always be using because of their convenience. It is a question, then, of how you get these ingredients into the cup, and good written directions must specify whether the cup is loosely or rather tightly packed with grated cheese or fresh bread crumbs, and whether the flour is scooped or sifted in. You cannot hope for the exactitude you would get by weighing on balance scales, but, again, for everyday home cooking the cup measures are accurate enough.

Because of these measurement variants, it's a good idea to establish your own tables of equivalents, and to start you out, I submit mine, that I've established through the years. I shall begin with flour, since flour is the most difficult item to translate if you are living abroad, or are using foreign books—or if you want to calculate our old friend, the ounce equivalent of ⅘ of 3¾ cups of flour. (Measurements in the following tables are based on the nearest convenient equivalents.)

FLOUR EQUIVALENTS

For all-purpose, cake flour, French flour, whole-wheat and rye flour, instantized (granular) flour, and so forth. Measure by dipping dry-measure cup into flour container and sweeping off excess with the flat edge of a knife; do not sift until after measuring.

CUPS AND SPOONS	OUNCES & POUNDS	METRIC
7–7½ cups	2.2 pounds	1 kilogram
		1,000 grams
3¾ cups	1.1 pounds	500 grams
3½ cups	1 pound	454 grams
1 cup	5 ounces	140 grams
⅔ cup	3½ ounces	100 grams
⅓ cup	1¾ ounces	50 grams
3 Tb	scant ounce	25 grams
1⅓ Tb	⅓ ounce	10 grams
1 Tb	¼ ounce	7½ grams (une cuillère)

FLOUR MEASURES IN VOLUME I OF "MASTERING"

When Volume I was first published, American flours were not presifted, and in all printings taken from the first edition the following flour measuring system is used: Sift flour directly into dry-measure cups, and sweep off excess with flat edge of a knife. Here is a table translating the cumbersome sifting-into-cup method to the far faster scoop-and-level system; you might like to jot it down in your copy of the book.

ALL-PURPOSE FLOUR *sifted into cup*	FRENCH FLOUR & CAKE FLOUR *sifted into cup*	ANY KIND OF FLOUR *Scooped and leveled (not sifted until after measuring)*	OUNCES	GRAMS
1 cup	1 cup plus 3 Tb	⅔ cup	3.5	100
¾ cup	1 cup	⅓ cup plus ¼ cup	2.8	80
½ cup	⅔ cup	⅓ cup	1.8	50
. . .	½ cup	¼ cup plus 1 Tb	1.4	40
⅓ cup	. . .	¼ cup	1.2	33
¼ cup	⅓ cup	3 Tb	0.9	25
. . .	¼ cup	Scant 3 Tb	0.7	20

OTHER MISCELLANEOUS MEASUREMENTS

ITEM	CUPS & SPOONS	OUNCES & POUNDS	METRIC
LIQUIDS	1 cup	8 ounces	225 grams
RAW MEAT & FISH	1 cup, tightly packed	8 ounces	225 grams
DICED OR SLICED RAW VEGETABLES	3½ cups, diced or sliced	1 pound, whole	450 grams
ALMONDS, ground	¾ cup, lightly packed	4 ounces	125 grams
APPLES	2⅔ to 3 cups peeled & sliced	1 pound (whole)	500 grams (whole)
BACON, raw	⅓ cup, diced, or in lardons	2 ounces	60 grams
BEANS, dry	2½ cups, raw 7 cups, cooked	1 pound	450 grams
CABBAGE, shredded	3 cups, shredded	½ pound	225 grams
CHEESE	½ cup, grated, lightly packed	2 ounces	60 grams
CHESTNUTS	5 cups (peeled)	2 pounds (whole)	900 grams
GLACÉED FRUIT	1 cup, diced	5½ ounces	150 grams
HERBS, fresh, leaves only	¼ cup (pressed down) 2 Tb (chopped)	½ ounce	15 grams
MUSHROOMS, fresh cultivated			
Whole	4 cups (1 quart)	10 ounces	300 grams
Diced	4 cups	10 ounces	300 grams
The above, squeezed dry	1 cup (pressed down)		
The above, cooked as *duxelles*	½ cup		
Whole	6–7 cups	1 pound	450–500 grams
Sliced	5 cups	1 pound	450–500 grams
NUT MEATS	2 cups	8 ounces	225 grams
PEAS, GREEN			
Small size, fresh	1 cup, shelled	1 pound, whole	450 grams
Large size, fresh	1½ cups, shelled	1 pound, whole	450 grams
Frozen package	1½ cups, cooked	10 ounce package	285 grams
POTATOES	2 cups, mashed	1 pound, whole unpeeled	450 grams
RAISINS, small seedless and currants	¾ cup	4 ounces	125 grams
RASPBERRIES	1⅓ cups whole Scant 1 cup, sieved	8 ounces whole	225 grams
RICE	1 cup, raw 3 cups, cooked	8 ounces	225 grams
SPINACH			
fresh	½ cup plus, cooked, squeezed, chopped	10 ounce package, raw	285 grams
frozen	½ cup, squeezed, chopped	10 ounce package, raw	285 grams

ITEM	CUPS & SPOONS	OUNCES & POUNDS	METRIC
STRAWBERRIES	4 cups, whole 2 cups, puréed	1 pound	450 grams
SUGAR (regular table sugar and instant superfine)	1 cup	6½ ounces	190 grams
	⅓ cup	2 ounces	65 grams
	1 Tb	⅓ ounce	12–15 grams
	5¼ cups	2.2 pounds	1,000 grams
Sugar lumps	¾ cup	4 ounces	125 grams
Confectioners' sugar	1 cup (sifted into cup)	2⅔ ounces	80 grams
TOMATOES, fresh	1½ cups peeled, seeded, juiced	1 pound whole	450 grams
Canned Italian	1¾ cups strained pulp	35 ounce can	1,000 grams
YEAST, package dry yeast	2½ tsp	⅔ ounce	20 grams
ZUCCHINI	3½ cups, sliced 2 cups grated, squeezed	1 pound whole	450 grams

Index

Page numbers in **boldface** *type indicate main references to an entry.*